Reference Guide to
Mystery and Detective Fiction

Reference Sources in the Humanities Series
James Rettig, Series Editor

The Performing Arts: A Guide to the Reference Literature. By Linda Keir Simons.

American Popular Culture: A Guide to the Reference Literature. By Frank W. Hoffmann.

Philosophy: A Guide to the Reference Literature. Second Edition. By Hans E. Bynagle.

Journalism: A Guide to the Reference Literature. Second Edition. By Jo A. Cates.

Children's Literature: A Guide to Information Sources. By Margaret W. Denman-West.

Reference Works in British and American Literature. Second Edition. By James K. Bracken.

Reference Guide to Mystery and Detective Fiction. By Richard Bleiler.

Linguistics: A Guide to the Reference Literature. Second Edition. By Anna L. DeMiller.

Reference Guide to
Mystery and Detective Fiction

Richard J. Bleiler

University of Connecticut

1999
Libraries Unlimited, Inc.
Englewood, Colorado

LIBRARIES UNLIMITED, INC.
P.O. Box 6633
Englewood, CO 80155-6633
1-800-237-6124
www.lu.com

Library of Congress Cataloging-in-Publication Data

Bleiler, Richard J.
    Reference guide to mystery and detective fiction / by Richard J.
Bleiler.
    xviii, 391 p. 17x25 cm. -- (Reference sources in the humanities series)
    Includes bibliographical references and indexes.
    ISBN 1-56308-380-9
    1. Detective and mystery stories--Bibliography. 2. Reference
books--Detective and mystery stories--Bibliography. I. Title.
II. Series.
Z5917.D5B59   1999
[PN3448.D4]
016.80883'872--dc21
                                                99-19091
                                                    CIP

Contents

Introduction xv

ENCYCLOPEDIAS and DICTIONARIES 1

READERS' GUIDES and GENRE BIBLIOGRAPHIES 4

General 4
Specific Genres 32
    African American Mysteries 32
    American Mysteries 33
    Asian American Mysteries 34
    Baseball Mysteries 34
    Bibliomysteries 34
    Blind-Accessible Mysteries 35
    Christmas Mysteries 36
    Classic British Mysteries 37
    Clerical Mysteries 37
    College Mysteries 39
    Courtroom Mysteries 40
    Cozy Mysteries 41
    Garden and Gardening Mysteries 41
    Gay and Lesbian Mysteries 41
    Golf Mysteries 43
    Gothic Mysteries 43
    Hard-Boiled Mysteries 44
    Historical Mysteries 46
    Law Mysteries 47
    Library Mysteries 47
    Locked Room Mysteries 48
    Married Protagonist Mysteries 49
    Men Detective Mysteries 49
    Mountie Mysteries 50
    Music Mysteries 51
    Nurse Mysteries 51
    Police Detective Mysteries 51
    Police Procedurals 52

READERS' GUIDES and GENRE BIBLIOGRAPHIES (*continued*)

Specific Genres (*continued*)
Private Eye Mysteries 52
Science Fiction and Fantasy Mysteries 55
Stamp Mysteries 56
Suspense Novels 57
Women Character Mysteries 58
Young Adult Mysteries 59

GENERAL BIBLIOGRAPHIES and LIBRARY CATALOGUES . . 60

General 60
Specific Libraries' Holdings 64

NATIONAL BIBLIOGRAPHIES 67

Australia 67
Belgium 68
Canada 68
Denmark 69
Finland 70
Germany 70
Ireland 72
Japan 73
Scandinavia 73
South Africa 73
Sweden 75

GEOGRAPHICAL GUIDES/MAPS 77

General Regional Guides 77
Specific Areas 78
American Cities 78
England 81
Other Countries 82

AWARDS LISTS 83

PUBLISHER BIBLIOGRAPHIES 86

Ace Books 86
Albatross Modern Continental Library 87
Avon 87
Boardman 88
Brown, Watson 89

Cherry Tree Books 89
Collins Crime Club 90
Collins White Circle. 91
Corgi 92
Curtis Warren/Grant Hughes 92
Dell 93
Detective-Club 94
Digit Books 95
Doubleday Crime Club 95
Four Square Books 96
Gollancz. 96
Gramol Group 97
Hamilton and Panther 98
Hodder and Stoughton 98
Hutchinson Group 99
Lion Books 100
R & L Locker/Harborough Publishing/Archer Press 101
Dennis McMillan 101
Modern Fiction 102
Mystery Book Clubs. 102
Pan Books 103
Penguin Books. 104
Piccadilly Novels/Fiction House 105
Série Noire/Gallimard. 105
Sexton Blake. 106
Viking/World Distributors/Consul. 107

MAGAZINE and ANTHOLOGY INDEXES 108
General 108
Magazine Indexes, General 113
Magazine Indexes, Specific Titles 122
    The Armchair Detective 122
    The Avenger 123
    Black Mask 124
    Dime Detective Magazine 125
    Doc Savage 126
    Ellery Queen's Mystery Magazine 127
    G-8 and His Battle Aces 128
    JDM Bibliophile 128
    Magnet Detective Library 128
    Mystery Fancier. 129
    New Magnet Library 130
    New Nick Carter Weekly 130
    Nick Carter Library 130
    Nick Carter Stories 131

MAGAZINE and ANTHOLOGY INDEXES (*continued*)

Magazine Indexes, Specific Titles (*continued*)
    Operator #5 132
    The Phantom Detective 132
    The Saint Magazine. 133
    Secret Agent 'X' 133
    The Shadow 134
    The Spider 136

BIOGRAPHICAL SOURCES

BIOGRAPHICAL SOURCES 137
General 137
Pseudonyms 146
Individual Authors. 147
    Margery Allingham 147
    Frederick Irving Anderson 148
    E. C. Ayres 149
    Marian Babson 149
    John Baker 149
    Pauline Bell 149
    Nicholas Blake. *See* C. Day-Lewis 149
    Robert Bloch 150
    Lawrence Block. 152
    Leigh Brackett 153
    Ernest Bramah 155
    Fredric Brown 156
    Rita Mae Brown 159
    Leo Bruce. 159
    James Lee Burke 159
    W. R. Burnett. 160
    Gwendoline Butler 160
    Carol Cail. 161
    James M. Cain 161
    John Dickson Carr 161
    Raymond Chandler. 162
    Leslie Charteris 164
    G. K. Chesterton 168
    Meg Chittenden. 171
    Agatha Christie 171
    Mary Higgins Clark. 179
    Liza Cody. 180
    Wilkie Collins. 180
    D. G. Compton. 182
    Patricia Cornwell 183
    Anthony Berkeley Cox 184
    Camilla Crespi 184

Edmund Crispin 185
James Crumley 185
Judith Cutler 185
Mary Daheim 185
Carroll John Daly 186
Barbara D'Amato 186
Avram Davidson 186
Diane Mott Davidson 187
Linda Davies 187
Lindsey Davis 187
Dianne Day 188
Marele Day 188
Cecil Day-Lewis 188
Jeffery Deaver 189
Lester Dent 189
August Derleth 190
Charles Dickens 195
Carole Nelson Douglas 195
Arthur Conan Doyle 196
Sarah Dreher 208
Stella Duffy 208
Martin Edwards 209
Ruth Dudley Edwards 209
James Ellroy 209
Loren D. Estleman 210
Janet Evanovich 210
Tony Fennelly 210
Bruno Fischer 211
Kate Flora 211
Dick Francis 211
R. Austin Freeman 212
Celia Fremlin 212
Kinky Friedman 212
Dale Furutani 213
Erle Stanley Gardner 213
Elizabeth George 215
Walter B. Gibson 216
David Goodis 217
Paula Gosling 217
Sue Grafton 217
Ann Granger 218
Kate Grilley 218
Martha Grimes 219
Terris McMahan Grimes 219
Frank Gruber 219
Jean Hager 220

BIOGRAPHICAL SOURCES (*continued*)

Individual Authors (*continued*)

Parnell Hall 220
Lyn Hamilton 220
Dashiell Hammett 221
Joseph Hansen 223
Cyril Hare 224
Carolyn G. Hart 224
Judith Hawkes 224
Sparkle Hayter 224
Lauren Henderson 225
Carl Hiaasen 225
Lynn S. Hightower 225
Reginald Hill 225
Tony Hillerman 226
Chester Himes 228
Edward D. Hoch 230
Matt Hughes 231
Evan Hunter. *See* Ed McBain 231
Elspeth Huxley 231
Michael Innes 232
P. D. James 232
Russell James 232
H. R. F. Keating 233
Alex Keegan 233
Harry Stephen Keeler 233
Jonathan and Faye Kellerman 234
Laurie R. King 235
Steven Knight 235
Joe R. Lansdale 235
Janice Law 236
Martha C. Lawrence 236
Elmore Leonard 236
Paul Levine 237
David Lindsey 237
Philip Luber 237
Ed McBain 238
Sharyn McCrumb 238
Val McDermid 238
John D. MacDonald 239
Ross Macdonald/Kenneth Millar 247
Jackie Manthorne 249
Ngaio Marsh 250
A. E. Marston 251
J. C. Masterman 251

Lia Matera 251
Catherine Lucille Moore and Henry Kuttner 252
John Mortimer 253
Walter Mosley 254
Marcia Muller 254
Magdalen Nabb 255
Sharan Newman 255
Maxine O'Callaghan 255
Carol O'Connell 256
Barbara Parker 256
Robert B. Parker 256
Barbara Paul 257
Michael Pearce 258
Anne Perry 258
Elizabeth Peters 258
Ellis Peters/Edith Pargeter 259
Talmage Powell 260
Bill Pronzini 261
Sandra West Prowell 261
Ellery Queen 261
Elizabeth Quinn 262
Ian Rankin 262
Ruth Rendell. *See* Barbara Vine 262
Paul Renin 262
Nicholas Rhea 263
Rick Riordan 263
Mike Ripley 263
Peter Robinson 264
Robert Rosenberg 264
Katherine Ross 264
Jay Russell 265
Nicole St. John 265
James Sallis 265
John Sandford 266
Walter Satterthwait 266
Dorothy L. Sayers 266
Sandra Scoppettone 270
Sharon Gwyn Short 271
Georges Simenon 271
Trish Macdonald Skillman 276
Barbara Burnett Smith 276
Enes Smith 277
Guy N. Smith 277
Troy Soos 277
Elizabeth Daniels Squire 277
Dana Stabenow 278

BIOGRAPHICAL SOURCES (*continued*)

Individual Authors (*continued*)

Vincent Starrett. 278
Shane Stevens. 279
Rex Stout 280
John Straley. 284
Penny Sumner 284
Julian Symons. 284
Andrew Taylor 285
Phoebe Atwood Taylor. 285
Ross Thomas 285
Jim Thompson 286
Aimée Thurlo and David Thurlo. 286
Elleston Trevor. 287
Wilson Tucker 287
Peter Turnbull 288
Arthur W. Upfield 289
Andrew Vachss. 289
Robert H. van Gulik 290
Jack Vance 291
Barbara Vine/Ruth Rendell 294
Hannah Wakefield 294
Mary Willis Walker 294
Peter N. Walker. *See* Nicholas Rhea 295
Edgar Wallace 295
Chassie L. West. 300
Christopher West. 300
Donald E. Westlake 300
Polly Whitney. 301
Denise Dietz Wiley. 301
Charles Willeford. 301
David Williams 302
Timothy Williams. 302
Barbara Wilson 302
Derek Wilson. 303
Robert Wilson 303
Mary Wings. 303
Steven Womack 303
Daniel Woodrell 304
Cornell Woolrich. 304
P. C. Wren 305
Rebecca York. 306

CHARACTER INDEXES and BIBLIOGRAPHIES 307
  General 307
  Specific Characters 321
    Black Bat 321
    Cherry Ames 321
    Dan Fowler 322
    Doc Savage 322
    The Hardy Boys 324
    Judy Bolton 325
    The Moon Man 326
    Nancy Drew 326
    The Phantom/Phantom Detective 327
    The Shadow 328

SECONDARY LITERATURE 329

CATALOGUING GUIDES 340

ARTIST STUDIES 342

MEDIA CATALOGUES and GUIDES 343
  General 343
  Specific Shows and Characters 351
    Alfred Hitchcock Presents 351
    Charlie Chan 351
    Hawaii Five-O 352
    Heartbeat 352
    Mystery! 353

CALENDARS 354

DIRECTORIES OF DEALERS and THEIR PRICE GUIDES . . 355
  Directories 355
  Price Guides 356

ELECTRONIC SOURCES 359

CORE PUBLICATIONS 363

PROFESSIONAL ORGANIZATIONS 366

Index 367

Introduction

Except through tautologies and generalities, it is not possible in the space of this introduction to provide a definition of either *detective fiction* or *mystery story*. The first term typically describes the activities of a detective, usually a person whose abilities at solving puzzles and interpreting evidence (clues) lead to a formal resolution of a problem, often a crime, frequently murder. The second generally involves a story in which a formally stated mystery and its equally formal resolution are central to the development of the plot. Of course, numerous exceptions can and should be made to these statements: more than one detective may be present and may provide a different but equally viable solution to the crime; or no crime may have been committed and the story is nothing more than an exercise in logic; or the detective may solve nothing and bungle everything; or the detective may not be human and, indeed, may not even be of this planet. Furthermore, the sense of mystery is not limited to those works in which a detective or detectives appear, and mysteries can be found in literary genres as distinct as weird fiction, science fiction, horror fiction, gothic fiction, espionage fiction, religious fiction, suspense fiction, and western fiction.

Despite the problems described above, there exists a substantial body of work that is commonly understood to be detective and mystery fiction, and there are numerous writers who have written and continue to write detective and mystery fiction. This volume addresses itself to this body of work and to the accomplishments of these writers. It is an annotated guide to the separately published reference works that document and describe the primary and secondary literatures of mystery and detective fiction. *Reference work* is here understood to include the encyclopedias, dictionaries, companions, vade mecums, bibliographies, biobibliographies, checklists, indexes, directories, handbooks, annotated editions, and guides intended and produced for an adult readership that were published prior to 1998. Reference works in languages other than English have not been cited, and no attempt has been made to describe the many biographies, essay collections, miscellaneous monographs, or general histories of the mystery and detective story. Also omitted from this volume are descriptions of the catalogues of book dealers, ephemeral in-house lists produced by libraries for their patrons, and works documenting materials intended for juvenile readers. I have not hesitated to make exceptions to those rules, especially when noteworthy publications might otherwise be omitted.

It is, of course, understood that the boundaries of literary genres are fluid and are generally established by outsiders, not its practitioners; one writer may well write in several different genres. Nevertheless, an arbitrary line has been drawn, and no efforts have been made to include works wholly devoted to the classical thriller, the adventure story, the espionage story, the gangster tale, the historical novel, the western, and the true crime story. This is not the source to use to locate works about such writers as Max Brand, John Buchan, Len Deighton, Ian Fleming, Geoffrey Household, and Robert Ludlum, though their works often contain crimes and mysteries awaiting resolution. Exceptions have, however, been made: Charles Dickens and Wilkie Collins are traditionally considered mainstream novelists, but Dickens's *The Mystery of Edwin Drood* and Collins's *The Woman in White*, *The Moonstone*, and *Armadale* are too famous to ignore and are as often as not interpreted as genre works. On an opposite note, most literary historians use Edgar Allan Poe as the start of the modern mystery, but despite Poe's enormous influence, as of this writing there exist no separately published bibliographies describing Poe solely as a writer of mysteries.

Also included in this guide are a number of sources that index and describe the pulp magazines, with particular attention paid to the works describing the hero pulps, a variety of pulp magazine that described the actions of a single heroic character and his assistants. The activities of these heroes were often set against backgrounds that amalgamated elements found in the adventure story, the science fiction story, and the mystery and detective story, but it must be stressed that, despite their frequently sensationalistic trappings and often fantastic overtones, many of the stories in the pulp magazines were structured as traditional mysteries and concluded with the hero—Doc Savage, the Phantom Detective, the Spider, or the Shadow—unmasking the true villain and providing a rational explanation to the hitherto baffling mysteries and murders.

It is fervently hoped that the citations will provide sufficient bibliographic data necessary to locate a publication. Entries begin by listing the author, authors, or editor(s); these are followed by the title, the place of publication, publisher, and year of publication of the first edition; pagination is provided, as are the series title and a statement as to whether an index or indexes are present. Works published only in paperback are so noted, and entries conclude with the work's Library of Congress number and its ISBN, when such are present. If the work was first published abroad, the primary publication data are noted, and the American edition is referenced, if such exists. If the work has been revised and updated, the earlier editions are listed and the most recent edition available is described, often with a note indicating that the later edition is described. Anonymous works are listed by title.

Following the above data are a description of each work's intent, organization, and content, and (when appropriate) an evaluative opinion. This latter may prove controversial, but although a reference book may be many things to many people and may contain data that are unique, it is ultimately—paramountly and inescapably—something that researchers must rely upon to answer their questions or to further their research. Compilers of reference works must thus strive to make their data as close to 100 percent accurate as possible and to present these data in such a way as to make them as readily accessible as possible. I have not hesitated to comment if these data cannot be obtained immediately and with ease, or if they cannot be relied upon. I do not, of course, believe that there is only one way to present material, but I feel it is important to comment if a volume does not contain an index when one would assist the user, if it indexes something without providing relevant pagination, or if it neglects or omits data while claiming to be comprehensive. In addition, I have commented when a volume is physically defective, poorly bound, badly printed, awkwardly laid out, or in some way idiosyncratic or frustrating in its presentation of data. These are relevant considerations when one is debating whether to purchase a volume.

In addition to describing and annotating paper publications, this volume describes and annotates a number of World Wide Web sites that are devoted to detective and mystery fiction and those who write it. No standard exists for websites, and well-done websites come in a variety of forms. An ideal website should nevertheless present material in an orderly fashion, without distracting backgrounds and Java aplets. When appropriate, a website should offer clearly accessible links to other websites. If the website is devoted to the life and work of a single author, or is an author's personal web page, it should provide reasonable biographical data, include a portrait or a photograph, give information about the writings, and provide reasonable bibliographic data on the works; references to secondary material are also helpful. Every attempt has been made to reference the personal web pages of the authors who have written more than three original novels; if these were not available, attempts were made to cite relevant websites, particularly those websites that are maintained as labors of love by enthusiasts and experts. I have not attempted to reference or describe the majority of the commercial websites (.com) currently available, for the primary intent of these tends to be the marketing of merchandise rather than the independent celebration of the author or genre.

The majority of the items described in this bibliography came from my own collections, but for obtaining those materials that I do not own, I am perpetually indebted to Bob Vrecendak, the wonderful Interlibrary Loan Librarian at the University of Connecticut's Homer Babbidge Library, and to his nonpareil assistants Lana Babbij, Judy DeLottie, and Lynn Sweet. These people work miracles, routinely obtaining the unobtainable.

For providing gracious assistance that is probably above and beyond the call of her duty, I would like to thank Ms. Monika Szakasits of the Interlibrary Loan Department in the Tarlton Law Library at the University of Texas at Austin School of Law.

For taking time from her studies to look for Polish publications, I would like to thank Joanna Koc.

For generously sharing their expertise, collections, and publications, I wish to express gratitude to noted bibliographers and scholars J. Randolph Cox, David Skene Melvin, Norbert Spehner, and Norman Stevens.

Special gratitude is due to my friend Sue Root, whose extensive knowledge of the used and rare book trade provided me with examination copies of items I would not otherwise have been able to obtain.

Finally, my very special thanks to my father E. F. Bleiler, who shared generously of his time and possessions, and to my dear Cheryl, who patiently reminded me when it was late and when I needed to eat, and who makes Connecticut a much nicer place to live.

All omissions and mistakes are of course my own responsibility. Corrections and additions should be sent to the author at the Reference Department, U-5RI, Homer Babbidge Library, University of Connecticut, Storrs, CT 06269-1005.

ENCYCLOPEDIAS and DICTIONARIES

SCOPE NOTE: This chapter includes publications that call themselves encyclopedias and the dictionaries of the vocabularies of mystery and fiction. Dictionaries and encyclopedias of specific subjects—authors, characters, motion pictures and television shows, and so forth—are listed under their respective subject headings later in this book.

1.　DeAndrea, William L. **Encyclopedia Mysteriosa: A Comprehensive Guide to the Art of Detection in Print, Film, Radio, and Television**. New York, London: Prentice-Hall, 1994. x, 405 p. Cloth. LC 94-2075. ISBN 0-671-85025-3.

Although nearly 20 years elapsed since Penzler and Steinbrunner compiled their *Encyclopedia of Mystery and Detection,* no comprehensive attempt has been made to update their efforts. DeAndrea—an award-winning author of mysteries—began this book because he saw a need for it: "A lot has happened since 1975. Writers so popular now as to seem forces of nature had not begun their careers then; there has been a decade and a half of (sometimes excellent) movies and TV shows, as well. It was time to get up-to-date." The result is a volume similar in appearance to the old *Encyclopedia*, an alphabetical list of approximately 1,400 entries containing numerous cross-references, a number of illustrations, and 11 separately signed essays on special aspects of the detective and mystery story. The volume concludes with three appendices ("Bookstores," "Organizations and Awards," and "Magazines and Journals"), and a glossary of terms specific to the mystery story.

Like the earlier *Encyclopedia,* DeAndrea's *Encyclopedia Mysteriosa* is a genuine encyclopedia, and its entries attempt an encyclopedic thoroughness. A number of thriller writers are profiled, as well as mainstream writers who contributed significantly to the genre, and writers more famous for their work in other genres. The *Encyclopedia Mysteriosa* differs significantly from its inspiration in that the majority of its entries are for the characters or for the "Film, Radio, and Television" presentations of crime and mystery. The first three pages of the volume contain 13 entries, of which 9 concern characters or media presentations, and this percentage remains consistent throughout the book.

Oddly enough, the most significant flaws in the *Encyclopedia Mysteriosa* are those that faced Penzler and Steinbrunner. First, because DeAndrea's concentration was on the more contemporary material, he failed to mention many of the older writers; a historian is likely to wonder, however, whether it was wise to neglect writers such as Archibald Clavering Gunter and Thomas Hanshew (to say nothing of John Collier and Thomas Cook) in favor of such television shows as the *A Team*. Next, though there are occasional entries for European writers, the *Encyclopedia Mysteriosa* focuses almost entirely on the literature produced in Great Britain and America; additional entries (or a companion volume) surveying the mystery and detective literature produced around the rest of the world are needed.

These caveats aside, the *Encyclopedia Mysteriosa* belongs on all reference shelves.

2. Denton, William. **Twists, Slugs and Roscoes: A Glossary of Hardboiled Slang**. http://www.vex.net/~buff/slang.html

This website provides definitions of slang words and terms commonly found in hardboiled detective fiction. A lighthearted introduction explains that "this is the language spoken by Philip Marlowe, Sam Spade, Mike Hammer and the Continental Op. When Cagney, Bogart, Robinson and Raft got in a turf war, this is how they talked." The list begins with "Ameche" (a telephone), concludes with "Zotzed" (killed), and includes definitions for such classics as "gunsel" and "gooseberry lay," as well as several hundred additional terms. Except in the case of e-mail submissions, attributions are provided for each term. The list of sources from which the terms were derived concludes the dictionary. A well-done and very helpful dictionary.

3. Steinbrunner, Chris, and Otto Penzler, eds. **Encyclopedia of Mystery and Detection**. New York, St. Louis, San Francisco: McGraw-Hill, 1976. 436 p. Cloth. LC 75-31645. ISBN 0-07-061121-1.

The *Encyclopedia of Mystery and Detection* was the first attempt at providing readers of what the editors call "the country's favorite literary genre" with a comprehensive reference work. It was partially inspired by the success of the *Detectionary* (q.v.), which was written by (among others) the editors of the *Encyclopedia*, but at 300,000 words, the *Encyclopedia* is more than five times the length of the *Detectionary*. It is a genuine encyclopedia, an alphabetical listing of nearly 600 articles, the majority concentrating on the authors of detective and mystery fiction, herein defined broadly enough to include writers of thrillers (John Buchan, Ian Fleming, and Geoffrey Household), writers traditionally considered mainstream (Theodore Dreiser, Fyodor Dostoevski, and Victor Hugo), and writers significant in other literary genres (John Collier, Arthur Machen, and Ann Radcliffe). Additionally, important characters are accorded entries of their own: Arthur Upfield's Inspector Napoleon Bonaparte and Ian Fleming's James Bond share a page, and other odd juxtapositions can be easily located. A significant number of the author entries include an author photograph and conclude with chronologically arranged "checklists" of the author's fiction and descriptions of significant motion picture, radio, and television adaptations. Character entries describe their earliest appearance as well as their media appearances, and often include checklists of publications in which the character appears and photographs of actors portraying the character. Finally, there are copious cross-references and a number of signed entries for such thematic subjects as "Collecting Detective Fiction," the "Had-I-but-Known School," "Locked-Room Mysteries," and "Pulp Magazines."

The two greatest flaws in the *Encyclopedia* are those of inclusiveness and consistency. The editors recognize the former problem in their introduction by stating, reasonably enough, that "this is a big book, by any reasonable standard, but a line had to be drawn somewhere. If the reader insists, 'But X is just as important as Y,' he may be right. There are scores of borderline entries in this book, and hundreds of borderline omissions." This is quite correct. The problem of consistency is less noticeable but equally relevant: The entry on Pierre Chambrun concludes with a list of the publications in which he appears, but the entry for the vastly more significant Charlie Chan does not. Additionally, it is to be regretted that the checklists provide merely title and publication date; more bibliographical data would have been welcome. Nevertheless, despite its age, the strengths of the volume far outweigh its weaknesses. The *Encyclopedia* defined a field of literature; it remains a landmark volume.

4. Turner-Lord, Jann. **Bob's Your Uncle: A Dictionary of Slang for British Mystery Fans**. Santa Barbara, CA: Fithian Press, 1992. 62 p. Paperback. LC 92-3858. ISBN 1-56474-022-6.

The cover of this slim paperback describes Jann Turner-Lord as "a confirmed anglophile and mystery-addict," and Turner-Lord's preface states that she was inspired to create this dictionary by reading Jonathan Gash, whose character Lovejoy "uses more slang than I've ever seen." Sources of inspiration aside, *Bob's Your Uncle* defines approximately 800 terms that Turner-Lord has located through her reading. None of her definitions provides attributions or sources, making the volume useless for determining whether a usage is historical or modern and for whether a word or phrase originated with a specific author. Furthermore, many of the terms defined by Turner-Lord are neither English slang nor limited to British mystery novels. A number of standard English abbreviations are defined, as are readily understandable terms such as "flummox," "petrol tin," "queue," "row," and "smarmy." *Bob's Your Uncle* was obviously a labor of love, but this does not excuse its deficiencies.

READERS' GUIDES and GENRE BIBLIOGRAPHIES

SCOPE NOTE: In this chapter are works that survey more than one genre or that are selective and general lists (i.e., lists of the 100 best books). Surveys of individual genres are listed separately. Furthermore, bibliographies intended to record an entire genre or subgenre or to document a nationality's literary output are listed in the genre and bibliography chapters, even when they are extensively annotated.

GENERAL

5. Barnes, Melvyn. **Best Detective Fiction: A Guide from Godwin to the Present**. London: Clive Bingley, 1975; simultaneously published: Hamden, CT: Linnet Books, 1975. 121 p. Index. LC 75-22344. ISBN 0-208-01376-8.

Best Detective Fiction differs from the other guides in this section by being a bibliographic essay describing the books that Barnes considers "key contributions to the genre." In his preface, Barnes states that his criteria for inclusion were "excellence of plot, writing and/or characterisation, or a degree of innovation that has established or enhanced a trend." He generally excluded thrillers and spy stories from his discussion, although he made exceptions for significant titles.

The essay, a chronological (rather than thematic) history, starts with discussion of two of the more significant pre-Poe detective stories, William Godwin's *Things as They Are; or, the Adventures of Caleb Williams* (1794) and the first English edition of Eugène François Vidocq's *Memoirs of Vidocq, Principal Agent of the French Police Until 1827* (1828–1829). Successive chapters discuss Arthur Conan Doyle and his contemporaries and imitators; the writers of the 1920s; the hard-boiled writers; and the writers of detective stories during the 1930s, 1940s, 1950s, and so forth. The essay concludes with mention of such writers as "Anthony Gilbert," Andrew Garve, Laurence Meynell, and Dick Francis. In all, about 125 authors and 225 books are mentioned, and for each of the latter Barnes cites the first English-language edition, citing also the first British edition

4

if there is a difference. A "checklist of books mentioned" that is effectively an author index concludes the volume; there is no title index.

Although Barnes's preface specifically states that his volume "is not intended as a complete history of detective fiction," students with no background in the subject may find Barnes a useful introduction, for his judgments are solid and conventional, likely to surprise neither critics nor scholars. On the debit side, *Best Detective Fiction* contains virtually nothing that cannot be found elsewhere, and his omissions are significant. The only work of Raymond Chandler mentioned is *The High Window*, and such vital writers as R. Austin Freeman, John Dickson Carr, Dashiell Hammett, and Erle Stanley Gardner have only two works (apicce) cited. Worst of all, *Best Detective Fiction* is lifeless, dated in a way that Barzun and Taylor's *A Catalogue of Crime* and Pronzini and Muller's *1001 Midnights* (q.q.v.) are not. Its successor (below) is superior.

6. Barnes, Melvyn. **Murder in Print: A Guide to Two Centuries of Detective Fiction**. London: Barn Owl Books, 1986. xii, 244 p. Index. ISBN 0-9509057-4-7.

Murder in Print was originally conceived as the 2d edition to Barnes's *Best Detective Fiction* (above), but while revising his book, Barnes realized that "the field [of detective fiction] has changed over the years to a degree that cannot be ignored. If the full picture is to be shown, there must be greater coverage of the modern crime novel in all its manifestations. Similarly, various subgenres, while mentioned in the earlier book, now warrant considerable sections of their own." *Murder in Print* thus presents "the result of further extensive research and an examination of the best authors to have emerged in the past twenty years. All material which appeared in the original volume has similarly been comprehensively revised, reorganized and expanded."

Like *Best Detective Fiction*, *Murder in Print* is a bibliographic essay, citing the first British and first American editions of the books it discusses. Nevertheless, *Murder in Print* contains a greater awareness of thematic developments than the first book, and its later chapters are thematic discussions rather than chronological lists. Like its predecessor, *Murder in Print* begins with the discussion of William Godwin's *Things as They Are* (1794) and the first English edition of Eugène François Vidocq's *Memoirs of Vidocq* (1828–1829). Later chapters discuss important mystery and detective stories written prior to the advent of Sherlock Holmes, and significant chapters discuss Arthur Conan Doyle and his contemporaries. Thematic discussions include women detective and mystery writers and the writers of hard-boiled detective stories, police procedurals, and historical mysteries. As before, thrillers and spy stories were generally excluded from discussion, although Barnes made occasional exceptions for significant titles. In all, approximately 260 authors and nearly 500 books are discussed. A "checklist of books featured," a select but useful bibliography, and a combined author/title index conclude the volume.

Murder in Print is vastly superior to *Best Detective Fiction* Authors neglected in the earlier volume are discussed at length in *Murder in Print*, and Barnes's critical assessments are sharper and shrewder. *Murder in Print* is substantially shorter than either Barzun and Taylor's *A Catalogue of Crime* and Pronzini and Muller's *1001 Midnights* (q.q.v.), but it has the virtue of offering its criticism in a historical context.

7. Barnett, Sandy, and Newfront Productions. **The History of the Mystery: An Interactive Journey**. http://www.mysterynet.com/history/

As its title indicates, this website provides an interactive history of the mystery, from the days of Cicero until the present. The material is very well presented and offers numerous illustrations. Unfortunately, it also contains entirely too many errors, including the misspelling of the name of Poe's pioneering detective, a claim that "The Purloined Letter" was a novel, assertions that Mickey Spillane wrote only six novels featuring Mike Hammer, and a statement that *The Mysterious Affair at Styles* featured both Poirot and Marple. One hopes for corrections.

8. Barzun, Jacques, and Wendell Hertig Taylor. **A Catalogue of Crime [Being a Reader's Guide to the Literature of Mystery, Detection, & Related Genres]**. New York: Harper & Row, 1971. xxxi, 831 p. Indexes. LC 75-123914. ISBN 0-06-010263-2.

9. Barzun, Jacques, and Wendell Hertig Taylor. **A Catalogue of Crime [Being a Reader's Guide to the Literature of Mystery, Detection, and Related Genres]**. Revised and enlarged edition. New York: Harper & Row, 1989. xxxvi, 952 p. Indexes. LC 88-45884. ISBN 0-06-015796-8.

The two editions of *A Catalogue of Crime* are among the most significant annotated bibliographies of detective and mystery stories. They are also among the most idiosyncratic of bibliographies, combining seemingly arbitrary inclusions, poorly presented citations, and most unhelpful and often frustrating layouts with intelligent, witty, and waspish opinions. The first edition differs significantly from the second not only in the number of citations but also because the first edition's final chapter is devoted to ghost stories, studies and reports of the supernatural, psychical research, and ESP.

This annotation concentrates on the *Catalogue*'s second edition, which contains the following sections: novels of detection, crime, mystery, and espionage; short stories, collections, anthologies, magazines, pastiches, and plays; studies and histories of the genre, lives of writers, and the literature of *Edwin Drood*; true crime: trials, narratives of cases, criminology and police science, espionage, and cryptography; and the literature of Sherlock Holmes: studies and annotations of the tales, nonfiction parodies, and critical pastiches. All entries are numbered, and in all, 5,045 works are annotated, an impressive 3,549 of these being "novels of detection, crime, mystery, and espionage." Each section is arranged alphabetically by the author's or editor's last name; when multiple books by an author are annotated, the titles are listed alphabetically. The annotations are of necessity terse, most being no more than 75–100 words and the briefest a mere two (Miles Burton's *Murder at the Moorings* is "Very Poor!"). A combined author-title index concludes the volume.

A Catalogue of Crime is an authoritative (one could say authoritarian) annotated bibliography. It is, however, more satisfactory for the quality of its annotations than as a reference book. Crucial bibliographical data are consistently abbreviated, necessitating frequent reference to nine pages of abbreviations at the book's beginning until such abbreviations as CCC, CCD, CUP, C&B, C&E, C&H, C&S, and C&W (to list but a few) are internalized. Furthermore, the names of individual authors are set in small capital letters but are not otherwise distinguished from the text, and the volume contains no running heads. In the case of prolific writers, this makes the location of information very difficult. Finally, Barzun and Taylor never state their methods for determining the contents of *A Catalogue of Crime*. Is this list based solely on the books they have read? based on their personal libraries? derived from the recommendations of friends and acquaintances?

Despite their idiosyncrasies and quirks, neither edition of *A Catalogue of Crime* may be dismissed. No other guide considered here offers anything approaching the breadth and depth of the *Catalogue*, and Barzun and Taylor's critical judgments remain models of perception and concision, expressing in but a few words what other critics need a page to say. The revised and expanded edition is a cornerstone of any reference collection and belongs in all libraries.

10.   Barzun, Jacques, and Wendell Hertig Taylor. **A Book of Prefaces to Fifty Classics of Crime Fiction 1900–1950**. New York: Garland, 1976. viii, 112 p. LC 76-26751. ISBN 0-8240-2425-7. (250 copies printed.)

This annotated bibliography began its existence as the prefaces to 50 classic mystery stories, originally published between 1900 and 1950, that Garland reprinted around the time of this book's publication. The contents are arranged alphabetically by author's name. Each annotation discusses the work, providing a brief but critical appreciation of its significance. As one would anticipate, the book lists familiar works by such authors as Chandler, Chesterton, Christie, Freeman, Gardner, Sayers, Stout, and Upfield (to name but a few), but it nevertheless contains surprises: Barzun and Taylor praise such lesser-known works as Gerald Bullett's *The Jury*, C. W. Grafton's *Beyond a Reasonable Doubt*, Thomas Kindon's *Murder in the Moor*, Dermot Morrah's *The Mummy Case*, and Henry Kitchell Webster's *Who Is the Next?* A brief biographical statement concludes each entry.

Genial though the annotations are, the research value of this book is unfortunately slight.

11.   Bourgeau, Art. **The Mystery Lover's Companion**. New York: Crown, 1986. 311 p. LC 86-4511. ISBN 0-517-55602-2.

In his introduction, Bourgeau, proprietor of Philadelphia's Whodunit? Bookstore, states that he is frequently asked to recommend mysteries, and to assist his customers, he compiled this annotated list of approximately 2,500 mysteries. The volume begins with an introduction in which Bourgeau briefly presents his criteria for determining quality ("a good mystery contains four vital elements: the main character, the plot, the action, and the atmosphere"). The body of the book contains four sections: The American Mystery; The English Mystery; The Thriller; and The Police Procedural. Each section begins with a brief essay defining the term, after which the annotations are arranged alphabetically by author's last name. Authors represented by more than one volume have their books listed chronologically. Apart from the publication year, bibliographic data are not given, and the annotations are terse, the longest being no more than 100 words. Finally, Bourgeau rates each book using daggers: one is the lowest ("only read this one when you're drunk") and five is the highest ("a true classic").

Bourgeau often writes engagingly, but this volume is unfortunately less than satisfactory as a reference work. It contains no indexes, effectively rendering it useless to a reader who remembers only a title, and it is far from comprehensive: Fredric Brown (here spelled Frederic Brown) is represented by only four books, such significant works as *The Screaming Mimi* (1949) being unmentioned. Because such authors as Trevanian wrote in more than one genre, cross-references are necessary, yet none have been provided. Most sadly, the book's contents are dated in a way that Barzun and Taylor's *A Catalogue of Crime* and Pronzini and Muller's *1001 Midnights* (q.q.v.) are not.

12. Cataio, Joseph. **Mystery Checklist**. Chicago: Reference Books, 1978. 57 p. Paperback. OCLC 5465563.

The *Mystery Checklist* lists the mystery books by 13 popular mystery writers: Raymond Chandler, Agatha Christie, Erle Stanley Gardner, Dashiell Hammett, John D. MacDonald, Ross Macdonald, Ngaio Marsh, Ellery Queen, Dorothy Sayers, Georges Simenon, Maj Sjöwall and Per Wahlöö, Mickey Spillane, and Rex Stout. The arrangement is alphabetical by author. Beneath each author's name are lists of that author's mystery novels, grouped by series character; there are two lists, one arranged alphabetically, the other chronologically. Nonseries books are listed after the lists. Short story collections are referenced in as many sections as necessary; anthologies and omnibus collections of separately published novels are excluded. In all cases, publishers, places of publication, pagination, and other bibliographic data have been omitted; titles are accompanied only by the date of first publication. In the case of Georges Simenon, only the English-language translations of the Inspector Maigret series are included; in the case of Ngaio Marsh, American and British titles are listed when they were published in the same year; and in the case of Ellery Queen, only those titles by Frederic Dannay and Manfred B. Lee are listed.

Though this title is well put together and attractively laid out, the similar work by Granovetter (q.v.) offers more.

13. Cooper, John, and B. A. Pike. **Detective Fiction: The Collector's Guide**. Lydeard, England: Barn Owl Books, 1988. x, 212 p. GB 88-32237. ISBN 0-9509057-5-5. 2d edition: Aldershot, England: Scolar Press, 1994. x, 341 p. ISBN 0-85967-991-8.

Unlike Eric Quayle's similarly titled *The Collector's Book of Detective Fiction* (q.v.), this volume is not so much a literary history as it is a handbook for collectors: Cooper and Pike arrange their guide by author and describe the works of 144 significant authors and writing partnerships. All entries follow a similar format. Each gives the author's name, followed by a brief biographical statement that includes relevant pseudonyms; these are followed by a sometimes lengthy bibliographic description of the author's detective and mystery fiction. Binding colors are noted, dustwrappers are described, and unique points of the first edition are mentioned. Entries conclude with chronological lists of the first editions of the writer's detective and mystery novels (occasionally arranged by detective) and of uncollected mystery stories. Each entry is accompanied by a black-and-white photograph of one of the author's books; a section of color plates occupies the middle of the volume. The volume concludes with 13 appendixes that offer a subject guide to the output of the profiled writers; list the anthologies of the CWA (Crime Writers' Association [of Great Britain]) and the MWA (Mystery Writers of America), list the CWA and MWA award-winners for the best novel(s) of each year from 1955 (CWA) and 1953 (MWA) until 1993; provide the names and addresses of specialist dealers in the UK and the US; provide a glossary of terms used by book collectors and dealers; offer a selective guide to publishers' practices for designating first editions; list the names and addresses of specialist journals; provide the addresses of societies, journals, and newsletters devoted to individual writers; and give brief information on dustwrapper artists.

Cooper and Pike state in their introduction that "we are amateurs in bibliography, with no training or specialized knowledge of this field." This lack of background is the book's greatest weakness, for the descriptions almost invariably concentrate on the external appearance of the book and not on the textual and typographical elements that distinguish a first edition. Similarly, although their discussions are generally thorough, Cooper and Pike occasionally miss relevant titles. Nevertheless, they obviously enjoy collecting and reading mystery and detective fiction, and their enthusiasm permeates this pleasurable volume.

14. **The Crown Crime Companion: The Top 100 Mystery Novels of All Time, Selected by the Mystery Writers of America**. Annotated by Otto Penzler. Compiled by Mickey Friedman. Introduction by Peter Ginna and Jane Cavolina. New York: Crown Trade Paperbacks, 1995. 190 p. Paperback. LC 94-43825. ISBN 0-517-88115-2.

Inspired by Susan Moody and the British Crime Writers' Association's *Hatchards Crime Companion* (q.v.), the Mystery Writers of America surveyed their members and compiled a list of their 100 best mystery novels of all time. The results of their survey, annotated by noted bibliographer Otto Penzler, are presented in the first section of *The Crown Crime Companion*. Accompanying these annotations are various lists that emerged during the compilation: favorite female/male writer, favorite female/male sleuth, favorite cities for murder, favorite murder weapon, favorite hiding place for a body, favorite animal in a mystery novel, and favorite mystery movie.

The second section assigns the mysteries to one of 10 categories, and an expert discusses the contents of each category: Classics (H. R. F. Keating), Suspense (Mary Higgins Clark), Hard-Boiled/Private Eye (Sue Grafton), Police Procedural (Joseph Wambaugh), Espionage/Thriller (John Gardner), Criminal (Richard Condon), Cozy/Traditional (Margaret Maron), Historical (Peter Lovesey), Humorous (Gregory Mcdonald), and Legal/Courtroom (Scott Turow).

The third section provides lists of the Edgar nominees: Grand Master, Best Novel, Best First Novel by an American Author, Best Original Paperback, Best Fact Crime, and Best Critical/Biographical Work. Data in this last section are current as of 1994; winners are listed in boldface type.

Surprisingly, the technical problems with this volume are identical to those of *Hatchards Crime Companion*. Nowhere do the creators provide simple alphabetical lists of the authors, titles, or detectives, and the volume is unindexed. Furthermore, the creators failed to define what they meant by a mystery or a novel, and as a result their lists include works that are neither mysteries nor novels (e.g., short story collections). Equally seriously, this list has been created by active writers, rather than scholars, and the preponderance of the titles listed are those published in the last half of the century, a number of which were bestsellers. One cannot fault the Mystery Writers of America for reading bestsellers (or wanting to write them), but when they include such works as Tom Clancy's *The Hunt for Red October*, Ira Levin's *Rosemary's Baby*, Jack Finney's *Time and Again*, and Bram Stoker's *Dracula*(!), while completely neglecting such writers as Margery Allingham, Lawrence Block, James Lee Burke, Fredric Brown, Dick Francis, R. Austin Freeman, Helen MacInnes, Ngaio Marsh, Robert B. Parker, Ellery Queen, Georges Simenon, and Cornell Woolrich, one is left wondering about the critical acumen of this supposedly august body.

The list of the top 100 mystery novels of all time is available via the Web: http://www.id-online.de/ufo/co3-crow.htm

15. Gorman, Ed, et al., eds. **The Fine Art of Murder: The Mystery Reader's Indispensable Companion**. New York: Carroll & Graf, 1993. x, 390 p. Paperback. Index. LC 93-21930. ISBN 0-88184-972-3.

This most enjoyable companion arranges its contents thematically, with 22 chapters offering what the back cover refers to as "the perfect accessory to any crime imaginable: a hefty, handsome, one-volume look at mystery fiction of all kinds, from the traditional mystery as written by Charlotte MacLeod and Lilian Jackson Braun, to the serial killer novels of Thomas Harris and Jim Thompson." The contents: American mysteries; traditional mysteries; the Black detective; religious mysteries; private eye mysteries; gay mysteries; British mysteries; dark suspense; women's suspense; police procedurals; hard-boiled mysteries;

thrillers and other mysteries; young adult mysteries; short stories; true crime mysteries; the writing life; fandom; television mysteries; comic books; nostalgia; organizations; and mystery bookstores. Illustrations are plentiful, and the volume concludes with a well-done author-title index.

At their lengthiest, the chapters contain significant essays, interviews, discussions, and appreciations. The sections on American mysteries and traditional mysteries, for example, contain 17 and 22 different subsections, respectively. On the other hand, the section devoted to the Black detective contains only an essay on "Chester Himes and the Black Experience" and a bibliography; and the chapters devoted to dark suspense, women's suspense, thrillers and other mysteries, young adult mysteries, and true crime mysteries contain but three sections apiece. The quality of the essays occasionally varies, but the contributors include Robert Bloch, Lawrence Block, Jon Breen, Simon Brett, Dorothy Cannell, Dorothy Salisbury Davis, Carolyn G. Hart, Joan Hess, Edward D. Hoch, H. R. F. Keating, Stephen King, John D. MacDonald, Charlotte MacLeod, Margaret Maron, Warren Murphy, Joan Lowery Nixon, Nancy Pickard, Bill Pronzini, and Margaret Yorke, and all entries have the virtue of being lively and readable.

On the debit side, there are some notable omissions. Homage is repeatedly paid to the hard-boiled masters, and the pulp magazine *Black Mask* is mentioned a few times, but almost nothing is said about the pulps per se. Furthermore, the focus is almost exclusively on Anglo-American mystery writers, with little said about mysteries and mystery writers from other cultures and traditions.

These complaints aside, the considerable strengths of *The Fine Art of Murder* far outweigh its weaknesses. It is a volume that will have something for most people.

16. Granovetter, Pamela. **The Copperfield Checklist of Mystery Authors: The Complete Crime Works of 100 Distinguished Writers of Mystery and Detective Fiction**. New York: Copperfield Press, 1987. 128 p. Paperback. (Copperfield Collection, vol. 1). ISBN 0-9617037-1-7.

17. McCallum, Karen Thomas, and Pamela Granovetter. **The Copperfield Checklist of Mystery Authors: The Complete Crime Works of 100 Distinguished Writers of Mystery and Detective Fiction**. 2d ed. New York: Copperfield Press, 1990. 160 p. Paperback. (Copperfield Collection, vol. 2). ISBN 0-9617037-1-7.

Intended as a checklist for the collector and reader rather than as a bibliography for the scholar, this slim volume lists the novels written by 100 of the most notable detective and mystery writers. Arrangement is alphabetical by the author's name; the book titles are listed chronologically beneath the name. Publication data include only the date of the first edition; the publisher is not given. Next to each title are three boxes that readers can check to indicate whether they have read the book, own the book, or are uncertain. Omnibuses and collections of shorter works are included, as are (often) the contents of omnibuses. References to known alternate titles, lists of pseudonyms, and books where the writer was a contributing author are given; award-winning titles are noted with a star. Uncollected short stories, the titles of individual short stories in collections, contributions to anthologies, edited works, and nonfiction titles are not given. Concluding the volume are blank pages for addenda and a directory of specialty dealers. The 2d edition updates all data through 1991.

Lovers and collectors of mystery and detective fiction will appreciate this checklist. It is portable, clearly arranged, and designed for use. Additional editions are anticipated.

18. Gribbin, Lenore S. **The Case of the Missing Detective Stories: A List of Books Desired in the Detective Fiction Collection of the University of North Carolina Library**. Chapel Hill, NC: University of North Carolina Library, 1966. [iv], 135 p. Paperback.

Despite its title, this is not merely a list of the books that the library at the University of North Carolina desired. It is, instead, a checklist of the first English and American editions of the fiction of 60 of the most significant writers of mystery and detective fiction. The list is arranged alphabetically by subject's name, given in capitals and often accompanied by dates of birth and death. The titles are listed alphabetically beneath the subject's name, each title accompanied by the place of publication, publisher, year of publication, and pagination; there are separate entries for British and American editions. The University of North Carolina's Library's holdings (as of 1966) are indicated with an unobtrusive asterisk. On the debit side, retitlings have not always been caught, and edited works have not been included.

Had this list been widely distributed, it could have been a significant reference work. It is now a historical document.

19. Grost, Michael E. **A Guide to Classic Mystery and Detection**. http:// members.gnn.com/MGrost/classics.htm

Grost describes his website as "an educational site containing reading lists and essays on great mysteries, mainly of the pre 1960 era." It is this and far more besides, for he has provided a guide that links hundreds of writers and their books by genre. The discussion begins with nineteenth-century mystery fiction and links to the writers and genres. There are sections and links devoted to turn-of-the-century mystery fiction and its writers and genres; Golden Age writers and genres; noted pulp fiction writers and genres; contemporary mystery fiction writers and genres; and general discussions of the canons of mystery fiction and observations on mystery writers. Subsections are used in the discussion of Golden Age writers, which has separate discussions of the groups in what Grost terms "the Intuitionist School," "the Van Dine School," "the Realist School," and "the Bailey School." Grost's bibliographic data are based on his readings rather than comprehensive lists, he provides no illustrations, and his prose occasionally flags, but his site nevertheless is an excellent guide to significant publications.

20. Haycraft, Howard, ed. **The Art of the Mystery Story: A Collection of Critical Essays**. New York: Simon & Schuster, 1946. ix, 545 p. LC 47-30017.

21. Haycraft, Howard, ed. **The Art of the Mystery Story: A Collection of Critical Essays**. New ed. New York: Biblo and Tannen, 1976. ix, 565 p. Index. LC 75-28263. ISBN 0-8196-0289-2.

Neither this collection of essays nor Haycraft's earlier *Murder for Pleasure* (q.v.) is, strictly speaking, a reference book akin to the other reference books in this section. Nevertheless, *The Art of the Mystery Story* is a landmark work, for it established not only that serious criticism could be written about what had hitherto been largely dismissed as a substandard literary genre, but also that critical standards could be applied to works in this genre, and that many of these works could withstand this critical scrutiny.

The Art of the Mystery Story contains eight sections and, in all, 53 chapters, several of which were written specially for Haycraft. The first section, "Mystery Matures: The Higher Criticism," consists of generally appreciative eight essays by important critics and writers: G. K. Chesterton, R. Austin Freeman, Dorothy L. Sayers, Marjorie Nicolson, H. Douglas Thomson, Vincent Starrett, and Haycraft himself.

The second section, "The Rules of the Game," reprints S. S. Van Dine's "Twenty Rules for Writing Detective Stories," Ronald A. Knox's "Detective Story Decalogue," and the semihumorous oath of The Detection Club. Lighthearted though these rules are, they nevertheless successfully criticize the way in which too many detective and mystery stories are written.

The third section, "Care and Feeding of the Whodunit," contains work by Erle Stanley Gardner, Dorothy Sayers, Raymond Chandler, Craig Rice, Anthony Boucher, James Sandoe, John Dickson Carr, and Ken Crossen, among others. These authors discuss what Haycraft terms "the craft of mystery fiction," and not only is their prose eminently readable, their conclusions are magisterial.

The fourth section, "The Lighter Side of Crime," contains poems by Ogden Nash and Richard Armour and reprints, among others, "Watson Was a Woman," Rex Stout's classic piece of silliness; Stephen Leacock's "Murder at $2.50 a Crime"; and Ben Hecht's "The Whistling Corpse." Other works in this section are by S. S. Veendam and Christopher Ward, Robert J. Casey, E. V. Lucas, and Pierre Véry.

The fifth section, "Critics' Corner," consists of discussions by professional critics and reviewers and is, with the possible exception of the third section, the strongest portion of the book. Not only are favorably inclined reviewers included (among them Will Cuppy, Anthony Boucher, Ellery Queen, and Nicholas Blake), but among the critics is Edmund Wilson, whose mordant "Who Cares Who Killed Roger Ackroyd?" remains one of the finest attacks on the genre.

The sixth section, "Detective Fiction vs. Real Life," contains only four articles, but one of them—Dashiell Hammett's delightful "From the Memoirs of a Private Detective"—does much to show that truth is often infinitely stranger, sillier, and more ominous than detective and mystery fiction, for truth need not follow the rational lines of a literary plot. The "Inquest on Detective Stories" by the pseudonymous R. Philmore examines the validity of complicated killings in five recent novels and examines the psychological motives for the fictional crimes.

The seventh section, "Putting Crime on the Shelf," offers an article on collecting detective fiction by John Carter, a historical survey of the detective short story by Ellery Queen, and a lengthy list by James Sandoe of works "designed to sketch the form's history, but even more to gather its excellencies and its varieties in puzzling, literacy, and vigor." Haycraft prefaces Sandoe's presentation with a lengthy essay, offering support for and disagreement with Sandoe's choices.

The concluding section, "Watchman, What of the Night?" contains predictions for the future of the detective and mystery story written by novelist Harrison R. Steeves, critic Philip Van Doren Stern, and Haycraft.

Despite its age, this work belongs in all libraries. The new edition has an introduction by Robin W. Winks. Later editions are indexed.

22. Haycraft, Howard. **Murder for Pleasure: The Life and Times of the Detective Story**. New York: D. Appleton-Century, 1941. xviii, 409 p. Index. LC 41-16907.

23. Haycraft, Howard. **Murder for Pleasure: The Life and Times of the Detective Story**. Newly enlarged and revised ed., with **Notes on Additions to a Cornerstone Library** and **The Haycraft-Queen Definitive Library of Detective-Crime-Mystery Fiction**. New York: Biblo and Tannen, 1968. xviii, [14], 409 p. Index. LC 68-25809. ISBN 0-8196-0216-7.

Neither general histories nor collections of miscellaneous essays have been included in this section, but exceptions have been made for this book and for Haycraft's later *The Art of the Mystery Story* (above). *Murder for Pleasure* is not the first book-length study of the genre, but it is the work that defined the genre, showing that it was a genuine form of literature and that its history and development were worthy of criticism and study. The 1974 edition contains the additional information promised by its title, and it moves to the end of the volume the illustrations that formerly accompanied the text.

For the first half of the book, Haycraft's approach is essentially historical. His coverage begins with the 1841 appearance of Poe's "The Murders in the Rue Morgue" and concludes with appreciative discussions of his significant numerous British and American contemporaries. Many of the writers he discusses are now forgotten, but few of his judgments have been seriously challenged or overruled.

The second part of *Murder for Pleasure* is more thematic in approach. Haycraft formulates the (hitherto largely unwritten) rules for writing a detective story, explaining structures and sources, the need for unity, the creation of the detective, whether there is a need for a sidekick, the viewpoint from which the story should be written, and so forth. In addition, he provides a lengthy list of the criticism written about the detective story, with separate sections for material in books and magazines, and he provides a briefer but still important list of significant books. Finally, he discusses the probable future of the detective story, offers a still-challenging quiz, and provides a "who's who in detection" (i.e., an alphabetical list of the detectives, sidekicks, and antagonists paired with their creators).

Many histories have since been written, but this one belongs in all libraries.

24. Keating, H. R. F. **The Bedside Companion to Crime**. London: O'Mara, 1989. 192 p. Index. GB-35501. ISBN 0-94839753-5. First American edition: New York: Mysterious Press, 1989. 192 p. Index. LC 89-43167. ISBN 0-89296-416-2.

Noted crime writer and critic Keating maintains that it is for enjoyment that people read crime fiction versus fiction with crime in it. In this sense of enjoyment—and to defend a genre that he sees as being attacked by people who want to make crime fiction into something it is not—he has assembled *The Bedside Companion to Crime*. It contains 11 chapters, their numbering beginning with 10 and counting down to 0. Numerous sidebars and rare photographs are present throughout.

The first chapter, "10 Little—Well, Ten Little Whats?" discusses Agatha Christie titles that were changed upon republication in America: *And Then There Were None* began its life as *Ten Little Niggers* and has also been titled *Ten Little Indians; The Sittaford Mystery* became *The Murder at Hazlemoor*, and so forth. "9 Sly Glances" discusses, among other topics, dull books ("dull, nicely dull, books are what we the reading public want for a great deal of the time"), round-robin novels, Keating's own errors, 20 great crooks, and some prolific authors (Leonard Gribble, Erle Stanley Gardner, Edgar Wallace, Leslie Charteris, Rex Stout, and John Creasey). "8 Kinds of Criminosity" surveys the genres that dominate mystery and detective fiction. "7 Songsters Singing" presents verse, in order of diminishing quality, by W. H. Auden, Ogden Nash, Reginald Hill, Julian Symons, John Heath Stubbs, Gawain Ewart, and Roger Woddis (whose "A Hell of a Writer" states that "The world has cause to celebrate / That day in 1888 / When Raymond Chandler was born"). "6 Beginnings" discusses the early careers of six writers. "5 Favourites" provides appreciations of five classic novels: *The Moonstone, The Hound of the Baskervilles, The Maltese Falcon, The Talented Mr. Ripley*, and *A Taste for Death*. "4 Good Old Boys" profiles R. Austin Freeman, Melville Davisson Post, Edgar Wallace, and Jacques Futrelle, whereas "3 Good Old Girls" profiles Mary Roberts Rinehart, Gladys Mitchell, and Margery Allingham. "2 into One" discusses the collaborative efforts behind Ellery Queen and Emma Lathen; and "1 Fearful Yellow" surveys the works of John D. MacDonald. The last chapter, "And Then There Were None," brings the companion full circle, analyzing the form and structure of the Agatha Christie novel. An excellent index concludes.

Whether or not this volume can be considered a reference book is debatable, but it shares the same spirit as Dilys Winn's *Murder Ink* and *Murderess Ink* (q.q.v.), and Keating's intelligence, literacy, and wit make it thoroughly enjoyable.

25. Keating, H. R. F. [ed.]. **Whodunit? A Guide to Crime, Suspense and Spy Fiction**. London: Windward, 1982. 320 p. Index. ISBN 0-711202-29-4. New York: Van Nostrand Reinhold, 1982. 320 p. Index. LC 82-8616. ISBN 0-442-25438-5.

With assistance from 22 leading novelists and critics, Keating has assembled one of the most enjoyable reader's guides, a volume that offers historical essays, critical discussions of genres, biocritical data on noted writers and their books, and information on some important characters in mystery, detective, and suspense fiction. The volume is illustrated throughout with pictures of authors, actors, manuscript pages, and renderings of noted characters.

Keating's introduction discusses the differences between crime fiction, crime fact, and mainstream fiction. The first section, "Crime Fiction and Its Categories," consists of essays from writers surveying the history and genres of detective and mystery fiction. Reginald Hill provides a pre-history of the detective story. Keating writes on "The Godfather and the Father"; Robert Barnard, on "The English Detective Story"; Julian Symons, on "The American Detective Story"; Hillary Waugh, on "The American Police Procedural"; Michael Gilbert, on "The British Police Procedural"; Eleanor Sullivan, on "The Short Story"; Jessica Mann, on "The Suspense Novel"; Jerry Palmer, on "The Thriller"; Michele Slung, on "The Gothic"; and John Gardner, on "The Espionage Novel." All writers are excellent as well as experts in their fields; their essays are brief and insightful, though not completely free from error. Symons, for example, states that "*Red Harvest* is the only Continental Op novel," neglecting *The Dain Curse*.

The second section, "How I Write My Books," is autobiographical, with statements from Stanley Ellin, P. D. James, Desmond Bagley, Dorothy Eden, Patricia Highsmith, Gregory McDonald, Lionel Davidson, Len Deighton, Eric Ambler, and H. R. F. Keating. Brief though these essays are, they nevertheless reveal unexpected similarities; for example, Ambler and McDonald make virtually identical statements regarding the importance of the Idea.

The third section, "Writers and Their Books: A Consumers' Guide," is the lengthiest. Written by Keating, Dorothy B. Hughes, Melvyn Barnes, and Reginald Hill, it provides biographical data on some 500 (predominantly) Anglo-American writers of some 1,500 books. Listed beneath each author are the titles of representative books "recommended as an introduction to the author in question." The characterization, plot, readability, and tension of each book are separately rated, with up to 10 stars awarded for each. This awkward rating system is unintentionally made more difficult by the small size of the stars. Furthermore, though one can argue about the choice of subjects and representative books—Jacques Futrelle is represented only by a 1973 collection, Robert Van Gulik by only *Necklace and Calabash*—the rankings are the most objectionable. One senses that the coauthors did not talk much among themselves, or else they would not have let *Arthur Reeve's The Poisoned Pen* rank higher in tension than Ruth Rendell's *Put on by Cunning*; nor would they have woefully undervalued R. Austin Freeman's tension, overrated Carter Brown's tension and readability, and similarly overrated the characterizations of Mary Higgins Clark. Nor is this section error-free. *Rogue Male* was not Geoffrey Household's second book; the first name of Fredric Brown is misspelled; and so forth.

Keating is sole author of the fourth section, "The People of Crime Fiction," an illustrated guide to 90 of the best-known detectives and criminal figures, from "Abner, Uncle" to "Wolfe, Nero." Each character is briefly and wittily described; each entry concludes with the name of the character's creator. The brief concluding section is by Philip Graham, Professor of Child Psychiatry at the Institute of Child Health, London, and Consultant Psychiatrist at the Hospital for Sick Children, Great Ormond Street. He attempts to address the subject of "Why People Read Crime Fiction." His theories, which involve releases of childhood fantasies and compulsive personalities, are debatable.

Despite the occasional errors and the weak final section, this is one of the better reader's guides. The concluding index is excellent.

26. la Cour, Tage, and Harald Mogensen. **The Murder Book: An Illustrated History of the Detective Story**. Foreword by Julian Symons. New York: Herder and Herder, 1971. 192 p. Index. LC 71-150304.

Originally published as *Mordbogen* (Copenhagen: Lademann Forlagsaktieselskab, 1969), this is far more than the coffee-table book it initially resembles. It is, instead, a well-illustrated history of the detective story, from Edgar Allan Poe to Georges Simenon. What makes it intriguing is that it is written from a Danish perspective. Many of its illustrations are by Scandinavian artists, and a number of its references are to English and European writers who have been either ignored or neglected by American historians. The foreword is by Julian Symons. The text is full of informed and intriguing commentary; Israel Zangwill, for example, "was the first writer to put a living personality into his book—no less a person, in fact, than Mr. Gladstone, the Prime Minister." The book concludes with a thoroughly international bibliography and a well-done index. Only slightly dated, this work remains relevant and enjoyable.

27. McLeish, Kenneth, and Valerie McLeish. **Bloomsbury Good Reading Guide to Murder, Crime Fiction, and Thrillers**. London: Bloomsbury, 1990. ix, 200 p. Paperback. Indexes. ISBN 0-7475-0732-5.

The first section of this guide describes the work of some 250 crime, thriller, and espionage writers, the majority of whom are from Great Britain or America. Arranged alphabetically by writer, each entry has the writer's birth year and nationality and provides a mildly critical but generally appreciative statement about the writer's oeuvre. Often an exemplary work is described in slightly more depth, though bibliographic data are generally confined to the book's title and its year of publication. Cross-references abound, and sidebars beside each author list other books by that author and related books by other authors. Some 66 "special menus" scattered throughout the book list authors and titles by genres ranging alphabetically from "The Art of Crime" to "War Stories" and including such diverse subject as "Big Money," "Christmas," "Filthy Rich," "Houses," "Junk Bonds," "Pensioners," "Special Skills Required," and "Unusual Locations." Following the first section, a two-page glossary defines eight related terms, and a "Who's Who" lists the name of the character and the name of his or her creator. The volume concludes with a capably done author/title index.

The contents of this guide were chosen because they reflected the enthusiasms of the McLeishes, and one cannot fault them for that. One can, however, argue that they should have cast their nets wider. A guide to good reading that mentions Michael Avallone and Tom Clancy but neglects Fredric Brown, R. Austin Freeman, Sue Grafton, Faye Kelleman, and Phoebe Atwood Taylor (to name but a few) cannot be considered definitive.

28. Mackler, Tasha. **Murder . . . by Category: A Subject Guide to Mystery Fiction**. Metuchen, NJ: Scarecrow Press, 1991. xiii, 470 p. LC 91-37638. ISBN 0-8108-2463-9.

Like Menendez and Olderr (q.q.v.), Mackler has compiled a subject index to mystery fiction; unlike them, she has annotated her bibliography, confining her focus "to mystery stories that are readily available as recently-released hardcovers and paperbacks, or as titles kept on a publisher's backlist." Mackler thus classifies and annotates approximately 2,400 titles, using subject headings ranging alphabetically from "Academics" to "Writers and Their Conventions." Geographic locations (Africa, Americans in England, Canada, Hollywood, etc.) are referenced, and Mackler's 80 subjects include "Anthropology and Archaeology," "Corruption," "Espionage, the Industrial Kind," "Libraries," "Manuscripts," "Old Crimes and Murders," "Psychics, with a Touch of Magic," "Suicide or Murder," and "Witches, Curses, and a Little Voodoo." Each citation provides publication data for the book's first hardcover and paperback editions; entries for paperback originals are distinguished by "PBO." Entries for books featuring series characters are numbered ("1st," "2nd," "3rd," etc.). Books that can be classified into more than one subject are cross-referenced, with the primary entry listing the secondary subject; the secondary subject references the primary entry. Concluding the volume are a list of British women mystery writers; a lengthier list of female detectives who are series characters; lists of the Edgar, Anthony, and Shamus Awards winners up to 1989; a brief bibliography; and an author index.

On the debit side, this volume is not error-free. Susan Moody's *Penny Black* and *Penny Dreadful* are both listed as the second volume in the Penny Wanawake series, and additional errors are readily discernible. Furthermore, Mackler's citations are occasionally frustrating in their use of cross-references, and she is often inconsistent in her revelation of pseudonyms. Reference is made to Erle Stanley Gardner writing as A. A. Fair, but a user knowing of only A. A. Fair will find no linking cross-reference because references to Fair occur only under Gardner. Similarly, nowhere is it stated that Barbara Michaels and Elizabeth Peters are the same person, and although the work cites titles by writers such as Ellis Peters and Dell Shannon, their real names are not listed. Most annoying, there is no title index.

These problems do not prevent the contents of this volume from being accessible, and that Mackler chose to annotate only recently published and generally available titles is simultaneously one of this book's major strengths and weaknesses. She provides contemporary readers with a readily accessible list of books, but a few years hence, the majority of Mackler's entries are likely to be utterly unobtainable, and this bibliography will be primarily of historical value.

29. Magill, Frank N., ed. **Critical Survey of Mystery and Detective Fiction**. Pasadena, CA: Salem Press, 1988. 4 vols. xii, 1,748, xliv p. Index. LC 88-28566. ISBN 0-89356-486-9 (set).

Critical Survey of Mystery and Detective Fiction provides biocritical surveys of the lives and prose of more than 270 authors chosen because they pioneered the development of the detective and mystery story, because they did their most notable work in the genre, or because they contributed to the genre while having significant reputations in fields of other literary endeavor. This last criterion is a dubious one, allowing for the inclusion of such figures as Arnold Bennett, Jorge Luis Borges, Fyodor Dostoevski, William Faulkner, W. W. Jacobs, Stephen King, and Frank R. Stockton. Also included are critical surveys of writers of gothic fiction, espionage fiction, the police procedural, the psychological thriller, the hard-boiled story, and the romantic suspense story.

The four volumes are arranged alphabetically by the subject's last name. Each article begins with ready-reference information that provides the subject's name, birth and death places and dates, notable pseudonyms, types of plot most commonly used, and the name of the author's principal series. This is followed by a section describing the principal series character(s). The next section provides a critical statement of no more than 200 words, detailing the subject's contribution to the genre; it is followed by a brief biography of the author that is also rarely more than 200 words. A section titled "Analysis" provides descriptions of the author's major contributions to the genre, the focus being (more often than not) on plot summary rather than criticism. Entries conclude with separate sections listing the subject's principal mystery and detective books, other major works, and a brief bibliography of secondary sources. All entries are signed; few are more than 2,500 words in length, though writers of exceptional importance warrant longer entries; and the entry format described above is not followed in the case of such writers as Ellery Queen and Nick Carter, whose names have "served as house names for a shifting and sometimes large number of authors." The fourth volume concludes with a glossary of mystery/detective terms, indexes for the plot genres and series characters, and a general author/title index.

The *Critical Survey* will satisfy most high school students and undergraduates, but its four volumes are far from flawless. One may object to an editorial approach that accords entries to such noninfluences as Dean Koontz but neglects such historical figures as T. S. Stribling and Carolyn Wells. The articles tend to overpraise their subjects, providing appreciations rather than analyses, and there are errors in the plot summaries that are sometimes significant. On occasion, the analyses focus exclusively on one series and neglect more worthy publications. The bibliographic data list only titles and dates of publication, and these are presented as a group; even if the author has written under a pseudonym or in collaboration, these publications are not separately identified. For example, the entry for Leslie Charteris states that "Charteris often contented himself with polishing and giving final approval to a story written largely by someone else," but one cannot locate these stories in this set. Finally, the glossary is woefully inadequate, failing to define even such basic terms as "cosy" and erring in its definition of such terms as "gunsel" and "hard-boiled."

30. Menendez, Albert J. **The Subject Is Murder: A Selective Subject Guide to Mystery Fiction. Volume 1.** New York: Garland, 1986. x, 332 p. Index. (Garland Reference Library of the Humanities, vol. 627). LC 85-45134. ISBN 0-8240-8655-4.

31. Menendez, Albert J. **The Subject Is Murder: A Selective Subject Guide to Mystery Fiction. Volume 2.** New York: Garland, 1990. x, 216 p. Index. (Garland Reference Library of the Humanities, vol. 1060). LC 85-45134. ISBN 0-8240-2580-6.

Recognizing that people collect, read, and sell mystery and detective fiction by the book's perceived subject, Menendez offers subject access to nearly 6,000 mystery and detective novels. More than 3,800 books are classified in the first volume, and nearly 2,100 are classed in the second. In the first volume, 25 subject classifications are used; the second volume uses 29, with subclassifications in such areas as "sports and hobbies," in which 25 subcategories have been identified. Both volumes are arranged alphabetically by the subject heading, with the citations listed alphabetically by author's name. Both volumes number their citations, which provide title, place of publication, publisher, and year of publication; both conclude with an index to the authors. The first volume, however, includes a list of stores specializing in detective and mystery fiction, whereas the second volume drops the list, provides a statistical ranking of books "by category," a cross-reference index to the first volume, and a title index. Neither volume identifies pseudonyms or offers internal cross-references.

There is a need for subject access to mystery fiction, but at best these volumes can be considered a beginning, for Menendez's subject headings are inadequate. Worse yet, each book is indexed only once. A reader thus hoping to find mysteries featuring cats (or dogs or pets) will find some of Lillian Jackson Braun's "Cat" volumes listed under "Journalism" and others classed under "Art," "Antiques," and "Christmas," but there is no subject access to Braun's most notable and recurring narrative device. Similarly, although Menendez's subjects include "Circuses and Carnivals," "Cooking," "Hotels and Inns," "Musical Murders," "Politics and Murder," and "Weddings and Honeymoons," those novels that use female detectives cannot be located, for there is no listing for "Women Detectives" (or any variant term). Finally, Menendez's classifications are occasionally erroneous. Why has he classed R. Austin Freeman's *The Uttermost Farthing* as an archaeological mystery? The story involves a doctor hunting for the murderer of his wife, a hunt that has the doctor capturing burglars and anarchists, shrinking their heads according to the best Mundurucús recipes, and mounting their skeletons in his personal museum. Archaeology plays no role in this gleefully black-humored novel.

A revised, expanded, and corrected edition of these volumes is needed.

32. Moody, Susan, ed. **The Hatchards Crime Companion: 100 Top Crime Novels Selected by the Crime Writers' Association**. London: Hatchards, 1990. xvii, 153 p. Paperback. GB 90-42224. ISBN 0-904030-02-4.

During the late 1980s, the Crime Writers' Association (CWA) of England voted on what they considered to be the 100 top crime novels of all time. The annotated list of their rankings occupies approximately the first third of this volume. The list begins with Josephine Tey's *Daughter of Time* and concludes with Edgar Wallace's *Four Just Men*; it includes such familiar names as Raymond Chandler, Dashiell Hammett, Dorothy Sayers, and P. D. James, but there are also some surprises. The CWA took a very broad view of their charge, and browsers of this section will find such titles as Richard Condon's *The Manchurian Candidate* and John Fowles's *The Collector*. The bibliographic data are limited, however; apart from the author, title, and publication year, the only information provided is the availability of a paperback or hardcover edition. Printed as sidebars throughout the annotated list are supplementary lists of the CWA's favorite male and female writers and favorite male and female detectives.

The second section consists of 10 essays that provide guides to the different genres of detective and mystery fiction, and the third section contains four essays on the nature of a good crime book. All the essays provide excellent introductions to their subjects; none will surprise anybody who has read substantially. The fourth and concluding section to the volume provides information about the CWA. A history is provided, as is an extensive list of the volumes that have won the awards issued by the Association: the Crossed Red Herrings Award, the Gold Dagger, the Silver Dagger, and the Diamond Dagger.

Despite its breeziness, this volume is inferior in organization and content to such "best of" lists as Maxim Jakubowsky's *100 Great Detectives* (q.v.). Nowhere does Moody provide simple alphabetical lists of the authors, titles, or detectives. The annotations are brief and not particularly insightful, and the volume is unindexed. Were it not for its information on the CWA and its distinguished awards, this book would be without value.

33. Olderr, Steven. **Mystery Index: Subjects, Settings, and Sleuths of 10,000 Titles**. Chicago: American Library Association, 1987. xiv, 492 p. LC 87-1294. ISBN 0-8389-0461-0.

Public librarian Olderr has indexed the authors, titles, detectives, subjects, and settings of approximately 10,000 British and American detective and mystery books. Why these and not others were selected for indexing is stated in neither Olderr's preface nor his acknowledgments, although many, if not all, of the books apparently came from the collections of the Riverside (Illinois) Public Library, Olderr's place of employment. The index is clearly reproduced from typed copy and is easy to use, but in its presentation of data and in its principles of compilation, this is an eccentric book, one for which every statement must be qualified.

A "Main Entry Section" lists the books by their author and also gives title, publisher, and date of publication. If the UK edition has a different title or publisher or both, these are provided. Each citation concludes with the name of the detective or the prime characters; a number after the character's name indicates the order of the character's appearance in a series. Although this material is not error-free, the worst problem with this section is that Olderr opted to index by only American titles, regardless of author's nationality or publication precedence, and did not include cross-references. In the case of prolific writers, this decision means that uncertain users must check the title index, for Olderr's lists are difficult to browse.

The title index lists all titles and retitlings, but it does not state which title the book has been indexed under, and occasionally it indexes titles that are nowhere present in the main entry section. A user curious about Agatha Christie's novel that began life as *Ten Little Niggers* will find an entry for that title, preceded by an entry for *Ten Little Indians*, but neither references the title under which the book has been indexed (*And Then There Were None*), and the entry for *And Then There Were None* does not mention *Ten Little Indians*.

The subject and setting index and the character index conclude the volume. The former is perhaps the best part of the book: The subject headings are well chosen and offer access to the novels by terms as varied and intriguing as "Burglars as Detectives," "Camels," "Postal Inspectors as Detectives," "Transsexuals," and "Witch Doctors as Detectives." The settings range alphabetically from the Adirondack Mountains to Zanzibar. There are numerous helpful cross-references. The character index lists the detectives by their last names, also giving the author. When the author used more than one detective or main character, individual titles are also given. Useful though this section could be, Olderr has been inconsistent in his indexing of detectives and main characters. Series detectives may be listed, but series narrators—those who observe and report on the activities of the detective—are not, with the exception of John Watson, MD. The researcher hoping to find the R. Austin Freeman stories narrated by Jervis, or Hercule Poirot stories narrated by somebody other than Hastings, will be thoroughly frustrated, for although these characters have the force, if not the status, of main characters, they (and thousands of other narrators) are nowhere mentioned.

If all Olderr offered were indexes by author, title, and detective, this flawed volume would have been thoroughly superseded by Hubin's monumental achievements (q.v.). Olderr's indexing of subjects and settings, however, is far superior to that offered by Hubin, and until such time as a superior subject and setting index is compiled for detective and mystery fiction, this book remains a necessary acquisition.

34. Ousby, Ian. **Guilty Parties: A Mystery Lover's Companion**. New York: Thames & Hudson, 1997. 224 p. Paperback. Index. LC 97-60242. ISBN 0-500-27978-0.

The title page of this lavishly illustrated guide states that it contains 195 illustrations, 31 in color. Indeed, the illustrations dominate the volume, which is in many ways reminiscent of la Cour and Mogensen's *Murder Book, Murder Ink* and *Murderess Ink* edited by Dilys Winn, and Waltraud Woeller and Bruce Cassiday's *The Literature of Crime and Detection* (q.q.v.).

Ousby's history is frequently gracefully written, but it is not without its share of factual errors. His discussion of the pulp magazines, for example, opens by stating that pulp magazines began "in the 1880s," that they sold largely by subscription, that their pages were gray, that Dr. Fu-Manchu was a creation of the dime novel, that the pulp series character the Shadow was Lamont Cranston, and that Dashiell Hammett first appeared in *Black Mask* in 1923: errors all. Similar errors exist throughout. Equally seriously, Ousby's history is unbalanced, mentioning such historically important writers as Edgar Wallace only in passing.

The reference material given by Ousby includes lists of material about Sherlock Holmes; Locked Room mysteries; Ronald Knox's 1929 "Ten Commandments"; mysteries set at Oxford, Cambridge, and Harvard; books about Agatha Christie; the first and last appearances of Golden Age detectives; a brief "hard-boiled" dictionary; books and movies about Simenon and Maigret; films connected with crime and mystery fiction; and notable women writers. A map of the United States indicates settings of private eye novels; sad to say, Ousby can find only one Philadelphia private eye. The volume concludes with lists of award-winning detective and mystery fiction produced in the United States, United Kingdom, and France. There are a brief and inadequate bibliography of secondary sources, a historical chronology, and a well-done index.

Though *Guilty Parties* is amiable, it is not the book it could and should have been. Ousby's *Bloodhounds of Heaven* (1976) shows that he is capable of superior work.

35. Pronzini, Bill. **Gun in Cheek: A Study of "Alternative" Crime Fiction**. Introduction by Ed McBain. New York: Coward, McGann & Geoghegan, 1982. 264 p. Index. LC 82-5172. ISBN 0-698-11180-X.

The majority of the reader's guides in this section list and describe the best writers and writings, but as Ed McBain's introduction makes immediately clear, this is not one of them. Pronzini's desire is to survey the truly terrible mysteries written by unashamedly bad writers, for these works have been neglected by both academics and aficionados. McBain cheerfully provides stultifying excerpts from his earlier works that Pronzini should have included (but did not). Pronzini's survey ranges wide, providing summaries of plots that should never have been hatched, samples of dialogue that should not have been written (and could not have been spoken), descriptions of behavior patterns that are improbable (and inimitable), and attitudes and approaches toward subjects that are perhaps best described as "politically incorrect." One chapter, "The Saga of the Risen Phoenix," assays the entire output of the low-budget Phoenix House, because "in less than twenty years, Phoenix published almost as many wonderfully bad novels as *all* the other publishers combined."

As in any guide, opinions are paramount and disagreements with them are inevitable. Pronzini is quite correct in stating that "what makes [William] Le Queux a classicist are his often-farfetched plots, his ability to pad them out interminably with description and repetitive conversation, and his unsurpassed ear for stilted dialogue." Pronzini is equally correct in damning Sydney Horler and Mickey Spillane (among others) for meretricious attitudes, impossible plotting, and generally poor writing. On the other hand, it is unfair to Michael Avallone, Robert Leslie Bellem, Carter Brown, and Richard Prather to include them here. All have styles uniquely their own and are in many ways self-parodic; indeed, critics such as S. J. Perelman recognized that Bellem's prose was unique, a cheerfully ribald parodying of all the pretensions and conventions of a genre. Avallone's mangling of metaphors and improbable plots and Prather's perpetual descriptions of tumescence (and equally improbable plots) are good-humored, lightweight, and intentionally silly.

Nor, alas, is *Gun in Cheek* free from error. In opening his discussion of the amateur detective ("AD"), Pronzini states that "beginning with Jacques Futrelle's Professor F. X. Van Duesen [sic], 'The Thinking Machine,' in this country, and, somewhat later, Chesterton's Father Brown in England, the AD has seen more bloodletting, faced more peril, and unraveled more mysteries than all professional detectives in public and private, combined." Futrelle most certainly did not invent the amateur detective, and the character of the Thinking Machine did not engage in physical activity but epitomizes the armchair detective. Nor (as Pronzini states elsewhere) was writer Tom Roan from Alabama; Pronzini undoubtedly meant Arizona.

Though these errors are jarring, they do not inhibit the pleasures of this book. Pronzini's first chapter states that "the purpose of this book is threefold: first, to rectify the neglect of these writers and their books, to give them the critical attention they deserve; second, to provide a different historical perspective on crime fiction—its detectives, its genres, its publishers—and on the social attitudes it reflects (which are often more pronounced in the bad mystery than in the good one); and third, to add a few chuckles—perhaps even a guffaw or two—to the heretofore sobersided field of mystery criticism." In all of these, he succeeds admirably.

36. Pronzini, Bill. **Son of Gun in Cheek**. New York: Mysterious Press, 1987. x, 229 p. Index. LC 87-7872. ISBN 0-89286-287-3.

A compilation in the same vein as *Gun in Cheek* (q.v.), this gleeful celebration of bad writing examines the output of Harry Stephen Keeler and works by

Sydney Horler, Anthony Rud, Murray Leinster, Peter C. Herring, Michael Avallone, and Arnold Grisman, to name but a few. The overwrought blurbs used to
promote these books are examined ("loaded to the gunwale with superpowered
quake-stuff to make your withers quiver," concludes one gem), and unintentional examples of bad writing by good writers are presented. Finally, as before,
Pronzini examines unintentionally hilarious sex scenes and the output of numerous (deservedly) unsuccessful presses.

The pulp writer Florence Mae Pettee in particular is excoriated. (States
Pronzini, "she seemed to believe that substituting big words for little words,
and/or colorfully offbeat words for common words, was the key to Good Writing.") Pettee's mystery, the 1929 *The Palgrave Mummy*, is described at (hilarious)
length, and a Locked Room mystery, "Death Laughs at Walls," is reprinted in its
entirety from the January 1930 *Detective Classics*. (States Pronzini: "I think I can
guarantee that after you've read it, you'll never again feel quite the same about
either the mystery short story or the English language.")

As before, there are a small number of errors that in no way inhibit the
pleasures given by the book, and as before, one might ask if it is wise to use the
same standards to compare Michael Avallone and Robert Leslie Bellem with
Sydney Horler and "Michael Morgan." Apart from this, *Son of Gun in Cheek*
should be read and enjoyed by all.

37.   Pronzini, Bill, and Marcia Muller. **1001 Midnights: The Aficionado's
       Guide to Mystery and Detective Fiction**. New York: Arbor House,
       1986. 879 p. LC 85-30817. ISBN 0-87795-622-7.

The introduction to *1001 Midnights* begins by stating that the book was
written by "aficionados, collectors, and students of this form of popular literature" to "provide other aficionados, collectors, as well as casual and new readers,
with a reference guide to one thousand and one individual titles; to additional
works by their authors; and to books of a similar type (whodunit, thriller, police
procedural, etc.) by other writers." It closes by stating that *1001 Midnights* is a
celebration of a genre, and this latter attitude—celebration—offers the key to
1001 Midnights. Unlike Barzun and Taylor, whose *A Catalogue of Crime* shows no
mercy to those books deemed inadequate, the 28 writers of the 1,001 entries
know how to appreciate the terrible. They realize that without bad books—
books that are "inspired nonsense" (those of Sidney Horler), that feature "creative butchery of the English language through phonetic spellings and some of
the weirdest idioms ever committed to paper" (those of James O'Hanlon), and
that are told through "one of the dullest, most annoying protagonists the genre
has yet produced" (those of H. F. Heard)—there would be no way to identify the
great books. The writers revel in the botched prose of such writers as Michael
Avallone and "Michael Morgan," even as they celebrate the finer efforts by the
genre's better writers.

The 1,001 annotations in *1001 Midnights* are arranged alphabetically by the
subject's name; when the writer is represented by more than one book (as is often the case), the arrangement is alphabetical by title; novels and collections are

represented. Bibliographic data are kept to a minimum, each citation listing only the first American edition (or the first British edition if no American edition exists). In addition, a simple code (e.g., *A* for Action and Adventure; *C* for Comedy; *E* for Espionage; *PP* for Police Procedural) classifies the contents; notable titles and cornerstone titles are identified with one and two asterisks, respectively. The annotations provide a brief plot synopsis and a critical commentary that places the work in the context of the author's other works; all annotations are signed with the initials of their writers. Anglo-American authors predominate, but Georges Simenon is represented, as are Robert van Gulik, Janwillem van de Wetering, and Maj Sjöwall and Per Wahlöö. Citations for translations list only first American publication and do not provide the name of the translator.

Though *1001 Midnights* has a few errors of fact—the entry for "Trevanian," for example, states that it is a pseudonym used by three writers—its most serious flaws lie elsewhere. First, Pronzini and Muller fail to state their basis for inclusions, and a user may well wonder why Robert Bloch's enormously important *Psycho* is mentioned only in passing, whereas *Psycho II* is excoriated at length. And if the deathly prose of Michael Morgan is accorded space, why were the Prince Zaleski stories, the lunatic lapidary creations of M. P. Shiel, neglected? Furthermore, the book lacks a title index, an oversight in a volume that is "a reference guide to one thousand and one individual *titles*." Nevertheless, any library that purchases *A Catalogue of Crime* would do well to locate and purchase the long-out-of-print *1001 Midnights* as a companion; it conveys the joy that comes from reading detective and mystery fiction.

38. Quayle, Eric. **The Collector's Book of Detective Fiction**. Photographs by Gabriel Monro. London: Studio Vista, 1972. 143 p. Index. LC 73-154663. ISBN 0-289-70263-1.

Sometimes listed as a reference work, this affectionate and heavily illustrated guide is reminiscent of Waltraud Woeller and Bruce Cassiday's *The Literature of Crime and Detection* (q.v.) in that it offers a roughly chronological history of the detective story. Where Quayle differs from his successors is that he remains constantly conscious of the financial worth of his books. "[I]t would be difficult to find a sounder financial investment than copies of some of the works I shall describe in the following pages," states Quayle's introduction. The numerous illustrations are taken largely from volumes in his own collection.

The Collector's Book of Detective Fiction is engagingly written and enjoyable reading; its illustrations are often fascinating, though sometimes they do not occur in conjunction with their text. Also on the debit side, Quayle provides no bibliographies apart from citations in his text, and some of his statements are inaccurate (i.e., Quayle states that "most of the 'S. S. Van Dine' tales are melodramatic in the extreme and crammed with the high-speed violence and blood-letting commonly found in American crime novels of this and later periods"). The last section of the book, "Collecting First Editions," warns of "the squirrel instinct," which occurs when "a consuming desire sometimes grips an otherwise quite rational bibliophile: he starts to hoard every edition of every procurable title in the various field of literature in which he maintains an avid interest."

39. Queen, Ellery. **Queen's Quorum: A History of the Detective-Crime Short Story As Revealed by the 106 Most Important Books Published in This Field Since 1845**. Boston: Little, Brown and Company, 1951. ix, 132 p. Index. LC 51-1258.

40. Queen, Ellery. **Queen's Quorum: A History of the Detective-Crime Short Story As Revealed in the 106 Most Important Books Published in This Field Since 1845**. 2d ed. Supplements through 1967. New York: Biblo and Tannen, 1969. ix, 146 p. Index. LC 68-56450.

Probably the most influential annotated bibliography in this section, *Queen's Quorum* began as a list published at the conclusion of *Twentieth Century Detective Stories*, edited by Ellery Queen (Cleveland: World Publishing, 1948.) From June 1949 through July 1950, it was reprinted as a series of columns in *Ellery Queen's Mystery Magazine*, after which it appeared in book form. The column was revived and continued in the November and December 1968 issues of *Ellery Queen's Mystery Magazine*, following which the 2d edition was published. The trivia-minded should note that the subtitle in both editions is in error. In the 1st edition it should be increased by one, for it contains entries numbered 73 and 73a; in the 2d edition, entries 73 and 73a remain, and the number of entries is 125. This annotation concentrates on the 2d edition.

Like many of the bibliographies and readers' guides that succeeded it, *Queen's Quorum* is simultaneously an appreciative history, a bibliographic essay, and an annotated bibliography of the most significant works published in the fields of detective, mystery, suspense, and criminal literature. Though it concentrates predominantly on Anglo-American writers, European writers are not slighted. The volume begins with a chapter titled "The Incunabular Period," which mentions the criminous elements in the works of writers from Cicero through Voltaire, and scattered throughout the bibliography are entries for Gaboriau's *Le Petit Vieux des Batignolles*, Maurice Leblanc's *Arsène Lupin, Gentleman-Cambrioleur*, and Balduin Groller's *Detektiv Dagoberts Taten und Abenteur*.

The annotations begin in the second chapter, "The Founding Father," which cites the 1845 edition of Poe's *Tales*. Thereafter the entries proceed largely chronologically, with chapters titled "The First Fifty Years," "The Doyle Decade," "The First Golden Era," "The Second Golden Era," "The First Moderns," "The Second Moderns," "The Renaissance," "Renaissance and Moderns," and "Renaissance and Moderns Continuing" annotating the most significant literature produced during these times. The last annotation is for Harry Kemelman's *The Nine Mile Walk* (1967), a collection of eight Nicky Welt stories.

Each citation provides publication data for the book's first edition and assigns each a code (H,Q,R,S) that indicates the book's historical significance, its quality (in terms of literary style and originality of plot), and the rarity or scarcity (or both) of the first edition. The annotations vary enormously in content, some being lengthy discussions of the detective, others being equally lengthy discussions of printing history, and still others citing other publications by the author; all are lively and well-written. The 1st edition concluded with a separate "check list" of the *Queen's Quorum* titles and an index merging authors, titles, and characters; the 2d edition maintains the index and checklist but offers separate indexes to the titles and characters listed in the supplement.

Though now somewhat dated, and rather cumbersome in its arrangement, this remains a landmark publication. Some of its conclusions may be debated, but few have been overturned.

41. Rennison, Nick, and Richard Shepard, eds. **Waterstone's Guide to Crime Fiction**. Brentford, England: Waterstone's, 1997. 171 p. Index. Paperback. ISBN 0-9527405-6-7.

In their brief introduction, the editors state that "the aim of the *Waterstone's Guide to Crime Fiction* is, primarily, to offer a generous selection of authors and titles currently available to those readers who enjoy reading novels that fall into the genre, broadly defined, of crime fiction."

The resulting volume lists nearly 200 historical and contemporary detective and mystery writers. Dead writers have their birth and death dates provided; no dates are given for living writers. A brief biocritical discussion of each author's influence, style, and recurrent themes is given, followed by an alphabetical list of their volumes available for sale in the UK; publishers, prices, and ISBNs are listed for approximately 1,400 books. Also present in the *Guide*, and making it more than merely an elaborate bookdealer's catalogue, are interviews with Elmore Leonard and Lawrence Block, articles by Nicholas Blincoe on British hard-boiled fiction and Val McDermid "on the rise of the dyke detective," and an article by Rennison about P. C. Doherty's historical mysteries. Finally, there are numerous illustrations and cover reproductions, and appendixes list winners of the Crime Writers' Association's Gold Dagger Award, significant crime anthologies available at Waterstone's, the authors arranged by 22 subgenres (e.g., pioneers, golden age of English crime fiction, modern British, psychological drama, American classics, contemporary American noir), and a list of the services and locations of the nearest Waterstone's.

Apart from the interviews and articles, the *Guide* has little that is likely to assist American researchers, but it is nevertheless an enjoyable work.

42. Stevenson, W. B. **Detective Fiction: A Reader's Guide**. London: Published for the National Book League by Cambridge University Press, 1949. 20 p. (Readers Guides). Paperback.

Like Julian Symons's list of eight years later (q.v.), this bibliography is hardly more than a pamphlet. Stevenson's bibliography, however, is prefaced with a 10-page introduction that provides a brief but still useful survey of the detective story. Stevenson's annotations are arranged alphabetically, with each citation providing the author's name in regular type, the book's title in capital letters, the publisher of the first edition in italics, and the year of publication in regular type. The annotations tend to be terse, one or two sentences in length. Significant and standard British and American authors are equally represented, though Stevenson's list is varied and includes such largely unfamiliar names as H. C. Branson, Mary Fitt, and David Frome, as well as such surprises as Frances and Richard Lockridge and Phoebe Atwood Taylor. A bibliography of books about detective fiction concludes the pamphlet. Unindexed and now virtually unobtainable, this work could, at one time, be purchased for one shilling.

43. Stilwell, Steven A. **What Mystery Do I Read Next? A Reader's Guide to Recent Mystery Fiction**. Detroit: Gale, 1997. xix, 545 p. Indexes. LC 96-47713. ISBN 0-7876-1592-7.

This is not an original catalogue but the cumulation of the detective and mystery data that appeared as part of the first seven editions of Gale's annual *What Do I Read Next?* Like its parent publication, *What Mystery Do I Read Next?* attempts to serve as a reader's adviser, "pointing the way to the best fiction in the genre published in the 1990s." The volume begins with lists of the winners (since 1990) of the Edgar Allan Poe Awards, the Shamus Awards, the Agatha Awards, the Anthony Awards, and the Macavity Awards. The data in these lists have not been integrated with the entries in the body of the volume.

The 1,799 entries in *What Mystery Do I Read Next?* are arranged alphabetically by author. Each entry is separately numbered, and the data presented include the book's title, place of publication, publisher, date of publication, series name (if any), story type within the genre, names and descriptions of up to three characters in the work, time period of the story, locale, a brief (three or four sentences) plot summary, and a list of up to five books that use similar themes. Pseudonyms and coauthors are identified. A series of indexes provide access to the stories by series name, time period, geographic setting, story type, character name, character description, author, and title. It should be mentioned that the index to story type uses some 16 different genres, ranging from "action/adventure" to "traditional" to classify its fiction; the index to character description includes occupation (actress, librarian, publisher, etc.) as well as plot function (e.g., counselor, cowboy, criminal); and the index to geographic location offers reference not only to countries and continents but also to specific cities and even to imaginary and fictional places.

As with any work of this size, there is much to debate. The public library orientation of the *What Do I Read Next?* series makes this volume perhaps unduly positive about all works described and unnecessarily chatty in its presentation of data. The section for plot summaries is titled "What the Book Is About," and the section offering links to other books is titled "Other Books You Might Like." Similarly, the limitations of the series mean that only works published since 1990 are described, though the books with similar themes are virtually all works from before 1990. Occasionally works that have nothing to do with the genre (e.g., those of Tom Clancy) are referenced and described. (And why describe Sharyn McCrumb's *Zombies of the Gene Pool* without mentioning the first novel in the series, *Bimbos of the Death Sun?*) Finally, there does not appear to have been significant proofreading of the text; readers curious to find works set in the Deep South will be partially disappointed, for the section devoted to Alabama has been dropped from the geographic index.

Public libraries will find *What Mystery Do I Read Next?* a necessary acquisition. Academic libraries supporting studies in popular culture may find that its indexing aids researchers.

44. Symons, Julian. **The Hundred Best Crime Stories**. London: Sunday Times, Kensley House, [1959]. 20 p. GB 59-8761. Paperback.

Though hardly more than a pamphlet, this annotated bibliography provides a solid and occasionally surprising list of the 99 books that Symons—"with the help of distinguished critics and crime novelists, who have contributed lists, made notes on books they admired, and generally helped to enlighten my own ignorance"—considered to be the finest or most representative of their genre. The hundredth volume was chosen by readers of the *Sunday Times*.

Symons's list contains four sections: "The Begetters," "The Age of the Great Detective," "Novels of Action," and "The Modern Crime Novel." The citations in each section are arranged chronologically, with each entry providing the book's title in capitals, year of publication, and publishers and costs of the first English hardcover and paperback editions; translators of such works as Dostoyevski's *Crime and Punishment* are not noted. Symons's annotations are terse but helpful, and the curious reader will find mentioned virtually every significant British and American mystery, detective, or crime story writer from the first century of the genre's existence, plus works by such authors as Arthur Machen and William Faulkner.

What is intriguing about *The Hundred Best Crime Stories* is that there is almost no overlap of contents between it and W. B. Stevenson's similar work of only 10 years earlier (q.v.). Had tastes changed so significantly in such a short time, or was Symons making a conscious attempt to be different from his predecessor? In any event, the work is unindexed and now virtually unobtainable, though at one time additional copies could be had by sending 2s. 10d. to the London *Times*. Its contents have been reprinted in *The Armchair Detective Book of Lists*, edited by Kate Stine (q.v.).

Note: The pamphlet is undated, and the publication date above is taken from that given in *Julian Symons: A Bibliography* (q.v.).

45. Winn, Dilys, et al. **Murder Ink: The Mystery Reader's Companion**. New York: Workman Publishing, 1977. xx, 520 p. Index. LC 77-5282. ISBN 0-89480-003-5 (hc); 0-89480-004-3 (pb).

A bestseller when it appeared, this heavily illustrated volume and its companion, *Murderess Ink* [below], are still useful. In part, this is because *Murder Ink* contains something for almost everybody. It has autobiographical reminiscences by people as diverse as Penelope Wallace (daughter of Edgar Wallace) and Ian Carmichael (television's definitive Lord Peter Wimsey); chapters on living with a mystery writer (by Abby Adams, whose husband is Donald Westlake) and on little old lady detectives; Peter O'Donnell reminiscences about creating Modesty Blaise; H. R. F. Keating writing about initials ("I.N.I.T.I.A.L.S."); and eight original limericks by Isaac Asimov ("Verses for Hearses"). In all, there are more than 150 original contributions, ranging from the lighthearted to the serious. This is certainly the only book to contain not only an article on forensic odontology written by one of the country's leading forensic dentists and illustrated with (mercifully faded) photographs of bitten homicide victims, but also illustrations of a disguised Freddy the Pig, useful rules for drafting poison-pen letters, a comparison of Oxford and Cambridge mysteries, a reprint of the 1951 Haycraft-Queen definitive library of detective-crime-mystery fiction, and a delightful table enabling the curious to tell Spade from Marlowe from Archer.

This is not to say that the volume is problem-free. There are occasional factual errors, the heavily illustrated table of contents is spread over 10 pages, and the arrangement of the 14 sections is neither intuitively obvious nor readily accessible. On the other hand, Winn and her co-perpetrators realized that mystery literature should not only be fun, it should be fun to read about, and this book was clearly assembled with that concept foremost in mind. The last pages contain a statement about the book's typeface (Baskerville, of course); the color of the endpaper "exactly matches the color of arterial blood"; and a tipped-in booklet reveals the solutions to 10 classic mysteries. The indexing is quite good.

46. Winn, Dilys, et al. **Murderess Ink: The Better Half of the Mystery**. New York: Workman Publishing, 1979. xiv, 304 p. LC 79-64783. ISBN 0-89480-108-2 (hc); 0-89480-107-4 (pb).

Following the success of *Murder Ink* (above), what could be more natural than to write a book devoted to the female of the species, one that (in the words of its dustwrapper) "proves, beyond a reasonable doubt, that women in the mystery are found dead as often as men, commit just as many murders as men, make just as many wisecracks as men, drink just as much booze as men, and that, in the final analysis, the female is not only deadlier than the male, but wackier." The resulting collection thus contains more than 100 pieces by more than 50 writers, on subjects as varied as the Gothic, the first women mystery and detective writers, female private eyes, and the wives of private eyes and detectives. As in the first volume, illustrations are plentiful and subject variety abounds. Stephen King writes on how to scare a woman to death, and Tabitha King writes about living with Stephen King; a pictorial shows Agatha Christie being measured for her waxwork at Madame Tussaud's; Jane Langton contributes illustrations of the clothing worn by Dorothy Sayers's characters; Jo April provides helpful hints for removing annoying (and incriminating) spots and marks; and Roger Lang provides illustrations for building a secret compartment.

Though some of this material is significant, this volume is by no means as useful as its predecessor. There are occasional factual errors, and the book has the same frustrating organizational problems, with eight thematic sections that are neither intuitive nor obvious and a heavily illustrated table of contents that is six pages in length. Equally serious, the book's tone comes across as calculatedly lightweight rather than irreverent. As before, the book is set in Baskerville, although this time the color of the endpaper "exactly matches the color of venous blood," and, as before, the indexing is quite good.

47. Woeller, Waltraud, and Bruce Cassiday. **The Literature of Crime and Detection: An Illustrated History from Antiquity to the Present**. New York: Ungar, 1988. 215 p. Index. LC 86-16040. ISBN 0-8044-2983-9.

First published in 1984 as *Illustrierte Geschichte der Kriminalliteratur* (not seen), this enjoyable and well-illustrated history offers a survey of detection and the detective story from classical antiquity to the writers of the early 1980s. Although it is more a history than a reader's guide, it is mentioned here because, like Tage la Cour and Harald Mogensen's *The Murder Book: An Illustrated History of the Detective Story* (q.v.), it is written from a German perspective. The nineteenth-century writers and texts discussed include those by the standard American and British writers, but Karl May's *Der verlorene Sohn oder der Fürst des Elends*, Annette von Droste-Hülshoff's *Die Judenbuch*, and Jodocus D. H. Temme's *Wer war der Mörder?* are also mentioned. The coverage concludes with lists of significant American writers of the 1980s, data on whom appear to have been added during the translation. Though containing some unfortunate typos (Dr. Thorndyke has become "Mr. Thorndyke") and too many exclamation points, and occasionally providing lists rather than discussions, this nevertheless remains a useful volume. A selective bibliography cites English and German sources, and the author index is annotated, providing biographical data in addition to paginations.

SPECIFIC GENRES

SCOPE NOTE: This section is for mysteries "about" a certain subject. Monographs surveying more than one subject are listed in the section devoted to readers' guides.

African American Mysteries

48. Daniels, Valarie L. **African American Mystery Page**. http://www.aamystery.com

This well-designed web page contains the following sections: Authors—bibliographies and book synopses; References—books about African American mystery fiction; "On the Shelf"—new, recent, and upcoming releases; Events—book tours, chats, etc.; Links—author websites and other sites of interest; Booklist—a comprehensive listing of books featured on this site; Photo Gallery; and a book excerpt (a changing feature). The layout is clear, with an attractive kente border. Although none of the site's sections is comprehensive, this is definitely a site to watch.

49. Lachman, Marvin. **A Reader's Guide to the American Novel of Detection**. New York: G. K. Hall, 1993. xii, 435 p. Indexes. (Reader's Guides to Mystery Novels). LC 92-25726. ISBN 0-8161-1803-5.

This volume is the second in a series that started with Susan Oleksiw's *A Reader's Guide to the Classic British Mystery* (q.v.), and like its predecessor, this is an oddly inconsistent collection. Lachman's preface states that his focus is on the amateur detectives, those who "do not earn a living by solving crimes," although there are some exceptions, Rex Stout's Nero Wolfe and Arthur Reeve's Craig Kennedy being the most notable. Lachman also states that his focus is on the detectives of North America, allowing him to discuss books by Canadian writers; that he generally includes all relevant novels by any author he discusses; and that he generally includes all the books in which a particular series detective appears. In all, he references "the work of 166 authors, many of whom also have one or more pseudonyms, and 1,314 books." However, the methodology Lachman used to choose these authors and titles remains questionable. Why, for example, is there no mention of Professor Augustus S. F. X. Van Dusen, the famous "Thinking Machine" created by Jacques Futrelle? Where are the writings of Margaret Maron?

Questions of content aside, the majority of the guide consists of the annotated bibliography to the North American novel of detection. Although the guide's initial arrangement is alphabetical by author, the titles are arranged neither alphabetically nor chronologically by publication date but by what Lachman deems to be their internal chronology. In the case of prolific writers, this system makes locating information on a particular title problematic; the dates of books featuring John Dickson Carr's Dr. Gideon Fell, for example, appear in the following order: 1941, 1938, 1940, 1938, 1939, 1944, 1941, 1946, 1947, 1949. Each citation provides the title in boldface type, place of publication, publisher, and date of publication; the major series detective is listed, as are the first British edition and subsequent retitlings. The annotations are well presented, stating the problem but not the solution.

In addition to the bibliography, the volume contains a list of pseudonyms and their users, an alphabetical list of creators and their most famous series character, an alphabetical list of the series characters, a list of the occupations of the series characters, a list by the story's chronological setting, a geographic locations index, and a settings index. An index for "miscellaneous information" provides thematic information about the novels; a holiday index lists books involving specific holidays; and the book concludes with Lachman's list of 100 notable novels of detection. There is no title index.

As with the other volumes in this series, a revised and expanded edition would be helpful.

Asian American Mysteries

50. Marple, Laura. **Asian American Mysteries List**.

Available as part of the archives maintained by the DorothyL listserv, and also through the Miss Lemon website (http://www.iwillfollow.com/lemon.htm), this list of mysteries featuring Asian Americans is arranged alphabetically by author. Each citation provides the name of the Asian American character, the titles in which he or she appears, and the setting. ISBNs are provided when relevant, as are references to websites.

Baseball Mysteries

51. Gants, Susan E. **Baseball Mysteries List**.

Available as part of the archives maintained by the DorothyL listserv, and also through the Miss Lemon website (http://www.iwillfollow.com/lemon.htm), this list of mysteries featuring the game of baseball (or baseball players as characters) is arranged alphabetically by author. Each citation provides the title of the book, year of publication, and publisher; the majority of citations are briefly annotated.

Bibliomysteries

52. Ballinger, John. **Biblio-Mysteries**. Williamsburg, VA: Bookpress, 1984. 88 p. Paperback. (Catalogue 8).

As a rule, dealer's catalogues have not been included in this work, but with *Biblio-Mysteries* an exception must be made, for despite an apparently sizable reader interest in bibliomysteries—mysteries that in some way make use of the worlds and arcana of librarianship, the used or rare book trade, or the publishing industry—this catalogue is apparently the only separately published bibliography of bibliomysteries.

Ballinger's catalogue cites 554 works, the majority of which are books. The arrangement is alphabetical by author; last names are given in boldface type and capitalized. Titles are in regular type. Publication data are italicized and include the place of publication, publisher, and year of publication. Furthermore, each title is briefly annotated, Ballinger's note indicating why the title is a bibliomystery. A few citations are to multiple editions and states of the work. The citation to Lawrence Block's *The Burglar Who Studied Spinoza*, for example, makes reference to the original typed manuscript and setting copy; the galley proofs corrected by the author, including master set, first and second passes, author's set and final set, the page proofs from which the book was photographed for printing, and the blue ink proof copy; and a presentation copy of the first edition.

Some years later Ballinger wrote *Collecting Bibliomysteries* (Williamsburg, VA: Bookpress, 1990), a history of his collection. This urbane and witty pamphlet culminates with Ballinger's account of selling his collection and writing *The Williamsburg Forgeries*, a bibliomystery published by St. Martin's Press.

53. McCurley, Marsha. **Bibliomysteries**. http://www.carol.net/dolphin/
     bibliomysteries/index.htm

The largest section of McCurley's well-designed website-in-progress is a substantial bibliography of bibliomysteries that is arranged alphabetically by author and gives the title, place of publication, publisher, and year of publication. In addition, different icons indicate whether the bibliomystery is set in a private, public, academic, or religious library; has a book-related plot; features an archive, archivist, or manuscript; and has as its main character a writer, bookstore bookseller, publisher, library detective, bibliodetective, or librarian. A bibliography of secondary sources is provided, as are separate lists of library detectives, bibliophilic detectives, library staff as murder victims, murder weapons used in libraries, quotations from bibliomysteries, and a discussion of collecting bibliomysteries. One hopes that McCurley will soon finish her site.

Blind-Accessible Mysteries

54. **Mysteries**. Washington, DC: Library of Congress, 1982. 205 p. Paperback. Indexes. LC 82-600158. ISBN 0-8444-0394-6. SuDoc: LC 19.11:M99. Also available on disc, on cassette, or in Braille.

55. **More Mysteries**. Washington, DC: National Library Service for the Blind and Physically Handicapped, Library of Congress, 1992. vi, 164 p. Paperback. Indexes. LC 92-30160. ISBN 0-8444-0763-1. SuDoc: LC 19.11:M9912. Also available on disc and in Braille.

Mysteries and *More Mysteries* are annotated bibliographies of the detective and mystery stories available through the network library collections provided by the National Library Service for the Blind and Physically Handicapped at the Library of Congress. *Mysteries* cites those works that are available through disc, cassette, and Braille up to 1982. *More Mysteries* lists the works available through cassettes and Braille that were produced after the 1982 publication of *Mysteries*. The paper form of each volume is in large print.

Both bibliographies begin with a section listing the mysteries of "Prolific Authors." In *Mysteries*, a prolific author has seven or more titles available through the National Library Service; in *More Mysteries*, a prolific author has six or more titles. These titles are separated by their medium and listed alphabetically. Each entry provides the work's title and order number in boldface type, (in regular type) describes the size of the work (e.g., two cassettes, three disks, three volumes), and provides a descriptive annotation with occasional evaluative comments (e.g., "strong language and explicit descriptions of sex"). The name of the detective is always included.

The second section of *Mysteries* is titled "More Mysteries", the second section of *More Mysteries* lists the works of "Other Authors"; and both list the works of less-prolific authors in the format described above. *Mysteries*, however, has a list of mystery anthologies, an index to "British-Sounding Narrators," and separate title indexes for the discs, cassettes, and Braille works. *More Mysteries* has a section listing single-author collections of short stories, lists its anthologies under the heading of "Multiple Authors," and has separate title indexes to cassettes and Braille publications. Both volumes conclude with an order form.

An updated volume is certainly needed, but with the ready accessibility of books on tape, it is improbable that one will be produced.

Christmas Mysteries

56. Christmas Mysteries. http://www.mysterynet.com/christmas

This congenial site provides an article about Christmas mysteries by Vicki Cameron; links to short mystery stories by Bill Pronzini, Marcia Muller, and Edward D. Hoch; links to classic Christmas mysteries by (among others) Arthur Conan Doyle, O. Henry, and Damon Runyon; and a list of Christmas mystery books that may be ordered.

57. Menendez, Albert. Mistletoe Malice: The Life and Times of the Christmas Murder Mystery. Silver Spring, MD: Holly Tree Press, 1982. 35 p. Paperback.

"There is a whole body of literature featuring assorted varieties of crime and mayhem at the Happiest Time of the Year," writes Menendez in his brief introduction to this cheerful study of mystery novels that in some way use Christmas. Menendez identifies the eight varieties of Christmas Murder Mysteries (CMM), describing them as the Country House Party Thriller, the Police Procedural (with its subcategory, the Lonely Cop), the Big-City Private Eye, the Village, the Department Store Glitter, the Spy Caper, the Lunatic on the Loose, and the Christmas as Background. The novels that exemplify these categories are annotated, and Menendez carefully refrains from providing the solutions. The pamphlet concludes with a checklist of 89 CMMs that lists the first American or British editions of each book.

A delightful achievement.

58. Wolfe, S. J. A Bibliography of Christmas Mysteries.

Approximately 60 novels and short stories are in this list, one of the bibliographies available through the archives maintained by DorothyL or through the Miss Lemon website (http://www.iwillfollow.com/lemon.htm). Arrangement is alphabetical by author or editor; no additional publication data are given, but the name of the detective is provided for the majority of the citations.

Classic British Mysteries

59. Oleksiw, Susan. **A Reader's Guide to the Classic British Mystery**. Boston: G. K. Hall, 1988. xiii, 585 p. LC 88-1735. ISBN 0-8161-8787-8. Also: New York: Mysterious Press, 1989. xiii, 585 p. Indexes. LC 88-43489. ISBN 0-89296-969-5 (hc); 0-89296-968-7 (pb).

A novice to the study of detective and mystery fiction is likely to be frustrated rather than enlightened by Oleksiw's effort, for although she describes and annotates more than 1,440 titles by 121 authors, nowhere does she define the criteria that make one book a classic British mystery and render its neighbor unfit for inclusion. Why, for example, does Oleksiw list Reginald Hill's thriller *Fell of Dark*, yet not cite its apparent model, John Buchan's *The Thirty-Nine Steps*?

Questions of definition aside, Oleksiw's bibliography references books published after 1900; the sole exception is Fergus Hume's *The Mystery of a Hansom Cab*. These citations are arranged alphabetically by author's last name. When the author wrote more than one volume, the entries are listed chronologically; when the author used more than one character, the entries are listed chronologically by series character. Pseudonyms and cross-references are provided. Each citation gives the title, publisher, and publication date for the book's first British and American editions and provides the name of the investigating detective. The annotations range in length from approximately 30 to more than 100 words, give away no plot twists, and reveal no endings.

The annotated bibliography dominates the volume, but there are indexes for characters and their creators, creators and their characters, occupations of series characters, time periods during which the stories are set, locations of stories occurring outside England, settings, and novels in which specialized technical information plays a significant role. A concluding list lists "one hundred classics of the genre," and there is an essay on the metropolitan police and local forces with a list of the ranks within the British class system. Oddly enough, there is no title index.

A revised and expanded edition of this study is needed.

Clerical Mysteries

60. Breen, Jon L., and Martin H. Greenberg, eds. **Synod of Sleuths: Essays on Judeo-Christian Detective Fiction**. Metuchen, NJ: Scarecrow Press, 1990. viii, 161 p. Index. LC 90-21025. ISBN 0-8108-2382-9.

Surveying Judeo-Christian detective and mystery stories, this collection of five bibliographic essays is less concerned about theological problems than Spencer's work on the same subject (q.v.). Breen contributes two of the essays, "Protestant Mysteries" and "Mormon Mysteries"; Edward D. Hoch discusses "Priestly Sleuths"; Marvin Lachman discusses "Religious Cults and the Mystery"; and in an essay titled "Is This Any Job for a Nice Jewish Boy?" James

Yaffe discusses Jews in detective fiction. The book's final chapter is a "symposium" consisting of transcripts to questions answered by Ellis Peters, William X. Kienzle, Harry Kemelman, and Sister Carol Anne O'Marie. The book concludes with a bibliography of the works discussed in the body of the book, and a well-done index.

Though some of the essays are dated, this is nevertheless a highly readable work, and the contributors—professional writers all—do not hesitate to judge the works they are describing. The concluding bibliography is especially useful, providing author, title, and place, publisher, and year of publication; separate sections list the works of fiction and drama discussed in the essays, anthologies, and secondary sources.

61.   Harper, Carol. **Nuns in Mysteries**.

Available as part of the archives maintained by the DorothyL listserv, and also through the Miss Lemon website (http://www.iwillfollow.com/lemon.htm), this list of crime-solving nuns is arranged by chronological setting of the story, the first references being to Peter Tremayn's "Sister Fidelma" series, which takes place in seventh-century Ireland. A separate section lists works featuring "Active Nuns"; it is followed by a list of "Retired Nuns." Citations to books tend to provide the author's name, the name of the nun, the publisher, and the year of publication; several short stories are also referenced. Data are current as of 1996.

62.   Kristick, Laurel. **Saintly Sleuths**.

Available as part of the archives maintained by the DorothyL listserv, and also through the Miss Lemon website (http://www.iwillfollow.com/lemon.htm), this list of crime-solving clerics is arranged alphabetically by author and references some 22 authors. Citations give only the name of the detective, not the title(s) in which he or she appeared. The more thorough bibliographies in the works by Spencer and Breen (q.q.v.) are preferable.

63.   Spencer, William David. **Mysterium and Mystery: The Clerical Crime Novel**. Ann Arbor, MI: UMI Research Press, 1989. xi, 344 p. Indexes. (Studies in Religion, no. 6). LC 88-39773. ISBN 0-8357-1936-7. Also: Carbondale, IL: Southern Illinois University Press, 1992. xi, 344 p. Indexes. LC 91-28207. ISBN 0-8093-1809-1.

It is debatable whether *Mysterium and Mystery* should be included here, for it is not a reference work in the way that the other works considered herein are. Nevertheless, this is one of only two substantial studies of its subject, the genre crime novel in which a clerical figure plays the role of the detective, and for this reason it warrants inclusion. Furthermore, it contains substantial bibliographies.

Mysterium and Mystery began its life as Spencer's Th.D., granted in 1986 from Boston University, and it is still as much a work of theology as it is a study of the clerical crime novel. It opens with a defense of the genre, Spencer stating in his first chapter that "if some Christians question whether a mystery story can be a Christian story, they do not know their own faith thoroughly enough. And every detective of the full implication of any mystery ends in the mysterium that comes from this great source, which is the well-spring of morality as well."

Following Spencer's defense, the volume is divided into three major sections. The first, "Rabbis and Robbers," begins with a discussion of the elements of crime and detection found in *Bel and the Dragon* and the story of *Susannah,* and concludes with a discussion of Harry Kemelman's "Rabbi Small" series. "Priests and Psychopaths" discusses the clerical crime novels of Umberto Eco, Ellis Peters, E. M. A. Allison, G. K. Chesterton, Anthony Boucher, Henry Catalan, Margaret Ann Hubbard, Leonard Holton, Ralph McInerny, Dorothy Gilman, Sister Carol Anne O'Marie, William X. Kienzle, and Andrew Greeley. Concluding the body of the book is "Ministers and Murderers," which analyzes the novels of Vicar Whitechurch, C. A. Alington, Margaret Scherf, Stephen Chance, Barbara Ninde Byfield, Isabelle Holland, Matthew Head, Charles Merrill Smith, and James L. Johnson. An appendix provides a graph of the clerical crime novel in English, and there are a lengthy bibliography and an index to fictional characters. A combined author/title/subject index concludes the volume.

This is a substantial contribution to the field, a scholarly examination of a hitherto disparate body of work, with the results presented in clear and cogent prose.

College Mysteries

64. Kramer, John E., Jr., and John E. Kramer III. **College Mystery Novels: An Annotated Bibliography, Including a Guide to Professorial Series-Character Sleuths**. New York: Garland, 1983. xvii, 356 p. Indexes. (Garland Reference Library of the Humanities, vol. 360). LC 82-48291. ISBN 0-8240-9237-6.

Many academics are fond of detective and mystery novels, and (perhaps coincidentally) many detective and mystery novels involve academics and have an academic setting. The college mystery novel is a direct descendant of the British "cozy," with the campus replacing the small British village and the large rural countryhouse. A campus setting allows the author to create a small, insular world with its own government and political systems and populate it with academic eccentrics, geniuses, and (frequently naive and nubile) young people. A crime then disrupts this world, exposing its political infighting and petty concerns to the investigators. Often there is a sense of satire, the author delighting in the depiction of academics feuding over the interpretation of a line of Milton or the "true" authorship of Shakespeare's tragedies.

After defining the college mystery novel as "a full-length work of mystery or suspense fiction which is set at an institution of higher education and/or has as a principal character a student, a faculty member, or an administrator at a college or university," the father-and-son team of the Kramers identify 632 titles published between 1882 and 1982 that fulfill their definition. These titles are divided into two groups: the "professorial series-character sleuths" and the "free-standing college mystery novels." Fifty-one series characters are identified and have their adventures described; each series character's entry concludes with the books in which he or she appears. The section devoted to "free-standing" college mystery novels annotates 308 volumes that do not have a series character. An appendix lists outstanding college mystery novels, and well-done indexes for authors, titles, and series characters conclude the volume.

Although the Kramers' annotations are critically perceptive, *College Mystery Novels* is irksome and inconsistent as a bibliography. For example, R. Austin Freeman's 1914 *The Uttermost Farthing* is listed in the "series-character" section despite being Freeman's only novel featuring Humphrey Challoner (a one-book series?). Furthermore, Challoner's connection with academe is at best tenuous. Long prior to the start of the story, he was involved with anthropology and has maintained a small museum of oddities. In both sections the citations are listed chronologically, effectively frustrating those users who do not know the date of the series character's first book appearance or first publication date of a book. (Nor are these dates consistent. Arthur B. Reeve's "Craig Kennedy" is listed as 1912, whereas the first book cited is dated 1911 [and, for what it is worth, Craig Kennedy appeared in magazine form in 1910].) Finally, historians and scholars can complain about omissions (Edwin Balmer and William MacHarg's "Luther Trant" is not among the detectives surveyed), typographical errors (Charlotte Armstrong's *A Dram of Poison* "won the Edgar Allen Poe Award," and Fredric Brown's first name is given as "Frederic"), and the lack of an index for campus locations.

Despite these problems, *College Mystery Novels* is not insignificant. It is the first book-length attempt at describing a recurrent genre in crime and mystery fiction, and because much of the book is very capably done, the flaws mentioned above are all the more noticeable. *College Mystery Novels* needs expansion, clarification, reorganization, and proofreading, but it merits another edition.

Courtroom Mysteries

65. Breen, Jon L. **Novel Verdicts: A Guide to Courtroom Fiction**. Metuchen, NJ: Scarecrow Press, 1984. xiv, 266 p. Index. LC 84-14110. ISBN 0-8108-1741-1.

After an introduction detailing his guidelines for classifying a book as courtroom fiction, Breen provides an annotated bibliography of 421 books that match his criteria. His citations are arranged by author's name and include title, place of publication, publisher, and date of the first British and American editions. Cross-references are provided for works that are jointly authored, for pseudonymous works, and for linking authors to the names under which their books were published. Breen's citations include a symbol indicating the proportion of the book devoted to the trial (i.e., "A" for all or more than three-quarters, "$\frac{1}{2}$" for one-half or more, "$\frac{1}{4}$" for one-quarter or more, "B" for less than a quarter, and "C" for a collection containing courtroom action). The annotations are brief, opinionated, entertaining, and informative: a delightful blend. A supplementary bibliography contains approximately 200 books that Breen knew about but was not able to include, although he hints that these, "along with other volumes not yet discovered or still to be published, may be included in a second volume a few years hence." An author-title index, a "cause of action" index, and a jurisdiction index conclude the volume.

Despite a few inaccuracies—mercilessly identified by Breen himself in *What About Murder? 1981–1991* (q. v.)—this is an exemplary volume, an excellent demonstration of what a knowledgeable writer can do with a specialized subject.

Cozy Mysteries

66. Androski, Helene. **Cozies: A Selective List**.

Available as part of the archives maintained by the DorothyL listserv, and also through the Miss Lemon website (http://www.iwillfollow.com/lemon.htm), this list of "cozies" is prefaced with a useful definition of the genre: "mysteries that contain . . . a minimum of violence, sex, and social relevance; the solution is arrived at by ratiocination or intuition rather than forensics and police procedure (or beating a confession out of someone); the murderer is indeed exposed and order restored at the end; the hero/ine is honorable and the other characters (often including the murderer) are well mannered and well-bred (except, of course, the servants); the setting is a closed community of some sort, such as a village, university, or stately home. Desirable, but not essential: a writing style graced by wit and literary allusion."

The list is arranged alphabetically by author; nationality and birth and death dates are often provided. In all, approximately 70 writers of cozies are profiled. Citations provide a description of the author's best-known series rather than lists of individual titles. A concluding note provides an annotated list of references from which to locate additional information. A nicely produced list.

Garden and Gardening Mysteries

67. St. Charles Public Library. **Digging for Clues: Mysteries in the Garden**. http://www.st-charles.lib.il.us/low/clues.htm

This list of 44 mysteries (or series) featuring gardens and gardening is arranged alphabetically by author and provides only the title of the book or series. The list is nevertheless cleanly presented.

Gay and Lesbian Mysteries

68. Slide, Anthony. **Gay and Lesbian Characters and Themes in Mystery Novels: A Critical Guide to over 500 Works in English**. Jefferson, NC: McFarland, 1993. vii, 199 p. Indexes. LC 92-56695. ISBN 0-89950-798-0.

Slide's introduction to this occasionally intriguing annotated bibliography begins by noting that "prior to the 1980s gay and lesbian characters and themes were introduced in only a small number of mystery novels, and that the portrayal of gay characters was generally unsympathetic." The remainder of his introduction speculates about the relationship between Nero Wolfe and Archie Goodwin, provides a historical survey of the use of homosexuals as characters in mysteries, and discusses the historical usage of the word "gay" to describe homosexuals.

The bibliography is arranged alphabetically by author's last name, given in boldface capitals; biographical data are occasionally provided. The annotations list the title of the work(s) in boldface italics and provide reasonably thorough descriptions of the gay characters or themes: Characters are named, themes are elaborated, plots are described, locations are specified. Endings and solutions are rarely revealed. When the author has written more than one work, the citations are arranged chronologically. Bibliographical data on the works are limited to parenthetical asides listing the publisher and publication year, and there are thematic entries for such subjects as AIDS. Numerous cross-references are provided to authors using similar themes and to subjects that Slide felt are relevant to the gay and lesbian communities: Some of these include Gay Activists Alliance, Gay/Lesbian Bars, Gay Pride Parades, Gays/Lesbians as Heroes/ Heroines, Gays/Lesbians as Murder Victims, Gays/Lesbians as Villains, Gays/Lesbians in the Military, Hairdressers—Male, and the Hollywood Entertainment Industry. The book concludes with a list of specialist publishers of gay and lesbian fiction, a brief bibliography, and indexes to gay and lesbian characters and titles. In all, approximately 500 works are cited.

Surprisingly, there are a number of readily apparent omissions whose presence might have added greater depth to the book. For example, gay characters can be found in the work of Mickey Spillane, and Slide should have included them, not merely dismissed Mike Hammer as a latent homosexual; similarly, the sympathetically presented lesbian in Trevanian's *The Main* deserves mention but receives none. Furthermore, if the relationship between Wolfe and Goodwin can be interpreted as homosexual, surely the more intriguing relationship between E. W. Hornung's Raffles and Bunny warrants examination. Finally, there are occasional errors; H. F. Heard's *Dopplegangers: An Episode of the Fourth, the Psychological, Revolution* is science fiction and does not feature Mr. Mycroft as a detective.

Worse, too often Slide can be accused of twisting evidence. His discussion of Philip Marlowe, for example, claims that Marlowe might be gay because "Philip Marlowe practises sexual abstinence, has longstanding friendships only with men, and often displays an almost ingrained repugnance for the women whom he encounters." This is no evidence of anything except a literary tradition common to detective stories, particularly those first published in pulp magazines. Similarly, in discussing *The Big Sleep*, Slide states that Marlowe's revulsion at finding the naked Carmen Sternwood in his bed "is the action only of a misogynist," a misreading of ludicrous proportions. Would Slide have Marlowe behave like Dan Turner? Marlowe declines to bed the disturbed Carmen Sternwood because he is not enslaved by his libido, because she is the daughter of his well-paying client (professional ethics and common sense govern his actions), and because he feels no sexual attraction to her (she is the most loathsome character in a novel filled with loathsome characters).

There remains a need for a reliable bibliography of gay and lesbian characters and themes in mystery novels.

Golf Mysteries

69. Leininger, John. **Golf Mysteries**.

Available as part of the archives maintained by the DorothyL listserv, and also through the Miss Lemon website (http://www.iwillfollow.com/lemon.htm), this list of mysteries in which the game of golf is featured is arranged alphabetically by author. Each citation provides the title, the date of first publication, and the name of the series character. In all, approximately 60 titles are given.

70. Taylor, Thomas. **The Golf Murders Collection: A Reader's and Collector's Illustrated Guide to Golf Mystery Fiction**. Westland, MI: Golf Mystery Press, 1997. (400 copies printed.)

Not seen.

Gothic Mysteries

71. Radcliffe, Elsa J. **Gothic Novels of the Twentieth Century: An Annotated Bibliography**. Metuchen, NJ: Scarecrow Press, 1979. xvi, 272 p. Index. LC 78-24357. ISBN 0-8108-1190-1.

The Gothic novel in its earliest state combined elements of crime with stronger elements of horror and fantasy, but the genre is more properly considered a branch of sensationalistic fiction and reference books surveying the "pure" Gothic are thus not considered here. Elsa Radcliffe's work concentrates not on the historical Gothic but on the crime novels of the twentieth century that traditionally feature young women in peril. Using criteria put forth by Montague Summers's *The Gothic Quest* (New York: Russell & Russell, 1938), Radcliffe's introduction divides the contemporary Gothic into five categories: the historical Gothic, the sentimental Gothic, the horror Gothic, the exotic Gothic, and the whimsical Gothic. In all of these works, states Radcliffe, there are elements involving the supernatural; a quest or a wrong to be righted; a setting that includes an old dwelling (a castle); a fantasy of wealth suddenly acquired or an inheritance; mystery, suspense, and intrigue; a fantasy of romantic love in some form; romanticism of the past and a historical setting; and confrontations between the forces of good and evil.

Radcliffe's bibliography is arranged alphabetically by author's last name (given in capital letters); biographical data are occasionally provided. Titles of works are underlined, and the place of publication, publisher, and year of publication are given; paperback series numbers are also listed. Many citations are annotated. When more than one title exists by the same author, the arrangement is alphabetical. Pseudonymous works tend to be listed under the author's original name, and cross-references abound. References are consecutively numbered, and the bibliography cites 1,973 books. The concluding index offers title access to the works.

Gothic Novels of the Twentieth Century is the only substantial work on its subject, but it is also a work riddled with the most egregious of errors. Errors abound in the biographical data, bibliographic citations, and annotations. Too often, Radcliffe includes works on the strengths of their titles (e.g., Frank Belknap Long's *The Goblin Tower* and *The Horror from the Hills*) when minimal research would have indicated that the former is poetry and the latter is a Lovecraftian horror novel. Also too often, Radcliffe knowingly includes works that are not Gothic, and although she states that they are not Gothic, what is their purpose in a bibliography devoted to the contemporary Gothic?

A comprehensive bibliography of the contemporary Gothic remains to be created.

Hard-Boiled Mysteries

72. Goulart, Ron. **An Informal Reading List**. http://www.vex.net/~buff/rara-avis/biblio/goulart_checklist.html

This list of the works of 15 authors of hard-boiled novels originally appeared as an appendix to Ron Goulart's fiction anthology *The Hardboiled Dicks* (Los Angeles: Sherbourne Press, 1965). No additional bibliographical data are given, but the list is clearly presented. Nevertheless, choose the lengthier list provided by O'Brien (q.v.)

73. O'Brien, Geoffrey. **The Hardboiled Era: A Checklist, 1929–1958**. http://www.vex.net/~buff/rara-avis/biblio/checklist.html

Reprinted from the appendix to Geoffrey O'Brien's *Hardboiled America* (New York: Van Nostrand Reinhold, 1981), this chronologically arranged list of hard-boiled novels published between 1919 and 1958 is designed to show that the hard-boiled detective novel is not a series of isolated works but belongs to a longstanding tradition. As many as 15 authors and the titles of their works are listed in each year. No additional bibliographical data are given, but the list is lengthy, clearly laid out, and well chosen.

74. Sandoe, James. **The Hard-Boiled Dick: A Personal Check-List**. Chicago: Arthur Lovell, 1952. 9 p. Paperback.

This pamphlet is historically significant as the first separately published reference work on its subject. It is a selective, annotated bibliography, with Sandoe using as his criteria for selection the concepts of literary quality: "The reader who, having Hammett and Spillane to choose between, prefers the former, may find some use in the titles and notes which follow. The list is selective, not comprehensive, and some celebrated names are absent by design, but I hope that none is absent by choice."

Sandoe's entries are arranged alphabetically by author's name and provide the book's title (underlined) and the year of first book publication (in parentheses). A brief annotation follows, and the entry concludes with the name of the detective. Only in the entries for Chandler and Hammett does this format differ, with Sandoe providing more detailed annotations and, in the case of the latter, a lengthy excerpt from Anthony Boucher's review in the *New York Times* of 10 August 1952. The majority of the entries are for novels, though S. J. Perelman's "Somewhere a Roscoe" and "Farewell, My Lovely Appetizer" are praised, and Joseph Shaw's *The Hard-Boiled Omnibus* is discussed. Sandoe concludes his annotations by stating (perhaps disingenuously) that "the writers and tales noted here are themselves of very unequal merit and it's quite possible that the quality which appeared to me to rescue an otherwise routine imitation from boredom will not affect another reader in the same way."

This important bibliography is now superseded with regard to its content and bibliographic data but not to its critical judgments. Because the original publication of this bibliography is now virtually impossible to obtain, it should be noted that this list has been reprinted in its entirety in *The Armchair Detective Book of Lists* (q.v.). A slightly revised version of Sandoe's list—prefaced with a significantly longer introduction—can be found in the chapter titled "The Private Eye," published in *The Mystery Story*, a collection of essays edited by John Ball (Del Mar, CA: University Extension, University of California, San Diego, in cooperation with Publisher's Inc., 1976).

75. Skinner, Robert E. **The New Hard-Boiled Dicks: A Personal Checklist**. San Bernardino, CA: Borgo Press, 1987. 60 p. (Brownstone Chapbook Series, vol. 2). ISBN 0-941028-04-6.

76. Skinner, Robert E. **The New Hard-Boiled Dicks: Heroes for a New Urban Mythology**. San Bernardino, CA: Brownstone Books, 1995. 192 p. Indexes. (Brownstone Mystery Guides, vol. 2). LC 93-16090. ISBN 0-941028-13-5 (hc); 0-941028-13-3 (pb).

The 1st edition of this survey of the writers of hard-boiled fiction was intended as a direct continuation of the work of Sandoe (q.v.) and consisted of essays on the ten authors and one artist that Skinner believed represented the best of the newer generation of hard-boiled writers. The authors thus profiled are Andrew Bergman, James Crumley, Loren D. Estleman, Stephen Greenleaf, Donald Hamilton, Chester Himes, Stuart Kaminsky, Elmore Leonard, Robert B. Parker, "Richard Stark" (Donald Westlake), and Ernest Tidyman. The artist is Jim Steranko.

The 2d edition revised and expanded the above essays, dropped the essay on Ernest Tidyman, and expanded the contents with the inclusion of studies of James Lee Burke, Robert Campbell, James Colbert, Michael Collins, Sue

Grafton, Joseph Hansen, Andrew Vachss, and Chris Wiltz. The introductory chapter has changed from the terse "Hard-Boiled Dick Past and Present" to the lengthier "Hard-Boiled Hero: Evolution of an Urban Myth." The 1st edition contains no indexes and brief bibliographies; the 2d edition contains indexes to the authors, titles, and characters and lengthier (though not comprehensive) bibliographies of the works of the authors studied. The essays in both editions tend to the appreciative rather than critical.

Though not as magisterial in judgment as Sandoe's work, and arguably not a reference work, the 2d edition of *The New Hard-Boiled Dicks* is nevertheless one of the first volumes to acknowledge the accomplishments of some of the finest contemporary writers of the hard-boiled genre.

Historical Mysteries

77. Heli, Rick. **The Detective and the Toga**. http://www.best.com/~heli/roman/romys.shtml

This well-designed website begins with links to newly published mysteries set in Ancient Rome, offers information on new editions of works, and provides information on forthcoming titles. The list is arranged by time period, starting with lists of mysteries set during the founding of Rome and concluding with mysteries set during the Byzantine era. The citations are to titles, each title being linked to information providing the author, publisher, year and place of publication, and ISBN; translations are also listed. These lists are international, mixing titles written in English with those in other languages, and Heli's site permits searchers to list the contents by writings in Dutch, English, French, German, Italian, Russian, and Spanish. There are links to profiles of the authors, to a publishing chronology of Roman mysteries, to Roman mysteries in anthologies (with a separate section for German anthologies), to Roman mysteries in magazines, to Biblical retellings, and to novels on audiotape.

78. James, Dean, and Soon Y. Choi. **Historical Mystery Bibliography**. http://uts.cc.utexas.edu/~soon/histfiction

This nicely arranged website offers a chronological approach to its subject, starting with mysteries set in the ancient world (Ancient Egypt, Ancient Greece, and Ancient Rome) and concluding with mysteries set during the World War II era. Following classification by time period, the arrangement becomes alphabetical by geographical location, after which the mysteries are listed in alphabetical order by their author. No publication data are provided, and retitlings are rarely indicated. Furthermore, espionage novels and Sherlock Holmes pastiches are not included. Though this is not a comprehensive bibliography, several hundred books are listed.

Note: this material is also accessible as one of the lists maintained in the archives maintained through the DorothyL listserv, and it is available through the Miss Lemon website (http://www.iwillfollow.com/lemon.htm).

79. Orgelfinger, Gail. **Medieval and Renaissance Mysteries**.

This is one of the lists maintained in the archives maintained through the DorothyL listserv; it is also available through the Miss Lemon website (http://www.iwillfollow.com/lemon.htm). Arranged alphabetically by author's (or editor's) name, this list contains approximately 100 titles. The year of first publication is provided, as is the name of the sleuth (if a series detective), and often a note indicates historical time frame.

80. Wittman, Pat. **Humorous Mysteries**.

This list of humorous mysteries is one of the lists available through the archives maintained by DorothyL or through the Miss Lemon website (http://www.iwillfollow.com/lemon.htm). In all, approximately 60 authors are listed. The list's arrangement is alphabetical by author; the main (series) character is named, as are the titles of some of the works the character appears in. Entries are incomplete for many authors, but this appears to be the only separate publication on its subject. Data are current as of 1993.

Law Mysteries

81. Campbell, Heather. **Legal Thrillers**.

This randomly arranged list of approximately 100 authors and the legal thrillers they have written is available through the archives maintained by DorothyL or through the Miss Lemon website (http://www.iwillfollow.com/lemon.htm).

Library Mysteries

82. Gwinn, Nancy E. **Library Mysteries: A Halloween Sampler**. Washington, DC: Center for the Book, Library of Congress, 1992 (Halloween). Unpaged. [8 p.]. Paperback.

Compiled by Gwinn to celebrate "Mystery at the Library of Congress," the Library of Congress's First Annual Halloween Mystery Celebration, this slim pamphlet lists a handful of detective and mystery books and short stories set in libraries. Gwinn's citations are arranged alphabetically; book titles are given in italics, followed by place of publication, publisher, and year of publication. Citations to periodical publications give the title in quotation marks, followed by the periodical title in italics, the volume, month and year of publication, and pagination. All citations are annotated.

Though incomplete and brief, Gwinn's is the only separate paper publication on its subject. Special and affectionate mention must be made of a book by Edward F. Ellis: *The British Museum in Fiction: A Check-List* (Portland, ME: Anthoensen Press, 1981), which attempts to list all the books in which the British Museum has been mentioned. Ellis cites the first British and first American edition of each book, indicating retitlings when necessary. The references to the British Museum are indicated not by page but by chapter, and are followed by the text in which the mention is made; the book concludes with a title index. Ellis does not limit his contents to detective and mystery stories, nor does he provide a subject index, but users can nevertheless readily find references to the British Museum in works by August Derleth, Arthur Conan Doyle, R. Austin Freeman, and Inez Haynes Irwin, among many others.

See also the section devoted to Bibliomysteries.

83. Hall, Alison. **Library Mysteries Bibliography**.

Available as part of the archives maintained by the DorothyL listserv, and through the Miss Lemon website (http://www.iwillfollow.com/lemon.htm), this list provides the authors, titles, places of publication, publishers, and years of publication for approximately 60 works that feature libraries. Though the list needs updating, it has not been superseded by the much lengthier bibliography on the same subject maintained by Candy Schwartz (q.v.).

84. Schwartz, Candy. **Mysteries Involving Libraries, Librarians, Etc**.

Available as part of the archives maintained by the DorothyL listserv, and through the Miss Lemon website (http://www.iwillfollow.com/lemon.htm), this bibliography begins with a scope note explaining that it is based on a collection held by the library of the Graduate School of Library and Information Science at Simmons College. It includes mysteries in which libraries of any kind, archives, publishing houses, or bookstores occupy a central role, or mysteries in which librarians, archivists, booksellers, and the like are protagonists (and, preferably, the location or occupation are important to the plot or theme). The scope note is followed by a bibliography of the secondary sources used to compile the list. The lengthy list is arranged alphabetically. Citations provide title, place, publisher, year of publication, and a note as to the nature of the contents; a lengthy wish list concludes the bibliography. Nicely done, but it needs updating.

Locked Room Mysteries

85. Adey, Robert. **Locked Room Murders and Other Impossible Crimes**. London: Ferret, 1979. 190 p. Indexes.

86. Adey, Robert. **Locked Room Murders and Other Impossible Crimes: A Comprehensive Bibliography**. 2d ed., revised and expanded. Minneapolis, MN: Crossover Press, 1991. xliii, 411 p. Indexes. LC 94-212600. ISBN 0-9628870-0-5.

Like a great many bibliographies, this one began as a labor of love. Adey wanted to document the stories he loved, and in 1972 he "hit upon the idea of listing all impossible crime novels and short stories known to me." The result was a bibliography of some 1,280 novels and short stories, all featuring crimes that could not have been committed but somehow were, all taxing the reader's ingenuity to solve the mystery before the investigator.

Following a lengthy and informative introduction, the first part of Adey's bibliography is arranged alphabetically by author; when the author contributed more than one work to the locked room genre, the arrangement becomes alphabetical by title. Each entry is numbered and provides the work's title (listing alternative titles when known) and place of publication, publisher, and year of publication. Publication data on the first British and American editions are provided; if a book was simultaneously published in England and America, the English edition is cited first. Concluding each entry are the detective's name and a brief (and frequently intriguing) statement of the nature of the locked room problem. The second part of the volume contains the solutions. Each solution is numbered and keyed to its counterpart in the first part of the bibliography. A brief list of "Foreign Language Books" concludes the volume.

Had Adey been content not to provide a 2d edition, the 1st edition would be inestimably useful and fascinating to browse. The second edition, however, is a tour de force, a list of 2,019 locked room stories. Although it is nearly three times as thick as the 1st edition and thoroughly supersedes the earlier volume, its arrangement is largely similar to the original edition. All sections have been expanded, and titles new to the second edition are indicated with a check mark. A section listing the contents of locked room anthologies has been added.

Neither edition of this book contains a title index, and a chronological index might have been helpful. These oversights aside, the 2d edition will assist researchers as well as those who enjoy reading by genre.

Married Protagonist Mysteries

87.   Griffith, Thomas H. **A List of Married (Fictional) Sleuths**.

Available as part of the archives maintained by the DorothyL listserv, and through the Miss Lemon website (http://www.iwillfollow.com/lemon.htm), this brief list provides the authors and sleuths in mystery novels in which "the protagonists (amateur and professional) are married; and see their families as being important to their profession."

Men Detective Mysteries

88.   Heising, Willeta L. **Detecting Men: Pocket Guide**. Dearborn, MI: Purple Moon Press, 1997. 144 p. Paperback. ISBN 0-9644593-4-5.

Detecting Men: Pocket Guide was created to accompany *Detecting Men* (not published as of 1997; appeared in 1998), but it contains none of the biographical data or indexes of the full-sized volume; it is merely an author-title list. Only living men who wrote series characters are listed, though several authors who died in 1996 are included, for new titles by them may yet appear. The *Pocket Guide* is arranged alphabetically by author's last name, given in boldface type; pseudonyms are indicated by the letter P, but the real name is revealed in *Detecting Men*. The series character's name is listed beneath the author's name, and the series titles are listed in order, with the year of publication given in parentheses; only series titles are listed, though retitlings are given. Starred titles indicate award-winners; solid stars are used for winners, open stars for nominees. A notepad is provided. Though this work is not free from error, collectors and those needing lists will find the *Pocket Guide* extraordinarily helpful.

Mountie Mysteries

89.   Drew, Bernard A. **Lawmen in Scarlet: An Annotated Guide to Royal Canadian Mounted Police in Print and Performance**. Metuchen, NJ: Scarecrow Press, 1990. xx, 276 p. Index. LC 90-8388. ISBN 0-8108-2330-6.

No separately published bibliography of Mountie detective and mystery fiction appears to exist, but the character of the Royal Canadian Mounted Policeman, frequently resplendent in his red coat, is documented in this annotated guide of more than 200 motion pictures and approximately 500 books. Although many of these books are simply adventures, romances, and "Northerns," a significant percentage of these books feature the Mountie as a detective, solving crimes and righting wrongs.

The bibliography is divided into two sections, the first referencing print sources and the second referencing dramatic adaptations. The entries in the former include books, magazine fiction, pulp magazines, comic books, comic strips, and Big Little Books. The initial arrangement is alphabetical by author's last name; titles are then listed alphabetically beneath the name. Citations include a biographical sketch, the book's title, publication data for the first North American and the first British editions, and frequently a lively annotation; titles that Drew was unable to examine are merely listed. All citations are keyed to a bibliography listing the references from which Drew derived his listings.

The dramatic adaptations cite motion pictures, television programs, radio shows, musicals, plays, and operas in which Mounties appear. Citations are arranged alphabetically by title, and the presented data vary according to the material being described; for example, motion picture citations include studio, year the film was released, major cast and credits, and a content annotation.

In his *Canadian Crime Fiction* (q.v.), David Skene Melvin characterizes this book as "regrettably flawed, for it could have been a valuable tool." Skene Melvin's work includes an excellent index to Mountie novels, but Drew remains the only separately published work on its subject.

Music Mysteries

90.   Boettcher, Bonna J. **Music/Musicians/Musical Mysteries**.

Available as part of the archives maintained by the DorothyL listserv, and also through the Miss Lemon website (http://www.iwillfollow.com/lemon.htm), this list consists of citations to mysteries that feature music or musicians. It is arranged alphabetically by author, and the citations tend to include the following: title, year of publication, ISBN (when available), publisher, source used for verification, and notes on possible discrepancies. Boettcher has used the CD-ROM version of *Books in Print*, OCLC, and several additional sources to verify her data. Though she does not reveal pseudonyms (e.g., the identity of the ghost who wrote *The Metropolitan Opera Murders* for Helen Traubel), her bibliography is well presented and current as of late 1992.

Nurse Mysteries

91.   Mikucki, Eleanor. **Nurse Sleuths**. http://www.geocities.com/Athens/ 3777/sleuths.html

More than a mere list of nurses who served as sleuths, this clearly produced website provides significant information on each of the nurses and their authors, and gives for each nurse an annotated list of the works in which she appeared. Arrangement is alphabetical by the name of the nurse; in all, arrangement of the bibliographies is chronological, but additional publication data are not provided. Cover reproductions are given, as are links to related sites. The author compiled the website devoted to nurse-sleuth Cherry Ames (q.v.), and this website is equally enjoyable.

Police Detective Mysteries

92.   Kristick, Laurel. **Police Detectives**.

This list of novels featuring police detectives is part of the archives maintained by the DorothyL listserv, and is also available through the Miss Lemon website (http://www.iwillfollow.com/lemon.htm). Arrangement is alphabetical by author; the detective's name is given, but no additional bibliographic data are provided. The list mixes works from all countries and time periods, fails to distinguish between ranks (i.e., it mixes constables, detectives, detective chiefs, chief superintendents, sheriffs, and police commissars), and is effectively useless.

Police Procedurals

93. Vicarel, Jo Ann. **A Reader's Guide to the Police Procedural**. New York: G. K. Hall, 1995. xiv, 402 p. (Reader's Guides to Mystery Novels). LC 94-33650. ISBN 0-8161-1801-9.

In her preface, Vicarel offers a definition of the police procedural, stating in part that "the main difference between a police procedural and a traditional mystery is that the procedural is a novel about police life and work first, and a mystery second. Sometimes the crime is secondary to the personal lives of the police. . . ." Using this definition as her basis, Vicarel provides an annotated bibliography of 1,115 police procedural novels written by 271 authors. Her entries are arranged alphabetically by the author's last name; when the author is present with more than one book, the entries are listed chronologically. Pseudonyms and cross-references are provided. Each citation gives the title, publisher, and publication date for the book's first edition and provides the name and rank of the investigating officer or officers. The annotations range in length from fewer than 20 to more than 100 words but give away no plot twists and reveal no endings.

Although the annotated bibliography dominates the volume, there are additional chapters listing pseudonyms and their users, series characters and their creators, and periods during which stories occur. In addition, there are indexes for story location, novels featuring serial killers, "lighter" books, and authors "who have been identified as ex-police officers, currently serve on a police force, or have a close working relationship with a department." An essay discussing the differences between the police agencies of the United States and the United Kingdom, and Vicarel's list of her favorite 100 police procedurals, conclude the volume.

The Reader's Guide to the Police Procedural has its flaws. Thomas Harris's *Red Dragon* is listed, but not his *The Silence of the Lambs*, yet the former's Will Graham is listed in the series character list (a one-book series?). More seriously, Vicarel's preface states "read *Sci Fi* or *The Far Away Man* to understand this literary technique [lightness]," yet she fails to include a title index, forcing curious readers to read every entry in the section devoted to "lightness" or to go elsewhere for the relevant information.

These complaints aside, *The Reader's Guide to the Police Procedural* is an impressive achievement. Vicarel's efforts permit the identification and location of a large and disparate body of work, and for this she deserves commendation.

Private Eye Mysteries

94. Baker, Robert A., and Michael T. Nietzel. **Private Eyes: One Hundred and One Knights: A Survey of American Detective Fiction 1922–1984**. Introduction by Bill Pronzini. Bowling Green, OH: Bowling Green State University Popular Press, 1985. vi, 385 p. LC 85-70857. ISBN 0-87972-329-7 (hc); 0-87972-330-3 (pb).

This is one of two significant volumes on the private eye to be published in 1985, the other being David Geherin's *The American Private Eye: The Image in Fiction* (q.v.). Though the contents of the two books overlap to some degree, Baker and Nietzel's is lengthier, and, perhaps more significantly, a significant percentage of their content is derived from a 1983 questionnaire that surveyed the membership of the Private Eye Writers of America (PWA). "The ratings of the PWA membership guided our selection of authors for this book," states the introduction to *Private Eyes*, adding a little later that "of the 80 questionnaires that were distributed, 27 were completed and returned." The results of this survey are presented in the first chapter, but the validity of data derived from such a minuscule group is never seriously questioned.

The metaphor of the private eye as knight errant dominates the book's arrangement and the chapter names, but statistics and nomenclature aside, *Private Eyes* is essentially a historical survey of significant private eye detectives. Starting with the writings of Hammett and Chandler, Baker and Nietzel discuss the private eyes created by Ross Macdonald, John D. MacDonald, Mickey Spillane, Fredric Brown, Erle Stanley Gardner, Rex Stout, William Campbell Gault, Bill Pronzini, Marcia Muller, George Chesbro, and scores of others. In all, 101 private detectives are described; an appendix cites 101 additional private eyes. The book concludes with useful indexes to authors and characters.

As a guide, *Private Eyes* has more than its share of typos, an occasional unattributed quote, some factual errors, and too much in the way of appreciation and not enough in the way of criticism. For Baker and Nietzel to praise Michael Avallone's "Ed Noon" as "the most James Bond-like of all our PIs," without mentioning Avallone's unique prose style, does a disservice to the series and to readers. Worse yet, in an apparent effort to be informal, Baker and Nietzel undermine their academic credibility through such sentences as "he exercises his one-eyed wonder worm at every opportunity and the opportunities abound" (p. 161).

Since 1983 many hitherto inaccessible pulp private eye stories have been reprinted, and many writers have created new and memorable private eyes. An updated, more comprehensive survey, and a correspondingly rewritten version of *Private Eyes*, might be in order.

95. Geherin, David. **The American Private Eye: The Image in Fiction**. New York: Frederick Ungar, 1985. xii, 228 p. Index. LC 84-15251. ISBN 0-8044-2243-5 (hc); 0-8044-6184-8 (pb).

One of two books on the private eye to appear in 1985—the other being *Private Eyes: One Hundred and One Knights* by Robert Baker and Michael T. Nietzel (q.v.)—this book surveys only 27 private eyes, but a number of these are not discussed by Baker and Nietzel. Unlike Baker and Nietzel, Geherin chose his writers not by survey but through personal knowledge "on the basis of their influence on the genre, their enormous popularity, or as in the case of several of the lesser-known writers, a desire to pay long overdue recognition to their creative contributions to the growth and vitality of the genre."

Geherin begins his study by discussing two of the earliest private eyes, Carroll John Daly's Race Williams and Dashiell Hammett's Continental Op. Following sections discuss six notable pulp private eyes, four private eyes who had a life beyond the pulps, five private eyes who became active following World War II, four private eyes who were "compassionate" in one way or another, and six contemporary private eyes. An appendix, "An Enduring Hero," offers a theoretical understanding of the enduring popularity of the private eye. The book concludes with a well-done index.

Geherin's decision to include private eyes who were active in the pulps allows him to discuss such figures as Robert Leslie Bellem's Dan Turner and John K. Butler's Steve Midnight, neither of whom is discussed by Baker and Nietzel. Geherin also provides a welcome appreciation of the four Paul Pine novels written by Howard Browne, another private eye writer neglected by Baker and Nietzel. Furthermore, Geherin is a lively and perceptive critic, and his assessments are cogently expressed. An updated survey would be welcome.

96. Niebuhr, Gary Warren. **A Reader's Guide to the Private Eye Novel**. New York: G. K. Hall, 1993. xv, 323 p. Indexes. (Reader's Guides to Mystery Novels). LC 93-22212. ISBN 0-8161-1802-7.

This is the third in a series that began with Susan Oleksiw's *A Reader's Guide to the Classic British Mystery* and continued with Marvin Lachman's *A Reader's Guide to the American Novel of Detection* (q.q.v.), and like its predecessors, this is an oddly inconsistent work. Following the preface, in which Niebuhr provides a reasonable series of criteria for defining a private eye novel, he provides an annotated bibliography of approximately 1,100 works by 90 authors published up to and during 1992. The overall arrangement is alphabetical by author. For each work, Niebuhr provides the title in boldface type and the names of the series characters in italics. Beneath the title are the place of publication, publisher, and publication year of the first American and first British editions. The annotations are in the 75–100 word range; collections of short stories are cited and listed, but their contents are not annotated. The citations are arranged by series character, after which they are ordered by what Niebuhr deems to be their internal chronology.

The annotated bibliography dominates the volume, but there are additional chapters listing pseudonyms and their users and series characters and their creators, and there are indexes for the periods during which the stories occur, locations, settings, and miscellaneous information. The volume concludes with a list of 100 classics and highly recommended titles. As with the other volumes in this series, there is no title index.

Although one can argue that Niebuhr should have chosen additional authors and works for annotation, the greatest weakness of *A Reader's Guide to the Private Eye Novel* is that it does not stand alone well. It is best used in conjunction with the other books published in this series, in particular Lachman's *A Reader's Guide to The American Novel of Detection* and Vicarel's *A Reader's Guide to the Police Procedural* (q.q.v.). It is nevertheless a useful volume. A revised and expanded edition would be helpful.

97.   Siegel, Jeff. **The American Detective: An Illustrated History**. Dallas, TX: Taylor Publishing, 1993. vii, 168 p. Index. LC 93-7189. ISBN 0-87833-829-2.

Although heavily illustrated, this history and discussion of significant American detectives manages to be more than a coffee-table book. Siegel's six chapters—"150 Years of Gumshoes," "The Shamuses," "The Snoops," "The Sheriffs," "The Shysters," and "The Spooks"—are lively and engagingly written and contain frequently thought-provoking linkages, as between Nick Carter and Meville Davisson Post's Uncle Abner. Siegel's text frequently contains sidebars offering definitions and explanations, and there are some amusing but reasonable lists, such as "The Gumshoe Hall of Fame" and "The Ten Silliest Cop Shows in Television History." Siegel's discusses detectives in film as well as literature, linking, for example, the original "Dragnet" to the police procedurals of Hillary Waugh, Lawrence Treat, and Ed McBain. Nor, despite his introductory claims, does Siegel succeed in limiting his discussion to American detectives; numerous references are made to the British detectives, and Rumpole in particular is praised: "he is such a marvelous character . . . that he deserves to be an American." (One suspects that John Mortimer could imagine a higher honor for his Q.C.!)

Following the text is a bibliographic essay, "Tracking the Sources," that describes and recommends the notable reference books about the genre, and there is a list of the winners of the Mystery Writers of America Edgar Allan Poe Awards from 1946 through 1993 (without explanations of the significance of the Raven, the Ellery Queen Award, and the Robert L. Fish Award). The book concludes with a capable index.

Like many popular histories, the book is weakest in documenting the material written between the creations of Poe and the advent of the pulp magazines. Virtually none of Siegel's quotations and references are documented, and the book contains no bibliography.

Science Fiction and Fantasy Mysteries

98.   Frants, Marina. **F and SF Mystery**.

Available as part of the archives maintained by the DorothyL listserv, and also through the Miss Lemon website (http://www.iwillfollow.com/lemon.htm), this list of works that blur the genres of mystery and science fiction/fantasy is arranged alphabetically by author. References to titles are only occasionally given; instead, the citations provide annotations for series. This list contains significantly fewer references than Herald and Lovisi's works on the same subject (q.q.v.).

99.   Herald, Diana Tixier. **Detection in Science Fiction & Fantasy**. http://www.mancon.com/genre/sfmys.html

Derived from *Genreflecting*, a work whose contents are by no means limited to mystery and detective fiction, this bibliography lists six anthologies, but the majority of the citations are to the more than 150 books by approximately 70 authors that offer a blend of science fiction and fantasy. The list is alphabetical; titles are italicized; and many entries are accompanied by ISBNs to permit easy ordering. Lengthier than the list compiled by Frants (q.v.) and briefer but more bibliographically reliable than the work of Lovisi (q.v.).

100. Lovisi, Gary. **Science Fiction Detective Tales: A Brief Overview of Futuristic Detective Fiction in Paperback.** Brooklyn, NY: Gryphon Books, 1986. 107 p. Paperback. ISBN 0-936071-01-X.

This is not a bibliography but an extended bibliographical essay, with Lovisi, a prolific writer of hard-boileds and paperback enthusiast, surveying the works that straddle the borders of science fiction and detective stories. For each work discussed, Lovisi provides the publisher, publication date, series number, price, and pagination of each of the editions that were available to him.

What could have been a worthwhile project is unfortunately a thoroughly botched job. The volume is reproduced from typed copy, the writing is amateurish, and the number of typographical errors is unbelievable. On the first page alone are references to Harold Q. Masur's "Scott Jordon," to "Earle Stanley Gardner," to "Hercule Periot," and to "Miss Marble." There is no separate list of the works discussed, and the volume lacks an index.

Readers interested in the intersection of the detective story and science fiction might wish to examine Hazel Beasley Pierce's *A Literary Symbiosis: Science Fiction/Fantasy Mystery* (Westport, CT: Greenwood Press, 1983). Though lacking a cumulative bibliography, it is capably written and well indexed.

Stamp Mysteries

101. Hedman, Iwan. **Detektiver på Frimärken.** Introduction by Sigurd Tullberg. Strangnas, Sweden: DAST Forlag AB, 1978. 48 p. (DAST Dossier Nr. 5). (500 copies printed.)

Though Swedish publications are generally beyond the scope of this section, Hedman's bibliography deserves mention as a unique achievement. In 1973, the Nicaraguan government issued 12 postage stamps of varying denominations to commemorate the 50th anniversary of Interpol; each stamp featured a different literary detective. Hedman lists these stamps alphabetically by their subject. Each entry reproduces the stamp (in enlargement), a picture of the author, and a dustwrapper from a Swedish edition of the book. Annotations (in Swedish) provide information on the detective, a brief bibliography of secondary literature about the author or the detective or both, and a two-column bibliography citing the first Swedish and English-language editions of the books featuring this detective.

As has been observed by others, Hedman does not provide information on the origin of the stamps, which were created on the basis of a poll conducted by the readers of *Ellery Queen's Mystery Magazine*, and he does not provide information about the backs of the stamps, which contained statements about the importance of the detective. These complaints aside, this is an oddly delightful little publication, but its research value is slight.

Suspense Novels

102. Jarvis, Mary J. **A Reader's Guide to the Suspense Novel**. New York: G. K. Hall, 1997. ix, 316 p. Indexes. (Reader's Guides to Mystery Novels). LC 96-40455. ISBN 0-8161-1804-3.

This volume is the fourth in the series that began with Susan Oleksiw's *A Reader's Guide to the Classic British Mystery* (q.v.); like its predecessors, this is an oddly balanced and somewhat inconsistent work. Jarvis offers annotated entries to some 750 suspense novels by 150 authors as diverse as James Hadley Chase, Mary Higgins Clark, Frederick C. Davis, Bruno Fischer, Patricia Highsmith, Henry James (!), Dean Koontz, Holly Roth, and Edgar Wallace. Surprisingly, names that one would anticipate finding in a work such as this—John Buchan, Ian Fleming, Ken Follett, Geoffrey Household, Alistair Maclean, Sapper, Shane Stevens, and Trevanian, to name but a few of the better-known writers of suspense—are not present.

The problematic contents aside, *A Reader's Guide to the Suspense Novel* contains 11 indexes: series characters and creators; creators and series characters; occupations of series characters; pseudonyms; suspense novels; period of story; location of story; setting; miscellaneous information and special subjects; the suspense event; and notable suspense novels.

The first four chapters are relatively brief, and chapter 5 dominates the volume. It is arranged alphabetically by author's name, given in boldface type; if the name is a pseudonym, the original name is listed below in parentheses. An asterisk by the author's name indicates if Jarvis has annotated only a portion of the author's output. The citations are arranged chronologically; each gives the title in boldface type, place of publication, publisher, and date of publication of the first British and American editions of the book. The major series detective is listed, as are retitlings. The annotations are brief and very well written.

The contents of the remaining chapters are largely routine, but chapter 10 deserves mention for attempting to codify and itemize the initial causes of the suspense in the novels. There is no title index.

An expanded edition of this guide would be welcome.

Women Character Mysteries

103. Androski, Helene. **Women Mystery Writers: Strong, Independent Female Lead Characters**.

Like the work of Dean James (q.v.), this bibliography of women mystery writers who feature strong, independent female lead characters in their fiction is available as part of the archives maintained by the DorothyL listserv and through the Miss Lemon website (http://www.iwillfollow.com/lemon.htm). It contains three sections. The first, "Mean Streets," cites works that feature "gritty realism or hard-boiled atmospherics"; the second, "Tea at the Vicarage," cites works that "feature a minimum of violence or other distressing subject matter"; and the third section, "Making a Statement," cites works that "comment about social or environmental issues." Citations in all sections are arranged alphabetically by author; often the author's nationality and birth date are given. The series character is named, and her profession is provided; the settings are given, as is the time; and the title and publication date of the first book in the series are indicated. Data are complete as of 1995. Very well done.

104. Heising, Willeta L. **Detecting Women 2: Pocket Guide: A Checklist for Mystery Series Written by Women**. Dearborn, MI: Purple Moon Press, 1996. 128 p. Paperback. ISBN 0-9644593-2-9.

The *Pocket Guide* was created to accompany *Detecting Women 2* (q.v.), but it contains none of the biographical data or indexes of the full-sized volume and is an author-title list. It is arranged alphabetically by author's last name, given in boldface type; pseudonyms are indicated by the letter P, but the author's real name is given only in *Detecting Women 2*. The series character's name is listed beneath the author's name, and the series titles are listed in order, with the year of publication given in parentheses. Retitlings are given, and starred titles indicate award-winners: Solid stars are used for winners, open stars for nominees. A notepad is also provided. Collectors and those needing lists will find the *Pocket Guide* extraordinarily helpful.

105. James, Dean. **The Feminine Perspective: Crime Fiction by and About Women**.

Available as part of the archives maintained by the DorothyL listserv, and through the Miss Lemon website (http://www.iwillfollow.com/lemon.htm), this list contains several sections: "Female Private Eyes," "Female Police Officers," "Other Female Amateurs/Professionals," "Women Authors with Male Detectives," and "Male Authors with Female Detectives." Each section is arranged alphabetically by author, each providing the title of the books in capital letters; no additional bibliographical data are provided. A very useful list.

Young Adult Mysteries

106. Aubrey, Irene E. **Mystery and Adventure in Canadian Books for Children and Young People/Romans Policiers et Histoires D'Aventures Canadiens pour la Jeunesse**. Ottawa: National Library of Canada, 1983. 18 p. Index. Paperback. ISBN 0-662-52484-5. C83-090083-7E.

Prepared to accompany a display of juvenile mystery and adventure books shown in the National Library of Canada, this brief bilingual catalogue contains no prefatory material but is divided into two sections, the first listing the English-language publications and the second listing the French-language publications. Both sections are arranged alphabetically by author's last name. Titles of books are in capital letters and underlined; illustrators are provided, as are place of publication, publisher, year of publication, and pagination. Translations are listed, and the names of translators are given. Beneath each citation are two columns of annotations—one in English, the other in French—describing the story and noting its awards (if any); the English annotation occurs first for the English publications, and the French annotation is given first for the French publications. An index to titles concludes the volume. Only about 40 titles are annotated.

GENERAL BIBLIOGRAPHIES and LIBRARY CATALOGUES

SCOPE NOTE: This section contains only books that reference the primary texts of detective and mystery fiction. National bibliographies, subject bibliographies, indexes to short stories, and publisher bibliographies are found under their respective subject headings.

GENERAL

107. Gribbin, Lenore S. **Who's Whodunit**. Chapel Hill, NC: University of North Carolina, 1969. x, 174 p. Paperback. (University of North Carolina Library Studies, no. 5). LC 68-65305.

Gribbin intended to list in this book the "names used by all American and British authors of book-length detective stories from 1845 [the year Poe's *Tales* was published] through 1961." Naturally, she fails in this attempt, but this does not diminish the ambitiousness of her effort.

Following an introduction in which Gribbin defines the scope of her work, the majority of the volume provides a list of the names of the authors of book-length detective stories. When the name is genuine, the pseudonyms used by that author are listed beneath it. When the name is a pseudonym, it is cross-referenced to the person who used it; joint pseudonyms are referenced to both authors. In all cases, Gribbin cites the source that indicated the author wrote detective stories; these are listed in a bibliography. Because several of these sources erred in their attributions (e.g., Henry Kuttner did not use the pseudonym Jack Vance), Gribbin perpetuates the errors. The most significant problems with the volume, however, are not factual but bibliographic, for Gribbin cites no titles, making it is impossible to determine which works by prolific authors (e.g., Georgette Heyer and Aldous Huxley) were detective stories. *Who's Whodunit* has been thoroughly superseded by such volumes as Hubin's (q.v.), and it is now best seen as a period piece.

108.   Hagen, Ordean. **Who Done It? A Guide to Detective, Mystery and Suspense Fiction**. New York: R. R. Bowker, 1969. xx, 834 p. Index. LC 69-19209. ISBN 0-8352-0234-8.

It is dangerous to attempt to be all things to everyone, and in the field of bibliography, it is equally dangerous to claim to be comprehensive. In this substantial volume Hagen does both, and the results are dire.

Who Done It? is divided into two sections, the first of which is titled "A Comprehensive Bibliography of Mystery Fiction, 1841–1967." This section is alphabetically arranged by author's last name, beneath which is an alphabetical listing of titles. The publisher of the first edition is given, as is the year of publication; reprint editions are sometimes cited. Beside each author's name is a classification: (D) for detective, (M) for mystery, and (S) for suspense. Despite having been partially compiled by Allen J. Hubin, the listings are far from comprehensive.

The second half of the volume is titled "A Bibliographic Guide to Mystery Fiction" and contains eight sections: a subject guide to mysteries; the mystery novel on the screen; mystery plays; the scene of the crime; heroes, villains, and heroines; anthologies and collections; award-winning mysteries; and writing about the mystery novel. An appendix offers "a murder miscellany" of material including a list of organizations and societies, pseudonyms, title changes, quotations, collaborations, a dictionary, pulp magazines, and the mystery novel abroad. A title index to the comprehensive bibliography concludes the volume.

None of these sections can be considered complete or thorough. The subject guide, for example, contains only 29 subject classifications, and although works of Helen Traubel and Dick Francis are cited in the introduction, there are no sections devoted to their fields of interest (respectively, opera and/or music, and horse racing), although Francis is mentioned by name in the subject classification for sports.

In a review titled "The Book, the Bibliographer and the Absence of Mind" (*The American Scholar*, Winter 1969–1970, pp. 138–48), Jacques Barzun pilloried *Who Done It?* and denounced Hagen for being insufficiently familiar with his material and with the concepts of bibliography. Barzun concluded his castigation by stating that "this would-be bibliography is a product of uncontrolled promiscuity among twenty-five thousand cards. Both the text and the compiler's acknowledgments to his family and friends suggest that the work was put together from notes absent-mindedly taken, then transcribed by amanuenses who were willing but uncomprehending slaves (see Cobblestone)."

Barzun's review cannot be considered unduly harsh, for Hagen simply attempted to do too much. There are substantial bibliographic errors in all sections. The book's first section fails to address the problems inherent in identifying the writers of detective, mystery, and suspense stories. Barzun states that "amid the promised (D) (M) (S), he [the putative user] will find technical criminology (Cherrill), sea stories (Hammond Innes), ghost stories, famous trials, adventure stories (*Beau Geste*), stories of ethical struggle (Balchin, Cozzens), as well as the bare listing of the complete works of O. Henry, Ambrose Bierce, Henry James and Jorges [sic] Luis Borges. Is this bibliography? But editorial insouciance does not stop there. Since, as is well known, everything in French literature is mysterious, we are given titles at random from the translated works of Michel Butor, Marcel Aymé and Alain Robbe-Grillet; and for good measure, the somber sex-and-religious tale by Georges Bernanos called in English *Crime*." Barzun elsewhere addresses the misidentifications of retitled works, inconsistencies in citations, and the problems inherent in classifying authors (rather than their works) as (D), (M), and (S).

Hagen died shortly before the publication of *Who Done It?* Had he lived, it is possible that later editions would have resolved the problems raised in the first edition. As it is, *Who Done It?* has been completely superseded by such works as Hubin's (q.v.) and Albert's (q.v.), and it remains at best a sadly flawed and dated volume, an unreliable series of lists that offer nothing that cannot be readily obtained elsewhere.

109. Huang, Jim, ed. **The Drood Review's 1989 Mystery Yearbook**. Boston: Crum Creek Press, 1989. Paperback. OCLC 21012436.

Although it appears to have lasted but one issue, *The Drood Review's Mystery Yearbook* was intended to list all of the mystery and detective books published during the previous year; short story collections and secondary studies were also included among the citations. The 1989 volume thus has as its focus the works published in 1988. In addition, it lists awards presented during 1988, bookstores specializing in mysteries (alphabetically and by state), and periodicals publishing mystery and detective fiction. Many of these data were derived from secondhand sources.

The *Mystery Yearbook* offers nothing that cannot be readily abstracted from other bibliographies, in particular the annual bibliographies appearing in *The Armchair Detective*.

110. Hubin, Allen J. **The Bibliography of Crime Fiction 1749–1975: Listing All Mystery, Detective, Suspense, Police, and Gothic Fiction in Book Form Published in the English Language**. Del Mar, CA: University Extension, University of California, San Diego, in cooperation with Publisher's Inc., 1979. xiv, 697 p. Indexes. LC 78-23929. ISBN 0-89163-048-1.

111. Hubin, Allen J. **Crime Fiction: 1749–1980: A Comprehensive Bibliography**. 2d ed. New York: Garland, 1984. xv, 712 p. Indexes. LC 82-48772. ISBN 0-8240-9219-8.

112. Hubin, Allen J. **Crime Fiction II: A Comprehensive Bibliography 1749–1990**. 3d ed., completely revised and updated. New York: Garland, 1994. 2 vols., xxix, 1,568 p. Indexes. LC 93-41230. ISBN 0-8240-6891-2.

Superlatives must be used to describe this, the most comprehensive bibliography of crime fiction in English. A remarkable bibliography, it changes significantly with each edition; the 3d edition is not merely the 1st edition with new entries. The following description concentrates on the 3d (1994) edition, whose introduction is exemplary, defining its subject—crime fiction—as "fiction intended for adult readers or featuring an adult protagonist and containing crime or threat of crime as a major plot element." It states that the bibliography includes "mystery, detective, suspense, thriller, gothic (romantic suspense), police, and spy fiction," and limits coverage to "all such fiction in the English language published in book form (both soft and hard covers) through the end of 1990. Magazine and dime novel fiction, juvenile and children's material, omnibus collections, and anthologies are not included."

The 3d edition contains eight sections: an author index; a title index; a settings index; a series index; a series character chronology; a film index; a screenwriters index; and a directors index. In all editions, the author index is the longest and most comprehensive section, and in the 3d, it comprises some 887 triple-column pages. Each entry lists the author's name in capital letters and provides (in regular type) reference to the sources from which further biographical data can be obtained. Also listed are the author's pseudonyms and birth and death dates; Collaborators are cross-referenced. Series characters are identified and assigned a code based on their initials. Beneath the author's name, citations are alphabetical; the publisher and publication year of the first edition in English are given. Retitlings are indicated, and similar publication data are given for them; cross-references link title changes to the original title. The series-character code indicates if the series characters appeared in the book, and a note indicates whether the work is a novel, play, or short story collection. In addition, the contents of short story collections are identified, as are the settings of novels. Finally, if the work was adapted for the motion pictures, the citation provides the year and title of the film, screenwriters, and director.

The other indexes are derived from the author index and are relatively brief. The title index lists only the book's author. The settings index begins with "Academia," concludes with "Zurich," and lists the books alphabetically by author and alphabetically by title beneath author. In all, approximately 150 settings are identified and scope-matched to the book; books set in Stockholm are not also indexed under Sweden, though cross-references are provided. The series index lists the series character's name and the name of the author or authors who used the character. The "series character chronology" lists the year in which the series character first appeared, the type of work done by the character, the country in which the character appeared, whether the character appeared primarily in hardcover or paperback books, the number of books in which the character appeared, and the authors who wrote about the character (the exception being Arthur Conan Doyle's Sherlock Holmes). The film index provides the title of the film, the studio in which it was made, the year in which the film was released, the names of the directors and screenwriters, the source author and work, and the series character. The screenwriters index lists the name of the screenwriter in capital letters and in regular letters beneath it the name of the motion picture, the author of the original work, and the title of the work if it differs from the motion picture. The director's index lists the director's name in capital letters and in regular letters beneath it the name of the motion picture, the author of the original work, and the title of the work if it differs from the name of the motion picture.

Crime Fiction is incontestably the most significant bibliography in its field, and it is a monumental achievement. Nevertheless, its very thoroughness raises several important and intriguing questions, most significant of which is, at what point does a work become "crime fiction"? The only work of Robert Graves to be cited is *They Hanged My Saintly Billy*, but this book in fact argues that William Palmer was innocent of the murders attributed to him. Similarly, F. Scott Fitzgerald's *The Apprentice Fiction of F. Scott Fitzgerald, Bits of Paradise*, and *The Mystery of the Raymond Mortgage* are cited, but surely *The Great Gatsby*—whose titular hero is a minor thug who consorts with gamblers and bootleggers, and is murdered by his mistress's husband—deserves inclusion under the guidelines Hubin established for himself.

All public and academic libraries should hold the 3d edition of Hubin.

113. Mercantile Library. **Bibliography of Mysteries from the 1920's and 1930's.** New York: Mercantile Library, [1984?]. 27 leaves. Index. OCLC 13490887.

Containing no prefatory material and perhaps never formally published, this bibliography lists mysteries published during the 1920s and 1930s. It is arranged alphabetically by author's name; titles are underlined and, when more than one title is listed, they are listed alphabetically. The place of publication, publisher, and year of publication are given. It is worth noting that the publication data provided are for the first American edition; though a number of writers included here were British, data for the first British editions are not indicated. A concluding list provides the author's name, dates of birth and death, and pseudonyms used, and lists the page on which the entries can be found. Despite its rarity, this list contains only familiar names, neglects to mention several major writers, and offers nothing that cannot be readily abstracted from other bibliographies.

SPECIFIC LIBRARIES' HOLDINGS

114. Osborne, Eric. **Victorian Detective Fiction: A Catalogue of the Collection Made by Dorothy Glover & Graham Greene.** Bibliographically arranged by Eric Osborne and introduced by John Carter, with a preface by Graham Greene. London, Sydney, Toronto: Bodley Head, 1966. xviii, 149 p. Indexes. (500 copies printed and signed by Dorothy Glover, Graham Greene, and John Carter.)

If one has money enough, energy enough, dedication enough, and (especially) time enough, a fine collection of anything can usually be assembled. The Dorothy Glover/Graham Greene collection of Victorian detective fiction is case in point: After rereading *The Moonstone*, Glover and Greene set themselves the goal of collecting all of the mystery and detective fiction published between 1841 (the advent of Edgar Allan Poe's "Murders in the Rue Morgue") and 1900/1901 (a convenient stopping point). In more than 20 years, Glover and Greene compiled a collection of 471 books and occasional periodical issues;

dime novels are not included, and although translations into English were acquired, Glover and Greene did not seek works initially published in languages other than English.

The catalogue begins with a delightful introduction by John Carter on the history of collecting of pre-modern detective fiction, followed by a brief bibliography of sources used for bibliographic attribution and verification. The entries are numbered and arranged alphabetically by the author's last name, given in boldface type; the title is given in bold italics. The publisher's name and the publication date are followed by an edition statement that provides the pagination, a description of the binding's color and salient points, and the illustrator; the name of the detective is given, as are whether the book is a translation and part of a series (when relevant). First edition data are given if the volume owned by Glover and Greene is not a first edition, and the entries note if the volume is not held in the British Museum and (when relevant) reference it to the sources listed in the initial bibliography. An appendix written by Eric Sinclair Bell discusses the publishing history of Fergus Hume's *The Mystery of a Hansom Cab*, whose first edition is one of the rarest books in detective and mystery fiction. Indexes to detectives, illustrators, and titles conclude the volume.

Although some of its inclusions are dubious (Jules Verne's *Around the World in Eighty Days* is listed among the detective novels), the catalogue is exemplary as a bibliography. Its descriptions are full and helpful, and its indexing is excellent. Despite its age, it has enduring reference value.

115.   [Randall, David A.?] **The First Hundred Years of Detective Fiction. 1841–1941. By One Hundred Authors on the Hundred Thirtieth Anniversary of the First Publication in Book Form of Edgar Allan Poe's "The Murders in the Rue Morgue" Philadelphia, 1843**. Bloomington, IN: Lilly Library, 1973. 64p. Paperback. Indexes. (Lilly Library Publication Number XVIII).

The First Hundred Years is the catalogue of an exhibition held at Indiana University's Lilly Library from July through September 1973; Randall's name does not appear on its title page but at the end of the foreword. The catalogue begins with the foreword and a list of authorities quoted. The exhibition part contains chronologically arranged sections on Edgar Allan Poe; Sherlock Holmes; Gaboriau to Simenon—France; England to 1914; England since 1914; America to 1920; and America since 1920. The work concludes with capably done indexes of authors and titles. The first item described is the April 1841 issue of *Graham's Lady's and Gentleman's Magazine,* in which Edgar Allan Poe's "The Murders in the Rue Morgue" was published.

Although the display was probably fascinating, its catalogue leaves something to be desired. Not only is the title inaccurate (the last work described is the 1943 edition of Raymond Chandler's *The Lady in the Lake*), but it is also inconsistent in its presentation of citations. Moreover, the annotations often are problematic. In several instances, they commit the unpardonable sin of revealing the identity of the criminal, and even more seriously, they reveal that they were written by somebody unfamiliar with both the history of the detective story and the book's contents. R. Austin Freeman's *The Red Thumb Mark*, for example, is described as "the first to use the new science of fingerprints," effectively ignoring the earlier contributions of Mark Twain and Freeman's point in writing *The Red Thumb Mark* to show that fingerprints alone are not sufficient evidence to convict a person. Similarly, the book version of "Maxwell Grant's" *The Living Shadow* is dated to 1931 (it was in fact published in 1934), and the annotation states (in its entirety) that it was "the first of the long-lasting adventures, in print and on radio, of *The Shadow*," a statement that is completely and demonstrably inaccurate.

116. Smith, Wilbur J. **The Boys in the Black Mask: An Exhibit in the UCLA Library, January 6–February 10, 1961**. Preface by Philip Durham. Los Angeles, CA: University of California Library, 1961. 12 p. Paperback. OCLC 7715258.

Perhaps not a reference item, but nevertheless a significant work, this may be the first separately issued catalogue of a display of mystery and detective works. As its title indicates, the exhibit focused on the writers for *Black Mask*, with a particular concentration on the writers who appeared during the editorship of Captain Joseph Shaw. Arrangement is alphabetical, the first items in the catalogue being three works by W. T. Ballard, the last being three works by Cornell Woolrich.

In the display were typescripts and manuscripts from Raymond Chandler, Lester Dent, Dashiell Hammett, Frederick Nebel, and Horace McCoy; works by Shaw himself are well represented. Chandler contributed significantly to this display; Smith's foreword states that "Raymond Chandler, a *Black Mask* contributor, gave us, along with his manuscripts, the issues in which his stories appeared." Annotations are provided for the majority of items displayed, and the bibliographic citations remain helpful.

117. Sutherland, Michael C. **Landmark Publications in Mystery and Detective Fiction**. Los Angeles, CA: Occidental College Library, 1987. 8 p. Paperback. OCLC 16006457.

This is the catalogue of an exhibition of books from the Guymon Detective and Mystery Fiction Collection held at the Occidental College Library from March through May 1987. The exhibition contained some 24 separate sections, and the catalogue is arranged chronologically. The first item listed is the 1770 edition of *The Lamentable and True Tragedie of M. Arden of Feversham, in Kent: Who Was Most Wickedlye Murdered, by the Means of His Disloyal and Wanton Wyfe, Who for the Love She Bare to One Mosbie, Hyred Two Desperat Ruffins, Blackwill and Shagbag, to Kill Him*, a work originally published in 1592. Additional works in the exhibition include a first English-language edition of *The Castle of Otranto*, the 1841 appearance in *Graham's Lady's and Gentleman's Magazine* of Poe's "The Murders in the Rue Morgue," a first edition of *The Mystery of Edwin Drood*, various dime novels, several works by Doyle including the 1887 *Beeton's Christmas Annual* containing *A Study in Scarlet*, and a first edition of Hammett's *The Thin Man* accompanied by its typescript. This would have been an exhibition worth seeing!

NATIONAL BIBLIOGRAPHIES

SCOPE NOTE: This section lists the monographs and websites that attempt to document all mystery and detective fiction published in a specific country.

AUSTRALIA

118.   Loder, John. **Australian Crime Fiction: A Bibliography 1857–1993**. Victoria, Australia: D. W. Thorpe, in association with the National Center for Australian Studies, 1994. xiv, 287 p. Indexes. ISBN 1-875589-51-1.

Drawing partly from a vast private collection, bibliographer and bibliophile Loder has assembled a bibliography of the crime and mystery fiction published in Australia from 1857 to 1993. Although his focus is on the separately published book, he has also noted a few serializations that were not published as books, and he has also provided data on a number of Australian pulp magazines. In all, more than 2,600 books by more than 500 authors have been recorded, many for the first time. As Loder's introduction states, "it came as a surprise, when the impressive crime fiction bibliography of Hubin was published, to find he had missed a third of the Australian titles. On analysis it was apparent he had missed authors who had not published in America or Great Britain."

The body of Loder's bibliography is alphabetical by the author's last name; magazines are listed alphabetically by their title. A typical author entry provides the author's name (in boldface type), indicating pseudonyms and providing significant biographical data. The title of the book is given in smaller boldface type. The place, publisher, and year of publication are provided in regular type, as are the pagination and a physical description of the book, including the existence and placements of plates. The existence of a dustwrapper is noted, as is whether or not the volume has been recorded by Hubin. Title changes are noted, and a significant number of entries conclude with a brief description of the volume's contents. Cross-references are plentiful. Successive sections provide a title index; an index to the book's illustrators, jacket artists, designers, and photographers; and an index to the investigators and criminals.

Australian Crime Fiction is in all respects an exemplary bibliography. Loder's biographical data are frequently inaccessible elsewhere, and his bibliographic data are, so far as can be ascertained, gratifyingly accurate and thorough. Indeed, Loder has noted when he has verified the existence of the work through other sources but has been unable to examine it himself. This is a difficult volume to obtain in the United States, but it is worth the effort.

BELGIUM

119.   Hermans, Willy. **Petit Dictionnaire des Auteurs Belges de Littérature Policière**. Liege: Librairie Version Originale, 1989. [iv], 93 p. Paperback. ISBN 2-87287-000-8.

Despite the implications of the title, no larger or more comprehensive dictionary to the mystery and detective stories written by Belgian writers seems to exist. This slim volume is arranged alphabetically by the writer's last name, given in boldface capitals. A brief biographical statement is provided; pseudonyms are identified, birth and death dates are given, and the first Belgian (or French) editions of the author's significant mystery and detective works are listed chronologically at the bottom of each entry. Citations include the year of publication and often the publisher and place of publication. An index to the names given in the biographical statement concludes the book.

CANADA

120.   Skeen, Melvin, L. David St. C., with Norbert Spehner. **Canadian Crime Fiction: An Annotated Comprehensive Bibliography of Canadian Crime Fiction from 1817 to 1996 and Biographical Dictionary of Canadian Crime Writers, with an Introductory Essay on the History and Development of Canadian Crime Writings**. Shelburne, Ontario: Battered Silicon Dispatch Box, 1996. xxxi, 440 p. Indexes. C96-930488-9. ISBN 1-896648-60-6.

Some 11 years in the compilation, this comprehensive bibliography of Canadian crime fiction is vast in its coverage, citing adventure, crime, detective, espionage, mystery, suspense, and thriller books written by Canadians, books by non-Canadians and set in Canada, or books somehow connected to Canada, that were published between 1817 and 1996. Also included, when relevant, are citations to published dramas; tales of intrigue, violence, and investigation; and juvenile novels with a criminous connection. The cited publications may be in English or French.

The volume begins with a lengthy history of the detective story and Canadian crime fiction; the bibliography opens with "Crime Fiction by Canadians." Author's names are given in boldface type, the last name in capital letters. A typical entry includes the author's birth and death dates, a sometimes lengthy biographical profile, and a list of the author's criminous publications giving the title, place of publication, publisher, year of publication, series, and setting. Often the protagonist's name is given, and frequently there is an annotation describing the importance of the work; lists of the author's other publications are often provided. Cross-references abound. Furthermore, every criminous work is keyed to a series of symbols (repeated on the bottom of each page): + (plus) indicates it is by a Canadian and set in Canada; * (asterisk) indicates it is by a Canadian and set elsewhere; ! (exclamation point) indicates it is fiction by a non-Canadian set in Canada; ? (question mark, rarely used) indicates the work is unidentified; and # (hash mark) indicates that there is a "Canadian connexion" (i.e., a criminous novel with a Canadian protagonist written by a non-Canadian and set outside of Canada; a novel that has a portion set in Canada, or that touches peripherally upon Canada with either a Canadian character or a mention of Canada or Canadians; or "authors that passed this way but once, but didn't use Canada as a setting for their work"). It should be mentioned that an enormous number of these documents are completely unobtainable through any other reference work.

The bibliography is followed by two appendixes also containing bibliographical data. The first cites the criminous works set in Canada but written by non-Canadians; the second cites the works that have the aforementioned "Canadian Connexions." Both of these appendixes follow the format established in "Crime Fiction by Canadians," and the data in these sections are frequently lengthy and unobtainable elsewhere.

Eighteen useful indexes and a bibliography conclude the volume. The indexes offer access to titles of crime fiction by Canadians, to titles by non-Canadians, and to titles with a Canadian connection. There are also chronological indexes to crime fiction by Canadians and to titles by non-Canadians set in Canada; the characters of Canadian authors are indexed, as are the settings used by the Canadian authors. Juvenile works (for children and young adults) are indexed, as are mysteries about Canada, Mountie novels, short story collections of crime fiction by Canadians, criminous plays, series, Canadian criminal *romans à clef*, cross-genre criminous titles by Canadians, and pseudonyms used by Canadian crime writers. The indexes conclude with lists of the winners of the Crime Writers of Canada's "Arthur Ellis" awards, and the Canadian winners of a Mystery Writers of America "Edgar."

Unlikely ever to be superseded, *Canadian Crime Fiction* is a monumental achievement; it belongs in all academic libraries.

DENMARK

121. Nielsen, Bjarne. **Hvem Begik Hvad? Dansk Kriminalliteratur indtil 1979: En Bibliografi København [i.e., Copenhagen]**. Antikvariat Pinkerton, 1981. 131 p. Paperback. Indexes. LC 82-112686. OCLC 9918644.

Offset from typed copy, this bibliography of Danish detective fiction published in book form prior to 1979 begins with an introduction providing the bibliography's principals and a brief history of the detective story in Denmark. Only Danish writers or writers of Danish extraction are cited; this is not the place to find the Danish publishing histories of Agatha Christie, Arthur Conan Doyle, or Edgar Wallace.

The first portion of the bibliography is arranged alphabetically by author. The author's name is given in capital letters and underlined, and is often accompanied by biographical dates; brief signed biographies of significant authors are occasionally provided. The titles of books are given in capital letters and are followed by the publisher, year of publication, and pagination. Pseudonyms are indicated, and numerous cross-references are provided.

The bibliography's second section cites collective and anonymous books, using the same procedures as in the first section. The third section indexes anonymous series books. Series names are given in capital letters and underlined, the publisher and year in which the series started are given, and each title in the series is numbered; the titles are given in regular type. As in the earlier sections, numerous cross-references are provided. The bibliography concludes with a title index. Very capably done.

FINLAND

122. Sjöblom, Simo. **Rikoskirjallisuuden Bibliografia, 1864–1984: Eli 120 Vuoden Aikana Suomeksi Limestyneet Jännitysromaanit**. Helsinki: Antikvaarinen Kirjakauppa Simo Sjöblom, 1985. 375 p. LC 87-117925. ISBN 951-99692-0-9.

The full text of this bibliography of detective and mystery fiction published in Finland between 1864 and 1984 was not available to me. Nevertheless, unlike Nielsen's bibliography of Danish detective and mystery fiction (q.v.), Sjöblom has concentrated on mystery and detective fiction published in Finland, and not only fiction written by authors from Finland or of Finnish extraction. The author's name is given in capital letters, accompanied by birth and death dates; the titles of the books are listed alphabetically beneath the name, with the original title (if any) following immediately in parentheses accompanied by the original publication date. These are followed by the name of the translator, publisher, place of publication, year of publication, pagination, and name of the Finnish series in which the book appeared.

GERMANY

123. Hillich, Reinhard, and Wolfgang Mittmann. **Die Kriminaliteratur der DDR 1949–1990: Bibliografie**. Berlin: Akademie Verlag, 1991. 240 p. Index. ISBN 3-05-001856-9.

Research on this bibliography began in 1988, when the two authors—Hillich, a literary historian, and Mittmann, a writer and collector of mysteries—realized the need for a work that documented the detective and mystery books and uncollected stories written by German authors. Following the introduction, a section titled "Reihen" describes the major series by significant hardcover and pocketbook publishers. Entries provide the publisher's location, its founder, the years during which the publisher remained in business, the typical publication size, the date of the first (and, when relevant, last) publication, and significant additional series. The two successive sections list the bibliographic sources used by Hillich and Mittmann and list their abbreviations.

The first portion of the bibliography is a two-column author list. Names are given in boldface type, followed by the title in regular type; pseudonyms are indicated. Entries for books provide an abbreviated note indicating the nature of the book's contents (e.g., *KR* for Kriminalroman; *KERz(n)* for Kriminalerzäungen; *KNov(n)* for Kriminalnovellen), and list place of publication, publisher, and year of publication. Pagination is given, series numbers are recorded, and the contents of short story collections are listed. Entries for periodical publications give the periodical's title, volume, year, and issue number.

The second section is a two-column chronological list that reprints the data given in the first section. Despite the limitations implied by the title, the list includes some publications from the first part of 1991. The bibliography concludes with a list of authors. Birth and death dates are given when available, as are pseudonyms.

The bibliography lacks a title index, but apart from this, it contains an enormous amount of original research. It is superior to the earlier effort of Klaus-Dieter Walkhoff-Jordan (q.v.) and will be welcome in research libraries.

124. Walkhoff-Jordan, Klaus-Dieter. **Bibliographie der Kriminalliteratur 1945–1984 im deutschen Sprachraum**. Mit einem Vorwort von Friedhelm Werremeier. Frankfurt/M: Ullstein, 1985. 547 p. Paperback. (Ullstein Krimi). LC 86-141552. ISBN 3-548-10325-1.

The first bibliography of mystery and detective fiction published in Germany, this title lists works by authors of other nationalities as well as those by German authors. Arrangement is alphabetical by author; names are given in boldface capitals. When employed, pseudonyms are listed beneath the name, as are the German title of their books (in small capital letters); when the work is not by a German author, parentheses contain the original title and its publication date. Entries conclude with the name of the German publisher given in abbreviated form and keyed to a list of abbreviations at the beginning, the work's series number, and the dates of the work's German editions.

A second section lists the German editions of detective and mystery series. The arrangement is slightly different: entries are alphabetical by series title and given in boldface capitals. Beneath this is the name of the author, after which come the publisher and years it published the series. Next are individually numbered entries that give the German title of the book in small capital letters followed by the year of its first German publication; beneath these in parentheses are the English title and the year of its first publication.

Though a lot of effort has clearly gone into the compilation of *Bibliographie der Kriminalliteratur 1945–1984*, it lacks a title index, has an occasional error, and is not as comprehensive as the later work compiled by Reinhard Hillich and Wolfgang Mittmann (q.v.). Walkhoff-Jordan has published a supplement extending coverage to 1990 (q.v.).

125. Walkhoff-Jordan, Klaus-Dieter. **Bibliographie der Kriminalliteratur 1985–1990 im deutschen Sprachraum**. Mit einem Vorwort von Friedhelm Werremeier. Frankfurt/M: Ullstein, 1991. 228 p. Paperback. (Ullstein Sachbuch). LC 92-180642. ISBN 3-548-34813-0.

As its title indicates, this bibliography is a continuation of Walkhoff-Jordan's earlier effort (q.v.), listing the detective and mystery fiction published in Germany from 1985 to 1990. The introduction notes that there are 4,684 entries, 1,805 of which are by foreign authors first published in Germany, 718 of which are German originals, 1,658 of which are reprints from foreign authors, and 503 of which are reprints from German authors. The bibliography's arrangement is alphabetical by author (given in boldface capital letters), often accompanied by dates of birth and death; pseudonyms are also frequently provided. In small capital letters beneath each name are the German titles of the books; these are followed by parentheses containing the English title and the date of first English-language publication. This in turn is followed by the name of the publisher (in highly abbreviated form), the book's series number, and the date of the German edition of the book. A brief concluding section lists the contents of anonymous detective and mystery series published between 1985 and 1990.

This bibliography lacks a title index. More seriously, Walkhoff-Jordan has included a number of books solely on the strengths of their titles and the fact that characters are killed in them. There are thus references to the German editions of works by such authors as Clive Barker, Stephen King, Tabitha King, and Somtow Sucharitikul. Furthermore, this volume is simply not as comprehensive as the effort of Reinhard Hillich and Wolfgang Mittmann (q.v.).

IRELAND

126. Ingravallo, Ciccio. **Irish Mystery**.

This appears to be the only separately published bibliography on its subject. It is available as part of the archives maintained by the DorothyL listserv, and also through the Miss Lemon website (http://www.iwillfollow.com/lemon.htm).

This list of mysteries that in some way involve Ireland and the Irish is arranged alphabetically by author. Each citation gives the book's title, place of publication, publisher, and year of publication. Often an annotation provides the name of the chief character and some information as to the book's contents. A lengthier bibliography would be welcome.

JAPAN

127. Nakajimi, Kawataro. **Nihon Suiri Shosetsu Jiten**. Tokyo: Tokyo Shup-pan, 1985. 422 p. Index. LC 86-217532. ISBN 4-490-10204-6.

Apparently the most comprehensive bibliography of Japanese detective stories available, this dictionary includes only Japanese writers, arranged in alphabetical by author's last name. For each writer, a biography is provided, as are a list of books and a brief description of each. A title index concludes the bibliography.

Note: Katsuo Jinka's *Gendai Kaigai Misuteri Besuto 100* (Tokyo: Shakai Shisosha, 1991) lists 100 "best" detective and mystery stories, but these are not by Japanese writers, and the titles include *Blue Belle, Tinker, Tailor, Soldier, Spy*, and *Presumed Innocent*. The same is true of *Sekai no Suiri Shosetsu Sokaisetsu* by Nakajima and Manji Gonda (Tokyo: Jiyu Kokuminsha, 1982). Nakajima's *Sengo Suiri Shosetsu Somokuroku* (Tokyo: Nippon Suiri Sakka Kyokai, 1970–1980), entry A202 in the second edition of Walter Albert's *Detective and Mystery Fiction* (q.v.), is described as "an index of mystery stories published in Japan since 1945 through 1979. It focuses on the stories which first appeared in magazines, and includes only the novels that were originally written in book form." It has not been seen.

SCANDINAVIA

128. Steffensen, Jan B. **Scandinavian Mysteries in English**.

Compiled by Steffensen, and accessible through his Mysterious Homepage (q.v.), as well being accessible through the archives maintained by the DorothyL listserv and through the Miss Lemon website (http://www.iwillfollow.com/lemon.htm), this list of Scandinavian mysteries available in English translation is arranged by the author's country of origin. Within each country, the citations are arranged alphabetically by author; English titles are provided along with a year (whether of original publication or date of translation is not made clear); the original title is provided.

SOUTH AFRICA

129. Miller, Anita. **Afrikaanse speurverhale uitgegee tot die einde van 1950: 'n Bibliografie**. Johannesburg: Universiteit van die Witwatersrand Departement van Bibliografie, Biblioteekwese en Tipografie, 1967. iv, 23 p. Indexes.

I have not generally included dissertations in this book, but Miller's bibliography of Afrikaans detective and mystery writers is the first and only bibliography on its subject, and one would be remiss not to acknowledge its existence and the existence of Susan Friedland's continuation (below). Both dissertations were compiled as a partial fulfillment for the requirements for the Diploma in

Librarianship at the University of the Witwatersrand, Johannesburg, Miller's, however, is entirely in Afrikaans.

Miller's two-page foreword gives no theoretical discussions or definitions of her subject, but she does provide four criteria she used for determining inclusions in her bibliography: "Die Bibliografie sluit die volgende in: 1. Ooorspronklike [sic] Afrikaanse speurromans, en wel slegs dié; 2. wat in die Africana-versameling van die Johannesburgee Openbare biblioteek aanwesig is; 3. wat in boekvorm uitgegee is; and 4. en wat voor en tot die einde van 1950 verskyn hat." (In English, these translate roughly to a statement that the bibliography includes bibliographic information about original Afrikaans detective novels, with specific references only to those novels; what was available in the Afrikaaner collections of the Johannesburg Public Library; what was published in book form; and that they were published before the end of 1950.)

The first section lists the books alphabetically, by giving the authors' names in capital letters; book titles are not underlined. In addition, each citation provides the book's place of publication, publisher, date of publication, pagination, and size. Series characters are identified, as are pseudonyms. In all, approximately 300 books are referenced. A one-page section lists Afrikaans articles published on the subject, and the concluding section is a title index to the works cited in the bibliography.

The information in this volume is utterly unique, but the bibliography is not without its share of misspellings, and several of these include names; Petrus J. Nienaber's name is given as "Bienaber," and additional typos are not difficult to find. Probably only specialists will need this and Susan Friedland's continuation.

130. Friedland, Susan. **South African Detective Stories in English and Afrikaans from 1951–1971**. Johannesburg: University of the Witwatersrand Department of Bibliography, Librarianship and Typography, 1972. ii, 46 p. Indexes.

This volume is a direct continuation and expansion of Anita Miller's *Afrikaanse speurverhale uitgegee tot die einde van 1950: 'n bibliografie* (above), and as its title indicates, it documents the South African detective stories published in English and Afrikaans from 1951 to 1971. Like Miller's work, this was compiled as partial fulfillment for the requirements for the Diploma in Librarianship at the University of the Witwatersrand, Johannesburg, but whereas Miller wrote in Afrikaans, Friedland uses English for her prefatory material.

Friedland begins her bibliography with a reasonable caveat: "since South Africa is still a young country and its population fairly mobile, it is dificilt [sic] to define as South Africans only those writers who were born here. Writers have therefore been included who spent a considerable part of their lives in South Africa and wrote at least some of their novels while being citizens or residents here." Successive sections list English authors, Afrikaans authors, English titles, Afrikaans titles, English series, and Afrikaans series. The citations in the sections devoted to the English and Afrikaans authors are numbered; in all, 451 works are listed. Each entry provides the author's name, the title, publication data for the first edition, and the volume's pagination; a brief annotation concerning the volume's contents concludes each entry. The volume ends with a highly selective bibliography of journal articles on the detective story.

Although lists of the writings of the English authors has been reprinted in *Mysteries of Africa*, edited by Eugene Schleh (Bowling Green, Ohio: Bowling Green State University Popular Press, 1991), the listing of Afrikaans mystery and detective story writers is apparently unique to this volume. Nevertheless, like Miller's work, this one is likely to interest only specialists.

SWEDEN

131.   Hedman-Morelius, Iwan. **Kriminallitteratur på Svenska 1749–1985**. Göteborg: Dast Förlag, 1986. 473 p. ISBN 91-85208-07-8.

This is apparently an expansion of Hedman-Morelius's (1974) *Dekare och Thrillers på Svenska, 1864–1973* (not seen). The present volume lists the detective and fiction books that were published in Sweden and Swedish between 1749 and 1985, regardless of the author's initial origins. A number of entries are for translations of works originally published in English.

The entries in *Kriminallitteratur på Svenska* are arranged alphabetically, but unlike the other national bibliographies herein considered, it does not contain a separate index to titles; rather, the title index is incorporated into the volume as part of the main sequence. Each author's entries give his or her name in boldface capital letters; birth and death dates are occasionally provided, as are pseudonyms and the names of significant series characters. The books are listed chronologically by the date of the first Swedish publication, each entry providing in truncated form the citation to the first Swedish edition of that volume; the key to the abbreviations occurs at the beginning of the book. When the referenced book has been reprinted from an English source, the publication data of the first British or American edition are given, also in highly abbreviated form.

In addition, motion picture and dramatic adaptations are listed beneath the relevant author, the reference to these providing only the years of the adaptations. Also cited are significant works of nonfiction: Raymond Chandler's letters are referenced, as are such volumes as Bo Lundin's *Salongsbödlarna* and *The Swedish Crime Story*. Finally, the volume contains numerous photographs, not all of them credited, and concludes with a list of the awards given by the Swedish Academy of Detection.

An enormous amount of effort went into the creation of this book, and like the work of Allen Hubin (q.v.), this one is likely to be superseded only by the author's updating of his earlier efforts.

132. Hedman-Morelius, Iwan. **Kriminallitteratur på Svenska 1986–1990.** Huskvarna: DAST, 1992. 475–580 p. (DAST Dossier, no. 9). ISBN 91-85208-08-6.

This is apparently a direct continuation of Hedman-Morelius's *Kriminallitteratur på Svenska 1749–1985* (above). It has not been seen.

133. Lingblom, Hans E. **1257 Förteckning över Deckare, Thrillers, Faktaböcker, Memoarer, Kolportageromaner.** Ostersund: Berntssons, 1979.

Not seen.

134. Tullberg, Sigurd. **O och A. Detektivromaner på Svenska under 1900–talet.** Stockholm: Bibliotekens Bokformedling, 1954. 95 p.

Not seen.

GEOGRAPHICAL GUIDES/MAPS

SCOPE NOTE: This chapter cites publications that relate mysteries to specific locations. Many of the indexes and readers' guides also provide indexes for locations.

GENERAL REGIONAL GUIDES

135.   King, Nina, with Robin Winks. **Crimes of the Scene: A Mystery Novel Guide for the International Traveler**. New York: St. Martin's Press, 1997. xi, 291 p. Index. LC 96-44225. ISBN 0-312-15174-8.

Crimes of the Scene offers lists and reviews of mystery novels set in countries or regions other than Great Britain and the United States. The book contains 21 chapters, each devoted to the mysteries of a country or a region, each using the same structure. There is a general introduction to the mysteries of that region, followed by an annotated bibliography of the region's mysteries that have been translated into English. The chapters conclude with a list of works that have been "noted but not reviewed." An author index rounds out the work.

There is much to praise in *Crimes of the Scene*, but it is also a work with idiosyncrasies. The authors have made no attempts to distinguish between genres; in addition to citations to mysteries, there are numerous references to thrillers and adventure novels. One finds here entries for nonmysteries written by Eric Ambler, Ian Fleming, Ken Follett, Frederick Forsyth, Thomas Harris, Jack Higgins, and Donald Westlake, to name but a few. Significant mysteries have nevertheless been omitted. For example, Jonathan Kellerman's bestselling *Butcher's Theater* has not been included although it is set almost entirely in a meticulously described Jerusalem. Equally seriously, some of the annotations are completely erroneous: A. E. W. Mason's *The Four Feathers* (another dubious inclusion) is described as "the kitsch classic where the Brits storm Khartoum in 1882 and avenge the slaughter of Chinese Gordon by the 'fuzzie-wuzzies,'" which is most certainly not the plot of Mason's 1902 novel. The indexing, too, is not comprehensive.

Crimes of the Scene is the only work devoted entirely to its subject; it is perfect for the armchair traveler. One hopes for a revised, corrected, and expanded edition.

136. Lawson, Janet, and Cynthia Orr. **Mystery by Region**. http://www.Poly-Web.com/BookBrowser/MystRegion/mystregion.htm

Though still in the formative stages, this easy-to-use website allows readers to pick a geographical location—Canada, Europe, Scandinavia, the United Kingdom, the United States, and so forth—and to find mysteries set in that region. Clickable maps are provided, as are the names of countries and all of the states. The search leads to authors who have used that area for their settings and the titles of their works. Minimal bibliographic data are provided, but updates are promised.

SPECIFIC AREAS

American Cities

Boston

137. Parker, Robert B. **Spenser's Boston**. Photographs by Kasho Kumagai. New York: Otto Penzler Books, 1994. 199 p. LC 94-17814. ISBN 1-883402-50-6.

Although it contains a map of Boston and surrounding areas, *Spenser's Boston* is not a walking tour of those parts of Boston that appear in Parker's Spenser series. Instead, the book begins with a short story in which Spenser, Susan, and Rachel Wallace walk around Boston and comment upon the city. Chapters titled "Summer," "Autumn," and "Winter" contain seasonal pictures of Boston, New England, and Parker. A chapter titled "Crossing Mystic River Bridge" provides photographs of some of the sights—small towns, autumn trees, harbors—that can be seen after crossing the Mystic River Bridge, and "108 Miles to Cape Cod" has photographs of Cape Cod, Hyannis, and Provincetown. Kumagai provides an appreciative afterword, and the concluding "Guide to Boston" lists 12 places of interest in Boston. Lovers of Spenser and Boston will appreciate Parker's prose and Kumagai's beautifully composed and rendered photographs.

Chicago

138. Dale, Alzina Stone. **Mystery Reader's Walking Guide: Chicago**. Maps by Ben Stone. Lincolnwood, IL: Passport Books, 1995. xii, 385 p. Index. LC 94-33414. ISBN 0-8442-9607-4.

Mystery Reader's Walking Guide: Chicago follows the same format as Dale's other books, identifying 10 walks that will take the reader through Chicago sites that have been featured in crime and mystery novels. Each walk is accorded a separate chapter. Each chapter begins with a historical introduction, a statement as to the length of the walk, and a list of the places of interest and the places to eat that can be seen and visited during the walk. The descriptions of the walks are agreeably informal, mixing descriptions of sites with discussions of the mysteries set in them. Each chapter is provided with a map drawn specifically for this volume; no distance keys are provided.

The book's second section, "Special Helps," lists the authors, books, and sleuths mentioned in each walk although restaurants, places of interest, theaters and concert halls, and shops mentioned in the body of the book are not repeated. A brief bibliography and very well done indexes conclude the book.

Los Angeles and Southern California

139. Stone, Carolyn K. **A Reading List for Mystery Lovers! Mysteries on Location. Scene of the Crimes.** Beverly Hills, CA; Montpelier, CT: Literate Traveller, Stone and Stone Travel Research Services, 1996. 6 leaves.

These guides to regional mysteries may not have been formally published, but they have been advertised on the World Wide Web and through the DorothyL discussion group, and they are available through the website of the Literate Traveller (http://www.literatetraveller.com). All guides are reproduced from laser-printed copy and were published in 1996; all cleave to the same format. The first five leaves of each are arranged alphabetically by author and provide title, place of publication, publisher, and first publication date for between 13 and 21 mystery novels set in that region. The authors of these mysteries tend to be among the living. Each novel is capably annotated; often, other works by the author are referenced. The sixth leaf provides a bibliography of bibliographies listing mysteries set in that region.

This list covers mysteries set in Los Angeles, Hollywood, and Southern California.

140. Ward, Elizabeth, and Alain Silver. **Raymond Chandler's Los Angeles.** Woodstock, NY: Overlook Press, 1987. 234 p. LC 86-18007. ISBN 0-87951-266-0.

Raymond Chandler's Los Angeles is not a walking tour or a guide to the city of Los Angeles in the way that Don Herron's *Dashiell Hammett Tour* (q.v.) offers a guide to San Francisco. It nevertheless deserves mention here because Ward and Silver identify the locations that Chandler used in his short stories and novels, and pair Chandler's descriptions with a black-and-white photograph or photographs of the site. In all, more than 100 black-and-white photographs are provided. Although the photographs are contemporary, Ward and Silver manage to make them look timeless and, occasionally, eerie and disturbing. On the debit side, there are no maps, making this "armchair tour of Raymond Chandler's Los Angeles" less than ideal.

Overlook Press reissued this book in 1997, and a selection of the images can be found at http://members.aol.com/chandlerla/index.htm.

New York City

141. Dale, Alzina Stone. **Mystery Reader's Walking Guide: New York**. Maps by Kenneth Herrick Dale. Lincolnwood, IL: Passport Books, 1993. xvi, 361 p. Indexes. LC 92-60398. ISBN 0-8442-9481-0.

In this enjoyable walking guide to a few of the hundreds of New York City sites that have been used in mysteries, the introduction is weak, managing to put three factual errors into its two opening sentences. Writes Dale: "New York City has been the center of the mystery novel since its inventor, Edgar Allan Poe, borrowed a NYC crime for his chilling tale, *The Mystery of Marie Roget*, published in 1841. A generation later, in 1878, New Yorker Anna Katherine Green's *The Leavenworth Case* was the first detective story written by a woman." Apart from the fact that Poe neither wrote mystery novels nor invented New York City, "The Mystery of Marie Roget" was first published in *Snowden's Ladies' Companion* in 1842, and to credit Anna Katherine Green with the first detective story is to ignore Metta Victor's 1867 *The Dead Letter*.

This guide concentrates on Manhattan mystery sites, providing 11 walks through such neighborhoods as Wall Street, the Lower East Side, Greenwich Village, Midtown West, the Upper East Side, and Central Park. Although each walk covers one neighborhood, some of the walks are split into two or three parts because so many sites have been used.

As in the other volumes in this series, each walk is accorded a separate chapter. Each chapter begins with a historical introduction, a statement as to the length of the walk, and lists of the places of interest and the places to eat that can be seen and visited during the walk. The descriptions of the walks are chatty and lively, mixing descriptions of New York sites with discussions of the mysteries set in them. A map drawn specifically for this volume is provided for each walk; however, no distance keys are provided, and the writing on the map tends toward the microscopic.

The book's second section, "Special Helps," lists the authors, books, and sleuths mentioned in each walk and does not repeat the lists of the restaurants, places of interest, theaters and concert halls, and shops that are given in the body of the book. Concluding the volume are a brief bibliography and a well-done index.

San Francisco

142. Derie, Kate. **SanFran Sleuths: San Francisco Bay Area Mysteries**.

This list of mysteries set in the San Francisco Bay area is available through the archives maintained by DorothyL and also through the Miss Lemon website (http://www.iwillfollow.com/lemon.htm). Its first section is arranged alphabetically by author, a number sign (#) indicating when the author also lives in the Bay Area. Citations provide the name of the character, his or her occupation, the location of the books, the first publication date, title, and publisher. An index lists the works by detective's profession and gives the detective's name, author, and location.

143. Herron, Don. **Dashiell Hammett Tour**. San Francisco, CA: Dawn Heron Press, 1982. 95 p. Paperback. (Heron's Literary Walks in San Francisco, no. 1). ISBN 0-939790-02-5.

From 1921 until 1930 Dashiell Hammett lived in San Francisco, a city he used as background in "The Whosis Kid," "Fly Paper," *The Dain Curse*, and *The Maltese Falcon*. Hammett's locations have been identified in a number of articles, but Herron's is the first separate publication to provide readers with a walking tour. Furthermore, Heron identifies (and provides numerous pictures of) the buildings in which Hammett is known to have lived.

Heron begins his 27-stop tour at the San Francisco Library (in which Hammett did research and work) and concludes it with Samuels Jewelers, at which Hammett worked as an advertising writer. (Albert S. Samuels was also the person to whom *The Dain Curse* was dedicated.) Notable sites visited include all of Hammett's rooms, Burritt Street (in which the body of Miles Archer is found), John's Grill (in which Sam Spade ate), and 891 Post (the apartment lived in by Hammett and—probably—by Sam Spade).

The volume contains five maps but lacks scales, distances, and (unfortunately) indexing. It is nevertheless lively, informative, and enjoyable.

144. Stone, Carolyn K. **A Reading List for Mystery Lovers! Mysteries on Location. Scene of the Crimes**. Beverly Hills, CA; Montpelier, CT: Literate Traveller, Stone and Stone Travel Research Services, 1996. 6 leaves.

This is a Literate Traveller guide to the mysteries set in San Francisco. See the entry under "Los Angeles and Southern California" for a brief description of this set of guides.

England

145. Dale, Alzina Stone, and Barbara Sloan Hendershott. **Mystery Reader's Walking Guide: England**. Maps by Alisa Mueller Burkey. Lincolnwood, IL: Passport Books, 1988. xv, 416 p. Indexes. LC 88-60300.

Significantly larger in scope than their earlier *Mystery Reader's Walking Guide: London* (q.v.), this walking guide to England nevertheless shares the same premise and arrangement. In the first section, Dale and Hendershott identify 14 towns and regions that can be associated with mysteries, and they plot walks ranging in length from 2.5 to 8.8 miles through them. All towns are accessible by British Rail, and each walk starts and ends at the British Railway Station. As in the earlier volume, each walk is accorded a separate chapter. Information provided includes not only authors and works that made use of the area but also ancillary places of interest (and their hours of operation) and recommended places to eat. Helpful details abound: "Serves pub lunches and dinners to nonresidents." As before, each walk includes a clearly drawn map plotted specifically for this volume, and each map identifies the locations on the walk but does not include a distance key.

The book's second section, "Special Helps," lists the authors, books, and sleuths by walk; the separate lists of restaurants and pubs, places of interest, shops, theaters, and concert halls are not repeated. The volume concludes with a brief bibliography and a very capable index.

146.   Dale, Alzina Stone, and Barbara Sloan Hendershott. **Mystery Reader's Walking Guide: London**. Maps by John Babcock. Lincolnwood, IL: Passport Books, 1987. xx, 294 p. Indexes. LC 86-60564. ISBN 0-8442-9550-7.

As its title indicates, this is a guide for those whose love of mysteries extends to visiting the places used as their settings. In the first section, Dale and Hendershott identify the London locales used by more than 50 mystery and detective writers and plot 11 walks—ranging in length from 3 to 6.2 miles—that take one through these areas. Each walk is accorded a separate chapter. The information given includes not only authors and works making use of the area but also ancillary places of interest (and their hours of operation) and recommended places to eat. Helpful details abound: "Eating places and pubs within the walk are open Monday-Friday during lunch hours only. (Toilet facilities are also limited.)" Finally, each walk includes a clearly presented map drawn specifically for this volume; each map identifies the locations on the walk but does not include a distance key.

The volume's second section is called "Special Helps" and consists of lists recapitulating the data given in the first section: places to eat, places of interest, theaters and concert halls, shops mentioned, and authors, books, and sleuths associated with each walk. Though redundant in content, this section nevertheless provides a convenient checklist of the highlights of each walking tour. A bibliography and an index to persons, places, and books conclude the guide. It is not only well done but also a browser's delight.

147.   Stone, Carolyn K. **A Reading List for Mystery Lovers! Mysteries on Location. Scene of the Crimes**. Beverly Hills, CA; Montpelier, CT: Literate Traveller, Stone and Stone Travel Research Services, 1996. 6 leaves.

This is a Literate Traveller guide to the mysteries set in England. See the entry under "Los Angeles and Southern California" for a brief description of this set of guides.

Other Countries

148.   Stone, Carolyn K. **A Reading List for Mystery Lovers! Mysteries on Location. Scene of the Crimes**. Beverly Hills, CA; Montpelier, CT: Literate Traveller, Stone and Stone Travel Research Services, 1996. 6 leaves.

This is a Literate Traveller guide to the mysteries set in Africa, France, Asia, and the Pacific Rim. See the entry under "Los Angeles and Southern California" for a brief description of this set of guides.

AWARDS LISTS

SCOPE NOTE: This section lists the separately published lists of the genre awards. Many of these awards are also listed in the encyclopedias and the reader's guides.

---

149. Foxwell, Beth. **Agatha Award Winners**.

Accessible through the archives maintained by the DorothyL listserv, and also through the Miss Lemon website (http://www.iwillfollow.com/lemon.htm), this list of the Agatha Award winners, presented by Malice Domestic, is arranged chronologically. Each year's entries have a separate line listing the best novel, best short story, best first novel, best nonfiction work, lifetime achievement award, and so forth. Data are only through 1995.

150. Pearsall, Jay. **Mystery & Crime: The New York Public Library Book of Answers. Intriguing and Entertaining Questions and Answers About the Who's Who and What's What of Whodunits**. New York, London, Toronto: Simon & Schuster, 1995. 175 p. Indexed. Paperback. LC 94-25127. ISBN 0-671-87237-0.

The New York Public Library sponsored this book of questions and answers about mysteries, and Jay Pearsall, the proprietor of Murder, Ink., compiled the book. According to the introduction, Pearsall intended it as a "gathering together of what is interesting, clever, astounding, and hilarious in the mystery genre. It's the kind of information that you have to share with someone. . . ." Its contents are Sherlock Holmes and Forerunners; The Golden Age; Schools and Rules; The Amateur Detective; Agatha; Private Eyes, Grifters, and Dames; Sisters in Crime; Rogues and Scoundrels; Candlesticks and Curare; On the Beat; Murder by Quotation; Questions of Character; The Writers; Pseudonyms; Espionage and Thrillers; Politics and Murder; First, Lasts, and Onlies; The Subject Is Murder; Exotic Locales; Murderous Miscellanea; Killer Titles; Now a Major Motion Picture; Mystery Writers of America Edgar Allan Poe Awards; Bibliography; and Index.

Pearsall has attempted to provide something for everybody, and this is simultaneously one of the book's strengths and weaknesses; one may find something of what one is looking for, but most of the time it is not comprehensive. Also, Pearsall presents his material in what seems to be a lighthearted manner, giving his information in a question-and-answer format. Thus, though the volume can be browsed with pleasure, it has no uses apart from providing instant fodder to the players of trivia games. Users of the New York Public Library and visitors to Murder, Ink., may indeed have wanted to know the name of the espionage novel in which a 14-year-old boy with total recall is recruited by the British Intelligence as a spy, but will anybody else care? A smattering of factual errors reduces the reliability of this work. Choose instead the lists of Strosser and Stine (q.q.v.).

151. Slavin, Charlie. **Edgar Awards**.

Based on a compilation by Patricia Ridgway, with assistance from Edward D. Hoch and Patricia Guy, and scanned from Mystery Writers of America material, this partial online list of the winners of the various categories of Edgar Awards is accessible through the archives maintained by the DorothyL listserv and also through the Miss Lemon website (http://www.iwillfollow.com/lemon.htm). It is arranged by award, with data being provided for the winners of the Grandmaster award, the Best Novel award, the Best First Novel award, and the Best Paperback Original award. Data in each award are listed in reverse chronological order; runners-up are also given. Data are current as of 1994.

152. Strosser, Edward, ed. **The Armchair Detective Book of Lists: A Complete Guide to the Best Mystery, Crime & Suspense Fiction**. New York: Armchair Detective, 1989. 266 p. Paperback. LC 90-105981. ISBN 0-89296-423-5.

153. Stine, Kate, ed. **The Armchair Detective Book of Lists: A Complete Guide to the Best Mystery, Crime, and Suspense Fiction**. 2d ed. New York: Otto Penzler Books, 1995. xv, 267 p. Paperback. LC 94-41794. ISBN 1-883402-98-0.

This annotation describes the second edition. Although a daunting 34 chapters are listed in the table of contents, this most useful compilation contains in essence only three sections. The first section provides information about genre awards; the second consists of lists; and the third provides information about mystery organizations, conventions, and publications. There are illustrations throughout.

The material in the first section occupies nearly half the book and begins with lists of the winners of the awards given by the Mystery Writers of America (MWA). The winners of the MWA's Grand Master Award are listed, followed by lists of the winners of the MWA's Edgar Allan Poe award for best novel, best first novel by an American author, best paperback original, best short story, best fact crime, best critical/biographical work, best young adult mystery, best juvenile mystery, best episode in a television series, best motion picture, best foreign film, best play, best radio drama, outstanding mystery criticism, the winners of the special Edgar, the Ellery Queen Awards, the Robert L. Fish Memorial Awards, and the Raven Awards. When relevant, the lists include the finalists, with the winner's name(s) in boldface type. The list of MWA winners is followed by lists of the Crime Writers' Association of Great Britain Award, the Crime Writers of Canada's Arthur Ellis Awards, the Independent Mystery Booksellers Association's Dilys Winn Award, the International Association of Crime Writers' Hammett Awards, the Wolfe Pack's Nero Wolfe Awards, the Bouchercon World Mystery Convention Anthony Awards, the Private Eye Writers of America Shamus Awards, the Mystery Readers International's Macavity Awards, and the Malice Domestic Agatha Awards. The most recent data are from 1994.

The lists include the Haycraft-Queen definitive library of detective-crime-mystery fiction, the Queen's Quorum (125 titles), Otto Penzler's top 100 Sherlock Holmes books, Robin W. Wink's personal favorites, *The Armchair Detective* Reader's Survey, *The Drood Review*'s Editor's Choice, the *Sunday Times* 100 best crime stories selected by Julian Symons in 1957–1958, Sandoe's *The Hard-Boiled Dick: A Personal Checklist*, H. R. F. Keating's 100 best crime and mystery books, Jon L. Breen's list of the 10 best mystery reference works, Marvin Lachman's list of the 10 best first mystery novels, William Deeck's list of James Corbett's 10 greatest lines, Douglas Greene's list of the most ingenious locked room and impossible-crime novels of all time, *Firsts* magazine's list of 25 rapidly appreciating mystery books, Ric Meyer's lists of 10 top mystery movies and television serials, and lists from various authors of their favorite mystery writers and novels.

The third section is the briefest, but it provides useful contact information and data on mystery organizations, author fan clubs and newsletters, mystery fan conventions, and mystery periodicals. As before, data are current as of 1994.

Much of this information is available through other sources, but these sources can be difficult to obtain. Although this book is a treasure trove for the browser as well as an essential reference work, it would have benefited enormously from an index.

PUBLISHER BIBLIOGRAPHIES

SCOPE NOTE: Included here are checklists, indexes, and encyclopedic guides to the publications of specific publishing houses. The arrangement is alphabetical by the name of the publishing house or, occasionally, by series put out by a publishing house if the book annotated focuses exclusively on that series.

ACE BOOKS

154. Jaffery, Sheldon. **Double Trouble: A Bibliographic Chronicle of Ace Mystery Doubles**. Mercer Island, WA: Starmont House, 1992. xvi, 150 p. Indexes. (Starmont Reference Guide, no. 12). ISBN 1-55742-119-6 (hc); 1-55742-118-8 (pb).

In the early 1950s, publisher A. A. Wyn of Ace Books hit upon the idea of marketing paperback "doubles," two books bound back to back, each with its own cover art. The formula proved successful, and Ace issued Mystery Doubles, Science Fiction Doubles, Western Doubles, and Romance Doubles. There are at least five indexes and checklists to the Science Fiction Doubles, but relatively little attention has been paid to the other Ace Doubles, and well-known popular culture scholar (and lawyer) Jaffery's annotated bibliography of the Ace Mystery Doubles was overdue as a publication. In all, Jaffery describes approximately 130 books, from the first of the 1952 "D" series (D-1: *Too Hot for Hell* by Keith Vining and *The Grinning Gismo* by Samuel Taylor) through the "F" and "G" series, the last of which appeared in 1963.

A typical entry includes the Ace Double number, title (in boldfaced italics), author's name (pseudonyms are revealed when known), year of publication, and pagination; prices are given at the beginning of each section. Because Ace Doubles typically reprinted a novel, data are provided to earlier publications, as are references to the bibliographical sources used for locating this information. Abridgments are noted, but cover artists, alas, are not. Jaffery's annotations range from lighthearted descriptions of the covers—"nice cover of a blonde holding a smoking gun in her right hand and wearing a backless, strapless gown cut down to bikini level in the rear and held up God-knows-how by a perky pair of whatchacallums. (Thank you, Robert Leslie Bellem.)"—to reprinting the "teasers" from inside the front covers and excerpts from the critical praise received by the first editions. The result is a delightful guide to a disposable form of entertainment. As Jaffery's introduction puts it: "I don't agree that Ace Mystery Doubles were, on the whole, trashy, though some may be so classified. Many just weren't very good." Well-done author-title and title indexes conclude the volume.

ALBATROSS MODERN CONTINENTAL LIBRARY

155. Williams, Richard, and Alastair Jollans. **Albatross Modern Continental Library 1932–1949**. Scunthorpe, England: Dragonby Press, 1996. 20 p. Stapled sheets. Index. (British Paperback Checklist, no. 48).

Founded in 1931 by a coalition of English and German publishers and businesspeople, the Albatross Modern Continental Library purchased copyright for areas outside the British Empire and the United States and sold their paperbacks throughout Europe. Their books all bore a notice that they were "NOT TO BE INTRODUCED INTO THE BRITISH EMPIRE OR THE U.S.A." The Albatross Crime Club was introduced in 1933, reprinting books—initially published in hardcover by the Collins Crime Club—by such authors as Herbert Adams, Nicholas Blake, Miles Burton, Agatha Christie, G. D. H. Cole, E. C. R. Lorac, Ngaio Marsh, and Edgar Wallace. In all, the Albatross Modern Continental Library published more than 500 titles before going out of business in 1949.

Williams's and Jollans's checklist lists the Albatross volumes in the order in which they appeared. Each citation provides the book's series number, author and title (as given on the title page), publication date, and dustwrapper (when such existed); pagination and printer are given for some volumes. Because Albatross initially had a different color for each of its series, a key listing the meaning of the color scheme is provided, and each citation also lists the volume's color. The checklist concludes with a cumulative author-title index.

The checklist lacks a separate title index, but it is clearly reproduced from word-processed copy and is easy to use.

AVON

156. Cox, J. Randolph. **Avon Mystery**.

Available as part of the archives maintained by the DorothyL listserv, and also through the Miss Lemon website (http://www.iwillfollow.com/lemon.htm), this list of the 38 paperback mysteries published by Avon between 1969 and 1971 is arranged in the order of their publication. After the 10th volume in the series, the publisher ceased using series numbers, making this list particularly useful. Each citation provides the book's author and title.

BOARDMAN

157. Greenslade, Lyndsey, Tom Lesser, and Richard Williams. **Boardman Crime and Science Fiction 1942–1967, A Checklist of the First Editions, with a Guide to Their Value by Ralph Spurrier**. Scunthorpe, England: Dragonby Press, 1991. 44 p. Paperback. (Dragonby Bibliographies, no. 8). ISBN 1-871122-08-2. (300 copies printed.)

The English publishing firm of T. V. Boardman lasted from 1942 until 1967, during which time it published 679 crime novels and author short story collections; only 18 of Boardman's titles were science fiction. The Boardman books were published in series, the "Boardman Bloodhound" being the most popular, appearing on 533 of the firm's titles. Among the authors who appeared under the Boardman imprint were Fredric Brown, Bruno Fischer, Robert L. Fish, William Campbell Gault, Bret Halliday, Ed McBain, Lawrence Treat, Donald E. Westlake, and Cornell Woolrich.

Boardman Crime and Science Fiction is similar in appearance to the previous books in the Dragonby Bibliographies series, being reproduced from reduced laser-printed copy. After a foreword giving a brief history of the firm and a discussion of artist Denis McLoughlin (who drew most if not all of the Boardman covers), the majority of the bibliography is devoted to an author-title index of the Boardman authors. Each citation provides the author's byline as it appeared on the title page. On the same line are listed the number of books appearing under that byline in Boardman hardback and the approximate number of books published in England in hardback under that byline. If a pseudonym was employed, the author's real name is given in italics. Beneath each name are listed the books that appeared under that byline; they are listed chronologically by the official publication date, which is given. All titles are capitalized, and all citations include the series in which the book was published, the book's pagination, and its original publication price. Changes in title and whether the book appeared first in the United States are indicated. Citations conclude with Spurrier's assessment of the value. Additional indexes list the books by the Boardman series in which they were published; there are separate indexes for Boardman hardcovers and Boardman paperbacks.

Apart from Spurrier's (now dated) prices, *Boardman Crime and Science Fiction* contains much that is unobtainable elsewhere. It does not, however, include any cross-references. Users of the bibliography must know in advance that Evan Hunter also wrote as Hunt Collins, Ed McBain, and Richard Marsten, and that Kendell Foster Crossen wrote as M. E. Chaber and Christopher Monig. In addition, it lacks a title index. These shortcomings aside, this work remains the only comprehensive attempt at documenting this publisher's output.

158. Williams, Richard. **T. V. Boardman 1942–1957**. Scunthorpe, England: Dragonby Press, 1988. 10 p. Stapled sheets. Index. (British Paperback Checklist, no. 37).

T. V. Boardman appears to have started as the British publisher of American crime stories, but as the company grew, it began to issue hardback first editions by British authors, and it issued numerous separate series: Bloodhound Books, TVB Books, TVB Pocket Reader, TVB Red Arrow, TVB Red Arrow Romance, TVB Red Arrow Western, and so forth. Among the authors to appear under this imprint were Fredric Brown, Norbert Davis, Bruno Fischer, William Campbell Gault, and Harold Q. Masur. In all, approximately 220 paperbacks appeared during the first 15 years of the company's existence, and it continued publishing until 1968 or 1969.

Williams has grouped his publications by the Boardman series in which they appeared. Each entry includes the book's series, author, title, date of publication, pagination, printer, and cover artist. An alphabetical code (C for Crime, R for Romance, W for Western, etc.) indicates the book's genre. A cumulative author index concludes the checklist.

The checklist appears to have been reproduced from word-processed copy. It lacks a title index and an index for cover artists.

BROWN, WATSON

159.   Holland, Stephen. **Brown, Watson 1945–1957**. Scunthorpe, England: Richard Williams, n.d. 8 p. Stapled sheets. (British Paperback Checklist, no. 28).

The firm of Brown, Watson published Digit Books (q.v.) and currently survives as Brown, Watson (Leicester), publishing only children's books. From 1945 until 1957 it published more than 260 paperback books, the majority of which were Westerns, but a percentage were crime and mystery. Among the authors published by Brown, Watson were G. D. H. Cole, Bruno Fischer, Sam Merwin, and Walter Standish.

Holland's checklist is an author index to the Brown, Watson publications. Each entry provides the volume's title, date of publication, pagination, and printer. The cover artist is noted when available, and an alphabetical code (B for Battle, Bf for Foreign Legion, C for Crime, etc.) concludes each entry.

As with the other bibliographies in this series, this one appears to have been reproduced from typescript rather than word-processed copy, and it is typographically cramped and unattractive. It contains neither title index nor cover artist index. It is, however, the only separately published record of this publisher's output.

CHERRY TREE BOOKS

160.   Williams, Richard. **Cherry Tree Books 1937–1953**. Scunthorpe, England: Dragonby Press, 1987. 12 p. Stapled sheets. Index. (British Paperback Checklist, no. 35).

In the 16 years of its existence, Cherry Tree Books published slightly more than 400 paperback books, a sizable percentage of which were crime and mystery. Among the authors to appear under the Cherry Tree imprint were Herbert Adams, John G. Brandon, Leo Bruce, J. S. Fletcher, Craig Rice, Arthur Somers Roche, and Edgar Wallace. The majority of these publications were reprints.

Williams has arranged his checklist by the order in which the volumes were issued. Each entry provides the book's series number, author, title (indicating previous title when such existed), publication date, pagination, printer, and whether the rear cover provides a list or an advertisement. An alphabetical code (BN for Battle Nonfiction, C for Crime Fiction, F for Fiction, etc.) indicates the book's genre, and an author index that identifies pseudonyms (when known) concludes the checklist.

The checklist appears to have been reproduced from word-processed copy. It lacks a title index and is typographically cramped, though the copy is legible. This appears to be the only separately issued record of this publisher's output.

COLLINS CRIME CLUB

161. Foord, Peter, and Richard Williams. **Collins Crime Club: A Checklist of the First Editions, with a Guide to Their Value by Ralph Spurrier**. Scunthorpe, England: Dragonby Press, 1987. 40 p. Paperback. (Dragonby Bibliographies, no. 1). (500 copies printed.)

The Collins Crime Club began in 1930 and by the end of 1986 had published approximately 1,700 books by authors as varied as "Anthony Abbott," Agatha Christie, Jonathan Gash, Reginald Hill, Ngaio Marsh, Ellis Peters, and Julian Symons. *Collins Crime Club*, which lists the books published under this imprint, appears to have been reproduced from reduced laser-printed copy. It also appears to have been the work of people intent upon supplying as much information as possible but uncertain as to the way in which they should provide it and unfamiliar with the compilation of bibliographies.

The volume begins with an introduction explaining its organizational principles. The checklist is arranged alphabetically by the name under which the book was published, with this name given in boldface type. On the same line are listed the number of books appearing under that byline in the Collins Crime Club and the approximate number of books that were published under that byline. If a pseudonym was employed, the author's real name is given in italics. Beneath each name are listed the books that appeared under that byline; they are listed chronologically by the official publication date, which is given. All titles are capitalized, and all citations include the book's pagination and its publication price. Changes in title and whether the book appeared first in the United States are indicated, and recent titles provide a truncated version of the ISBN. Each entry concludes with Spurrier's selling price for that volume.

Apart from Spurrier's now dated prices, *Collins Crime Club* contains much that is unobtainable elsewhere. It does not, however, include any cross-references. Thus, users of the bibliography must know in advance that Edith Caroline Rivett used the pseudonyms Carol Carnac and E. C. R. Lorac and that Phoebe Atwood Taylor wrote as Alice Tilton. In addition, the work lacks a title index and provides no information on dustwrapper artists. These shortcomings aside, it remains the only comprehensive attempt at documenting this important series.

COLLINS WHITE CIRCLE

162. Williams, Richard. **Collins White Circle Books 1936–1959**. 3d ed. Scunthorpe, England: Dragonby Press, 1995. 24 p. Stapled sheets. Index. (British Paperback Checklists, no. 1).

The Collins White Circle paperback books were published from April 1936 until September 1959. In all, approximately 720 books appeared under this imprint. Although Collins White Circle published Westerns, romance novels, nonfiction, and newsbooks, nearly 500 of its paperbacks were crime or mystery. The Collins White Circle paperbacks distinguished their different series by color: The nearly 200 paperbacks appearing in the Crime Club series were green, whereas the nearly 200 volumes appearing in the Mystery series were mauve. Among the crime and mystery authors to appear in the White Circle Paperbacks were Anthony Abbot, Peter Cheyney, Agatha Christie, Mignon Eberhart, Elizabeth Ferrars, Sydney Horler, Hammond Innes, Philip Macdonald, Hugh Pendexter, Rex Stout, and Edgar Wallace. So far as is known, all of these paperbacks had prior publication, often by the Collins Crime Club (q.v.).

Like the other bibliographies in the Dragonby Press's series devoted to British paperbacks, this publication consists of stapled-together sheets. After a brief introduction containing statistical information about the press, the bibliography begins by arranging the paperbacks into the series in which they appeared, then listing the volumes by series number. Each entry provides the author's name, identifying pseudonyms when possible. The title is provided, with previous and additional titles noted. The date of publication is given, as are pagination, printer, and price. Paperbacks with dustwrappers are identified; cover artists are noted, as are the existence of advertisements on the rear cover. An author index concludes the bibliography.

The bibliography lacks indexes for title and artist, but it nevertheless succeeds admirably in recording this significant British paperback series. Note: the prior editions of this publication have not been seen.

CORGI

163. Williams, Richard. **Corgi and Scottie Books 1951–1960**. Scunthorpe, England: Richard Williams, 1986. 30 p. Stapled sheets. Index. (British Paperback Checklists, no. 26).

Until it published the British paperback edition of Vladimir Nabokov's *Lolita* in 1961, the paperbacks issued by the Corgi publishing house had not been terribly successful, for their competitors for British paperback rights were the well-established firms of Penguin and Pan. Nevertheless, in the years prior to 1960, Corgi—a subsidiary of the American Bantam Books—provided the British paperback editions of crime and mystery books by such notable authors as Leigh Brackett, Fredric Brown, John Dickson Carr, and Erle Stanley Gardner.

Williams's bibliography begins by listing the books in the various series appearing under the Corgi imprint: the Corgi Main series, the Corgi Bantam Series, the Corgi Pennant Series, the Scottie series, and the Scottie Special series. Each entry provides the series number, author's name (identifying the pseudonym when known), title (indicating if the volume appeared under a previous title), first edition status, publication date, pagination, date, and printer. Cover artists are noted, and an alphabetical code (B for Battle Fiction, BN for Battle Nonfiction, Bio for Biography, C for Crime Fiction, etc.) indicates the genre in which the book was marketed. An author index concludes the bibliography.

Like the other bibliographies in this most useful series, this appears to have been reproduced from typed rather than word-processed copy. It is cramped and typographically unattractive, and it lacks an index for titles and cover artists. It is, however, apparently the only separately published index to this significant publisher's output.

CURTIS WARREN/GRANT HUGHES

164. Holland, Stephen. **Curtis Warren and Grant Hughes**. Scunthorpe, England: Richard Williams, n.d. 16 p. Stapled sheets. (British Paperback Checklists, no. 21).

The publishing firm of Curtis Warren—which ended its days as the publishing firm of Grant Hughes—was one of the many paperback publishers that flourished briefly in postwar England. During the eight years of its existence (1946–1954), it published just over 500 books, more than 100 of which were crime stories. Like the other paperback publishers documented in this series, its line was written primarily by a small number of hacks. Among these were William Henry Fleming Bird, Brian Holloway, Dennis Hughes, Norman Lazenby, and John Russell Fearn.

Holland's index is arranged alphabetically by the author's name; when possible, he reveals pseudonyms. Each entry provides the book's title, copyright date (if such is given in the book), price, and total pagination. When known, the printer is listed, as is the cover artist; and the book's genre is indicated by a letter or letters (e.g., A for Adventure, B for Boxing, C for Crime).

As with the majority of British paperbacks published during this time, the history of the publishing firm is probably more interesting than the books that were published. This aside, this bibliography is typographically cramped and unattractive; it appears to have been reproduced from typescript rather than word-processed copy. There is no index to titles or cover artists. On the other hand, this appears to be the only separately published record of the output of this publisher.

DELL

165. Lyles, William H. **Dell Paperbacks 1942 to Mid-1962: A Catalog-Index**. Westport, CT: Greenwood Press, 1983. xxxv, 471 p. Indexes. LC 82-25505. ISBN 0-313-23668-2.

A sizable percentage of Dell Publishing's paperbacks published between 1943 and mid-1962—971 of 2,168 books—were mysteries, and in any given year between 1943 and mid-1962, Dell published more mysteries than it did Westerns, romances, science fiction and fantasy, and nonfiction and humor titles. Crime and mystery fiction was Dell's mainstay; the first Dell paperback was Phillip Ketchum's *Death in the Library*, and George Harmon Coxe's *Four Frightened Women* was the first of the enormously popular Dell "map back" series (paperbacks whose back covers provided a map or architectural re-creation of the crime scene).

Dell Paperbacks 1942 to Mid-1962 is an extraordinarily comprehensive and thorough catalogue-index to the paperbacks published by Dell during this time span. The volume begins with a series of statistical tables surveying the Dell paperbacks, followed by a brief but informative history of Dell and a lengthy explanation of how to use the catalogue-index and what to expect from it. The catalogue-index is broadly arranged by Dell series, with separate sections listing Dell reprints, Dell first editions, Dell Laurel editions, and volumes that were not part of these series: Dell Visual Books, Dell Special Student Editions, and Dell Digest-Sized Books. Each series is further divided by Dell's series letter and the accompanying changes in cover price.

Each entry provides the paperback's issue number, author, title, subtitle, and pagination. Also given are the front and back cover artist, cover blurbs, printing date, publication date (when it differed from the printing date), print run, and number of books that were sent to Canada. Reprints are listed chronologically, each entry including printing date, publication date, and print run. Abridgments are noted, changes in title are provided, ghost writers and ghost editors are identified, and the "head-of-title" notes contained in the Dell paperbacks published prior to 1952 are included. Concluding the volume are indexes for authors, anonymous titles, book subjects, cover artists, maps, special series, advance blurbs featured on the Dell first editions, and motion picture, television, and play "tie-ins." So detailed are these latter indexes that they list the actors and actresses featured on the motion picture, television, and play tie-ins.

Dell Paperbacks 1942 to Mid-1962 is reproduced from what appears to be reduced laser-printed copy. Its bibliographical data are frequently cramped, and the uninitiated must make constant reference to the explanatory section at the beginning of the book. Physical flaws aside, the book is by any standard a monumental achievement, an example of what a dedicated and scholarly researcher can do. It has a companion volume, *Putting Dell on the Map: A History of the Dell Paperbacks* (also 1983). Both volumes belong in all academic libraries.

166. Cox, J. Randolph. **The Dell Great Mystery Library**.

Available as part of the archives maintained by the DorothyL listserv, and also through the Miss Lemon website (http://www.iwillfollow.com/lemon.htm), this list of the 29 Dell Great Mystery books published between 1957 and 1960 is prefaced by a note explaining the differences between first and later printings and a description of the editorial board responsible for selection of titles. The list arranges the books in order of their publication and provides author and title. Much more information on the Dell Great Mystery Library is available in the catalog-index to Dell Paperbacks compiled by William Lyles (q.v.), but this information is accessible through the catalog-index only with the greatest of difficulty, for the Dell Great Mystery Library was a subseries, and Lyles does not separately index it.

DETECTIVE-CLUB

167. Baudou, Jacques, and Jean Jacques Schleret. **Les Metamorphoses de la Chouette**. Paris: Futuropolis, 1986. 192 p. Indexes. Paperback. ISBN 2-7376-5488-2.

Although French publications are generally beyond the scope of this work, one would be remiss not to mention this annotated bibliography of the Detective-Club, whose logo, an owl, was the "Chouette" of the title. The majority of the writers published by the Detective-Club were British and American, and the first section of this volume consists of bio-bibliographical data on them. Each entry begins with a sometimes lengthy biography of the writer, followed by a description of the works that were published in the Detective-Club series. The series number is given, as are the French title and the original English title (and significant retitlings); the name of the translator is also provided, as are data on reprintings. Following this, the work is annotated; Baudou and Schleret are careful not to reveal solutions. Successive (and significantly briefer) sections provide lists of the Detective-Club books in series order, and information on additional publications and series published under the Chouette logo. The volume concludes with a filmography providing data on Chouette publications that were filmed.

DIGIT BOOKS

168. Holland, Stephen, and Richard Williams. **Digit Books 1956–1966**. Scunthorpe, England: Richard Williams, 1986. 28 p. Stapled sheets. Index. (British Paperback Checklists, no. 27).

Digit Books was not a separate publishing firm but a series published by Brown, Watson (q.v.), a company that still exists as Brown, Watson (Leicester), though it is currently a publisher of children's books. Until 1966, when Brown, Watson discontinued Digit Books, the series published crime and mystery fiction by authors including Michael Avallone, Gil Brewer, "Nick Carter," and Edgar Wallace.

Because Digit Books initially published books in an unnumbered series, Holland and Williams's bibliography begins with an alphabetical listing of these volumes. Each entry includes the author, identifying pseudonym when known, title, price on the book, and month and year in which the book was published. An alphabetical code (B for Battle, C for Crime, E for Esoteric, etc.) indicates the book's genre. Printer and cover artist are identified when possible.

The next section lists the books by the Digit series in which they appeared. The information provided is the same as above, with the addition of the Digit series number. An author index concludes the checklist.

As with the other bibliographies in this series, this one appears to have been reproduced from typescript rather than word-processed copy. It is typographically cramped and unattractive. It is, however, the only separately published record of this publisher's output.

DOUBLEDAY CRIME CLUB

169. Nehr, Ellen. **Doubleday Crime Club Compendium 1928–1991**. Martinez, CA: Offspring Press, 1992. xxi, 682 p. Index. ISBN 0-9634420-0-7.

During its 62 years, the Doubleday Crime Club published more than 2,000 crime and mystery volumes by authors as diverse as Margery Allingham, Isaac Asimov, George Bagby, H. C. Bailey, Anthony Berkeley, Leslie Charteris, Doris Miles Disney, E. X. Ferrars, Frank L. Packard, Ruth Rendell, Georges Simenon, Arthur Upfield, and Edgar Wallace. In addition, during the early 1930s the Crime Club Radio Show offered radio dramatizations and adaptations of the volumes being published by the Doubleday Crime Club.

Doubleday Crime Club Compendium is a year-by-year listing of the books published by the Doubleday Crime Club. Within each year, the titles are listed alphabetically by author's last name. Nehr prefaces each year's entries with a description of the significant Doubleday Crime Club events of that year; taken cumulatively, they present a reasonably detailed history of the series. Following her history are the citations, each of which provides (at the very least) the author's name in boldface type, title of the book, name of its series or lead characters, setting, pagination, and a broad subject description (e.g., "murder of a playboy," "illegal sale of liquor during Prohibition," "werewolf in swamps—or *is* it a werewolf? Locked Room," "army life pre–World War II"). Reprint editions are documented in a note that also lists changes in titles and the form of the author's name. When the dustwrapper and the original binding are available, Nehr describes the binding's salient features and reprints the dustwrapper's complete blurb. (A doubtless unanticipated result of the latter is that the *Compendium*'s user is intrigued, teased—and all too often frustrated.) Also included, as an unpaginated slick-paper insert, are 24 pages of color reproductions of the more interesting Crime Club dustwrappers. Concluding the volume is a list of the Crime Club Radio Programs.

Doubleday Crime Club Compendium contains so much that is unavailable elsewhere and is so obviously a labor of love that it is almost ungrateful to complain about its shortcomings. Nevertheless, although there is a well-done author index, there are no indexes for titles, series characters, settings, or dustwrapper artists. Given Nehr's thoroughness in mentioning these in the body of the volume, it seems probable that the publisher decided to save money by omitting these indexes, a shortsighted and mercenary decision. One hopes for a 2d edition that includes these features.

FOUR SQUARE BOOKS

170. Williams, Richard. **Four Square Books 1–322 (1957–1960)**. Scunthorpe, England: Dragonby Press, 1993. 12 p. Stapled sheets. Index. (British Paperback Checklists, no. 39).

Although Four Square Books was a reprint house and never a major publisher of crime and mystery books, the authors who appeared under its imprint included Dorothy L. Sayers and Georges Simenon. Williams's checklist lists the books by their series number. Each entry provides author, title (indicating previous title when applicable), publication date, pagination, printer, and cover artist. An alphabetical code (C for Crime Fiction, F for Fiction, N for Nonfiction, etc.) indicates the book's genre, and an author index concludes the checklist.

The checklist lacks a title index and an index for cover artists, and like the other checklists in this series, it appears to have been reproduced from word-processed copy. It is the only record of this publisher's output.

GOLLANCZ

171. Williams, Richard, and Ralph Spurrier. **Gollancz Crime Fiction 1928–1988, a Checklist of the First Editions, with a Guide to Their Value**. Scunthorpe, England: Dragonby Press, 1989. 42 p. Paperback. (Dragonby Bibliographies, no. 4). ISBN 1-871122-04-X. (400 copies printed.)

Victor Gollancz began publishing detective and mystery fiction in 1928, categorizing their books as "Detective Stories and Thrillers." By the end of 1988 nearly 1,300 such volumes had appeared, and the categorization had changed to "Thrillers and Crime." The authors who appeared under the Gollancz imprint included Joan Aiken, H. C. Bailey, "Tucker Coe" (Donald Westlake), Edmund Crispin, Amanda Cross, Ellery Queen, Dorothy L. Sayers, Dell Shannon, Hillary Waugh, and Charles Willeford. Like the previous volumes in this series, *Gollancz Crime Fiction* appears to have been reproduced from reduced laser-printed copy and to have been the work of people intent upon giving as much information as possible, but uncertain as to the way in which they should provide it, and unfamiliar with the compilation of bibliographies.

The volume begins with an introduction explaining its organizational principles, and a two-page foreword by Spurrier provides a brief history of Gollancz. The checklist is arranged alphabetically by the name under which the book was published, with this name given in boldface type. On the same line are listed the number of books published under that byline by Gollancz and the estimated total number of books published in Great Britain under that byline. If a pseudonym was employed, the real name is given in italics. Beneath each name are listed the books that appeared under that byline; they are listed chronologically by the official publication date, which is given. All titles are capitalized, and all citations include the book's pagination and its publication price. Changes in title and whether the book appeared first in the United States are indicated, and recent titles provide a truncated version of the ISBN. Each entry concludes with Spurrier's selling price for that volume.

The references to the values are out of date, but *Gollancz Crime Fiction* contains much that is unobtainable elsewhere. It does not include any cross-references, and it lacks a title index. It nevertheless remains the only comprehensive attempt at documenting the output of this important publisher.

GRAMOL GROUP

172. Holland, Stephen, and Richard Williams. **The Gramol Group 1932–1937**. Scunthorpe, England: Dragonby Press, 1990. 20 p. Stapled sheets. Index. (British Paperback Checklists, no. 44).

One of the first British publishers of paperbacks, the Gramol Group appears to have been started by Arthur Gray and F. A. Mowl in 1927. Although the Gramol Group initially published a numbered series of "Sexy" books, in 1931 they began to publish a series of Thriller Novels; in 1933 they expanded their line to include the Gramol Mystery Novels. By the time they went out of business in 1937, approximately a sixth of the Gramol Group's roughly 600 paperbacks were crime and mystery novels.

Holland and Williams have arranged their bibliography by the name of the Gramol series, although the names are listed neither alphabetically nor chronologically. Each entry provides the book's series number, author, title, date of publication, and pagination. Cover artists are listed when available. The checklist concludes with a cumulative author index and a separate index of anonymously published books.

In addition to lacking a title index and an index for artists, the checklist is most confusingly arranged, and its title is belied by the inclusion of data from years prior to 1932. Like other checklists in this series, it appears to have been reproduced from word-processed copies. It is the only record of this publisher's output.

HAMILTON AND PANTHER

173. Holland, Stephen, and Richard Williams. **Hamilton and Panther Books 1945–1956.** Scunthorpe, England: Dragonby Press, 1987. 18 p. Stapled sheets. Index. (British Paperback Checklists, no. 31).

In the 11 years of its existence, Hamilton and Panther published slightly more than 500 paperbacks, about a fifth of which were crime and mystery. The majority of these books were published under such house names as Jeff Bogar, Ross Carni, and Duff Johnson.

Holland and Williams have divided their checklist into two sections. The first is an author list of titles under the Hamilton imprint, and the second is an author list of titles under the Panther imprint. Each entry provides series number, title of the book (indicating simultaneous hardback publication and an original title if such existed), date of publication, pagination, printer, cover artist, and price. An alphabetical code (B for Battle, C for Crime, E for Erotic, etc.) indicates the book's genre. A cumulative author index that identifies pseudonyms (when known) concludes the index.

As are many of the later publications in this series, this checklist appears to have been reproduced from word-processed copy and is rather clear. It lacks indexes for title and cover artist, but it is nevertheless the only separately issued record of this publisher's output.

HODDER AND STOUGHTON

174. Williams, Richard. **Hodder and Stoughton 1926–1960.** Revised ed. Scunthorpe, England: Dragonby Press, 1990. 22 p. Stapled sheets. Index. (British Paperback Checklists, no. 6).

Between 1926 and 1960, Hodder and Stoughton published approximately 600 paperbacks, all except a few appearing in two major series: the ninepenny Yellow Jackets and the postwar Two Shilling Yellow Jackets, which later were renamed Hodder Pocket Books. A sizable percentage of these publications were crime fiction, and the authors whose books were published by Hodder and Stoughton included Francis Beeding, Leslie Charteris, Gerald Fairlie, J. S. Fletcher,

Sydney Horler, William Le Queux, E. Phillips Oppenheim, the Baroness Orczy, and Edgar Wallace.

Like the other separately published bibliographies in Dragonby Press's series devoted to British Paperbacks, *Hodder and Stoughton 1926–1960* consists of stapled-together sheets. After a brief introduction, the bibliography begins with an author index to the Hodder and Stoughton ninepenny Yellow Jackets; the titles are listed alphabetically beneath the author. In parentheses beside each title is the month and year of publication. Author lists of the books appearing in the short-lived Hodder and Stoughton "New at Ninepence" and "Crown Octavo" series occur next; in their content they duplicate the earlier section, although pagination of the books is occasionally given.

The following sections list the volumes appearing in Hodder and Stoughton's Two Shilling Yellow Jackets and Hodder Pocket Books. These volumes, however, are listed by their series. Each entry provides author's name, title, month and year of publication, pagination, printer, price, and cover artist; a "valuation" is given for many of the later volumes. An author index to these sections concludes the publication.

The bibliography lacks an index to title and cover artists, and as the above description implies, its arrangement can be frustrating. It nevertheless succeeds in documenting the paperbacks published by Hodder and Stoughton, and collectors and libraries will need it. Note: The first edition has not been seen.

HUTCHINSON GROUP

175. Williams, Richard. **Hutchinson Group Post-War Numbered Series, Later Arrow Books 1949–1960**. Scunthorpe, England: Dragonby Press, 1988. 18 p. Stapled sheets. Index. (British Paperback Checklists, no. 38).

Before becoming Arrow Books in 1953, the Hutchinson Group included the publishers of Hurst and Blackett, Hutchinson, Jarrolds, Leisure Library, John Long, Melrose, Stanley Paul, Rich and Cowan, and Skeffington. Frequently these publishers had their own series devoted to racing, romance, and Westerns; a sizable percentage of the books published by the Hutchinson Group were crime and detective fiction. Among the authors appearing under the Hutchinson Group/Arrow Books imprint were James Hadley Chase, John Creasey, Brett Halliday, F. Van Wyck Mason, and Edgar Wallace.

In attempting to list the Hutchinson Group, Williams had a daunting task, for numbering was not used for the first three years of the imprint and was highly erratic when it was instituted; some books were reissued with lower numbers than the original. Nevertheless, his bibliography is arranged in series number, when such exists. Each entry includes author's name, title (identifying previous titles when such exist), publication date, pagination, printer, and publisher. A cumulative author index that identifies pseudonyms (when known) concludes the checklist.

The checklist lacks a title index and the genre code used in so many of the other checklists in this series. Like these other checklists, this one appears to have been reproduced from word-processed copy. It is nevertheless the only record of this publisher's output.

LION BOOKS

176. Stephens, Christopher P. **Lion Books and the Lion Library: A Checklist.** Hastings-on-Hudson, NY: Ultramarine Publishing, 1991. 662 p. Paperback. ISBN 0-89366-173-2.

Between 1949 and 1957, some 402 paperbacks appeared under the imprints of Lion Books, the Lion Library, and Red Circle Books. Relatively few of these books were detective and mystery stories, but the authors with early work published by these imprints included David Goodis, Harold Q. Masur, and Jim Thompson, and one would thus be remiss to ignore this publisher and this publication.

The checklist begins with a numerical list of the publications of Lion Books and Lion Library. It lists the book's series number, author's name, and title. The second section uses this format to list the few publications of Red Circle Books.

The majority of the checklist consists of a cumulative alphabetical list of the books appearing under the three imprints. Each citation gives the author's last name in capital letters, underlines the title, and lists the book's series number, publication year, cover price, and pagination. A note indicates the book's content (Western, mystery, a novel, humor, etc.) and the name of the cover artist. When the book was a reprint, the original publication data are provided. The publishers of Lion Books and the Lion Books obviously wished to appeal to an audience interested in sex, and whenever possible, they changed the titles on their reprints, making them more risqué: Ralph Ingersoll's *Wine of Violence* became *The Naked and the Guilty*; Anthony Scott's *Mardi Gras Madness* became *Carnival of Love*; Victor Wolfson's *The Lonely Steeple* became *The Passionate Season*; and so forth.

Stephens's checklist would have benefited from the addition of indexes for titles and illustrators, but his is the only separate publication on its subject. It should be noted that the publications of Lion Books, Lion Library, and Red Circle Books have been indexed in Robert Reginald's and M. R. Burgess's *Cumulative Paperback Index, 1939–1959* (Detroit, MI: Gale, 1973), which also includes a title index. Unfortunately, Reginald and Burgess do not provide a checklist of books by publisher, nor do they include data on content, title changes, and reprints. Collectors of early paperbacks should have both books; specialists will be satisfied with Stephens's work.

R & L LOCKER/HARBOROUGH
PUBLISHING/ARCHER PRESS

177.   Holland, Stephen. **R. & L. Locker/Harborough Publishing Co.
Ltd./Archer Press (1944–1954)**. Scunthorpe, England: Richard Williams, n.d. Stapled sheets. 10 p. (British Paperback Checklists, no. 29).

The British paperback publisher R & L Locker was established in 1944 by Raymond and Lilian Locker. In 1948, the Lockers acquired Harborough Publishing; also in 1948, they established Archer Press. From 1944 to 1954 the three presses published nearly 300 books, the majority of which were soft-core erotica but approximately 17 percent of which were crime and mysteries. Only Harborough Publishing survived, starting publication (in 1957) of Ace Books.

Holland's checklist is an author index to the volumes issued by Locker, Harborough, and Archer. Each entry provides the volume's title, date of publication, pagination, printer, and cover price. The cover artist is noted when available, and an alphabetical code (C for Crime, E for Esoteric, R for Romance, etc.) concludes each entry.

As with some of the other bibliographies in this series, this one appears to have been reproduced from typescript rather than word-processed copy, and it is typographically cramped and unattractive. It contains neither a title index nor a cover-artist index. It is, however, the only separately published record of this publisher's output.

DENNIS McMILLAN

178.   Stephens, Christopher P. **A Checklist of the Publications of Dennis McMillan**. Hastings-on-Hudson, NY: Ultramarine Publishing, 1992. 19 p. Index. Paperback. ISBN 0-89366-202-X.

Dennis McMillan is a specialty publisher, perhaps best known for its multivolume reprinting of the works of Fredric Brown. He began publishing in 1983 with the original publication of Brian Hodel's *The Brazilian Guitar* and reprints of Arthur Upfield's *The House of Cain* and Philip Jose Farmer's *Love Song*. This bibliography was reproduced from laser-printed copy. The arrangement is chronological, concluding its coverage with the 1991 publication of Brown's *The Gibbering Night* and *The Pickled Punks*. The author's last name is given in capital letters, the title is underlined, and the number of copies and pagination are listed, as are data on original publications and names of the writers of introductions. An index to titles concludes the pamphlet.

The contents of McMillan's publications and a history of the press can be found in the 3d edition of *The Science-Fantasy Publishers: A Critical and Bibliographic History* by Jack L. Chalker and Mark Owings (Westminster, MD: Mirage Press, 1991), but collectors of McMillan's publications will probably be satisfied with Stephens's inexpensive checklist. An updated edition is needed.

MODERN FICTION

179. Holland, Stephen. **Modern Fiction 1945–1958**. Scunthorpe, England: R. A. H. Williams, n.d. 8 p. Stapled sheets. (British Paperback Checklists, no. 20).

Although a few of its titles might have been reprints, Modern Fiction published primarily original paperbacks written by a variety of generally pseudonymous authors. Among the writers known to have contributed to this series are Raymond Buxton, Frank Dubrez Fawcett, Ernest L. McKeag, and Alistair Paterson. The names under which these authors contributed "American Gangster" books included "Griff" (underworld slang for an informant or a newspaper reporter), Hava Gordon, Spike Gordon, Don Rogan, and Ben Sarto. The ownership rights to this last pseudonym were the subject of a lawsuit between Modern Fiction and Fawcett, and although Fawcett won, Modern Fiction continued to issue books under the Sarto name, probably paying Fawcett to use it.

Holland has compiled an author index to the paperbacks appearing under the Modern Fiction imprint. When possible, pseudonyms are revealed. Titles and pagination are provided, as are data on original publication. The cost of the book is given, as are the month and year of publication. The printer is frequently identified.

Although Holland's introduction does not say so, it seems probable that the history of Modern Fiction is substantially more interesting than the books they published. In any event, the bibliography lacks a title index, and it is typographically cramped, appearing to have been reproduced from typescript rather than word-processed copy. It is nevertheless the only record of this publisher; and fly-by-night though it was, Modern Fiction nevertheless lasted nearly 13 years.

MYSTERY BOOK CLUBS

180. Cook, Michael L. **Murder by Mail: Inside the Mystery Book Clubs—With Complete Checklist**. Evansville, IN: Cook, 1979. 109 p. Index. LC 79-106640. (25 hardbound copies, the rest paperbound.)

181. Cook, Michael L. **Murder by Mail: Inside the Mystery Book Clubs with Complete Checklist**. Revised, expanded, and updated edition. Bowling Green, OH: Bowling Green State University Popular Press, 1983. viii, 222 p. Index. LC 83-82013. ISBN 0-87972-265-7 (hc); 0-87972-264-9 (pb).

The self-published 1st edition of this checklist lists the publications of the three most important mystery book clubs: the Detective Book Club, the Mystery Guild, and the Unicorn Mystery Book Club. A brief history of each book club is provided, and the publications of each club are listed chronologically, concluding with material published in early 1979; titles are listed in capital letters, and regular type is used for all other information. An intriguing point of this checklist is that Cook's citations are not uniform in appearance and content; each section presents different data. The entries for the Detective Book Club are separately numbered and present their information in three columns. The first column lists date of publication; the second, book titles; and the third, authors' names. The citations for the Mystery Guild are divided into years and use six columns. The first column lists month of release by the club; the second, title; the third, author; the fourth, original publisher; the fifth, original date of publication; and the sixth, price of the original publication. The Unicorn Mystery Book Club's data are also grouped by years but present data in four columns. The first lists month of publication and number of the book in order of its appearance; the second, title; the third, author; and the fourth, original publisher. An author index concludes the volume.

The 2d edition documents the publications of the three clubs described above and adds data on the publications of Ellery Queen's Mystery Club, the Masterpieces of Mystery Library, the Mystery Library, and the Raven House Mystery Book Club. As before, Cook provides a brief history of each book club and lists its publications chronologically; in this volume, the citations extend well into 1983. Also as before, the content of Cook's citations differs from club to club. The entries for Ellery Queen's Mystery Club, the Masterpieces of Mystery Library, and the Raven House Mystery Book Club merely list the book titles and authors, whereas the contents of the 12 books published in the Mystery Library are completely described, with Cook including the names of editors, bibliographers, and illustrators; descriptions of maps and essays that were included; obituary notices; and information on each book's first edition. Because the 2d edition of this checklist is substantially smaller than its predecessor, Cook abandoned his use of columns and listed his bibliographic data beneath the titles of the books. This change is not necessarily an improvement, for it frequently makes information harder to locate. New to this volume is a list of the current addresses of the two extant mystery/detective book clubs. The book concludes with an author index.

Researchers and collectors will want this checklist, but it is very specialized.

PAN BOOKS

182. Williams, Richard. **Pan Books 1945–1966. A Bibliographical Checklist with a Guide to Their Value.** Scunthorpe, England: Dragonby Press, 1990. 72 p. Paperback. Index. (Dragonby Bibliographies, no. 6). ISBN 1-871122-06-6. (200 copies printed.)

Pan Books was registered as a corporation in 1944, published three books in 1945 and 1946, and then found its niche as a publisher of mass-market paperbacks. By the end of 1966, Pan Books had issued nearly 1,700 different titles, approximately 750 of which were mystery and detective stories. The authors appearing under the Pan Books imprint included Leslie Charteris, Peter Cheney, Agatha Christie, John Creasey, Erle Stanley Gardner, John D. MacDonald, Ellery Queen, Georges Simenon, Arthur Upfield, and Edgar Wallace.

Pan Books 1945–1966 is similar in appearance to the previous books in the Dragonby Bibliographies series, being reproduced from what appears to be reduced laser-printed copy. Its arrangement, however, differs radically. Williams arranges his bibliography by the series given above, then lists his citations by their serial number, a largely chronological listing. Each citation provides author, title, publication date, pagination, printer, whether a dustwrapper was used, book's price, and cover artist. Pseudonyms are identified when they are known; changes in title are given; and differences between announced and actual publication date are recorded. Each citation concludes with a price that "a collector would pay for a Very Good copy (complete with Very Good dustwrapper where called for)," and the bibliography concludes with an author index that lists the titles, the Pan series in which they appeared, and the year of publication.

The prices listed by Williams are probably dated, but the information contained in *Pan Books 1945–1966* is largely unobtainable elsewhere. The volume lacks a title index, but it successfully documents the output of this significant British publisher.

PENGUIN BOOKS

183. Williams, Richard, with others. **Penguin Crime Fiction 1935–1990: A Bibliographical Checklist with a Guide to Their Value**. Scunthorpe, England: Dragonby Press, 1991. 66 p. Stapled sheets. Index. (British Paperback Checklists, no. 22; Dragonby Bibliographies, no. 5).

By the end of 1990 the redoubtable Penguin Books had published approximately 13,000 titles, approximately 2,000 of which were crime fiction. The authors whose detective and mysteries fiction appeared under the Penguin imprint were as varied as Margery Allingham, E. C. Bentley, Anthony Berkeley, John Dickson Carr, Agatha Christie, Erle Stanley Gardner, Elmore Leonard, Oriana Papazoglou, Robert Parker, Georges Simenon, and Donald Westlake.

Although it was separately published and sold, *Penguin Crime Fiction 1935–1990* differs from the earlier bibliographies in the Dragonby Bibliographies series by being stapled-together sheets rather than a pamphlet. In its thoroughness, however, it is every bit the equal of the earlier volumes. Following an introductory key, the body of the bibliography is arranged chronologically by the Penguin Books sequence number. Each entry provides author, title, date of publication, total number of pages, and printer; also recorded are existence of the dustwrapper, book's price, dustwrapper's color, book's format, a statement about the advertisements appearing on the rear cover (plain covers are so noted), and cover artist. Retitlings are noted, as are the names of translators, and each entry concludes with Williams's now somewhat dated appraisal of their value.

Successive sections provide an author-title index, an index to the cover artists, and a list of simultaneous publications by specific authors. There is, however, no separate index to the titles, and the ISBNs are not noted. These shortcomings aside, this publication belongs in academic libraries with the other volumes in the series.

PICCADILLY NOVELS/
FICTION HOUSE

184. Holland, Stephen. **Piccadilly Novels**. Scunthorpe, England: Richard Williams, n.d. 8 p. Stapled sheets. (British Paperback Checklists, no. 25).

The Piccadilly Novels, an English paperback series, were published by Fiction House from approximately 1935 through 1950. In all, nearly 300 Piccadilly Novels were published, with two of the more notable authors being John Creasy (under the name of Margaret Cooke) and Arlton Eadie. The majority of the Piccadilly Novels are originals rather than reprints; most of them were undated.

Holland's checklist contains two sections. The first is an author index to the Piccadilly Novels. Each entry lists the title, the book's Piccadilly number, and the year in which it was published; when possible, Holland reveals pseudonyms. The second section lists the Piccadilly Novels in the order in which they appeared; each entry provides author's name, title, pagination, and probable date of publication.

The bibliography appears to have been reproduced from typed rather than word-processed copy; it is typographically cramped, unattractive, and contains neither a title index nor an index to cover artists. It is, nevertheless, apparently the only separately published record of this publisher's output, and Holland has demonstrated considerable resourcefulness in obtaining the dates of publication.

SÉRIE NOIRE/GALLIMARD

185. Mesplède, Claude. **Les Années "Série Noire." Bibliographie, Critique, d'Une Collection Policière**. Volume 1: 1945–1959; Volume 2: 1959–1966; Volume 3: 1966–1972; Vol. 4: 1972–1982. Amiens: Editions Encrage, 1992–1995. Index. LC 92-228124. ISBN vol. 1: 2-906389-34-X; vol. 2: 2-906389-43-9; vol. 3: 2-906389-53-6; vol. 4: 2-906389-63-3. (299 copies printed.)

Publications in French are generally beyond the scope of this work, but one would be remiss not to mention this monumental bibliography of the Série Noire, a paperback series published by Gallimard that was devoted primarily to reprinting in French the works of British and American detective and mystery writers. Conceived of by mystery lover Marcel Archard in 1945, and edited by Archard's friend Marcel Duhamel, the Série Noire by 1982 contained some 1,866 books, providing the first French editions of works by authors as diverse as Raymond Chandler, Peter Cheyney, Harold Q. Masur, John D. MacDonald, Dick Francis, Ed McBain, Carter Brown, Donald E. Westlake, "K. R. Dwyer," Robert B. Parker, and Stuart Kaminsky.

Mesplède has arranged his bibliography chronologically, the first entry being the October 1945 publication of Peter Cheyney's *La Môme Vert-de-Gris* [*Poison Ivy*]; the last entry is the April 1982 publication of Stuart Kaminsky's *Pour qui Sonne le Clap* [*High Midnight*]. All citations are numbered and provide the author's name and French title in boldface type. Immediately following these are parentheses containing the original title in small capital letters and the year of the first publication. The name of the French translator is given, and separate paragraphs provide the book's setting, year in which the action occurs, and name of the principal character. A lengthy annotation describes the action of the novel, placing it in context with other works featuring that character. Each entry concludes with separate sections providing information on later editions and reissuings of the title, data on film and theater adaptations, and a quote from the teaser on the book.

Each volume is separately indexed and contains indexes for authors, French titles, original titles, themes, main characters, settings, and translators. Furthermore, each volume reproduces publicity material that includes unique pictures and letters from the authors. The first volume, for example, contains letters from David Goodis and Raymond Chandler; the former describes being badly beaten while doing research on the Philadelphia waterfront, while Chandler begins in French, lapses into English, mentions the death of his wife, and states that "I have been having a rather wild time with certain lovely ladies who seem, enormously to my surprise, to be willing to be fondled. By me, why? I am neither young nor beautiful."

Future bibliographers will be thoroughly indebted to Mesplède for this splendid achievement.

SEXTON BLAKE

186.   Holland, Stephen, and Richard Williams. **The Sexton Blake Library (Third and Fifth Series)**. Scunthorpe, England: Dragonby Press, 1988. 18 p. Stapled sheets. Index. (British Paperback Checklists, no. 40).

The enormously popular Sexton Blake first appeared in a story titled *The Missing Millionaire* that was written by Harry Blyth (under the name of Hal Meredith) and published in the 20 December 1893 issue of *The Halfpenny Marvel*. Since then, more than 200 different authors have written more than 3,500 Sexton Blake stories. The first issue of the Sexton Blake Library appeared in 1915 and ran for more than 380 issues; the second series contained more than 744 issues. The third and fifth series contained 526 and 45 titles, respectively; they were published from 1941 to 1963 and 1965 to 1968, respectively.

Holland's and Williams's checklist lists the books in their series order. Each entry provides the book's series number, author, title, and date of publication;

pagination is not given because the majority of the books were 64 pages in length. A cumulative author index reveals many of the pseudonyms.

One wishes that the apparently indefatigable Holland and Williams had provided a comprehensive index to the Sexton Blake series, but although aspects of the series have been discussed in numerous publications and at some length in such books as *Boys Will Be Boys*, a separately published bibliography does not seem to exist. As it is, the checklist lacks a title index but is clearly arranged and easy to use.

VIKING/WORLD DISTRIBUTORS/CONSUL

187. Holland, Stephen, and Richard Williams. **Viking/W[orld] D[istribu-tors]L[td.]/Consul 1949–1966.** Scunthorpe, England: Dragonby Press, 1987. 36 p. Stapled sheets. Index. (British Paperback Checklists, no. 30).

The nature of the relationship between the English paperback publishers of Viking, World Distributors, and Consul is not known, but from 1949 until 1966 the three firms published nearly 1,500 books, many of which were the reprints of works first appearing in hardcover. Among the crime and mystery writers appearing under these three imprints were "Dale Bogard," George Harmon Coxe, Erle Stanley Gardner, Brett Halliday, Evan Hunter, Sax Rohmer, and Charles Willeford.

Holland and Williams have arranged their bibliography by series, beginning with World Distributors and continuing with Viking, though a new series listing is provided with each change of publisher's address. Each entry provides series number; author's name (identifying pseudonyms when possible); title (listing previous titles); whether the book was a first edition, issued simultaneously in hardback, or a reissue; copyright date; pagination; printer; cover artist; and price. An alphabetical code (B for Battle, C for Crime, E for Erotic, etc.) provides an indication of the book's genre, and a cumulative author index concludes the checklist.

In its internal arrangement, this bibliography is most frustrating, for it is impossible to determine the books published under a single imprint without a tremendous amount of work. This aside, this bibliography appears to have been reproduced from word-processed copy, and although it is typographically cramped, its data are reasonably accessible.

MAGAZINE and ANTHOLOGY INDEXES

SCOPE NOTE: Included here are checklists, indexes, and encyclopedic guides to mystery and detective fiction anthologies and to fiction and nonfiction magazines. The monographs referencing the anthologies are listed first, after which the indexes to magazines are listed. Indexes to individual magazines are listed in alphabetical order by magazine name.

GENERAL

188.   Contento, William G., and Martin H. Greenberg. **Index to Crime and Mystery Anthologies**. Boston: G. K. Hall, 1991. xvi, 736 p. LC 90-43578. ISBN 0-8161-8629-4.

This enormous volume indexes more than 1,000 different crime and mystery anthologies published from 1875 through 1990. More than 12,500 different short stories, 3,700 novelettes, 500 novellas, 70 novels, and 300 articles by more than 3,600 different authors are accessible through this massive index. Definitions of terms and explanations of indexing procedures are provided in a helpful user guide, after which the volume contains the following sections: author list: books; title list: books; author list: stories; title list: stories; and book contents. The first brief section lists the books alphabetically by their author, editor, or (if published anonymously) title; publisher and publication date are given, as are Library of Congress number, ISBN, price, pagination, and binding. Cross-references are provided to coauthors, coeditors, and pseudonyms; data on changes in title and alterations in the contents of different editions are also given. In addition to listing the books by their titles, the second section (also brief) includes the names of the editor or compiler and whether the book is an anthology, an original anthology, or a novel.

The third section is the core of the book, listing the contents of the anthologies alphabetically beneath author name or by title if the stories were published anonymously. The original publication data are listed beneath each story, indicated by an asterisk (*), followed by a list of the books and major genre magazines that have reprinted the story. This information includes the book's author and/or editor, publisher, and date of publication. Coauthors and coeditors are indicated by a plus (+), and links to pseudonyms and notes on title changes are provided.

The concluding sections are reasonably brief. The fourth section lists the contents of all the anthologies, each entry providing the work's author, type (i.e., short story, novelette, novella, novel, or article), and original source of publication. As before, notes on title changes are provided, as is the identification of pseudonymous material. The fifth section lists the complete contents of the anthologies alphabetically by their author or editor, after which are given the volume's title, publisher, publication date, Library of Congress number, ISBN, price, pagination, and binding. The author or authors, title, and original publication are given; the story's pagination is frequently provided. Notes on title changes are provided, and an asterisk (*) beside a story's title indicates that it is original to the book. Concluding the volume are a combination errata/addenda sheet that lists one error and the contents of five anthologies that arrived too late to be indexed.

The *Index* is in all respects an exemplary reference work: friendly, accessible, and containing a wealth of data. It is the definitive index to crime and mystery anthologies and belongs in all libraries.

189. Denton, William. **Anthology Listings**. http://www.vex.net/~huff/rara-avis/biblio/anthologies.html

This website lists the contents of six significant anthologies of hard-boiled fiction. The site is arranged alphabetically by editor. Titles are italicized; publisher and year of publication are given. Paginations are not provided, but the short stories are listed in the order in which they appeared in the anthology. More would be welcome.

190. la Cour, Tage. **The Short Detective Story 1925–1982: A Personal Checklist**. Copenhagen: Pinkertons Antikvariat, 1983. (200 copies printed.)

Not seen.

191. Mundell, E. H. **A Checklist of Detective Short Stories**. Portage, IN: [N.P.], 1968. xiv, 337 p. Indexes. LC 68-3329.

As its title indicates, this is a checklist of the detective short stories that appeared in collections and anthologies. The stories in these works that do not feature detectives or detection are not mentioned. In arrangement, the *Checklist* is a thoroughly idiosyncratic work; it does not use alphabetical headings and does not number its approximately 1,100 citations. The contents include "Detective Short Stories," "Detective Experiences," "Secret Service Stories," "Problems," "Addenda," indexes, and book sizes.

The section on detective short stories contains two parts, one listing single-author collections of short stories, the other listing the contents of anthologies. Each entry in the single-author collections provides the author's name in regular letters, the book's title in capital letters, and bibliographic data on the first American and British editions; a code is used to identify the volume's size. If a series detective is featured in the stories, his or her name is given, and the story titles are listed. The listings of the contents of detective story anthologies is selective; only stories not included in author collections are listed, and only the story's first appearance is noted. Furthermore, listings under an anthology's title do not indicate if the stories are reprints. Additionally complicating this section is the arrangement of entries. Anonymous titles are listed first, after which books are listed by their editor's name. Entries provide the author's last name (in italics), title of the story, and name of the detective.

"Detective Experiences" references British yellow-backs and American dime novels whose titles indicate that they include autobiographical reminiscences. The entries in "Secret Service Stories" provide the author's name in regular letters, the book's title in capitals, and bibliographic data on the first American and British editions; a code is used to identify the volume's size. If a recurrent or series detective is featured in the stories, his or her name is given, and the story titles are listed. "Secret Service" anthologies are listed using the same system used in listing the detective story anthologies.

"Problems" lists collections of solve-it-yourself crimes; "Addenda" lists the volumes Mundell was unable to examine or were examined too late for inclusion. The indexes offer access by authors and detective, and the volume concludes with the key to Mundell's code for book sizes. There is no index to titles.

In many respects, this bibliography appears to be a rough draft for Mundell's later collaboration with Rausch (q.v.). Neither this volume nor its separately published supplement (below) are necessary for locating detective and mystery short stories.

192. Mundell, E. H. **A Checklist of Detective Short Stories: Supplement One**. Portage, IN: [N.P.], 1968. 34 p. Indexes.

A continuation of Mundell's 1968 *A Checklist of Detective Short Stories* (q.v.), this volume lists 58 titles that supplement the earlier volume. There is no table of contents, and the arrangement is as idiosyncratic as that in the first volume. The first section lists detective and spy stories, with each entry providing the author's name in regular letters, the book's title in capital letters, and bibliographic data on the first American and British; a code is used to identify the volume's size. If a recurrent detective is featured in the stories, his or her name is given, and the story titles are listed.

The section for "Experiences" is one page in length; the section for "Addenda" is three pages; and the volume concludes with separate indexes for authors and detectives. The key listing the explanation of the size codes is not provided, thus necessitating reference to the earlier volume.

As with the previous volume, this is not a necessary adjunct for research.

193. Mundell, E. H., Jr., and G. Jay Rausch. **The Detective Short Story: A Bibliography and Index**. Manhattan, KS: Kansas State University Library, 1974. v, 493 p. Index. (Bibliography Series, no. 14). LC 74-181860.

According to its preface, this sizable volume began as separate projects, with the authors merging their manuscripts in 1972. The resulting volume, clearly reproduced from typed copy, is an impressive but somewhat eccentric listing of more than 1,400 mystery and detective fiction collections and approximately 7,500 mystery and detective short stories. The contents include detective stories – author collections; Sherlockiana & Poeiana; detective story anthologies; Secret Service stories—author collections; Secret Service anthologies; problems—puzzles; Detective experiences; and titles not examined. There are an index of detectives and agents and an author index. The sections are not clearly delimited, and without constant recourse to the table of contents, locating a specific section can be difficult.

The arrangement and format of each section is similar. The overall arrangement is alphabetical by author or editor, when such is listed on the title page; works with no editor listed on the title page are listed alphabetically by title under "anonymous." Every work is given a unique number, and each entry provides on separate lines the author's (or editor's) name and dates, the book's title in capital letters, and bibliographic data for the first American and British editions. The detective's name is given, and the individual story titles are listed. The first index references only the author of the story, necessitating reference to the second index, which lists book titles in capitals and story titles in lowercase letters, and is keyed to the unique number given by each citation.

Despite its difficult arrangement and some factual errors, this index remains occasionally useful.

194. Queen, Ellery. **The Detective Short Story: A Bibliography**. Boston: Little, Brown, 1942. 146 p. LC 42-23794.

195. Queen, Ellery. **The Detective Short Story: A Bibliography**. With a new introduction by the author. New York: Biblo and Tannen, 1969. 146 p. LC 73-79517.

Despite its title, this is not a bibliography of detective short stories but a bibliography of the anthologies in which the short stories appeared. It is a thoroughly idiosyncratic work, lacking a table of contents and numbering for its citations, which amount to approximately 600. A brief explanatory note provides Frederic Dannay and Manfred Lee's basis for selection: "a detective story is a tale of ratiocination, complete with crime and/or mystery, suspects, investigation, clues, deduction, and solution; in its purest form, the chief character should be a detective, amateur or professional, who devotes most of his (or her) time to the problems of detection" and (more dubiously) " 'crook' stories have been considered eligible for the logical reason that whenever a story is concerned primarily with a criminal, it is concerned also, openly or by implication, with the forces of law operating against the criminal."

The bibliography records books published in Great Britain and the United States between 1841 and 1941. Single-author collections and anthologies are listed in separate sections. The collections are arranged alphabetically by author's name; when the author published more than one collection, the arrangement becomes chronological. The author's name is in boldface type, the title is in small capital letters, and the place of publication and the publisher are treated routinely. The presentation of the publication date, however, takes into consideration the placement of the date on the title page and the copyright page. In addition, the first edition's paper size is given (e.g., 8vo, 12mo, 16mo, 18mo), as is a description of its binding. Occasionally lengthy notes discuss publication histories of landmark collections and comment on the differences between British and American editions. If the collection features a single detective or a recurrent criminal, this name is given. Finally, there are two subsections; "Chinese Detective Stories" (compiled by Vincent Starrett) and "Incunables" (detective stories published prior to 1841) are listed under their respective letters.

The citations to anthologies are essentially similar to those of the single-author collections, although the anthologies are listed chronologically and the notes tend to comment on unique aspects of the contents. Each entry concludes by listing the name of the editor or editors.

The bibliography contains two indexes. The "Index of Detectives and Criminals" lists the names of detectives in upper- and lowercase and the names of the criminals in italics; characters who are both (e.g., Arsene Lupin) have their names given in large and small capital letters. The "Index of Anthology Editors" is routine. There is no title index.

Though their work is occasionally frustrating, the Queens deserve commendation for compiling the first bibliography of its kind. Furthermore, and more important, the citations tend to be accurate, and they often contain substantially more detail than do the citations of later bibliographers. Despite its age and some errors, this book remains useful.

196. Thom, William. **Hero Pulp Reprint Index**. Seymour, TX: Fading Shadows, 1997. 62 p. Paperback.

This bibliography lists the book appearances of the characters originally featured in the single-character ("hero pulp") magazines. Its contents include a hero pulp reprint index, an index of previously unpublished stories, and an index of new stories in the pulp tradition. There are also appendixes listing magazine title abbreviations, publisher name abbreviations, format abbreviations, artist name abbreviation, and notes.

The majority of the work consists of the hero pulp reprint index, which for each hero provides the title of the work and the name of the book that republished it; abbreviations list the name of the republisher, size (format) of the book, publication date, and cover artist. Also given are the original date and title of the story's publication, and entries conclude with the volume and number of the work's original publication. Similar information is given in the successive sections, although (of course) original publication data are not given.

The arrangement of the entries is idiosyncratic and can be frustrating, for Thom has listed his entries alphabetically by the first part of the fullest name under which the hero is known: the Phantom Detective is listed under "P," but so too are Phil Towne, Philip Strange, Prester John, Prince Raynor, and Purple Scar; similarly, Mr. Chang, Mr. Death, and Mr. Wong are all listed under "M." Cross-references have not been provided.

The majority of the data in the *Hero Pulp Reprint Index* cannot be located through any reference sources, and Thom deserves commendation for his efforts, which are accurate and will assist not only the fans of the hero pulps but also the scholars of popular culture.

Note: Earlier versions of this index were originally serialized in *Echoes* 58, 59, 60, and 85; all entries have been updated and corrected for this edition.

MAGAZINE INDEXES, GENERAL

197.   Contento, William G. **Mystery Magazine Index: 1980–1997**. http://www. best.com/~contento/mags

A direct continuation of the work started by Michael L. Cook in *Monthly Murders* (q.v.), this website offers author, title, and issue-by-issue indexes to some 23 magazines published since 1980. It also offers yearly indexes to mysteries appearing in nongenre publications since 1990. The magazines indexed include *Alfred Hitchcock's Mystery Magazine* and *Ellery Queen's Mystery Magazine*, as well as such relative newcomers as *Hardboiled* and *Mary Higgins Clark Mystery Magazine*. Several of the titles (e.g., *New Mystery* and *Scientific Detective Annual*) are indexed neither through *Monthly Murders* nor through other sources.

An exemplary website; an example of what the Web can do.

198.   Cook, Michael L. **Monthly Murders: A Checklist and Chronological Listing of Fiction in the Digest-Size Mystery Magazines in the United States and Canada**. Westport, CT: Greenwood Press, 1982. xviii, 1,147 p. Index. LC 81-6986. ISBN 0-313-23126-5.

The first digest-sized mystery magazine was the Fall 1941 issue of *Ellery Queen's Mystery Magazine*. Dozens of digest-sized mystery magazines have since been published, most lasting but a few issues. Until recently, very few of these magazines have been collected by academic libraries, and even private collectors have tended to shun them. As Cook states in his introduction, "digest-size mystery magazines have not been as popular among collectors as the pulp-magazines, digest-size mystery novels, or the paperback books for some reason. They are collected even less in England, yet many of these are far more scarce than is realized. It is estimated by several avid collectors that less than 25 copies of some still exist."

Monthly Murders is not a comprehensive index to the contents of digest-sized mystery magazines; it does not cumulate in the way that other indexes do, nor does it index nonfiction. Rather, it is a listing of the stories appearing in more than 100 British and American digest-sized mystery magazines, the best-known being *Alfred Hitchcock's Mystery Magazine*, *Ellery Queen's Mystery Magazine*, and *The Saint Detective Magazine*; less familiar titles include *All Mystery* (one issue, 1950), *Bizarre! Mystery Magazine* (three issues, 1965–1966), *The Craig Rice Mystery Digest* (one issue, 1945), *Strange* (three issues, 1952), *Sleuth Mystery Magazine* (two issues, 1958), *Verdict Crime Detection Magazine* (two issues, 1956), and *Whodunit* (one issue, 1967). Chronologically, coverage of *Monthly Murders* begins with the Fall 1941 issue of *Ellery Queen's Mystery Magazine* and concludes with the contents of the digest-sized mystery magazines being published at the end of 1980.

Cook begins each magazine's entry by providing the publisher's name and address, citing changes when they can be documented, though introductory prose is kept to a minimum. The arrangement is issue-by-issue chronological, each entry citing the magazine's publication date, volume and issue number, and newsstand cost. Only the fictional contents of the magazines are given; they are listed in no particular order, and their pagination is not included. An alphabetical list of magazines is followed by an author index that reveals occasional pseudonyms, provides some cross-references, and lists the stories alphabetically.

Apart from being somewhat mistitled—several of the digest-sized mystery magazines appeared bimonthly, and at least one was quarterly—*Monthly Murders* is an ambitious achievement with some curious and all too readily noticeable flaws. One cannot fault Cook for being unable to obtain certain issues, or for neglecting to indicate reprints and stories that were reprinted under different titles, but why, for example, did he choose to alphabetize his magazines by an arbitrarily chosen system of abbreviations rather than by the magazine's name? In just the first letter of the alphabet, the reliance on abbreviations leads to the following idiosyncratic arrangement of magazines: *American Agent*, *Alfred Hitchcock's Mystery Magazine* (British edition), *Accused Detective Story Magazine*, *Alfred Hitchcock's Mystery Magazine* (American edition), *All Mystery*, *Avon Modern Short Story Monthly*, and *Avon Detective Mysteries*. More seriously, the lack of a title index means that the contents of *Monthly Murders* are effectively inaccessible to those who know neither magazine nor author.

Like Cook's *Mystery Fanfare* and his *Mystery, Espionage, and Detective Magazines* (q.q.v.), *Monthly Murders* is a flawed monument. It deserves revising, correcting, expanding, and updating.

199. Cook, Michael L. **Mystery, Detective, and Espionage Magazines**. Westport, CT: Greenwood Press, 1983. xxiv, 795 p. Index. (Historical Guides to the World's Periodicals and Newspapers). LC 82-20977. ISBN 0-313-23310-1.

A companion of sorts to Cook's *Mystery, Detective, and Espionage Fiction* (q.v.), this monumental book has a larger focus than the other volume. Not only does it describe the pulp magazines indexed in the previous volume, but it also describes numerous fan publications and foreign, academic, and nonfiction magazines, and it provides lengthy appendixes and a first-rate index.

The first and largest section of the volume focuses on the magazines published in the United States and provides histories that describe the significant events and personalities in the publication's lifetime. These profiles are at times lengthy and are generally proportionate to the magazine's significance. The longest is that received by *Ellery Queen's Mystery Magazine* (ten pages), but it is followed closely by *Black Mask* (seven pages), *The Spider* (six), and *The Shadow* and *Doc Savage* (five and a half apiece).

The profiles are by such experts as Walter Albert, J. Randolph Cox, Bernard Drew, E. R. Hagemann, Will Murray, Robert Sampson, and Albert Tonik. Their prose is lively, informative, and very often superior to the stories and publications being described. Sampson in particular appears to have enjoyed his writing assignments, lavishing the trashiest of pulp magazines with the most exuberant of prose. His essay on *Scarlet Adventuress* opens by stating that "the annals of unrepentant trash contain few examples more sleazy than *Scarlet Adventuress*," and continues by stating that "the story was usually told from what passed for the woman's point of view. The prose is unbelievable. The word *exotic* appears about six times per page, never correctly used. *Alluring* is used once per paragraph. The story lines, such as they are, support descriptions of feminine undressing and sly mention of other various mysteries."

Each entry has two concluding sections. A bibliography references the articles and books that discuss the magazine, cites indexes to the magazine (if any), and lists the libraries in which the magazine can be found. The second section provides bibliographical information on the publication: its official title and title changes (if any), volume and issue data, publisher, editor, price per issue, size and pagination, and publication status as of 1983.

Successive sections use the same format to provide overviews of foreign magazines and to profile mystery book clubs. These are followed by appendixes listing the magazines by category for the United States, Canada, and Great Britain; certain key writers in the Golden Age, their most common pseudonyms, and the magazines with which they were commonly associated; a year-by-year chronology of the magazines; lists of American and Canadian true-detective magazines; lists of Sherlock Holmes Scion Society Periodicals; and a list of other periodicals of interest to the collector. A two-page bibliography and a thorough index conclude the volume.

Mystery, Detective, and Espionage Magazines is deservedly acclaimed as a landmark volume, and complaints about it tend to the trivial: Fredric Brown's name is given once as "Frederick"; E. Hoffmann Price's middle name is given consistently as "Hoffman"; and a ghost is inadvertently created when Lawrence G. Blochman is cited as Lawrence Blackman.

This volume belongs in all academic libraries.

200. Cook, Michael L. **Mystery Fanfare: A Composite Annotated Index to Mystery and Related Fanzines 1963–1981**. Bowling Green, OH: Bowling Green State University Popular Press, 1983. 441 p. Index. LC 82-73848. ISBN 0-87972-229-0 (hc); 0-87972-230-4 (pb).

Although science fiction fanzines have been published since the early 1930s, it is Michael Cook's contention that the first regularly published mystery and detective fanzines not solely devoted to Sherlock Holmes did not appear until the 1960s. Fifty-two of these fanzines are indexed in *Mystery Fanfare*, the chronologically oldest being the Winter 1963 (vol. 60) issue of *The Pulp Era*. Other fanzines indexed by Cook include *The Armchair Detective*, *The August Derleth Society Newsletter*, *The Bony Bulletin*, *Clues*, *The Gazette: The Journal of the Wolfe Pack*, *The Mystery Fancier*, *The Mystery Lover's Newsletter*, *The Mystery Readers Newsletter*, *The Poisoned Pen*, and *The Thorndyke File*. In all, nearly 600 different issues and approximately 2,400 articles are indexed by author, title, and subject, with a concluding appendix listing the reviews of films, stage productions, and television programs that were published in these fanzines. Book reviews are included in the major indexing sequence; unless they contained something significant, letters published in the fanzines are indexed by only the name of their writer. Especially useful is the introductory "Guide and Chronology of Magazines Indexed," which provides not only a brief prose history of each magazine but also includes such data as the publication history of the issues indexed, the fanzine's usual size and pagination, its status, editor, publisher, and frequency of publication. Each bibliographic citation provides the article's author and title and, in abbreviated form, the fanzine's name, volume, issue, and relevant pages.

The fanzines indexed in *Mystery Fanfare* frequently contained original and significant information, and Cook's ambition to make their contents more widely known is a laudable one. Nevertheless, Cook's desire too often outweighed his indexing skills, for *Mystery Fanfare* has severe methodological problems. Because it is a composite index, Cook assigned each fanzine a one- or two-letter code that is not intuitively obvious; users must constantly check the alphabetical list of code designations at the beginning of the volume. More seriously, Cook failed to maintain adequate intellectual control over his material; he used a computer to compile and sort his data without examining and questioning the integrity of the output. Because of this, articles whose titles begin with "A" and "An" are indexed under the letter "A," which leads to separate sections for titles beginning with "An interview with . . . " and "Interview with . . ."; makes such titles as "A John Creasey Bibliography," "A John Dickson Carr Checklist," and "A Simon Ark Bibliography" virtually inaccessible; and splits such series as "A Report on Bouchercon": the title for Report IV apparently did not possess the initial article and is thus listed under "R." Furthermore, because Cook occasionally miskeyed his data, the computer sorted according to its own internal logic: The entries entitled "A. D." (an article on August Derleth) and "A. Merritt's Mysteries" occur out of alphabetical sequence because (in Cook's typing) the "A" in the former is followed by a period and no space and in the latter the "A" is (erroneously) followed by a comma. Titles beginning with "The," however, occur in their correct alphabetical sequence, for the initial article is transposed to the end of each title entry. Cook's usage of subject headings is equally idiosyncratic (e.g., different entries occur under "bibliography" and "checklist").

None of this is to say that *Mystery Fanfare* cannot be used. If one is willing to endure the frustrating arrangement, *Mystery Fanfare* can be considered a monumental achievement. It preserves the contents of publications that have been too often discarded as ephemeral, and it has something to offer virtually all researchers on detective and mystery literature. It is clearly reproduced from legible copy, and it exemplifies the concept of "labor of love." Still, a revised, corrected, and updated edition of *Mystery Fanfare* is badly needed.

201. Cook, Michael L., and Stephen T. Miller. **Mystery, Detective, and Espionage Fiction: A Checklist of Fiction in U.S. Pulp Magazines, 1915–1974**. New York: Garland Publishing, 1988. 2 vols. xvi, 1,183 p. Index. (Garland Reference Library of the Humanities, vol. 838). LC 88-7190. ISBN 0-8240-7539-0.

In a project that took more than four years, Cook and Miller indexed the fiction that appeared in every mystery, detective, and espionage pulp magazine published between 1915 and 1974. An incredible 58,000 stories appearing in nearly 9,000 issues of more than 360 different magazine titles are indexed in these two volumes.

Both volumes contain two columns per page. The first volume lists the magazines alphabetically, then lists the contents in chronological order by volume and issue number. The authors' names are given in capital letters, titles are given in regular type, and joint authors are listed separately. In addition, each magazine is assigned a two-letter code, and to this code are added numbers signifying the magazine's volume and issue number. *The Illustrated Detective Magazine*, for example, is HJ, and volume 3, no. 4, of the magazine is 3HJ4. The first volume concludes with an alphabetical index providing publication data for the magazines and an index listing the magazines by their commencement dates.

The second volume indexes the stories by author. As before, the author's name is given in capital letters, and the story's title is given in regular type. Each story title is keyed to the coding system described above.

In intended scope, this index is awe-inspiring; in execution, it is thoroughly frustrating. At its most basic, the index is badly laid out, for approximately a quarter of each page is blank; had correct formatting been used, this could have been a one-volume work. Layout aside, the author index has severe problems. First, it appears that Cook's and Miller's computer made all of the indexing decisions, and several of its sort routines were inadequately defined. A sorting problem put some of the names beginning with "Mac" and "Mc" at the beginning of the letter "M," but (in a break with tradition), the majority of the "Mac" and "Mc" entries occur at the *conclusion* of the letter "M." Stories by Alan MacDonald, William B. MacHarg, and Donald MacGregor (among others) appear in both locations. Other entries—as in the case of Frank Gruber—occur out of their proper alphabetical sequence and are thus inaccessible except by chance.

As if these problems were not enough, Cook and Miller appear to have made no attempts to establish a consistent or standardized spelling for any of the authors' names or even to verify that an author's name does not repeat itself on the page. E. Hoffmann Price's name occurs 18 times on two pages, and beneath each occurrence is a (different) alphabetical list of stories. Nor are any of these lists of titles particularly accessible, for although they are alphabetical, initial articles have been used in their indexing. Researchers must not only look under each variant and repetition of an author's name, they must then look to see if a particular title has been given as "A Night for Murder," "The Night for Murder," or "Night for Murder." As if this were not enough, the index contains no separate index to story titles, and the entries do not provide pagination.

None of this is to say that this index cannot be used. If one is willing and able to ignore the above problems, enormous amounts of information can sometimes be located. No other index does what this one attempts to do; the indexed publications are frequently surpassingly rare, surviving only on microfilm or in the hands of private collectors. Thus, however defective this index is, it provides a means to locate original magazine work by many writers who have since become significant. A thoroughly revised, corrected, and expanded edition of this index is badly needed.

Note: There is some overlap with the indexes compiled by Leonard Robbins (q.v.), but Robbins's work does not supersede that of Cook and Miller.

202. Gunnison, John P. **Street & Smith's Hero Pulp Checklist**. Upper Marlboro, MD: Pulp Collector Press, 1991. Unpaged. Paperback. (Pulp Collector Press Checklist Series, no. 1).

In 1931, Street & Smith, the largest publisher of pulp magazines, started a pulp magazine called *The Shadow* to capitalize on the success of "Detective Story Magazine," a radio program narrated by a mysterious voice known as the Shadow. Written by Walter Gibson, *The Shadow* became the first of the hero pulps, the pulp magazines devoted to describing the heroic activities of one recurrent series character.

Gunnison's checklist is arranged alphabetically by names of the pulp heroes. Illustrations appear throughout. Each entry is prefaced by a brief discussion of the character and authors known to have written about the character. Entries for specific magazines are chronologically arranged and list the volume and issue number, date of publication, story's title (in capital letters), and house name assigned to the work. When the hero was no longer featured in a separate magazine named for him but remained active—as happened with the Avenger, Bill Barnes, Pete Rice, the Skipper, and the Wizard—a separate entry lists the magazine issues in which the stories were published.

Collectors of Street & Smith's hero pulps will find this a useful publication.

203. McKinstry, Lohr, and Robert Weinberg. **The Hero Pulp Index**. Hillside Park, NJ: Robert Weinberg, 1970. 54 p. Index. Paperback. LC 70-24788. (250 copies printed.)

204. Weinberg, Robert, and Lohr McKinstry. **The Hero Pulp Index**, 2d revised ed. Evergreen, CO: Opar Press, 1971. 48 p. Paperback. Index.

The Hero Pulp Index attempts to index every major hero pulp magazine published, as well as heroic series characters who never had pulp magazines devoted to their activities but who were prominently featured in other magazines; pulp antiheroes and supervillains are also described. This description concentrates on the revised (2d) edition, which is reproduced from typed copy.

The first section of the *Index* is an issue-by-issue listing of the contents of the hero pulp magazines. The contents are arranged alphabetically by heroes' crimefighting names, though cross-references to and from heroes' ordinary names are not provided. Citations list the hero's name and the magazine in which he appeared; also given are the house name under which the stories were published, and many pseudonyms are revealed. The arrangement of citations is chronological. Each entry is separately numbered and lists the story title, volume, issue, and month and year of publication. Entries indicate when the hero no longer warranted a pulp of his own but became resident in another pulp (e.g., "Kenneth Robeson's" *The Avenger*).

The second section of the *Index* lists some noted authors of hero pulp stories and some of the pen names and house-names they were known to have used. Listed after each name are the magazines for which the author wrote and the number of stories written for that magazine.

A third section has information on book appearances and reprints of the pulp characters. The concluding section, "A Guide to the Pulp Heroes," provides a biographical description of the hero or villain; e.g., for *Doctor Yen Sin* Weinberg and McKinstry write, "attempting to imitate Sax Rohmer's Fu Manchu, Popular Publications presented Dr. Yen Sin, an Oriental genius who plotted to become emperor of the world. Yen Sin fought the usual group of troubleshooters in the Rohmer pattern. The Doctor, who used super forces, was known as 'The Invisible Peril.' The series was written by pulpster, [sic] Donald Keyhoe, who was going to gain notoriety many years later with the flying saucer craze."

Though some entries have errors, and the *Index* as a whole needs updating and a title index, this remains one of the more useful indexes to a specialized genre of pulp magazine.

205. Mundell, E. H. **Detective Mystery Crime Magazines**. Portage, IN: [N.P.], 1971. 47 p.

Mundell has compiled an alphabetical list of all of the detective, mystery, and crime magazines in his personal collection or whose titles he found listed in the Copyright registers issued by the Library of Congress during the years from 1915 until 1953. Each citation gives the magazine's title, its publisher, and the date of its first issue; terminal dates are occasionally given, as are changes in title and publisher. The titles of magazines not seen by Mundell are in italics. In all, basic bibliographic information is given about nearly 300 magazines, many of which are not accorded mention in either the works of Michael Cook or Leonard Robbins (q.q.v.).

According to Mundell's brief introduction, this is the third such list he has compiled. One regrets that none of these lists appears to have been widely distributed.

206. Robbins, Leonard A. **The Pulp Magazine Index: First Series**. Mercer Island, WA: Starmont House, 1989. 3 vols. x, 467, 882, 810 p. Index. LC 88-20056. ISBN 1-55742-111-0 (set).

207. Robbins, Leonard A. **The Pulp Magazine Index: Second Series**. Mercer Island, WA: Starmont House, 1989. viii, 583 p. Index. LC 89-34752. ISBN 1-55742-162-5.

208. Robbins, Leonard A. **The Pulp Magazine Index: Third Series**. Mercer Island, WA: Starmont House, 1990. Index. xii, 639 p. Index. ISBN 1-55742-204-4.

209. Robbins, Leonard A. **The Pulp Magazine Index: Fourth Series**. Mercer Island, WA: Starmont House, 1991. xi, 567 p. Index. ISBN 1-55742-241-9.

A monumental achievement that is largely unknown outside the insular world of pulp magazine collectors, these enormous books cumulatively index several hundred pulp magazines from all genres. Thousands of issues of mystery and detective, romance, Western, adventure, aviation, war, hero, science fiction, sports, and shudder pulps are listed issue-by-issue, then indexed by their authors, titles, illustrators, and various forms of the characters' names. Most of these data do not exist in any other source.

Though individual volumes have a similar arrangement, *The Pulp Magazine Index* is not always an easy work to use, perhaps because of the unique nature of its content. Each series begins with a section titled "Special Remarks" that offers commentary on numbering and table of contents errors or particularly desirable data in the magazines. These comments, which will convey nothing to the uninitiated, are arranged by the one- or two-letter code that Robbins has assigned each magazine to facilitate computer sorting. Unfortunately, these codes are not intuitively obvious and follow no discernible order: AO is *Air Trails*, AP is *Triple Detective*, AQ is *The Angel Detective*, and AR is *Captain Hazzard Magazine*; conversely, *Thrilling Mysteries* is BD, *Thrilling Spy Stories* is DW, and *The Thrill Book* is GS.

The next sections are titled "Magazine File Report: Listed by Magazine" and "Magazine File Report: Listed by Code." The former is an alphabetical listing of the magazines by title; accompanying data provide the magazine's price, size, pagination, frequency, publisher, editor(s), and the letter code Robbins has assigned the magazine. The latter section contains the same data as the previous section, but the magazines are arranged alphabetically by the letter code rather than alphabetically by title. Users of the index must make constant reference to these sections.

Successive divisions are confusingly titled "Magazine Data File Report: Listed by Code," "Magazine Data File Report: Listed by Title," "Magazine Data File Report: Listed by Author," "Artists File Report: Listed by Artist," "Character File Report: Listed by Character," "Special Zero Character Data," and "Character File Report: Special Zero Code Data." These are, respectively, the issue-by-issue indexes to the magazines arranged by their assigned code, the title index to the stories in magazines, the author index to the stories in the magazines, the artist index to the magazines, and the indexes to various forms of the characters' names. Entries in the issue-by-issue index provide the magazine's publication date (in the form of 08-1935 for August 1935), volume and issue number, story's page number, title, and author; these data are rearranged to create the title and author indexes. Entries in the "Artists File Report" list the artists by last name, the code for the magazine for which the artwork was done, and the magazine's volume and issue number, and a note as to whether the artwork was a cover or an "int"[erior illustration]. If the artist contributed more than one interior illustration, the number is given.

Entries in the "Character File Report: Listing by Character" list the names of the characters in the story, the code for the magazine, volume and issue number, and title of the story in which the character appeared. The "Special Zero Character Data" provide three symbols: * is used to signify the hero's aides; # is used to signify the hero's antagonists; and + is used to signify aliases and nicknames. These symbols appear after the names in the "Character File Report: Listing by Character" and the "Character File Report: Special Zero Code Data." Entries in this last section list the names of the aliases, nicknames, and antagonists and cross-reference them to the character's name. "Ham+," for example, is linked as the nickname of Theodore Marley Brooks.

Apart from the frustrating use of codes to identify magazines, *The Pulp Magazine Index* has only one serious shortcoming: Robbins used a computer to sort his data, and in a computer sort, numbers precede words, as do nonalphanumeric characters. In this index, all titles that have numbers and symbols as the first word are listed separately at the beginning of their section. Similarly, humans alphabetizing titles beginning with "A," "An," or "The" would know to disregard them and index using the first significant word. In this index the listings have not been integrated, and the titles beginning with "A" and "An" appear alphabetically in section A, and the titles beginning with "The" are listed alphabetically in the T section.

Because of the magnitude of Robbins's accomplishment, the above shortcomings can be dismissed as idiosyncrasies. The indexes are clearly reproduced from computer-generated copy, and they belong in all research libraries. Robbins was preparing indexes to the long-lasting *Short Stories* and to a number of additional pulp magazines when the owner of Starmont House died, effectively leaving Robbins without a publisher willing to take a project of this magnitude. Given the specialized nature of these indexes, it is improbable that additional volumes will be published in paper. The loss will not be noticed by most, but it will be enormous nevertheless.

MAGAZINE INDEXES,
SPECIFIC TITLES

The Armchair Detective

210. Stilwell, Steven A. **The Armchair Detective Index, Volumes 1–10, 1967–1977**. New York: Armchair Detective, 1979. 64 p. Paperback. LC 79-90556. ISBN 0-89296-051-X.

Though indexes to the early issues of *The Armchair Detective* were published in the even-numbered volumes, this is the first separately published index to this long-running and influential magazine. The index has been clearly reproduced from word-processed copy. It is alphabetical by author, title, and subject, listing in one alphabetic sequence all the articles, reviews, and letters published in *The Armchair Detective* between October 1967 and October 1977. Titles of books, plays, and films are capitalized; subjects are underlined and are in regular type; and titles of short stories are given in quotation marks. Symbols and abbreviations have been kept to a minimum: (R) after the title means "reviewed," (MN) means "movie note," and (L) means "letter." Each entry concludes with the volume, issue number, and page on which the piece appeared. The format in which these data are presented is initially unclear—a typical entry looks like 8/4/303—but this is merely an inconvenience. There are occasional problems in alphabetization, the index being derived from a computer sort that put articles about *Pulps* before a discussion of *Pulp Tradition in Mystery Novels*. Nevertheless, this index offers far greater access to *The Armchair Detective* than does Michael Cook's *Mystery Fanfare* (q.v.). Now, however, it has been completely superseded by the index compiled by Deeck and Stilwell (q.v.).

211. Deeck, William F., and Steven A. Stilwell. **The Armchair Detective Index, Volumes 1–20, 1967–1987**. New York: Armchair Detective, 1992. iii, 178 p. LC 92-54768. ISBN 1-56287-043-2 (hc); 1-56287-044-0 (pb).

Although Stilwell assisted in the compilation of this volume, it is here considered a separate publication rather than merely a 2d edition because there have been significant changes made to the original publication. Many of these changes have to do with improved computer technology. The first edition placed *Coxe, George Harmon* before *Cox, J. Randolph* and interfiled compound names such as *Van Dine* and *Van Gulik* with such words as *Vance* and *Vanishers*. These and other errors have been silently corrected.

The *Index* is alphabetical by author, title, and subject, listing in one alphabetic sequence all of the articles, reviews, and letters published in *The Armchair Detective* between October 1967 and October 1987. Titles of books, plays, television shows, and films are capitalized; subjects are italicized; and the titles of short stories are given in quotation marks. Individual reviews of books, short stories, and plays are indexed under the author of the work, the title of the work, the subject, and the author for the review, but movie and television reviews are listed under the title alone. Reviews in columns are listed only under the author and title of the review, the exception being the contents of Charles Shibuk's "The Paperback Revolution," which have not been separately indexed.

Symbols and abbreviations are the same as those in Stilwell's solo effort: (R) after the title means "reviewed," (MN) means "movie note," and (L) means "letter." Letters from individuals are listed in their alphabetical sequence, and those letters related to a subject are also grouped at the conclusion of each subject entry.

Entries conclude with the volume, issue number, and page on which the piece appeared. As in the other index, the format in which these data are presented is initially unclear—a typical entry looks like 12/3/203—but this is at most a minor inconvenience.

An essential index for all academic and research libraries.

The Avenger

212. Finnan, R. W. **The Avenger.** http://members.aol.com/Hardyboy02/avenger.html

This website provides a list of *The Avenger* stories, indicating the titles and issues of the magazines in which they appeared as well as their reprint status. Information on authors of specific stories is briefly given. Some cover reproductions of the paperbacks are provided. A complete list of the titles in *The Avenger* on radio is also given.

213. Hopkins, Howard. **The Gray Nemesis.** Scarboro, ME: Golden Perils Press, 1992. 148 p. Paperback.

Introduced in 1939, *The Avenger* was the one of Street and Smith's last attempts to create a major pulp hero. Protagonist Richard Henry Benson was intriguingly presented: He was an adventurer whose wife and daughter vanished mysteriously on an airplane trip, so shocking him that his hair turned white and his features became an emotionless mask, thereby enabling him to become a master of disguise. However, the magazine lasted a mere 24 issues, dying in 1942. In 1974 the Warner Paperback Library reprinted the magazines in paperback form and reintroduced the character in a series of original paperbacks that failed.

Clearly reproduced from word-processed copy, *The Gray Nemesis* is a loving tribute to one of the less successful pulp magazines. The first part of the book consists of descriptions of the world of Benson and of his assistants. While most of the latter were standard pulp types, two of them—Joshua Elijah and Rosabel Newton—are reasonably sympathetic portraits of African Americans, and the early magazines contain hints that another character was also intended to be a minority. This section has lists of the radio dramatizations of *The Avenger*, summarizes all *The Avenger* stories (pulp magazines as well as paperback), and concludes with a chronological list of all *The Avenger* stories that provides the title under which the story was published, the date the story was submitted, the story's original title, and the date the story was published. This material occupies less than half of the volume; the rest of the book consists of reproductions of illustrations from the magazines.

214. Vaisala. **The Avenger/Justice, Inc**. http://www.cs.uku.fi/~vaisala/AVENGER/Avenger.htm

This website provides a complete index to *The Avenger*, using much of the information appearing in Hopkins's *The Gray Nemesis* (q.v.). The title of each issue is given, as are author, date of publication, and series number. When *The Avenger* was forced to appear in other magazines, their titles are also indicated. Lists of the comic-book issues of *The Avenger* are given, as are the radio shows in which *The Avenger* was featured. Finally, cover reproductions of the paperback reprints of *The Avenger* are given. A very nicely done site.

Black Mask

215. Hagemann, E. R. **A Comprehensive Index to** *Black Mask*, **1920–1951: With Brief Annotations, Preface, and Editorial Apparatus**. Bowling Green, OH: Bowling Green State University Popular Press, 1982. 236 p. LC 82-81824. ISBN 0-87972-201-0 (hc); 0-87972-202-9 (pb).

For an astoundingly long time, *Black Mask* set the standard. Other pulp magazines could try to emulate it, but only rarely could they beat it, and it remains a legend, having lasted for some 31 years and publishing in its 340 issues approximately 2,500 stories by approximately 640 authors. Although numerous anthologies have been drawn from its pages, surprisingly few indexes to *Black Mask* have been compiled. Hagemann's is but one of two known. Others are rumored to exist, but their existence cannot be confirmed.

Despite its title, this is not so much a comprehensive index as it is an author index. The volume opens with a "Register of *Black Mask*" that lists the holdings of the British Library, the library at UCLA, the Library of Congress, the University of Louisville, and private collectors. This is followed by data on the magazine's issuance, editorship, title, and price, and a list of editors, writers (arranged by debut), frequency of appearance, and series characters.

These facts occupy only 15 pages; the remainder of the volume is the author index. For each author Hagemann lists alphabetically the stories contributed, numbering each story and including in each citation the volume, issue number, and month and year in which the story was published. The story's pagination is given, as are the names of major series characters appearing in the story and, occasionally, an editorial comment (e.g., "unusually well-plotted"). All of this material is clearly presented and admirably accessible.

Had Hagemann continued in this vein and provided indexes listing the contents of the magazine, the titles of the stories, and the illustrators, he would have produced the definitive index to *Black Mask*. As it is, there is still a need for a truly comprehensive index, but given the rarity of the magazine—two complete sets are known to exist—it is improbable that such will ever be compiled.

Hagemann's index thus remains the only viable means for accessing the contents of this most important pulp.

216. Mundell, E. H. **An Index of Black Mask**. Portage, IN: [N.P.], 1973. 164 p.

According to Mundell's brief preface, this is the second index of the *Black Mask* that he compiled, the first being an issue-by-issue index. This earlier index has not been seen and cannot be located. The contents include indexes of authors, editors, and cover illustrators.

Arrangement in the first section is alphabetical, but authors' names are not reversed for alphabetization. The names are given in capital letters; beneath each, in regular type, are two columns. The first lists the titles of the author's stories; the second, the month and year in which the story was published. Only the last two digits of the year are given. When the author contributed more than one story, the arrangement is chronological. Not provided are the story's pagination and the volume and issue number of the magazine in which the story appeared. Nor are cross-references provided to reveal pseudonyms.

The second section lists the editors of *Black Mask* in chronological order, and the third lists the cover artists alphabetically. The entries for the artists are not separated into columns but are lumped together as a paragraph, the year occurring only at the end of each listing of months.

This is not a discreditable effort, but one nevertheless wishes that Mundell had included with it his issue-by-issue index and had indexed nonfiction and editorial material. This aside, although the author index has been superseded by Hagemann's *A Comprehensive Index to* Black Mask, *1920–1951* (q.v.), the list of cover artists is unique to this volume.

Dime Detective Magazine

217. Traylor, James L. **Dime Detective Index**. New Carrollton, MD: Pulp Collector Press, 1986. 124 p. Paperback.

Dime Detective Magazine was Popular Publication's imitation of *Black Mask*, but it never captured *Black Mask*'s readership. Indeed, it would probably not be included in most lists of the most important pulp mystery and detective magazines; its stories were frequently tinged with horror, and the covers tended toward the (delightfully) lurid. It nevertheless proved to be Popular Publication's most durable mystery title, lasting from November 1931 until August 1953, a total of 273 issues. Among its more notable authors were Cornell Woolrich (31 stories), Carroll John Daly (53 stories), and John D. MacDonald (35 stories). Raymond Chandler is present with seven stories, including "The Lady in the Lake."

Traylor's index begins with a brief history of the magazine that discusses its contents, authors, series characters, and artists and their artwork. Following are an issue-by-issue index, an author index, an index to the author profiles and pictures that appeared in the magazine, and an alphabetical list of the story characters, their authors, and the number of stories in which they appeared. Concluding the volume are indexes ranking the frequency of the character's appearance and a brief discussion of two magazine features, "Crossroads of Crime" (a crossword puzzle) and "Ready for the Rackets" (a factual discussion of confidence games). Not included in the table of contents or the pagination are two sections providing black-and-white reproductions of magazine covers.

Dime Detective Index is clearly reproduced from word-processed copy and does much to make accessible the contents of a largely overlooked pulp magazine. It lacks a title index, however, and its entries do not provide pagination. These oversights make the Dime Detective Index less than comprehensive. Researchers interested in only the fiction published in Dime Detective Magazine should know that the magazine is also indexed in Leonard Robbins's Pulp Magazine Index: Third Series (q.v.). Traylor's introduction, tabular data, and indexes to the author profiles and pictures are, however, unique to his index.

Doc Savage

218. Brown, Michael Rogero. **Doc Savage**. http://sflovers.rutgers.edu/archive/bibliographies/doc-savage.txt

Doc Savage is sometimes classified as a science fiction magazine, but the majority of its stories were structured and plotted as traditional mysteries, the last chapter revealing the identity of the villain responsible for all the misdeeds and misdirections. The first section of Brown's index is an issue-by-issue of the story's title, followed by the initials of its author, date of its publication, volume and number of the magazine, and Bantam reprint number. These are followed by a key to the authors' full names, textual information on the reprints, and Doc Savage's appearances in comic books, radio shows, motion pictures, television, newspaper syndication, and works by other authors. More information and additional indexing would have been welcome, but this website is very well done.

219. Clark, William J. **The Author Index to the Doc Savage Magazine**. Los Angeles, CA: M & B Publications, 1971. 21 p. Paperback. [Note: On the cover, the title is "An Author Index to the Doc Savage Magazine."]

Clark's index to the 181 issues published between March 1933 and Summer 1949 is alphabetical by author; within each author, the stories are listed chronologically. Each entry also provides the story's publication date and its page count within the magazine (not its pagination). Stories featuring series characters have the series character's name given in parentheses, and when they are known, pseudonyms and house names are listed in italics. In all, this is an exemplary author index to an important pulp magazine. One wishes that Clark's energies had extended to providing issue-by-issue, title, and illustrator indexes as well.

Note: Lengthy discussions of the character of Doc Savage may be found in Philip Jose Farmer's Doc Savage: His Apocalyptic Life, Rick Lai's The Bronze Age: An Alternate Doc Savage Chronology, and Rob Smalley's Doc Savage: The Supreme Adventurer (q.q.v.)

220. Finnan, R. W. **Doc Savage**. http://members.aol.com/Hardyboy02/savage. html

This impressive website is more of an index to the publication of Doc Savage's adventures (as they appeared in *Doc Savage*) than it is a discussion of the character. The adventures are separately numbered and listed in chronological order by their original publication date; the number, month, volume, and issue number are given. Also given are the adventure's author, original hardcover appearance (if any), Bantam Books reprint number and date of republication, adaptation for comic books (if any), and notes; in addition, the material from the backs of the Bantam editions is reprinted. There are links to other sites, including a list of Doc Savage's radio adventures. A very well done site, though its dark background is an occasional impediment, and a title index would also be helpful.

Ellery Queen's Mystery Magazine

221. Nieminski, John. **EQMM 350: An Author/Title Index to Ellery Queen's Mystery Magazine Fall 1941 Through January 1973**. White Bear Lake, MN: Armchair Detective Press, 1974. 116 p. Paperback. Index.

As its title indicates, this is an index to the contents of the first 350 issues of the American newsstand edition of *Ellery Queen's Mystery Magazine*. Nicminski has omitted only newspaper item fillers and what his introduction describes as "a few short 'guest' story introductions," and has indexed all the stories, poems, articles, and features that appeared in this popular and long-running digest-sized magazine. The publication is reproduced from clearly typed copy. The contents include a user's guide, a checklist of issues indexed, an author index, a title index, and appendixes.

The user's guide provides explanations of Nieminski's methodology, and the checklist of the issues indexed lists the magazine's volume, number, whole number, date of publication, and overall pagination. The author index lists all names in capital letters (except for such compound names as de la Torre and de Ford) and arranges the titles alphabetically beneath it, providing each with a unique number. The citation provides the story's publication date and pagination within that issue, and frequent headnotes link stories by their series characters and locale and reveal pseudonyms. The title index lists the titles and their unique numbers (thus necessitating reference to the first section). Eleven appendixes list title changes; series characters and their creators; articles, essays, and features; true crime essays; book reviews; poems and verse; quizzes and puzzles; cartoons; translations; Sherlockiana; and "non-Sherlockian parodies, pastiches, burlesques, satires, take-offs and other genre-related narrative fiction."

Although *EQMM 350* lacks an issue-by-issue index, Nieminski's index is an exemplary job. It is accessible and thorough and provides an enormous amount of data. It is the definitive work on its subject and deserves to be updated.

Note: An index to the fiction in *Ellery Queen's Mystery Magazine* appears in Michael Cook's *Monthly Murders* (q.v.).

G-8 and His Battle Aces

222.   Carr, Nick. **The Flying Spy: A History of G-8**. With an introduction by Jack Deveny and a biography of Robert Jasper Hogan by Sid Bradd. Oak Lawn, IL: Robert Weinberg, 1978. 160 p. Paperback. (Pulp Classic, no. 18). Also: Mercer Island, WA: Starmont House, 1989. 160 p. Paperback. (Starmont Pulp and Dime Novel Studies, no. 3). LC 75-26231. ISBN 0-930261-72-0 (hc); 0-930261-75-5 (pb). ISSN 0885-0658.

G-8 and His Battle Aces was a hero pulp, its predominant focus being descriptions of the aeronautical deeds of derring-do that repelled a series of increasingly baroque invaders determined to conquer the world. Because reference to the magazine is often made in the standard checklists of detective and mystery magazines, one would be remiss to ignore Carr's account and index to it.

Reproduced from typed copy and heavily illustrated with cover reproductions, *The Flying Spy* is written from the perspective of a believer in the reality of G-8. Different chapters describe the author of the 110 issues of the magazine (Robert J. Hogan), the character of G-8, his three stalwart companions, the recurrent villains, and the frequently incredible inventions employed by the villains. A chronological list gives the year and month of publication and the title of the G-8 novel. Though written with affection, this remains an item for completists.

JDM Bibliophile

223.   Shine, Walter, and Jean Shine. **An Index to the JDM Bibliophile**. 1982. 33 p.

Not seen.

Magnet Detective Library

224.   Cox, J. Randolph. **Magnet Detective Library**. Fall River, MA: Edward T. LeBlanc, 1985. 48 p. (Dime Novel Round-Up: Bibliographic Listing). Supplement No. 51: vol. 54, no. 6, December 1985. Index. Paperback.

Though not the first paper-covered crime novel series, Street & Smith's *Magnet Detective Library* was one of the most successful. It began life in 1897 and lasted for 483 issues until 1907, at which point it was retitled *New Magnet Library*. This index concentrates on the 483 volumes of the *Magnet Detective Library*; an index to the *New Magnet Library* was separately published and is described under that heading (q.v.).

The arrangement of the index is simple and effective: The books are listed in the order in which they were published. Each entry is numbered and includes the author's name as it appears on the book, author's real name (if known), title, subtitle (if known), pagination, publication date, reprint data, and notes on points of interest. The exception to this rule is for books signed "Nicholas Carter"; for these, only the real author's name is given, in parentheses.

An author index concludes the volume and deserves mention, for it indexes not only the stories in the *Magnet Detective Library* but also the stories in *Nick Carter Library*, *Nick Carter Weekly*, and *Nick Carter Stories*. The authors whose names appeared on the title page or covers of the *Magnet Detective Library* have their names given in capital letters.

A title index would have been helpful, as would an index to the numerous retitlings in this series, but this is an exemplary work.

Mystery Fancier

225. Deeck, William F. **The Mystery Fancier: An Index to Volumes I–XIII, November, 1976–Fall, 1992**. San Bernardino, CA: Brownstone Books, 1993. ix, 169 p. (Brownstone Mystery Guides, vol. 9). LC 93-341. ISBN 0-941028-11-9 (hc); 0-941028-12-7 (pb).

Edited and published by writer and critic Guy M. Townsend, *The Mystery Fancier* lasted for some 70 issues over 16 years. Each issue was a lively blend of fannish and academic criticism, with often pungent reviews of books, conventions, movies, and television programs. Though *The Mystery Fancier* never achieved the success of *The Armchair Detective*, it had a readership that was equally loyal and vociferous.

Deeck's index to *The Mystery Fancier* begins with a checklist of the issues indexed and a small section listing the cover artists (when known). The body of the book lists the authors and titles of every article featured in the magazine; the names and titles of all the books, movies, and television programs that were reviewed; and the authors of the letters and (frequently) the contents of their letters. Many reviews are also indexed by subject; biographies of Agatha Christie, for example, are listed under her entry as well as being accessible under the names of their authors. Book titles are given in capital letters, as are the titles of films and television programs; short story titles are given in quote marks. Eleven abbreviations—(L) for letters, (IAC) for It's About Crime, (TAR) for The Armchair Reviewer, (TCITC) for The Curmudgeon in the Corner, and so forth—provide the name of the department in which the item appeared, with the rest of the citation providing volume number, issue number, and page numbers on which the item began and ended. Numerous cross-references are provided.

This is an exemplary index to an important small publication. It is accessible and thorough and presents its data concisely and accurately. Though specialized, this index belongs in research libraries, as of course do the 70 issues of *The Mystery Fancier*.

New Magnet Library

226. Cox, J. Randolph. **New Magnet Library**. Supplemental notes on *Magnet Detective Library* by Victor A. Berch. Fall River, MA: (Dime Novel Round-Up/Edward T. LeBlanc), 1991. xiv, 115 leaves. Paperback. Index.

New Magnet Library lasted from 1907 until 1932 and published nearly 900 paperbound novels, many of them featuring Nick Carter. It is the continuation of *Magnet Library* (q.v.), which lasted 483 issues, and its numbering thus begins with issue no. 484.

The index *New Magnet Library* lists the stories by the order in which they appeared. Entries appear only on the rectos of the sheets; versos are blank. Each citation includes the name of the author as it appears on the book, the real name of the author (if known) in parentheses, title, and subtitle (underlined); pagination, publication date, reprint information, and notes on points of interest conclude the entries. Victor Berch's "Supplemental Notes on *Magnet Detective Library*" follows the major index and contains information that updates the entries in the 1985 index to the *Magnet Detective Library*. An author/detective index to *New Magnet Library* concludes the volume.

As with the index to the *Magnet Library*, a title index would have helped trace the retitlings, but this is an exemplary work.

New Nick Carter Weekly

227. Cox, J. Randolph. **New Nick Carter Weekly**. Fall River, MA: Edward T. LeBlanc, 1975. 64 p. (Dime Novel Round-Up: Bibliographic Listing). Supplement: vol. 44, no. 9, December 1975. Whole No. 516. Paperback.

New Nick Carter Weekly was one of the most popular dime-novel detective weeklies, with 819 issues published from January 2, 1897, until September 7, 1912. After a lengthy introduction to the character of Nick Carter and the publications in which he appeared, Cox provides a chronological list of the publications. Each entry is numbered and includes the author's real name (if known) in parentheses, title and subtitle, date of publication, and reprint information. Some of the stories were printed in book form prior to appearing in the *New Nick Carter Weekly*; these are noted. A title index would have been useful, as would an index to the retitlings and reprintings, but as with the other volumes in this series, this is an exemplary publication.

Nick Carter Library

228. Cox, J. Randolph. **The Nick Carter Library (with Notes and Commentary on the Rest of the Saga)**. Fall River, MA: Edward T. LeBlanc, 1974. 40 p. (Dime Novel Round-Up: Bibliographic Listing). Supplement: vol. 43, no. 7, July 15, 1984, Whole No. 502. Paperback.

The first issue of the *Nick Carter Library* appeared on August 8, 1891, and it continued as a weekly publication for 282 issues, the last being dated December 26, 1896. The index to this series comprises slightly less than half the volume, the majority of which is devoted to Cox's history of the series and an account of the other publications in which the character of Nick Carter appeared. The index lists the publications chronologically, with each entry being numbered and including the author's real name (if known) in parentheses, title and subtitle, publication date, and reprint data. A title index would have been helpful, as would an index to the retitlings and reprintings, but in all, this is an exemplary publication.

Nick Carter Stories

229. Cox, J. Randolph. **Nick Carter Stories and Other Series Containing Stories About Nick Carter: Part I: Nick Carter Stories**. Fall River, MA: Edward T. LeBlanc, 1977. 20 p. (Dime Novel Round-Up: Bibliographic Listing). Supplement: vol. 46, no. 4, August 1977. Whole Number 526. Index. Paperback.

230. Cox, J. Randolph. **Nick Carter Stories and Other Series Containing Stories About Nick Carter: Part II: Nick Carter Magazine, Detective Story Magazine, New York Weekly, and Others**. Fall River, MA: Edward T. LeBlanc, 1980. 56 p. (Dime Novel Round-Up: Bibliographic Listing). Supplement: vol. 49, no. 2, April 1980. Whole No. 542. Paperback.

Although they were published some years apart, the two volumes constitute one work—Cox's documentation of the dime novels that published stories about Nick Carter. The first volume provides a chronological listing of *Nick Carter Stories*, which lasted for some 160 issues published from 1912 through 1915. Each entry is numbered and includes the author's real name (if known) in parentheses, story title and subtitle, date of publication, and reprint information; separate indexes list the serial stories and the known authors.

The second volume provides a chronological index to the dime novels and pulp magazines that published Nick Carter stories. These include *Nick Carter Magazine, Detective Story Magazine, New York Weekly, Ainselee's, Shield Weekly, Old Broadbrim Weekly, Rough Rider Weekly, New Medal Library, Clues—Detective, Crime Busters,* and *The Shadow*. For each publication, Cox provides the author's name (when known) in parentheses, and lists the story's title and subtitle, date of publication, and reprint information. Separate indexes list the issues of dime novels that were eventually rewritten as Nick Carter adventures. As with the other volumes in this series, title indexes would have been useful, but these two publications represent a monumental achievement.

Operator #5

231.   Brown, Michael R. **Operator #5**. http://sflovers.rutgers.edu/archive/bibliographies/operator5.txt

The 48 issues of *Operator #5* are sometimes classed as detective and mystery fiction, but it would be more apt to consider them a hero pulp, for in each issue, Operator #5—proclaimed by the majority of the covers to be "America's Undercover Ace" singlehandedly, or almost singlehandedly, saved the United States from invasion and destruction by increasingly bizarre agents of foreign powers. Nevertheless, the magazine is occasionally referenced in the standard checklists of detective and mystery magazines, and one would be remiss to ignore this index.

The arrangement is chronological by magazine issue. Each entry provides the title of the lead story, initials of the author, date of publication, magazine's volume and number, and a note as to reprint. Following the list are the authors' full names and notes. Given the magazine's general rarity, one would have hoped for more comprehensive information about its contents, but Brown's list is very well done.

Note: A fuller index to *Operator #5* can be found in the first series of Leonard Robbins's *The Pulp Magazine Index* (q.v.).

232.   Carr, Nick. **America's Secret Service Ace: The Operator #5 Story**. Oak Lawn, IL: Robert Weinberg, 1974. 63 p. Also: Mercer Island, WA: Starmont House, 1985. 63 p. (Starmont Pulp and Dime Novel Studies, no. 2). LC 85-26269. ISBN 0-930261-70-4 (hc); 0-930261-73-9 (pb). ISSN 0885-0658. Also: San Bernardino, CA: Borgo Press, 1985. 63 p. Paperback. LC 85-31413. ISBN 0-89370-564-0.

Reproduced from typed copy and heavily illustrated with cover reproductions, *America's Secret Service Ace* is written as though Operator #5 (real name: Jimmy Christopher) and his associates existed. Different chapters describe major characters, villains, supporting characters, invasions, inventions, and authors of the magazine. A chronological list gives the month and year of publication and the title of the novel.

As with all of Carr's works on the pulps, this one is written with affection. Nevertheless, as a reference work, it remains an item for completists.

The Phantom Detective

233.   Sauer, Nicholas, and Michael R. Brown. **The Phantom Detective**. http://sflovers.rutgers.edu/archive/bibliographies/phantom-detective.txt

The Phantom Detective was one of the more popular pulp magazines, with 170 issues published between 1933 and 1953. Sauer and Brown's list is chronological by issue. Each entry provides the lead story's title, initials of its author, date of its publication, volume and number, and reprint information. Following the list are the authors' full names and notes, and information on the comic book appearances of the Phantom Detective. Information on the rest of the magazine's contents would have been welcome, but this list is well done.

Note: Fuller indexes to *The Phantom Detective* can be found in Michael Cook and Stephen T. Miller's *Mystery, Detective, and Espionage Fiction* and the first series of Leonard Robbins's *The Pulp Magazine Index* (q.q.v.). A lengthy discussion of the character of the Phantom Detective can be found in Tom Johnson's *Phantom Detective: The Original Masked Marvel* (q.v.).

The Saint Magazine

234. Nieminski, John. **The Saint Magazine Index, Authors and Titles, Spring 1953–October 1967**. Evansville, IN: Cook & McDowell, 1980. 68 p. Paperback. (Unicorn Indexes to the Mystery/Detective Magazines).

With the exception of the purely editorial matter and filler, this index lists the authors and titles of all material published in the 141 issues of *The Saint Magazine* from Spring 1953 until October 1967. All stories, articles, quizzes, and features are clearly indicated. Following a user's guide that explains the layout and arrangement of this index, and a checklist of issues indexed, the index contains an author index, a title index, and a series of eight appendixes.

The names of the authors are given in capital letters, and minor variations (e.g., George H. Coxe and George Harmon Coxe) are ignored and interfiled. Joint authors are listed once, by the first name on the byline, with appropriate cross-referencing. All titles are listed alphabetically beneath the author's name and are numbered; each title is followed by its date of appearance expressed in numbers (e.g., 7/59 for July 1959) and its pagination. Series characters are identified by the code "SC" and the name of the character is underlined; reprints are indicated by the letter "R"; and "OT" and "BT" identify, respectively, "other titles" (i.e., retitlings) and book titles.

The title index links the story titles to their unique numbers, and the appendixes list title changes; series characters; articles, essays, and features; true crime features; book reviews; quizzes and puzzles; translators; and Sherlockiana published in *The Saint Magazine*.

Note: A partial index to *The Saint Magazine* is provided by Michael Cook in his *Monthly Murders* (q.v.).

Secret Agent 'X'

235. Brown, Michael Rogero. **Secret Agent 'X'**. http://sflovers.rutgers.edu/archive/bibliographies/secret-agent-x.txt

Brown's index lists the lead stories of 41 issues of *Secret Agent 'X'* in chronological order. Each entry gives the magazine's issue number, story's title, initials of the author, date of publication, magazine's volume and number, and information on reprints. Following the list, the authors' full names are given. In formation on the contents of the rest of the magazine would have been welcome, but this list is well done.

Note: Fuller indexes to *Secret Agent 'X'* can be found in Michael Cook and Stephen T. Miller's *Mystery, Detective, and Espionage Fiction* and the first series of Leonard Robbins's *The Pulp Magazine Index* (q.q.v.).

The Shadow

236. Brown, Michael Rogero. **The Shadow**. http://sflovers.rutgers.edu/ archive/bibliographies/shadow.txt

Brown's index to *The Shadow* lists only the lead story of each issue. Its arrangement is chronological; the story's title is given, followed by the initials of the author, date of publication, magazine's volume and number, and reprint information. Following the list are the authors' full names, information on reprints, and the appearances of the Shadow in comic books, radio shows, newspaper syndication, and motion pictures. This is a very capable index, but one wishes Brown had provided information on the contents in the rest of the magazine.

Note: A fuller index to *The Shadow* can be found in Michael Cook and Stephen T. Miller's *Mystery, Detective, and Espionage Fiction* and the first series of Leonard Robbins's *The Pulp Magazine Index* (q.q.v.).

237. Eisgruber, Frank, Jr. **Gangland's Doom**. Preface by Robert Weinberg. Oak Lawn, IL: Robert Weinberg, 1974. 64 p. Paperback. Also: Mercer Island, WA: Starmont House, 1985. 64 p. Paperback. (Starmont Pulp & Dime Novel Studies, no. 1). LC 85-26069. ISBN 0-930261-71-2 (hc); 0-930261-74-7 (pb). ISSN 0885-0658. Also: San Bernardino, CA: Borgo Press, 1985. 64 p. Paperback. LC 85-31407. ISBN 0-89370-563-2.

238. Gibson, Walter B. **The Shadow Scrapbook**. Preface by Chris Steinbrunner. New York: Harcourt Brace Jovanovich, 1979. v, 162 p. Paperback. LC 78-22277. ISBN 0-15-681475-7.

239. Murray, Will. **The Duende History of** *The Shadow* **Magazine**. Greenwood, MA: Odyssey, 1980. 128 p. Paperback. ISBN 0-933752-21-0.

240. Sampson, Robert. **The Night Master**. Chicago, IL: Pulp Press, 1982. 216 p. LC 81-82237. ISBN 0-934498-08-3.

None of these books about the Shadow, supremely lethal hero of the long-lasting *The Shadow Magazine*, is, strictly speaking, a reference book. Each nevertheless contains lists of Shadow novels and illustrations and offers additional critical material.

Gangland's Doom is the weakest of the volumes. Reproduced from typed copy and intended primarily for a fannish audience, it is written from the conceit that the Shadow and his assistants were real. Different chapters describe the Shadow's identities, his agents and allies, notable and recurrent villains, The Shadow's sanctums, and the Shadow's travels. Appendixes discuss the Shadow in light of theories put forth by Philip Jose Farmer, describe the writers of *The Shadow*, and provide a chronological list of the issues of the magazines, indicating when the writer was Theodore Tinsley or Bruce Elliott rather than Walter Gibson.

The Shadow Scrapbook is not a scrapbook but a history by Walter B. Gibson, the man who wrote the majority of *The Shadow* stories. It begins with "Introducing the Shadow," a historical essay in which Gibson discusses the origin and gradual development of the Shadow and which contains a chronological list of Shadow novels. Gibson explains his use of plot outlines and provides his outline for "The Mask of Mephisto" (published in *The Shadow Magazine* in July 1945), and he discusses the evolution of *The Shadow Magazine*'s covers, agents of the Shadow, and codes used by the Shadow. Anthony Tollin provides an article on the illustrations of *The Shadow Magazine* and a lengthy discussion of the Shadow on radio. A chronology of broadcasts is given (including the date of the broadcast, names of the readers, sponsor's name, and names of individual episodes during the various seasons), and the script for "The Death House Rescue" (broadcast 26 September 1937) is reprinted in virtually its entirety (the conclusion was lost and Gibson wrote another). Also provided are accounts of treatments of the Shadow in motion pictures and comic books and the various collectibles associated with the magazine.

The Duende History of The Shadow is slightly mistitled. In addition to providing the history of the magazine, it contains lengthy biographies of all connected with the creation and writing of *The Shadow Magazine*, and an excellent chronological index to the magazine. Will Murray and Robert Sampson provide a history and description of Lester Dent's "Golden Vulture," which, written in 1932, appeared in *The Shadow Magazine* in 1938 only after being rewritten by Walter Gibson. Sampson discusses the character of the Shadow as written by Theodore Tinsley and by Bruce Elliott, and there are lengthy interviews with Tinsley and Gibson. Finally, Gibson provides a short account of the Shadow's girasol and a short story ("Blackmail Bay") written especially for this volume.

The Night Master is a lengthy and affectionate study of the Shadow, with a lively history connecting the pulp series to the events of the real world as well as to the world of publishing. Eleven lists (here referred to as "Tables") provide descriptions of the characters in the Shadow Series by time period; a chronology of "certain major events" in the career of Kent Allard, the Living Shadow; lists of the editors of *The Shadow Magazine*; variations in the magazine's title between 1931 and 1949; approximate word counts in Shadow novels; descriptions of the magazine's major departments; and lists of the artists and illustrators for *The Shadow Magazine*. Appendixes describe variations in the magazine's size, pagination, and cost; list reprint appearances of the Shadow; and provide a chronological list of all of *The Shadow Magazines* (reprinted from *The Duende History of the Shadow*). Though unfortunately unindexed (stated Sampson, "I squalled and howled for an index and got overruled because of the extra expense"), and oddly laid out (Sampson: "the printer was the one who laid it out. That's the reason the type floods over the illustrations and wanders so about the page in an innocent and simple way, like a little country girl gathering posies"), this remains one of the finest books done on an influential pulp magazine and its series character.

Libraries fortunate enough to be able to purchase *The Shadow Scrapbook*, *The Duende History of the Shadow,* and *The Night Master* should acquire all; they provide insight into the creation and actions of one of the most durable characters of the pulp magazines.

Note: The bibliography documenting Walter Gibson's enormous output is described in the section devoted to the authors of detective and mystery stories, and a lengthy discussion of the character of the Shadow may be found in Rick Lai's *Chronology of Shadows* (q.q.v.).

The Spider

241. Brown, Michael Rogero. **The Spider.** http://sflovers.rutgers.edu/archive/bibliographies/spider.txt

Brown's index to *The Spider* is arranged by issue. The title of the lead story featuring the Spider is given, followed by the initials of its author, date of its publication, issue's volume and number, and reprint availability. At the conclusion of the list, the authors' full names are given, and Brown provides information on the Spider's appearance in comic books and movie serials. Information on the other works appearing in the magazine and additional indexes would have been welcome, but this is a very usable index.

Note: A fuller index to *The Spider* can be found in Michael Cook and Stephen T. Miller's *Mystery, Detective, and Espionage Fiction* (q.v.). Robert Sampson's *Spider* (Bowling Green, OH: Bowling Green State University Popular Press, 1987) contains appendixes providing a checklist of *The Spider* novels, a checklist of short fiction appearing in the magazine, and a checklist of the writers publishing short fiction in the magazine.

BIOGRAPHICAL SOURCES

SCOPE NOTE: Included here are who's-whos, bio-bibliographical directories, and literary dictionaries. Additional biographical data can be found in many different sources, including encyclopedias, readers' guides, and works dealing with specific authors.

GENERAL

242. Bakerman, Jane S., ed. **And Then There Were Nine . . . More Women of Mystery**. Bowling Green, OH: Bowling Green State University Popular Press, 1985. 218 p. LC 84-72822. ISBN 0-87972-319-X (hc); 0-87972-320-3 (pb).

A successor to *10 Women of Mystery* (below), *And Then There Were Nine* contains biocritical essays on Daphne du Maurier (by Jane S. Bakerman), Margery Allingham (by Rex W. Gaskill), Anne Morice (by Martha Alderson and Neysa Chouteau), Dorothy Uhnak (by George N. Dove), Lillian O'Donnell (by Neysa Chouteau and Martha Alderson), Craig Rice (by Peggy Moran), E. X. Ferrars (by Susan Baker), Patricia Highsmith (by Kathleen Gregory Klein), and Shirley Jackson (by Carol Cleveland). As in the earlier volume, bibliographic data are minimal and are presented in notes concluding each chapter. Also as before, the essays vary in length and quality, and in some cases they reveal conclusions. There are no indexes.

243. Bargainnier, Earl F., ed. **10 Women of Mystery**. Bowling Green, OH: Bowling Green State University Popular Press, 1981. 304 p. Indexes. LC 80-86393. ISBN 0-87972-172-3 (hc); 0-87972-173-1 (pb).

This volume and its sequel (*And Then There Were Nine* [above]) are included because their biographical essays are significant. In this work are essays on Dorothy Sayers (by Kathleen Gregory Klein), Josephine Tey (by Nancy Ellen Talburt), Ngaio Marsh (by Earl F. Bargainnier), P. D. James (by Nancy C. Joyner), Ruth Rendell (by Jane S. Bakerman), Anna Katharine Green (by Barrie Hayne), Mary Roberts Rinehart (by Jan Cohn), Margaret Millar (by John M. Reilly), Emma Lathen (by Jeanne F. Bedell), and Amanda Cross (by Steven F.

Carter). Each essay provides a photograph of its subject, and each chapter is followed by brief and selective bibliographies of the subject's works. The volume concludes with indexes listing the names of the characters and the names of the titles mentioned in the body of the book.

Several of the essays warrant updating, but the writers are generally successful in providing an understanding of the lives and prose of their subjects.

244. Bargainnier, Earl F., ed. **Twelve Englishmen of Mystery**. Bowling Green, OH: Bowling Green State University Popular Press, 1984. 325 p. LC 83-72499. ISBN 0-87972-249-5 (hc); 0-87972-250-9 (pb).

Though it is similar in format and approach to Bargainnier's *10 Women of Mystery* (q.v.), the contents of this volume are more idiosyncratic. There are essays on Wilkie Collins (by Jeanne F. Bedell), A. E. W. Mason (by Barrie Hayne), G. K. Chesterton (by Thomas E. Porter), H. C. Bailey (by Nancy Ellen Talburt), Anthony Berkeley Cox (by William Bradley Strickland), Nicholas Blake (by Earl F. Bargainnier), Michael Gilbert (by George N. Dove), Julian Symons (by Larry E. Grimes), Dick Francis (by Marty Knepper), Edmund Crispin (by Mary Jean DeMarr), H. R. F. Keating (by Meera T. Clark), and Simon Brett (by Earl F. Bargainnier). Each essay begins with a picture and a brief chronology of its subject; each concludes with brief and selective bibliographies of its subject's works. There are no indexes.

In addition to the somewhat puzzling choice of subjects, the quality of the essays varies. The weakest is probably Knepper's discussion of Dick Francis. Not only are conclusions occasionally revealed, but statements such as "even persons who are not enamored of the hard-boiled mystery genre are reading and enjoying Francis's novels" reveal little awareness of either Francis's writings or the world of mysteries.

Choose instead the vastly more comprehensive work of Benstock and Staley (below).

245. Benstock, Bernard, and Thomas F. Staley, eds. **British Mystery Writers, 1860–1919**. Detroit: Gale, 1988. xi, 389 p. Index. (Dictionary of Literary Biography, vol. 70). LC 88-11465. ISBN 0-8103-1748-6.

246. Benstock, Bernard, and Thomas F. Staley, eds. **British Mystery Writers, 1920–1939**. Detroit: Gale, 1989. xi, 414 p. Index. (Dictionary of Literary Biography, vol. 77). LC 88-30048. ISBN 0-8103-4555-2.

247. Benstock, Bernard, and Thomas F. Staley, eds. **British Mystery and Thriller Writers Since 1940, First Series**. Detroit: Gale, 1989. xi, 419 p. Index. (Dictionary of Literary Biography, vol. 87). LC 89-12021. ISBN 0-8103-4565-X.

These three volumes of the Dictionary of Literary Biography provide bio-bibliographical and biocritical information on 105 British writers of mystery and detective fiction. Each volume follows the pattern of the series as a whole.

The entries are arranged alphabetically by subject's surname; the name and affiliation of the critic is given at the top of the article. Each entry begins with a chronologically arranged bibliography listing the first separate British and American editions of the subject's published works; these are followed by selective lists of the subject's uncollected short prose. The biocritical essays that follow the bibliography range in length from 1,000 to 5,000 words; they are frequently illustrated with photographs of the subject and the subject's works. Concluding each essay is a selective bibliography of secondary sources; concluding each volume is a bibliography listing additional sources for reading, a list of the contributors' affiliations, and a cumulative index to the other volumes in the series. There are 35 entries in *British Mystery Writers, 1860–1919*, 45 in *British Mystery Writers, 1920–1939*, and 25 in *British Mystery and Thriller Writers Since 1940, First Series*.

The first two volumes are particularly useful because major and minor writers for each time period are profiled. The first volume, for example, contains entries on such writers as Mary Elizabeth Braddon, John Buchan, Wilkie Collins, Charles Dickens, Sir Arthur Conan Doyle, and Edgar Wallace. There are also entries for such lesser luminaries as M. McDonnell Bodkin, J. S. Fletcher, Fergus Hume, Angus Reach, and Victor L. Whitechurch. The second volume has entries for Margery Allingham, Eric Ambler, Agatha Christie, John Creasey, Ngaio Marsh, Dorothy L. Sayers, and Josephine Tey, as well as Winston Graham, Richard Hull, C. B. Kitchen, Gladys Mitchell, Helen Simpson, and Henry Wade. The expanded focus of the third volume allows the inclusion of essays on Ian Fleming, Ken Follett, Geoffrey Household, John le Carré, and Peter O'Donnell, all of whom are known for their thrillers and espionage fiction.

The three volumes edited by Benstock and Staley can be compared to *The St. James Guide to Crime and Mystery Writers* (q.v.), which contains the same primary bibliographies and, in return for offering significantly less biographical data, provides entries on many more writers. Nevertheless, such a comparison does neither series justice; the volumes are intended for different audiences. The volumes of the Dictionary of Literary Biography offer structured and organized criticism that the *St. James Guide* cannot, whereas the latter offers what are essentially brief encyclopedic entries on a wider variety of contemporary writers. Neither series is inexpensive, but both should be held by academic and public libraries.

248. Breen, Jon L., and Martin Harry Greenberg, eds. **Murder off the Rack: Critical Studies of Ten Paperback Masters**. Metuchen, NJ: Scarecrow Press, 1989. x, 178 p. LC 89-33085. ISBN 0-8108-2232-6.

Murder off the Rack provides extensive bio-bibliographical discussion of 10 significant crime and mystery writers whose fate it was to have their work appear primarily (or entirely) in paperbacks. In alphabetical order, these authors are Marvin Albert (by George Kelley), Donald Hamilton (by Loren D. Estleman), Ed Lacy (by Marvin Lachman), Warren Murphy (by Dick Lochte), Vin Packer (by Jon L. Breen), Don Pendleton (by Will Murray), Peter Rabe (by Donald E.

Westlake), Jim Thompson (by Max Allan Collins), Harry Whittington (by Bill Crider), and Charles Williams (by Ed Gorman). Each chapter concludes with a partial bibliography of the author's works, and the volume concludes with separate indexes listing the book titles and the personal names mentioned in the essays.

As with the rest of Breen's works, this is a well-conceived and generally well-executed volume. The 10 essays are critical, but the criticism is tempered by affection and compassion. The indexing is well done. The volume's greatest flaws lie in the bibliographies, which are deliberately incomplete, concentrating only on the crime and mystery fiction written by the subject. This is thoroughly understandable, but it is nevertheless frustrating to learn that Vin Packer's first story appeared under the name "Laura Winston" in a 1951 *Ladies' Home Journal*, but the story's title and the issue in which it appeared are never given.

Murder off the Rack presents its subject admirably. Indeed, one wishes that Breen and his fellow contributors had included additional profiles.

249. Budd, Elaine. **13 Mistresses of Murder**. New York: Ungar, 1986. xiii, 144 p. LC 86-1459. ISBN 0-8044-2086-6.

During the first part of the 1980s Budd interviewed 13 notable women writers of mystery and detective fiction: Mary Higgins Clark, Amanda Cross, Dorothy Salisbury Davis, Lady Antonia Fraser, Lucy Freeman, Dorothy B. Hughes, P. D. James, Emma Lathen, Margaret Millar, Shannon O'Cork, Ruth Rendell, Dorothy Uhnak, and Phyllis A. Whitney. The results of these interviews became *13 Mistresses of Murder*, and it is mentioned here as a thematic companion to the works of Bakerman, Bargainnier, and Breen (q.q.v.).

Budd provides the edited interview in each chapter, then a lengthy summary of the author's best-known works. There is occasional criticism in the summaries; plot holes are mentioned, as are weaknesses in the presentation of characters. The volume concludes with notes and brief selective primary bibliographies. Still occasionally useful.

250. Heising, Willetta L. **Detecting Women: A Reader's Guide and Checklist for Mystery Series Written by Women**. Dearborn, MI: Purple Moon Press, 1995. 256 p. Paperback. Index. LC 95-221452. ISBN 0-9644593-0-2.

251. Heising, Willetta L. **Detecting Women 2: A Reader's Guide and Checklist for Mystery Series Written by Women**. Dearborn, MI: Purple Moon Press, 1996. 384 p. Paperback. Index. ISBN 0-9644593-1-0.

Like so many reference books, *Detecting Women* began as a labor of love. Heising wanted to document the mystery series being written by women writers and began compiling lists. She received assistance from mystery lovers, and her lists became increasingly lengthy and elaborate. At the time the first volume was published, Heising had recorded information on the authors of more than 2,340 titles in 479 mystery series published between 1900 and 1995. The second volume expands these data, offering information on nearly 600 women authors of 681 series—nearly 3,600 titles—published between 1878 and 1996. (Incomplete data for 1997 are provided.)

Detecting Women 2 contains 13 chapters: the master list, mystery types, series characters, settings, mystery chronology, alphabetical title list, pseudonyms, short stories, awards and organizations, other resources, a glossary, a bibliography, and an index. Appendix A offers a preview of future editions, and appendix B contains changes to the pocket guide that accompanies the book.

The master list is arranged alphabetically by author's last name, given in boldface type. A biographical profile is provided for each author, and beneath the profile, the name of her series character is listed in boldface type, along with a brief description of the character. The titles in which the series character appears are numbered and listed chronologically; the date of first publication is given. When a book is known by more than one title, both are listed, with a note indicating whether the second title is American, British, or a paperback retitling. When a book was nominated for or received a major mystery award, its title is boldfaced and marked with a star and the name of the award. When the author has more than one series detective, the characters are listed in alphabetical order by first name.

Chapters 2 through 7 rearrange the data presented in the first chapter. "Mystery Types" separates the books into three categories: police procedurals, private eyes, and amateur detectives. The traditional mystery series are further classified using 47 subject categories, a few of which are "Academics," "Animals," "Art and Antiques," "Ecclesiastical and Religious," "Gay and Lesbian," "Medical," "Theatre and Performing Arts," and "Travelers." Beneath each of these categories, the books are listed alphabetically by author, and the publication year, series number, series character name and occupation, and setting are given. "Series Characters" lists the characters alphabetically by first name; each entry provides the author's name, the book's publication year, its series number, the character's occupation, and the setting. The fourth chapter rearranges this data to provide a settings index, with entries listing the author, book's publication year, series number, and character's name and occupation.

The mystery chronology begins with a prose discussion of the explosion of mystery series titles written by women and published since 1980; several helpful figures are given. The first volume listed in the chronological list is Anna Katherine Green's *The Leavenworth Case* (1878), and from 1900 until 1989, the books are grouped by decade, then listed by year. From 1990 forward, the titles are listed by year. Within each year, entries are alphabetical by author; citations provide the title, and the author's name is in parentheses. First books in series are marked with a "1."

The material in the remaining chapters is only occasionally unique to this volume. Chapter 8 indexes 25 short story anthologies containing more than 350 short stories written by 188 women; author entries are cross-referenced to the previous sections. The information on awards and organizations in chapter 9 provides explanations, definitions, and contact information. The "other resources" of chapter 10 are annotated lists discussing relevant magazines and newsletters, along with contact information, and an annotated list of reference books. The glossary (chapter 11) defines awards, types of detectives, and some terms used by collectors of books; the bibliography (chapter 12) lists in alphabetical order the entries given in chapter 10. The index offers access to authors, series characters, and the contents of the entries in chapters 8–12.

Detecting Women won the 1995 Macavity Award for best critical/biographical book. It is a monumental achievement.

252. Herbert, Rosemary. **The Fatal Art of Entertainment: Interviews with Mystery Writers**. Foreword by Antonia Fraser. New York: G. K. Hall, 1994. xx, 351 p. LC 93-22862. ISBN 0-8161-7279-X.

During the early 1990s Herbert talked with 13 notable British and American mystery and detective writers: Julian Symons, Sue Grafton, P. D. James, Tony Hillerman, John Mortimer, Patricia Cornwell, Jonathan Gash, Reginald Hill, Jane Langton, Robert Barnard, Jeremiah Healy, Catherine Aird, and Barbara Neely. The transcripts of these conversations became *The Fatal Art of Entertainment.*

Herbert begins each chapter with a photograph and a brief discussion of her subject's writing, and then provides the transcripts of her conversation; the dates of these conversations are not given. The transcripts do not appear to have been edited, and the conversations thus appear unstructured and spontaneous. This is simultaneously the book's greatest strength and weakness, for asking each writer the same structured series of questions might have eliminated the spontaneity but led to greater depth in the responses. As it is, the authors discuss their lives, families, and works, occasionally with introspection, often with the pride of creation. Solutions are occasionally revealed: Reginald Hill, for example, reveals that the death in *A Clubbable Woman* was inspired by a childhood memory. John Mortimer discusses his father, and Sue Grafton mentions her parents, stating that her father wrote; Herbert does not follow up on this, and it is left to readers to be aware that Grafton's father, C. W. Grafton, was a well-regarded mystery novelist in his own right.

Frustratingly, the volume contains neither bibliographies nor index.

253. Herman, Linda, and Beth Stiel. **Corpus Delecti of Mystery Fiction: A Guide to the Body of the Case**. Metuchen, NJ: Scarecrow Press, 1974. viii, 180 p. Index. LC 74-16319. ISBN 0-8108-0770-X.

Although this volume begins with a series of chapters offering a brief history and a defense of mystery fiction and definitions of various terms, the majority of the book consists of bio-bibliographic sketches of "fifty representative authors and their works" chosen "because their writings form a balanced collection within our present scope." These authors range alphabetically from Margery Allingham and Eric Ambler to Arthur Upfield and S. S. Van Dine, and they include such stalwarts as Raymond Chandler, Agatha Christie, Dashiell Hammett, John D. MacDonald, Ngaio Marsh, Ellery Queen, and Dorothy L. Sayers. Each author's entry provides a brief biographical profile, cites a few secondary sources, and concludes with a chronological list of titles. The book has name and title indexes.

There is nothing in this book that cannot be readily obtained elsewhere. Herman and Stiel's choice of authors is weak, including many espionage and thriller writers while neglecting such significant talents as Fredric Brown and R. Austin Freeman. International writers are particularly neglected and are represented by only Robert van Gulik (whose last name is indexed under "G"), Maurice LeBlanc, and Georges Simenon. Finally, Herman and Stiel fail to provide even the publishers of the books in their bibliographic citations.

254. Klein, Kathleen Gregory, ed. **Great Women Mystery Writers: Classic to Contemporary**. Westport, CT: Greenwood Press, 1994. xxi, 432 p. LC 94-16123. ISBN 0-313-28770-8.

In arrangement, this guide is similar to the various editions of the *Twentieth Century Crime and Mystery Writers* (q.v.), consisting of alphabetically arranged signed bio-bibliographical essays. In content, however, the focus is tighter, for *Great Women Mystery Writers* surveys 117 (predominantly) Anglo-American women writers. These essays range in length from 500 to 1,500 words, provide excellent introductions to the totality of the writer's output, discuss her series and series characters, attempt to put her into a greater literary context, and conclude with a primary bibliography and (when relevant) a secondary bibliography.

Following the biocritical discussions are seven appendixes. A) lists the Edgar Awards won by women writers; B) lists the Agatha Awards and their winners; C) discusses the organization Sisters in Crime; D) discusses activities for mystery fans; E) discusses DorothyL, the electronic discussion group for fans of mysteries; F) lists the names, addresses, and telephone numbers of approximately 100 North American booksellers specializing in crime and mystery fiction; and G) offers 14 categories of mystery fiction into which the 117 writers discussed may be classified. The volume concludes with an author/pseudonym index and a title index to the works discussed in the essays.

On the debit side, the discussion of historically important women writers is lacking. Mary Elizabeth Braddon is the only woman writer from the nineteenth century to be discussed, and the discussion of twentieth-century women writers is not all that it could be; one looks in vain for such figures as Leigh Brackett, Lillian de la Torre, Mignon Eberhart, and Carolyn Wells. Among the moderns, Sandra Scoppettone and Janice Law have been overlooked. In addition, one wishes that the editor had included more international writers, for apart from discussions of one South African and two Japanese writers, all subjects profiled are Anglo-American. Finally, one wonders whether the editor should have unilaterally excluded discussion of collaborations; collaborative partnerships such as Frances and Richard Lockridge, Maj Sjöwall and Per Wahlöö, and Sarah and Peter Dunant probably warrant discussion.

The above criticisms in no way detract from the usability and importance of Klein's efforts; she deserves nothing but praise for this book. Not only is it almost everything that a reference book should be (but rarely is), but its contents are timely and of enormous importance.

255. Swanson, Jean, and Dean James. **By a Woman's Hand: A Guide to Mystery Fiction by Women**. New York: Berkley Books, 1994. 254 p. Paperback. Index. ISBN 0-425-14143-8.

256. Swanson, Jean, and Dean James. **By a Woman's Hand: A Guide to Mystery Fiction by Women**. 2d ed. New York: Berkley Prime Crime, 1996. Paperback. Index. ISBN 0-425-15472-6.

Unlike the other guides considered in this section, these books include minimal biographical data. Instead, they serve as readers' advisers, with brief essays discussing and describing the series characters and recurrent themes in the best-known works written by Anglo-American women mystery writers of the late twentieth century. The 1st edition profiles the work of approximately 200 such writers; the 2d edition revises and expands the entries in the 1st edition and profiles nearly 300 women writers. This review focuses on the 2d edition.

The introductory material is largely reprinted from the 1st edition. The volume begins with an alphabetical list of the authors whose works have been profiled. The essays are listed alphabetically by the name of the profiled authors and are typically between 200 and 400 words in length. More important, these essays are selective in their presentation of data; only two of Patricia Highsmith's five "Tom Ripley" novels are listed, for example. Furthermore, these essays tend toward the appreciative rather than the critical, and their arrangement is occasionally questionable: Oriana Papazoglou's entry can be found under her "Jane Haddam" pseudonym, though the majority of the entries are given under the author's real name. Each essay concludes with advisory tips that on occasion are surprising but effective.

A brief list of important short story anthologies of women mystery writers follows, and indexes pair the series character with the author, list authors by the geographical settings of their books, and offer access by detective's profession.

By a Woman's Hand contains significantly fewer entries than does Willetta L. Heising's *Detecting Women* (q.v.), but the entries are longer, and mystery lovers are likely to welcome its concluding advisories.

257. Reilly, John M., ed. **Twentieth-Century Crime and Mystery Writers**. New York: St. Martin's Press, 1980. xxiv, 1,568 p. (Twentieth-Century Writers of the English Language). LC 79-92844. ISBN 0-312-82417-3.

258. Reilly, John M., ed. **Twentieth-Century Crime and Mystery Writers**. 2d ed. Chicago: St. James Press, 1985. xx, 1,094 p. Index. (Twentieth Century Writers Series). LC 87-37779. ISBN 0-912289-17-1.

259. Henderson, Lesley, ed. **Twentieth-Century Crime and Mystery Writers**. 3d ed. Chicago: St. James Press, 1991. xxxi, 1,294 p. Index. (Twentieth-Century Writers Series). LC 90-63662. ISBN 1-55862-031-1.

260. Pederson, Jay P., and Taryn Benbow-Pfalzgraf, eds. **St. James Guide to Crime & Mystery Writers**. 4th ed. Detroit: St. James Press, 1996. xiv, 1,264 p. Index. LC 96-18661. ISBN 1-55862-178-4.

The four editions of this work are part of a larger series that provides bio-bibliographical information on significant twentieth-century writers whose work can be readily classified into a genre. There are companion volumes devoted to novelists and poets, science fiction writers, writers of Westerns, children's writers, and romance and historical writers. Each volume in these series has had multiple editions and often multiple publishers and title changes. Each edition is more comprehensive in content and physically larger than its predecessor; each is in its own right a monumental achievement and essential as a reference; and each contains crucial flaws that a firmer editorial hand and greater bibliographic control would not have permitted. The following description concentrates on the fourth (1996) edition, which profiles approximately 650 authors.

A typical entry begins with who's-who biographical information. At its fullest, this includes pseudonyms, place and date of author's birth, education, military service, marriage date(s), spouse's name(s), number of children, significant places of employment, and notable awards. Entries for the dead conclude with the death date, whereas entries for the living tend to conclude by providing the subject's literary agent's name and address and the subject's address.

Lengthy bibliographies often follow the biographical information. Mystery and detective novels are listed first; the principal series characters (if any) are named at the head of the list, and entries indicate the works in which those characters appear. Citations to mystery and detective short story collections follow; these do not indicate the presence of series characters. If the subject has written in multiple genres, a section devoted to "other publications" lists novels, short story collections, plays, screenplays, radio plays, nonfiction, and edited works. If the subject used more than one name, the works are listed beneath the respective names. Citations in all sections are arranged chronologically and provide the publication data for the first British and American editions; retitlings are indicated, and first edition publication data are provided for them. After the bibliography are selective references to uncollected short stories and media adaptations.

After the bibliography comes a listing of locations of the author's manuscripts, and there are selective references to significant biocritical studies. If the author has chosen to provide a brief biographical comment, it is given; the comment is dated if the author made it for an earlier edition and has chosen not to revise it or has since died. Finally, a signed article provides a biocritical statement of the author's major works and themes. The volume concludes with separate indexes to the nationalities of the subjects and to the titles of the publications that were cited in the bibliographies, and offers a lengthy reading list that does not distinguish between criticism, bibliographies, and coffee-table books.

The 4th edition has corrected a number of the typographical errors found in the earlier editions, and its bibliographies have been updated and compressed (the previous editions in this series tended to provide exhaustive lists of uncollected short works). A number of errors introduced in the earlier volumes nevertheless remain, as in the case of Gil Brewer. Though Brewer's birthdate is given, the bibliographer has confused his output with that of a (probably pseudonymous) pulp writer. (Common sense should dictate that Brewer was not writing for *Zeppelin Stories* at age seven.) Additional complaints may be made with regard to the biocritical statements, which tend to the adulatory rather than the acute, and to the volume's editorial balance. The entries for Agatha Christie and Dashiell Hammett are barely one column in length, Arthur Conan Doyle is discussed in one and a half columns, and Raymond Chandler and Dorothy L. Sayers merit but two columns; the thrillers of Tom Clancy, on the other hand, have been accorded four full columns of space. Furthermore, why have thriller writers such as Clancy and Ian Fleming been accorded entries, when such talented crime and mystery writers as Thomas Cook and Sandra Scoppettone (to name but two) have not?

It must be stressed that no other one-volume work attempts to do so much, and the strengths of this book far outweigh its weaknesses. This series is indispensable for research, and its editors deserve commendation rather than censure. All editions of this book should be held by academic and public libraries.

PSEUDONYMS

SCOPE NOTE: This section includes works that are only lists of pseudonyms and real names of mystery writers. Partial lists can be found in many readers' guides and biographical dictionaries.

---

261.   Bates, Susannah. **The Pendex: An Index of Pen Names and House Names in Fantastic, Thriller, and Series Literature**. New York: Garland, 1981. xii, 233 p. Index. (Garland Reference Library of the Humanities, vol. 227). LC 80-8486. ISBN 0-8240-9501-4.

Although Bates's focus is on the literature of the fantastic, a sizable percentage of the approximately 950 authors and their 1,700 pseudonyms listed in this volume belong to mystery and detective writers.

The contents of the sections and appendixes are as one would expect. The first section lists in capital letters the author's name and beneath it, indented two spaces and in regular type, the pseudonyms he or she has used; birth and death dates are often given, as are whether the name is a collaborative pen name (CPN), a house name (HN), or a name used in the Stratemeyer Syndicate (SSN). The second section lists the pseudonym in capital letters and, beneath it, indented two spaces, in regular type and prefaced with RN:, the real name of the writer or writers who used it. The third section lists collaborative pseudonyms, providing the pseudonym in capital letters and beneath it, in regular type, the names of the writers who used it. The fourth section lists house names in capital letters, provides a brief description of the type of publication in which the name was used, and concludes with a list of the names of the writers who are known to have used the house names. The fifth section lists the names of the writers known to have worked in the Stratemeyer Syndicate, an organization whose thousands of juvenile and young adult titles appeared under hundreds of pseudonyms.

A number of sources have pilloried Bates. First, the book is rife with misspellings: "Frank Aubray" instead of Frank Aubrey, "Algerdas Budrys" instead of Algirdas Jonas Budrys, "Greya La Spina" instead of Greye La Spina, and so forth. Next, the volume contains such errors as "Catherine Louise Moore" instead of Catherine Lucille Moore, and such misattributions as Julian Chain being May Dikty. Worst of all, it is incomplete. When Bates does list a name, her lists of pseudonyms are grossly inadequate. Harlan Ellison is known to have used in excess of 20 pseudonyms; Bates lists but three. Similarly, Hugh Cave's famous "Justin Case" and Dashiell Hammett's "Peter Collinson" are not mentioned.

In the fields of science fiction, fantasy, and horror fiction, superior pseudonym indexes exist, and Bates's work is considered negligible. In the field of detective and mystery fiction, however, she holds a more important position. Though works such as Hubin's and Contento's (q.q.v.) reveal many pseudonyms, such is not their primary purpose. Users of Bates are cautioned to verify her data elsewhere.

262. Kenner, Pat. **File of Mystery Authors and Their Pseudonyms**.

Available in the archives maintained by the DorothyL listserv, and through the Miss Lemon website (http://www.iwillfollow.com/lemon.htm), this list of names mixes pseudonyms and real names; the real name is followed by the pseudonym, and the pseudonym is followed by the real name. Though obviously compiled with the best of intentions, the list nevertheless contains numerous errors. For example, the entry for John Creasy does not cite his writing as "J. J. Marric," whereas the entry for "Marric" references Creasy. There are significant problems in the assignation of pseudonyms for series books, and the titles of pseudonymous works are not given. One hopes that Kenner will correct, expand, and update this list.

INDIVIDUAL AUTHORS

Margery Allingham

263. "Father Brown." **Campion List**.

Available as a list maintained in the archives of the DorothyL listserv and through the Miss Lemon website (http://www.iwillfollow.com/lemon.htm), this list of Margery Allingham's Campion books is derived from the 1st edition of Barzun and Taylor's *A Catalogue of Crime* (q.v.). It lists the books alphabetically, giving titles and date of publication; title changes are indicated. Two short stories published in *Ellery Queen's Mystery Magazine* are also referenced, but this is a very incomplete list. More information on Allingham is available in such bio-bibliographies as *Twentieth Century Crime and Mystery Writers* (q.v.).

Frederick Irving Anderson

264. Fisher, Benjamin Franklin, IV. **Frederick Irving Anderson (1877–1947): A Biobibliography.** Madison, IN: Brownstone Books, 1987. 43 p. (Brownstone Chapbook Series, vol. 4). LC 88-34112. ISBN 0-8095-6403-3 (hc); 0-941028-07-0 (pb).

Today remembered only by specialists, Frederick Irving Anderson (1877–1947) created a versatile con man (the Infallible Godahl), vividly described a queen of crooks (in *The Notorious Sophie Lang*), and wrote a number of detective short stories noted for their craftsmanship, style, and local color. Although his work appeared in a number of magazines, particularly the *Saturday Evening Post*, Anderson apparently left few personal records, and he would probably be entirely forgotten were it not for Ellery Queen, whose *Queen's Quorum* (q.v.) cites Anderson's *The Book of Murder* (1930) as item 82 on its list of the 125 most important books of detective-crime-mystery short stories. Fisher's biography presents the few known facts of Anderson's life, corrects a few erroneous beliefs about Anderson, and discusses Anderson's works.

The bibliography begins by listing Anderson's works. The first citations are for Anderson's nonfiction and "semi-fiction"; these are followed by citations listing Anderson's fiction books and short fiction. Each section is arranged chronologically; all citations are consecutively numbered.

Citations to publications in periodicals provide the title in quotations, list the periodical title in italics, and give its month, volume, and pagination. Reprints are cited in the same fashion. The citations to Anderson's five books list their titles in italics and place, publisher, and year of publication; reprints are noted by listing the year of the reprint edition. The collections of Anderson's short fiction include cross-references to the story's original appearance. Pagination is not provided. All citations are annotated.

The secondary bibliography begins by citing contemporary reviews of Anderson's books. These are followed by a lengthy list of "additional secondary material" that in some way discusses or describes Anderson and his work. These citations are arranged alphabetically by author and are documented using the formats described above. As before, all citations are annotated.

Indexes to titles and periodical names would have benefited researchers, but apart from this lack, this work belongs in collections with a historical focus.

E. C. Ayres

265. Ayres, E. C. **E. C. Ayres Homepage**. http://members.aol.com/ecayres/home.htm

Ayres's home page provides images from his books, along with sample chapters and summaries and synopses from the dustwrappers. A brief biography and a picture of Ayres are provided, as are excerpts from positive reviews. Enjoyable though the site is, Ayres never reveals the meaning of the initials "E. C."

Marian Babson

266. Tangled Web. **Marian Babson**. http://www.twbooks.co.uk/authors/mbabson.html

Available through the Tangled Web, this website contains a photograph and a brief biography of its subject and reproduces the covers and jacket material from two of her books. Excerpts from positive reviews and the text of a full review are given. The site concludes with a chronological bibliography of her works that cites the publisher, publication year, and series detective appearing in the book.

John Baker

267. Tangled Web. **John Baker**. http://www.twbooks.co.uk/authors/jbaker.html

This website contains a photograph and a brief biography of its subject, and it reproduces the covers and jacket material from his two books. Excerpts from positive reviews and the text of a full review are given. The concluding bibliography cites the publisher and publication year.

Pauline Bell

268. Tangled Web. **Pauline Bell**. http://www.twbooks.co.uk/authors/pbell.html

Although Bell has written a number of police procedurals, a cover image of only one is given. The books are listed in chronological order and briefly described, and the site concludes with a two-sentence biographical statement.

Nicholas Blake. *See* C. Day-Lewis

Robert Bloch

269.   Flanagan, Graeme. **Robert Bloch: A Bio-Bibliography**. Canberra, Australia: Graeme Flanagan, 1979. 64 p. Paperback.

Although he is probably better known for his cheerfully macabre fantasies and horror fiction, Robert Bloch wrote a number of detective and mystery stories and warrants inclusion here. This bio-bibliography was compiled with Bloch's assistance and with the assistance of Randall D. Larson, who was later to compile his own Bloch bibliography (q.v.). It contains the following sections: an introduction; "Robert Bloch: a few words of friendship by Harlan Ellison"; a biography; the Robert Bloch Collection; "Mr. Weird Tales" by Robert Weinberg; Interview One: Mostly Concerning *Weird Tales*; "When Screwballs Meet . . ." by Fritz Leiber; Interview Two; a bibliography; radio, television, and motion pictures; and "My Weird Little Brother, Bob," by Mary Elizabeth Counselman. In addition, there are numerous photographs.

The biography is a reprint from that appearing in the Summer 1949 issue of *The Fanscient*. The bibliography contains the following sections: short stories—first magazine printings; nonfiction published in magazines; novels; collections—short stories; collections—nonfiction; short stories and nonfiction published in anthologies; short stories and nonfiction reprinted in magazines; foreign translations; and miscellanea. The entries in the first two sections are arranged chronologically; the title is given, followed by pseudonym (if any), magazine in which it appeared, and month and year of publication. The citations in the third, fourth, and fifth sections are arranged alphabetically; the book's title is given in capital letters and is underlined, and listed beneath them are the publisher, place of publication, year of publication, pagination, and original cost of all known printings of the book. The contents of collections are provided. The anthology citations in are listed chronologically; the magazine citations are listed alphabetically. The translation section is an alphabetical listing of titles followed by the language into which the work has been translated; full publication data are not provided. The section devoted to miscellanea references Bloch's introductions and afterwords, printed speeches, interviews, and sources of biographical data.

The bibliography of Bloch's radio, television, and motion pictures lists the titles of Bloch's radio series, with a subsection listing titles, stations, and air dates of pieces for which Bloch provided only the story. The section devoted to Bloch's television writing lists teleplays, the shows for which they were written, and the years in which they appeared; casts are occasionally provided. The section on Bloch's motion pictures lists studio, year of release, producer's name, and cast.

Though this work is a very worthy effort, Bloch's fan writings are not cited, and Flanagan's accomplishment has been superseded by Larson's (below).

270. Hall, Graham M. **Robert Bloch Bibliography**. Tewksbury, England: Graham M. Hall, 1965. 32 p. Paperback.

Not seen. Referenced in Michael Burgess's *Reference Guide to Science Fiction, Fantasy, and Horror* (Englewood, CO: Libraries Unlimited, 1992).

271. Larson, Randall D. **The Complete Robert Bloch: An Illustrated, International Bibliography**. Sunnyvale, CA: Fandom Unlimited Enterprises, 1986. x, 126 p. Paperback. LC 85-82410. ISBN 0-96071-81-1. Also: San Bernardino, CA: Borgo Press, 1987. x, 126 p. Index. LC 87-20858. ISBN 0-8095-6106-9.

Like the earlier Bloch bibliography compiled by Graeme Flanagan (above), this heavily illustrated title was compiled with Bloch's assistance; Bloch even provides a brief introduction. This bibliography, however, largely eschews the biographical data offered by Flanagan and concentrates on providing what Larson's brief preface describes as the "first *complete* and comprehensive bibliography of all the work of Robert Bloch, including international appearances in print, radio, television and film, both professional and amateur." It contains the following sections: a preface; an introduction by Robert Bloch; "Robert Bloch: The Man with the Heart of a Small Boy," by Larson; the main bibliography; the fanzine bibliography; supplemental bibliographies; and "Themes and Variations: A Categorical Guide to the Short Stories and Novels of Robert Bloch." The main bibliography contains the following sections: short stories; novels; collections; nonfiction; introductions and forewords; verse; radio, television, and motion pictures bibliographic and biographic material; and miscellany. The supplemental bibliographies are a series of indexes: selected story index by magazine; a chronology of first appearances; unanthologized stories; Lefty Feep stories; collaborative stories; and pseudonymous stories.

The entries in the first six sections are alphabetical by title. Entries for short stories provide the title in boldface type, the story's wordage, title and date (month and year) of the magazine in which it first appeared, and all known subsequent appearances, including international publications and anthologizations. Magazine titles are underlined; book titles are in capitals. Retitlings are cross-referenced to the original title; stories that appeared under pseudonyms are indicated; and stories that were adapted for television and motion pictures are also indicated. Finally, Bloch's popular "Lefty Feep" stories are marked with an [LF] by their title. The sections devoted to Bloch's books provide the place of publication, publisher and year of publication, and translated title for all known editions; wordage is provided for Bloch's novels, and the contents of Bloch's collections are listed. In no section are paginations provided. The sections devoted to the media adaptations are arranged chronologically. The title or program titles are given in boldface type, accompanied by date of broadcast or release, production company or broadcasting network, and director (for motion pictures). International rebroadcasts of television shows are also indicated, though the data are sketchier.

The indexes in the "Supplemental Bibliographies" rearrange much of the data presented in the earlier sections. In addition to listing the stories by the magazines in which they appeared, the first index provides a series of abbreviations that indicate whether the work is a cover story [c], a reprinted story [r], a nonfiction article [n], a Lefty Feep story [LF], or a story that appeared under a pseudonym. The chronology of the second index indicates whether the piece is nonfiction or a Lefty Feep story. The entries in the unanthologized stories are listed alphabetically; a note indicates if the piece was anthologized only in a foreign publication, reprinted only in an American magazine, or reprinted only in a fan magazine.

Though still the most comprehensive bibliography of Bloch available, this work is now outdated. As Bloch has since died, a comprehensive bibliography of his work is possible. One hopes that Larson manages to create one, adding paginations and, perhaps, references to the increasing body of literature about Bloch.

Lawrence Block

272. King, David J. **Lawrence Block**. http://www.dcs.gla.ac.uk/~gnik/
crime-fiction/block/block.html

King's website offers a brief biography of Block, and the bibliography arranges Block's work by series, with different sections listing the works featuring Bernie Rhodenbarr, Matt Scudder, Leo Haig, Evan Tanner, Chip Harrison, and others. A filmography is given, but short stories and limited editions are not cited. The contents of each section are arranged chronologically, but no bibliographic data are provided apart from the publication date. Though his bibliography is incomplete, King nevertheless references material not to be found in Seels's bibliography of Block (q.v.).

273. Seels, James T., ed. **Lawrence Block: Bibliography 1958–1993**. Introduction by Wendy Hornsby. "Pen Names and Other Subterfuge" and "One Thousand Dollars a Word" by Lawrence Block. An Appreciation by Charles Ardai. Afterword by Philip Friedman. Royal Oak, MI; Mission Viejo, CA: ASAP/Airtight-Seels Allied Production, 1993. 103 p. Paperback. Indexes. (30 copies in cloth slipcases; 50 copies in acrylic slipcases; 420 trade copies.)

Despite being compiled with the assistance of Block, this bibliography is less than satisfactory; it is certainly less than comprehensive. Block's introduction states forthrightly that "there are other pseudonymous books that I feel more kindly towards. Some thought and care went into their composition, and I remain pleased with the way they turned out. I thought about allowing some of them to be listed in this bibliography, and I decided against it." What is present is awkwardly designed, difficult to use, and does not follow a known form of bibliographic citation.

Following an introduction by Wendy Hornsby and Block's history of his use of pseudonyms, the first section of the bibliography is a chronological list of the books appearing under Block's name. Titles are listed in boldfaced capital letters; beneath each title is a statement indicating whether the work is a short story, a novel, or nonfiction. The bibliographic information includes the book's place of publication, publisher, publication year, stock number, and format (paperback or hardcover). Statements of printing are provided for each edition, as are information on later publications and retitlings. Occasional notes on the series to which the book belongs are also given. Following this section, and using the same format, are lists of Block's works as Chip Harrison and Paul Kavanagh. Concluding this section are alphabetical lists of Block's works and a list of his works by series. These do not include the year in which the work was published, making them useless except as lists.

The bibliography's second section is a chronological list of the short stories written by Block. Titles are set in quotation marks in boldface capital letters, and the citation lists the magazine's place of publication, title (in italics), and month and year of publication. If the story was collected or anthologized, the citation includes place of publication, title (in small boldface capital letters), and year of publication. Notes indicate title changes and occasionally the series character featured in the story. An alphabetical list of the short stories concludes the bibliography, and the volume concludes with Block's short story "One Thousand Dollars a Word" and an afterword by Philip Friedman.

A comprehensive bibliography—one that lists all of Block's work, provides information on pagination and dustwrappers, contains indexes, and uses a recognizable system of bibliographical citation—remains to be done.

274. Tangled Web. **Lawrence Block: Bernie Rhodenbarr and Evan Tanner**. http://www.twbooks.co.uk/authors/authorpagelist.html

This British website contains a photograph and a brief biography of its subject, and reproduces the covers and jacket material from several books. Excerpts from positive reviews and the text of a full review are given; there is also a link to the Lawrence Block newsletter that Block self-publishes. The concluding bibliography is chronologically arranged and cites the publisher, publication year, and series character appearing in the book; there is a separate section listing Block's writings as "Paul Kavanagh."

Leigh Brackett

275. Arbur, Rosemarie. **Leigh Brackett, Marion Zimmer Bradley, Anne McCaffrey: A Primary and Secondary Bibliography**. Boston: G. K. Hall, 1982. xlviii, 277 p. Indexes. LC 81-4216. ISBN 0-8161-8120-9.

All three authors are best known for their science fiction and fantasy works. All have written detective and mystery stories, but only Brackett's work in this genre achieved any fame. Arbur provides lengthy introductions to the writers, giving general biographical data on them and simple comparisons and contrasts of the themes found in their writing (e.g., "both Bradley and McCaffrey chose for the science part of their science fictions the relatively soft science of psychology"). Following the introduction, the bibliography is tripartite, with separate sections for each writer. Each of these sections uses a similar arrangement in its presentation of material: fiction, miscellaneous media, nonfiction, and critical studies. The data in each section are similarly numbered; for example, Brackett, Bradley, and McCaffrey each have sections beginning A1, A2, A3, and so forth. Each section is chronologically arranged.

In the fiction section, book titles are underlined, and the place of publication and publisher are given. Titles of short stories are in quotations. Publication data include periodical name, volume, number, month, and story's pagination. Beneath each citation are lists of additional appearances of the work; these reprints are also separately numbered and cited in their chronological sequence, with cross-references to their first appearance. Paginations of books are not provided.

The material listed in the miscellaneous media section includes lengthy lists of Brackett's screenplays, short poems by Bradley, and spoken recordings by McCaffrey. The citations for the majority of Brackett's materials are based on materials in the Brackett Collection at Eastern New Mexico University Golden Library. Entries provide title of the piece (underlined), name of the production company, date of original broadcast, whether screenplay was original or based on somebody's work, and a note as to the format of the screenplay (e.g., "original and carbon typescript of final draft, 500 leaves").

The material listed in the other sections is very capably annotated and follows the arrangement of the first section. The volume concludes with six separate indexes, offering author and title access to works by and about the author.

Brackett died in 1978 and her section is essentially complete. Bradley and McCaffrey are alive at this writing and have continued to write. (Indeed, Bradley and McCaffrey have had their greatest successes in the years following the publication of this book.) This nevertheless remains a useful bibliography. It has an unnecessarily redundant system of documenting primary publications, and the six indexes are cumbersome, but these problems aside, the work offers data that cannot be found elsewhere. There is now academic interest in all three authors, and significant research has been produced on each. One hopes that this bibliography can be expanded and updated.

276.   Benson, Gordon, Jr. **Leigh Douglas Brackett and Edmond Hamilton: A Working Bibliography**. Leeds, England; Albuquerque, NM: Galactic Central, 1988. i, 25 p. Paperback. (Galactic Central Bibliographies for the Avid Reader, vol. 20). ISBN 0-912613-05-X.

277.   Benson, Gordon, Jr. **Leigh Brackett & Edmond Hamilton: The Enchantress & The World Wrecker: A Working Bibliography**. 2d revised ed. Polk City, IA; Leeds, England: Galactic Central, 1988. 25 p. Paperback. (Galactic Central Bibliographies for the Avid Reader, vol. 20). ISBN 0-912613-05-X.

Leigh Brackett is generally remembered as a writer of science fiction and fantasy, but she worked on the screenplay of *The Big Sleep* and wrote several fine detective novels, including the noir classic, *No Good from a Corpse*. (Though several of his short stories appeared in the mystery and detective pulp magazines, her husband Edmond Hamilton was predominantly a science fiction writer.) Pages 1–9 in this bibliography cite Brackett's work; the remainder (pages 10–25) cite Hamilton's. Each section begins with the subject's name in capital letters and a double underline, followed by the dates of their birth and death. Their awards are listed, as are citations to biographical data appearing in specialized publications. The data for both authors are arranged by subject, with separate sections for stories, books, and series. Entries in each section are separately numbered and arranged alphabetically; the titles of all books and magazines are capitalized. Each citation lists all known appearances and publications of that work. For stories, Benson lists the magazine's name and provides the date of publication in abbreviated form (e.g., 7-41 for July 1941); reprints are listed beneath. Paginations for short stories are not provided. For books, Benson lists the publisher, series number, year of publication, pagination, initial price, and cover artist of all known editions. Title changes are indicated and cross-referenced.

The bibliographic data in Hamilton's section are preceded by a lengthy list of the abbreviations used to reference the magazines in which he was published. The references to Hamilton's short stories exclude his work for Captain Future. The 27 Captain Future tales are listed in chronological order in the section devoted to Hamilton's series, followed by separate sections listing Captain Future books and "other" books.

The arrangement of Hamilton's work is unnecessarily baroque, the bibliography lacks a title index, and the periodical citations fail to provide paginations. Worse, it is incomplete, lacking the data on screenplays provided by Arbur (q.v.). Nevertheless, this remains an inexpensive and useful introduction to a pair of significant and too-often neglected writers. One hopes for a revised and expanded edition.

Ernest Bramah

278. Berro, Mike. **Ernest Bramah Bibliography: Books.** http://www.massmedia. com/~mikeb/bramah/index.html

This excellent website contains a comprehensive list of Bramah's publications, with separate (but linked) sections offering lists of Bramah's books, his appearances in periodicals and anthologies, biography and criticism about him, and a list (complete as of 1958) of reviews of his books. The data in each section are gratifyingly thorough. The section for books provides (in tabular form) place of publication, publisher, year of publication, pagination, and original price. Contents of short story collections are given, and reprints are listed. Furthermore, title-page transcriptions are provided for first editions, and significant bibliographic notes are often given (e.g., "the first issue of the first edition measures

1.5″ thick outside the covers, and has a list of recent fiction on the verso of the half title. The second issue is in dark green cloth, it measures 1.25″ thick outside the covers, has no half-title"). Finally, images of the title pages are provided for most of Bramah's works.

The section devoted to Bramah's appearances in periodicals and anthologies is arranged alphabetically by story title. Citations provide month, year, pagination, volume number, and illustrator for the original publication, and offer links to book publications. The section with Bramah's biography and criticism is arranged alphabetically by critic; full bibliographic data are provided for each book, and citations are briefly annotated. Similarly, the section devoted to reviews of Bramah's books lists the reviews chronologically beneath the book titles. As before, bibliographic data are thorough and include reviewer's name, title of the periodical, volume, date of publication, page on which the review was published, and number of words in the review. In all, an exemplary website.

Fredric Brown

279. Ahearn, Allen, and Patricia Ahearn. **Author Price Guides: Fredric Brown**. Rockville, MD: Quill & Brush, 1996. 7 leaves. (APG 153).

This Author's Price Guide lists the writings of Fredric Brown from the 1947 publication of the uncorrected proof of *The Fabulous Clipjoint* to the 1991 appearance of *The Pickled Punks*.

The Author Price Guides include a facsimile of the author's signature, a brief biographical sketch, a list of the author's first British and American editions with separate entries for limited and trade editions, the number of copies printed, how to identify the first edition, and estimated value. Each guide presents the bibliographical information chronologically; each separate publication is numbered, with different editions indicated by lowercase letters.

The first entry in each citation is the title, given in capital letters. The second is the publisher's name as it appears on the title page; if the name does not appear there, it is enclosed in parentheses. The third entry is the place of publication, and the fourth is the date of publication; as before, parentheses enclose these data if they are not listed on the title page. The fifth entry is a code providing information on how to identify the first printing (first edition) of the particular book. Notes indicate when there is more than one issue of a particular first edition; page and line numbers are provided if it is necessary to identify issues. First editions appearing in paper are so indicated.

The Author Price Guides are inexpensive and useful bibliographies for those collecting separate publications. On the debit side, separately published pieces in anthologies are not identified, published letters are not traced, dramatic works are only sporadically recorded, and the contents of short story collections are not noted.

280. Baird, Newton. **A Key to Fredric Brown's Wonderland: A Study and an Annotated Bibliographical Checklist with Reminiscences by Elizabeth Brown and Harry Altshuler and "It's Only Everything" by Fredric Brown**. Georgetown, CA: Talisman Literary Research, 1981. 63 p. Index. LC 81-52422. (275 copies paperbound; 85 copies hardcover.)

One of the few authors equally adept at short stories and novels, and noted for detective and mystery fiction as well as science fiction, fantasy, and weird fiction, Fredric Brown unfortunately remains largely unstudied. Baird's introduction to this excellent bibliography acknowledges Brown's originality, linking him to writers as diverse as Ayn Rand, Mickey Spillane, William Campbell Gault, and Lewis Carroll: "His 'wonderland,' like Carroll's, is full of wonder and curiosity, created from what he saw in reality, and he shared Carroll's sense of the fantastic and delight with word inventions and puzzles. But no other author, including Lewis Carroll, became a prototype for Fredric Brown. He is one of the most original writers of all time."

Prior to the bibliography, the *Key* contains separate sections providing a chronology of Fredric Brown and two reminiscences of Brown from *Les Amis du Crime*: "Fredric Brown, My Husband," by Elizabeth Brown, and "The Early Career of Fredric Brown" by Harry Altshuler; and "It's Only Everything" by Fredric Brown. Elizabeth Brown was Fredric's wife; Altshuler was his first literary agent and his friend; and "It's Only Everything" is a brief, thought-provoking essay discussing atheism, Christianity, and the need for conviction.

The bibliography itself contains the following sections: A) books; B) foreign anthologies not published in the United States; C) parts of books; D) short stories; E) poetry: books and periodicals; F) other contributions to periodicals; G) radio adaptations of short stories; H) television adaptations of fiction; I) film adaptations of fiction (other than films made for television); J) phonograph recordings of fiction; K) parts of books; and L) articles, parts of articles, and published letters about Fredric Brown. An appendix contains "A Few Supplemental Matters," and an index to the entire *Key*—prefatory material and biographical reminiscences, as well as the bibliography—concludes the volume.

With the exception of the material in sections K and L, which are listed alphabetically, the citations in each section are arranged chronologically. The book citations list the book's title in italics and provide publication data—publisher, place and year of publication, and pagination—for all known editions of the work. The annotation provides the names of the character and a clear statement of the plot without revealing the climax, and includes a note on Brown's narrative style (e.g., "third person narration with nine points-of-view, including 'Death.'") Each citation concludes with a list of the contemporary reviews.

The citations in the other sections vary in their comprehensiveness. The listing for Brown's short stories provides the name, month, and year of the periodical in which the piece appeared, as well as the titles of the books in which they were reprinted. Oddly, the story's original pagination is not given. Worse, Baird's data were undoubtedly as complete as could be hoped for in 1981, but a great many additional short stories by Brown have since been discovered.

Though it is not recent or as comprehensive in its listings of short stories as Christopher Stephens's *A Checklist of Fredric Brown* (q.v.), this work nevertheless contains much that cannot be obtained elsewhere, and it presents its material well. Baird should revise and update his *Key* and print a larger quantity of copies.

281. Stephens, Christopher P. **A Checklist of Fredric Brown**. Hastings-on-Hudson, NY: Ultramarine Publishing, 1992. 83 p. Paperback. Index. ISBN 0-89366-225-9.

One of the longest of the Ultramarine bibliographies, this is also one of the more thorough. It contains three chronologically arranged sections: books written by Fredric Brown, books edited by him, and short stories written by him. In the first section, each citation is numbered, and publication data are provided on the first American and first British edition and the first paperback edition of each. Titles are underlined; retitlings are indicated; and information on paginations, dustwrapper artists, prices, and identifying points is given. The citations for the short stories are also arranged chronologically. Story titles are given in quotation marks, magazine names are underlined, publication date is provided, and reprint information is also given. Original paginations, however, are not given. An index to all works concludes the checklist.

Stephens lists far more short stories by Brown than does Baird (q.v.), and his entries are significantly more recent than Baird's. However, Stephens's format for listing his citations is thoroughly unattractive, to the point of impeding rather than enhancing access. Flaws of appearance aside, this is the most comprehensive bibliography of Fredric Brown's short works available, and most researchers will find its listings of Brown's novels quite adequate.

282. Williams, Richard, ed. **Fredric Brown: British and American Books and Films: A Checklist**. Scunthorpe, England: Dragonby Press, 1991. 4 p. Collated sheets. (British Author Checklists, no. 2).

Despite its title, this brief bibliography contains almost no information on Brown's films; it is an alphabetical listing of Brown's books. Each title is given in boldface capitals. A note indicates whether the book is one of short stories or a novel, and a list provides data on all of the American and British editions of the book. These data are presented in abbreviated form but usually include publisher's name and date of publication; pagination is sometimes provided, as is the artist for the paperback editions of the book. Despite its brevity, this bibliography cites some British paperback editions that are not listed in Baird's or Stephens's bibliographies of Fredric Brown (q.q.v.), but it contains little else that is not readily accessible elsewhere.

Rita Mae Brown

283. Wicker, Gene. **Rita Mae Brown**. http://www.iwillfollow.com/rmb/

This website contains a photograph of its subject, a bibliography of Brown's nonmysteries that includes "samplings" from all of Brown's work, and lengthy descriptions and cover reproductions of Brown's mystery novels featuring Sneaky Pie Brown. Very capably done.

Leo Bruce

284. Kobayashi, Susumu. **Leo Bruce Homepage**. http://www.freepage.total. co.jp/LeoBruce/LeoBruce.htm

Leo Bruce was the pseudonym of Rupert Croft-Cooke (1903–1979). This web page provides a picture of its subject, a biographical statement, and a chronological list of Bruce's works. Several links lead to indexes of the contents of Bruce's short story collections. Additional publication information, cover reproductions, and story summaries are not provided.

James Lee Burke

285. Ahearn, Allen, and Patricia Ahearn. **Author Price Guides: James Lee Burke**. Rockville, MD: Quill & Brush, 1993. 2 leaves. (APG 133).

This Author's Price Guide lists the work of James Lee Burke from the 1965 publication of *Half of Paradise* to the 1993 appearance of *In the Electric Mist with the Confederate Dead.*

For a thorough description of the format of Author Price Guides, see the entry under Fredric Brown.

286. Steffensen, Jan B. **The James Lee Burke Internet Guide**. http://www. webfic.com/jlb/jlb.htm

This well-designed website provides a photograph of its subject and links to a James Lee Burke bibliography, a biography, information about Burke's best-known character, Dave Robicheaux, secondary material about Burke, television and film adaptations, and what Steffensen refers to as various "Burkian" stuff: newsletters, information about the French Creoles, the Cajuns, and Louisiana. The bibliography provides a chronological list of the Dave Robicheaux stories, a list of Burke's other books, and a list of Burke's short stories. There are cover reproductions for a number of Burke's works; often there are links to reviews. The 1996 adaptation of *Heaven's Prisoners* is linked to numerous reviews, articles, and picture and sound files. A dark background occasionally makes for difficult reading, but the amount and quality of material included are gratifying.

287. Tangled Web. **James Lee Burke and Dave Robicheaux.** http://www.twbooks. co.uk/authors/jburke.html

By no means as complete as Steffensen's website on the same subject (q.v.), this British website contains no photograph, but it has brief biographical data and offers reproductions of several cover illustrations and the information from their covers. Excerpts from positive reviews and the full text of a few reviews are also given. The site concludes with a list of books by Burke, only four of which are accompanied by dates or bibliographical data.

W. R. Burnett

288. Denton, William. **W. R. Burnett.** http://www.vex.net/~buff/rara-avis/ biblio/burnett.html

This clearly designed site contains sections covering Burnett's books, short fiction, screenplays, and adaptations. Each section lists Burnett's works in chronological order. Book titles are italicized and include publishers and year of publication. Short stories are given in quotation marks, periodical titles are italicized, and the date of publication is provided. Screenplays are italicized, and the year the film was released is given, as are the names of collaborators. Adaptations have titles italicized and the year of adaptation. Though derived from data compiled by Harper (q.v.), this site is much clearer in its presentation.

289. Harper, Katherine. **W. R. Burnett.** http://ernie.bgsu.edu/~kharper/ index.html

This site contains a biographical sketch of Burnett, a small portrait, and links to Burnett's work, grouping it by crime novels; Westerns; experimental, historical, other adult, and juvenile novels and nonfiction; and short stories, book reviews, and articles. In each section a brief description of the work and the publisher and publication year are provided. Apart from the paucity of data, this is a potentially useful site on a writer who is only now starting to get attention. The site compiled by Denton (q.v.) is, however, more clearly presented.

Gwendoline Butler

290. Tangled Web. **Gwendoline Butler.** http://www.twbooks.co.uk/authors/ gbutler.html

This website provides a photograph and a brief biography of its subject, and it reproduces the covers and jacket material from several of her books. Excerpts from positive reviews and the text of a full review are given. A concluding bibliography is chronologically arranged and cites the publisher and publication year; there is also a link to her work as Jennie Melville.

Carol Cail

291. Cail, Carol. **Carol Cail's Home Page**. http://www.starsend.com/authors/
cc/cailhome.htm

The author's home page contains a picture of herself, a brief biography,
and some quite outdated information about a book signing. Although Cail has
written at least five novels, this page mentions only her 1995 *Unsafe Keeping*, providing publisher and ISBN along with an excerpt from the book.

James M. Cain

292. Denton, William. **James M. Cain**. http://www.vex.net/~buff/rara-avis/
biblio/jmcain.html

Brief biographical information on Cain is accessible through a link, but
this site provides a well-presented bibliography of Cain's writings, with different
sections listing Cain's books, short fiction, short nonfiction, plays, screenplays,
and adaptations. Each section lists Cain's works in chronological order. Book
titles are italicized, and publishers are mentioned, as is year of publication; contents
of short story collections are listed. Titles of short stories are given in quotation
marks, periodical titles are italicized, and the date of publication is provided.
Screenplays are italicized, and the year the film was released is given, as are the
names of any collaborators. Play titles and titles of adaptations are italicized; the
latter list the year of adaptation and collaborators. Though the section devoted to
Cain's nonfiction is incomplete, this remains an excellent bibliography.

293. King, David J. **James M. Cain**. http://www.dcs.gla.ac.uk/people/personal/
gnik/crime-fiction/cain/cain.html

King's website offers a link to a brief biography of Cain, and his bibliography arranges Cain's work by genre, with different sections listing Cain's novels,
short story collections, plays, screenplays, and other publications. The website
concludes with a Cain filmography. The contents of each section are arranged
chronologically, but no bibliographic data are provided apart from the publication date; publication data are not provided for individual short stories. Consult
instead Denton's more comprehensive website (q.v.).

John Dickson Carr

294. Shortling, Grobius. **Grobius Shortling's John Dickson Carr Page**.
http://members.aol.com/grobius/carr.htm

Shortling's web page has no picture of its subject and almost no biographical information, but it contains a reasonably full list of Carr's books, arranged in chronological order by series. In each group, the major series character

is described, and the titles of the books are listed and briefly annotated. Shortling's prose is occasionally clumsy, but this appears to be the only web page devoted to its subject.

Raymond Chandler

295. Ahearn, Allen, and Patricia Ahearn. **Author Price Guides: Raymond Chandler**. Rockville, MD: Quill & Brush, 1992. 5 leaves. (APG 124).

This Author's Price Guide to Raymond Chandler lists his work from the 1939 advance publication copy of *The Big Sleep* to the 1990 publication of *Poodle Springs*.

For a thorough description of the format of Author Price Guides, see the entry under Fredric Brown.

296. Bruccoli, Matthew J. **Raymond Chandler: A Checklist**. Kent, OH: Kent State University Press, 1968. ix, 35 p. (Serif Series: Bibliographies and Checklists). LC 68-16892.

Bruccoli's introduction begins by stating that this slim volume is not a bibliography but a checklist. Nevertheless, the book lists "all editions of the books, first periodical appearances only, and first book appearances only of short pieces. For the first printing of the first edition of a Chandler book it supplies a short form title-page transcription, pagination, and signature collation." That these do not make the work a bibliography are because (in Bruccoli's words) it "fails to provide the detailed descriptive and analytical information about paper, type, binding, printing, and text—especially text—that a true bibliography, no matter how digressive, must provide."

The checklist begins with a chronological list of Chandler's books. Separate sections provide chronological lists of Chandler's first book appearances, stories, articles, reviews, columns, letters, poems, and blurbs. Other sections contain an interview with Chandler, a statement by Chandler, and a brief list of references (three items cited).

Though Bruccoli is accurate in his presentation of his material, Chandler wrote far more than he is here given credit for, and this volume has been thoroughly superseded by Bruccoli's later work on the subject (q.v.).

297. Bruccoli, Matthew J. **Raymond Chandler: A Descriptive Bibliography**. Pittsburgh: University of Pittsburgh, 1979. xv, 146 p. Index. (Pittsburgh Series in Bibliography). LC 78-4280. ISBN 0-8229-3382-9.

As if to make amends for his earlier *Raymond Chandler: A Checklist* (q.v.), Bruccoli presents this comprehensive bibliography of the works of Raymond Chandler. The bibliography contains six lettered sections: A) Separate Publications; B) First-Appearance Contributions to Books; C) First Appearances in Magazines and Newspapers; D) Keepsake; E) Dust-Jacket Blurbs; and F)

Motion-Picture Work. The citations in each of these sections are arranged chronologically and are separately lettered and numbered.

Section A, the longest in the book, comprises the first 106 pages. Each citation reproduces the title page of the first edition of all British and American hardcovers and paperbacks. Each entry provides an exhaustive analytical bibliographical description of the first edition, with collation, pagination, contents, typography and paper, binding, dust jacket, publication, and printing noted and described at length. A section called "notes" provides additional information and cross-references to other sections, and a section for "locations" provides not only a list of the holdings of libraries but also the dates on which the major copyright libraries received the volume. Additional printings and editions are also noted and described, though the descriptions of these of necessity terser; the title and copyright pages are described at length. A supplement (Section AA) lists collections of Chandler's writings using the same principles of bibliographical description.

The concluding sections provide similarly detailed bibliographical data. Retitlings of short stories are indicated, as are unsigned works. Section D contains one citation; Section E contains two citations. Section F lists the motion pictures written by Chandler as well as those based on his work; it contains 17 citations. Appendixes list the compiler's notes and provide a brief list of the principal works about Chandler, and the volume concludes with a comprehensive index.

Though the concluding sections could well have been compressed, this remains the definitive bibliography of Chandler.

298. Denton, William. **Raymond Chandler.** http://www.vex.net/~buff/rara-avis/biblio/chandler.html

A biography of Chandler is accessible through a link, but the above URL provides a comprehensive list of Chandler's works, with different sections listing the first printings of his books, short fiction, short nonfiction, screenplays, and adaptations. A bibliography of material about Chandler concludes this section. The contents of each section are arranged chronologically. Book titles are italicized, and the publisher and year of publication are given. Contents of short story collections are listed. The titles of individual short stories and short nonfiction pieces are in quotation marks, and the titles of the periodicals that published them are italicized; publication month and year are given. The titles of Chandler's screenplays and adaptations are also italicized; both are accompanied by year of release, and the names of Chandler's screenplay collaborators are given. Though a number of posthumously published titles are not cited, this bibliography remains clearly presented and accessible.

299. King, David J. **Raymond Chandler.** http://www.dcs.gla.ac.uk/~gnik/crime-fiction/chandler/chandler.html

King's website offers a link to a brief biography of Chandler, and its bibliography arranges Chandler's work by series. Different sections list Chandler's

Philip Marlowe novels, short story collections, screenplays, and other publications. The site concludes with a filmography. The contents of each section are arranged chronologically, but no bibliographic data are provided apart from the publication date; publication data are not provided for individual short stories. Though King presents his material clearly, a better choice is Denton's more comprehensive website (above).

300. Lovisi, Gary. **Dashiell Hammett and Raymond Chandler: A Checklist and Bibliography of Their Paperback Appearances**. Brooklyn, NY: Gryphon Books, 1994. 82 p. Paperback. LC 96-134119. ISBN 0-936071-36-2. (500 copies printed.)

After an appreciation of the two authors and the section devoted to the paperbacks of Dashiell Hammett, the paperback appearances of Raymond Chandler are listed. The citations are arranged alphabetically by title and then alphabetically by publisher, a reasonable arrangement that quickly develops problems when Lovisi cites international editions without any familiarity with the languages. The paperback editions of Ullstein Verlag's publication of *The Big Sleep*, for example, are listed under the words "Allgemeine Reihe." The citations include the book's series and year of publication; often there is a note on cover artist, cover price, and pagination. The section concludes with the following disturbing statement: "there are also various German editions, mostly from Ullstein Verlag in the 1970's and 1980's that collect Chandler stories under titles usually not used in the English language editions. These I've omitted as some combine stories from different collections and only serve to complicate matters bibliographically. Besides, as I don't know German it's impossible to decipher these editions."

Separate sections discuss paperbacks on and about Hammett and Chandler, collecting Hammett and Chandler in paperback, and collecting the foreign editions of their works. Lovisi includes significantly more listings of Chandler's paperback appearances than does Bruccoli, but this remains a discreditable bibliography.

Leslie Charteris

301. Ahearn, Allen, and Patricia Ahcarn. **Author Price Guides: Leslie Charteris**. Rockville, MD: Quill & Brush, 1993. 10 leaves. APG 135.

This Author's Price Guide lists the publications of Leslie Charteris from the 1927 *X Esquire* to the 1983 collection *The Saint: Five Complete Novels*.

For a thorough description of the format of Author Price Guides, see the entry under Fredric Brown.

302. Alexandersson, Jan, and Iwan Hedman. **Leslie Charteris och Helgonet under 5 Decennier en Bio-Bibliographi**. Stockholm, Sweden: Strängnäs, 1973. 124 p. Paperback. Index. (DAST Dossier, no. 2). ISBN 91-85208-01-9.

A reading knowledge of Swedish is not necessary to appreciate this bio-bibliography of Leslie Charteris. Following a brief biography of Charteris, a lengthy seven-column bibliography lists the British, American, and Swedish editions of Charteris's publications. Each citation is numbered, followed by the publication date in reverse order (i.e., 2 February 1929 is listed as 29.03.02). The following column lists the title of Charteris's work; short stories are listed in regular type, whereas book titles are in capital letters. The first appearance of a work is underlined. Retitlings are indicated in this column, as are media adaptations. Successive columns list the publisher's or magazine's name in highly abbreviated form, the nature of the work, pagination (given only for books), and price (also given only for books). Publications through 1971 are covered, and one 1972 publication is listed.

The next section provides significantly greater bibliographic data on the first editions of Charteris's English-language and Swedish books. Each citation is separately numbered and cross-referenced to the bibliography in the first section. Arrangement is chronological. There are two columns: The left describes the first English-language edition, and the right describes the first Swedish edition. Each citation lists the book's title in underlined capital letters. The publisher of the first edition is given, as are the place of publication, year of publication, printer, book's size, number of chapters in the book, pagination, a description of the binding, price, and dedication.

The third section provides publication data on Charteris's short fiction. Each citation is separately numbered and cross-referenced to the bibliography in the first section. The publication date is given in the same format as the first section. The title is underlined, and the place of publication is given. Magazine titles are listed in regular type, whereas book titles are in capital letters. A list at the conclusion of this section provides retitlings and original titles for Charteris's short fiction.

The fourth section lists Charteris's Swedish publications. As before, citations are arranged chronologically, separately numbered, and cross-referenced to the bibliography in the first section. The Swedish title is given followed by the original English title, and the publication data lists magazine titles in regular type and capitalizes the names of book titles.

A fifth section selectively lists Charteris's nonfiction, and lengthy lists of the cast and credits of motion picture and television adaptations follow. Included are the names of actors and actresses and the characters they portray, the production company, producer, distributor, distribution company, director, author of the screenplay, camera operator, music director, running time, and name of the work by Charteris from which the work is adapted. A well-done index concludes the book.

Though dated, this work is superior to the effort by W. O. G. Lofts and Derek Adley (q.v.), but fans of the Saint will be more satisfied with Burl Barer's 1993 *Saint* (q.v.).

303. Barer, Burl. **The Saint: A Complete History in Print, Radio, Film and Television of Leslie Charteris's Robin Hood of Modern Crime, Simon Templar, 1928–1992.** Jefferson, NC: McFarland, 1993. xii, 419 p. Index. LC 92-53509. ISBN 0-89950-723-9.

Like the bio-bibliography compiled by Lofts and Adley (q.v.), the first part of this book describes Leslie Charteris's life and career. The bibliography is contained in seven appendixes: I) *The Saint* radio script synopses; II) Episode and players guide to *The Saint*, starring Roger Moore; III) *Return of the Saint* Script Synopses and Credits; IV) "Mystery Wheel of Adventure" press releases and feature stories; V) The Saint's automotive icon; VI) Chronology of the Saint Writings; and VII) The Saint Club. In the case of the radio scripts, each script is numbered by the week in which it aired, with air dates and (in most cases) the name of the writer. Although the actors playing the Saint are identified at the beginning of the appendix, the casts are not given. Gimmicks are revealed, though not the names of the villains.

The episodes of *The Saint* starring Roger Moore provide the episodes' original promotional "log lines," written by ITC for newspaper listings; production numbers; acting credits for principal actors and actresses; and opening lines spoken by the Saint. The section concludes with a lengthy list of the actors and actresses from the Roger Moore series and the episodes of *The Saint* in which they appeared. This list is not keyed to the production numbers, necessitating use of the index.

The synopses in *The Return of the Saint,* 24 television films that starred Ian Ogilvy, are longer than those in the previous sections, provide lengthy lists of casts and credits, and are listed in the order in which they were sold for syndication.

The material surveying "The Mystery Wheel of Adventure," six television films that starred Simon Dutton as Simon Templar, were drawn largely from the promotional material released by one of the co-producers, DLT Entertainment. The annotations are lengthy but do not provide separate lists of casts and credits.

The appendix devoted to the Saint's automobile provides its history in its various incarnations, from the 5,000-pound (weight) Hirondel of the early novels to the Volvo P1800 used by Roger Moore, to the white Jaguar XJ-S piloted by Ian Ogilvy.

The "Chronology of *The Saint* Writings" contains three sections. The first section lists original publication information for all short stories and novels. The second section provides publication histories on the books about *The Saint*; it too is arranged chronologically. The book data in these sections include the title in italics, publisher, and month and year of publication. The short story information lists the title in quotation marks and the publishing periodical in italics, and gives date of publication and (when relevant) original title. Contents of short story collections are listed. Data on Charteris's numerous collaborators and ghostwriters are provided in each entry. The third section is devoted to the French printing of Charteris's books, several of which were not published in English. Citations are listed chronologically and follow the same format as above. However, they give the original (English) title when one exists and include series number, date of the French copyright, and contents of short story collections.

The volume concludes with information on contacting the fan club devoted to the Saint and a well-done index. The bibliography of Charteris's writings leaves a bit to be desired, but the book is as up-to-date and comprehensive as one could hope for in its treatment of Charteris's life and the media adaptations of his writing.

304. Bodenheimer, Daniel. **The Saint and Leslie Charteris: A Collection**. [Santa Cruz, CA?]: [University of California, Santa Cruz?], 1993. 4 v. OCLC 28155273.

Although this work is unobtainable in its entirety, photocopies indicate that this is a bibliography of commendable complexity and comprehensiveness. "The Saint Books" lists in boldface type the titles and retitlings of Charteris's works. Elaborate publication data are provided beneath each title, including the publisher of the first British and American editions, publishers of serializations and condensations, and publishers of retitlings and paperback editions. The contents of collections are given, as are the authors of the ghost-written volumes; all citations are separately numbered. Paginations, however, do not appear to be provided.

305. Lofts, W. O. G., and Derek Adley. **The Saint and Leslie Charteris**. London: Hutchinson Library Services, 1971. 134 p. ISBN 0-09-304800-9.

The first half of this book (pages 11–67) consists of biographical data on Charteris and appreciations of Charteris's writings. The bibliography begins with a list of "Leslie Charteris in Book Form." This chronologically arranged list provides the book's title in italics, publisher, and year of publication; data are current as of 1969. Entries in "Leslie Charteris in Book Form" are cross-referenced to a section titled "The Books of Leslie Charteris," but before this section is reached, two sections intervene. A section titled "The Saint's Travels" lists chronologically the novels featuring the Saint and provides setting and year of publication; an asterisk indicates if the story was adopted for television. In the chronologically arranged section titled "The Saint Films," titles are listed in italics, followed by issuing studio, film's director, length, time, and major cast.

Entries in "The Books of Leslie Charteris" are arranged alphabetically. Each entry provides the book's title in italics, followed by publisher's name, location of the copyright date (e.g., dated reverse to the title page), and copyright date. A brief physical description is given (e.g., *Cr. 8vo* for *crown octavo*), as are the pagination and the color of the cover. The dedication is reprinted, and the rest of each citation indicates serialization and reprint data, which are linked to the bibliography's concluding section, "Stories by Leslie Charteris Appearing in Magazines and Newspapers." First sentences are provided for all separately published sections; alternate titles and retitlings are also given.

"Leslie Charteris Stories Included in Collections of Short Stories" gives publication data for two titles. It is followed by "Books about The Saint by Other

Authors," which contains data (in the form of the citations in "The Books of Leslie Charteris") on three titles.

"Stories by Leslie Charteris Appearing in Magazines and Newspapers" is arranged by the title of the publication, beneath which, listed chronologically, are the title of the story, first sentence, and successive reprintings, also listed chronologically. Cross-references indicate when the story received book publication.

Although compiled with the assistance of Charteris, this bibliography is virtually impossible to use and lacks that most basic of bibliographical necessities, an index to titles. Choose Alexandersson and Hedman or Barer (q.q.v.) for superior treatments of a similar subject.

306.   Mechele, Tony, and Dick Fiddy. **The Saint**. London: Boxtree, 1989. 176 p. Paperback. Index. ISBN 1-85283-259-2.

This bibliography contains separate chapters on the Saint's adventures in radio, film, television, and comic books. There is also a chronological list of Charteris's books. Place of publication, publisher, and date of publication are indicated, as are retitlings and reissuings. Most chapters begin with a prose history of the Saint in that medium and contain numerous stills.

The section devoted to radio lists broadcasting station, actors and actresses, director, scriptwriters, producer, adapter of Charteris's stories, title of the play, date on which it was first broadcast, and a brief annotation that is probably superior to the original broadcast. One would be hard put to improve upon, "The Saint crosses swords with a mad scientist and his giant ant."

The sections on the Saint in the visual media list the year of release and the title of the production in a gray box; entries for motion pictures also include the issuing studio. Each entry lists cast, screenplay writers, director, and producer. Annotations range from 250 to 500 words and include the running time and the book or story upon which the adventure was based.

The chapter on comic book adaptations of the Saint contains virtually no data; it consists primarily of reproductions of the covers of U.S. and British books. Those interested in the thespians who appeared in the various adaptations of the Saint will find the index dismal, for it covers only the material in the prose histories. Completists interested in the media versions of the Saint will find similar annotations and better indexing—but far fewer illustrations—in Burl Barer's *The Saint* (q.v.).

G. K. Chesterton

307.   Chesterton, G. K. **The Mask of Midas, with a Father Brown Bibliography by John Peterson**. Edited and with a preface by Geir Hasnes. Illustrated by Noralf Husby. Trondheim, Norway: Classica Forlag AS, 1991. 62 p. ISBN 82-7610-000-7 (leather edition); 82-7610-001-5 (standard edition). (1,000 copies printed.)

The first half of *The Mask of Midas* consists of the first publication of a previously unpublished Father Brown story; Hasne's introduction provides its complex history. The latter half of the volume is a three-part bibliography listing Chesterton's Father Brown stories, his writings on the concept of crime and mystery fiction and Father Brown, and studies of Father Brown and Chesterton's crime and mystery fiction.

The first section lists the Father Brown stories in chronological order. Each citation is numbered and lists the story title in boldface type; its first publication date is given, as is the name of the periodical in which it was first published Entries indicate in which Chesterton collections the story was published and if it was retitled for book publication.

The second section is alphabetical by the title of the article, printed in boldface type. Names of the periodicals and books are given in italics. Periodical publication data include the page on which the article appeared; book publication data include place of publication, publisher, date of publication, and page on which the article appeared. Reprints and retitlings are also indicated.

The third section is alphabetical by author and covers reference books, chapters in books, articles, and miscellaneous materials. It includes a number of references that are not listed in either Sullivan's three volumes of Chesterton bibliography (q.v.) or the standard indexes to literary criticism.

Though *The Mask of Midas* is difficult to obtain, it repays the effort, for the material is well presented, accurate, and helpful. Serious scholars of Chesterton's mystery fiction will wish to examine it, and fans of Chesterton's Father Brown will rejoice in the volume's first part.

308. Sullivan, John. **G. K. Chesterton: A Bibliography, with an Essay, on Books, by G. K. Chesterton.** Epitaph by Walter de la Mare. London: University of London Press, 1958. 208 p.; New York: Barnes & Noble, 1958.

Only a small percentage of G. K. Chesterton's enormous output was mystery and detective stories, but that percentage remains historically significant and justifies the inclusion of these bibliographies.

The first volume of Sullivan's comprehensive Chesterton bibliography contains eight sections: A) books and pamphlets by Chesterton; B) contributions to books and pamphlets; C) contributions to periodicals; D) books and periodicals containing illustrations by Chesterton; E) books and articles about Chesterton; F) collections and selections; G) translations into foreign languages; and H) a G. K. C. miscellany. Except in the cases of sections C and G, the entries in each section are chronologically arranged and separately numbered. In section C, the entries are alphabetically ordered by periodical title and then listed chronologically beneath each title. In section G, the entries are alphabetically ordered by the language into which they were translated, then listed chronologically. The 954 citations are continuously numbered and are current as of 1957.

The citations in section A provide a full description of the first British editions of all works by Chesterton and of his works published in the United States that contained material not in the British editions. The title page of each work is transcribed in the quasi-facsimile method; a collation statement is provided; the contents are given; illustrations are detailed; the binding is described; and dust-jackets or wrappers are described. The first publication date is given, as is the date of the copy held in the British Museum, and notes indicate the source of original publication (if any). Later editions are referenced if their contents are different.

The citations in sections B–G are equally thorough, though paginations are not provided for the secondary materials listed in section E, and section G does not always provide the translated titles. A thorough index concludes the volume.

309. Sullivan, John. **Chesterton Continued: A Bibliographical Supplement, Together with Some Uncollected Prose and Verse by G. K. Chesterton**. London: University of London Press, 1968. xiv, 120 p. Index. LC 72-370814. ISBN 0-340-09457-5.

The second volume of Johnson's G. K. Chesterton bibliography uses the same arrangement as the first for its citations, and its citations are numbered and are keyed to the entries in the first volume. It corrects errors and expands upon the data presented in the first volume, and continues its documentation of material by and about Chesterton. Section G is lengthy, bespeaking international interest in and awareness of the writings of Chesterton. Entries are current as of 1966.

310. Sullivan, John. **Chesterton Three: A Bibliographical Postscript**. Bedford, England: Vintage Publications, 1980. 46 p. Paperback.

Reprinted from articles appearing in *The Chesterton Review*, this slim volume corrects and updates the data published in Sullivan's 1958 and 1968 bibliographies of Chesterton (q.q.v.). The notes follow the arrangement and numbering system introduced in the previous two volumes. The section containing the most citations is G, which lists the translations into foreign languages of books by Chesterton. The data in all sections are complete as of 1978. Owners of the first two volumes of Sullivan's Chesterton bibliography will want *Chesterton Three*, but it does not stand on its own.

311. Ward, Martin. **G. K. Chesterton**. http://www.dur.ac.uk/~dcs0mpw/gkc

Though not focusing on Chesterton's mysteries, this nevertheless provides a well-written biography of Chesterton, links to Chesterton's works on the Web, links to pictures of Chesterton, and links to related subjects including the American Chesterton Society, Hilaire Belloc, C. S. Lewis (and the Inklings), and Christian resources.

311a. G. K. Chesterton Society
1437 College Drive
Saskatoon, SK
Canada S7N 0W6

Meg Chittenden

312. Chittenden, Margaret. **Meg Chittenden's Web Page**. http://www.techline.com/~megc/

Author Meg Chittenden's personal web page provides information about the setting of her Charlie Plato series on the San Francisco Peninsula. There are links to a biography (with photograph) and information about Chittenden's books (cover reproductions, publication date, ISBN, a summary, the first chapter, and quotations from approving critics). In addition, there are links to other home pages of other writers, information on square dancing, and tips for mystery writing. Enthusiastically written, with great graphics, and quite enjoyable.

Agatha Christie

313. Ahearn, Allen, and Patricia Ahearn. **Author Price Guides: Agatha Christie**. Rockville, MD: Quill and Brush, 1995. 14 leaves. APG 082.2.

This Author's Price Guide to Agatha Christie documents her work from the 1920 publication *The Mysterious Affair at Styles* to the 1991 publication of *Problems at Pollensa Bay*.

For a thorough description of the format of Author Price Guides, see the entry under Fredric Brown.

314. Fitzgibbon, Russell H. **The Agatha Christie Companion**. Bowling Green, OH: Bowling Green State University Popular Press, 1980. ix, 178 p. LC 78-61075. ISBN 0-87972-137-5 (hc); 0-87972-138-3 (pb).

Despite its title, this is not a companion to the works of Agatha Christie in the way that the books with similar titles by Saunders and Lovallo and Riley and McAllister are (q.q.v.). The first half of the book contains essays in which Fitzgibbon discusses the history of the detective story, Christie's life and accomplishments, and her detectives.

The second half of the book begins with a lengthy bibliography of Christie's work. Only the first British publications are included, and the emphasis and arrangement concentrates on Christie's detective and mystery stories. Each citation is separately numbered. Bibliographic information includes title (in italics), place of publication, publisher, and year of publication for each known edition. Contents of short story collections are listed; title changes are noted.

The next section provides a comprehensive list of all detective and mystery book and short story titles. Entries in italics refer to books; entries in roman type refer to short stories. All entries are keyed to the imprint of first publication listed in the previous bibliography.

A list of alternate Christie book titles follows, after which a grid lists the contents of Christie's short story collections. Collections of short stories are listed at the top of the grid, chronologically from left to right, with each keyed to its entry in the bibliography. Story titles are listed at the left side of each page; in parentheses following each title are the initials of what Fitzgibbon describes as Christie's "central detective." An X indicates whether the story appeared in the collection listed at the top of the page.

A selective but lengthy list of Christie's characters concludes the book. Each character's function is defined, and his or her appearance is keyed to the bibliography. The lists do not include Christie's detectives.

This work contains nothing that cannot be found elsewhere.

315. Haining, Peter. **Agatha Christie: Murder in Four Acts. A Centenary Celebration of "The Queen of Crime" on Stage, Film, Radio, and Television**. London: Virgin Books, 1990. 159 p. GB 90-24438. ISBN 1-85227-273-2.

Although occasionally described as a reference book, this heavily illustrated work is an amiable prose survey of Christie's works that have been adapted for the stage, film, radio, and television. Separate chapters survey the works that appeared in each medium and describe ten actors who have played Hercule Poirot, six actresses who have played Miss Jane Marple, and four couples who have played Tuppence and Tommy Beresford. The volume contains neither lists nor documentation and is unindexed, effectively preventing researchers from using it.

316. Ho, Dora. **The Christie List**.

This list of the works of Christie is available as part of the archives maintained by DorothyL and through the Miss Lemon website (http://www.iwillfollow. com/lemon.htm). It contains three sections. The first lists Christie's short story collections; the second, Christie's plays; and the third, Christie's novels. The arrangement of each section is chronological, the year of publication followed by title of the work and name of the detective(s) featured in it. Retitlings are indicated, though the original title of *And Then There Were None* is not given.

317. Jonasson, Ragnar. **Agatha Christie**. http://www.hi.is/~ragnaj/

Offering its data in English and Icelandic, this site provides a biography of its subject and offers several reasonably thorough chronological lists of her publications in tabular form. "Mysteries" provides title of the book, year of publication, and series characters appearing in it; the original title of *And Then There Were None* is not given. Critical information on Hercule Poirot and Miss Jane Marple is provided. The site has lists of Christie's works written as Mary Westmacott and as Agatha Christie Mallowan. Her plays are listed in chronological order. A lengthy tabular list provides information on Agatha Christie adaptations for movies and television; the adaptation title is given, as are the title of the work on which it was based, the year it was broadcast, whether it was made for television, and the name of the leading actor or actress. Related works are also listed. Despite some spelling errors, this is the most thorough Christie bibliography and the best Christie site available via the Web.

318.   Morselt, Ben. **An A to Z of the Novels and Short Stories of Agatha Christie**. Hertfordshire, England: Phoenix Publishing, 1985. 255 p. Indexes. LC 86-16678. ISBN 0-9465-7649-1 (hc); 0-9465-7643-2 (pb).

Morselt provides plot summaries for Christie's work, with separate chronologically arranged sections for the 66 novels and 143 short stories. Virtually no bibliographical data are provided. Entries in both sections list the work's title in boldface capital letters, provide a summary of rarely more than one page, and conclude with an entry number and the year of publication. An occasional section titled "Remarks" lists alternative titles and title changes without indicating preferences.

Following the summaries, a section titled "Whodunnits" provides the names of Christie's criminals (when such exist) keyed to the entries in the first two sections. The book contains numerical and alphabetical lists of all of the works summarized, a list of Christie's short story collections whose contents are keyed to the numerical lists (but whose titles are not revealed), and numerical lists of the works in which Miss Jane Marple, Hercule Poirot, Tommy and Tuppence, Parker Pyne, Colonel Race, and Superintendent Battle appear as characters.

Lacking in significant detail (Poirot's nonexistent brother Achille surely merits mention but is accorded none), by no means free from typos (*N or M?* is cited as *N of M?*), poorly arranged, and occasionally missing the point of the story (Morselt fails at providing a solution to *The Murder on the Orient Express*), this is a work only completists will want.

319.   Riley, Dick, and Pam McAllister, eds. **The Bedside, Bathtub & Armchair Companion to Agatha Christie**. Introduction by Julian Symons. New York: Frederick Ungar, 1979. xviii, 330 p. Index. LC 79-4822. ISBN 0-8044-5971-3 (hc); 0-8044-6733-1 (pb).

320.   Riley, Dick, and Pam McAllister, eds. **The New Bedside, Bathtub & Armchair Companion to Agatha Christie**. 2d ed. Foreword by Julian Symons. Additional material edited by Pam McAllister and Bruce Cassiday. New York: Ungar Publishing, 1986. xviii, 362 p. Index. LC 86-6960. ISBN 0-8044-5803-0 (hc); 0-8044-6725-0 (pb).

The expanded and revised 2d edition is described.

This heavily illustrated and highly frustrating guide provides signed synopses of every Christie novel and original play and many of the short stories, occasionally in conjunction with Christie's comments from her autobiographical writings. The arrangement is chronological by British book publication date. Each entry is prefaced with symbols indicating whether the work is a novel, play, or short story collection, and whether it features Hercule Poirot, Jane Marple, Ariadne Oliver, or Tuppence and Tommy Beresford. The entries provide the book's year of publication and a lengthy summary in which situations, characters, and motivations are described, but the solution is left unrevealed. Retitlings are also indicated.

If the *Companion* had contained only synopses, the book would be usable, though by no means as comprehensive as Saunders and Lovallo's work on the same subject (q.v.), but making this work unique are several dozen original essays on Christie-related topics. Murder weapons and victims are described; the history of the British police is expounded; motion picture adaptations are detailed; and English dishes are listed. A map shows key crime locations in Christie's fiction set in southern England, and there are crossword puzzles and double-crostics featuring the names of Christie's characters. Bruce Cassiday describes being murdered at an Agatha Christie weekend; there are descriptions of the events in the Detective Club that led to Christie contributing to "round robin" novels; and the filming of *Agatha*, the movie, is discussed.

Most of this material is unfortunately inaccessible, for the essays are in no discernible order. Summaries of *Death in the Air* and *The A. B. C. Murders* are interrupted by an appreciation of the movie version of *Murder on the Orient Express* and a "word-find" using the names of Christie's characters. Similarly, between the summaries of *N or M?* and *The Body in the Library* are a lengthy essay on Christie's writings as Mary Westmacott and a discussion of the history of the title and the motion picture adaptations of the work now known as *And Then There Were None*.

The volume concludes with lists of Christie on video, Christie editions in print, Christie's books arranged by detective, Christie's plays and short story collections, and a title index. (And interrupting these is a verse about Agatha Christie.) Devout fans and desperate researchers may want to use the *Bedside, Bathtub, and Armchair Companion*, but its value as a reference work is unfortunately low, and it contains little that is not better presented elsewhere.

321. Ryan, Richard T. **Agatha Christie Trivia**. Boston: Quinlan Press, 1987. Reprint: New York: Bell Publishing, 1990. 185 p. LC 89-18165. ISBN 0-517-69917-6.

Though sometimes listed as a reference book, this collection of trivia questions about Christie's writings has no research value. Its 12 sections each contain two parts: The first asks the questions, the second provides the answers. The book is superior to Andy East's *Agatha Christie Quizbook* (New York: Drake Publishers, 1975) in that there are more multiple-choice questions, but it contains no lists, no index, and nothing to benefit the student or researcher.

322. Santangelo, Elena. **Christie in Order**.

This chronologically arranged list of the works of Agatha Christie is available as a list maintained in the DorothyL archives and through the Miss Lemon webpage (http://www.iwillfollow.com/lemon.htm). The year of first publication is followed by the title of the work (in capital letters); alternative titles are given, as are the names of the detectives and a note indicating whether the work was a collection of short stories, a romance, or an original play. The original title of *And Then There Were None* is not provided.

323. Saunders, Dennis, and Len Lovallo. **The Agatha Christie Companion: The Complete Guide to Agatha Christie's Life and Work**. New York: Delacorte Press, 1984. xxvii, 523 p. Index. LC 83-5167. ISBN 0-38529285-6.

324. Saunders, Dennis, and Len Lovallo. **The Agatha Christie Companion: The Complete Guide to Agatha Christie's Life and Work**. Revised ed. New York: Berkley Books, 1989. xxviii, 498 p. Paperback. Index. LC 89-218325. ISBN 0-425-11845-2.

With thorough descriptions and evaluations of virtually all of Christie's prose, as well as equally thorough descriptions and evaluations of the dramatic adaptations of those works, *The Agatha Christie Companion* is one of the most comprehensive guides to Agatha Christie's works currently available.

Following a biographical sketch of Christie, the first section of the *Companion* contains a chronologically arranged list of Christie's books. Each book is accorded a separate chapter and given a number that reflects its publication order. The first British title is then listed, followed by any additional titles the book might have been given. The contents of each chapter describe the role that the book occupied in Christie's career and the circumstances surrounding its composition and reception. Poems and songs that inspired Christie are quoted at length, as are numerous contemporary reviews. A separate section describes the plot of the book, providing situations without revealing solutions; another section lists the names of the characters who play a role in the work. Data on the first British and American editions are provided. Each entry lists the place of publication, publisher's name, year of publication, pagination, retitling (if any), and original cost. Each book's entry concludes with a section listing the dramatic adaptations of the work; cast and credits are not provided, but there are enough details to locate the adaptation in the *Companion*'s second section, which provides data on the stage, motion picture, and television adaptations of Agatha Christie's works. Each medium is treated separately, but all entries provide the year in which the work was first performed, the circumstances behind the adaptation, contemporary reviews, and the casts of the first British and American performances. Numerical cross-references are provided, linking the title of the work to the description given in the first section of the *Companion*.

The third section of the *Companion* contains lists: alphabetical lists of Christie's books and short stories, and lists of books and short stories featuring Hercule Poirot, Jane Marple, Tommy and Tuppence Beresford, Mrs. Ariadne Oliver, Captain Arthur Hastings, Chief Inspector James Japp, Superintendent Battle, Colonel Johnny Race, Mr. Parker Pyne, and Mr. Harley Quin. A select bibliography and a Christie chronology follow. The *Companion* concludes with an excellent index to names and works.

The *Companion* is generally an exemplary achievement, but it is not without a few typographical errors. For some reason, it omits discussion of the work Christie wrote as a member of the Detection Club. More seriously, Sanders and Lovallo occasionally express critical judgments that are undeservedly harsh, assigning to the author sentiments that are expressed by her characters. In their discussion of *Cards on the Table*, for example, they assume that certain references to a "damned dago" are expressions of Christie's attitudes, and state that "it is not unusual while reading the early Christie novels to come across some racial and ethnic slurs. Christie was a product of her times, reflecting the middle- and upper-middle class English attitude towards foreigners."

These objections aside, the *Companion* is a superb achievement.

325. Sova, Dawn B. **Agatha Christie A to Z: The Essential Reference to Her Life and Writings**. Foreword by David Suchet. Introduction by Mathew Prichard. New York: Facts on File, 1996. xv, 400 p. Index. LC 95-48326. ISBN 0-8160-3018-9.

A volume that unfortunately delivers less than its title promises, *Agatha Christie A to Z* contains more than 2,500 encyclopedic entries, a majority of which consist of descriptions of Christie's characters and the works in which they appear. In addition, there are entries for significant people in Christie's life, a description of the facts known about Christie's disappearance in 1926, chapter-by-chapter synopses of all her mystery novels, summaries of all her stories, and references to stage, screen, and television adaptations of Christie's works. Furthermore, there are a number of illustrations, and the volume includes a separate list of Christie's works, a chronological list of the works, a bibliography of suggested readings, and a "categorical appendix" that lists the works by their detectives and by their murder methods. An excellent index concludes the volume.

Agatha Christie A to Z is a work with significant flaws. It is especially weak in providing adequate bibliographical data; the list of Christie's works is merely an alphabetically arranged hodgepodge whose purpose here is pointless. Similarly, only minimal first edition information is provided for the books; original publication data are not provided for the short stories; and retitlings are inadequately indicated. Only through careful reading of the entry for *And Then There Were None* can one learn Christie's original title for that novel, for Sova does not include a cross-reference from Christie's original title. The references to the stage, screen, and television adaptations provide neither casts nor credits, and the entries provide none of the data routinely given by Saunders and Lovallo in *The Agatha Christie Companion* (q.v.). Finally, Sova's facts occasionally leave something to be desired. She states that "The Blue Geranium" appeared "under the title, *The Tuesday Club Murders*, by Dodd, Mead and Company in New York," but this is simply not so; it was merely one story in the collection.

One longs for an expanded and corrected edition of this work.

326.   Toye, Randall. **The Agatha Christie Who's Who**. New York: Holt, Rinehart, and Winston, 1980. 264 p. Indexes. LC 80-14148. ISBN 0-03-057588-5.

Undoubtedly a labor of love, this most enjoyable guide provides biographical and identifying data on more than 2,000 of the memorable and significant characters created by Agatha Christie in her 66 novels and 147 short stories. Toye's delightful introduction explains that his initial catalogue contained more than 7,000 listings, but that he pared them down, eliminating "such miscellaneous characters as cousins and aunts, postmistresses and innkeepers, and chauffeurs and cooks." Toye thus refrained from citing Jane Marple's "village parallels," the people "who have experienced situations similar to the one Miss Marple is currently investigating and who indirectly help her find the solution to the problem," but he has cited the victims "who have died before the action of the story begins and who, though they do not actually appear, are important to the plot and therefore warrant an entry."

The names of the characters are in boldface type and are listed alphabetically by surname, followed by their first name. Nicknames are cited in parentheses, and if the character was also known by another name, an "also known as" note (AKA) and a cross-reference are provided. The function and identifying features of the character are listed, and each entry concludes with the name of the work in which the character appeared, the exception being Christie's most famous series characters. The works in which Arthur Hastings, Jane Marple, Ariadne Oliver, and Hercule Poirot appeared are listed in Appendix A.

The book concludes with a chronological listing of Christie's mystery novels and short stories. Differences between British and American titles are indicated, and stories in collections not published in the United States are cross-referenced to their subsequent appearances in U.S. collections. A separate index provides a title index to the bibliography, and Appendix B lists the works by Agatha Christie (plays, her romantic novels as Mary Westmacott, autobiographies, and children's titles) that have not been indexed.

In all, this is an exemplary work, enlivened by a number of illustrations and by Toye's obvious affection for his subject. Jon Breen's comment, that "there is at least one glaring omission: there is no entry on Mr. Parker Pyne, just a 'see' reference to a criminal who once disguised himself as Pyne" (*What About Murder*, p. 137), is in error: Parker Pyne's entry is to be found under "Parker Pyne, Christopher."

327.   Underwood, Lynn, ed. **Agatha Christie: Official Centenary Edition, 1890–1990**. England: Belgrave Publishing for Agatha Christie Centenary Trust, 1990. 98 p. Paperback. LC 90-51017. ISBN 0-006-37675-4. Also: New York: HarperCollins, 1990. 98 p. Paperback. ISBN 0-06-100126-0.

Not a reference book, this glossy, heavily illustrated work deserves to be mentioned for several reasons. It contains a chronological list of Christie's novels and short story collections; a complete list of her plays that includes directors, casts, and premiere dates; a complete list of her films that includes directors and stars; and information about her characters. Although this information is engagingly presented, none of this information is unique to this volume. Nevertheless, a surprising depth is achieved through brief essays on the world in which Christie matured, examinations of Christie's notebooks that reveal the writer's mind at work, and an account of her only child Rosalind. Reprinted in this volume is "Trap for the Unwary," a short story previously published in 1923 in a short-lived periodical called *The Novel*, and published for the first time is an article by Christie on her relationship with her paperback publisher Allen Lane. Although predictions by Christie's grandson end the book, the volume effectively concludes with the moving funeral speech delivered by Sir William Collins, Christie's publisher for 50 years.

328. Wilson, Michael. **St. Mary Mead Public Library: An Agatha Christie Booklist.** http://ccwf.cc.utexas.edu/~kmwilcox/Agatha/

Containing neither a picture of nor biographical data about Christie, this chronological list offers a reasonably lengthy but not complete or accurate bibliography of Christie's detective and mystery books. British titles are listed first, with a note mentioning the American title. The contents of short story collections are given, as is a note indicating when the British edition differed from the American edition. Appearances of Christie's major series characters are noted. A significant problem is that bibliographic data are not reliable. Unpleasant though it is to our sensibilities, there is no denying that one of Christie's finest novels was first titled *Ten Little Niggers*, and to list the book *And Then There Were None*, mentioning only the other title *Ten Little Indians*, is to evade bibliographic responsibility. Choose instead the sites by Jonasson, Strong, and Woodbury (q.q.v.).

329. Woodbury, Roger. **The Web Companion to Agatha Christie.** http://www.nd. edu/~rwoodbur/christie/christie.htm

It is Woodbury's goal to provide a website that contains a chronology of Agatha Christie's mystery novels, plays, and short story collections. Ultimately it will provide for each novel a complete list of major and minor characters, a brief synopsis of the plot, and a spoiler, revealing the identity of the criminal. As of this writing, a chronological list of Christie's works is available, lists of Christie's works by detective are given, and several of Christie's novels have been annotated.

330. Wynne, Nancy Blue. **An Agatha Christie Chronology.** New York: Ace Books, 1976. 266 p. Paperback.

The first reference book devoted to Agatha Christie, the *Chronology* has obviously been assembled as a labor of love by a passionate devotee whose knowledge of the history of mystery and detective stories is minimal. The first page of the first entry states that "prior to 1920, the detective story was almost purely a short story form," revealing the author's ignorance of the presence of thousands of novels. Soon thereafter comes a comment that R. Austin Freeman "wrote only in the short story form," which will come as a surprise to those who love his many novels.

The first section of the *Chronology* consists of chronologically arranged appreciations of Christie's work; each book is accorded a separate chapter. Titlings and retitlings are not consistently applied. Unpleasant though it is to modern sensibilities, there is no denying that one of Christie's finest novels was first titled *Ten Little Niggers*, and to list the book first as *And Then There Were None* is to evade bibliographic responsibility. Wynne's appreciations are virtually uniform in praise of Christie's work; they are chatty and filled with exclamation points and demonstrate no critical acumen. Worse, they occasionally reveal the gimmick or solution.

Following sections link Christie's short stories to their first book publication; list her short stories published in anthologies between 1928 and 1973; list all her titles in chronological order; list the books in which Poirot, Marple, Tuppence and Tommy, Ariadne Oliver, and Superintendent Battle appear; list Christie's nonmystery books, omnibus volumes, and plays; and provide a bibliography of her works. The latter is arranged alphabetically and provides place of publication, publisher, year of publication, and pagination for all English-language hardcover editions known to exist. Determining first edition and/or priorities is impossible. The *Chronology* concludes with a brief biography of Christie.

Dated and worthless to researchers.

331.   Yaffe, Ben. **Agatha Christie**. http://www.dalton.org/students/bkyaffe/wwwac/achome.html

Contains a few photographs and a brief biography of Christie, and offers a link to a selective secondary bibliography. Yaffe now runs a Christie discussion group at http://www.books.com.

331a. **Agatha Christie Society**
       P.O. Box 985
       London, SW1X 9XA
       England

Mary Higgins Clark

332.   Clark, Mary Higgins. **Mary Higgins Clark**. http://www.simonsays.com/mhclark/

Clark's official website is produced by her publishers, Simon and Schuster. It provides an interview with Clark ("friendly interrogations"), biographical information, a few pictures of Clark, and significant information on her books. The titles are listed alphabetically, with connections to information about the paperback edition, audiobook edition, and movie tie-in. Citations provide the publisher, year of publication, pagination, cost, and ISBN. A summary is provided, as are a text excerpt and excerpts from positive reviews area, setting, and principal characters and their roles. Finally, there are connections to a bulletin board for Clark fans and to a mailing list that provides information on forthcoming titles and as a way to learn about Clark. Would that all publishers served their authors so well.

Liza Cody

333. Tangled Web. **Liza Cody: Anna Lee & Eva Wylie**. http://www.twbooks. co.uk/authors/lcody.html

This website provides a brief biography but no photograph of its subject. Cover reproductions and jacket information are given, as are excerpts from positive reviews and indications when the work has won an award. A list of Cody's works concludes the bibliography, but there are no bibliographical data. Moreover, Cody's real name is not revealed.

Wilkie Collins

334. Andrew, R. V. **Wilkie Collins: A Critical Survey of His Prose Fiction with a Bibliography**. New York: Garland, 1979. 358 p. (Fiction of Popular Culture). LC 78-60801. ISBN 0-8240-9667-3.

Sometimes cited as a reference book, this work began its life in 1959 as a thesis presented at the Potchefstroom University for C. H. E. in South Africa; the Garland edition is the offset typed thesis. The vast majority of the book is Andrew's observations about Collins; the bibliography does not commence until page 338. The first part of the bibliography lists its citations alphabetically, the second chronologically. In both sections, titles of books, short stories, and journals are given in capital letters, making locating a reference quite difficult; nor are paginations provided. Furthermore, Andrew's typing was not of the highest quality, and the bibliography contains a number of overstrikes. Though Andrew's work was once significant, the full-length bibliographies compiled by Beetz and Parrish and Miller (q.q.v.) are better.

335. Beetz, Kirk H. **Wilkie Collins: An Annotated Bibliography, 1889–1976**. Metuchen, NJ: Scarecrow Press, 1978. viii, 167 p. Index. (Scarecrow Author Bibliographies, no. 35). LC 77-26609. ISBN 0-8108-1103-0.

Beetz's contribution to Collins studies begins with a capable 21-page bibliographical essay; each of its 82 paragraphs is numbered and separately indexed. The bibliography contains three sections: The first cites Collins's works, the second lists criticism and scholarship about Collins, and the third covers selected book reviews. Primary and secondary citations are continuously numbered; in all, 688 articles, books, chapters, dissertations, and book reviews are cited. Book citations are underlined and provide place of publication, publisher, year of publication, series, and pagination. Citations to articles are generally by author, with the title of the article in quotations, the journal name underlined, and the volume, month, publication year, and pagination given. Anonymous articles are listed under the journal's name. The volume concludes with separate indexes for authors, editors, illustrators, and subjects.

Though its contents are as thorough as can be reasonably hoped, the arrangement and layout of this book can be frustrating. The primary bibliography starts by listing different editions of Collins's collected works. This list is followed by an alphabetical list of the different editions of his novels and other book-length works, a list of his plays, a list of his short works and correspondence (with books devoted solely to Collins and works in collections not devoted solely to Collins separated), and lists of his collaborations with Charles Dickens. The arrangement of the secondary bibliography is even more cumbersome, with separate sections for books, periodical articles, and dissertations. The section for books arranges its citations into the following sections: biographical, bibliographical, assessments of Collins's life and works, discussions of individual works, influences on Collins, Collins's reputation and influence, correspondence (written by and to Collins), and other scholarship.

The primary bibliographies provided by M. L. Parrish and Elizabeth V. Miller in their *Wilkie Collins and Charles Reade: First Editions Described with Notes* (q.v.), as well as those of Michael Sadleir in his *Excursions in Victorian Bibliography* (London: Chaundy & Cox, 1922) and his *XIX Century Fiction: A Bibliographic Record Based on His Own Collection* (London: Constable; Berkeley: University of California Press, 1951), are significantly clearer those provided by Beetz, and they have the added blessing of being chronologically arranged. Nevertheless, Beetz offers comprehensiveness in his citations, whereas Parrish and Miller, and Sadleir, do not. In addition, Beetz's secondary bibliography and annotations make this a useful acquisition. It is to be preferred to the work of R. V. Andrew (q.v.).

336. Grigg, David R. **Wilkie Collins Appreciation Page**. http://www.ozemail. com.au/~drgrigg/wilkie.html

One of two excellent websites devoted to Victorian writer Wilkie Collins (1824–1889), this site contains a photograph of its subject, a biography, and an incomplete bibliography. Books about Collins are listed and annotated, and information on electronic editions of Collins's work is given, as is information about Wilkie Collins societies, media adaptations of Collins, illustrations from his work, and links to other sites. This site complements the Wilkie Collins site of Paul Lewis (below).

337. Lewis, Paul. **Wilkie Collins**. http://www.deadline.demon.co.uk/wilkie/ wilkie.htm

The second of two fine websites devoted to Wilkie Collins, this one offers a photograph of its subject, a brief biography, and links to the full text of Collins's will, electronically available texts of some of Collins's lesser-known works, and photographs and prose descriptions of the houses in which Collins lived. In addition, there are excerpts of Collins's writings about his friend Charles Dickens, details about Collins's first novel *Iolani*, and a selective annotated list of books about Collins. The bibliographic data in this last include author, title, publisher, place and year of publication, ISBN, and data on reprint editions. Finally, there is a large image of Collins, information on his monogram, and a useful guide to Victorian money and coins. This site complements the Wilkie Collins site of David Grigg (above).

338. Parrish, M. L., with Elizabeth V. Miller. **Wilkie Collins and Charles Reade: First Editions (with a Few Exceptions) in the Library of Dormy House, Pine Valley, New Jersey**. London: Constable, 1940. x, 355 p. Index. LC 41-19254. (150 copies printed.) Reprinted as: **Wilkie Collins and Charles Reade: First Editions Described with Notes**. New York: Burt Franklin, 1968. x, 355 p. Index. LC 68-4143.

The first 161 pages of this well-done bibliography describe Collins's writings with exemplary thoroughness, the majority of the citations being derived from the Wilkie Collins collection privately held in Dormy House, New Jersey. The citations in the bibliography are not numbered, but this in no way impedes its usefulness.

The book is divided into four lettered sections, the first of which is a Collins biography; it reprints several letters by Collins that contain extensive biographical data. The bibliography is a chronological list of all separately published first English-language editions in the collection. Each entry provides an exhaustive analytical bibliographical description of these books, transcribing their title pages, noting number of volumes and size of paper, and giving the books' collation, pagination, contents, illustrations, binding, publication, and printing. Variant editions are noted, and a section called "Notes" provides additional information about the publication histories and contents of the books. Letters inlaid in these books are transcribed in full, and reproductions of title pages are provided in several instances.

The third section is "Errata in Works of Wilkie Collins" and contains lengthy lists of all of the typographical errors in the editions described in the first section. The concluding section, "Posters and Programmes of the Plays of Wilkie Collins," describes the posters and theater programs that advertised Collins's dramatic works. Reproductions of several of these posters and programs are provided. A very thorough index concludes the volume.

Though somewhat dated, this remains the most thorough Collins bibliography extant.

D. G. Compton

339. Tangled Web. **D. G. Compton and Alex Duncan**. http://www.twbooks. co.uk/authors/dgcompton.html

Concentrating on Compton's mysteries rather than his science fiction, this site provides a two-sentence biography and has no photograph of its subject. Dustwrapper images are provided, as are jacket material and excerpts from positive reviews. The site concludes with a list of Compton's mysteries, publishers, years of publication, and names of starring detectives.

Patricia Cornwell

340. Ahearn, Allen, and Patricia Ahearn. **Author Price Guides: Patricia Cornwell**. Rockville, MD: Quill & Brush, 1996. 3 leaves. APG 155.

This Author's Price Guide documents Patricia Cornwell's publications from the 1983 *A Time for Remembering* to the 1996 *Cause of Death*.

For a thorough description of the format of Author Price Guides, see the entry under Fredric Brown.

341. Junot, Jim. **The Patricia Cornwell Web Site**. http://www.louisville.edu/ ~jsjuno01/pc.html

Not quite as comprehensive as the Cornwell site maintained by Birger Nielsen (q.v.), this one nevertheless includes a photograph and biographical data on its subject and offers lengthy information on the Kay Scarpetta books. Links offer access to Cornwell's publisher's website, lists of her bestsellers, reviews of her books, sites with information on Cornwell's audiobooks, sound files containing excerpts from the Scarpetta novels, and secondary sources offering information about Cornwell. There are numerous links.

342. Nielsen, Birger. **Patricia Cornwell Bibliography**. http://hjem.get2net.dk/ bnielsen/cornwell.html

Following a picture and a capably written biography of Cornwell, this website offers descriptions and summaries of Cornwell's novels (as of July 1996). The victims in each book are named, and the date of their deaths are given. A list of inconsistencies in the novels is provided (e.g., "In *Body of Evidence* pages 320–22 Kay Scarpetta is in her home during a power black out. Nonetheless her answering machine keeps working") and is followed by a probable chronology for the life of Kay Scarpetta. Descriptions of Cornwell's series characters are provided, as are links to quotations about Scarpetta's background, unusual abbreviations used in the novels, and selected reviews of each of her novels, profiles of the author, and lists of places that might have additional information on Cornwell. Finally, the dedication in each of Cornwell's novels is given, and there is a list of the real-life models for a number of Cornwell's characters. A gratifyingly thorough site, somewhat unusual in that it admits that its subject's prose is occasionally less than perfect.

343. Tangled Web. **Patricia Cornwell**. http://www.twbooks.co.uk/authors/ pcornwell.html

The weakest of the three Cornwell websites considered here, this British site provides a photograph of its subject, a brief biography, and cover reproductions and jacket information from only two of her books. A few excerpts from positive reviews are provided. The concluding bibliography lists titles and publishers but does not provide year of publication.

Anthony Berkeley Cox

344.   Johns, Ayresome [George Locke]. **The Anthony Berkeley Cox Files: Notes Towards a Bibliography**. London: Ferret Fantasy, 1993. 32 p. Paperback. (300 copies printed.)

The only separately published bibliography of the works of Anthony Berkley Cox (1893–1971), this volume is cleanly offset from word-processed copy and contains the following sections: A) British first editions; D) dustjackets of British first editions; B) contributions to books; C) contributions to periodicals; CB) contributions to periodicals: "Brenda" stories; CD) contributions to periodicals: "Down Our Road"; M) a catalogue of manuscripts; MB) a catalogue of manuscripts: "Brenda" stories; MD) a catalogue of manuscripts: "Down Our Road" stories; P) plays, radio, films, and other media; and an unlettered section titled "Who Was Francis Iles?—The Debate." The entries in each section are separately numbered and lettered; in sections A and D, the book's title is given in boldface capital letters. The contents of all sections are chronologically arranged.

Descriptions of the British first editions provide a transcription of the title page of the book, a collation of its pagination and contents, a description of its binding, a reference to the description of its dustjacket, the date upon which the British Museum Library's copy was accessioned, and notes about the contents of the work. If the book had an American edition, it is cited. The description of the dustjackets of the British editions is equally thorough, with each citation transcribing the contents of the spine, front panel, rear panel, front flap, and rear flap.

The majority of this bibliography is devoted to describing Cox's contributions to periodicals and his numerous extant manuscripts. The former provide the name of the work, title of periodical that published it, and date of publication, and include a cross-reference to its publication in book form or the existence of its manuscript or both. The descriptions of the manuscripts provide the title of the work, length, and whether a carbon or a ribbon copy, and include a cross-reference to its original publication.

Although the contents are often cramped, and a title index would have been helpful, the bibliography is reasonably easy to use and thorough. Each copy of this bibliography has the typescript of one of Cox's manuscripts tipped into it.

Camilla Crespi

345.   Crespi, Camilla T. **The Trouble with Simona Griffo**. http://members.aol. com/camcrespi/Intro.html

Camilla Crespi is one of the names used by Camilla Trinchieri, whose best-known mystery series feature Simona Griffo, a transplanted Italian who works in a New York advertising agency; all titles featuring Griffo start with *The Trouble with . . .* and conclude with an Italian recipe. Crespi's website provides an autobiography, a picture of herself, and descriptions of each of her books. Cover art is provided, as are year of publication, publisher, ISBN, a statement about where Crespi got her ideas, story's setting, plot, an excerpt, and excerpts from positive reviews. A cheerful site, enhanced by the presence of the original recipes from each book.

Edmund Crispin

346. Nedblake, William. **The Edmund Crispin Archive.** http://www.kc.net/~nedblake/RootDocs/crispin.html

Provides biographical data on Crispin, the name under which talented writer and composer Bruce Montgomery wrote nine mysteries and two short story collections featuring Gervase Fen. A list of these works is given as are their synopses, and links to reviews and bibliographic data are present.

James Crumley

347. Ahearn, Allen, and Patricia Ahearn. **Author Price Guides: James Crumley.** Rockville, MD: Quill & Brush, 1995. 3 leaves. APG 032.3.

This Author's Price Guide to James Crumley documents his work from the 1969 appearance of *One to Count Cadence* to the 1995 publication of *The Mexican Tree Duck*.

For a thorough description of the format of Author Price Guides, see the entry under Fredric Brown.

Judith Cutler

348. Tangled Web. **Judith Cutler.** http://www.twbooks.co.uk/authors/jcutler.html

This site contains a photograph of its subject and provides a brief biography, cover illustrations, and jacket information from Cutler's two novels. Excerpts from positive reviews are given. The concluding bibliography is chronologically arranged and provides publisher and year of publication, and the detective's name.

Mary Daheim

349. Daheim, Mary. **Mary Daheim Page.** http://members.aol.com/ktbooks/daheim.htm

Mary Daheim's web page provides a picture of her, a biography, and information about her two series set in and around the Pacific Northwest. The books are listed chronologically by series, and viewers can read an excerpt from the latest novel in each of the series. Some cover illustrations are provided, but more illustrations and excerpts would certainly be welcome.

Carroll John Daly

350. Pulp Fiction Central. **Carroll John Daly Online!** http://www.vintagelibrary. com/pulp/daly/daly.htm

Commercial sites are not generally included in this work, but this site is mentioned because it contains information on Carroll John Daly, the man who can be said to have established the hard-boiled detective story. A biographical statement provides little information about Daly but mentions his importance. The site includes links to Daly stories available in electronic format—for a price.

Barbara D'Amato

351. D'Amato, Barbara. **Books by Barbara D'Amato**. http://www. barbaradamato.com/

D'Amato's home page provides a picture of her, a biographical sketch, and images of her books, complete with ISBNs. Each image tale is linked to a summary, the book's first chapter, questions and answers about the books, a biographical profile, and extracts from positive reviews. The biographical profile includes a picture and a chronological list of D'Amato's currently available books that includes paperback editions as well as hardcovers. This is a nicely done site.

Avram Davidson

352. Wessells, Henry. **Avram Davidson**. http://www.kosmic.org/members/ dongle/henry/

It is debatable whether Avram Davidson was better known as a writer of fantasies or as a writer of mysteries, but as Davidson won both the Queen's Award and the Edgar Award for the latter, this website deserves mention. It is gratifyingly thorough, containing links to a short list of books by Davidson, material about him, information on the Davidson Award (given to "The Best Beloved Out-of-Print Works of Imaginative Fiction"), Davidson ephemera, useful information and resources, detailed bibliographic information, and an index to the author's writings. The list of Davidson books provides title, place of publication, publisher, and year of publication, with a note indicating whether the work was a paperback. Often its series number is provided, changes of title and retitlings are indicated, and ISBNs are occasionally provided, as are references to reviews. Davidson's ephemera includes images and bibliographic data on the unauthorized Russian editions of Davidson's writings. The list of Davidson's publications is a comprehensive alphabetical list of his work, providing title of the work and date and place of its first publication. Anthologizations and reprintings of short fiction are noted, as are the lengths of the unpublished stories existing in manuscript form.

Davidson lovers will appreciate this thorough and well-produced site.

Diane Mott Davidson

353. Reid, Sharon. **The Unofficial Diane Mott Davidson Webpage.** http://
members.aol.com/biblioholc/goldy.html

This appears to be the only site devoted to Diane Mott Davidson. It contains a chronological list of five Davidson mysteries published from 1990 to 1995. The publisher, year of publication, and ISBN for each are given, as are a summary of the mystery and a critical comment. The site concludes with brief biographical information about Davidson. The wood-grain background occasionally makes reading difficult

Linda Davies

354. Davies, Linda. **Financial Thrillers by Linda Davies.** http://www.ex.ac.uk/
~RDavies/arian/linda.html

Linda Davies's website provides her photograph, a biographical statement, and links to magazine and electronic profiles about her and to information about her books. The latter provide a cover illustration, a summary of and an extract from the novel, and a thorough bibliography of every known edition and every known translation. This very capably done site is maintained by Linda's brother Roy.

355. Tangled Web. **Linda Davies.** http://www.twbooks.co.uk/authors/
ldavies.html

Containing far less information than Davies's own page (q.v.), this site provides a photograph, a brief biography, and cover reproductions of her books. Excerpts from positive reviews are given. Prefer the author's own page.

Lindsey Davis

356. Tangled Web. **Lindsey Davis.** http://www.twbooks.co.uk/authors/
ldavis.html

This site is unique among the Tangled Web sites in that it offers an autobiographical statement in place of the usual anonymous sketch. A photograph of Davis is provided, as are reproductions of the covers of some of her books and their accompanying dustwrapper information. Excerpts from positive reviews are also provided as are a biographical sketch of detective Marcus Didius Falco. The concluding bibliography is chronologically arranged. It provides the publisher and year of publication (most of the time) and lists the books in which Falco appears.

Dianne Day

357. Day, Dianne. **Fremont Jones: A Few Words from the Author.**
http://members.aol.com/dianneday/

The author's home page provides a photograph and biographical data. A list of her works, including those done under pseudonyms Madelyn Sanders and Diana Bane, is provided, and much space is devoted to Day's best-known character, Fremont Jones, a young woman who left Boston to go to San Francisco during the nineteenth century. There are links to her titles that offer cover reproductions, descriptions, and critics' comments. Earlier versions offered images of the historical photographs that helped Day in her research and contained links to "The Anachronistic Women's Page," which provides documentation about women who were considered "ahead of their time." One hopes they are restored.

Marele Day

358. Tangled Web. **Marele Day and Claudia Valentine PI.** http://www.twbooks.co.uk/authors/mareled.html

This site provides a brief biography of Day and offers information about her novels featuring private investigator Claudia Valentine. Cover reproductions are accompanied by descriptions of the contents and excerpts from reviews. The concluding bibliography is more thorough than the majority of the usual Tangled Web efforts, providing publication data for hardcover as well as paperback editions.

Cecil Day-Lewis

359. Handley-Taylor, Geoffrey, and Timothy D'Arch Smith. **Day-Lewis, the Poet Laureate: A Bibliography.** With a Letter of Introduction by W. H. Auden. Chicago and London: St. James Press, 1968. xii, 42 p. Index. LC 73-1604. ISBN 0-900997-00-1.

From 1968 until his death in 1972, Cecil Day-Lewis was the Poet Laureate of England. In addition, from 1935 until 1968, using the pseudonym Nicholas Blake, Day-Lewis wrote some 20 detective novels featuring Oxford graduate Nigel Strangeways as detective, apparently modeled on Day-Lewis's friend, poet W. H. Auden. This bibliography of the works of C. Day-Lewis begins with a delightful letter from Auden, whose penultimate sentence states that the bibliography "does, however, make reference to that secretive character N******* B****, who has given more pleasure to more people than, in our age, any writer of verses can ever hope to give." This is followed by acknowledgments, a "bibliographical note" that explains the principles used to compile the body of the volume, and a poem by Day Lewis, "Sunday Afternoon," which is original to this book.

The bibliography itself contains three sections: books and pamphlets by C. Day-Lewis; books and pamphlets with contributions by C. Day-Lewis; and detective stories by C. Day-Lewis under the pseudonym of Nicholas Blake. The data in the first two sections are very thorough. Each item is separately numbered. Titles are given in capital letters; in smaller capitals are listed the place of publication and the publisher, and the publisher's address appears in italics. Also provided are paper size, pagination, a description of the book's binding, the exact publication date, and references to American editions and to locations of the manuscripts of the poems. References to periodical publications are not included.

The final section, however, is merely a chronological list of the titles of Day-Lewis's mysteries, accompanied only by the dates of their first publications. Day-Lewis's most popular and enduring writings are thus marginalized and dismissed, an indefensible action on the part of the bibliographers.

This is the only book-length bibliography of Day-Lewis. A comprehensive and sympathetic bibliography remains to be done.

Jeffery Deaver

360. Tangled Web. **Jeffery Deaver**. http://www.twbooks.co.uk/authors/jdeaver.html

This site provides a photograph of Deaver, a brief biography, cover reproductions, and the prose from the covers of his books. Excerpts from positive reviews and the full text of selected reviews are given. The concluding bibliography provides data on the first British editions of Deaver's books.

Lester Dent

361. Cannaday, Marilyn. **Bigger Than Life: The Creator of Doc Savage**. Bowling Green, OH: Bowling Green State University Popular Press, 1990. 201 p. Index. LC 89-085739. ISBN 0-87972-471-4 (hc); 0-87972-472-2 (pb).

362. McCarey-Laird, M. Martin. **Lester Dent: The Man, His Craft and His Market**. West Des Moines, IA: Hidalgo Publishing, 1994. 104 p. Paperback. Index. LC 94-076268. ISBN 0-9641004-9-5.

363. Weinberg, Robert, ed. **Lester Dent: The Man Behind Doc Savage**. Cover Ttitle: **The Man Behind Doc Savage: A Tribute to Lester Dent**. Oak Lawn, IL: Robert Weinberg, 1974. 127 p. Paperback.

Lester Dent wrote the majority of the 181 *Doc Savage* novels, a number of lively mysteries, and numerous short stories published in pulp magazines ranging from *Argosy* and *Black Mask* to *Nation's Business* and the *Saturday Evening Post*. It is thus surprising that, as of this writing, there is no comprehensive and separately published bibliography of his writings. The three books discussed below are among the most widely accessible studies of Dent, but others exist, in particular a series of booklets written by Will Murray and published by Odyssey Publications of Massachusetts.

Marilyn Cannaday's biography of Dent is a lengthy and affectionate tribute. It contains illustrations, though these tend to be of Dent and his relations, and it reprints "The Pulp Paper Master Fiction Plot" (also in Weinberg) and an article by Dent ("Wave Those Tags") first published in the 1940 *Writer's Digest Yearbook*. Particularly useful is a partial checklist of Dent's published fiction. Arranged chronologically, it lists the title of the work and the place of publication. Titles of stories appearing in *Doc Savage* are capitalized. On the debit side, the book is not without error; for example, Dent did not write boys' series books for Grosset and Dunlap under the name John Baine. Furthermore, Cannaday's discussion of Dent's "Oscar Sail" stories is surprisingly (and perhaps uncomfortably) reminiscent of the discussion by Robert Sampson first published in *Lester Dent: The Man Behind Doc Savage*.

Lester Dent: The Man, His Craft and His Market began its life as a 1979 master's thesis by Margaret Gwinn of Northeast Missouri State University in Kirksville, MO. It was revised for publication, but the revisions did not redress numerous factual errors, and McCarey-Laird's writing is distressingly poor. Dent's vital personality occasionally reveals itself through quoted interviews, letters, and articles, but he would have been hard put to praise this amateurish effort.

Lester Dent: The Man Behind Doc Savage is reproduced from typed copy and is heavily illustrated with black-and-white reproductions of the covers of magazines in which Dent appeared. It contains eight chapters of criticism. Three by Will Murray discuss aspects of *Doc Savage*; three by Robert Sampson discuss Dent's writings apart from *Doc Savage*; one by Robert Weinberg provides a biographical profile of Dent; and one by Philip José Farmer provides an account of Farmer's *Doc Savage: His Apocalyptic Life*. There are also chapters reprinting Dent's formula for plotting ("The Pulp Paper Master Fiction Plot") and two of Dent's lesser-known short stories. Although riddled with typos and unfortunately amateurish in appearance, the work is not without its uses, for its contents are valuable and not readily accessible elsewhere.

August Derleth

364. Derleth, August. **August Derleth: Twenty Years of Writing, 1926–1946**. Sauk City, WI: Arkham House, 1946. 20 p. Paperback.

365. Derleth, August. **August Derleth: Twenty-Five Years of Writing, 1926–1951**. 2d ed. Sauk City, WI: Arkham House, 1951. 24 p. Paperback.

366.   Derleth, August. **August Derleth: Thirty Years of Writing, 1926–1956**. 3d ed. Sauk City, WI: Arkham House, 1956. 30 p. Paperback.

367.   Derleth, August. **100 Books by August Derleth**. [4th ed.] Foreword by Donald Wandrei. Sauk City, WI: Arkham House, 1962. 121 p. LC 63-4567. (1,225 copies: 200 hardbound, 1,025 paperbound.)

During his lifetime, Derleth was noted as a regionalist writer and acclaimed for his mysteries and weird fiction. Today his mysteries are all but forgotten, and he is remembered largely for his posthumous collaborations with H. P. Lovecraft and for establishing Arkham House, the oldest and finest specialty publisher of weird fiction, in 1939. Because the first three versions of this bibliography were never advertised for sale but were given gratis to the regular customers of Derleth's Arkham House, it is debatable whether they were formally published; in any event, they have not been seen. There is no doubt, however, that the 4th edition was formally published; indeed, the 200 hardbound copies were intended primarily for the library market.

Following a foreword by Donald Wandrei (cofounder of Arkham House and a talented writer in his own right), *100 Books by August Derleth* contains the following sections: "Biographical" (autobiographical as well as excerpts from reference books); "Bibliographical" (a listing of the titles of the publications that have published Derleth's short stories, essays, reviews, poetry, and miscellaneous prose since 1 April 1926); "A Checklist of Published Books" (a chronological listing of 102 of Derleth's cloth or board-bound volumes, with the exception of hardcover reprints); "Awaiting Publication" (14 books); "Work in Progress" (9 books); "Summary" (Derleth's books listed by series [e.g., the Judge Peck mysteries] and broad subject [e.g., "Books for younger readers"]); "Recordings" (two recordings are cited; the contents of one are given); "Compilations" (lists of the works compiled by Derleth or that have Derleth introductions or both); "Anthologies/Textbooks" (citations to the anthologies and textbooks that have published Derleth's short stories, poems, and miscellaneous prose); "Publications" (a list of the Arkham House books that have not been cited in the preceding sections of this bibliography); "Films" (the titles of 15 of Derleth's short stories that were adapted for television); "Lectures" (titles of the nine subjects upon which Derleth delivered occasional lectures); "Appraisals" (excerpts from the favorable criticism of notable writers); "From the Reviews" (excerpts from favorable reviews); and "Self-Appraisal" (Derleth's list of his 10 best works). A reproduction of a diploma from "Miskatonic University" concludes the publication.

The "Checklist of Published Books" occupies the majority of this bibliography and contains the fullest data. Each citation is numbered. The titles are given in capital letters and provide publisher, place, and year of publication; pagination; and initial cost. Title changes are indicated, as are names of illustrators and dustwrapper designers and data on international editions known to Derleth. The contents of Derleth-edited anthologies are also given, an invaluable list. Oddly enough, Derleth neglected to number his original paperback appearances, and such works as his *Some Notes on H. P. Lovecraft* (Sauk City, Wisconsin: Arkham

House, 1959) appear in their chronological sequence without being counted. (A more accurate title for this publication would be *105 Books by August Derleth*.)

The other sections contain far less data and, more often than not, are mere lists of titles, arousing curiosity without satisfying it. The section titled "Bibliographical," for example, lists only titles of publications in which Derleth's work appeared, not the publication data for Derleth's appearance, and it is prefaced with a headnote that speaks of "the byline of August Derleth or one of his pen names." The pen names, however, are given nowhere.

Lacking a title index, incomplete (Derleth continued producing virtually until his death in 1971), and reminiscent of a vanity publication, *100 Books by August Derleth* is nevertheless more than the product of an oversized ego. Derleth's remarkable achievements and versatility make him a significant figure in several distinct areas, and that he was not a trained bibliographer in no way invalidates the importance of this work.

Note: *100 Books by August Derleth* was also reprinted in 1974 by E. V. A. Publishers of Sauk City, Wisconsin (LC 74-162941), but this is a facsimile of the 1962 edition and contains no new data.

368. Dutch, William, and others. **August Derleth (1909–1971): A Bibliographical Checklist of His Works**. Shelburne, ON: Battered Silicon Dispatch Box/George A. Vanderburgh, 1996. 76 p. Paperback. Index. LC 96-86124. ISBN 1-896648-14-2.

The cover of this book has as its subtitle "A Selective Checklist of His Books and Assorted Commentary by Many Hands," an assessment of the book's contents more accurate than that found on the title page, for this is not intended to serve as a comprehensive bibliography of Derleth's works. It contains the following sections: "An Autobiography" by August Derleth; "August Derleth: Storyteller of the Sac Prairie" by Norbert Blei; *A Bibliographical Checklist of the Books of August Derleth*; "Addenda: Derleth Bibliography" by Alison M. Wilson; *About August Derleth: The Writings about the Writings*; *The August Derleth Society Newsletters*; and *August Derleth Society Newsletters* [New Series]. In addition, there are two appendixes: "Abbreviations for The Solar Pons Canon" by Peter Ruber, Ronald B. de Waal, and George A. Vanderburg, and *August Derleth: The Writings by Genre*. There is an index to titles.

The chronologically arranged "Bibliographical Checklist" cites the books written by and edited by Derleth. Titles are listed in italicized boldface type, and the place of publication, publisher, and year of publication are provided for all known editions. Data are current into 1997 and each citation concludes with a one- or two-word description of the book's contents. Alison Wilson's addenda to her bibliography (q.v.) is alphabetical in arrangement and provides reprint data for more than 100 of Derleth's writings. Each citation provides the title in boldface type, gives its original publication, and lists beneath it the sources in which the reprint appeared. Book titles are given in italics; editor's names are listed, and the publisher, place of publication, and year of publication are given.

The titles of periodicals are also italicized, and the month and year of publication are given.

"The Writings about the Writings" cites 11 books about Derleth; articles are not listed. The sections devoted to the different series of the August Derleth Society's *Newsletter* consist of an issue-by-issue listing of the contents of the 65 issues published to date (52 issues in the first series, 13 issues in the new series).

Researchers interested in Derleth and the areas in which he worked and published will want this publication, but it is an item for specialists.

369. Wilson, Alison M. **August Derleth: A Bibliography**. Metuchen, NJ: Scarecrow Press, 1983. xxvi, 229 p. Index. (Scarecrow Author Bibliographies, no. 59). LC 82-24020. ISBN 0-8108-1606-7.

Wilson conceived of this bibliography while writing an entry on Derleth for Gale's Dictionary of Literary Biography and initially planned to annotate all of Derleth's published work. The size of Derleth's published output made her reconsider her goal, but she has nevertheless annotated virtually everything cited in this volume. After providing an introduction and a chronology to Derleth, Wilson divides the author's output into two broad sections: "The Fantasy World: Mystery, Science Fiction, and Horror"; and "Sac Prairie and the Real World." Each of these sections is in turn subdivided. The first contains the following sections: "Short Stories," "Anthologies of Derleth's Own Work," " 'Posthumous Collaborations' with H. P. Lovecraft," "Collaboration with Mark Schorer," "Collaborations: Books," "The Pontine Canon," "Judge Peck," "Miscellaneous Mysteries," "Books Edited by Derleth," and "Derleth Introductions." The contents of the Sac Prairie and the Real World are "Sac Prairie Saga: Short Stories"; "Sac Prairie Saga: Collections"; "Sac Prairie Saga: Novels"; "Sac Prairie Saga: Miscellaneous Prose"; "Sac Prairie Saga: Steve-Sim Juvenile Mysteries"; "Wisconsin Saga"; "Other Juvenile Literature"; "Poetry"; "Nonfiction: Books"; "Nonfiction: Articles, Reviews, Introductions"; and "Representative Published Letters." An index to titles concludes the bibliography.

Despite the plethora of sections, the 736 citations are numbered consecutively, but additional problems are caused by the individual arrangement of each section. Wilson arranged her entries alphabetically rather than chronologically, and chronological lists are nowhere given. Derleth wrote 10 Judge Peck novels, but the first citation is to the last one, and it is up to the reader to put the works into the order in which they appeared. This problem is exacerbated in the sections devoted to Derleth's mainstream fiction.

Apart from the arrangement of the work, the contents are accurate but occasionally lacking in necessary data. Entries for short stories have the title of the story in quotations, an annotation, and the publication. Periodical titles are underlined, and the volume and numbering are given, as are month, year, and pagination. When the story was anthologized in one of Derleth's own works, the book's title is given in capital letters and the story's pagination is listed. When a story was reprinted elsewhere, the book's title is given in roman type and under-lined, and the publisher, date and place of publication, and pagination are given. Retitlings are noted. Citations for books underline the book's title and (on a separate line) provide publisher and date and place of publication. Each citation is annotated and concludes with citations to the major reviews. Reprints and title changes are noted, and the contents of Derleth's collections and collaborations are listed. The contents of the Derleth-edited anthologies are not listed, and paginations for novels, collections, collaborations, and anthologies are nowhere provided.

Researchers interested in Derleth will get a better sense of Derleth's achievements from his own publications (q.v.), but Wilson's bibliography pro-vides a foundation upon which scholars can build. A comprehensive and accessi-ble Derleth bibliography nevertheless remains to be done.

For the curious: Wilson's biographical article appeared in *American Novel-ists, 1910–1945* (Dictionary of Literary Biography, vol. 9), edited by James J. Martine (Detroit: Gale, 1981). A supplement appears in Dutch (above).

370.   Smith, Ralph B., Jr. **The Solar Pons Page**. http://www.clysmic.com/ pons/index.html

Solar Pons is the Sherlock Holmes-inspired character created by Derleth. This web page contains links to Web and ASCII versions of an annotated Solar Pons bibliography, plus links to the August Derleth Society, an Arkham House Publications Listing, various Sherlock Holmes discussion groups and home pages, and a scanned dustjacket of one of Derleth's non-Pons novels.

The bibliography is lengthy and strives to be comprehensive, offering citations to all known books and periodicals containing Solar Pons stories. Cita-tions for books provide place of publication, publisher, year of publication, re-print editions (including hypertext editions), and the contents of the books. Notes by each title indicate a previous publication and the year in which it ap-peared. Cover reproductions of some of the readily accessible paperback edi-tions are provided. Citations to periodicals are arranged chronologically and give the title of the periodical, month and year of publication, and occasionally vol-ume and issue number. Contact information to Pons organizations, lists of pub-lishing houses publishing Pons, and notes conclude this useful site.

370a. August Derleth Societies

Kay Price, Executive Secretary
c/o The August Derleth Society
P.O. Box 481
Sauk City, WI 53583

Praed Street Irregulars
c/o Dr. George A. Vanderburgh
P.O. Box 204
Shelburne, ON Canada L0N 1S0

Charles Dickens

371. Jacobson, Wendy S. **The Companion to the Mystery of Edwin Drood**.
London: Allen & Unwin, 1986. xvii, 209 p. Index. (Dickens Companions).
LC 85-22855. ISBN 0-04-800063-9.

Charles Dickens's *The Mystery of Edwin Drood* is probably the most famous
unfinished work in the English language, but as of this writing, a separately published bibliography of the criticism has not been compiled. Jacobson's *Companion*
deserves mention here because it explicates *The Mystery of Edwin Drood* in the
same way that Jack Tracy's *Encyclopaedia Sherlockiana* or Christopher Redmond's
The Sherlock Holmes Handbook (q.q.v.) explicate their sources.

Using as text the 1972 Clarendon Dickens edited by Margaret Cardwell,
the *Companion* presents a chapter-by-chapter explication of the novel. (Jacobson
has also consulted Dickens's manuscripts and has discovered a number of significant variants not mentioned by Cardwell.) As the general preface notes, each
annotation identifies Dickens's "allusions to current events and intellectual and
religious issues, and supplies information on topography, social customs, cos-
tume, furniture, transportation, and so on. Identifications are provided for allusions to plays, poems, songs, the Bible, the Book of Common Prayer, and other
literary sources." Similarly, Dickens's illustrators are discussed, as are those texts
that represent Dickens's experiences and those that directly influenced the
works of other writers. An appendix discusses and annotates the "Sapsea Frag-
ment." There are a lengthy bibliography and an index.

An encyclopedic format might have made many of Dickens's references
more accessible, but *The Companion* can be used with no trouble. It will assist all
readers not intimately versed in Victorian culture and Dickens's life and habits.

Carole Nelson Douglas

372. Douglas, Carole Nelson. **Midnight Louie, Esq**. http://www.fastlane.net/
homepages/cdouglas/cnd_bio.html; http://www.fastlane.net/cdouglas

Douglas's home page provides biographical data and a photograph, and
offers links to her mysteries, romances, fantasy, and science fiction. Her mysteries are of two kinds. She has written a number of Sherlock Holmes pastiches
featuring Irene Adler; a cover illustration for each of these books is provided,
along with the publisher and ISBN, excerpts from positive reviews, and summaries of the books. Furthermore, Douglas is very fond of cats, is concerned about
homeless cats, and has written a series partially narrated by Midnight Louie, a
large (19 pound) tomcat living in Las Vegas. Cover illustrations from each of
these books are provided, as are the publisher, ISBN, summaries, and excerpts
from positive reviews. *Midnight Louie's Scratching-Post Intelligencer* is available at:
http://www.fastlane.net/cdouglas.

Arthur Conan Doyle

SCOPE NOTE: More has been written about Arthur Conan Doyle's Sherlock Holmes than about any other detective, real or imagined. This section is highly selective in its contents, listing only a few of the many reference sources available. The entries have been chosen for their comprehensiveness, significance, provision of unique material, and probable availability in most libraries.

Primary Bibliographies

373. Goldscheider, Gaby. **Conan Doyle Bibliography: A Bibliography of the Works of Sir Arthur Conan Doyle, M.D., LL.D. (1859–1930).** Windsor, England: Gaby Goldscheider, 1977. 40 p. Paperback.

Prior to Goldscheider's bibliography, the most comprehensive listing of the works of Sir Arthur Conan Doyle was H. Locke's *A Bibliographical Catalogue of the Writings of Sir Arthur Conan Doyle, 1879–1928* (Tunbridge Wells, England: D. Webster, 1928). Enterprising individuals had updated Locke's effort, but it remained for Goldscheider to prepare a comprehensive catalogue of the writings of Doyle, incorporating the additions of the other bibliographers into the effort. Its contents: The works of the master; biographies & critical writings; Holmesiana; and "What the Press Said." The entries in the first three sections are consecutively numbered; there are 1,158 citations.

The first section dominates the book and contains 1,063 citations. It is divided into three sections: Doyle's works, his contributions to the works of others, and his collected works. The entries in each section are alphabetically arranged by title; short story titles are in boldface type, book titles are in capitals. Beneath each the citations provide the date (in boldface type) and list in chronological order the work's appearances. Citations to periodical publications are uniformly inadequate, only occasionally providing the month of the periodical and never providing the story's pagination. Citations to books are more thorough, providing publisher, place and date of publication, illustrator, pagination, binding color, and paper size; the contents of books are not given.

The second and third sections list primarily monographs and are alphabetical by the author's name. The concluding section provides snippets of praise culled from contemporary reviews. Apart from the name of the periodical in which the review appeared, no bibliographic data are provided.

The more comprehensive bibliography of Green and Gibson (below) is preferable.

374. Green, Richard Lancelyn, and John Michael Gibson. **A Bibliography of A. Conan Doyle**. Foreword by Graham Greene. Oxford: Clarendon Press, 1983. xvi, 712 p. Index. (Soho Bibliographies, XXIII). LC 82-3541. ISBN 0-19-818190-6.

This gratifyingly thorough bibliography lists all the works of Arthur Conan Doyle published in English during his lifetime. Translations are not listed, and citations to reprints are confined to listing the colonial, Canadian, American, and copyright editions that appeared during Doyle's life.

The bibliography is divided into five lettered sections, the first of which lists all known British, Canadian, American, and continental editions; copyright pamphlets; plays; *belles-lettres*; poetry; collected editions; sets; and omnibus volumes. Each citation is numbered, and many of the cites are accompanied by an illustration of the cover of the first edition. Each entry provides an exhaustive analytical bibliographical description of the various editions of the book, starting with a transcription of the title page and followed by the book's collation and pagination, and descriptions of its contents, typography, paper, binding, dustjacket, printing, and publication. The date of publication is given, as are the initial cost and data on the serialization of the text. A section titled "Notes" provides additional information about the composition of the book and comments on the texts. The last work cited in this section is the *The Crowborough Edition*, a 24-volume set of 760 copies, published in 1930, that was intended to be a complete and definitive edition of Doyle's works. Doyle died before he could revise his texts, write new prefaces, and arrange the stories in a meaningful order.

Section B, "Miscellaneous Works," lists Doyle's histories, speeches, offprints, propaganda, autobiography, psychic books, pamphlets, and open letters. As in the first section, the bibliographical data are thorough: Citations are numbered, and many are accompanied by an illustration reproducing the cover of the first edition. Entries provide exhaustive analytical bibliographical descriptions of the various editions of the work, beginning with a transcription of the title page and followed by the book's collation, pagination, contents, typography, paper, binding, dustjacket, printing, and publication. The date of publication is given, as are the initial cost and data on the serialization of the text. As before, "Notes" contains additional information about the composition of the book and comments on the texts. The last citation in this section is to the 1963 *Strange Studies from Life*, a reprinting of three uncollected studies that first appeared in the *Strand Magazine* in 1901.

Section C, "Minor Contributions," documents Doyle's prefaces, forewords, collaborations, translations, and appearances in symposia; special anthologies of Doyle's work, a selective list of important anthologies, and ephemera are also cited. Although posthumous reprints are occasionally included (e.g., the 60-copy edition of "How Watson Learned the Trick" published in 1947), the majority of the citations are to materials published during Doyle's life.

Section D, "Periodical and Newspaper Contributions," lists Doyle's uncollected miscellaneous fiction and poetry and also includes a chronological list of Doyle's fiction with information on the first serial publication of each item. The section concludes with a section listing Doyle's miscellaneous writings: medical, photography, and travel articles; his published letters; contributions to symposia, and translations.

Section E, "Biographical Sources," provides a lengthy but selective list of important interviews, reports of speeches, biographical references, and articles on Doyle's life, work, and opinions that were published in newspapers and periodicals during Doyle's life. The section concludes with the 1978 publication of an article in *Blackwood's Magazine*. A special section lists the different editions of the book-length biographies of Doyle and books and other publications of biographical, bibliographical, and critical interest.

An appendix contains publisher listings for Doyle's British, colonial, continental, Canadian, and American publications, including references to the "unauthorized and cheap American editions." In addition there are references to a vocal score and Doyle's poetry set to music, information on his dramas (first performances and unpublished and unfinished plays), misattributions to Doyle, his dedications, bibliographies, checklists, and other material of bibliographical interest, and shorthand editions of Doyle's works. The index is thorough, referencing all books, periodicals, short stories, articles, and letters, and providing access by page and citation number.

This bibliography belongs in all academic libraries.

375. Lovisi, Gary. **Sherlock Holmes: The Great Detective in Paperback**. Introduction by John Bennett Shaw. Brooklyn, NY: Gryphon Books, 1990. 151 p. Index. ISBN 0-936071-15-X (hc); 0-936071-14-1 (pb).

Reproduced from clearly typed copy, this extended bibliographic essay on the paperback editions of Sherlock Holmes had its origins in a booklet titled *Sherlock Holmes; Fifty Years of The Great Detective in Paperback* (New York: Fantasia Books, 1983). The present work begins with an appreciative essay by Baker Street Irregular John Bennett Shaw, and contains the following unnumbered chapters: Collecting Sherlockian Paperbacks; British and Other Foreign Paperbacks; Before the Mass-Market: Dime Novels and Proto Paperbacks; The Doyle Tales: The Official Books; The Doyle Tales: Publishers Compilations [sic]; Sherlock Holmes: The Pastiches and Others; Books Yet to Appear; The Solar Pons Series; Small Press Items; Specialty Items; Some Juvenile Paperbacks; and Afterword. There are separate indexes to the works by Doyle and to those by other authors.

Lovisi's citations tend to provide the title of the work and list beneath it all known printings of all known paperback houses. Series numbers are usually provided; so too are paginations and cover prices. Reproductions of numerous rare covers are often given, and there are many useful annotations differentiating between editions. However, misspellings are rife ("separate" is consistently misspelled), and Lovisi's arrangement occasionally makes it difficult to locate specific references. A title index would be welcome.

376. Redmond, Donald A. **Sherlock Holmes Among the Pirates: Copyright and Conan Doyle in America 1890–1930**. Westport, CT: Greenwood Press, 1990. xviii, 286 p. Index. (Contributions to the Study of World Literature, no. 36). LC 89-27280. ISBN 0-313-27230-1. ISSN 0738-9345.

Not intended to be as comprehensive as the work of Green and Gibson (q.v.), this monograph contains two sections. The first provides a prose history of the appearances of Arthur Conan Doyle's earliest American editions, which (due to the absence of an international copyright law) were pirated by dozens of publishers. The second section is a publishing history of the different printings and editions of *A Study in Scarlet* and *The Sign of the Four* published between 1890 and 1930. The various plates from which the texts were printed are described, and successive publications from these plates are described in thorough bibliographical detail. The title page is transcribed; measurements, pagination, and signature markings are given; the bindings are described, with variants noted; and textual variations and individualities are likewise noted and described at length. Entries conclude by indicating whether the copy has been cited in the bibliographies of Green and Gibson or de Waal (q.q.v.). The book contains an appendix reprinting Jay Finley Christ's 1952 bibliographic study, "Sherlock Comes to America," and it concludes with tables listing the appearances of the different editions of *A Study in Scarlet* and *The Sign of the Four.*

Though intended for a very specialized audience, this nevertheless remains an exemplary textual bibliography and is also an excellent publishing history. In 1991 this book won the Crime Writers of Canada Arthur Ellis Award for Best Genre Criticism/Reference Book.

Secondary Bibliographies

377. de Waal, Ronald Burt. **The World Bibliography of Sherlock Holmes and Dr. Watson: A Classified and Annotated List of Materials Relating to Their Lives and Adventures**. New York: New York Graphic Society, 1974. xvi, 526 p. Indexes. LC 72-80900. ISBN 0-821204-20-3.

378. de Waal, Ronald Burt. **The International Sherlock Holmes: A Companion Volume to the World Bibliography of Sherlock Holmes and Dr. Watson**. Hamden, CT: Archon Books, 1980. 621 p. Indexes. LC 79-24533. ISBN 0-208-01777-1.

379. de Waal, Ronald Burt. **The Universal Sherlock Holmes**. Foreword by John Bennett Shaw. Illustrated by Betty and George Wells. Edited by George A. Vanderburgh. Shelburne, ON: Metropolitan Toronto Reference Library, 1994–1995. 5 vols. Index. C93-095453-X. ISBN 1-896032-00-1 (Cerlox bound); 1-896032-01-X (set not yet bound). Volume 5 is titled: **The Indexes to The Universal Sherlock Holmes**.

The first volume of this monumental set records every known publication of the "Sacred Writings" (i.e., the 56 short stories and four novels featuring Sherlock Holmes) and of the "Apocrypha" (works that do not feature Holmes but otherwise resemble the Sacred Writings), together with citations to the translations of these tales into 50 languages. In addition, all critical writings about

Sherlock Holmes are cited, as are the films, musicals, plays, radio and television programs, recordings, parodies, pastiches, and miscellaneous uses of Holmes in popular culture (e.g., Christmas cards). Despite the enormity of this undertaking, the volume contains only 10 sections: 1) The Sacred Writings; 2) The Apocrypha; 3) Manuscripts; 4) Foreign-Language Editions (Translations, English Readers, Parodies, and Pastiches); 5) The Writings About the Writings; 6) Sherlockians and the Societies; 7) Memorials and Mementos; 8) Games and Competitions; 9) Criticism; and 10) Parodies, Pastiches, Burlesques, Travesties, and Satires. Each of these sections contains numerous subdivisions; in all, there are 6,221 citations to materials published between 1887 and 1971. De Waal's bibliographical data are gratifyingly thorough, and many of his citations are annotated. An appendix provides abbreviations, a directory of the collections used for compiling the volume, and contact information for Sherlock Holmes societies. Finally, there are separate indexes for names and titles.

The International Sherlock Holmes contains a list of Sherlockiana published between 1971 and 1979 as well as references to earlier publications that de Waal missed in his first volume. The section devoted to manuscripts has been dropped; Sections 7 and 8 have been retitled as "Memorials and Memorabilia" and "Games, Puzzles, and Quizzes"; and lengthy sections devoted to "Actors, Performances, and Recordings" and to "Cartoons, Comic Strips, and Comic Books" have been added. In all, there are 6,135 citations; and, as before, de Waal's bibliographic data are thorough, and many of his citations are annotated. A directory of Sherlock Holmes Societies is provided, and the volume concludes with separate indexes for names and titles.

The Universal Sherlock Holmes was conceived as a four-volume work that cumulated the two editions above, added references to earlier publications that had been missed, and listed the materials published up through 7 January 1994. Despite its size, its arrangement is essentially similar to the earlier volumes; a section devoted to "The Literary Agent" has been added, and several sections have changed titles. Furthermore, the fourth volume contains a "selective concordance," a list of some 55,000 words that effectively indexes the keywords appearing in the set's 24,703 citations. As before, many of these citations are annotated.

The separately published fifth volume of The Universal Sherlock Holmes provides indexes to the names and titles appearing in the four volumes. There are separate indexes for headings and classifications, pseudonyms, personal names, titles, thespians appearing in Sherlock Holmes adaptations, and reviewers of books and dramas. In addition, there is an index of the "imposters" of Holmes. The volume concludes with conversion tables that permit the entries in The World Bibliography of Sherlock Holmes and The International Bibliography of Sherlock Holmes to be matched with the entries in The Universal Sherlock Holmes.

Superlatives do not do justice to this obsessively comprehensive labor of love. Sherlock Holmes is one of a few literary figures to have achieved global recognition, and de Waal documents his every known appearance, in every known venue, with unparalleled thoroughness. The Universal Sherlock Holmes was produced in a very short print run, but it belongs in all academic libraries. One hopes that an electronic version becomes available.

Encyclopedias and Character Dictionaries

380. Bullard, Scott R., and Michael Leo Collins. **Who's Who in Sherlock Holmes**. New York: Taplinger Publishing, 1980. 251 p. LC 79-66638. ISBN 0-8008-8281-4 (hc); 0-8008-8281-4 (pb).

Who's Who in Sherlock Holmes has references to places and significant objects in the short stories and novels and contains significantly more than its title implies. The entries begin with "Abbas Parva" and conclude with a reference to a Signor Zamba from "The Adventure of the Red Circle." In all, approximately 1,600 definitions are given, all keyed to the two volumes of Baring-Gould's *The Annotated Sherlock Holmes*. There are no illustrations, and media adaptations are not discussed.

As a reference work, *Who's Who in Sherlock Holmes* is inferior. Bullard and Collins's definitions are frequently self-referential and utterly useless. For example, the definition for "Crimean War" states in its entirety that "The ill-fated *Gloria Scott* left England from Falmouth, bound for Australia with her cargo of criminals, at the height of the Crimean War," forcing those who would know anything of the Crimean War to look elsewhere. Internal cross-references are not provided, and definitions are often oddly placed (e.g., the references to the hotels Cosmopolitan, Dulong, Escurial, and National are listed under "H" with no corresponding entries under their respective letters of the alphabet) or are missing. There are no entries for the stories (indeed, no separate list of the works is ever given) or for such significant creatures as "Swamp Adder."

The encyclopedic works of Tracy and Bunson (q.q.v.) are superior.

381. Bunson, Matthew E. **Encyclopedia Sherlockiana: An A-to-Z Guide to the World of the Great Detective**. New York: Macmillan, 1994. xxi, 326 p. LC 94-10714. ISBN 0-671-79826-X.

The *Encyclopedia Sherlockiana* contains approximately 1,500 articles and more than 100 illustrations relating to the life, achievements, and world of Sherlock Holmes. The book begins with "A Chronology of Sherlockiana," which chronicles events in the lives of Holmes and Watson; lists the works in "The Canon"; and presents the results of a 1927 poll by the *Strand Magazine* in which readers and Doyle answered the question, "Which Sherlock Holmes stories are the best?" This is followed by a list of "Unchronicled Cases of the Canon," which provides the names of cases referenced but not described in the texts.

The *Encyclopedia*'s entries begin with "Abbas Parva" (a small village in Berkshire mentioned in "The Adventure of the Veiled Lodger") and conclude with a reference to "Zucco, George," who acted in some of the early motion pictures. Significant characters, places, and incidents are described; all the stories and a number of notable pastiches are summarized; notable actors and actresses who have played in adaptations of the works are profiled; the appearances of Holmes on screen and television are listed; and aliases, codes, and disguises used by Holmes are given. There are entries for subjects as varied as "Dog-Cart" and "Dogs of the Canon," for the titles of the books carried by Holmes while he was disguised as an old bibliophile in "The Adventure of the Empty House," and for people who figured notably in Doyle's life (e.g., George Edalji.)

The *Encyclopedia* concludes with a list of the writings of Holmes, names of noted artists who portrayed Holmes in early publications and the works for which their illustrations were made, a lengthy list of Sherlock Holmes in film, and an even lengthier list of the names and addresses of more than 300 Sherlock Holmes societies around the world. A biographical account of Doyle reproduces his bookplate but (somewhat surprisingly) the book nowhere contains a picture of Doyle.

One can always complain about depth and balance in a work such as this—is there a need for so many references to actors and actresses, when the fine pastiches of John Dickson Carr and Adrian Conan Doyle are mentioned but in passing? when cross-references are not always adequate?—but the *Encyclopedia Sherlockiana* is enjoyable and generally useful.

382.   Park, Orlando. **Sherlock Holmes, Esq., and John H. Watson, M.D.: An Encyclopaedia of Their Affairs**. Evanston, IL: Northwestern University Press, 1962. viii, 205 p. LC 62-17805. Reprinted as: **The Sherlock Holmes Encyclopedia [A Complete Guide to the People, Towns, Streets, Estates, Railway Stations, Objects—in Fact, Everything]**. New York: Carol Publishing, 1994. 205 p. LC 93-42779. ISBN 0-8065-0764-0.

The oldest of the Sherlock Holmes encyclopedias considered here, this is also the weakest. It is unillustrated, and its approximately 2,000 entries are unexceptional and frequently contain less information than the corresponding entries in the other volumes. Like Bullard and Collins's *Who's Who in Sherlock Holmes* and Bunson's *Encyclopedia Sherlockiana* (q.q.v.), Park begins his entries with "Abbas Parva," but although Park correctly cites the significance of the place, there is no explanation of meaning. Similarly, although Park concludes his entries with "Zoo," his definition mentions only the story in which the word was used; Jack Tracy's *Encyclopaedia Sherlockiana* (q.v.) gives a significantly superior definition, citing not only the story but also the Zoological Gardens in Regent's Park in London.

Park provides no separate list of the stories and no chronologies, fails to comment upon such animals as "Swamp Adder," and provides cross-references at the end of each article that are meaningless unless one has internalized the full title of the story. For example, *vampire* refers to "The Adventure of the Sussex Vampire," which is listed under the letter *S*, but there is no cross-reference under the letter *V*. Choose Tracy or Bunson instead.

383.   Tracy, Jack. **The Encyclopaedia Sherlockiana; or, A Universal Dictionary of the State of Knowledge of Sherlock Holmes and His Biographer John H. Watson, M.D**. Garden City, NY: Doubleday, 1977. xv, 411 p. LC 75-13394.

The most comprehensive of the Sherlock Holmes encyclopedias examined here, *The Encyclopaedia Sherlockiana* contains more than 3,500 entries and 8,000 story citations, as well as nearly 200 period illustrations. Where it differs from such works as Bunson's *Encyclopedia Sherlockiana* and Park's *The Sherlock Holmes Encyclopedia* (q.q.v.) is that its references and entries are limited to Doyle's world and background; there are no lists of media adaptations and no entries for the actors and actresses who have performed in motion picture adaptations of Doyle.

Tracy begins his *Encyclopaedia* with an entry for the letter A, the volume of the *Encyclopaedia Britannica* out of which Jabez Wilson spent eight weeks copying entries ("The Red-Headed League"), and concludes with an entry for "Zoology" (which figures in *The Hound of the Baskervilles* and "The Adventure of the Creeping Man"). All characters, places, and incidents are described. There are entries for subjects such as the names of the newspapers that figure in the Canon; historical figures as varied as Charles Darwin, Edgar Allan Poe, Brigham Young, and Count Ferdinand von Zeppelin; regions and locations in which the stories are set; principal railway stations of London; and references that might have meant something to one of Doyle's readers but whose meanings are today largely lost, such as crystal palace, dark lantern, doctor's commons, Sepoy, and student lamp. The illustrations are well chosen, support the text, and include one of Doyle. A lengthy bibliography concludes the book.

The Encyclopaedia Sherlockiana has its faults. Although the story titles are listed, the list does not provide complete names and neglects to distinguish collections from short stories. In addition, definitions are occasionally dubious: It is most improbable that the sheet of royal cream paper received by Mycroft Holmes measured 19" x 24". And why are there no entries for the periodicals in which the Canon was first published? Contemporary readers would benefit from knowing the significance of a Christmas Annual or the general editorial approach of the *Strand Magazine*. Furthermore, the volume is so prodigiously cross-referenced that the user must often check four or five entries before finding the complete data. Nevertheless, Tracy successfully gives a sense of the world in which the Sherlock Holmes stories take place, and his *Encyclopaedia* is thoroughly useful.

Handbooks, Companions, and Text Explications

384. Doyle, Arthur Conan. **The Annotated Sherlock Holmes: The Four Novels and Fifty-Six Short Stories Complete, with an Introduction, Notes, and Bibliography by William S. Baring-Gould; Lavishly Illustrated with Maps, Diagrams, Photographs, and Drawings**. New York: Crown for Clarkson Potter, 1967. 2 vols. 688 p., 824 p. Indexes. LC 67-22406. Many later editions.

The contents of the two volumes of *The Annotated Sherlock Holmes* are arranged chronologically. Accompanying the text of each work are explanations of

Doyle's references, frequently accompanied by illustrations from period publications. Baring-Gould's annotations are useful and will benefit readers new to Doyle and the world in which Holmes operated, but as Barzun's *Catalogue of Crime* (q.v.) notes, they are "marred by many misprints, errors of fact, and errors of judgment." A corrected and expanded edition of this work would be welcome.

385. Redmond, Christopher. **A Sherlock Holmes Handbook**. Toronto: Simon & Pierre, 1993. 251 p. Index. C 93-094437-2. ISBN 0-88924-246-1.

Redmond's brief introduction explains that he intended *The Sherlock Holmes Handbook* to be used by two kinds of people: those curious about Holmes, and those who know a lot about Holmes. It is possible that the second group will not need a work such as this, but a novice to the worlds of Arthur Conan Doyle and Sherlock Holmes will more than likely find something of use in the nine lively chapters in the *Handbook*.

Redmond—son of the Donald Redmond whose works are also discussed in this chapter—begins by explaining the concept of the Canon, a discussion that presents in "Canonical order" (the order in which the pieces are usually published in collected editions) concise summaries of the stories; first publication data are also provided. The successive chapters survey and discuss the characters and adventures, Sherlock Holmes in print, Sir Arthur Conan Doyle, the Victorian backgrounds of the stories, crime and punishment, modern media adaptations of Holmes, the fans and followers of Holmes, and the influence of Holmes. An appendix lists the 60 tales and provides the commonly used abbreviations for them, along with dates of first publication and volumes and pages of the 1967 *The Annotated Sherlock Holmes* in which they are discussed. An excellent index concludes the book.

All chapters contain an enormous amount of information. On occasion strange juxtapositions occur. The chapter on crime and punishment discusses British law of the late nineteenth and early twentieth centuries, and policing and detection in the late nineteenth and early twentieth centuries; it also has statements on the history of the detective story, including a number of stories that owe debts to Doyle. Redmond's opinions in this latter section are occasionally waspish and highly debatable. For example, R. Austin Freeman's Dr. Thorndyke is dismissed as a "humourless polymath"; Agatha Christie's output consists of "dozens of enjoyable but forgettable novels"; and for Redmond to state that "there is detection in such books [as Chandler's *The Big Sleep* and Hammett's *Red Harvest* and *The Maltese Falcon*], but primarily there is violence, usually accompanied by sex," is simply incorrect. Furthermore, his discussion of electronic resources has dated badly.

Nevertheless, in all sections Redmond's writing is admirably clear, and his enthusiasm for the character of Holmes and the writings of Doyle is infectious. An audience that has missed reading Doyle or that wants to know about the world in which Doyle lived and worked will find the *Handbook* extraordinarily helpful.

Character Dictionaries

386. Redmond, Donald A. **Sherlock Holmes: A Study in Sources**. Kingston and Montreal: McGill-Queen's University Press, 1982. xviii, 357 p. Index. C 82-094628-1. ISBN 0-7735-0391-9.

A somewhat mistitled volume, *Sherlock Holmes: A Study in Sources* does not concentrate on the sources used by Doyle but on the names in Sherlock Holmes, focusing on the probable significance and derivation of each name. Although the names are organized by the stories in which they first appeared, this nevertheless remains a "who's who" to the characters, of whom (states Redmond) "there are 763 named characters of whom 269 are allusions or 'mentioned characters' who are named but do not appear in person or in eyewitness narration. Add to these forty-nine aliases, maiden names and subordinate titles of nobility, at least twenty-one real persons, and forty-eight firm names compounded of personal names; ships, real firms, etcetera, and the total appears to be over 890."

Redmond has devoted an enormous amount of effort to identifying sources likely to have inspired Doyle, working through contemporary newspapers, histories of banks and banking, clerical directories, biographical dictionaries, library catalogues, military lists, registries of ships, alumni directories, regional directories, place-name indexes, obituary indexes, and cricketing yearbooks, to name but a few. His derivations and accounts of origins are generally reasonable and acceptable, though taken collectively they have the (probably unintentional) effect of diminishing Doyle's achievements by making him appear to have been entirely derivative rather than creative.

On the debit side, Redmond does not indicate pronunciations, and in the case of a name such as "Lestrade," this would be helpful: Is it "Lestrahd" or "Lestrayed"? Furthermore, Redmond's discussion of Lestrade mentions "Bleiler, speculating on its pronunciation," an apparent reference to critic E. F. Bleiler's "Marmelahd or Marmelade" (*The Armchair Detective* vol. 13, no. 4 [Fall 1980]: 334–35), but nowhere is this article referenced in Redmond's bibliography. Apart from the questions of pronunciation and documentation, this remains a thoroughly useful work, on the level of Christopher Redmond's helpful *A Sherlock Holmes Handbook* (q.v.). It belongs in academic libraries.

Television and Motion Picture Adaptations

387. Haining, Peter. **The Television Sherlock Holmes**. London: W. H. Allen, 1986. 224 p. Paperback. LC 86-235166. ISBN 0-49103055-X.

388. Haining, Peter. **The Television Sherlock Holmes**. 2d ed. London: Virgin Publishing, 1991. 238 p. Paperback. GB 92-20231. ISBN 0-86369-537-X.

389. Haining, Peter. **The Television Sherlock Holmes**. 3d ed. London: Virgin Books, 1994. 255 p. Paperback. LC 93-44613. ISBN 0-86369-793-3.

The third edition is described here.

This elaborately illustrated volume provides a history of all the known television adaptations of Sherlock Holmes, although many earlier motion picture adaptations are also described. Sherlock Holmes first appeared on television in 1937, and Haining provides stills from and an account of the first production, an adaptation of "The Three Garridebs" that starred Louis Hector as Holmes and William Podmore as Doctor Watson. Dozens of additional adaptations are described, often accompanied by photographs of the actors playing Holmes (these have been as physically diverse as Peter Cushing, John Cleese, Christopher Lee, Stewart Granger, Peter Cook, and Frank Langella). A sizable percentage of the book is devoted to describing the Granada Television adaptations of the stories starring Jeremy Brett as Holmes and having either David Burke or Edward Hardwicke as Watson. Casts and credits of all television shows are provided, though the lengthiest descriptions are accorded to those starring Brett et al. This is an enjoyable book to browse, but alas, it is unindexed.

Websites

390. Carroll, David. **Baker Street Connection: A Sherlock Holmes Collection.** http://www.citsoft.com/holmes.html

The Baker Street Connection provides an electronically available collection of Sherlock Holmes-related material, and electronic versions of all of the Canon, with the exception of the 12 stories appearing in the 1927 *The Case Book of Sherlock Holmes*, which is still covered by copyright. Though numerous other sites also offer electronic versions of the works, the simplicity of the arrangement facilitates access.

391. Newbury, Jenny. **Sherlock Holmes International.** http://www.sherlock-holmes.org/

Available in English, French, German, Spanish, Italian, Danish, and Japanese versions, this monumental site contains sections for and links to major Sherlockian resources, the Canon online, useful information, multimedia Holmes, specialized sites, Granada's TV Series with Jeremy Brett, Sherlockian publications, Holmesian societies, Sherlockians' Holmes pages, essays and scholarly ramblings, pastiches and fan fiction, museums and restaurants, and Sherlockian items for sale. There are numerous subdivisions.

The layout is clear and accessible and facilitates access to the information. One can only wish that other detectives were so beloved.

392. Redmond, Chris. **A Sherlockian Holmepage.** http://watserv1.uwaterloo.ca/~credmond/sh.html

Noted Sherlockian scholar Redmond's well-done page begins with a hyperlinked table of contents that permits users to access electronic texts of the Canon; major electronic Sherlockian resources; multimedia files accessible via

FTP; specialized Sherlockian sites; Sherlockian societies (with a list of the home pages of individual Sherlockians); Granada Television and Jeremy Brett; Sherlockian things for sale; additional material by and about Arthur Conan Doyle; sites devoted to mysteries in general; sites devoted to England and the Victorian era; sites devoted to science fiction, horror, and kindred fields; sites of collateral interest; lists of companies called Sherlock; and Sherlockian-related oddities. An exemplary achievement.

393. Sherman, Michael. **221B Baker Street**. http://members.tripod.com/ ~msherman/holmes.html

Sherman's website provides links to electronic versions of 48 of the 60 works that feature Holmes; the 12 stories that do not have electronic versions are the stories that appeared in *The Case Book of Sherlock Holmes*, which is still under copyright. In addition, there are links to pictures from the original periodical publications and to other organizations. A useful site, and one that is available through Chris Redmond's *Sherlockian Holmepage* (q.v.).

393a. Sherlock Holmes Fan Clubs and Societies

Hundreds of fan clubs and Holmes societies exist, and contact information for many of these can be found in the different editions of Ronald de Waal's bibliographies or through the websites cited above, in particular http://www. sherlock-holmes.org/. Nevertheless, one would be remiss not to mention the Baker Street Irregulars, established in 1934 and still flourishing:

Baker Street Irregulars
P.O. Box 2189
Easton, MO 21601
(410) 745-5553

Their "irregular quarterly of Sherlockiana" is:

Baker Street Journal
c/o Sheridan Press
Box 465
Hanover, PA 17331-5172
ISSN 0005-4070

Numerous additional periodicals exist, and the following is nothing more than a selective list. Additional names can be found in the different editions of Ronald de Waal's bibliographies or through the websites cited above.

A C D, The Journal of the Arthur Conan Doyle Society
c/o Christopher Roden
Ashcroft
2 Abbotsford Drive
Penyfford, Ches. CH4 0JG
England
ISSN 0966-0763

The Battered Silicon Dispatch Box
P.O. Box 204
Shelburne, Ontario, LON ISO
Canada
ISSN 1188-0449

The Musgrave Papers
c/o Northern Musgraves Sherlock Holmes Society
69 Greenhead Road
Huddersfield, W. York, HD1 4ER
England
ISSN 1351-1890

Sherlock Holmes Gazette
46 Purfield Drive
Wargrave, Berks RG10 8AR
England
ISSN 0965-5549

Sherlock Holmes Journal
c/o R. J. Ellis
13 Crofton Ave.
Orpington, Kent BR6 8DU
England
0037-3621

Sherlockian Tidbits
42 Melrose Place
Montclair, NJ 07042-2028
ISSN 1040-4937

Sarah Dreher

394. Tangled Web. **Sarah Dreher and Stoner McTavish.** http://www.twbooks. co.uk/authors/sdreher.html

A two-sentence biography, cover reproductions, the prose from the back covers of Dreher's books, and excerpts from positive reviews are given at this website. The concluding bibliography provides publisher and publication year. No photograph of the author appears.

Stella Duffy

395. Tangled Web. **Stella Duffy and Saz Martin.** http://www.twbooks.co.uk/ authors/sduffy.html

This site provides a brief biography of the author (no photograph, however), and cover reproductions are accompanied by ISBN, publisher, and price. The material from the back cover is printed, accompanied by excerpts from positive reviews. The concluding bibliography lists publisher and year of publication.

Martin Edwards

396. Tangled Web. **Martin Edwards.** http://www.twbooks.co.uk/authors/medwards.html

This site is unique among the Tangled Web sites in that it begins with the bibliography and provides the author's e-mail address. Apart from these idiosyncrasies, it is similar to the other web pages in this series; it provides a picture of Edwards, cover reproductions from a number of his works, excerpts from positive critical reviews, and a biographical statement.

Ruth Dudley Edwards

397. Tangled Web. **Ruth Dudley Edwards.** http://www.twbooks.co.uk/authors/rdedwards.html

This site provides a photograph of Edwards, a brief biography, cover reproductions of two of her novels, and prose from the covers of her books. Excerpts from positive reviews are given. The concluding bibliography lists the titles and occasionally provides publication data for Edwards's novels.

James Ellroy

398. Perani, Jérôme. **Ellroy Confidential.** http://www.geocities.com/Paris/1906/ellroy.htm

Available in English and French versions, this well-done French site provides numerous photographs of its subject, information on Ellroy's works, his works as adapted for motion pictures and television, interviews, sound and image files, and miscellaneous links to Ellroy material. The bibliography provides publication year, publisher, and publisher's location for the first American and French editions of Ellroy's books. The date of the story's setting is given, a comment is provided (when necessary), and there are links to full-text reviews. Finally, there is a lengthy list of websites devoted to Ellroy and Ellroyiana.

399. Tangled Web. **James Ellroy.** http://www.twbooks.co.uk/authors/jellroy.html

The least consequential of the Ellroy sites considered in this publication, this one provides a picture of Ellroy, a brief biographical sketch, cover illustrations of several of his works, excerpts from positive critical reviews, and prose from the covers of those books included here. The bibliography lists titles by Ellroy and occasionally provides additional publication data.

Loren D. Estleman

400. Stephens, Christopher P. **A Checklist of Loren D. Estleman**. Hastings-on-Hudson, NY: Ultramarine Publishing, 1991. 16 p. Index. Paperback. ISBN 0-89366-176-7.

Apparently offset from typed copy, this bibliography lists the books written by Loren Estleman, from the 1976 *Oklahoma Punk* until the 1991 publication of *Motown*; the 1992 *King of the Corner* and the 1993 *The Witchfinder* are listed as forthcoming. Each numbered citation provides publication data on the first American and first British editions of the book. Titles are underlined; retitlings are indicated; and information on dustwrapper artists, prices, and identifying points are occasionally also given. Following the bibliography of primary texts, a section lists the works edited by Estleman; as before, titles are underlined, though as two of the three books in this section are listed as forthcoming, data are minimal. An index to the titles and retitlings concludes the pamphlet. Though this pamphlet is a useful starting point for collectors, it does not list Estleman's nonbook writings, and he has of course been active since 1991. An updated edition is needed.

Janet Evanovich

401. Evanovich, Janet. **Janet Evanovich Online**. http://www.evanovich.com/

Evanovich's home page offers a biographical statement, a picture, cover reproductions of her novels, a schedule of her tours, and information about her forthcoming books. Summaries of and excerpts from each novel are provided, as are excerpts from positive critical attention. Cover reproductions of paperback editions are also provided; bibliographic data include price, pagination, and ISBN. Similar information is given on audio versions of the books, the cover reproductions being accompanied by data detailing reader, price, running time, and ISBN. Finally, Evanovich provides instructions on obtaining signed bookplates.

Tony Fennelly

402. Tangled Web. **Tony Fennelly**. http://www.twbooks.co.uk/authors/tfennelly.html

This site provides a photograph of Fennelly, a brief biography, cover reproductions from her novels, and prose from the covers of her books. Excerpts from positive reviews are given. The concluding bibliography lists the titles of her books, indicating whether they feature Matt Sinclair or Margo Fortier as their detective.

Bruno Fischer

403. Williams, Richard. **Bruno Fischer**. Scunthorpe, England: Dragonby Press, 1990. 4 p. Stapled sheets. (British Author Checklists, no. 1).

Despite the implications of the series title, Bruno Fischer (1908–1992) was an American, one of many who began his writing career in the pulp magazines. This brief checklist cites only Fischer's books. The first section is a chronological listing of American first editions; the entries provide year of publication, title (in capital letters), and publisher. The second section lists Fischer's American paperback editions. Arranged alphabetically by publisher, it provides series number, title (in capital letters), and year of publication (in parentheses). The third section lists Fischer's British first editions. The entries in this section are arranged chronologically, with the year and month of publication given, title (in capital letters), pagination, price, and publisher. The fourth section, arranged like the second section, lists Fischer's British paperback editions. An index lists the books and their publishers. A comprehensive Fischer bibliography remains to be done.

Kate Flora

404. Flora, Kate. **Kate Flora's Home Page/Kate's Lair**. http://www. kateflora.com

Kate Flora's website provides a picture of her, an amusing biographical statement, and cover illustrations of her novels featuring Thea Kozak. Links lead to a summary of the work, excerpts from positive reviews, the book's first chapter, and recipes that Kozak has prepared. The website has excellent graphics.

Dick Francis

405. Ahearn, Allen, and Patricia Ahearn. **Author Price Guides: Dick Francis**. Rockville, MD: Quill & Brush, 1997. 8 leaves. APG 096.2.

This Author's Price Guide to Dick Francis lists his work from the 1957 publication of *The Sport of Queens* to the 1996 appearance of *To the Hilt*.

For a thorough description of the format of Author Price Guides, see the entry under Fredric Brown.

406. Carter, D. F. **Francis Listing**.

Available through the DorothyL archives and through the Miss Lemon website (http://www.iwillfollow.com/lemon.htm), this chronologically arranged list gives the book's title, publication date, and description from the dustwrapper or the back of paperbacks. References are given to four additional works written or edited by Francis. Data are complete as of 1994.

407.   Messall, Mary. **Dick Francis**. http://www.mindspring.com/~mmessall/ francis

Messall's website offers a picture of and biographical about Francis, and Messall provides summaries of each work, brief excerpts, and snippets from reviews. Adding depth to the site are a sound file containing a clip of the radio coverage of one of his rides in the Grand National and a JPEG image of a letter Messall received from Francis. The summaries of the novels tend to be derived from the back covers of the Fawcett Crest editions of Francis's work and do not provide bibliographic data. There are no summaries of Francis's short stories, but very thorough bibliographic data are given. Finally, there are links to the few other websites devoted to Francis.

R. Austin Freeman

408.   Grost, Michael. **R. Austin Freeman**. http://members.aol.com/MG4273/ freeman.htm

The only significant source of information on Freeman currently available via the Web is through A Guide to Classic Mystery and Detection (http://members.aol.com/MG4273/classics.htm), written and maintained by Michael Grost. A partial Freeman bibliography is provided, as are discussions of several of Freeman's novels and short story collections.

A list of the R. Austin Freeman-Vincent Starrett correspondence held at Kent State University is available through http://www.library.kent.edu/ speccoll, and Gerry Howe of England maintains a sporadically available Freeman page at http://www.sidwell.demon.co.uk/freeman.html.

Celia Fremlin

409.   Tangled Web. **Celia Fremlin**. http://www.twbooks.co.uk/authors/ cfremlin.html

In this site, a photograph of Fremlin is provided, as are a brief biography, selected cover reproductions, and the prose from those covers. Excerpts from positive reviews and the full text of selected reviews are given. The concluding bibliography provides the titles of Fremlin's works.

Kinky Friedman

410.   Kemper, Lisa. **The Kinky Friedman Site**. http://www.kinkyfriedman.com/

Kemper's web page provides a biography of her subject, numerous photographs, and information about Friedman's books, music, and lyrics. The full text of some articles about and interviews by Friedman is given, along with information about joining the Kinky Friedman Crime Club and obtaining Friedman memorabilia. The bibliography is a table listing in chronological order the first American editions of Friedman's books; publisher and year of publication are given, as are ISBN and estimated street price. Links from the titles provide a reproduction of the cover and the book's first paragraph. The website is well designed and has a lighthearted approach that befits its subject.

411. Kuilder, Gerrit. **Kinky Friedman**. http://www.yours-untildeath.demon.nl/ kinkster.html

Although less comprehensive than the Kinky Friedman site maintained by Lisa Kemper (q.v.), this site deserves mention for providing pictures of Friedman and his New York settings that cannot be found on other websites. It also contains some quotations from Friedman, but the sources from which these were taken are not attributed.

Dale Furutani

412. Furutani, Dale. **Dale Furutani**. http://members.aol.com/dfurutani/ index.html

Furutani's personal web page includes a family history, pictures of his relatives, several pictures of himself at various ages, and an autobiographical statement. Information on his Ken Tanaka mystery series is provided; cover illustrations are given, as are descriptions of the series from the publisher and Furutani's own perceptions. The text of an interview is provided, as are excerpts from positive reviews and a guide to Furutani's first novel. Furthermore, there are a number of links to sites exploring aspects of the Japanese culture featured in Furutani's works; topics of these range from personal seals to Japanese card games, swords, the Yakuza (the Japanese Mafia), daily life, and the language. A very well-presented page.

Erle Stanley Gardner

413. Miller, John Anthony. **The Erle Stanley Gardner Home Page**. http://www. phantoms.com/~phantom/gardner/

Miller operates the Phantom Bookshop in Ventura, California, across the street from the place where Gardner wrote his first Perry Mason mysteries. His website provides information on Gardner and his use of Ventura sites in his writings, information on the Temecula group that is trying to get the library's name changed to reflect Gardner's influence, Gardner's recipe for Podunk Candy, a Gardner quiz, and information on a Gold Coast Virtual Bus tour, wherein one can visit some of the places Gardner visited. In addition, there is a comprehensive list of Gardner's book publications; the fiction is arranged by series, with titles listed chronologically. In addition, there are illustrations of the covers of Gardner's books and advertisements for Richard L. Senate's *Erle Stanley Gardner's Ventura: The Birthplace of Perry Mason* (Ventura, CA: Charon Press, 1996), a paperback account of Gardner and Ventura, whose contents do not quite justify giving it a separate entry. One hopes Miller continues to maintain this site.

414. Moore, Ruth. **Bibliography of Erle Stanley Gardner**. Publisher unknown, 1970. 115 leaves. LC 79-23856.

Not seen. Moore was one of three sisters who worked with Gardner and was with him at his death in 1970. It would appear that the *Bibliography of Erle Stanley Gardner* is the copied manuscript of the Gardner bibliography by Moore that appeared on pages 311–41 of *Erle Stanley Gardner: The Case of the Real Perry Mason* by Dorothy B. Hughes (New York: William Morrow, 1978). This bibliography is arranged chronologically. Titles of all pieces are given in boldface capitals. Data included are a note indicating whether the work was a letter, short story, article, pamphlet, television adaptation, or novel; whether it featured one of Gardner's series characters (i.e., Speed Dash, Paul Pry, Fish Mouth McGinnis, the Patent Leather Kid, Mr. Manse, Lester Leith, and, of course, Perry Mason); and whether it appeared under one of Gardner's pseudonyms. Serialization data are provided. Periodical titles are given in italics and are followed by date of publication. Book publications provide publisher and month and year of publication for the first hardcover and the first paperback editions. Data are reasonably comprehensive until 1970. Lacking are indexes to titles, publications, and series characters, but as far as listing most of Gardner's output is concerned, this remains the most comprehensive Gardner bibliography currently available.

415. Mundell, E. H. **Erle Stanley Gardner: A Checklist**. Portage, IN: [N.P.], 1968. 80 p. Indexes. LC 78-111.

Apparently only the second book-length work on Erle Stanley Gardner, this self-published and often frustrating checklist contains five sections: short fiction, book fiction, magazine nonfiction, book nonfiction, and miscellaneous print appearances. Each section is arranged chronologically.

Coverage of the short fiction starts with the appearance of "Chas. M. Green's" "The Shrieking Skeleton" in the 15 December 1923 *Black Mask* and concludes with a publication from 1965; there is also a list of seven stories (including a 1921 *Breezy Stories*) about which publication data are uncertain. Story pagination and volume and issue numbers are not given, and magazine names are not typographically distinguished. Title changes are not acknowledged, and a number of stories are listed twice, with no indication that they are reprints.

The citations for the books provide the book's title and an indication of the number of foreign editions it had. Because all the volumes were first published by William Morrow of New York, none of the book citations lists the publisher's name. Paperback editions are not included. This section concludes with a list of the titles that were condensed in Canadian periodical publications; publication dates are not provided.

The section devoted to Gardner's magazine nonfiction provides neither pagination nor volume and issue numbers for the magazines that published Gardner's prose, and the names of the magazines are not distinguishable from their surroundings.

The section for book-length nonfiction lists the title of the book and indicates the number of foreign editions the publication went through. The name of the publisher is not provided (presumably it was William Morrow). Finally, the miscellaneous section mentions the television adaptation of Perry Mason ("Perry Mason appeared in 270–80 television plays") and mentions syndicated comic book adaptations of Gardner's work. A series of indexes provide title keyword access to Gardner's fiction, a subject index to Gardner's nonfiction, and a selective list of Gardner's series characters (exclusive of Perry Mason, Bertha Cool, and Donald Lam) and the titles of some of the stories in which they appeared.

A somewhat revised edition of this book is described below.

416. Mundell, E. H. **Erle Stanley Gardner: A Checklist**. Kent, OH: Kent State University Press, 1970. 91 p. Indexes. LC 70-97619. ISBN 0-87338-034-7.

Although this bibliography is in a great many ways defective, it is nevertheless a substantial improvement over the first edition. The arrangement is essentially the same as the first edition, with five chronologically arranged sections listing Gardner's short fiction, book fiction, short nonfiction, book nonfiction, and miscellanea.

Coverage of the short fiction starts with two appearances in *Breezy Stories* of 1921 and concludes with a publication from 1965. Volume and issue numbers are not given; paginations are not provided; magazine titles are not typographically distinguished; and stories that were retitled and reprinted are listed without any indication of their status.

Apart from some typographical changes, the data in the first four sections are essentially unchanged from their earlier appearances. Publishers are not provided; paperback editions are not cited; publication dates of periodical appearances have not been given; magazine names are not distinguished; and pertinent publication data are not provided.

The section devoted to miscellanea has been expanded to include a selective list of Gardner's series characters (exclusive of Perry Mason, Bertha Cool, and Donald Lam) and titles of some of the stories in which they appeared. The indexes still include the keyword listing of title words from Gardner's fiction, and it now offers access to Gardner's series characters and his pseudonymous work. An index to Gardner's nonfiction concludes the book.

Elizabeth George

417. Bantam Doubleday Dell. **Elizabeth George**. http://www.bdd.com/ prev_featured_authors/authors/f293.html

One of the "A Visit With" series produced by Bantam Doubleday Dell, this site provides a picture of George and offers links to her new book, her previous books, a profile, a place to write to the author, tours and appearances, related links, and other authors in the series. The section devoted to books provides a cover reproduction for each title, a summary of the contents, purchasing information, and excerpts of critical praise.

Walter B. Gibson

418. Cox, J. Randolph. **Man of Magic and Mystery: A Guide to the Works of Walter B. Gibson**. Metuchen, NJ: Scarecrow Press, 1988. xxiv, 382 p.

Though he is today largely unknown, Walter B. Gibson (1897–1985) wrote at least 20 million words for the pulp magazines, including (as "Maxwell Grant") some 283 pulp novels, two short stories, and one paperback original featuring the Shadow. Gibson was also a noted magician, a friend to magicians including Houdini and Blackstone, an astrologer, a pioneer in the history of comic books, a lover of mysteries, and an enthusiastic games player; in all these areas he had numerous publications. Finally, he was a professional ghost, responsible for the novelization (as "Harry Hershfield") of the script of Preston Sturges's *The Sin of Harold Diddlebock*; for the historical novel (as "Douglas Brown") *Anne Bonny, Pirate Queen* ("She could fight like the devil and love like an angel," reads the cover); for books on yoga, the martial arts, and true crime; and for numerous articles, one of which—"A Million Words a Year for Ten Straight Years"—appeared in 1941, when Gibson's writing career was barely 20 years old and had another 44 years to run.

Librarian and scholar Cox was a friend of Walter Gibson's, and his *Guide* is an account of Gibson as well as a documentation of Gibson's prodigious output. It contains the following sections: Books and pamphlets by Walter B. Gibson, contributions to periodicals, contributions to books and pamphlets by other writers, syndicated features, comic books and newspaper strips, and radio scripts and miscellaneous works. Each of these sections contains biographical data on Gibson and citations to Gibson's publications. Citations are arranged chronologically, each entry having a section letter and a separate number. Book titles are given in boldface type, followed by place of publication, publisher, year of publication, pagination, whether it was illustrated, and if it appeared in paperback. Periodical publications give the title in quotation marks, publication's name in boldface type, volume, date of publication, and pagination of Gibson's story. When the title of an entry does not explain its contents, Cox provides an annotation ranging from one to several dozen words.

Five appendixes provide a list of Walter Gibson's pseudonyms, a list of the magazines in which Gibson was published, information on the other writers and writings to appear under the Maxwell Grant name, three comic book series and six movies adapted from Gibson's writings, and a list of secondary sources about Gibson and his works. The *Guide* concludes with a "checklist" of the 187 books written by Gibson, an index to the titles mentioned in *The Guide* that indicates whether the piece is an independent unit or part of a larger unit, and a list of the names, including Gibson's pseudonyms, found in section A and the appendixes about the other Maxwell Grants and the comic book/motion picture adaptations.

This is an exemplary bio-bibliography about a fascinating figure.

David Goodis

419. Stephens, Christopher P. **A Checklist of David Goodis**. Hastings-on-Hudson, NY: Ultramarine Publishing, 1992. 16 p. Index. Paperback. ISBN 0-89366-233-X.

Like many authors, David Goodis (1917–1967) got his start in the pulp magazines and moved into producing paperback originals, with an occasional hardcover. Offset from laser-printed copy, this bibliography contains separate sections listing Goodis's books and short stories. The overall arrangement in each section is chronological. Book citations are numbered and provide publication data on the first American and first British edition. Titles are underlined; retitlings are indicated; and information on paginations, dustwrapper artists, prices, and identifying points is also given. The citations for the short stories are also arranged chronologically. Story titles are given in quote marks; pulp magazine names are underlined; volume and issue numbers are given; and the publication date is provided. Pagination, however, is not given. An index to the titles and retitlings concludes the pamphlet. The data on Goodis's books are accurate, but less than half of his short fiction has been cited, and an occasional typo (e.g., *"Crace" Detective* instead of *Crack Detective*) does not help its credibility. A new and updated edition is badly needed.

Paula Gosling

420. Tangled Web. **Paula Gosling**. http://www.twbooks.co.uk/authors/pgosling.html

No photograph of Gosling is provided, but this website has a brief biography and a cover reproduction; it is accompanied by excerpts from positive critical reviews. A chronological bibliography concludes the website. Titles are accompanied by publisher and year of publication.

Sue Grafton

421. Ahearn, Allen, and Patricia Ahearn. **Author Price Guides: Sue Grafton**. Rockville, MD: Quill & Brush, 1993. 3 leaves. APG 140.

This Author's Price Guide lists Sue Grafton's works from the 1967 appearance of *Keziah Dane* to the 1993 publication of *J Is for Judgment*.

For a thorough description of the format of Author Price Guides, see the entry under Fredric Brown.

422. Grafton, Sue. **Sue Grafton's Web Site**. http://www.suegrafton.com

Grafton's own website contains a biography, photographs of her and her cats, links to reviews and sites for reader commentary, and cover illustrations and data about all of her books. Features include a sample chapter, a biography of Kinsey Millhone, and a trivia contest about Millhone, the answers of which appear at the bottom of the screen. The section devoted to her books provides a cover illustration, publisher and year of publication, ISBN, initial cost, excerpts from positive reviews, and a summary of the book. Nicely designed and cleanly presented.

423. King, David J. **Sue Grafton**. http://www.dcs.gla.ac.uk/~gnik/crime-fiction/grafton/grafton.html

King's website offers a link to a brief biography of Grafton. His bibliography arranges Grafton's work by genre, with different sections listing Grafton's Kinsey Millhone novels, other works, uncollected short stories, and plays. The website concludes with a Grafton filmography. The contents of each section are arranged chronologically, but no bibliographic data are provided apart from the publication date; publication data are not provided for individual short story publication. The section providing the filmography is unique to this website, but for other material, Grafton's official website (above) is preferable.

Ann Granger

424. Tangled Web. **Ann Granger**. http://www.twbooks.co.uk/authors/agranger.html

No photograph of Granger appears, but this website provides a brief biography and a cover reproduction accompanied by excerpts from positive critical reviews. A chronological bibliography concludes the website; titles are accompanied by publisher and, often, the year of their publication.

Kate Grilley

425. Grilley, Kate. **Welcome to Kate Grilley's Web Site**. http://ourworld.compuserve.com/homepages/Kate_Grilley/

Grilley's home page has references about her work, photographs of Egypt and island life, a picture of her cat, and a list of other websites. More information would be welcome.

Martha Grimes

426. Ahearn, Allen, and Patricia Ahearn. **Author Price Guides: Martha Grimes**. Rockville, MD: Quill & Brush, 1997. 4 leaves. APG 097.2.

This Author's Price Guide to Martha Grimes lists her works from the 1981 publication of *The Man with a Load of Mischief* to the 1996 publication of *Hotel Paradise*.

For a thorough description of the format of Author Price Guides, see the entry under Fredric Brown.

Terris McMahan Grimes

427. Grimes, Terris McMahan. **Terris McMahan Grimes Presents Sister Sleuth**. http://vme.net/dvm/sister-sleuth

Grimes's site provides a photograph, an interview, and selected synopses and illustrations of the covers of her books. Publication data including publisher, year of publication, and ISBN. Biographical data are weak, but Grimes does reveal that she is well read in the genre, drives a six-year-old Toyota, and has never been in a fight, "not even when I went to Tompkins Elementary School in Oakland, California."

Frank Gruber

428. Clark, William J. **The Frank Gruber Index**. Los Angeles, CA: William J. Clark, 1969. 18 p. Stapled sheets.

Compiled largely from the information contained in Frank Gruber's own files, this index (reproduced from typed copy) contains three sections. The first lists the books by Gruber; the second lists his fiction; the third, his nonfiction.

The first section is chronological. The book's publication date is given, followed by title and publisher. Although this section is but one page in length, it contains a few surprises: Gruber's first book, *The Dillinger Book*, was published in 1934, but *The Pulp Jungle*, Gruber's 1967 autobiography, makes no mention of it—Gruber describes the events of 1934 largely in terms of his rejected short stories and his acceptance by *Operator #5*.

The second and third sections are arranged alphabetically by the title of the publication in which Gruber appeared, with Gruber's appearances listed chronologically. Publication titles are given in capital letters and underlined. Gruber's titles are listed in regular type followed by a parenthetical note giving the number of pages in the story or the number of columns in the piece; serializations are indicated by (S) followed by the number of parts in the serialization. The series character's name appears in parentheses. A (+) indicates that the work appeared in book form. Entries conclude by providing additional reprint information, including if the work appeared under a pseudonym.

Although Gruber died in 1969, this is the only separate list of his work, and it is incomplete, failing to mention his writing for motion pictures and television. He is now largely forgotten except for devotees of the pulp magazines, but a full bibliography of the man once dubbed "The American Edgar Wallace" would be helpful.

Jean Hager

429. Hager, Jean. **Jean Hager**. http://www.imt.net/~gedison/hager.html

Hager's personal website provides a picture, an autobiographical statement, and information about her three mystery series: Mitch Bushyhead, Molly Bearpaw, and Iris House Bed and Breakfast. Cover illustrations are selectively provided, but every book is accorded a synopsis. Publisher and ISBN are given for in-print titles, as are excerpts from positive critical reviews. Finally, the page contains an interview with Hager, information about her book signing tours, and links to other sites.

Parnell Hall

430. Hall, Parnell. **Parnell Hall's Mystery Page**. http://pathfinder.com/twep/mysterious_press/authors/parnell_hall/index.html

At one time Hall's home page contained two quizzes, links to his work in progress, information about his previous works, biographical information on his nonexistent friend J. P. Hailey (the name under which Hall writes courtroom drama), sound bites and video clips of Hall, information on the movies in which Hall has appeared, critical responses to Hall's work, a story about the world's worst copyeditor, and links to other mystery sites. Sample chapters from the novels of Hall and his character Stanley Hastings were provided; bibliographic data cited publisher, year of publication, and ISBN for first editions, and publisher and year for later editions. The present site contains significantly less, but it may expand once again.

Lyn Hamilton

431. Hamilton, Lyn. **Lyn Hamilton**. http://www.interlog.com/~avebury/

Hamilton's personal website provides a photograph of her, an interview, reproductions of the covers of her novels, and synopses of and chapters from her books. Additional bibliographic data are not provided, but the website provides an effective introduction to the author and her work.

Dashiell Hammett

432. Denton, William. **Dashiell Hammett**. http://www.vex.net/~buff/rara-avis/
biblio/hammett.html

The above URL provides a comprehensive list of Hammett's works, with
different sections listing the first printings of his books, short fiction, short nonfiction, poetry, screenplays, and adaptations. A list of movies about Hammett
and a selective bibliography conclude the site. There is a link to a biography of
Hammett.

The contents of each section are arranged chronologically. Book titles are
italicized, and publisher and year of publication are given. Contents of short
story collections are listed, and titles featuring the Continental Op are indicated.
The titles of individual short stories, short nonfiction pieces, and poems appear
in quotation marks, and titles of periodicals that published them are italicized;
publication month and year are given. The titles of screenplays and adaptations
are also italicized; both are accompanied by year of release. Though a number of
posthumously published collections are not cited, this bibliography is clearly presented and accessible.

433. **Hammett and His Continental Op**. http://nanaimo.ark.com/~wilted/
home.html

One of the best sites devoted to Hammett, this concentrates on Hammett's Continental Op. Its first page asks, "Who is this nameless, somewhat
overweight, slightly balding forty-something sleuth?" Other pages provide a
biography and a picture of Hammett, more information on the Continental Op,
lists and descriptions of the short stories and novels in which the Continental Op
appeared, and a selection of quotes from the "Op."

434. Johnson, Joseph M. **The Hammett-List WWW Page**. http://www.
cigarsmokers.com/hammett/hammett.html

This useful site provides a picture of Hammett and offers links to many of
the numerous Hammett bibliographies, websites, and discussion groups, including those listed elsewhere in this section.

435. Layman, Richard. **Dashiell Hammett: A Descriptive Bibliography**.
Pittsburgh, PA: University of Pittsburgh Press, 1979. xiii, 185 p. Index.
(Pittsburgh Series in Bibliography). LC 78-53600. ISBN 0-8229-3394-2.

This fine volume is without doubt the most comprehensive bibliography
of the writings of Dashiell Hammett likely to appear. Oddly, its compiler does
not seem to have been aware of Mundell's earlier effort (q.v.), or he would not
have opened his acknowledgments by stating that "Hammett bibliography
started with William F. Nolan. His *Dashiell Hammett: A Casebook* (Santa Barbara:
McNally & Loftin, 1969) has been the sole book-length study of Hammett. . . ."
Apart from this oversight, Layman's work is exemplary.

The bibliography contains six lettered sections: A) Separate Publications, B) First-Appearance Contributions to Books, C) First Appearances in Periodicals, D) First Appearances in Newspapers, E) Movies, and F) Miscellanea. Each of these sections is arranged chronologically, and the citations in each are separately lettered and numbered.

Section A is 112 pages in length. Each citation reproduces the title page of the first edition of all British and American hardcovers and paperbacks. Each entry then provides an extensive analytical bibliographical description of the first edition, describing collation, pagination, contents, typography and paper, binding, dustjacket, publication, and printing. A section called "Notes" provides additional information and cross-references to other sections. A section for "Locations" has not only a list of the holdings of libraries but also the dates on which the major copyright libraries received the volume. Additional printings and editions are also noted and described; though the descriptions of these are of necessity brief, the title and copyright pages are described at length. A supplement (section AA) lists collections of Hammett's writings, using the same principles of bibliographical description.

Section B, C, D, and E are equally thorough, the citations referencing pseudonymous works, public letters or petitions signed by Hammett, and the movies for which Hammett provided the original story or script material. (Only six movies are cited, but a footnote makes intriguing reference to four unpublished typescripts at the MGM studios in Culver City, California.) Section F contains only two citations, one referencing a dustjacket blurb Hammett provided for Nathanael West's *The Day of the Locust*, and the other describing a copy of a typed form letter in the F. Scott Fitzgerald archives at Princeton University Library.

Six appendixes list the advertising copy that Hammett might have written for the Albert S. Samuels Jewelry Company in San Francisco between 1922 and 1926; radio plays based on Hammett's work; television plays, movies, and stage plays based on Hammett's work; the syndication of previously published work by Hammett; notes by the compiler; and a brief bibliography. A comprehensive index lists all titles and names mentioned in the book.

436.   Lovisi, Gary. **Dashiell Hammett and Raymond Chandler: A Checklist and Bibliography of Their Paperback Appearances**. Brooklyn, NY: Gryphon Books, 1994. 82 p. Paperback. LC 96-134119. ISBN 0-936071-36-2. (500 copies printed.)

See the entry under Raymond Chandler for a description of this book.

437.   Mundell, E. H. **A List of the Original Appearances of Dashiell Hammett's Magazine Work**. Portage, IN: [N.P.], 1968. 52 p. Index. LC 71-41.

Not seen, but presumably the first edition of the work below (q.v.).

438.   Mundell, E. H. **A List of the Original Appearances of Dashiell Hammett's Magazine Work**. Kent, OH: Kent State University Press, 1968. 52 p. Index. (Serif Series: Bibliographies and Checklists, no. 13). LC 75-97620. ISBN 0-87338-033-9.

As its title indicates, this is a list of the first magazine appearances of Dashiell Hammett's short stories, poetry, and letters; Hammett's nonfiction, which includes numerous book reviews, is not treated. The list is arranged chronologically. Each citation provides title and issue of the magazine in which the piece appeared; often the opening sentence is quoted. Mundell indicates when he was unable to obtain the original publication data. A number at the bottom of each citation indicates when the material has been collected and/or reprinted; these numbers are keyed to a section near the book's conclusion. Indexes list the stories by title, Hammett's books, verse, letters to *Black Mask*, pseudonyms, magazines in which he published, and names of his detectives and the cases in which they appeared.

The opening sentences are unique to this bibliography, but the publication has been effectively superseded by Richard Layman's *Dashiell Hammett: A Descriptive Bibliography* (q.v.).

439.   Nolan, William F. **Dashiell Hammett: A Casebook**. Introduction by Philip Durham. Santa Barbara, CA: McNally & Loftin, 1969. xvi, 189 p. Index. LC 68-8393.

Although cited by Layman (q.v.) as the first bibliography of Hammett, it would be more accurate to refer to this pioneering work as the first book-length study of Hammett. Nolan's life of Hammett comprises pages 1–127; the bibliography does not begin until page 132. Called "A Dashiell Hammett Checklist," the bibliography has separate sections for books, magazine fiction, articles, introductions, poetry, reviews, letters, newspaper work, radio work, motion pictures (written by Hammett), and Hammett's anthology appearances. Unlike the other bibliographies in this section, Nolan documents secondary literature. The checklist concludes with a bibliographic essay describing books relating to the hardboiled school of literature.

The checklist is not as comprehensive as either Mundell's or Layman's work, but Nolan's life of Hammett, apparently written without the assistance of Lillian Hellman, is sympathetic and worth reading.

Joseph Hansen

440.   Tangled Web. **Joseph Hansen and Dave Brandstetter**. http://www.twbooks. co.uk/authors/josephhansen.html

Although it lacks a photograph of Hansen, this website provides a brief biography, and cover reproductions from several of his mysteries featuring gay sleuth Dave Brandstetter. These are accompanied by excerpts from positive critical reviews. A chronological bibliography concludes the website; titles are accompanied by publisher and year of publication.

Cyril Hare

441. Tangled Web. **Cyril Hare (1900–1958)**. http://www.zubooks.co.uk/authors/ authorpagelist.html

Posting a photograph of English mystery writer Cyril Hare, this website discusses two of his better-known novels, *An English Murder* (1951) and *He Should Have Died Hereafter* (1958). A brief biography is given, as is a cover reproduction of the Penguin edition of *An English Murder*; excerpts from positive critical reviews are provided. A chronological bibliography concludes the website; titles are accompanied by publisher and year of publication. Hare's real name (Alfred Alexander Gordon Clark) is mentioned.

Carolyn G. Hart

442. Johnston, Gerald H. **Carolyn G. Hart List**.

Available from the archives maintained by DorothyL, and also through the Miss Lemon website (http://www.iwillfollow.com/lemon.htm), this list of the writings of Carolyn G. Hart is arranged chronologically. Each title is accompanied by place of publication, publisher, and year of publication; series are indicated, and Hart's nonmystery publications are listed separately. This list appears to have been compiled in 1992.

Judith Hawkes

443. Tangled Web. **Judith Hawkes**. http://www.twbooks.co.uk/authors/ jhawkes.html

No photograph of Hawkes is provided, but this website does have a brief biography of her and cover reproductions from her two novels, *Julian's House* (1996) and *My Soul to Keep* (1996). These are accompanied by excerpts from positive critical reviews and a link to the full text of a review. The titles in the concluding bibliography are accompanied by publisher and year of publication.

Sparkle Hayter

444. Hayter, Sparkle. **Planet Sparkle**. http://members.aol.com/SHayter370/ index.html

This is Hayter's official home page; it is frequently updated and invariably whimsical, with a recent version presenting information on Hayter's Robin Hudson series, listing titles, ISBNs, publishers, cost, and publication dates, and providing teasing summaries of the contents and excerpts from positive critical reactions. Cover images are given, and there are links to an interview with Hayter, her diary, tours, rants, men, and the pages of her friends.

Lauren Henderson

445. Tangled Web. **Lauren Henderson.** http://www.twbooks.co.uk/authors/lhenderson.html

A photograph of Henderson is given, and this website provides a brief biography of her and cover reproductions from her novels. These are accompanied by the full text of positive critical reviews. In the concluding bibliography, titles are accompanied by publisher and year of publication.

Carl Hiaasen

446. Zelzer, Marcus. **The Unofficial Carl Hiaasen Webpage.** http://studbimb.tuwien.ac.at/~e9225468/hiaasen.html

This site contains a picture of Hiaasen and cover images to selected British paperback editions. Each of the latter is accompanied by the text of the back cover, ISBN, publisher, and publication year. A link to the *Miami Herald* provides additional information about Hiaasen.

Lynn S. Hightower

447. Tangled Web. **Lynn S. Hightower.** http://www.twbooks.co.uk/authors/lshightower.html

A photograph of Hightower is provided, as are cover reproductions from *Eyeshot* (1996) and *Flashpoint* (1996); these are accompanied by excerpts from positive critical reviews A brief biography is given, followed by some autobiographical notes. The concluding list of titles provides publisher and year of publication.

Reginald Hill

448. Tangled Web. **Reginald Hill and Dalziel & Pascoe.** http://www.twbooks.co.uk/authors/rhill.html

This site provides a brief biography of Hill, a picture of Hill, and cover images to selected British paperbacks that feature Hill's series characters Pascoe and Dalziel. All images are accompanied by the text appearing on the book's back cover, with excerpts from positive reviews, and information about television adaptations of the novels. There is also a chronological list of Hill's works.

Tony Hillerman

449. Ahearn, Allen, and Patricia Ahearn. **Author Price Guides: Tony Hiller-man**. Rockville, MD: Quill & Brush, 1996. 7 leaves. APG 158.

This Author's Price Guide lists the works of Tony Hillerman from the 1970 publication of *The Blessing Way* to the 1996 appearance of *Finding Moon*.

For a thorough description of the format of Author Price Guides, see the entry under Fredric Brown.

450. Greenberg, Martin, ed. **The Tony Hillerman Companion: A Compre-hensive Guide to His Life and Work**. New York: HarperCollins, 1994. viii, 375 p. LC 93-49507. ISBN 0-06-017034-4.

Despite the title, this is not a comprehensive guide to Hillerman's life and works but a seven-chapter miscellany, the last two chapters of which print three of Hillerman's short stories and six of his articles. The book contains maps of the Southwest as its endpapers and opens with a two-page chronology of Hiller-man's life and career. The first five chapters focus on Hillerman's writing; the first two are by Jon L. Breen. In "The Detective Fiction of Tony Hillerman: A Book-by-Book Guide," Breen provides lengthy, appreciative, and intelligent de-scriptions of Hillerman's novels (as of 1993), and Breen's "Interview with Tony Hillerman" is exactly as its title indicates and has not had prior publication.

The third chapter, George Hardeen's "The Navajo Nation," is reprinted from APA Publication's 1991 *Insight Guide: Native America*. It was recommended by Hillerman as being the finest account by a Navajo available, and it vividly de-scribes "Navajoland," the physical area in which the Navajo live. The fourth chapter, "Native American Clans in Tony Hillerman's Fiction: A Guide" is co-authored by Elizabeth A. Gaines and Diane Hammer. The clans are arranged alphabetically within tribes, and under each clan are listed the names of the char-acters belonging to it. Each name is followed by "p" (indicating paternal clan) or "m" (indicating maternal clan), and an abbreviation indicates the name of the book in which the relationship is revealed. Clans that are named but for which no characters are identified are listed at the conclusion of this section.

The fifth chapter, also by Gaines and Hammer, lists and describes all the people who have appeared as characters or who are mentioned in Hillerman's 13 novels and three short stories. Each entry provides character's name, works in which s/he appeared, clan, history, and function within the work. Characters known only by a descriptive name (e.g., Blue Policeman, Fly on the Wall) are listed under the first letter of that name.

Hillerman has continued to write, and a comprehensive guide to Hiller-man's life and works still remains to be done. Nevertheless, this solidly written and pioneering effort will be welcome to those wanting information about a sig-nificant, popular, and deservedly honored writer.

451. Hieb, Louis A. **Collecting Tony Hillerman: A Checklist of the First Editions of Tony Hillerman, with Approximate Value and Commentary**. Santa Fe, NM: Vinegar Tom Press, 1992. Unpaged. (275 copies printed.)

Not seen.

452. Hieb, Louis A. **Fifty Foreign Firsts: A Tony Hillerman Checklist**. Santa Fe, NM: Parker Books of the West, 1991. 16 p. (50 copies printed.)

Not seen, but apparently superseded by *Tony Hillerman Abroad* (q.v.).

453. Hieb, Louis A. **On Collecting Hillerman**. Tucson, AZ: University of Arizona, 1990. Unpaginated [5 p.]

Though occasionally cited as a reference publication, this pamphlet consists of prose discussions of Hillerman's works. Hieb discusses Hillerman's first editions, nonfiction, juvenile fiction, advance reading copies, paperback reprints, British editions, other challenges, foreign-language editions, and reading and collecting. Each of those subjects is accorded one paragraph. The Hillerman completist may want this pamphlet, but it has been thoroughly superseded by Hieb's book-length bibliography (q.v.).

454. Hieb, Louis A. **Tony Hillerman: A Bibliography**. Tucson, AZ: Gigantic Hound, 1988. 18 p. Gigantic Hound Keepsake. (100 copies printed.)

Not seen.

455. Hieb, Louis A. **Tony Hillerman: From the Blessing Way to Talking God: A Bibliography**. Tucson, AZ: Press of the Giant Hound, 1990. 88 p. Cloth. (1,000 copies printed.)

Tony Hillerman: From the Blessing Way to Talking God is apparently an expansion of Hieb's 1988 *Tony Hillerman: A Bibliography*. Following a biographical introduction and a two-page chronology of Hillerman's life, this well-done bibliography contains seven lettered sections: A) Novels, B) Short Fiction, C) Non-fiction, D) Contributions to Books, E) Contributions to Periodicals, F) Works about Hillerman, and G) Audio Recordings. The arrangement of citations in each section is chronological, with each entry separately lettered and numbered.

Section A describes the first American and British editions of all printings of Hillerman's novels; illustrations are provided for many of these books. Each entry has a title page transcription; a description of the pagination, collation, and page size; a description of the content; a description of the binding using the Inter-Society Color Council of the National Bureau of Standards method of designating colors; notes about publication and the novel's first price; and notes regarding the novel's setting, awards it has won, and unusual features of the book. Although the focus is on the American and British first editions, later editions and translations are nevertheless listed, though extensive bibliographic data are not provided for them. Though they are briefer, sections B-G are equally thorough.

Hieb's citations are clear and well presented. At this writing, this is the most accessible and comprehensive bibliography of Hillerman. One hopes for updated editions that maintain the thoroughness of this edition but have wider distribution.

456.   Hieb, Louis A. **Tony Hillerman Abroad: An Annotated Checklist of Foreign Language Editions**. Santa Fe, NM: Parker Books of the World, 1993. 45 p. (75 copies printed.)

Not seen, but apparently an expansion of the material first presented in *Fifty Foreign Firsts: A Tony Hillerman Checklist* (q.v.).

457.   PBS Adult Learning Service. **PBS Adult Learning Service Presents an Online Q&A with Tony Hillerman**. http://www.pbs.org/als/feature/hillerman

This online interview is undated, and the dozen questions never achieve any depth. Nevertheless, the questions that Hillerman answers concern his knowledge and use of the Navajo culture, his writing habits, and the spiritual depth in his books, and these are likely to be subjects that are of some interest to the general reader.

Chester Himes

458.   Ahearn, Allen, and Patricia Ahearn. **Author Price Guides: Chester Himes**. Rockville, MD: Quill & Brush, 1995. 4 leaves. APG 059.3.

This Author's Price Guide to Chester Himes documents his work from the 1945 publication of *If He Hollers Let Him Go* to the 1995 publication of *Conversations with Chester Himes*.

For a thorough description of the format of Author Price Guides, see the entry under Fredric Brown.

459.   Daniels, Valarie. **Chester Himes**. http://www.aamystery.com/authors-list.html

Daniels provides a chronological list of Himes's "Harlem Domestic Series," starting with the 1957 *For Love of Imabelle* and concluding with the 1993 *Plan B*. The data are clearly presented, though more bibliographical data would be desirable. The comprehensive Himes bibliography is that of Fabre, Skinner, and Sullivan (below).

460. Fabre, Michel, Robert E. Skinner, and Lester Sullivan. **Chester Himes: An Annotated Primary and Secondary Bibliography**. Westport, CT: Greenwood Press, 1992. xxvi, 216 p. Index. (Bibliographies and Indexes in Afro-American and African Studies, no. 30). LC 92-18316. ISBN 0-313-28396-6.

This solid bibliography begins by providing an introduction and a chronology to the life and career of Chester Himes, a man worthy of study. A precocious child from Ohio's African American middle class, Himes entered Ohio State University at age 16; was soon expelled for a prank; and following an abortive armed robbery, was sentenced to 20 years at hard labor in the Ohio State Penitentiary. He began to write while in prison and, like Richard Wright and James Baldwin, explored in his work the problems of racial identity. After his release, Himes worked for the WPA and labor organizations and became an expatriate; he did not start his career as a writer of crime fiction until 1953. When he died in 1983, his work was out of print in the United States but was enormously popular in Europe, in particular France.

The publications in all sections are listed in chronological order. The primary bibliography contains separate sections for Himes's fiction, nonfiction, manuscript materials, and a filmography. Citations to the fiction and nonfiction are continuously numbered; entries begin with "P" and a number, and the manuscripts and filmography are numbered with "M" and "F," respectively. Novel titles are given in italics, followed by place of publication, publisher, publication year, pagination, and (when relevant) paperback series number for all known American, French, and British editions; names of translators are provided. Data on titles first appearing in French are listed ahead of the subsequent printings in England and America, and because most of Himes's French publications appeared in a designated series, the series title appears in italics between the publisher's name and the publication date.

The section describing Himes's short fiction contains two sections. The first lists first periodical appearances and gives story titles in quotation marks, publication titles in italics, and the magazine's month, year, volume number, and pagination. The second lists the contents of short story collections; it uses the same citation format as the section listing Himes's novels, but the contents are listed and cross-referenced to their previous appearances as short fiction and nonfiction.

Himes's nonfiction is listed according to the principles described above. Entries for his manuscripts are to those that are documented in OCLC and the *National Union Catalog of Manuscript Collections*. The filmography provides the cast and credits of the three motion pictures that have thus far been made of Himes's writings.

The citations in the secondary bibliography are continuously numbered with "S" and a number, and reference French publications as well as American and British criticism. In all, some 680 reviews, articles, chapters, and full-length books are cited using the citation formats and principles described above.

Anonymous works are listed at the start of the chronological sequence, and all citations are helpfully annotated. Indexes to critics and to the titles of Himes's works conclude the volume.

Though alternative arrangements might have made the secondary bibliography less cumbersome, this remains a solid and usable work.

Edward D. Hoch

461. Moffatt, June M., and Francis M. Nevins, Jr. **Edward D. Hoch Bibliography, 1955–1991**. Introduction by Marvin Lachman. Van Nuys, CA: Southern California Institute for Fan Interests, 1991. xii, 112 p.

Hoch has published at least one short story in every issue of *Ellery Queen's Mystery Magazine* since May 1973, and he is perhaps the most prolific writer of mystery short stories currently alive. This bibliography documents an impressive output that rarely disappoints. Compiled for Bouchercon 22, the 22d Annual Anthony Boucher Memorial Mystery Convention held in Pasadena, California, in 1991, this bibliography begins with an appreciative introduction by fellow crimewriter Marvin Lachman. This is followed by a guide to abbreviations, which explains the abbreviations used in the bibliography and defines the attributes of Hoch's 24 series characters. The bibliography itself contains the following sections: novels, story collections, and anthologies; short fiction as Edward D. Hoch; short fiction as Anthony Circus; short fiction as Stephen Dentinger; short fiction as R. L. Stevens; short fiction as Mr. X; short fiction as Pat McMahon; short fiction as Irwin Booth; novels and short stories as Ellery Queen; contest novels under pseudonyms; nonfiction as Edward D. Hoch; nonfiction as Stephen Dentinger; nonfiction as Irwin Booth; nonfiction as R. E. Porter; stories on audiotape; and film adaptations of stories by Hoch. Following this listing are 24 indexes providing access to Hoch's works by series character.

In all sections, titles of books are given in italic capital letters, and magazine titles are given in italics; titles of short stories are given in regular type. Citations to Hoch's books provide publisher and year of publication. When relevant, the contents are given, with cross-references to the original magazine publications. Citations to Hoch's magazine appearances are arranged chronologically within each magazine; story titles are cross-referenced to their later book appearances. Paginations are not provided for either books or magazine publications, and citations to magazine publications do not include the magazine's volume number.

In addition to the above shortcomings, the volume does not include a comprehensive chronological list of Hoch's works, and it lacks a title index. It nevertheless remains a useful publication.

Matt Hughes

462.   Hughes, Matt. **Matt Hughes**. http://mars.ark.com/~mhughes/

Hughes's website provides an autobiographical statement, a photograph, and links to his books that include a synopsis, the first chapter, and a cover illustration. Hughes provides ISBN, publisher, and publication date for his published works, and he gives descriptions of his (as yet) unsold books.

Evan Hunter. *See* **Ed McBain.**

Elspeth Huxley

463.   Cross, Robert S., and Michael Perkin. **Elspeth Huxley: A Bibliography**. Foreword by Elspeth Huxley. New Castle, DE: Oak Knoll Press; Winchester, England: St. Paul's Bibliographies, 1996. xix, 187 p. Index. (Winchester Bibliographies of 20th Century Writers). LC 95-26301. ISBN 1-8847-1817-5.

Compiled with the assistance of Huxley and current as of 1995, this fine bibliography uses a format reminiscent of the Pittsburgh Series in Bibliography. The bibliographical citations are arranged into five sections, each separately lettered, with each citation separately numbered: A) books and pamphlets by Elspeth Huxley, including translations; B) books edited or with contributions by Elspeth Huxley; C) contributions to newspapers and periodicals; D) radio and television appearances; and E) miscellanea. There are also a chronology of Huxley's life, numerous reproductions of dustwrappers and bindings, and a fine index.

The data in each section are gratifyingly thorough. In section A, the title page is transcribed in the quasifacsimile method, and there is information about collation statement, contents, illustrations, binding cases and their colors, dustjacket or wrappers, and the paper on which the book was printed. The bibliographer's notes also indicate which copy or copies were used for the description and provide notes on the printing history (number of copies printed, prices, textual changes, cancellations, author's agreements, etc.). Each entry concludes by citing contemporary reviews received by the book. Corrected editions and first American editions are also accorded this bibliographical treatment.

The citations to Huxley's material in the other sections are equally thorough and detailed, though (oddly) paginations are only sporadically provided for Huxley's contributions to newspapers and periodicals. The index thoroughly covers sections A, B, and E; sections C and D are indexed only by the name of the periodical or radio or television station. These minor lacunae in no way invalidate the usefulness of this bibliography, which remains comprehensive and accessible.

Michael Innes

464.   McAllister, Jill. **Comprehensive Michael Innes List**.

Available from the archives maintained by the DorothyL listserv, and through the Miss Lemon website (http://www.iwillfollow.com/lemon.htm), this comprehensive list of the books of Michael Innes is arranged chronologically. Novels are listed first, then collections of short stories. Changes in titles are referenced.

P. D. James

465.   Ahearn, Allen, and Patricia Ahearn. **Author Price Guides: P. D. James**. Rockville, MD: Quill & Brush, 1992. 2 leaves. APG 116.

This Author's Price Guide lists the work of P. D. James from the 1962 publication of *Cover Her Face* to the 1990 publication of *Devices and Desires*.

For a thorough description of the format of Author Price Guides, see the entry under Fredric Brown.

Russell James

466.   James, Russell. **The Russell James Website**. http://dspace.dial.pipex.com/found/rj.htm

James's website offers a picture of him and information about his books and news about his writing. The site, however, contains no illustrations of the books, minimal biographical data, and less-than-adequate bibliographical data. On the plus side, several sample chapters are provided as are excerpts from positive critical reviews. Best used in conjunction with the site maintained by the Tangled Web (q.v.).

467.   Tangled Web. **Russell James**. http://www.twbooks.co.uk/authors/rjames.html

A photograph of James is provided, as are a brief biography and cover reproductions from four of James's thriller/mysteries. These are accompanied by excerpts from positive critical reviews. A chronologically arranged bibliography concludes the website; titles are accompanied by publisher and year of publication. There is also a link to James's personal home page (q.v.).

H. R. F. Keating

468.   Tangled Web. **H. R. F. Keating**. http://www.twbooks.co.uk/authors/
hrfkeating.html

A photograph of Keating is provided, as are a biography and cover images
from a number of his books, including several of his Inspector Ghote mysteries;
these are accompanied by excerpts from positive critical reviews. A chronologically arranged bibliography concludes the website. Titles are accompanied by
publisher and year of publication and indicate whether the work features Inspector Ghote.

Alex Keegan

469.   Keegan, Alex. **The Official Alex Keegan Home Page**. http://www.
btinternet.com/~alex.keegan1/

Keegan's home page provides links to his novels: Cover illustrations, the
opening chapter, and information about the characters are provided. In addition,
Keegan posts a different short story every week, and he offers numerous links to
other crimewriting and literary fiction sites and much helpful advice on creative
writing. On the debit side, his choice of background colors is unpleasant, and the
extracts from his novels are in a font so large that reading is difficult.

Harry Stephen Keeler

470.   Polt, Richard. **Harry Stephen Keeler Society**. http://xavier.xu.edu:8000/
~polt/keeler.html

This tribute to Keeler includes a picture and a biography of its subject,
several excerpts from Keeler's writings, and numerous photographs of the covers of his books, the latter in a section referred to as the Keeler Dustjacket Vault.
Information on joining the Harry Stephen Keeler Society is also given, and there
is a link to the home page of William Poundstone (q.v.).

471.   Poundstone, William. **Harry Stephen Keeler Home Page**. http://users.
aol.com/bigsecrets/Keeler.html

This website provides a biography of Keeler and discussion of some of
the eccentric Keeler's recurrent themes. Because Keeler's works are not yet electronically available, there is a lengthy plot summary of *The Man with the Magic Ear-
drums* (1939), a work in which Keeler's eccentricity clearly reveals itself. Also
included are an account of Poundstone's correspondence with the blind and eld-
erly Thelma Keeler, and Poundstone's failed attempt at getting congressional
support for a postage stamp commemorating the centennial of Keeler's birth
(1990). Finally, there is a link to the Harry Stephen Keeler Society's home page
(q.v.).

Jonathan and Faye Kellerman

472. Seels, James T., ed. **Jonathan and Faye Kellerman: American and English Publications, 1972–1996**. Foreword and short story "Malibu Dog" by Faye Kellerman. Afterword by Jonathan Kellerman. Royal Oak, MI: Mission Viejo, CA: ASAP/Airtight-Seels Allied Publication, 1994. 54 p. Indexes. Paperback. (60 copies in acrylic slipcases and 240 limited copies.)

Despite being compiled with assistance from the Kellermans, this bibliography is quite disappointing. Following an introduction by Faye Kellerman (in which she discusses Jonathan), the bibliography provides a chronologically arranged list of her publications, the first citation being a 1986 novel, *The Ritual Bath*. Titles of books and short stories are listed in capital letters, the latter in quotations; beneath each title is a statement indicating whether the work is a short story or a novel. The publication data list place of publication, publisher's name, and year of publication. When the publisher identified works with the words "first edition" or with numbers indicating printing, these too are listed; the data are current through 1995. Pagination, paperback reprints, dustwrapper information, and commentary about texts are not provided. An index to titles concludes this section.

The second section is also chronological in arrangement, the citations beginning with the statement that between 1972 and 1985 "Jonathan Kellerman wrote and edited numerous articles in peer-review psychology and medical journals. He also wrote articles in newspapers and magazines." None of these are listed; the first complete citation is to Kellerman's 1977 short story, "The Questioner." As in the previous section, titles of books and short stories are listed in capital letters, the latter distinguished by quotations. A statement indicates whether the work is a short story, a novel, a children's book, or nonfiction, and the publication data list place of publication, publisher's name, and year of publication. When the publisher identified works with the words "first edition" or with numbers indicating printing, these are listed. International and limited editions are listed, though paperback reprints are not; data extend through 1996. Pagination, dustwrapper information, and commentary about texts are not provided. A title index lists the cited works.

An afterword by Jonathan Kellerman (in which he discusses Faye) and Faye Kellerman's 1990 short story "Malibu Dog" conclude the book. The Kellermans are talented, versatile, and enormously popular writers, and a comprehensive and thorough bibliography of them remains to be done.

473. Bantam Doubleday Dell. **Jonathan Kellerman**. http://www.bdd.com/bin/featured_author/authors/f388.html

One of the "A Visit With" series produced by Bantam Doubleday Dell, this site provides a picture of the author and offers links to Kellerman's new book, his previous books published by Bantam/Doubleday/Dell, a profile, a place to write to the author, tours and appearances, related links, and other authors in the series. The section devoted to books provides a cover reproduction for each title, a summary of the contents, purchasing information, and excerpts of critical praise.

Laurie R. King

474. Tangled Web. **Laurie R. King.** http://www.twbooks.co.uk/authors/lrking.html

A photograph of King is provided, as are a brief biography and cover reproductions from most of her mysteries; these are accompanied by excerpts from positive critical reviews. A chronologically arranged bibliography concludes the website; titles are accompanied by publisher and year of publication.

Steven Knight

475. Tangled Web. **Steven Knight.** http://www.twbooks.co.uk/authors/sknight.html

No photograph of Knight has been posted, but this website provides a brief biography of him. Cover reproductions from two of his mysteries are given; these are accompanied by excerpts from positive critical reviews. A chronological bibliography concludes the website; titles are accompanied by publisher and year of publication.

Joe R. Lansdale

476. Lansdale, Joe. **The Orbit: The Official Drive-in Theatre of Champion Mojo Storyteller Joe R. Lansdale.** http://www.joerlansdale.com

Joe R. Lansdale's own site. The opening page of this amusing and well-designed site is designed to look like the marqee of a drive-in theater. Inside the theater, there are images of four movie posters. "Horror!" connects to one of Lansdale's short stories, which is changed frequently. "The Brute Man" provides a Lansdale biography and a Lansdale bibliography that is reasonably thorough but not comprehensive: Several of Lansdale's pseudonymous collaborations are not listed. "The Mask of Shen Chuan" provides information about Lansdale's school of martial arts, and "The Orbit Now Playing!" provides news about Lansdale's writings and offers connections to his publishers and several of his favorite sites. An earlier version of this site included an interview with Hap Collins and Leonard Pine, Lansdale's series detectives. There is as yet no image of Lansdale.

477. Tangled Web. **Joe R. Lansdale.** http://www.twbooks.co.uk/authors/jrlansdale.html

A photograph and a brief biography of Lansdale are provided, as are cover reproductions from the British editions of his novels featuring Hap Collins and

Leonard Pine and for the British edition of *Cold in July*. These are accompanied by excerpts from positive critical reviews. The selective bibliography provides year of British publication and British publisher. More would be welcome.

Janice Law

478. Law, Janice. **Janice Law**. http://www.sp.uconn.edu/~en291is1/ lawhomepage.html

Janice Law is the name under which Connecticut author Janice Law Trecker has written numerous short stories and nine mystery novels, most of the latter involving the series character Anna Peters. Her home page provides cover reproductions of several of the novels along with material from the back cover/dustwrapper and excerpts from positive critical reviews. First chapters from two novels are given, as is one of her short stories, and there are links to other websites. A photograph of the author would be nice, as would more information about her books, but this is a cleanly done site.

Martha C. Lawrence

479. Lawrence, Martha C. **Martha C. Lawrence**. http://www.mlawrence.com

This is the home page of the author of two novels featuring Dr. Elizabeth Chase, a parapsychologist-turned-private eye. Cover images of the novels are given, as are the prologues and the first chapters of the books and excerpts of positive critical notices. Lawrence provides a picture of herself, a message discussing her psychic experiences, additional biographical data, lists of forthcoming appearances, and information on ordering autographed copies of her works. A cleanly done site.

Elmore Leonard

480. Ahearn, Allen, and Patricia Ahearn. **Author Price Guides: Elmore Leonard**. Rockville, MD: Quill & Brush, 1995. 7 leaves. APG 036.4.

This Author's Price Guide to Elmore Leonard begins with a brief bibliography citing secondary references. It documents Leonard's work from the 1954 publication of *The Bounty Hunters* to the 1995 appearance of *Riding the Rap*.

For a thorough description of the format of Author Price Guides, see the entry under Fredric Brown.

481. Stephens, Christopher P. **A Checklist of Elmore Leonard**. Hastings-on-Hudson, NY: Ultramarine Publishing, 1991. 17 p. Paperback. Index. ISBN 0-89366-215-1.

Apparently offset from laser-printed copy, this bibliography lists the books written by Elmore Leonard, from his earliest days as a Western writer until the 1992 publication of *Rum Punch*. Each numbered citation provides publication data on the first American and first British editions. Titles are underlined; retitlings are indicated; and information on dustwrapper artists, prices, and identifying points are occasionally also given. An index to the titles and retitlings concludes the bibliography. Though this pamphlet is a useful starting point for collectors, it lists neither Leonard's nonbook writings nor his short fiction, and he has of course remained active beyond 1992. A comprehensive bibliography of the writings of Elmore Leonard would be welcome.

482. Tangled Web. **Elmore Leonard**. http://www.twbooks.co.uk/authors/ eleonard.html

A photograph and a brief biography of Leonard are given, as are cover reproductions from the British editions of *Get Shorty* and *Out of Sight*; these are accompanied by excerpts from positive critical reviews. The concluding bibliography lists all of Leonard's titles but provides no additional bibliographical data.

Paul Levine

483. Levine, Paul. **Paul Levine**. http://www.booktalk.com/PLevine/

Levine, author of a series featuring Jake Lassiter, a linebacker-turned-lawyer, provides a photograph, a biographical sketch, and information on his books: a synopsis, cover illustrations, publisher, cost, and ISBN. There is a separate chronologically arranged bibliography. A cleanly produced site.

David Lindsey

484. Lindsey, David. **David Lindsey: On-line with the Best Selling Author**. http://www.lnstar.com/davidlindsey/

Lindsey's web page provides a picture of him, news about him, and biographical data, and offers information about his books that include character descriptions, synopses, and excerpts from positive reviews. Clear cover images are provided. Nicely done.

Philip Luber

485. Luber, Philip. **Philip Luber's Home Page**. http://www.ultranet.com/ ~luber/home.htm

A licensed psychologist specializing in the area of forensic psychology, Luber has written four novels. His website has images of the books, and for each he provides a synopsis, excerpts from positive reviews, the first chapter (or two), and information on ordering autographed copies. He provides a photograph of himself and the text of a recent interview. A capably done site.

Ed McBain

486. King, David J. **Ed McBain**. http://www.dcs.gla.ac.uk/~gnik/crime-fiction/mcbain/mcbain.html

King's website offers a link to a brief biography of McBain and provides information about the 87th Precinct. The bibliography arranges McBain's work by series and genre, with different sections listing McBain's 87th Precinct novels, his Matthew Hope novels, other works, plays, screenplays, and children's works. The website concludes with a McBain filmography. The contents of each section are arranged chronologically, but no bibliographic data are provided apart from publication date; publication data are not provided for individual short stories or limited editions.

487. Stybr, Denise. **87th Precinct**.

Available as part of the archives maintained by the DorothyL listserv, and also through the Miss Lemon website (http://www.iwillfollow.com/lemon.htm), this chronologically arranged list gives the titles of McBain's novels set in the 87th Precinct of New York. No additional bibliographic data are provided; short stories are not referenced. The list is complete until 1995.

Sharyn McCrumb

488. **The Official Sharyn McCrumb Website**. http://www.swva.net/aphill/index.html

This well-designed website provides photographs of McCrumb, her family, and biographical data. Information on her different series is provided. Each book is accompanied by a cover reproduction; the ISBN of the first edition is given, accompanied by a statement about the book's origins. Also included are lists of the awards won by McCrumb and names of those owning international rights, audio rights, book club rights, and film rights. Information on McCrumb's work in progress and her tour and speaking schedule are given, as are links to other sites.

Val McDermid

489. Tangled Web. **Val McDermid**. http://www.twbooks.co.uk/authors/valmcdermid.html

This site provides a picture of McDermid and information on her dramas, short stories, and novels and nonfiction. Numerous cover illustrations appear; bibliographic data include publication month and year, publisher, and changes of title. This site is closely allied with "Val McDermid and Lindsay Gordon" (http://www.thenet.co.uk/~hickafric/lindsayg.html), which discusses Lindsay Gordon, McDermid's best-known series character. Summaries of the Lindsay

Gordon books are provided, accompanied by a cover illustration; a brief biography of McDermid is also given.

John D. MacDonald

490. Ahearn, Allen, and Patricia Ahearn. **Author Price Guides: John D. MacDonald**. Rockville, MD: Quill & Brush, 1993. 14 leaves. APG 143.

This Author's Price Guide lists John D. MacDonald's works from the 1950 appearance of *The Brass Cupcake* to the 1987 publication of *Reading for Survival*.

For a thorough description of the format of Author Price Guides, see the entry under Fredric Brown.

491. Branche, Cal. **The John D. MacDonald Homepage**. http://innet.com/ ~cbranche/jdm.html

The text is occasionally ragged and needs reorganizing, but this website provides a significant amount of information about MacDonald. There are data on the *JDM Bibliophile*, and there are links to bookstores selling MacDonald's works, to a list of his novels, and to the list of his books in the University of Florida Special Collection at Gainesville [sic]. In addition, the rumor of the "black McGee" is squelched; there is a copy of the letter received by MacDonald for his first sale; there is information on Plymouth Gin and a recipe for one of McGee's favorite drinks involving it; and there are links to other MacDonald websites.

492. Campbell, Frank D., Jr. **John D. MacDonald and the Colorful World of Travis McGee**. San Bernardino, CA: Borgo Press, 1977. 64 p. Paperback. (Milford Series. Popular Writers of Today, vol. 5). LC 77-773. ISBN 0-89370-208-0.

Arguably not a reference book, this slim volume contains virtually nothing about MacDonald but provides chatty plot summaries of 16 of MacDonald's Travis McGee novels, from the 1964 *Deep Blue Good-By* to the 1975 *The Dreadful Lemon Sky*. The arrangement of the summaries is chronological, and each chapter has as its title the color used in MacDonald's title. The book concludes with a one-page bio-bibliography that lists the Travis McGee books. There is no table of contents, and users not intimate with MacDonald's bibliography must either consult the bibliography for the publication year and then endeavor to locate the summary by its relative position in the bibliography, or page through the book in the hopes of finding the essay. Neither approach is satisfactory, and Campbell's often facetious comments make it difficult to take this publication seriously.

493. Caribbean Soulman. [Marty Warble]. **Slip F-18/John D. MacDonald's Travis McGee**. http://pages.prodigy.net/mwarble/slipf18/mcgee/

Named for the yacht basin where Travis McGee moored his houseboat, the *Busted Flush*, this website reprints Carl Hiaasen's 1994 introduction to *The Deep Blue Good-By* and lists the 21 McGee novels in chronological order. Following this, the contents of the back covers of the McGee novels published by Fawcett Gold Medal Books are given. There are links to a number of MacDonald/McGee sites and to related Florida sites.

494. Denton, William. **John D. MacDonald**. http://www.vex.net/~buff/rara-avis/ biblio/jdmacdonald.html

The above URL provides a comprehensive chronological list of the first printings of MacDonald's books; his more than 600 short stories are not listed, nor are adaptations. The titles of his books are italicized; the publisher and year of publication are given, as is often the book's series number. The contents of short story collections are listed, and an asterisk by the title indicates that the book features Travis McGee. No data after 1987 are given. A biography of Mac-Donald is accessible through a link.

495. MacLean, David C. **John D. MacDonald: A Checklist of Collectible Editions and Translations with Notes on Prices**. Decatur, IN: Americana Books, 1987. 32 p. Paperback. Index. ISBN 0-917902-06-8.

Concerned only with those works of John D. MacDonald that appeared in book form under his own name—the one exception is so noted—this bibliography is arranged chronologically. Titles are listed in capital letters and separately numbered. Beneath each title are listed the editions known to MacLean. English-language editions are listed first followed by references to editions in French, Swedish, German, and so forth. Each citation provides place of publication, publisher, year of publication, height (in centimeters), pagination, and series and stock number. Reprint editions and large-type editions are also referenced. A note by the title indicates whether the book was part of MacDonald's Travis McGee series. A guide to the price cross-references the citation number to the price offered by various dealers. The bibliography concludes with a title index.

MacLean forthrightly states that many of his entries are "from catalog card entries and not from books actually seen," and his citations contain far fewer data than the bibliographies done by Walter and Jean Shine (q.v.). Nevertheless, this checklist is capably done—portable, lean, and well-arranged. One wishes that MacLean had found the energy to document MacDonald's short stories.

496. Moffatt, Len, June Moffatt, and William J. Clark. **The JDM Master Checklist: A Bibliography of the Published Writings of John D. MacDonald**. Downey, CA: Moffatt House, 1969. xii, 42 p. Paperback. Index. LC 71-7688.

Based upon a bibliography serialized in the *JDM Bibliophile*, the *JDM Master Checklist* is apparently the first separately published bibliography devoted to John D. MacDonald; it is reproduced from clearly photocopied material and printed on blue paper. The *Master Checklist* begins with an introduction to Mac-Donald's life and works, and contains the following sections: 1) Magazine Stories and Articles (American); 2) Stories in Anthologies; 3) Books: U. S. A.

Editions; 4) A Special List of Fawcett Editions; 5) Books: British Editions; 6) Stories Reprinted in British Magazines; 7) Books (international editions); and 8) Stories Reprinted in Japanese Magazines. The data in each section are complete until 1968, though titles projected for 1969 are listed.

The first section is arranged alphabetically by magazine. Beneath each magazine's title is a chronologically arranged list of MacDonald's appearances that includes publication date, story's title, word count or number of pages, and name under which the title was published. Reprints, retitlings, and stories that were part of a series are indicated. This format is also used in the sixth section.

Sections 2 through 5 are chronological in arrangement, though not consistent in format. In the second section, book titles are capitalized; year of publication, publisher, and names of editors are given; and MacDonald's contribution is in quotations and capital letters. In the third section, titles are in capital letters, beneath which are given publisher and year of first publication. Reprint data are provided, as are lists of the contents of MacDonald's short story collections. In the fourth section, the data include book's stock number, title, price, and original publication date. Those books that were out of print when this list was compiled have an "X" in the column for the price. In the fifth section, the title, publication date, and name of the publisher are given.

The section on MacDonald's international publications is alphabetical by language. Within each language, titles are listed chronologically, accompanied by publisher's name and date of publication; the translated title is followed by parentheses containing the original title. In the case of MacDonald's Japanese translations, the original title is given in parentheses, followed by a romanized version of the title, Japanese title in Japanese characters, magazine's name, and date of publication. The bibliography concludes with a comprehensive title index.

This title has been superseded by the work of Walter and Jean Shine, in particular *A Bibliography of the Published Works of John D. MacDonald, with Selected Biographical Materials and Critical Essays* (q.v.). However, the use of Japanese characters is unique to this bibliography.

497. Rufener, S. **JDM Quotations**. http://home.earthlink.net/~rufener

Containing neither biographical nor bibliographical data, this site provides thematic excerpts from the Travis McGee novels and thus serves as a quotations database. The quotations are grouped thematically on the following subjects: economics, population, development, law enforcement, danger and coping, psychology, love and sex, fitness, and "Interesting Facts." A significant number of quotations are provided, but because no linking narrative is present, more often than not MacDonald/McGee appears sententious and pretentious rather than thoughtful and poetic. See http://www.letters.com/~gray/quotes/macdonald.html for nonthematic excerpts from each novel.

498. Shine, Walter, and Jean Shine. **A Bibliography of the Published Works of John D. MacDonald, with Selected Biographical Materials and Critical Essays**. Gainesville, FL: Patrons of the Libraries, 1980. xiv, 209 p. Spiralbound. Index. LC 80-22673.

Unlike the Shines' 1988 *MacDonald Potpourri* (q.v.), which concentrates exclusively on MacDonald's book publications, this bibliography lists all the published works by John D. MacDonald, from the January 1946 appearance of "Conversation on Deck" through November 1980, although the 1981 *Free Fall in Crimson* is listed. The bibliography is heavily illustrated, provides enormous amounts of data, and is far too long. It is nevertheless described here in some detail, for its data are important and are often unique to this volume.

The bibliography begins by listing MacDonald's publications chronologically, each entry providing the month and year in which the piece was published, title, and word/page count. Titles of books are given in uppercase letters; titles of short publications are in quotation marks; and nonfiction, science fiction, and sports stories are indicated by (nf), (sf), and (sp). References to MacDonald's letters, speeches, and nonprofessional writings are not included in this section.

The second section documents MacDonald's books, starting with a chronological checklist. Seventy titles are numbered and listed in capital letters, an asterisk indicating whether the first printing was in hardcover. This material is followed by lists of the Travis McGee series, an alphabetical checklist of Mac-Donald's books, and the contents of his short story collections. Book titles are given in capital letters, followed by place of publication, publisher, year of publication, and a list of the stories; an asterisk indicates if the story had no prior publication. Next comes a lengthy list of the publishing histories of MacDonald's American editions. Books are arranged alphabetically, with the first line beneath each title providing original place of publication, publisher, and year of first printing. Each entry then repeats the year of first printing and lists the number of interim paperback printings or the number of hardcover printings with the date of the most recent printing as of November 1980; publisher's stock number, ISBN, or Library of Congress card number; and prices of the first and latest printings. Paperback publishers are indicated by lowercase type; hardcover publishers, by uppercase. The section concludes with data on books in Braille and on cassettes and discs, and a list (with addresses) of MacDonald's U.S. publishers.

Similar publication data for MacDonald's British editions are provided; this section concludes with a list (with addresses) of MacDonald's British publishers. These data are followed by a list of MacDonald's translations into other languages. The titles are listed alphabetically; the languages into which the work was translated are listed beneath. The foreign title is underlined, and translator's name, country of publication, publisher, year of publication, and series (if any) in which the book appeared are given. Titles appearing in non-Romantic languages are romanized. This section concludes with a list of translations of MacDonald's magazine stories published as books and addresses for MacDonald's international publishers.

The next section lists MacDonald's appearances in magazines and newspapers. The publications in which MacDonald appeared are arranged alphabetically, their titles capitalized. Beneath each title is a chronologically arranged list of MacDonald's contributions that includes publication date, MacDonald's title (in quotation marks), magazine's volume and issue, and page on which the item was published.

The following section records MacDonald's appearances in anthologies and collections. MacDonald's stories are listed alphabetically, with titles underlined and in quotation marks. The titles of the collections are capitalized; citations include editor, place of publication, publisher, and year of publication.

Listings for MacDonald's nonfiction "et al." come next. Citations reference his articles on the art and business of writing and on the environment, articles of general interest, published letters to the editor, speeches, interviews and public appearances, and early nonprofessional writings.

Next are data on the adaptations of MacDonald's writings for motion pictures, television, and radio. The section begins with a chronological checklist of MacDonald's adaptations for television and motion pictures. This is followed by more thorough data on the television adaptation. Entries provide show's air date, title of MacDonald's story, television sponsor and show's name, and cast and credits. Data on MacDonald's motion picture adaptations include year in which the movie was released, title of MacDonald's work, producing studio, and cast and credits.

The next section provides a biographical sketch of MacDonald; a chronological list of various biographical and autobiographical articles; honors, awards, and prizes given to (or won by) MacDonald; his professional and civic activities; and summary data on his education, military service, and employment.

The final section lists critical articles about MacDonald, cites book reviews, and concludes with information about the *JDM Bibliophile*. These listings form the core of the material documented at much greater length in the Shines' 1993 *Rave or Rage* (q.v.). The bibliography concludes with indexes listing MacDonald's titles in English and in translation.

As stated above, this work is too long, but it is the only comprehensive bibliography of the works of John D. MacDonald. It thoroughly supersedes the earlier checklist produced by Len and June Moffatt and William J. Clark (q.v.). A revised edition citing the publications from MacDonald's last years is rumored to be forthcoming and would be most welcome.

499. Shine, Walter, and Jean Shine. **John D. MacDonald: A True Bibliophile**. North Palm Beach, FL: Walter and Jean Shine, 1985. ix, 54 p. Paperback.

Reproduced from typed copy, this semiannotated list examines the books that John D. MacDonald is known to have read and, in many cases, reviewed. MacDonald's reading and comments are described in chapters titled "Fiction in the Early Years" and "Non-Fiction Reading," but much of the volume consists of excerpts from MacDonald's reviews. In "Recent Reading and Reviews," the books read and reviewed by MacDonald are listed alphabetically by title, and an annotation provides an indicative excerpt from MacDonald's assessment. "Caustic, Critical Comments" provides excerpts from MacDonald's often mordant reviews, but these (unfortunately) are not matched to the work, although a list of the works which MacDonald reviewed negatively (and from which the reviews are taken) is given at the end of the section. "Detective & Mystery Fiction—and Views" provides further indication of MacDonald's views on writing. This work concludes with a list of MacDonald's reviews and introductions.

MacDonald may have been a perceptive reviewer, but this volume does him a disservice. It is amateurish in presentation and riddled with typographical errors. Because it contains nothing in the way of bibliographic citations, it is useless for research purposes.

500. Shine, Walter, and Jean Shine. **A MacDonald Potpourri . . . Being a Miscellany of Post-Perusal Pleasures of the John D. MacDonald Books for Bibliophiles, Bibliographers and Bibliomaniacs.** Gainesville, FL: University of Florida Libraries, 1988. xii, 219 p. LC 88-14419. ISBN 0-929595-00-9.

Far from being the potpourri promised by the title, this lengthy bibliography is a comprehensive list of all MacDonald books published in the United States, Great Britain, and internationally. Sprawling, often frustrating to use, and extraordinarily thorough at times, this is the only bibliography in this section that provides comparative charts of its subject's appearance on the bestseller lists compiled by *Time*, *Publisher's Weekly*, and the *New York Times*.

After an introduction, the volume distinguishes between "printing" and "edition," and describes the various symbols used by MacDonald's publishers to distinguish first printings of first editions from later printings and later editions. Publisher in-house numbers are detailed, as are Fawcett's "dot device," the end print number, Library of Congress numbers, the Standard Book Number System, the International Standard Book Number System, the printing key, and other features that can be (and are) used to identify different editions.

The bibliography begins with two checklists of MacDonald's work, one chronological, the other alphabetical. The chronological checklist indicates whether the book appeared first in hardcover, if it was a short story collection, if it contained Captain John Kilpack, if it was part of the Travis McGee series, and if it was edited and introduced (or merely introduced) by MacDonald. The posthumously published *Reading for Survival* is identified as such.

The next checklist is an alphabetical list of MacDonald's first printings in paperback. The publishers are listed, as are the book's in-house number and date of publication. Next comes a list of MacDonald's U.S. publishers and those of his books they published. There are separate sections for paperback publishers, hardcover publishers, book club publishers, and large-print editions.

Following are sections describing the contents of MacDonald's trilogies and omnibus editions and the contents of his short story collections. The former provides the book's title and standard bibliographical data—place of publication, publisher, and year of publication—and its Library of Congress number, pagination, book club number, and ISBN. The section on his short story collections merely lists the contents of the books.

In the comparative charts of MacDonald's bestsellers, entries list the number of weeks the book spent on the bestseller list, the highest position it reached, the number of weeks it spent at the highest position, and its weekly position on the list of bestsellers.

There is a lengthy list of the total copies of MacDonald's books printed or sold by publishers in the United States. The list is arranged alphabetically. Each entry provides publisher, number of printings the book received, and total number printed or sold. Columns permit comparison of the sales of paperback and hardcover printings. These are followed by lists of MacDonald's foreign editions arranged by language. Citations provide only the English-language title of MacDonald's work and an English translation of the foreign title—in the German publications, *The Deceivers* becomes *Adultery*, *The Dreadful Lemon Sky* becomes *Death Casts Yellow Shadows*, and the like.

The next section is an alphabetical list of MacDonald's typographical errors and inappropriate word choices. Entries provide the page and line number for the paperback and hardcover editions, the word or phrase in question, how MacDonald wanted it to be, and how many printings this error appeared in before it was corrected. (It is perhaps worth noting that, like many of us, MacDonald occasionally confused "infer" and "imply.")

An alphabetical reprinting of the epigraphs in MacDonald's books is followed by a list of MacDonald's original working titles and published titles, a reprinting of his dedications, a list of the photographers of MacDonald and the books in which their photographs appeared, reproductions of the photographs, lists of the cover artists and jacket designers of his books and the books they illustrated, and reproductions of all English-language covers of each edition.

The bibliography concludes with a lengthy list of every printing of every one of MacDonald's books. Arranged alphabetically, each entry provides printing number, book number, cost, photographer responsible for MacDonald's picture, cover artist, end print number, dot device or printing key, pagination, issue date, and miscellaneous data on the mail ads, lists, and colors of back covers.

A must for MacDonald collectors and dealers, but the unnecessarily baroque arrangement does not facilitate access to the data.

501. Shine, Walter, and Jean Shine. **Rave or Rage: The Critics & John D. MacDonald.** Gainesville, FL: University of Florida, George A. Smathers Libraries, 1993. xv, 261 p. Index. LC 93-19930. ISBN 0-929595-02-5.

This comprehensive annotated bibliography of the criticism of John D. MacDonald begins with a statement of the necessity for such a bibliography, acknowledgments, and an explanation of the style and abbreviations used. The book contains the following sections: A) critical essays and articles, and awards (with a special section listing obituaries and posthumous tributes); B) book reviews; C) books about John D. MacDonald or his work; D) miscellaneous articles and parodies; E) a selected list of essays and reviews of particular merit; and F) an afterword by John D. MacDonald.

The material in sections A and B is arranged chronologically, the coverage ending with publications in late 1992. Citations provide author's name in regular type, title of the article or book review in quotation marks, publication's name in boldface capital letters, issue number and/or date of publication, and (often) pagination. Annotations are printed in smaller type and are pithy, informative, and full of surprises. For example, Pablo Neruda praised MacDonald, as did figures as diverse as Kingsley Amis, Anthony Boucher, Harry Reasoner, Charles Willeford, and Carl Sagan.

The third section cites only eight items, five of which are by the Shines. Arranged chronologically, all citations give author's name in regular type, title of the publication in boldface capital letters and quotations, place of publication, publisher, year of publication, ISBN, pagination, and arrangement of contents. Reviews of the publications are listed, and the Shines provide comments on the publications of others.

Sections D and E contain few citations and could probably have been integrated into the previous sections with no loss. MacDonald's "afterword" is a reprint of that from a 1945 publication. The book concludes with an index of the books and a numerical list of the reviews received by each book.

Essential for MacDonald scholars, and given the overall quality of MacDonald's writing, their number is bound to increase.

502.   Shine, Walter, and Jean Shine. **The Special Confidential Report**. Tampa, FL: JDM Bibliophile, 1979. 34 p. Paperback.

503.   Shine, Walter, and Jean Shine. **Special Confidential Report: Subject: Travis McGee**. 2d ed. Fort Lauderdale, FL: Florida Center for the Book and Literary Landmarks Association, 1987. 32 p. Paperback.

504.   Shine, Walter, and Jean Shine. **Special Confidential Report: Subject: Travis McGee**. 3d ed. Fort Lauderdale and North Palm Beach: Bahia Mar Resort and Yachting Center and Shines' Cottage Industry, 1992. 66 p. Paperback.

The first two editions have not been seen.

Written as a confidential report from a series of private detectives who have been shadowing MacDonald's Travis McGee, the character's life, friends, possessions, and personality are described at length through quotations from MacDonald's publications. Each "detective" has been assigned a code name based on the color used in the title of MacDonald's novel from which the "evidence" has been derived. Descriptions of McGee and his military record, criminal record, education, background, Bahia Mar friends, longtime friends, and other acquaintances are provided as lists, with page references indicating the source of the data. McGee's personality is described at some length in a separate section, with subsections profiling his special and professional talents; hobbies;

cultural interests; clothing, food, restaurant, and drink preferences; personal effects; sexual experiences; travel records; and adversaries. Separate "Exhibits" prepared by the detectives describe Meyer, *The Busted Flush*, the *Muñequita*, and "Miss Agnes."

A labor of love, but necessary only for MacDonald obsessives.

Ross Macdonald/Kenneth Millar

505. Ahearn, Allen, and Patricia Ahearn. **Author Price Guides: Ross Macdonald [Kenneth Millar]**. Rockville, MD: Quill & Brush, 1993. 7 leaves. APG 144.

This Author's Price Guide lists Ross Macdonald's writings from the 1944 appearance of *The Dark Tunnel* (as Kenneth Millar) to the 1982 publication of *Early Millar: The First Stories of Ross Macdonald & Margaret Millar*.

For a thorough description of the format of Author Price Guides, see the entry under Fredric Brown.

506. Bruccoli, Matthew J. **Kenneth Millar/Ross Macdonald: A Checklist**. Detroit: Gale, 1971. xvii, 86 p.

A compiler's note by Bruccoli introduces this slim volume and states that it is a checklist and not a bibliography of the works of Kenneth Millar/Ross Macdonald. Those who would know the difference are referenced via footnote to Bruccoli's 1968 *Raymond Chandler: A Checklist* (q.v.), in which Bruccoli states that a checklist "fails to provide the detailed descriptive and analytical information about paper, type, binding, printing, and text—especially text—that a true bibliography, no matter how digressive, must provide."

Questions of nomenclature aside, this book lacks a table of contents and any sense of organization, but it has been compiled with Millar's assistance and contains a fine autobiographical essay by Millar. It lists all editions of Millar's books; his contributions to books; his stories, articles, verse, reviews, letters, blurbs, interviews, references, "ana," and apocrypha; and sketches, reviews, and verse in the Toronto *Saturday Night* between 1939 and 1942. (Reproductions of pages from Millar's notebooks and term papers are also provided.)

The bibliographic data in this checklist tend to be given on the right (even-numbered) page, and the left (odd-numbered) pages tend to be reserved for reproductions of the title pages of Millar's books. Citations for books are arranged chronologically and give the title in boldface capital letters next to which, in parentheses, is the publication year. Following are a statement of edition from the copyright page, pagination, collation, and exact date of first publication. Separately numbered citations list each known printing and paperback edition, including stock number; retitlings are indicated, as are periodical appearances.

Citations for first book appearance list the title of the book in italics and provide editor, place of publication, publisher, and year of publication; Millar's contributions are listed in quotation marks. The citations for Millar's stories and verse provide the title of his contribution in quotation marks; periodical title in italics; volume, month, and year of publication; and pagination. In some cases, as in the publications from the Toronto *Saturday Night*, a majority of the data are not available, and the citations are only to the title of the work.

Frustrating in arrangement and poorly laid out, this checklist has been thoroughly superseded by Bruccoli's 1983 *Ross Macdonald/Kenneth Millar: A Descriptive Bibliography* (q.v.).

507. Bruccoli, Matthew J. **Ross Macdonald/Kenneth Millar: A Descriptive Bibliography**. Pittsburgh, PA: University of Pittsburgh Press, 1983. xv, 259 p. Index. (Pittsburgh Series in Bibliography). LC 83-1398. ISBN 0-8229-3482-5.

A completely new work rather than a revision of Bruccoli's earlier checklist, this descriptive bibliography is a comprehensive and analytical list of all English-language editions of all works in which Kenneth Millar has in some way been involved. Millar, whose early books are signed "John Macdonald" and "John Ross Macdonald," dropped the "John" in order to avoid being confused with John D. MacDonald.

The bibliography contains four lettered sections: A) Separate Publications; B) First-Appearance Contributions to Books; C) First Appearances in Magazines and Newspapers; and D) Blurbs. The citations in each of these sections are arranged chronologically and are separately lettered and numbered.

Section A, the longest section, occupies the first 204 pages of the book. Each citation reproduces the title page of the first edition of all British and American hardcovers and paperbacks. Each entry provides an exhaustive analytical bibliographical description of the first edition, with collation, pagination, contents, typography and paper, binding, dustjacket, publication, and printing noted and described at length. A section called "Locations" lists whether the book may be found in the holdings of six research libraries and/or Bruccoli's own collections; the entry for the Library of Congress lists the book's deposit date. Additional printings and editions are also noted and described; though the data given are briefer, the title and copyright pages are described at length. Section AA lists the collections of Millar/Macdonald's novels using the same principles of bibliographical description.

Sections B, C, and D are equally thorough, referencing previously unpublished material, unsigned works, and retitled works. Two appendixes—the compiler's notes and a selective, brief list of books and articles about Millar/Macdonald—follow; an excellent index concludes the book. As Millar/Macdonald is now dead, an updated edition would be useful.

508. Denton, William. **Ross Macdonald**. http://www.vex.net/~buff/rara-avis/biblio/rossmacdonald.html

This site provides a comprehensive list of Macdonald's works, with different sections listing the first printings of his books, short fiction, short nonfiction, and adaptations; a bibliography of material about him concludes this section. The contents of each section are arranged chronologically. Book titles are italicized, and the publisher and year of publication are given. Contents of short story collections are listed; titles that were not published under the name "Ross Macdonald" list the name under which they appeared; and an asterisk indicates when the title featured the character Lew Archer. The titles of individual short stories and short nonfiction pieces are in quotation marks, and titles of the periodicals that published them are italicized; publication month and year are given. The titles of adaptations are italicized and are accompanied by year of their release. A link provides a biography of Macdonald. The most recent citation is one from 1982; an updated list would be desirable.

509.   King, David J. **Ross Macdonald**. http://www.dcs.gla.ac.uk/~gnik/crime-fiction/macdonald/macdonald.html

King's website offers a link to a brief biography of Macdonald. The bibliography arranges Macdonald's work by series, with different sections listing Macdonald's Lew Archer novels, Chet Gordon novels, other works, and nonfiction. The website concludes with a Macdonald filmography. The contents of each section are arranged chronologically, but no bibliographic data are provided apart from publication date; publication data are not provided for individual short stories. For more comprehensive data on Macdonald, examine Denton's website or that of Karl-Erik Lindkvist (q.q.v.).

510.   Lindkvist, Karl-Erik. **The Ross Macdonald Files**. http://hem1.passagen.se/caltex/

The finest of the Macdonald websites considered here, the home page of this Swedish site provides a picture and biography of Macdonald. It has sections on books, short stories, articles, odds and ends, and the Archer M. O. The section devoted to books provides a chronological list of the first editions of Macdonald's books, listing also place of publication, publisher, and publication year for the first American and British editions. Retitlings are indicated, and numerous titles are linked to images of the covers of paperback editions. The material from the back of paperbacks is given, as are notes about the composition and contents of the book. The sections for short stories and articles are equally thorough, and there are links providing casts and credits of motion pictures and television adaptations of the Archer novels. An exemplary tribute to a major author.

Jackie Manthorne

511.   Manthorne, Jackie. **Jackie Manthorne**. http://www.geocities.com/WestHollywood/8551

Manthorne's home page contains neither a photograph nor cover illustrations. Instead, there are an autobiographical statement and discussion of her Harriet Hubbley mystery series, which Manthorne cheerfully describes as "gripping mysteries with a lesbian twist and a dash of sly humor." An engaging site, but cover illustrations and photographs would be nice.

Ngaio Marsh

512. Gibbs, Rowan, and Richard Williams. **Ngaio Marsh: A Bibliography of English Language Publications in Hardback and Paperback, with a Guide to the Value of the First Editions**. Scunthorpe, England: Dragonby Press, 1990. 51 p. Paperback. (Dragonby Bibliographies, no. 7). ISBN 1-871122-07-4. (300 copies printed.)

As its title indicates, this bibliography lists the English-language book publications of New Zealand writer Ngaio Marsh. In all, she wrote some 32 detective novels, eight short stories (six of which were criminous), a number of playscripts, much incidental material, and her autobiography. The bibliography is reproduced from what appears to be dot-matrix printout and is surprisingly complex in its arrangement. It begins with a "main index," an alphabetical listing of all of the books by Marsh. Each title is given in boldface capital letters; beneath it are listed the first editions of all hardbacks and paperbacks in the approximate order of their publication. Data in this list include country of publication, publisher's name, book's series number, and year and month of publication.

The second section describes Marsh's British hardbacks. This list is arranged chronologically, and as before, titles are given in boldface capital letters. The data include the book's pagination, a description of the binding and dustwrapper, size, dedication, and original price and value as of 1990. Later editions and their distinguishing points are also listed. This section concludes with listings of British Book Club editions, British Large Print editions, and British Audio editions.

The third, fourth, and fifth sections are arranged by publishers. The third section lists British paperback editions of Marsh's work. Beneath each publisher's name is a chronological list of paperbacks. Each citation gives the book's title in capital letters, series number, date of publication, pagination, cover artist (when available), and ISBN (when available). The fourth section lists the American hardbacks of Marsh's work; when the title is a first American edition, the citation provides publication data, pagination, a description of the binding and the dustwrapper, size, and original price and value as of 1990. Later editions and their distinguishing points are also listed. (When the title is not a first edition, it is merely listed alphabetically beneath its publisher.) This section concludes with listings of American Book Club editions and American Large Print editions. The fifth section lists Marsh's American paperback editions. Beneath each publisher's name is a chronological list of the paperbacks; each citation gives the book's title in capital letters, series number, date of publication, pagination, original price, and ISBN (when available).

Significantly briefer sections list Marsh's Australian, Canadian, New Zealand, and European editions. A separate section lists her short stories alphabetically and provides data on their original publication and subsequent anthologization. Another section lists Marsh's plays and films, providing information on the production and the director.

The primary bibliography concludes with a section listing articles and pamphlets by Marsh. The list is alphabetical; titles are in capital letters, and publication data are provided. The volume concludes with a lengthy selected bibliography of sources used in the compilation of this bibliography.

Though the volume lacks a cumulative index and has an unnecessarily baroque and convoluted arrangement, Gibbs and Williams deserve commendation. One hopes for a revised and simplified edition.

513. Tangled Web. **Ngaio Marsh**. http://www.twbooks.co.uk/authors/nmarsh.html

This tribute to Marsh provides a picture of her, a biographical sketch, reproductions of the covers of several of her novels, and excerpts from positive critical comments. It concludes with a chronological listing of all titles featuring Inspector/Superintendent Roderick Alleyn.

A. E. Marston

514. Tangled Web. **A. E. Marston**. http://www.twbooks.co.uk/authors/aemarston.html

Neither a photograph nor the names behind Marston's initials are provided (his first name is apparently Alwyn), but this site provides descriptions and cover reproductions of two of Marston's novels, excerpts from positive criticism, and a chronological listing of his mystery novels featuring Gervase Bret and Ralph Delchard.

J. C. Masterman

515. Tangled Web. **J. C. Masterman**. http://www.twbooks.co.uk/authors/jcmasterman.html

John Cecil Masterman (1891–1977) was a don at Christ Church, Oxford; his last mystery novel appears to have been published in 1957. This tribute to him reproduces the cover of the 1939 (Penguin) edition of his 1933 *An Oxford Tragedy*. A photograph of Masterman, a brief biography, and a briefer bibliography conclude this site. Neither Masterman's first and middle names nor his death date are provided.

Lia Matera

516. Matera, Lia. **Lia Matera's Web Site**. http://www.scruz.net/~lmatera/LiaMatera.html

The author's home page starts with a deep blue background, and it is well-done, attractive, and gratifyingly complete. Icon-based links lead to sample pages from Matera's books and short stories, to passages being read by Matera, to her research bibliographies, to lists of her books, and to websites she might have used in her writings. In addition, text-based links lead to a preview of a forthcoming novel and to her works by series, to foreign editions, and to excerpts from positive book reviews. The section listing Matera's books provides title, publication date, publisher, year of publication, ISBN, initial cost for all editions, and a brief summary. The section devoted to Matera's short stories has a picture of the cover of the book, title and page on which the story appeared, publisher, year of publication, ISBN, and cost. It offers visitors the opportunity to read a portion of a story.

Catherine Lucille Moore and Henry Kuttner

517.   Utter, Virgil, Gordon Benson, Jr., and Phil Stephensen-Payne. **Catherine Lucille Moore and Henry Kuttner: A Marriage of Souls and Talent**. 4th ed. Leeds, England: Galactic Central, 1996. x, 142 p. Paperback. (Galactic Central Bibliographies for the Avid Reader, vol. 21). ISBN 1-871133-44-0.

C. L. Moore and Henry Kuttner had separate careers writing for the pulp magazines, but they began to collaborate after their 1940 marriage, producing not only the science fiction, fantasy, and weird fiction for which they are renowned but also a number of well-crafted detective and mystery stories. This collaboration lasted until Kuttner's untimely death in 1958, after which Moore turned her attention to television writing. She died in Hollywood, California, in 1987. The very demanding Jacques Barzun stated that it was "a pity the author [Kuttner] did not live to write more, for he was fully aware of the demands of physical objects, time, and space."

An explanatory introduction and a list of bibliographical sources used begin the bibliography, following which it contains three major sections: I) C. L. Moore solo; II) Henry Kuttner solo and with C. L. Moore; and III) secondary material. Each of these is further divided, the first two sections containing the date and place of the author's birth and death, a list of awards and pseudonyms used, and the following divisions: A) prose fiction, B) prose fiction books, C) series, D) poetry and drama, E) poetry and drama books, F) articles, G) miscellaneous, H) nonfiction books, and I) publications edited. The third section contains the following: J) other media, K) articles on Henry Kuttner and C. L. Moore, L) reviews, M) books about Henry Kuttner and C. L. Moore, N) phantom and forthcoming titles, O) related items by other authors, P) textual variations and other notes, and Q) a chronological index of prose fiction.

The sections citing the primary literature are arranged alphabetically, with each citation in each section given a separate letter and a number. Entries for the prose fiction provide the story's title and the name of the publication in regular type; month and year of publication are given, and if the story was accompanied by an internal illustration or featured on the cover, the artist's name is provided. A brief note indicates whether the story was a short-short story (sss), short story (ss), novelette (NT), novella (NA), or short novel (SN). Paginations are not given. Reprints of the stories are listed alphabetically beneath the initial citations. The titles of the books are given in capital letters, the editor's name is listed, and the publication data cite the publisher and year of publication. Book prices and translations are also referenced, but the names of translators are given only sporadically.

The sections listing books are comparable to the sections listing the prose fiction. Entries list the book's contents by referencing the citation letters and numbers given in the section for prose fiction. Titles are given in capital letters; editors' names, stock numbers, and prices are given; and the publication data cite the publisher and year of publication. Reprints and republications are noted, as are translations, and the names of translators are sometimes given. As before, pagination is not given.

The data in other sections tend to be less thorough. The listing for series lists the series by title, then lists beneath each title the works comprising the series, but contains no cross-references to the section for short fiction. The sections listing poetry and drama by Moore and Kuttner are empty; no such works are known. (One wonders why Utter et al. did not simply note the absence of these works in the introduction to this bibliography.)

The listing of secondary sources is arranged alphabetically and references fan publications as well as a number of international publications. The section devoted to textual variations and other notes is somewhat mistitled, for it has nothing to do with textual variations but lists sometimes intriguing background data on the stories. Did Kuttner use the name "Leslie Charteris" for some radio plays? (A section devoted to correcting and acknowledging misspellings and variant titles is buried in the chapter on phantom and forthcoming titles.)

Though lacking an index to titles and unfortunately incomplete in documenting Moore's writing career following Kuttner's death, this is one of the best of the Galactic Central bibliographies. It is clearly reproduced from word-processed copy, and its data are current through 1995. Researchers interested in two of the finest pulp writers will need this book.

John Mortimer

518. Briggs, Matt. **John Mortimer Page**. http://wxgods.cit.cornell.edu/mortimer.html

This website provides cover images of the American editions of some of Mortimer's works; a title list of his works; a biography and news; and links to sites from which his works can be obtained, to the Rumpole Usenet discussion group, and to the Rumpole Home Page (q.v.). An affectionate page, though more would be desirable.

519. Schott, Brian. **The Rumpole Home Page**. http://www.cs.umbc.edu/~schott/rumpole/index.html

This pleasant site provides an amusing rendition of Rumpole and offers links to a brief description of Rumpole and his creator, frequently asked questions concerning Rumpole and Mortimer, a list of definitions of Rumpolean terms, and a number of Rumpolean quotations. A sound file containing a Rumpole joke is provided in the section about Rumpole, and the section devoted to Rumpolean quotations offers links to the full texts of Rumpole's favorite authors (Wordsworth, Keats, Shakespeare, and Percy Bysshe Shelley). Additional links are offered to Rumpole lists, to the John Mortimer Home Page (q.v.), and to the *Mystery!* home page (q.v.), but bibliographic data—a listing of the works in which Rumpole appears, for example—are not provided.

Walter Mosley

520. Daniels, Valarie. **Walter Mosley**. http://www.aamystery.com/authors-list.html

Daniels provides a chronological list of Mosley's Easy Rawlins mysteries, starting with the 1990 *Devil in a Blue Dress* and concluding with the 1997 *Gone Fishin'*; the name of the publisher of the first edition is also given. The data on the site are clearly presented.

Marcia Muller

521. **Marcia Muller: Mystery and Suspense Writer and Editor**. http://www.hycyber.com/MYST/muller_marcia.html

Although it contains no images, this site provides a reasonably accurate bibliography of Marcia Muller's writings. Her novels are listed first, with separate sections listing the novels featuring Sharon McCone, Joanna Stark, and Elena Oliverez. These are followed by lists of her collaborations, her original short fiction, collections of short fiction, sources of biographical and bibliographical information, and her reference works (i.e., her nonfiction and edited works). Citations are arranged chronologically. The bibliographical data are inconsistently presented; some citations provide only year of publication, while others provide place of publication, publisher, year of publication, and ISBN.

522. Tangled Web. **Marcia Muller and Sharon McCone**. http://www.twbooks.co.uk/authors/mmuller.html

Neither a photograph nor a biography of Muller is provided, but a number of cover reproductions are given, along with synopses from the back covers and excerpts from positive critical reviews. A chronologically arranged bibliography indicates whether the novel features Sharon McCone, Elena Oliverez, or Joanna Stark, and provides the date of publication and the publisher.

Magdalen Nabb

523. Tangled Web. **Magdalen Nabb**. http://www.twbooks.co.uk/authors/mnabb.html

A photograph of Nabb is provided, as are a biographical sketch and reproductions from the covers of her books. The material from the back covers and excerpts from positive reviews are posted. The chronologically arranged concluding bibliography indicates which titles belong to Nabb's Marshal Guarnaccia series; publishers and years of publication are indicated.

Sharan Newman

524. Newman, Sharan. **Sharan Newman Home Page**. http://members.aol.com/senewman/Homepage/Levendeur.html

Sharan Newman's home page provides minimal biographical data and contains no photograph; she discusses instead her Catherine Levendeur series. Cover illustrations are provided for each book, along with a synopsis, publisher, year of publication, ISBN, and cost. A comprehensive bibliography cites foreign editions for novels and provides publication data for Newman's short stories, and there are links to pages of other authors, organizations, and websites containing information about the Middle Ages.

Maxine O'Callaghan

525. Seels, James T., ed. **Maxine O'Callaghan: Bibliography 1974–1995**. Introduction by Maxine O'Callaghan. Appreciation by Marcia Muller. Short stories "A Change of Clients" and "Deal with the Devil" by Maxine O'Callaghan. Afterword by Wendy Hornsby. Royal Oaks, MI; Mission Viejo, CA: ASAP/Airtight-Seels Allied Publication, 1994. 51 p. Paperback. (50 collectors copies in acrylic slipcase and 200 limited copies.)

In 1974 Maxine O'Callaghan created Delilah West, one of the first female private investigators. O'Callaghan has since written half a dozen mystery novels, four horror/dark suspense novels, one pseudonymous romance novel, and a handful of short stories. O'Callaghan's output is thus relatively small; only six pages of this bibliography are necessary to document it. The rest of the book consists of an introduction by O'Callaghan, two of her short stories (one first published here), an appreciation by Marcia Muller, and an afterword by Wendy Hornsby.

The bibliography lists O'Callaghan's works in chronological order, with separate sections listing her mystery novels, horror/dark suspense novels, and short fiction. Beneath each year, the book's title is listed in boldface capital letters, and a note indicates whether the work is a novel or a short story. The publication data list the place of publication, publisher, and year of publication; when the publisher identified works with the words "first edition" or with numbers indicating printing, these too are listed. The data are current through 1994, though information on some 1995 titles is provided. Pagination, paperback reprints, dustwrapper information, and commentary about texts are not provided. There is no index to titles.

A disappointment as a bibliography.

526. O'Callaghan, Maxine. **Maxine O'Callaghan's Home Page**. http://users. aol.com/maxineoc/max1.htm

The author's home page provides a biography and a photograph, a bibliography, information on her book signings and events, and a link to an interview. Her series featuring Dr. Anne Menlo and Delilah West (one of the first female private eyes) are listed. Year of publication, publisher, price, and ISBN are given, as are a summary and excerpts from critical praise. A short story can be downloaded, and there are links to other websites and to the Berkely-Putnam website, where cover reproductions can be found. A congenial effort, though more would be welcome.

Carol O'Connell

527. Tangled Web. **Carol O'Connell and Kathy Mallory**. http://www.twbooks. co.uk/authors/coconn1.html

No photograph of O'Connell is provided; nor are reproductions from the covers of her successful novels featuring Sergeant Kathy Mallory of the New York Police Department. Nevertheless, the material from the back covers is given, accompanied by excerpts from positive reviews. The concluding bibliography lists the titles in chronological order.

Barbara Parker

528. Parker, Barbara. **Barbara Parker**. http://www.booktalk.com/BParker/

Barbara Parker's website provides a photograph of her, a brief biographical sketch, and information about her novels. Cover illustrations are provided, as are synopses and excerpts; publishers are listed, as are ISBNs. Finally, there is a chronologically arranged bibliography.

Robert B. Parker

529. Ahearn, Allen, and Patricia Ahearn. **Author Price Guides: Robert B. Parker**. Rockville, MD: Quill & Brush, 1995. 7 leaves. APG 010.3.

This Author's Price Guide to Robert B. Parker documents his work from the 1970 appearance of *The Personal Response to Literature* to the 1995 publication of *Thin Air*.

For a thorough description of the format of Author Price Guides, see the entry under Fredric Brown.

530. Loux, Mike. **Bullets and Beer: The Spenser Home Page**. http://www. neca.com/~mloux/spenser/Spenser.html

One of the finest single-author websites, and certainly one of the most elaborate, Bullets and Beer provides information on all aspects of Robert Parker's writings—in particular, Parker's novels about Spenser.

The first screen provides eight buttons that offer connections to information about the Parker/Spenser books, television shows, movies, links to biographical data on the actors, updates, aids, literary sources used by Parker, and reviews of the books. In addition, a frequently updated introduction provides late-breaking news about Parker and Spenser. Each of the Spenser novels is listed, and the English-language editions are described. Data are given for publisher, place of publication, copyright date, ISBN, dedication, information from the dustwrapper, and recurring characters. Unanswered questions are presented for the reader's delectation, and a chapter-by-chapter list provides the origins of Spenser's literary references. Inconsistencies from book to book are given, as are favorite lines. Each section concludes with notes and commentary. The section devoted to motion picture adaptations links only to the Internet Movie Database, but Loux promises additional information in the future. Finally, there are links to related subjects and genres.

There are surprisingly few illustrations and unfortunately no sound files, but "Bullets and Beer" is a well-designed labor of love.

Barbara Paul

531. Paul, Barbara. **Barbara Paul's Home Page**. http://www.eskimo.com/ ~bpaul/

The author's own website contains a well-designed table that provides links to her Marian Larch mysteries, opera mysteries, other mysteries, science fiction, and short stories; to "odds and ends"; to upcoming events; to mystery websites; and to book-ordering sites. The site for the Marian Larch mysteries explains the origins of the character, and the site for the opera mysteries contains an essay, "How I Got Hooked on Opera." There are cover illustrations for each book, anecdotes and information about the efforts that went into researching the backgrounds, excerpts from positive reviews, and publication data that include place of publication, publisher, year of publication, and ISBNs for all editions. Finally, two short stories are available for downloading. A well-designed and enjoyable site.

Michael Pearce

532. Tangled Web. **Michael Pearce**. http://www.twbooks.co.uk/authors/
mpearce.html

A photograph of Pearce and a brief biography are given, as are cover reproductions from several of Pearce's Mamur Zapt novels plus material from the
back covers and excerpts from positive reviews. The concluding bibliography is
arranged chronologically; titles featuring Mamur Zapt are indicated, and publisher and year of publication are given.

Anne Perry

533. Tangled Web. **Anne Perry and Charlotte and Thomas Pitt**. http://
www.twbooks.co.uk/authors/aperry.html

A photograph of Perry is given, as is a brief biography that makes no mention of the crucial events that occurred in her formative years. Reproductions of
covers from several of her historical mysteries are given, accompanied by material from the back covers and excerpts from positive reviews. The chronologically arranged bibliography lists only her novels featuring Charlotte and Thomas
Pitt; publisher and date of publication are given.

534. **Anne Perry's Pitt Series**.

Available through the archives maintained by the DorothyL listserv, and
also accessible through the Miss Lemon website (http://www.iwillfollow.com/
lemon.htm), this list of the titles in Anne Perry's Pitt Series is apparently given in
chronological order, but no additional bibliographical data are provided. According to an opening note, this list was "contributed by several members of
DorothyL" and was last updated in early 1994.

Elizabeth Peters

535. James, Dean. **Elizabeth Peters**.

Available as a list maintained in the DorothyL archives, and accessible also
through the Miss Lemon website (http://www.iwillfollow.com/lemon.htm), this
list of the writings of Elizabeth Peters is grouped by series character. Beneath the
name of each Peters character is a list of the works in which the character has appeared. No additional bibliographic data are provided. The websites done by Margie Knauff and Lisa Speckhardt, and Monica Sheridan (q.q.v.), are better.

536. Knauff, Margie, and Lisa Speckhardt. **Another Shirt Ruined: The Amelia Peabody Page**. http://www.eaglenet.com/amelia/

Devoted to Amelia Peabody, the intrepid archaeologist/detective/Egyp-
tologist created by Elizabeth Peters (whose real name is Barbara Mertz and who

has also written as Barbara Michaels), this site provides synopses of each of the Amelia Peabody volumes and amusing excerpts of Amelia's thoughts on and reactions to other characters and institutions. Only minimal biographical data on Peters are provided, and there are no bibliographic data, but the site gives an idea of the flavor of Peters's novels, and there are links to the Peters/Michaels sites created by Monica Sheridan (q.v.).

537. Sheridan, Monica. **The Unofficial Elizabeth Peters Page/The Unofficial Barbara Michaels Page/The Unofficial Barbara Mertz Page**. http://www.autopen.com/elizabeth.peters.shtml

This site contains no photograph of the author and no separate bibliographical data, but it nevertheless provides an appreciation of the major themes in the works of Peters/Michaels/Mertz. This site also provides the address for the free Elizabeth Peters/Barbara Michaels newsletter.

537a. **Elizabeth Peters Fan Club**
Elizabeth Peters / Barbara Michaels
MPM
P.O. Box 180
Libertytown, MD 21762-0180

Ellis Peters/Edith Pargeter

538. Johnston, Gerald. **Ellis Peters/Edith Pargeter**.
Available through the archives maintained by the DorothyL listserv, and also accessible through the Miss Lemon website (http://www.iwillfollow.com/lemon.htm), this list of the writings of Peters/Pargeter is grouped by author. The section for the works of Peters begins by listing the Brother Cadfael series in chronological order; this is followed by a chronological list of Peters's Felse Family Series, and her nonseries titles. The section for the works of Pargeter is selective, though chronological lists of her Brothers of Gwynedd Quartet and the Heaventree Trilogy are given. Finally, miscellaneous works are mentioned, including *The Cadfael Companion* (q.v.). Titles are nearly always accompanied by dates; other bibliographic data are not given. Data are complete as of 1992, and as no further titles are forthcoming, one would hope for a comprehensive list.

539. Whiteman, Robin. **The Cadfael Companion: The World of Brother Cadfael**. Introduction by Ellis Peters. London: MacDonald, 1991. 288 p. GB 91-91175. ISBN 0356200523.

540. Whiteman, Robin. **The Cadfael Companion: The World of Brother Cadfael**. Revised ed. Introduction by Ellis Peters. New York: Mysterious Press/Warner Books, 1995. 412 p. LC 95-15435. ISBN 0-89296-513-4.

This large, well-illustrated volume is a guide to the characters and locations appearing in the 20 novels and one short story collection chronicling the cases of Brother Cadfael, the twelfth-century merchant/warrior/lover turned Benedictine monk and herbalist who remains one of Ellis Peters's (Edith Pargeter's) finest creations. There are approximately 1,200 entries, and the volume is thoroughly cross-referenced, indicating such with small capital letters. Headings and entry names are given in boldface Gothic. Pronunciation keys are not provided.

Entries for geographical locations provide a brief history of the location, its significance in the twelfth century, and excerpts from Peters's fiction in which the location is mentioned. Location entries conclude with a key to Peters's works that indicates the page on which the location is mentioned. Entries for historical characters provide the character's birth and death dates (when known), their significance in the twelfth century, excerpts from the fiction in which they appear or are mentioned, and a key to Peters's works that indicates the page on which the character is mentioned. Entries for fictional characters are indicated with (fict.) but are otherwise identical in format to the entries of historical characters, although roles of the fictional characters are described in some detail.

The volume concludes with four appendixes. The first lists the plants and herbs mentioned in *The Chronicles of Brother Cadfael*, provides each plant's Latin name, and references the works in which it appeared. The second appendix is a list of the brothers and sisters of Cadfael's Shrewsbury Abbey; the third appendix lists the eleventh- and twelfth-century kings of England, France, and Jerusalem, the Emperors of the Holy Roman Empire and the Byzantine Empire, the Popes (excluding Anti-Popes), and the Archbishops of Canterbury. The fourth appendix is a glossary to words that have special meaning in *The Chronicles of Brother Cadfael* (e.g., "banker" is "a stone bench used by masons to cut stone").

Enthusiasts of the Cadfael novels will delight in this book.

540a. Ellis Peters Fan Club
Ellis Peters Appreciation Society
c/o Sue Feder
7815 Daniels Ave.
Parkville, MD 21234

Talmage Powell

541. Powell, Talmage. **Talmage Powell, Author.** http://www.main.nc.us/~tpowell

In his website, Powell provides a picture of himself and lists his work by genre. Novels are in capital letters and accompanied by the publisher of the first edition. Individual appearances of short stories are not listed individually, nor are Powell's numerous appearances in anthologies. Translations are mentioned, but citations to translated titles are not given. Neither the contents of short story collections nor the numerous screenplays written by Powell are listed. Powell does not list his individual pieces of nonfiction, though he reveals that he wrote for a daily newspaper in St. Petersburg, Florida.

Bill Pronzini

542. Bill Pronzini: Mystery and Suspense Writer and Editor. http://www.hycyber.com/MYST/pronzini_bill.html

Although it contains no images, this site provides a partial list of Bill Pronzini's writings. His novels are listed first, with the citations arranged chronologically and a parenthetical note indicating when the book features the Nameless Detective. The bibliographical data are inconsistently presented; some citations provide only the year of publication, while others provide place of publication, publisher, year of publication, and ISBN. These are followed by lists of Pronzini's collaborations, his original short fiction, collections of short fiction, sources of biographical and bibliographical information, his reference works, and his edited collections. More data would be welcome.

Sandra West Prowell

543. Prowell, Sandra West. **The Book Binder, Author Sandra West Prowell.** http://www.imt.net/~gedison/prowell.html

The author's own home page provides a photograph, a biographical statement, an interview, and information about her series character, Montana private investigator Phoebe Siegel. A cover illustration, a story summary, and excerpts from positive reviews are provided for each novel, and the publisher, year of publication, and ISBN are also given. Very capably done.

Ellery Queen

544. Gideon, David. **Ellery Queen.** http://members.aol.com/davdgideon/dannay.html

This website contains no cover images and offers very little in the way of information about its subjects. It does, however, provide a bibliography of resources for use on the various aspects of the life and career of Ellery Queen, and it offers links to the few sites that contain information about Queen.

545. Sullivan, Eleanor. **Whodunit: A Biblio-Bio-Anecdotal Memoir of Frederic Dannay, "Ellery Queen."** New York: Targ Editions, 1984. 45 p. LC 85-134154. (150 copies.)

Containing no table of contents or index, this slim volume has a first section that provides a biographical account of the two writers who wrote as Ellery Queen, beginning with the 12-year-old Frederic Dannay's discovery of Sherlock

Holmes and continuing with a brief account of his cousin Manfred Lee's childhood. The bibliographical section begins on page 40 with sections listing the novels, short story collections, and short story anthologies edited by Queen. Each section is arranged chronologically; book titles are italicized and accompanied by the year of first publication. Additional publication data are not given for books, and publication data for individual short stories are not provided. Dannay and Lee were important as writers, editors, and publishers, and although Sullivan's tribute is affectionate, it does not do them full justice, nor is it complete. A comprehensive bibliography of the works of Ellery Queen is needed.

Elizabeth Quinn

546. Quinn, Elizabeth. **Elizabeth Quinn's Homepage**. http://www.magick. net/~ebarnard/index.html

Quinn's home page provides pictures of her, biographical data, and information on her series character Lauren Maxwell. There are links to cover images, a synopsis, and the book's first chapter. Bibliographic data provided include publisher, date of publication, cost, and ISBN. In addition, Quinn provides similar information about her nonmystery backlist, listing the characters and their roles, and she offers numerous links to other locations, including various park and wildlife systems.

Ian Rankin

547. Tangled Web. **Ian Rankin in His Own Words**. http://www.twbooks. co.uk/authors/irankin.html

Rankin provides a chatty discussion of his novels featuring Detective Inspector John Rebus. The backgrounds and events in each novel and cover illustrations for each book are provided. A "potted biography" is given, and there are links to a subsite providing additional information about the books: a summary, a cover illustration, excerpts from positive reviews, cost, ISBN, and publisher. The site concludes with a chronological list of Rankin's books that includes information on works that were retitled for U.S. publication.

Ruth Rendell. *See* Barbara Vine

Paul Renin

548. Holland, Stephen, and Richard Williams. **Paul Renin: A Bibliographical Checklist**. Scunthorpe, England: Dragonby Press, 1990. 8 p. Stapled sheets. Index. (British Paperback Checklists, no. 43).

Under the names of "Paul Renin," "John Courage," and his own name, Richard Goyne (1902–1957) wrote at least 40 mysteries. This checklist concentrates on the books written under the name of Renin, works that predominantly concerned what Holland and Williams describe in their brief foreword as "naughty ladies."

The checklist begins with the index, an alphabetical list that gives the title of the book in capital letters; beneath each title are the publisher and the year in which it was published. Following the index is an alphabetical list of the publishers. Beneath each publisher are the titles of the books in capital letters, the year of publication in parentheses, and pagination.

A comprehensive bibliography of the works of Richard Goyne remains to be done.

Nicholas Rhea

549.   Tangled Web. **Nicholas Rhea (Peter N. Walker)**. http://www.twbooks. co.uk/authors/nrhea.html

As this site reveals, Nicholas Rhea is one of a number of pseudonyms used by the prolific Peter Walker. A picture of Walker (as Rhea) is provided, as are a brief biographical sketch and cover illustrations for several of his many novels. Material from the backs of covers and excerpts from positive reviews are given. The bibliography is arranged idiosyncratically and repetitively, listing titles by the pseudonym under which they appeared and further dividing them by series. Publication dates and sometimes publishers are given.

"Rhea" is also the author of a number of novels featuring the adventures and misadventures of a young constable in Yorkshire. These novels have been turned into the popular British television drama series *Heartbeat*. A description of the web pages devoted to this series can be found in the section on media and television (q.v.).

Rick Riordan

550.   Riordan, Rick. **Rick Riordan**. http://www.flash.net/~huisache

Riordan's personal website provides a photograph and information on his Tres Navarre mystery series. The books are described and illustrated with cover reproductions. Although bibliographic data are minimal, there are links to the Riordan site at Bantam Doubleday Dell, which provides costs, ISBNs, and excerpts from the books.

Mike Ripley

551.   Tangled Web. **Mike Ripley and Fitzroy Maclean Angel**. http://www. twbooks.co.uk/authors/mikeripley.html

A picture of Ripley is provided, as are a brief biographical sketch and cover reproductions from several of his comic novels featuring the cab-driving, trumpet-playing Fitzroy Maclean Angel. Material from the back covers of

Ripley's novels is given, as are excerpts from positive reviews. The bibliography lists the titles in the Angel series and indicates the awards they have won but provides no additional publication data.

Peter Robinson

552.   Robinson, Peter. **Peter Robinson**. http://www.interlog.com/~peterob/home.html

In his website, Robinson provides a picture of himself and an autobiographical statement, and offers links to his published works and a bibliography. The links to his published works provide a synopsis and excerpts from positive reviews; excerpts from Robinson's most recent books are also provided. Robinson's bibliography consists of chronological lists and publication data about his novels, short stories, poetry, and articles. The publisher's name, year of publication, and a note indicating whether the work appeared in hardcover or paperback is provided for each known edition of each book. A capably done site. For an additional Peter Robinson site, see the Tangled Web site (below).

553.   Tangled Web. **Peter Robinson and DCI Alan Banks**. http://www.twbooks.co.uk/authors/authorpagelist.html

This site provides a picture of Robinson that differs from the picture used at Robinson's personal site (above). A brief biography and the cover material from each of his novels are posted, accompanied by excerpts from positive reviews. The bibliography is quite thorough, providing full publication data (place, publisher, date of publication) for each known edition of each book.

Robert Rosenberg

554.   Rosenberg, Robert. **The Avram Cohen Mystery Series**. http://www.ariga.com/cohen/

Rosenberg's site provides almost no information about him but discusses his series character Avram Cohen and the composition of the books in which Cohen appears. Cover illustrations are provided, and the first two Avram Cohen mystery novels—*Crimes of the City* and *The Cutting Room*—are completely online. Numerous links permit browsers to order books, and there are links to sites devoted to promoting peace. This is a clean and well-designed site.

Katherine Ross

555.   Ross, Katherine, and Gene Wicker. **The Katherine Ross Home Page**. http://www.iwillfollow.com/kjr

Compiled partially as a tribute to Katherine Ross, author of the popular Julian Kestrel series, and partially with Ross's assistance, earlier versions of this site included photographs, basic biographical information, cover illustrations, and synopses of her novel. Cover reproductions were given, as were excerpts from positive critical reviews, a schedule of signings, and links to Ross's favorite mystery sites. At one time, the site contained Wicker's marriage proposal.

Ross died young of cancer in early 1998. The site is now maintained as a tribute, offering the above information and providing a link to Ross's obituary in a Boston newspaper.

Jay Russell

556. Russell, Jay. **Jay Russell**. http://www.sff.net/people/jrussell

Russell's personal website provides cover reproductions of his novels *Burning Bright*, *Celestial Dogs*, and *Blood* and synopses of these books; the first chapter of *Blood*, excerpts from *Celestial Dogs*, and the full texts of several short stories are also provided. News about Russell's writing career is given, as are the full text of reviews and excerpts from positive reviews. A picture of Russell is hidden but can be found.

557. Tangled Web. **Jay Russell**. http://www.twbooks.co.uk/authors/jayrussell.html

A photograph of the author is provided, and there are a brief biography of Russell and cover reproductions of his three fantastic crime novels, *Burning Bright*, *Celestial Dogs*, and *Blood*, accompanied by text from the back covers. There are also links to an interview and the full text of reviews as well as excerpts from positive reviews. A link to Russell's personal web page is offered (q.v.).

Nicole St. John

558. St. John, Nicole. **Nicole St. John/Norma Johnston**. http://www.blaze.net/chipmunkcrossing/

St. John is primarily a writer for juveniles and young adults. Her website provides a self-portrait, lists her pseudonyms (half a dozen in addition to Norma Johnston), and gives an autobiographical sketch. A bibliography of her writings under each name is given, and a number of cover illustrations are provided. Additional information about St. John's writings is promised.

James Sallis

559. Tangled Web. **James Sallis**. http://www.twbooks.co.uk/authors/jamessallis.html

A photograph of Sallis is posted, and illustrations from five of Sallis's Lew Griffin novels are given, accompanied by the material from the back cover, excerpts from positive reviews, and a brief biographical sketch. A concluding bibliography lists the Lew Griffin works.

John Sandford

560.   Camp, Roswell Anthony. **John Sandford**. http://www.rehov.org/sandford/

The most comprehensive of the John Sandford websites currently available, this well-designed site is maintained by the author's son. (Sandford is the pseudonym of Pulitzer Prize-winning journalist John Camp.) In a slightly earlier version of this site, Roswell Camp stated, "as the son of the author, I have a somewhat closer perspective to the hows and whys and wherefores of the books than people, as well as knowledge of many of the in-jokes, blunders, cameo appearances, and, well, *weirdisms* that are otherwise just not immediately visible to the casual reader."

The site provides a photograph of its subject, the text of a lengthy interview, and information about Sandford's books, each of which is accorded a separate page. On each book's page is the text of the material from the inside dustjacket of the first American hardcover edition accompanied by a reproduction of the cover of that edition. This is followed by excerpts from positive as well as negative reviews, which are accompanied by a reproduction of the cover of the first American paperback edition of the novel. A concluding section offers often amusing and always intriguing comments.

561.   Jacovetty, Vincent L. **John Sandford**. http://www.goldengate.net/ ~vincentj/JohnSand.html

This capably done website provides a picture of its subject, links to the text of an interview (the same interview available through Camp's site [q.v.]), and links to other John Sandford websites. For each of Sandford's books, Jacovetty provides a reproduction of the cover of the first American hardcover edition and the text from the dustwrapper of that edition.

Walter Satterthwait

562.   Satterthwait, Walter. **The Walter Satterthwait Homepage**. http://freenet. vcu.edu/education/literature/Walter_Satterthwait.html

Satterthwait's home page provides an autobiographical statement and a picture, and offers links to his more recent works as well as to a short story, "One of a Kind." The links to his recent publications provide a reproduction of the book's cover, its first two chapters, and the full texts of various reviews; the book's ISBN and cost are given. There is also a chronological list of Satterthwait's publications that provides publisher, date of publication, ISBN, cost, and a note that indicates whether the book was published in paperback or hardcover. A nicely done site.

Dorothy L. Sayers

563. Clarke, Stephan P. **The Lord Peter Wimsey Companion**. New York: Mysterious Press, 1985. [ix], 563 p. Indexes. LC 85-060072. ISBN 0-89296-850-8.

Though this enormous book contains some 7,509 numbered entries, it has but one goal: to explain the references used by Dorothy L. Sayers or, in the words of Clarke's introduction, "to make the Peter Wimsey stories accessible to more readers who choose to participate in the stories at some level beyond that of simple entertainment." To make the stories and novels accessible, Clarke combed them for names, events, references, and allusions that readers of a later generation would not necessarily recognize. For each he provides an explanatory definition as well as a citation (in abbreviated form) to the work in which the reference was found. Furthermore, the names and roles of all characters are given, and there are a number of illustrations of sights—photographs of buildings, streets, people, and landmarks—that are mentioned in the stories. The *Companion* concludes with an eight-page bibliography of secondary sources, an index to the references by cited work, and several undated and unkeyed maps of Great Britain and London.

Like Jack Tracy, whose *Encyclopaedia Sherlockiana* (q.v.) similarly explicates the works and world of Doyle, Clarke has explained much that is obscure, clarifying references that would be largely lost on a contemporary audience. His writing is clear; cross-references abound, and the book, though weighty and reproduced from typed copy, is easy to use. Clarke is to be commended for what surely must have been a more than arduous labor of love. If he is to be faulted, it is on the grounds of overspecialization, but each year enables a specialized work such as this to grow in usefulness.

564. Gilbert, Colleen B. **A Bibliography of the Works of Dorothy L. Sayers**. Hamden, CT: Archon Books, 1978. 263 p. Indexes. LC 78-18795. ISBN 0-2080-1755-0.

Five years in the compilation and unquestionably the definitive bibliography of the works of Dorothy L. Sayers, this volume is an exemplary achievement. Intended as a comprehensive description of Sayers's works, it contains seven sections: books, pamphlets, cards, and ephemera by Dorothy L. Sayers alone or in collaboration; contributions to books, pamphlets, and miscellanea; contributions to newspapers and periodicals; book reviews; broadcasts, play productions, films, and records; lectures; and manuscript collections. Entries in all sections are chronologically arranged and separately numbered.

In the first and second sections, descriptions begin with a quasifacsimile transcription of the title page and are followed by a statement of collation, pagination, book's length and width (in centimeters), and bulk of the sheets and endpapers with and without the binding (in centimeters). Paper, endpapers, binding, original price, print run, and official date of publication are given, as are any textual variants or typographic idiosyncrasies that distinguish the state of a first edition from later states. Finally, the first section provides numerous reproductions of title pages and book bindings.

Entries in the third and fourth sections provide complete citations to the periodicals that published Sayers's original work and her reviews. Periodical titles are italicized, and bibliographic data include volume, issue number, month, year, and page upon which the work was published. In the third section, a concluding note indicates whether Sayers's piece was a poem, a letter to the editor, or an essay; reprint data are provided, as are occasional notes on the nature of Sayers's contribution. In the fourth section, a note provides authors' names and titles of the books reviewed by Sayers.

The entries in the fifth and sixth sections provide exact date and title of the play or lecture. A note indicates the nature of the broadcast or lecture; a star by an item indicates that it was published as well as broadcast.

The entries in the last section are grouped by repository. Each citation provides the title of the work and number of pages (or leaves), and indicates whether it is an AMS (autograph manuscript), a TMS (typed manuscript), a TCC (typed carbon copy), an ALS (autograph letter signed), or a TLS (typed letter signed). As in the preceding two sections, a star by an item indicates that it was published.

An excellent index concludes the volume, which belongs in all academic libraries.

565.   Harmon, Robert B., and Margaret A. Burger. **An Annotated Guide to the Work of Dorothy L. Sayers**. New York: Garland, 1977. x, 286 p. Index. (Garland Reference Library of the Humanities, vol. 80). LC 76-57952. ISBN 0-8240-9896-X.

The introduction to this, one of two book-length Sayers bibliographies published in 1977, reveals a bias toward Sayers akin to hero worship. This might not be objectionable if Harmon and Burger expressed their adulation without cliché and with some recognition of literary history. Instead, readers get such sentences as "in the 1920's and 1930's, Miss Sayers established herself as one of the few who could give a new look to the detective novel. Her recipe was to deftly mix [sic] a plot that kept readers guessing with inside information, told without tears, about some fascinating subject. . . ." The conclusion to the introduction begins "Dorothy L. Sayers was definitely no fly-by-night writer of thrillers" and is lifted word for word (and without acknowledgment) from the writings of Carolyn Heilbrun.

The bibliography contains the following sections: novels, short stories, essays, dramatic works, poetry, translations, miscellaneous works, criticism, sources, and adaptations. Each section contains numerous subdivisions; the first section, for example, has listings for novels written by Sayers, novels written in collaboration with others, and novels collected in omnibus editions. Miscellaneous works lists addresses, lectures, speeches, bibliographies in which Sayers's name appears, book reviews of her works, children's books by her, series edited by her, published letters, and pamphlets by her. Entries in all sections and subsections are arranged alphabetically and are separately numbered. The titles of novels are underlined. Beneath each title are bibliographical data for all known Anglo-American editions: place of publication, publisher, year of publication, and pagination. A lengthy (and adulatory) annotation concludes each entry. Entries for short stories underline the title, provide an annotation, and list all known appearances of the story, cross-referencing titles to collections. Entries in other sections are similarly arranged.

The sections presenting the secondary sources also contain numerous subdivisions; sources, for example, lists bibliographies, biographies, indexes, obituaries, portraits, and reviews in which Sayers's name or image appears. As before, annotations tend to be adulatory, downplaying the work of those critics who have not been enchanted by Sayers's prose. Their entry for Edmund Wilson states in its entirety that "on pages 339 to 341, Mr. Wilson criticizes Miss Sayers' ability as a detective fiction writer as exemplified in her novel *The Nine Tailors*." In actuality, Wilson was far more caustic, stating in part that "I have heard people say that Dorothy Sayers wrote well, and I felt that my correspondents had been playing her as their literary ace. But, really, she does not write very well: it is simply that she is more consciously literary than most of the other detective-story writers and that she thus attracts attention in a field which is mostly on a sub-literary level. In any serious department of fiction, her writing would not appear to have any distinction at all." (Wilson dismisses *The Nine Tailors* as "one of the dullest books I have ever encountered in any field. The first part of it is all about bell-ringing as it is practiced in English churches and contains a lot of information of the kind that you might expect to find in an encyclopedia article on campanology.")

A Sayers chronology, a checklist of her papers at Wheaton College, and a capable author-title index conclude the *Guide*. As a primary bibliography, this is inferior to Colleen B. Gilbert's *A Bibliography of the Works of Dorothy L. Sayers* (above). As a secondary bibliography, it is inferior to Ruth Youngberg's *Dorothy L. Sayers: A Reference Guide* (below).

566. Youngberg, Ruth Tanis. **Dorothy L. Sayers: A Reference Guide**. Boston: G. K. Hall, 1982. xxii, 178 p. Index. LC 81-6992. ISBN 0-8161-8198-5.

This "reference guide" is in fact a well-done annotated bibliography of the literature about Dorothy L. Sayers. Following a lively and well-written introduction, Youngberg provides a selective bibliography of Sayers's writings, listing only the works by Sayers that have received critical attention. This is nevertheless quite a sizable number, and different sections list Sayers's novels, collaborative novels, short stories, collected short stories, collected novels and short stories, short story collections edited by Sayers, Sayers's poems, plays, collected plays, films, miscellaneous essays and nonfiction, collected essays, translations by Sayers, biographies by Sayers, children's books by Sayers, and books reprinting selections of Sayers's writings. Each section provides title of the work (underlined), place of publication, publisher, and year of publication for the first British and American editions. Retitlings are clearly indicated.

The secondary bibliography is chronologically arranged, each year's entries being separately numbered and alphabetically arranged. Citations are given for the books, chapters, journal articles, significant newspaper articles, speeches, and dissertations written in English and published in the United States and England. All entries list the critic's name in capital letters and are otherwise consistent and clear; anonymous works are listed under "ANON" rather than by title. Youngberg's annotations are pithy and accurate; her description of Edmund Wilson's famous dismissal of Sayers's work is a model of abstraction: "Following a series of letters in response to his article 'Why Do People Read Detective Stories?' in the 14 October 1944 issue [of the *New Yorker*], tells of his attempt to give detective fiction another trial. Since Sayers's *The Nine Tailors* was urged on him, he skimmed it, picking up the thread of the story. Criticizes her writing adversely on the strength of this incomplete reading." (Compare with the milquetoast annotation given by Harmon and Burger [above].) Although three publications from 1981 are cited, the bibliography effectively ceases its coverage as of September 1980.

A nicely done author/title index concludes the bibliography, which is clearly reproduced from typed copy. An updated edition would be welcome.

567. **The Dorothy L. Sayers Society**: http://www.sayers.org.uk/

Secretary
Lenelle Davis
6 Constantius Court
Brandon Road
Church Crookham Shropshire
GU13 0YF
England

Chairman
Christopher Dean
Rose Cottage
Malthouse Lane
Hurstpierpoint
West Sussex
BN6 9JY
England

Sandra Scoppettone

568. Scoppettone, Sandra. **Sandra Scoppettone**. http://www.imt.net/~gedison/scoppett.html

Scoppettone's home page provides a picture of herself and a synopsis of her novels that offers links to cover illustrations. A brief bibliography of her works includes ISBNs. The text of an interview is posted, as are excerpts from positive reviews. A different arrangement might have facilitated access to the data, but it remains an informative site.

Sharon Gwyn Short

569. Tangled Web. **Sharon Gwyn Short**. http://www.twbooks.co.uk/authors/sgshort.html

No picture of Short is provided, but this website provides cover reproductions from her two novels. These are accompanied by the prose from the back of the book and excerpts from positive critical reviews. A brief biography is given, and the bibliography provides ISBNs and prices.

Georges Simenon

570. Arens, Arnold. **Das phänomen Simenon: Einführung in das Werk: Bibliographie (Verzeichnis der Werke und der Sekundärliteratur)**. Stuttgart, Germany: Franz Steiner Verlag Wiesbaden, 1988. 166 p. Index. ISBN 3-515-05243-7.

German-language publications are generally beyond the scope of this work, but the elaborate secondary bibliography makes *Das phänomen Simenon* deserving of mention. Following an introduction, the first section of this bibliography lists Simenon's pseudonymous works, grouped alphabetically by the pseudonym under which Simenon wrote them. Each of the 16 sections contains chronologically arranged but unnumbered citations. Titles are given in italics, and place of publication, publisher, and year of publication are listed. The second section lists Simenon's Maigret novels; the third, non-Maigret novels; the fourth, Simenon's autobiographical works; the fifth, novellas and short stories; the sixth, Simenon's introductions; the seventh, Simenon's theatrical works; the eighth, Simenon's published letters; and the ninth, collected editions of Simenon. Data in these sections are also arranged chronologically. Citations are not numbered, titles are given in italics, and place of publication, publisher, and year of publication are provided. The first German and Swiss editions are also cited in this format.

The primary bibliography occupies the first 70 pages of this volume. The remainder is occupied by an extensive bibliography of secondary literature on Simenon. Arranged chronologically, then listed alphabetically by author's last name, the entries begin with publications from 1932 and conclude with publications of 1985. In all, some 815 separately numbered citations to books, chapters in books, journal articles, and dissertations are given. Furthermore, although a few of these citations are to works published in English, the majority are from European publications unindexed by standard reference sources.

Research libraries supporting serious studies in the twentieth-century French novel and scholars doing research on Simenon will find that Arens's secondary bibliography justifies purchasing this book.

571. Foord, Peter. **Georges Simenon: A Bibliography of the British First Editions in Hardback and Paperback and of the Principal French and American Editions, with a Guide to Their Value, edited by Richard Williams and Sally Swan**. Scunthorpe, England: Dragonby Press, 1988. 85 p. Paperback. Index. (Dragonby Bibliographies, no. 3). ISBN 1-871122-03-1.

As its title indicates, this bibliography lists the British first editions and many of the French and American editions of the books of the prolific Georges Simenon. The French section of the bibliography cites some 371 works, of which 240 were translated into English. The bibliography is reproduced from what appears to be dot-matrix printout and is quite elaborate in its arrangement, containing the following sections: main index: Maigret titles in English, alphabetically; main index: non-Maigret titles in English, alphabetically; French first editions: Maigret, in order of publication; French first editions: non-Maigret, in order of publication; French title index: Maigret alphabetically (with subsections listing translated works with original English titles and short stories and collections not translated); French title index: non-Maigret alphabetically (with subsections listing translated works with original English titles and short stories, other works, and collections not translated); British first editions: Maigret, in order of publication; British first editions: non-Maigret, in order of publication; British paperback editions: serially by imprint; other British editions: by publisher and date; American first editions: Maigret, in order of publication; American first editions: non-Maigret, in order of publication; American paperback editions: serially by imprint; other American editions: by publisher and date; British and American anthologies in which Simenon short stories appear; and British, American, and French magazines in which Simenon short stories appear. Finally, there are lists of printer abbreviations and the translators of Simenon, and a selected bibliography.

The data provided differ from section to section. At their fullest, however, entries include the book's title (in capital letters), exact date of publication, publisher, pagination, binding, and dustwrapper and its artist. Translated editions provide the translator's name and the book's original title. The 1988 value of the book (in English pounds) is provided.

Though it is overly complex in its arrangement and thus occasionally frustrating, this is more substantial than Trudee Young's earlier bibliography (q.v.) and is the most comprehensive English-language bibliography of Georges Simenon available.

572. Haining, Peter. **The Complete Maigret: From Simenon's Original Novels to Granada's Much Acclaimed TV Series**. London: Boxtree Limited, 1994. 128 p. Index. Paperback. 94-20780. ISBN 1-85283-447-1.

Though not a reference book, this heavily illustrated appreciation of the media adaptations of Simenon's Maigret novels nevertheless deserves mention. The book opens with a description of Maigret and provides surveys of the adaptations of Maigret in the cinema and on television; the films that were made with Budapest serving as Paris are described and praised at some length. The book concludes with a chronological listing of the films and television series in which Chief Inspector Jules Maigret appeared. The principal entry, however, is the name (capitalized and in boldface type) of the actor who portrayed Maigret. This is followed by the adaptation's title in italics; non-English titles are followed by a parenthetical translation into English. The names of the production company, producer, director, scriptwriter, release/transmission date, and leading co-stars are also given.

573. Lemoine, Michel. **Index des Personnages de Georges Simenon.** Bruxelles: Editions Labor, 1985. 695 p. Index. ISBN 2-8040-0119-9.

French-language publications are generally beyond the scope of this work, but one would be remiss to ignore Lemoine's monumental index to and description of all of the named characters (and a few of the unnamed but readily identifiable characters) appearing in the collected works of Georges Simenon.

The first section of the index lists the characters. Each name is given in small capital letters; the name of the work or works in which the character appears is given in italics. A few key words and occasionally a sentence or two identify the character's gender and describe his or her role in the novel. In the case of enormously important characters (e.g., Paul, Lucas, and Henriette and Louise Maigret), the descriptions are substantially longer.

The index to character names is followed by three appendixes, both using the format of the first section. The first lists the named animals in Simenon's collected works; the second, the named boats. The third indexes the cited works.

Maigret lovers will delight in this well-done index, but it is unlikely to be used in most American libraries.

574. Menguy, C. **Bibliographie des Éditions Originales de Georges Simenon y Compris les Oeuvres Publiées sous des Pseudonymes.** Brussels: Le Livvre et l'estampe, 1967. Extrait de la revue "Le Livre et L'Estampe." Numéro 49–50, Premier numéro, double, de 1967. 100 p. Paperback. Index.

The first section of this separately published fascicle of *Le Livre et L'Estampe,* "Oeuvres publiées sous des pseudonymes," contains a thorough and accessible bibliography of Simenon's early pseudonymous publications. The arrangement of this section is alphabetical by pseudonym. Citations are separately numbered and listed chronologically. Each entry lists the title in italics and provides place of publisher, publisher, and date of publication. Series titles and series numbers are given, as are pagination, book size, a description of the cover, and original price. Retitlings and reissues are listed and cross-referenced to the original work. In all, more than 100 publications under 18 pseudonyms are documented.

The second section, "Oeuvres publiées sous son patronyme," lists Simenon's works under his own name. It is chronological in arrangement, with the 1967 *Le Voleur de Maigret* being the last title cited. The data included are the same as in the first section. Separate title indexes to the pseudonymous and acknowledged work conclude the bibliography.

Although the list of acknowledged publications is superseded by Menguy's later work (q.v.), the thoroughly documented and easily accessible list of Simenon's pseudonymous works makes this quite a useful bibliography.

575. **Le nouvelisste et le conteur**. Bruxelles: Les Amis de Georges Simenon, 1993. 133 p. Paperback. Index. (Cahiers Simenon, 6).

The first section of this volume consists of appreciations and discussions of Simenon, but the last 50 pages are Claude Menguy's "Inventaire raisonné des nouvelles de Georges Simenon." French publications are largely beyond the scope of this work, but Menguy's bibliography deserves mention for the currency of his citations and the clarity of his presentation.

Like Piron before him, Menguy divides Simenon's output into two chronologically arranged sections: the "Séries Policières" and the "Nouvelles Diverses." Though the content for individual entries varies, at their fullest both sections list the story's title in boldface type, date of composition, date of first periodical publication, first book publication, later French publications, position it holds in Simenon's *Oeuvres Complètes* (Éditions Rencontre, 1967–1973), and position it holds in the *Tout Simenon* (Presses de la Cité, 1988–1992). For book publications, Menguy provides publisher's name, location, date of publication, and pagination. For the periodical publications he provides volume, month, and year. The index is by title.

Researchers and collectors of the French editions of Simenon will find Menguy's data are clearly presented and accessible.

576. Piron, Maurice. **L'Univers de Simenon: Guide des Romans et Nouvelles (1931–1972) de Georges Simenon**. Paris: Presses de la Cité, 1983. 490 p. Paperback. Index. LC 83-147085. ISBN 2-258-01152-3.

French publications are generally beyond the scope of this work, but one would be remiss to ignore this comprehensive annotated bibliography of the works of Georges Simenon. The volume is dominated by two sections: "Les romans de la destinée" and "Les romans de Maigret." Each of these is arranged chronologically, and all citations are separately numbered and occupy two facing pages. The book's title is given on the top of the right page; at the top of the left page are the date of composition and minimal publication data (publisher's name and date of publication). Each entry begins with a statement of the time and place of the work in a section titled "Cadre spatio-temporel." This is followed by a section describing the protagonists; for example, the description in "Les romans de la destinée" is titled "Statut du héros" and provides the protagonist's full name, profession, marital status, and age. The description in "Les romans de Maigret" is essentially the same, with "Status de Maigret, héros du roman" providing Maigret's name, rank, and marital status, and "Statut du héros" providing the full name, profession, marital status, and age of other significant characters.

Each entry has a section titled "Autres personnages principaux" that lists the names, marital status, profession, and age of the other principal characters. This is followed by "Aspects particuliers du roman," a statement of the noteworthy incidents in the work, and each citation concludes with a lengthy summary of the contents ("Résumé").

Following the descriptions of the novels are descriptions of Simenon's shorter work. As before, there are two sections, each arranged chronologically. The first concentrates on Simenon's non-Maigret works. Each citation occupies one page; provides periodical title, month and date of initial publication, and title of its first book appearance; and concludes with a summary of the story. The second section concentrates on Simenon's Maigret stories and uses the same arrangement. None of these citations in either section is numbered.

Indexes to the titles, side-by-side chronological lists of non-Maigret and Maigret publications, and indexes to the settings conclude this volume. Though the bibliographical data are not comprehensively presented, readers of French will find the annotations thorough and helpful. An English edition of this book would be welcome.

577. Trussel, Steve. **Georges Simenon's Inspector Maigret**. http://www.trussel. com/f_maig.htm

A number of websites devoted to Simenon's Maigret exist, but this one has been selected because of the comprehensiveness of its contents and because it contains links to many other websites. There are links to a Simenon bibliography, Maigret statistics, a Maigret bulletin board, an online Maigret, cover reproductions, Maigret films and videos, and books for sale. The bibliography is thorough. Trussel provides the following links: Maigret in English (with French original editions); Maigret in Danish, Dutch, Finnish, German, Italian, Norwegian, Spanish, and Swedish; a multi-language Maigret list; a French and English title list; and a list of "The Other Maigrets," eight titles that Trussel has not seen.

The information on Maigret's appearances in English is arranged chronologically by French original edition. The French titles are given in light purple italics, followed by series, pagination, place of publication, and publisher; each French citation is separately numbered. English-language editions are listed beneath the French title and include publication year, English title (in light blue italics), translator, pagination, place of publication, and publisher. Paperback editions and retitlings are indicated; ISBNs are provided when relevant. A hyperlink in this file permits title searching.

Trussel's site is gratifyingly comprehensive.

578. Young, Trudee. **Georges Simenon: A Checklist of His "Maigret" and Other Mystery Novels and Short Stories in French and English Translation**. Metuchen, NJ: Scarecrow Press, 1976. iii, 153 p. Index. (Scarecrow Author Bibliographies, no. 29). LC 76-14410. ISBN 0-8108-0964-8.

Despite the limitations apparently imposed by its title, this bibliography does not restrict itself to Simenon's Maigret and other mystery novels and short stories, although it does refrain from documenting his juvenilia, pseudonymously published hackwork, and uncollected publications.

In arrangement, this bibliography is roughly chronological, with Young having arranged Simenon's output by the decade in which it was first published. These data are presented in sections titled "Titles First Published in the 1930s," "Titles First Published in the 1940s," and so forth, the last section being "Titles First Published in the 1970s." Within each of these sections, however, the citations are arranged alphabetically. Each citation is separately numbered and begins by listing the title of the first French edition (in capital letters), followed by place of publication, publisher, year of publication, and pagination. Additional French editions are listed beneath this entry, using the same format. They are followed by English translations, with data on British editions preceding that of the American editions. The format is essentially the same as that used for citing the first French edition, though the translator's name is provided. The contents of Simenon's anthologies and collections are not distinguished by a separate section and are also listed in this format. Concluding the bibliography are separate indexes for French titles and English translations. In all, some 222 works are listed.

Although typographically much clearer than Foord's later work (q.v.), Young's bibliography is substantially more frustrating. There is no reason to divide Simenon's work by decade other than convenience, but then to list the output of each decade alphabetically rather than chronologically prevents access to the work and necessitates constant use of the indexes. Researchers wanting comprehensiveness in a Simenon bibliography will prefer Foord.

Trish Macdonald Skillman

579. Skillman, Trish Macdonald. **Trish Macdonald Skillman**. http://www.cyberstation.net/skillmantm/trish.htm

Skillman's personal website provides a picture of her, an autobiographical statement, and cover illustrations of her works. Synopses of each book are given, as is a brief chronologically arranged bibliography that provides publisher, year of publication, and ISBN.

Barbara Burnett Smith

580. Smith, Barbara Burnett. **Welcome to Purple Sage**. http://www.io.com/purple_sage/

Barbara Burnett Smith's website contains neither a photograph of her nor autobiographical data, but it provides information about her books set in the town of Purple Sage. An excerpt from each is given, as are publisher and ISBN.

Furthermore, the site provides a detailed map of Purple Sage, with various locations linked to their descriptions in Smith's books; for example, clicking on the image of Sage Lake provides an excerpt from Smith's *Dust Devils of the Purple Sage*.

Enes Smith

581. Smith, Enes. **Enes Smith**. http://www.kmxnet.com/ehs/

Enes Smith's website has no photograph and contains minimal autobiographical information. Links provide cover illustrations of each of Smith's novels, a synopsis of each book, excerpts from positive reviews, and publication data, including the address of the publisher, year of publication, and ISBN.

Guy N. Smith

582. Tangled Web. **Guy N. Smith**. http://www.twbooks.co.uk/authors/gnsmith.html

Though a prolific writer of low-grade horror novels, Smith has also written numerous thrillers and crime novels as well as a series featuring detective Dixon Hawke. This web page concentrates on Smith's horror, but its concluding bibliography provides a short list of his crime and thriller novels.

Troy Soos

583. Soos, Troy. **Troy Soos Home Page**. http://members.aol.com/TroySoos/index.html

Troy Soos's website provides news, autobiographical information, several photographs of him (including one at age 11 in a Little League game), and cover illustrations from his novels. A synopsis of each book is given, as are excerpts from positive reviews. A "publishing history" provides for each edition the date of publication, publisher, ISBN, and cost; audiobooks are also cited.

Elizabeth Daniels Squire

584. Squire, Elizabeth Daniels. **Elizabeth Daniels Squire**. http://www.booktalk.com/edsquire

Squire's website provides a photograph and an autobiographical statement. Cover illustrations for her books are given, as are a synopses of each; excerpts from positive reviews and from each book are also provided. A list of Squire's books in print is provided; it includes publisher, year of publication, and ISBN.

Dana Stabenow

585. Stabenow, Dana. **Dana Stabenow's Home Page**. http://www.stabenow. com/

Stabenow's home page provides a picture and an autobiographical statement, and offers access to information about her Star Svensdotter science fiction series and her Kate Shugak mystery series. The latter provides information about Shugak and has links to the various books in the series. A cover illustration, publisher, year of publication, ISBN, and position in the series are provided for each book, as are also a synopsis, the dedication (and an explanation of its meaning), a note from the author, and a lengthy excerpt. Finally, there is a list of frequently asked questions and information on recent developments ("All the Latest News") in Stabenow's career. This is a well-designed, informative, and useful site.

Vincent Starrett

586. Honce, Charles. **A Vincent Starrett Library: The Astonishing Result of Twenty-Three Years of Library Activity**. Mount Vernon, NY: Golden Eagle Press, 1941. 81 p. LC 41-15879. (100 copies printed.)

Not seen.

587. Norfolk-Hall. **A Vincent Starrett Catalogue: First Editions, Books By and About, Fine Association Copies & Ephemera**. Oakville, MO: Norfolk-Hall, 1979. 38 p.

Dealers' catalogues are not generally included here, but like the work of Enola Stewart (below), this one must be mentioned. Items in it are separately numbered and arranged chronologically; items published prior to 1941 have their number in Honce's bibliography (above) given. References to books list place of publication, publisher, year of publication, and significant features; references to fascicles are also provided. More is listed in this catalogue than in Stewart's, but its arrangement is less felicitous.

588. Ruber, Peter. **The Last Bookman**. New York: Candlelight Press, 1968. 115 p. LC 72-44.

589. Ruber, Peter. **The Last Bookman**. 2d ed. Toronto: Metropolitan Toronto Reference Library, 1995. 172 p. (Vincent Starrett Memorial Library, vol. 3). CN 95-931571. ISBN 1-89603266-4.

This tribute to Starrett contains a partial bibliography compiled by Esther Longfellow. The bibliography contains the following sections: novels, short stories, juveniles, poetry, critical studies and essays by Starrett, books edited, and "About Vincent Starrett." Citations in each section are chronologically arranged, and bibliographic data for each include place of publication, publisher, year of publication, pagination, paper size (e.g., 16mo.), and, when relevant, notes on the size of the edition.

A comprehensive Starrett bibliography remains to be compiled, but given Starrett's prolixity, it is unlikely such will ever be attempted.

590. Stewart, Enola. **Vincent Starrett: A Catalogue of First and Variant Editions of His Work, Including Books Edited by Him and Those with Introductions, Prefaces, Afterwords, or Anthologized Contributions**. Pocono Pines, PA: Gravesend Books, 1975. 26 leaves. (300 copies.)

Although dealers' catalogues are not generally included here, this one must be mentioned. Reproduced from typed copy and compiled by the owner of Gravesend Books, it offers a cover illustration by Mathew Zimmer and contains 10 sections: first and variant editions of books and pamphlets written by Starrett; books edited by Starrett; books and pamphlets containing introductions, prefaces, forewords, and afterwords by Starrett; books and pamphlets containing contributions by Starrett; books and pamphlets containing information pertaining to Starrett and his books; magazines and journals containing stories and articles written by Vincent Starrett; books once in the possession of Starrett; ephemera; reference books used in preparing this catalogue; and terms. Citations are continuously numbered and chronologically arranged in each section; in all, 139 items are listed. In all citations, the publication's title, publisher, and place of publication are given in capital letters and followed by the date of publication.

As Stewart's foreword explains, Starrett wrote far more than is listed in this bibliography, and "the catalogue . . . although by no means complete, is a representative sampling of his work." Affectionate though Stewart's sampling is, it is inadequate as a bibliography, and one regrets that Starrett, who died in 1974, was unable to assist in its compilation.

Shane Stevens

591. Legg, John. **Collecting Shane Stevens a.k.a. J. W. Rider**. Charleston, WV: Black Diamond Books, 1995. 88 p. Paperback. LC 94-96663. ISBN 0-9644069-0-X.

Though he is hardly well known, Shane Stevens has a devoted core of fans, and no less a writer than Stephen King has appropriated the names of Shane Stevens's characters. This affectionate tribute to the elusive thriller/mystery writer Shane Stevens/J. W. Rider contains nine chapters, the first of which is a biographical recounting of the few facts known about the reclusive Stevens. Chapter 2 describes Stevens's magazine and newspaper contributions; chapter 3 describes the Shane Stevens novels. Chapter 4 discusses the two pseudonymous novels Stevens has written as J. W. Rider. Chapter 5 discusses book collecting basics; Chapter 6 provides a checklist of Shane Stevens, and chapter 7, a J. W. Rider checklist. Chapter 8 presents illustrations of letters written by and books inscribed by Stevens. Chapter 9 lists booksellers specializing in modern first editions. The book concludes with a glossary of bookselling terms and a quick reference checklist of Stevens's/Rider's works. There are numerous illustrations throughout.

The largest sections in the book are chapters 6 and 7, which describe all known English-language editions of Stevens's books. The arrangement in these chapters is chronological, and each edition is separately numbered. The distinguishing features of each edition are described; bibliographic data include place of publication, publisher, and month of publication. When relevant, ISBNs are also provided, as are the name of the dustjacket artist, pagination, and measurements of the book. Finally, changes in printings and covers are detailed, and the approximate worth of the book (as of late 1995) is given.

The bibliographic data in the other chapters are less comprehensive, and in the case of chapter 2, they appear to be incomplete, for Stevens's autobiographical accounts mention publications not referenced by Legg. This aside, the volume's organization is occasionally frustrating, for it follows no pattern and mixes chapters containing useful book-collecting hints with chapters documenting publications. Nevertheless, *Collecting Shane Stevens* can be used with ease, and it is the only significant publication on an intriguing and quietly influential writer. Legg is reportedly working on a second volume titled *In Search of Shane Stevens*.

Rex Stout

592. Ahearn, Allen, and Patricia Ahearn. **Author Price Guides: Rex Stout**. Rockville, MD: Quill & Brush, 1995. 9 leaves. APG 076.2.

This Author's Price Guide to Rex Stout documents his work from the 1929 publication of *How Like a God* to the 1987 publication of *Under the Andes*; the Nero Wolfe pastiches by Robert Goldsborough are also listed.

For a thorough description of the format of Author Price Guides, see the entry under Fredric Brown.

593. Barkocy, Muffy. **Nero Wolfe**. http://www.fish.com/~muffy/pages/books/rex_stout/nero_wolfe.html

This engaging website provides a picture (uncredited) of Wolfe and a brief biography. A link to the novels provides a chronological list in a three-part table. The first part provides the year of publication; the second, the exact date or dates; and the third, the publication event that transpired on those dates. Additional links provide blueprints to the four-story brownstone on West 35th Street and to two sketches of Wolfe's office. There is information on joining the Wolfe Pack, and a list of respondents who have information about *The Nero Wolfe Cookbook*. On the debit side, the background is a mix of colors, the type is yellow, and viewing is occasionally difficult.

594. Gotwald, Frederick G. **The Nero Wolfe Companion**. Salisbury, NC: Rev. Frederick G. Gotwald, 1996– . 9 vols. Paperback.

Inspired by William S. Baring-Gould's annotations to Sherlock Holmes (q.v.), the introduction to each volume of this nine-volume guide to the Nero Wolfe novels of Rex Stout states that "it is the conclusion of the author that the setting of the Wolfe adventures were in real time. Over four hundred and thirty names of real persons are name-dropped. Events of the day are noted and even become the topic of an adventure. Rex Stout's attitudes about social and political issues of the time are revealed through his primary characters Nero Wolfe and Archie." To provide biographical data on these names, explanations of these events, and explications of these attitudes is the purpose of these self-published guides.

Here is a list of the volumes and the works they annotate:

Volume 1: *Fer-de-Lance, The League of Frightened Men, The Rubber Band, The Red Box,* and *Too Many Cooks*

Volume 2: *Some Buried Caesar, Over My Dead Body, Where There's a Will, Bitter End, Black Orchids,* and *Not Quite Dead Enough*

Volume 3: *The Silent Speaker, Too Many Women, And Be a Villain, The Second Confession,* and *In the Best Families*

Volume 4: *Trouble in Triplicate, Three Doors to Death, Curtains for Three, Triple Jeopardy,* and *Murder by the Book*

Volume 5: *Three Men Out, Prisoner's Base, The Golden Spiders, The Black Mountain,* and *Three Witnesses*

Volume 6: *Before Midnight, Three for the Chair, And Four to Go, Might as Well Be Dead,* and *If Death Ever Slept*

Volume 7: *Champagne for One, Three at Wolfe's Door, Homicide Trinity, Plot It Yourself,* and *Too Many Clients*

Volume 8: *Trio for Blunt Instruments, The Final Deduction, Gambit, The Mother Hunt, A Right to Die,* and *The Doorbell Rang*

Volume 9: *Death of a Doxy, The Father Hunt, Death of a Dude, Please Pass the Guilt,* and *A Family Affair*

Each volume is reproduced from typed copy. Each entry begins with a reproduction of the cover or title page (or both) of the first edition and an account of its publication. Stout's references are explicated in the order in which they occur, with Gotwald's left column listing the chapter in which the reference is located and the right column providing explanatory data. The majority of the explications are accompanied by (occasionally grainy) illustrations. Concluding each chapter are reprints of contemporary reviews.

Gotwald has performed yeoman service in his explications, which are concise and generally helpful. On the debit side, he has not indicated the sources from which he has derived his data; there are occasional misspellings (including Hemingway's name); and the lack of a cumulative index prohibits researchers from locating similar references in different novels. Readers new to Stout and Nero Wolfe may nevertheless find these volumes quite helpful.

595. **List Nero.**

Available in the archives maintained by the DorothyL listserv and through the Miss Lemon website (http://www.iwillfollow.com/lemon.htm), this list of Stout's Nero Wolfe novels is arranged chronologically. Brief "rude notes" accompany each title, noting the introduction of specific characters. The site has typos. Barkocy's site is superior (q.v.).

596. Townsend, Guy M., and others, eds. **Rex Stout: An Annotated Primary and Secondary Bibliography.** New York: Garland, 1980. xxvi, 199 p. Index. (Garland Reference Library of the Humanities, v. 239). LC 80-8507. ISBN 0-8240-9479-4.

This excellent bibliography lists every available item by or about Rex Stout written in English and published in the United States, Great Britain, and Canada, with the exception of newspaper stories: In these, it is selective. The volume begins with a lively biography of Stout, who can be said to have had three writing careers but who did not start seriously writing detective and mystery stories until 1934, when he was in his late 40s—and who then wrote some 72 novels and novellas before his death at age 89 in 1975. Near the conclusion of this section, Townsend (et al.) offer a statement that simultaneously explains Stout's technique, rationalizes his popularity, and justifies his enormous importance: "One of the chief reasons why the Nero Wolfe stories command so extraordinary a following is that in them Stout reconciled the formal detective story with the hard-boiled detective story at a time when the steadily widening breach separating them threatened the dissolution of the genre." To this one might add that despite occasional deficiencies in plot, Stout's stories were lively and witty; his characterizations and settings were vivid and exact; and his sense of the rights of the individual and the importance of humanity was pervasive and appealing.

The bibliography contains the following sections: novels; short stories; short story collections; omnibus volumes; articles; forewords, introductions, prefaces, afterwords, and jacket essays; reviews; jacket blurbs; edited volumes; poetry; broadcasts in print; movies; Nero Wolfe radio broadcasts; pastiches; interviews; and criticism. The contents of each of the sections are arranged chronologically and are exemplary in their presentation of data. The section devoted to novels contains separately numbered citations, each of which provides information on all known appearances of the work, starting with the original serialization of the piece. Data presented for serializations include the magazine's date of publication, volume, and pagination. Citations for books list place of publication, publisher, date of publication, pagination, and all known reprint editions. The annotations are lively, providing plot elements without revealing conclusions. Finally, each entry concludes with a list of significant reviews received by the book upon original publication.

The citations for Stout's short stories are also individually numbered. Each lists every appearance of the story, from its first periodical publication to its later appearance in Stout's collections and its eventual anthologization. As before, the data are gratifyingly comprehensive. Periodical publication data include magazine's name, volume, and story's pagination, and the references to the story's anthologization provide the book's editor, anthology's title, publisher, place of publication, year of publication, series number, and pagination. As in the earlier section, the annotations are models at stimulating interest in the story. Furthermore, cross-references are provided throughout this section, linking the story to its appearances in the short story collections and omnibus volumes. The successive sections of the primary bibliography are equally comprehensive and well done, revealing a man of extraordinary energy and versatility.

The secondary bibliography indexes and annotates some 112 articles, chapters in books, and books. Though many of these publications appeared in (virtually inaccessible) fan magazines, a gratifying number are from sources as varied and accessible as the *London Times*, *Nation*, *English Studies*, and *The Practitioner*. An excellent author/title index concludes the volume, which belongs in all academic libraries.

597.   Van Dover, J. Kenneth. **At Wolfe's Door: The Nero Wolfe Novels of Rex Stout**. San Bernardino, CA: Borgo Press, 1991. 120 p. Index. (Milford Series Popular Writers of Today, vol. 52). LC 88-34363. ISBN 0-89370-189-0 (hc); 0-89370-289-7 (pb). ISSN 0163-2469.

At Wolfe's Door provides a synopsis of every mystery novel and each short story published by Stout between 1934 and 1975; such posthumously published works as *Death Times Three* (1985) are also summarized. Because Nero Wolfe is by far Stout's best-known creation, the first section of the volume surveys those works in which Wolfe appears, and the volume's second section surveys the rest of Stout's writings. Both sections are arranged chronologically; when more than one work appeared in a particular year, the arrangement is alphabetical. Each entry is numbered, the title of the work appearing in boldface type with the date of publication beside it; when the work is a short story, its first book appearance is indicated. Each entry lists the name and identifying activity of the victim(s), the client(s), and the principal(s). A synopsis of the plot follows, though the murderer's identity is never revealed, and each entry concludes with a critical comment on the merits of the work. In all, 85 works are summarized. An essay comparing Stout with Erle Stanley Gardner follows the summaries, and the volume concludes with an index.

Apart from titles and dates of publication, Van Dover provides no bibliographic data, and in summarizing only the mysteries, Van Dover deliberately neglects Stout's early novels and much ephemeral work, including poetry and articles that occasionally contain themes that prefigure his later work. Nevertheless, Van Dover should not be faulted for limiting his focus to Stout's criminous work; the 85 annotations are well written and clear, and his concluding essay is insightful.

597a. Rex Stout Fan Clubs
   The Wolfe Packe
   PO Box 822
   Ansonia Station
   New York, NY 10023

John Straley

598. Tangled Web. **John Straley and Cecil Younger, PI**. http://www.twbooks.co.uk/authors/authorpagelist.html

A picture of Straley is provided, as are cover reproductions of his novels featuring Alaskan detective Cecil Younger. The material from the back covers is given, accompanied by reviews and excerpts from positive reviews. Book titles are accompanied by their ISBN and prices (in pounds).

Penny Sumner

599. Tangled Web. **Penny Sumner and Victoria Cross**. http://www.twbooks.co.uk/authors/psumner.html

A brief biography of Sumner is given, accompanied by a cover reproduction of *Crosswords*, starring Victoria Cross, archivist-turned-investigator. There are links to two other titles by Sumner, *Reader, I Murdered Him* and *Reader, I Murdered Him Too*.

Julian Symons

600. Walsdorf, John J., and Bonnie J. Allen. **Julian Symons: A Bibliography with Commentaries and a Personal Memoir by Julian Symons and a Preface by H. R. F. Keating**. New Castle, DE: Oak Knoll Press; Winchester, England: St. Paul's Bibliographies, 1996. xliii, 296 p. Index. (Winchester Bibliographies of 20th Century Writers). LC 96-12092. ISBN 1-8847-1822-1.

Compiled with the assistance of Symons, who died two years prior to its publication, this fine bibliography uses a format reminiscent of the Pittsburgh Series in Bibliography. The contents: A) Fiction, B) Poetry, C) Nonfiction, D) Works Edited, E) Contributions to Books, F) Contributions to Anthologies, G) Selected Contributions to Periodicals, and H) Contributions to *Ellery Queen's Mystery Magazine*. Entries in all sections are chronologically arranged and separately numbered. In addition, there are also a lengthy autobiographical statement by Symons (reprinted from the Contemporary Authors Autobiography Series from Gale), introductions by H. R. F. Keating and John Walsdorf, and a brief reminiscence by Kathleen Symons (reprinted from *Mystery Writers Annual*, 1987). Finally, a chronology of Symons's life is provided, as are numerous reproductions of title pages, an appendix, and an epilogue. The volume concludes with a well-done index.

The data in each section are gratifyingly thorough. In sections A–C, the title page of each work is transcribed in the quasifacsimile method; a collation statement is provided; the contents are given; any illustrations are detailed; the binding cases and their colors are described; the dustjacket or wrappers are described, and the paper on which the book was printed is detailed. The bibliographer's notes provide statements on the printing history (number of copies printed, prices, textual changes, author's agreements, etc.). Corrected editions and the first American editions are also accorded this bibliographical treatment. Furthermore, Symons has provided notes on many of the titles.

The citations to Symons's material in the other sections are equally thorough and detailed. The appendix lists selected biographical and critical material about Symons, and the epilogue lists the dates on which obituaries of Symons appeared in major publications. The indexes contain separate sections listing titles, publishers, printers, designer/illustrators, photographers, poems (by title), and short fiction (by title); they conclude with names and titles not listed in the previous sections.

Andrew Taylor

601.   Tangled Web. **Andrew Taylor.** http://www.twbooks.co.uk/authors/ataylor2.html

Though predominantly a writer of thrillers, Taylor has written several novels of detection, in particular the well-received *Caroline Minuscule* (1982) and *Our Fathers' Lies* (1985). This website begins with a photograph of Taylor and a biography that concludes by listing the addresses of his U.S. and U.K. agents and the whereabouts of his manuscripts. Cover reproductions of several of Taylor's works are given, accompanied by brief histories of the composition of the works. Excerpts from positive reviews are provided. The concluding bibliography lists the first British and American publishers and the dates of publication for each of Taylor's series. A well-presented site.

Phoebe Atwood Taylor

602.   Chester, John. **Phoebe Atwood Taylor.**

Available as a list through the archives maintained by the DorothyL listserv, and also accessible via the Miss Lemon website (http://www.iwillfollow.com/lemon.htm), this list of the writings of Phoebe Atwood Taylor is divided into three sections, each alphabetically arranged. The first lists Taylor's writings under her own name that feature the character Asey Mayo; the second lists Taylor's writings (as "Alice Tilton") that feature the character Leonidas Witherall; and the third lists Taylor's other pseudonymous work. Each title is accompanied by the publication date.

Ross Thomas

603.   Ahearn, Allen, and Patricia Ahearn. **Author Price Guides: Ross Thomas.** Rockville, MD: Quill & Brush, 1995. 4 leaves. APG 022.3.

This Author's Price Guide to Ross Thomas documents his work from the 1966 appearance of *The Cold War Swap* to the 1994 publication of *Ah, Treachery!*

For a thorough description of the format of Author Price Guides, see the entry under Fredric Brown.

604. Stephens, Christopher P. **A Checklist of Ross Thomas**. Hastings-on-Hudson, NY: Ultramarine Publishing, 1992. 13 p. Paperback. Index. ISBN 0-89366-228-3.

Apparently offset from typed copy, this brief checklist lists the books written by Ross Thomas under his own name as well as those he wrote under the pseudonym Oliver Bleeck. Each numbered citation provides publication data on the first American and first British editions. Titles are underlined; retitlings are indicated; and information on dustwrapper artists, prices, and identifying points is given. There is an index to the titles and retitlings, and pagination is inconsistently provided. Though this pamphlet is a useful starting point for collectors, it does not list Thomas's nonbook writings; a comprehensive bibliography is needed.

Jim Thompson

605. Furlong, Leslie. **The Killer Beside Me: The Jim Thompson Resource Page**. http://www.geocities.com/SoHo/Lofts/6439/intro.htm

This website contains a brief and somewhat sanitized biography of Thompson, references to the two book-length Thompson biographies, and links to sites with information about the movies made from Thompson's books. A few cover reproductions are provided, but the site unfortunately contains no additional resources about the author.

Aimée Thurlo and David Thurlo

606. Thurlo, Aimée, and David Thurlo. **Aimée and David Thurlo**. http://www.comet.net/writersm/thurlo/home.htm

The website of the husband-and-wife writing team provides some biographical data on the authors, some information on their *Four Winds* romance trilogy, and significant information on their series featuring Navajo investigator Ella Clah. Cover reproductions are given, as are excerpts and positive critical comments. In addition, a section titled "Summaries of Our Published Mysteries" provides title, publisher, year of publication, ISBN, a summary, and ordering information for each book. There are links to reviewers' critical comments and to websites the Thurlos find interesting.

Elleston Trevor

607. Peralez, Jon. **The Unofficial Quiller Web Site**. http://home.earthlink. net/~quiller/quiller.html

Elleston Trevor wrote a number of mystery novels, but his espionage novels featuring Quiller, written under the name Adam Hall, gained him a loyal following and are the focus of this website. Peralez provides bio-bibliographical information about the author that links to other sources when appropriate. These include a picture of Trevor, a biographical statement, tributes, and cover images. The bibliographic section provides a chronological list of the Quiller novels, each accompanied by two buttons. The left button provides a synopsis of the book taken from its jacket and bibliographic data (publisher, year of publication, date of publication, and dustjacket design); the dedication is also given. The right button provides images from all known editions of that book. The site is well designed, and one hopes that Peralez will expand his coverage to include the rest of Trevor's writings.

Wilson Tucker

608. Stephens, Christopher P. **A Checklist of Wilson Tucker**. Hastings-on-Hudson, NY: Ultramarine Publishing, 1991. 18 p. Paperback. Index. ISBN 0-89366-211-9.

Wilson Tucker is traditionally considered a writer of science fiction, but more of his work is detective and mystery stories than it is science fiction. This checklist begins with a chronologically arranged listing of his books, from the 1946 *The Chinese Doll* to the 1982 *The Best of Wilson Tucker*. Each of the citations is separately numbered and provides data on the first American and first British editions. Titles are underlined, and there is information on pagination, retitlings, dustwrapper artists, prices, and identifying points. The second section lists Tucker's short stories, from the 1941 publication of "Interstellar Way-Station" in *Super Science Stories* to the 1978 publication of "The Near Zero Crime Rate on JJ Avenue" in *Analog*; the citations provide only the month and year of the magazine. An index to the books and short stories concludes the bibliography.

In science fiction circles, Tucker is something of a legend, and stories about his youthful behavior still circulate. Unfortunately for his fans and collectors, this checklist is far from comprehensive. Not only does it neglect to provide Tucker's full name (Arthur Wilson Tucker), but it neglects to cite his semiprofessionally published works in fanzines. The bibliography of Stephensen-Payne and Benson, Jr. (q.v.), is a superior work.

609. Stephensen-Payne, Phil, and Gordon Benson, Jr. **Wilson "Bob" Tucker: Wild Talent**. 4th revised edition. Leeds, England; Albuquerque, NM: Galactic Central, 1994. 29 p. Paperback. (Galactic Central Bibliographies for the Avid Reader, vol. 8). LC 94-51091. ISBN 1-871133-41-6

The earlier editions have not been seen.

This bibliography attempts to cite all the published works in English by or about Wilson Tucker and as many foreign-language items as can be located. It contains the following sections: stories, books, series, poems and songs, poem and song collections, articles, miscellaneous, nonfiction books, edited books, media presentations, articles on the author, reviews, books about the author, phantom and forthcoming titles, related works by other authors, textual variations, and a chronological listing of fiction. Several of these sections contain no data, making the bibliography less formidable than it appears in description.

In each section, entries tend to follow a chronological order, with each section having its own numbering. Entries for "Stories" reference all professionally published fiction that appeared as part of a larger publication (e.g., a magazine or a collection). An abbreviation ("sss" for short-short story or vignette, "NT" for novelette, "N" for novel, etc.) indicates the approximate length of item, and serialization is indicated. Paginations are not given.

The entries for books list all separate publications, excluding poetry. Each entry provides title, publisher, ISBN, date of publication, pagination, original price, and artist. Reprints and reissues by the same publisher are listed chronologically beneath the first edition. When ISBNs were not available, the publisher's stock number, the number given by the Library of Congress, or the number given by the British Library General Catalogue—or some combination of these three—is listed. The contents of collections are given, and editions in languages other than English are cited when they are known.

"Articles on the Author" references all known articles that relate to the author and his work, excluding book reviews. In the case of Tucker, who has been enormously visible in fan circles, the secondary literature concentrates primarily on the professionally published material, and Stephensen-Payne's and Benson's introduction states forthrightly (and optimistically) that "there are bound to have been many secondary items (particularly in fanzines) that have been omitted. These omissions will hopefully be corrected in future editions of this bibliography."

Despite the unnecessarily cumbersome arrangement, this is the most comprehensive bibliography of Wilson Tucker available.

Peter Turnbull

610. Tangled Web. **Peter Turnbull**. http://www.twbooks.co.uk/authors/pturnbull.html

A photograph of Turnbull is given, as are a brief biography, synopses of his novels, several cover reproductions, and excerpts from positive reviews. The concluding bibliography lists his works in chronological order and provides publisher, year of publication, and series for each title.

Arthur W. Upfield

611. Asdell, Philip T. **A Revised Descriptive Bibliography of First Editions of Arthur W. Upfield: Australian, British, and U.S.** Frederick, MD: P. T. Asdell, 1988. 32 p. Paperback. LC 88-165213.

Not seen. Apparently a revision of an earlier publication, the 1984 *Provisional Descriptive Bibliography of First Editions of the Works of Arthur W. Upfield*.

612. Stephens, Christopher P. **A Checklist of Arthur Upfield**. Hastings-on-Hudson, NY: Ultramarine Publishing, 1991. 18 p. Paperback. Index. ISBN 0-89366-135-X.

Arthur Upfield was born in England, thrice failed to pass his examinations for professional advancement, and was sent to Australia by his father. Following a stint in the armed forces, he returned to Australia and, in his second novel, created the character of Inspector Napoleon Bonaparte (Bony to his friends), a half-caste educated at Brisbane University and employed by the Queensland Police Department. Stephens's bibliography, apparently offset from typed copy, lists chronologically the books by Upfield. Each citation is numbered; the title is underlined; and publication data on first British, American, Canadian, and Australian editions are given. Retitlings are documented. Pagination is provided (when available), as is information on the dustwrapper artist. An index to the titles (including the retitlings) concludes the pamphlet. Though not complete—Upfield wrote a fair amount of incidental material, including numerous articles, none of which have been reprinted—and containing an occasional typo (*Wings Above the Diamantina* has become *Wings Above the Diamantia* in the index)—this is nevertheless a helpful listing.

613. Rauch, Nancy V. **Upfield Mysteries**.

Available as a list through the archives maintained by the DorothyL listserv, and also accessible via the Miss Lemon website (http://www.iwillfollow.com/lemon.htm), and derived partially from a bibliography published by Betty Donaldson in the November 1974 *The Armchair Detective*, this list of Arthur Upfield's books is arranged chronologically. Each title is followed by a note indicating setting, whether it features Detective-Inspector Napoleon Bonaparte, and alternative titles. Very capably done.

Andrew Vachss

614. Vachss, Andrew. **The Zero: The Official Home Page of Andrew Vachss**. http://www.vachss.com

Vachss's own website contains an introduction to his work and a list of frequently asked questions, offers news about his life and projects, and provides a gratifyingly thorough bibliography, with separate sections listing his nonfiction texts, novels, short stories, comic books, special projects, plays, introductions to the works of others, and articles, essays, and editorials. The bibliographic data provided include publisher and year of publication for the first appearance of the work, and data are occasionally offered on paperback reprintings. Dates of publication are provided for articles. Furthermore, articles are offered as full text, a note indicating the format in which they are available for downloading. The site is well designed and informative, though somewhat surprisingly it contains neither cover reproductions nor references to reviews.

Robert H. van Gulik

615. **Bibliography of Dr. R. H. van Gulik (D. Litt).** [N.P.] Compiled for the Benefit of the Boston University Libraries - Mugar Memorial Library "Robert van Gulik Collection." Undated. 82 p. Paperback.

Though undated, this pamphlet was almost certainly compiled shortly after van Gulik's death in 1967, perhaps in early 1968. It is not merely a bibliography but an account of a the life of an extraordinarily versatile man. The volume begins with a curriculum vitae for van Gulik. Separate sections list data on his education and career, family background, marriage and children, decorations, memberships, pen names, and theses. Chinese characters are given when applicable, as are romanizations of Chinese names.

The bibliography contains sections for van Gulik's books, pamphlets, essays, articles, book reviews, vocabularies, encyclopedia entries, lectures, necrologies, and translations of Chinese and Japanese poems. The data include the book's title (with an English translation as necessary), the language in which the book was written, printer, and publisher. Paginations are occasionally given, as are citations to reviews.

The documentation of van Gulik's own work begins with citations to his poetry, each reference listing the poem's title, English equivalent, year in which the poem was published, language in which the poem was written, and place of its publication; unpublished (typescript) poems are also listed. This material is followed by citations to the justly famous Judge Dee stories; separate sections list all first editions of the works in all languages. Lists of the comic strip syndication in the Dutch and Scandinavian newspapers and lengthy series of miscellaneous notes conclude the pamphlet.

The bibliography appears to have been offset from photocopied typescript and would have benefited immensely from better printing. Moreover, it lacks a table of contents and a title index. These complaints aside, the bibliography is quite usable and seemingly comprehensive. It remains a substantial achievement and deserves to be better known.

616. Nielsen, Birger. **Robert van Gulik Bibliography.** http://jhem.get2net.dk/bnielsen/gulik.html

Concentrating on van Gulik's mysteries, this website begins with a complete list of the English-language editions of the Judge Dee books; dates of publication arc occasionally provided. A lengthy section ("when, where, titles & information") provides a chronology of the life of Judge Dee and matches it to the books in which Dee appeared. Links to some of van Gulik's drawings and sites occasionally offering van Gulik's books for sale are given. Mention is made of Janwillem van de Wetering's 1987 van Gulik biography and a Dutch bibliography of van Gulik (not referenced here for language reasons). Finally, there is a list of the Danish editions of van Gulik's titles with their English counterparts.

Jack Vance

617. Levack, Daniel J. H., and Tim Underwood. **Fantasms: A Bibliography of the Literature of Jack Vance**. San Francisco, CA; Columbia, PA: Underwood/Miller, 1978. 91 p. (1,000 copies, 100 clothbound.)

Fantasms attempts to provide a complete listing of Vance's English-language publications, including a complete printing history of his books and a list of all his English-language periodical, anthology, and collection appearances through early 1978. It is heavily illustrated with numerous black-and-white reproductions of Vance's works.

The first section lists Vance's book publications in alphabetical order, separately numbering each citation. Titles are given in boldface capital letters; prior periodical publication data are listed on the next lines, as are the contents of short story collections and the name of the series (if any) to which the work belongs. Separate lines provide a chronological list of the book's different editions. Publication data include publisher, stock number (for paperbacks), year of publication, and whether the work appeared in paperback or cloth.

The second section is an alphabetical list of Vance's short stories. It too is arranged alphabetically, with its entries separately numbered. Each citation contains a chronological list of the story's appearance in periodicals and books; series names are indicated, as is occasionally the story's length (in number of words).

The next sections list Vance's works by series, his pseudonyms (and the works written under each name), his works chronologically, and his works that have been adapted for television.

In many respects, *Fantasms* appears to be an early draft that was rushed to print. It lacks such minimal data as the publisher's location and pagination; the names of cover illustrators are not provided; the television adaptations provide no data about the shows; and worst of all, the bibliography provides no sense of the author's varied accomplishments. It is now outdated and has been thoroughly superseded by the work of Hewett and Mallett (q.v.).

618. Cockrum, Kurt, Daniel J. H. Levack, and Tim Underwood. **Fantasms II: A Bibliography of the Works of Jack Vance**. Canoga Park, CA: Kurt Cockrum, 1979. xiii, 83 p. (Approximately 100 copies issued.)

Not seen.

619. Hewett, Jerry, and Daryl F. Mallett. **The Work of Jack Vance: An Annotated Bibliography & Guide**. Introduction by Robert Silverberg. San Bernardino, CA: Borgo Press; Penn Valley, CA; and Lancaster, PA: Underwood-Miller, 1994. xxiv, 293 p. Indexes. (Bibliographies of Modern Authors, no. 29). LC 92-28056. ISBN 0-8095-0509-6 (hc); 0-8095-1509-1 (pb); 0-88733-165-3 (trade cloth); 0-88733-166-1 (limited edition).

Although he is best known as a science fiction author, Jack Vance has written a number of mysteries under his full name, John Holbrook Vance, and under several pseudonyms, including that of Ellery Queen, as whom he ghostwrote several novels. This gratifyingly comprehensive and elaborate bibliography of Vance was compiled with the assistance of Jack and Norma Vance and with the compilers' desire to rectify the inadequacies of the previously published bibliographies. The volume begins with Robert Silverberg's introduction, "The World of Jack Vance." This appreciation is followed by a lengthy Vance chronology, whose contents were assembled by Norma Vance using information derived from personal journals.

The bibliography contains the following sections: A) Books; B) Short Fiction; C) Verse and Poetry; D) Nonfiction; E) Other Media; F) Interviews; G) Maps and Drawings; H) Phantom Editions and Works; I) Unpublished Manuscripts; J) Honors and Awards; K) Guest of Honor Appearances; L) Interviews with Vance; M) Secondary Sources; N) Miscellanea: "The Genesee Slough Murders: Outline for a Novel" by Jack Vance; Afterword: "Jack Vance: The Man and the Myth" by Tim Underwood; and Index. The contents of the first six sections are chronologically arranged, with each citation being separately lettered and numbered.

The first section is the longest and dominates the bibliography. The title of each work is given in boldface type, followed by the place of publication, publisher, year of publication, pagination, and publisher's series number. The book's contents are itemized. Short story paginations are provided and cross-referenced to the contents of the other sections. The collation, binding measurements (in centimeters), notes about the contents, cover illustrator, original price, and ISBN are given. Similar data are provided for all English-language reprint editions and for the international editions; the titles of international editions are also in boldface type, and the name of the translator is given. When relevant, retitlings are indicated. Following the bibliographic descriptions of each work is an alphabetical list of secondary sources and the reviews that discuss the work.

In "Short Fiction," the title of each story is given in boldface type and quotation marks. The publication data italicize periodical titles and provide the periodical's volume and publication date and the story's pagination. Book titles are also italicized. Publication data include name of the editor, place of publication, publisher, date of publication, and pagination. All reprints of every story are listed. When relevant, retitlings are indicated and cross-references link these items to other sections.

Less needs to be said about the other sections, whose titles indicate their contents. The section documenting Vance's nonfiction begins by listing the editorials Vance wrote while a student at the University of California, Berkeley. "Other Media" provides production data on Vance's radio and television adaptations that include broadcast date, cast, and notes on the availability of the work. "Phantom Editions and Works" lists titles that appear to have been published. "Interviews with Jack Vance" cites radio interviews as well as those that have been published.

The bibliography concludes with eight separate indexes. The first indexes Vance's works by their titles; book titles are italicized. The second lists the artists who have illustrated Vance's work; the third, the editors of works in which Vance has appeared or has been discussed; the fourth, Vance's translators; the fifth, the titles of the magazines and anthologies in which Vance has appeared; the sixth, Vance's publishers; the seventh, the titles of the secondary works that have discussed Vance; and the eighth, the names of critics and reviewers of Vance.

A table listing the retitlings of Vance's publications would have been useful, but apart from this minor lacuna, *The Work of Jack Vance* is a thoroughly impressive achievement.

620. Stephensen-Payne, Phil, and Gordon Benson, Jr. **Jack Vance: A Fantasmic Imagination**. Albuquerque, NM: Galactic Central, 1988. 46 p. Paperback. (Galactic Central Bibliographies for the Avid Reader, vol. 28).

621. Stephensen-Payne, Phil, and Gordon Benson, Jr. **Jack Vance: A Fantasmic Imagination, A Working Bibliography**. 2d revised ed. Leeds, England; Polk City, IA: Galactic Central, 1990. 61 p. Paperback. (Galactic Central Bibliographies for the Avid Reader, vol. 28). ISBN 1-871133-02-5.

Though not as comprehensive as the Vance bibliography compiled by Hewett and Mallett (q.v.), *Jack Vance: A Fantasmic Imagination* is nevertheless a reasonably thorough list of the British editions of Vance's work. Like most of the publications of Galactic Central, its introduction states that it contains the following sections: A) Stories; B) Books; C) Series; D) Poems, Songs, and Plays; E) Poem, Song, and Play Volumes; F) Articles; G) Miscellaneous; H) Nonfiction Books; I) Edited Books; J) Media Presentations; K) Articles on the Author; L) Reviews; M) Books about the Author; N) Phantom and Forthcoming Titles; O) Related Works by Other Authors; P) Textual Variations; and Q) a Chronological Listing of Fiction. And, as in many publications of Galactic Central, several of these sections contain no material whatsoever.

The contents of the first three sections are alphabetically arranged, each citation being separately lettered and numbered. In the first section, beneath each story's title are the places in which it has seen print. Book titles are capitalized and often accompanied by the names of the editors. Journal titles are given in regular type, and the original publication date is given in abbreviated form (e.g., 8-52 for August 1952). An abbreviation indicates whether the piece is a short-short story or vignette, short story, novelette, novella, short novel, or novel. Cross-references are provided for retitlings and alternative titles. The titles for Vance's books are given in capital letters. Each citation lists publisher, series number, pagination, ISBN, original price, and cover artist. All known English-language editions are cited.

Less needs to be said about the other sections, whose titles indicate their contents; sections E, H, I, and O are empty. The section on media presentations provides only the title and year in which the work appeared, and Vance's radio interviews are not listed. There are no indexes.

A useful introduction, but no more.

Barbara Vine/Ruth Rendell

622. Tangled Web. **Barbara Vine**. http://www.totalweb.co.uk/tangledweb/authors/authorpagelist.html

Despite Ruth Rendell's enormous popularity, this site, devoted only to her writings as Barbara Vine, appears to be the only Rendell website available. It provides a photograph of Rendell, a brief biography clearly identifying Vine with Rendell, the cover illustrations of two her books, and the material from the back covers with by excerpts from positive reviews. The bibliography is in two sections. The first lists Rendell's works as Vine but provides only their publication years and the awards they have won. The second section is a list of Rendell's titles to 1996. Arranged chronologically, this list gives the publisher and the series detective appearing in the book.

Hannah Wakefield

623. Tangled Web. **Hannah Wakefield and Dee Street**. http://www.twbooks.co.uk/authors/hwakefield.html

No photograph of Wakefield is provided, but a brief biography and cover illustrations from her books are given, accompanied by material from the back covers and excerpts from positive reviews. The concluding bibliography lists titles but does not provide publishers.

Mary Willis Walker

624. Tangled Web. **Mary Willis Walker**. http://www.twbooks.co.uk/authors/mwwalker.html

A photograph of Walker is provided, as are cover reproductions from Walker's novels accompanied by reviews and excerpts from positive reviews. The concluding bibliography lists publishers, publication year, and the detective's name.

Peter N. Walker. *See* Nicholas Rhea

Edgar Wallace

625. Kiddle, Charles. **A Guide to the First Editions of Edgar Wallace**. Morcombe, Dorset: Ivory Head Press, 1981. 88 p. Index. Paperback. LC 82-100973. ISBN 0-903639-05-X.

This bibliography describes the first editions of Edgar Wallace published in the United Kingdom and the United States. Wallace's plays, poems issued as broadsides, and United Kingdom collections of stories are not included, nor are the data on original periodical publications of the contents of Wallace's books that occupy so much space in the Wallace bibliography done by Lofts and Adley (q.v.). In all, Kiddle describes 183 books. (A laid-in errata sheet describes a 184th book and corrects some small typographical errors.)

The bibliography is arranged alphabetically by English title. Citations begin with a "first edition reference number" and the book's title in boldface type. A second line provides publisher, date of publication, initial cost, size of the book (in inches), color of the binding, and "rarity factor." The rarity factor allows comparison between different first editions. For example, Wallace's extremely rare *Smithy and the Hun* and *The Tomb of Ts'in* have rarity factors of 400 and 275 respectively, whereas his *Again the Ringer* and *The Frightened Lady* have rarity factors of 2 and 5. A section entitled "Identification" provides the points used to identify a first edition; these include pagination and descriptions of advertisements and contents. A section called "Notes" lists retitlings and title changes, mentions variant bindings, and contains such comments as "a book at 7/6d dated 1925 without a catalogue is not a First Edition." Each entry concludes with a citation to the first U.S. edition that includes publisher and year of publication, binding color, pagination, and other data allowing for the identification of a first edition.

A chronological index provides the year and month in which the book appeared, title, and publisher. (Wallace's busiest year appears to have been 1929; 25 titles appeared, including five in April.) Separate sections list the titles of the first U.K. editions and the titles under which they were later reprinted, American collections of Wallace that have no British equivalent, and American retitlings listed next to their U.K. originals.

This bibliography would have been easier to use had the title cross-references been within the body of the book rather than being separately listed at the conclusion. However, this feature does not significantly mar the usability of this bibliography, which is clear and helpful. It belongs in all libraries, next to the earlier effort of Lofts and Adley.

626. Kiddle, Charles, and Richard Williams. **Edgar Wallace: First American Editions**. Scunthorpe, England: Dragonby Press, 1992. 4 p. Stapled sheets. (Edgar Wallace Monographs, no. 4).

Some 91 titles are listed in this bibliography of the first American editions of Edgar Wallace. The data are arranged chronologically by date of publication and provide title (as given on the title page), position of the publication dates in the book ("t" indicates that the date appeared on the title page; "v," that it appeared on the verso of the title page), color of the cloth binding, publisher, highest numbered page, original price, a valuation price, and (when relevant) original British title in italics and a note indicating that the American edition preceded the first British edition. Finally, an alphabetical list of publishers' names states the number of Wallace titles they published and provides notes on their indications of first editions.

Reproduced from word-processed copy and cramped, this work offers little that cannot be extracted from Kiddle's earlier *A Guide to the First Editions of Edgar Wallace* (q.v.).

627. Lofts, W. O. G., and Derek Adley. **The British Bibliography of Edgar Wallace**. London: Howard Baker, 1969. [xv], 246 p. LC 74-426863. ISBN 0-09-394760-6.

In his introduction Lofts states that he and Adley decided to compile a bibliography of the works of Edgar Wallace published in the United Kingdom, thinking that "the task would not be too difficult." Soon after, Lofts says that "I could not have been more wrong. It has proved to be a most laborious business. For Wallace's output was truly prodigious, and he himself kept few records, and of the few that he did keep none is anywhere close to being complete." Worse, writes Lofts, the "favoured recourse of the British bibliographer, the British Museum, has been unable to assist authoritatively in this instance either, since many of its files of the popular magazines of the Twenties, which contained the bulk of first publications of Wallace's work, were destroyed in the Blitz." Worse yet: "unfailing sources of irritation along the way have been the erroneous, and often downright misleading, brief bibliographies contained in all too many of the multitudinous books about Edgar Wallace. A little more care on the part of their authors would have saved Derek Adley and I [sic] many hours of fruitless research."

Thus plaintively introduced, the resulting bibliography contains the following sections: A) Books by Year of Publication, B) Short Stories, C) Rare Editions, D) First Editions, E) Works Published in Book Form, F) Autobiographies and Biographies, G) Collections of Stories, H) Stories in Short Story Collections, I) Plays, J) True Crime Articles, K) Miscellanea, L) Works Contained in Magazines and Newspapers, and M) First London Magazine Stories.

"Books by Year of Publication" lists chronologically the 172 books by Wallace documented in this bibliography. Each entry provides the year of publication, a boldface reference number keyed to sections D and E, the title of the book in capital letters, and the publisher's name. "Short Stories" lists titles of short stories known to exist but "they did not appear in book form—nor have they been traced in magazines." "Rare Editions" is an essay mentioning the rarest Wallace items.

"First Editions" begins with a lively essay detailing the frustrations involved in documenting Wallace. A lengthy "classification of first editions" follows: Books are listed alphabetically, each one assigned a boldface reference number. Titles are listed in capital letters, giving book's publisher and year of publication, paper size (e.g., Cr 8vo for "Crown Octavo"), pagination, and dedication. Cover designs and interior illustrations are so noted.

"Works Published in Book Form" expands the data presented in "First Editions." Wallace's 172 books are listed alphabetically, each entry prefaced with a note that indicates whether the work is V (verse), HF (historical fiction), NF (nonfiction), SS (short stories with central character), CSS (collected miscellaneous short stories), LSS (long short stories), BK (book), MG (magazine), N (newspaper), and/or published in the *EWMM* (*Edgar Wallace Mystery Magazine*). The reference number and title are given in boldface type and are followed by publisher and publication date, dates of later editions, and series. The contents of collections are listed; when stories were previously published, citations provide title under which the story was published, name of the publishing magazine and its volume, and date of original publication. The opening phrases of short stories and novels are given.

The sections devoted to "autobiographies and biographies, collections of short stories, stories in short story collections, plays, true crime articles, and miscellanea are brief, generally making reference to the material documented in the previous sections. The listings of Wallace's appearances in magazines and newspapers, however, are quite lengthy. This section begins with an alphabetical list of periodicals containing Wallace's work and a note as to whether the work is a serial, short story, article, poem, or true crime publication. Next comes a list of Wallace's periodical contributions arranged by periodical title. Entries are arranged chronologically and provide periodical's number, date in which Wallace's contribution appeared, and title and opening phrase of Wallace's contribution. A note indicates if the contribution appeared in book form and if Wallace used a pseudonym.

More Wallace titles have since surfaced, but despite this volume's sometimes baroque arrangement and the lack of a cumulative title index, it remains the most accessible list of Wallace's books available.

628. Williams, Richard. **Edgar Wallace: A Filmography.** 2d ed. Scunthorpe, England: Dragonby Press, 1990. 21 leaves. Stapled sheets. Indexes. (Edgar Wallace Monographs, no. 1).

This filmography lists all the films based on Edgar Wallace's writings or on characters created by Wallace, as well as those films in which Wallace played a role in the production. In all, some 176 films and five variants are listed and described, the most recent being from 1976. The filmography is international in scope, referencing films made in Great Britain, Germany, and the United States.

The first section of the filmography arranges the films by titles, using as the principal entry the title given the film in the country of its production. Where two or more countries were involved in production, the British title is given preference, then the American, then the German.

All alternate titles are indicated, and cross-references are provided when the film was shown in another country under a different title. The film script's source is given, a note indicating whether it was one of Wallace's novels or short stories or whether the film was adapted "freely from Wallace." Additional data list the name of the production company, country of production, whether the film was in color or black-and-white, year of release, and running time. The names of the scriptwriters and directors are given, and a list of the sources from which data were derived appears at the bottom of each entry.

The filmography's second section is a chronological index to the films. Release date, title, production company, and country in which the film was made are listed. The third section of the filmography lists the production and distribution companies responsible, and an abbreviation indicating the company's nationality.

Though easy to use and containing a wealth of data not readily available elsewhere, this work is likely to be too specialized for all but the most comprehensive of academic libraries or the most determined of Edgar Wallace collectors.

629. Williams, Richard. **Edgar Wallace British Magazine Appearances (Fiction)**. Scunthorpe, England: Dragonby Press, 1988. 18 p. Stapled sheets. (Edgar Wallace Monographs, no. 2).

A revision of the data first published in Lofts and Adley's *British Bibliography of Edgar Wallace* (q.v.), this bibliography lists all the fiction written by Edgar Wallace that appeared in British magazines, newspapers, and periodicals. The contents are arranged alphabetically by publication name, and under each publication stories are listed in chronological order. Numeration and/or volume and issue number are given, as is the story's title. An abbreviation indicates the work's category ("n" for novels, "sn" for serialized novel with the number of episodes in the serial, "s" for short story, and "ss" for short story collection with the number of stories given in the collection), and entries conclude with date of publication.

Reproduced from word-processed copy, the bibliography is cramped and would have benefited enormously from a title index. It nevertheless remains the most comprehensive list of Wallace's British periodical publications currently available.

630. Williams, Richard. **Edgar Wallace Index**. 2d ed. Scunthorpe, England: Dragonby Press, 1986. 8 p. Stapled sheets. (British Paperback Checklists, no. 17).

This list of Edgar Wallace titles appearing in paperback is clearly reproduced from typed copy. The citations are arranged alphabetically by book title. Data presented include previous title (when such exists), date and publisher of the original hardback edition (when such exist), an abbreviation indicating the book's genre (e.g., NF for nonfiction, Poe for poetry), another abbreviation indicating whether the book is short stories (ss) or stories and novelettes (s), and if the work appeared in more than one volume. Finally, the paperback's publishers are listed chronologically, the publisher's name abbreviated and keyed to a note on the first sheet and accompanied by date of publication.

Collectors of Edgar Wallace paperbacks will find this work well arranged and useful, but all save the most comprehensive research libraries will be able to do without it.

Note: This publication also serves as the title index to the later *Edgar Wallace Paperbacks* (below).

631.   Williams, Richard. **The Edgar Wallace Index (Books and Fiction)**. Scunthorpe, England: Dragonby Press, 1996. 76 p. Stapled sheets. (Edgar Wallace Monographs, no. 5).

Containing data cumulated from Dragonby Press's monograph series devoted to Edgar Wallace, and reproduced from word-processed copy, *The Edgar Wallace Index (Books and Fiction)* uses a single alphabetical index to provide citations to all of Wallace's books and short stories. References to Wallace's uncollected articles, verse, and other nonfiction are not included.

All titles are listed in capital letters, a category note indicating whether the work is an anthology, novel, twosome (two novels in one binding), omnibus (three or more novels in one binding), nonfiction, short story collection, play, short story, soldier-oriented short story, or verse. Additional notes indicate if Wallace's piece was based on work by somebody else and if the work was announced for publication under a different title. The opening words for all pieces are provided. Citations for books provide publisher and date of the first British edition. Citations to the first British hardcovers are often followed by citations to additional British hardcovers, British paperback editions, and the first American and Tauchnitz editions. The contents of short story collections are listed.

Citations to short stories give periodical, volume, issue, month, day, and year and list the books by Wallace in which the story was published; the name of the illustrator is provided if the periodical was illustrated. Additional notes indicate abridgments, revisions, and whether the work was filmed.

An index to periodical titles, pagination, and a citation numbering system would have strengthened the bibliography, but it is easy to use and does a very good job in making an enormous amount of data readily accessible. Academic libraries holding Lofts and Adley, and Kiddle (q.q.v.), will find this a very useful addendum.

632.   Williams, Richard, and Charles Kiddle. **Edgar Wallace Paperbacks: A Bibliographic Checklist by Imprint. With Valuations**. Scunthorpe, England: Dragonby Press, 1990. 17 p. Stapled sheets. (Edgar Wallace Monographs, no. 3).

As its title indicates, this is a bibliography of all Edgar Wallace books issued in paperback (or in light card covers). The bibliography is arranged alphabetically by the publisher's series name. The beginning of each series entry provides publisher's name and address, size of the books in the series (in millimeters), a brief description of the cover, price, and notes about the series. Individual citations provide the book's series number, title (indicating retitling), edition status (whether first book publication or first paperback appearance), date of publication, number of copies printed, pagination, printer (in abbreviated form), price, dustwrapper (if such existed), cover artist, and price a collector would pay for a very good copy.

The checklist is clearly reproduced from word-processed copy, but it lacks a title index. Those wishing to learn if a Wallace title has appeared in paperback must consult the separately published *Edgar Wallace Index* (above).

Wallace completists will want this work, but unless it is used in conjunction with other publications, it is unlikely to be of significant use to libraries or researchers.

632a. Edgar Wallace Fan Club
Kai Jorg (KJ) Hinz, Director
The Edgar Wallace Society
Kohlbergsgracht 40
6462 CD Kerkrad

Chassie L. West

633. West, Chassie L. **Chassie L. West, Author**. http://www.softaid.net/bobwest/

Although she is often classed as a writer of romantic suspense, Chassie (pronounced Chay-see) West has been a recent nominee for the Edgar Award for Best Original Paperback Novel, and she has authored several of the updated Nancy Drew Files.

West's website provides a picture of her, biographical information, an image of the Edgar Certificate of Nomination, images of her books, the names and series under which they appeared, the date of publication, and the information from the books' back covers. This is an engaging site.

Christopher West

634. Tangled Web. **Christopher West**. http://www.twbooks.co.uk/authors/cwest.html

A photograph of West is provided, along with a brief biography and cover illustrations from his novels. There is a link to information about Chinese puzzles. Excerpts from positive reviews are provided. The bibliography lists publisher, publication year, and detective's name.

Donald E. Westlake

635. Blixt, Johan. **Donald E. Westlake**. http://www.chem.uottawa.ca/blixt/westlake.html

This site has five columns. The first indicates the year of a novel's publication. The second provides initials of the name under which the work appeared, when Westlake used a pseudonym (e.g., "RS" for Richard Stark). The third uses a one-letter abbreviation to indicates the name of the lead series character (e.g., "D" for Dortmunder, "P" for Parker). The fourth provides the title of the novel in English, and the fifth provides the Swedish title. There are links to a picture of Westlake and a few reproductions of cover titles. One hopes for more information for an author of Westlake's stature.

Polly Whitney

636. Whitney, Polly. **Polly Whitney**. http://members.aol.com/Mystfield/Kitchen/polly.html

Whitney's personal home page provides a photograph of her and a brief biography; excerpts from positive reviews are listed as "Criminally Blatant Self-Promotional Blurb." There are links to her cyberbook, to excerpts featuring rollerblading from her Ike and Abby novels, to the consensual mystery novel *Mystfield Hall*, and to miscellaneous sites of personal interest (e.g., to Skates Away, "the Web's premier skate shop"). The cyberbook deserves mention, for it is a witty and acute series of lists that successfully describe and parody all of the conventions of the various genres of detective and mystery fiction. There are no cover images.

Denise Dietz Wiley

637. Wiley, Denise Dietz. **Denise Dietz Wiley**. http://www.eclectics.com/denise/

Wiley's site provides a picture, a brief biographical statement, and information about her novels: a cover reproduction, a summary, and links to positive reviews. The publisher, ISBN, and year of publication are provided for each work. As of this writing, these data are presented in one long file rather than smaller interlinked files, but this site is still quite usable.

Charles Willeford

638. Denton, William. **Charles Willeford**. http://www.vex.net/~buff/rara-avis/biblio/willeford.html

The above URL provides a comprehensive chronological list of the first printings of Willeford's books and references his screenplays, adaptations, and Willeford's appearance in motion pictures. A biography of Willeford is available through a link. The titles of his books are italicized; publisher and year of publication are given, as is often the book's series number. The contents of short story and poetry collections are listed; an asterisk by the title indicates when the book features Hoke Moseley. Data are complete as of 1993. Although there is a reference to it, none of Willeford's short fiction is listed. This nevertheless remains a useful list and is superior to the Willeford website offered by the Tangled Web (q.v.).

639. Tangled Web. **Charles Willeford**. http://www.twbooks.co.uk/authors/
cwilleford.html

No photograph of Willeford is provided; the biography describes Willeford's life and mentions that he "died some years ago," without providing the terminal date. Cover reproductions of the British editions of several of Willeford's novels are given, accompanied by the material from the back covers. The concluding bibliography is highly selective and incomplete, listing only recent British editions. The Willeford website offered by Denton (q.v.) is superior.

David Williams

640. Tangled Web. **David Williams**. http://www.twbooks.co.uk/authors/
davidwilliams.html

A photograph of Williams is provided, accompanied by a brief biography and cover reproductions from several of his novels. The text from the back covers is given, as are excerpts from positive reviews. The chronologically arranged bibliography gives the publisher and year of publication, and indicates whether the book features series characters Mark Treasure or DCI Parry and DS Gomer Lloyd.

Timothy Williams

641. Tangled Web. **Timothy Williams**. http://www.twbooks.co.uk/authors/
twilliams.html

No photograph of Williams is given, but the site provides a brief biography and reproductions of the covers from several of his novels. The material from the back covers is given, as are excerpts from positive reviews. The concluding bibliography lists publishers and whether the book features series character Trotti; publication dates are occasionally given.

Barbara Wilson

642. Tangled Web. **Barbara Wilson**. http://www.twbooks.co.uk/authors/
bwilson.html

A brief biography of Wilson is given, as are reproductions of the covers of several of her novels, the material from the back covers, and excerpts from positive reviews. There is, however, no photograph of the author. The concluding bibliography is arranged chronologically; citations occasionally indicate publisher and the series detective featured in the book.

Derek Wilson

643. Tangled Web. **Derek Wilson's Tim Lacy Artworld Mysteries**. http://www.twbooks.co.uk/authors/dwilson.html

A photograph of Wilson is given, as is a general summary of the concept of the "artworld," "a galaxy where the exotic, the beautiful and the priceless draw into their gravitational fields eccentric collectors, ruthless dealers, bent auctioneers, forgers, thieves, and murderers." A brief biography and cover illustrations from several of Wilson's artworld mysteries are provided, accompanied by synopses of the books; excerpts from positive reviews are given. The concluding bibliography is chronologically arranged and provides publisher in addition to year of publication.

Robert Wilson

644. Tangled Web. **Robert Wilson**. http://www.twbooks.co.uk/authors/rwilson.html

A photograph of Wilson is posted, as are a brief biography and cover reproductions from two of his novels. Material from the back covers is provided, accompanied by excerpts from positive reviews. The chronologically arranged concluding bibliography lists publishers as well as year of publication.

Mary Wings

645. Tangled Web. **Mary Wings and Emma Victor**. http://www.twbooks.co.uk/authors/mwings.html

No photograph of Wings appears, but there are a brief biography, cover reproductions from several of her novels, the material from the back covers, and excerpts from positive reviews. The chronologically arranged concluding bibliography lists only the publication date.

Steven Womack

646. Womack, Steven. **The Womack Web**. http://users.aol.com/dfblooz

Womack's personal home page contains five links. "Background" provides bio-bibliographic information, and the titles of "book excerpts," "in the works," and "upcoming events" are self-explanatory, as is "favorite websites."

"Book excerpts" offers cover reproductions, the book's publisher, price, publication year, ISBN, and first chapter. Positive critical reviews are accessible. Womack's site is engaging and accessible.

Daniel Woodrell

647. Tangled Web. **Daniel Woodrell**. http://www.twbooks.co.uk/authors/
dwoodrel.html

No photograph of Woodrell is provided, but a brief biography is. Cover
reproductions from several of his novels are accompanied by the material from
the back covers and excerpts from positive reviews. The concluding bibliography is selective and inconsistent in its presentation of data.

Cornell Woolrich

648. Stewart, Enola. **Cornell Woolrich (William Irish, George Hopley). A
Catalogue of First and Variant Editions of His Work, Including An-
thology and Magazine Appearances**. Pocono Pines, PA: Gravesend
Books, [1975]. v, 30 leaves. Paperback. (250 copies.)

Although dealers' catalogues are not generally included here, this sale
catalogue, compiled by the owner of Gravesend Books, must be mentioned, as it
is the only separately published bibliography of Cornell Woolrich issued to date.
Reproduced from typed copy, it contains five sections: first and variant editions
of books written by Cornell Woolrich, magazines containing stories by Woolrich, anthologies containing stories by Woolrich, miscellaneous works containing information pertaining to Cornell Woolrich and his books, and reference
books used in preparing this catalogue. Entries in all sections are numbered and
chronologically arranged; data are provided on only one side of each sheet. An
unnumbered sheet reprints Jack Gaughan's illustration of Woolrich.

The entries in the first section give the book's title, publisher, place of
publication, and publication date in capital letters. A note on the book's condition follows. Entries conclude with pagination and asking price. Paperback, variant, and reprint editions are cited; stock numbers are given for the former.
Occasionally, lengthy notes are provided on Woolrich's significant novels; for
example, the entries for the different editions of *The Bride Wore Black* describe the
dedication, title page quote, dustwrapper of the first hardcover edition, and appearance of the first Dell edition at some length.

Citations to Woolrich's short fiction have the story's title in parentheses
and the title, publication, and date in capital letters. Entries describe the magazine's condition and conclude with the pagination of Woolrich's contribution
and Stewart's asking price. Citations to Woolrich's anthology appearances have
the book's title, editor, publisher, and place of publication in capital letters. Entries describe the book's condition, list the title of Woolrich's contribution in
capital letters and its pagination, and conclude with Stewart's asking price.

The final two sections are perhaps unduly brief, occupying one leaf
apiece.

Despite some typos and omissions, this is not a wholly discreditable attempt, but it is a work necessary only to completists. A more recent and accessible bibliography may be found at the conclusion of Francis Nevins's *First You Dream, Then You Die* (New York: Mysterious Press, 1988), which updates Nevins's bibliography published in *Darkness at Dawn* (Carbondale, IL: Southern Illinois University Press, 1985), which is in turn an updating of Nevins's bibliography first published in *Nightwebs* (New York: Harper and Row, 1971).

The primary bibliography in *First You Dream, Then You Die* contains sections devoted to Woolrich's novels, separately published short novels, collections of short stories, short fiction (listed chronologically by the magazine in which it was published), short stories first published in collections of Woolrich's short fiction, short stories first published in anthologies, and articles. Successive sections provide full cast and credit information on Woolrich adaptations for movies, U.S. radio, and television. The bibliography concludes with a lengthy list of secondary sources, each annotated. As bibliographies go, it is well done, though more data in citations would be helpful. However, a separately published and comprehensive bibliography of Woolrich is still desirable.

P. C. Wren

649. Stephens, Christopher P. **A Checklist of Percival Christopher Wren**. Hastings-on-Hudson, NY: Ultramarine Publishing, 1991. 18 p. Paperback. ISBN 0-89366-178-3.

Best known for writing *Beau Geste* and other stirring stories of the French Foreign Legion, P. C. Wren wrote a number of works in which crime and mystery figured in the background and motivated the characters. This checklist of Wren's books is chronologically arranged, beginning with the 1912 *Dew and Mildew* and concluding with the 1949 *Dead Men's Boots*. Each citation is separately numbered and provides data on the first American and British editions. Titles are underlined and include information on pagination, retitlings, dustwrappers, original prices, and identifying points, though not always consistently. A title index concludes the checklist.

Though Wren's books are documented, data on his short stories and other publications have not been provided. A revised and expanded edition of this bibliography is to be hoped for, but given the general lack of interest in Wren, it will not be surprising if such a work never materializes. Researchers determined to find a more thorough bibliography of Wren's works are referenced to H. C. Arbuckle, III, "Bibliography, Chronological Listing, and Comments on the Works of Major Percival Christopher Wren, I.A.R.," *Taius* (December 1972), n.p. It is difficult to obtain and is also far from complete, but Arbuckle provides more data and a useful biographical sketch of Wren.

Rebecca York

650. Glick, Ruth, and Eileen Buckholtz. **Meet Rebecca York**. http://www. lightst.com/meetreb.html

Rebecca York is the shared pseudonym of Ruth Glick and Eileen Buckholtz. This website provides biographical data and pictures for both writers and offers a link to Rebecca York's 43 Light Street Home Page. The plot of the books in 43 Light Street is revealed in the opening sentence ("If you rent an office at 43 Light Street, you're going to have a thrilling adventure, meet a fantastic soul mate, almost get killed trying to solve an intriguing mystery, and live to tell about it"). Links provide a complete list of the books in the series and a schedule for book signings and appearances. Several cover reproductions are provided, as are excerpts from positive reviews. Even if one's taste does not run to romantic mysteries, this is a cleanly written and nicely produced site.

CHARACTER INDEXES and BIBLIOGRAPHIES

SCOPE NOTE: This chapter references only general works, works surveying the characters of more than one author, and works documenting series characters. Indexes to the characters created by specific writers—as in the characters created by Christie, Doyle, Simenon, etc.—will be found under their respective authors.

GENERAL

651. Amos, William. **The Originals: An A-Z of Fiction's Real-Life Characters**. Boston: Little, Brown, 1985. xx, 614 p. Index. LC 85-81298. ISBN 0-316-03741-9.

652. Amos, William. **The Originals: Who's Really Who in Fiction**. London: Jonathan Cape, 1985. xx, 614 p. Index. LC 86-191609. ISBN 0-2240-2419-5.

This entertaining collection identifies nearly 3,000 people who inspired the creation of fictional characters. Irene Adler, the Baskervilles, Dr. Gideon Fell, Sherlock Holmes, Miss Marple, Nigel Strangeways, and Lord Peter Wimsey are but a few of the fictional detectives who have been linked to human models.

The book's arrangement is alphabetical by the character's full name or the name by which the character is commonly known, given in boldface type; the Continental Op, for example, is profiled under the letter "C." The entry identifies the author who created the character, names the work in which the character first appeared, and provides the identity of and basic biographical data about the person (or people) on whom the character was based. The book concludes with a selective bibliography of the sources Amos used to identify the originals and an index to the people who were named in the volume. There are several sections of black-and-white photographs of the people who were turned into characters. Though this is a specialized volume, it is well written and presents its data well; it remains consistently helpful.

653. Brown, Michael Rogero, and Nicholas Sauer. **Index of Small Hero Pulps from Dell [and others]**. http://sflovers.rutgers.edu/archive/bibliographies/small-hero-pulps.txt

The title of this website refers not to the size of the heroes but to their importance and duration: Few of the pulps listed by Brown and Sauer appeared for more than a few issues, and their heroes were often equally short-lived. The pulps listed include *Doctor Death, Terence X. O'Leary's War Birds, Public Enemy, Captain Satan, Doctor Yen Sin, Dusty Ayers and His Battle Birds, The Octopus, The Scorpion, The Secret Six, The Mysterious Wu Fang, The Ghost—Super Detective*, and *The Masked Detective*. The characters listed include Anthony Hamilton, Doc Harker, Don Diavolo, the Green Lama, Matalaa, Captain V, the Crimson Mask, the Domino Lady, and Captain Danger.

The arrangement is by issue of appearance. For each hero, Brown lists the title of the lead story, author initials, publication date, magazine volume and number, and reprint information. These data are followed by the authors' full names and information on the characters' appearances in other venues. Though fuller indexes to these pulps can be found in Michael Cook and Stephen T. Miller's *Mystery, Detective, and Espionage Fiction* and the first series of Leonard Robbins's *Pulp Magazine Index* (q.q.v.), these works are increasingly difficult to find. Brown and Sauer's website is useful and well done.

654. Carr, Wooda Nick. **The Other Detective Pulp Heroes**. Chicago, IL: Tattered Pages Press, 1992. 96 p. Paperback. Index. (Pulp Vault Pulp Study, no. 1).

A comprehensive description of the detectives that appeared in series in the pulp magazines would be lengthy, so Carr has limited himself to describing just 40 of them. These 40 include police, secret agents, private eyes, lawyers, millionaire playboys with secret identities, and encyclopedia sellers with quick memories and quicker fists. The volume is illustrated with numerous illustrations reprinted from the pulp magazines showing these characters in action.

Carr's list is arranged alphabetically by author, starting with Seven Anderton's Edna Pender and Steve Ware and concluding with Jean Francis Webb's Kimo. Additional authors having their detectives described include Robert Leslie Bellem's Dan Turner, Carroll John Daly's Satan Hall, John Dickson Carr's Dr. Gideon Fell, Erle Stanley Gardner's Edward Jenkins and Barney Killigen, Frank Gruber's Oliver Quade, Louis L'Amour's Kip Morgan, and Theodore Tinsley's Terry "Bulldog" Black and Major John T. Lacy.

A checklist of pulp appearances follows Carr's descriptions. It too is alphabetical by author, listing the pulp magazine(s) in which the character appeared and giving the magazine's date and story's title. Reprints and book appearances of these stories are not noted.

One can cavil that some of the more interesting pulp detectives (including some mentioned in Carr's introduction) are not described. Furthermore, Carr's enthusiasm is often stronger than the stories would seem to warrant. Nevertheless, by describing several dozen detectives who are rarely considered in genre surveys, Carr has performed a considerable achievement.

655.   Conquest, John. **Trouble Is Their Business: Private Eyes in Fiction, Film and Television, 1927–1988.** New York: Garland, 1990. liii, 497 p. Index. (Garland Reference Library of the Humanities, vol. 1151). LC 89-33039. ISBN 0-8240-5947-6.

In 1985 the Bowling Green State University Popular Press published Robert A. Baker and Michael T. Nietzel's *Private Eyes: One Hundred and One Knights, A Survey of American Detective Fiction 1922–1984* (q.v.), a prose study dealt with elsewhere in this volume and mentioned here because it stands directly behind Conquest's monumental achievement. Baker and Nietzel provided generally appreciative surveys of private investigators, but it was Conquest's more ambitious goal to document "all private eye writers and their creations published in English since 1927 plus films and television and radio shows in which PIs are the main characters; nine hundred fifty-two authors, one hundred seventy-six feature films, one hundred sixty-four television series, pilots and films, fifty six radio programs and a grand total of 1563 PIs are listed." In general, Conquest's 952 authors are novelists; short stories, unless somehow notable, are not listed.

A lengthy, excellent introduction defines and discusses the private investigator, providing a lively history of the genre and a survey of some of the more notable subgenres of private eye: homosexual detectives, ethnic detectives, the unbaptized private investigator, wounded heroes, animal private eyes, the science fiction private eye, and so forth.

The next section of the volume is devoted to the 952 authors and their creations. It is arranged alphabetically by the author's last name, given in boldface capitals, and the private investigator's name, given in boldface upper- and lowercase. Entries for the private investigators reference users to the author's entry, which describe the investigator. These descriptions do not mince words and are witty and accurate; one author's works are described as "aspiring to mediocrity, they never quite achieve it," while the private investigator of another "keeps reminding the reader how confusing everything is and wanders around dark houses at night." Entries conclude with references to media adaptations (given in boldface capitals) and a brief bibliography listing the titles in which the investigator appeared and the year in which the book was published. A date by itself is always for a first American edition, and dates prefaced by UK, Aus, and Can are for the first British, Australian, and Canadian editions. In the case of certain important writers (e.g., Raymond Chandler), bibliographic data are provided not only for Chandler's novels but also for his short stories, the entries listing each story's original publication and (when relevant) the novel it later became. Finally, a section devoted to private eye anthologies lists their contents, providing details under the author's heading.

Successive sections list television, motion picture, and radio shows featuring private investigators. The entries list the shows' years, premise, the actor playing the private investigator, authors and titles of novelizations, and the names of notable scriptwriters. A "Yellow Pages" provides a geographic index to the investigators; a "Check List of Authors & Titles" recapitulates the contents of the first section. The volume concludes with a capably done title index and a "Stop Press" section listing late additions.

It is possible to fault Conquest for being too catholic in his contents, for he includes references to a number of works in which the private investigator is actually an amateur detective, but this criticism is readily dismissed, for the comprehensiveness of this book is one of its strengths. Conquest's data are accurate, and his arrangement and organization are exemplary. Its physical appearance is unprepossessing, for Conquest uses so much boldface type that he occasionally inhibits access to the data. This aside, the volume is a monumental achievement and belongs in all libraries.

656. DellaCava, Frances A., and Madeline H. Engel. **Female Detectives in American Novels: A Bibliography and Analysis of Serialized Female Sleuths**. New York: Garland, 1993. xiv, 157 p. Index. (Garland Reference Library of the Humanities, vol. 1685). LC 93-30644. ISBN 0-8153-1264-4.

The first 50 pages of this guide discuss the series character heroine, analyzing similarities and differences and surveying such social issues as sexism, gay and lesbian rights, racism, anti-Semitism, homelessness, illegal aliens, substance abuse, crimes involving women and children, and conservatism as they are addressed in the series novels featuring American female sleuths. In all, 161 American female sleuths in 636 books by 147 authors are analyzed.

The second half of the volume provides bibliographic data and profiles of the works discussed above, with the data presented in chronological groupings for the female sleuths of the nineteenth century, the early twentieth century to the mid-1960s, the mid-1960s to 1979, and 1980 to the present. The profiles in each section are arranged alphabetically by author's name. The titles of works in which the character appears are listed chronologically, with the title in italics and the place and year of publication and publisher provided. The profile describes the main character and often names her friends, helpers, and the social themes addressed in the mystery. The volume concludes with indexes to the authors, sleuths, and book titles.

Though clearly written and containing some original research, *Female Detectives in American Novels* lacks the thoroughness and comprehensiveness of Victoria Nichols and Susan Thompson's *Silk Stalkings* and Willeta Heising's *Detecting Women* (q.q.v.).

657. Drew, Bernard A. **Heroines: A Bibliography of Women Series Characters in Mystery, Espionage, Action, Science Fiction, Fantasy, Horror, Western, Romance and Juvenile Novels**. New York: Garland, 1989. 400 p. Index. (Garland Reference Library of the Humanities, vol. 878). LC 89-34233. ISBN 0-8240-3047-8.

As its title indexes, this volume lists the women series characters in a number of fictional genres. Nearly 1,200 series are listed, of which approximately 350 are detective and mystery fiction. No attempt has been made to distinguish between women series characters created by men and those created by women, nor does Drew attempt to provide a literary evaluation of these series.

Drew begins his listings with an index to the authors that lists both pseudonyms and real names. Each name is followed by the name of the series that is listed in the main section of the bibliography. The main section is arranged alphabetically by series character's name or by series name. Each series is separately numbered. The author (or authors) of the series is listed below, followed by an extremely brief annotation and a chronological list of the books in the series. Each title is followed by the name of the first publisher and year of publication. Retitlings are not indicated. Indexes (here called appendixes) provide access to the series by the genres named in the title as well as by such subjects as "Miscellaneous Domestic, Humor and Literary Titles" and "Comic Book and Comic Strip Reprints and Related Prose Series." A title index concludes the volume.

Drew attempts too much in *Heroines*, and the book is rife with problems. The listings in the main section are often frustrating in their arrangement. For example, the series featuring Nancy Drew can be located without any difficulty, but in the case of the series created by Laura Ingalls Wilder that featured Mary and Laura Ingalls, the entry is under neither Ingalls nor Wilder but under "Little House on the Prairie," with no cross-references. Similarly, Drew's annotations are uninformative and repetitive; one shudders to see how often he has used "this is a girls' book series." Finally, Drew lists a number of women characters who appeared in but one book, thus vitiating his stated purpose of listing women series characters.

Readers and researchers interested in the detective and mystery stories featuring women as series characters would be better served by using Victoria Nichols and Susan Thompson's *Silk Stalkings* (q.v.). Those interested in the subject of mystery series written by women will find that Willetta Heising's *Detecting Women* (q.v.) offers superior access to the subject.

658. Green, Joseph, and Jim Finch. **Sleuths, Sidekicks and Stooges: An Annotated Bibliography of Detectives, Their Assistants and Their Rivals in Crime, Mystery and Adventure Fiction, 1795–1995**. Aldershot, England; Brookfield, VT: Scolar Press, 1997. 874 p. Index. LC 95-49334. ISBN 1-85928-192-3.

The most thorough work considered in this section, *Sleuths, Sidekicks and Stooges* contains nearly 8,000 entries on the sleuths, their sidekicks and their rivals appearing in British and American mystery and detective fiction published between 1795 and 1995. It is a monumental work, but it is not always easy to use, and it is unfortunately not always reliable. The contents: a preface, an introduction, a guide to "The Detectives," the detectives, the authors, the books, the sidekicks, and the stooges. There are three appendixes: sources, source discrepancies, and Sherlock Holmes parodies.

The fourth section, on the detectives, constitutes the majority of the volume and is arranged alphabetically by detective. The detective's name is given in boldface type with the last name capitalized. The entry for each detective, however, can have up to 18 parts. A prose description of the character is given, followed by a line (in italics) providing the detective's nationality, sex, location of operations, and type (i.e., police, professional amateur, private detective, professional investigator, secret agent, amateur, pulp, or sleuth). Following this, the name(s) of the detective's sidekick(s) and stooge(s) are noted as such, their last names printed in capital letters; these are occasionally accompanied by a description providing details of their relationship to the detective. Next, the author's name is given in boldface type, with the last name capitalized, along with a biography of the author. Following this are names and biographies of other authors who have used the same character, also using the above format. Other bylines of the primary author are listed, with reference made to other detectives created by the primary author, and the other detectives are listed, with reference given to the bylines under which they appeared. In addition, a "citation record" lists the frequency of the detective's appearances, excluding radio, television, and motion picture appearances. The title, publisher, and year of publication of the first and last book in which the detective appeared are given (and noted as such), occasionally accompanied by an explanatory narrative of their own. Pairs and multiple detectives are listed under the name for which the most biographical information can be given; cross-references are provided.

As can be inferred, the arrangement of the main section is confusing and repetitive, albeit detailed. Although pages are numbered and letter-tabbed and have the name of the detective printed in the upper right-hand corner, the layout of entries is frequently unclear; this is especially so in the case of the stories featuring Sherlock Holmes. Furthermore, perhaps because the authors attempted to do so much, numerous errors have crept in, often in the entries for the older writers. As examples, Jacques Futrelle's *The Diamond Master* does not feature the Thinking Machine as detective; Nevada Alvarado, sidekick to Cleve Adams's Violet McDade, is not a Hispanic male; Chester Himes did not graduate from Ohio State University; T. S. Stribling's Henry Poggioli is a character in 36 short stories, not 20; Carroll John Daly's Race Williams did not surface in 1927, nor was "he fairly moderate in his activities and not widely imitated"; Doc Savage's full name is not given, nor are the names of any of his sidekicks; and the correct identity of the Shadow is not revealed. The cross-referencing system is frequently frustrating. A user looking at James Bond finds an entry for Robert Markham, author of a James Bond pastiche; the user is then referenced to Peter Furneaux, and only then can it be discovered that Markham was a pseudonym for Kingsley Amis. One may also take the authors to task for equating dime novels and pulp magazines and for demonstrating familiarity with neither.

None of this is to say that *Sleuths, Sidekicks, and Stooges* cannot be used, but too often it must be used with caution rather than confidence. One longs for a revised 2d edition.

659. Hullar, Link, and Frank Hamilton. **Amazing Pulp Heroes**. Brooklyn, NY: Gryphon Books, 1988. 58 p.

660. Hamilton, Frank, and Link Hullar. **Amazing Pulp Heroes: A Celebration of the Glorious Pulp Magazines**. 2d ed. Brooklyn, NY: Gryphon Books, 1996. 201 p. Paperback. ISBN 0-936071-68-0 (pb); 0-936071-69-9 (limited ed.).

Though its contents are not limited to the detectives appearing in the pulp magazines, a sizable percentage of the entries appearing in *Amazing Pulp Heroes* are either detectives (the Phantom Detective, Nick Carter, Secret Agent X, Operator # 5, etc.) or serve a detective's function (Doc Savage, the Shadow, the Avenger, etc.). Approximately 50 characters are described and portrayed, Hullar providing the prose and Hamilton the illustrations. In addition, there is commentary on subjects as diverse as Doc Savage and American history, the Bama Doc Savage covers, women in the bloody pulps, men's action/adventure magazines, and so forth.

Unlike such similar works as Wooda Nick Carr's *The Other Detective Pulp Heroes* (q.v.), the contents of *Amazing Pulp Heroes* are in no discernible order. Furthermore, though Hullar writes enthusiastically about the characters, the volume contains occasionally significant typos ("Grant Stickbridge" rather than "Grant Stockbridge" for the entry on *The Spider*), and the entries more often than not fail to provide any bibliographic data. Hamilton's artwork is generally excellent.

661. Jakubowsky, Maxim, ed. **100 Great Detectives; or, The Detective Directory**. London: Xanadu, 1991. 255 p. GB 91-16041. ISBN 1-95480-025-6; New York: Carroll & Graf, 1991. 255 p. ISBN 1-85480-025-6.

It seems like a great marketing ploy: Get 100 of the best-known mystery writers and ask each to contribute a brief essay on his or her favorite detective, with the editor making certain that duplications do not occur. The resulting book could then be sold to collectors (known for their obsessiveness), detective and mystery readers (known for their voraciousness), and to libraries (known for their indiscriminate acquisitiveness). And thus it was nearly so: Each writer contributed an essay of somewhere between 250 and 500 words, though one of the essays discussed the detectives of different authors (Anthony Berkeley's Roger Sheringham and Philip MacDonald's Anthony Gethryn), and several essays discussed detectives who operate in teams (e.g., Joe Leaphorn and Jim Chee, Ed and Am Hunter, Dalziel and Pascoe). Further, several of the essays were jointly authored, and several of the contributors have reputations in areas other than mystery and detective fiction. Because the volume is focused on the detectives (rather than on the writers), the essays are arranged alphabetically by the name of the detective; each essay concludes with a brief bibliography listing the books in which the detective appeared. The approaches range from the uncritically appreciative to the acute.

Like all "best" lists, the contents of the volume are debatable; and a list of the best detectives that mentions Sax Rohmer's Morris Klaw but which neglects such giants as Judge Dee, Travis McGee, Dr. John Evelyn Thorndyke, and Napoleon Bonaparte (to name but a few) can hardly be considered as unbiased. On the other hand, Jakubowsky does not appear to have striven for evenhandedness. This is a list meant to be enjoyed and discussed, and the enjoyment value of the book lies in its very idiosyncrasy, for it is a volume replete with surprises. Writer Michael Moorcock writes glowingly of Margery Allingham's Albert Campion ("he's a joy to live with, and so, incidentally are the many recurring characters of the series"), and graphic novelist Neil Gaiman provides a thought-provoking analysis of G. K. Chesterton's Father Brown. Many writers offer discussions of favorite characters that provide insights into their own writings; Reginald Hill, for example, turns out to be a devotee of Anthony Trollope's *Eustace Diamonds*.

On the debit side, the book is unindexed, and its value as a reference/ research tool is almost nil.

662. Madden, Cecil, ed. **Meet the Detective**. London: G. Allen & Urwin, 1935. 142 p.; New York: The Telegraph Press, 1935. 158p. LC 36-533.

Note: Madden's name does not appear on the title page but appears at the conclusion of an introduction.

Like Otto Penzler's *The Great Detectives* (q.v.), *Meet the Detective* is not traditionally considered a reference work but should be. Its title, however, is not strictly accurate, for although this book consists of essays by authors describing the genesis and creation of their literary characters, one of the characters we are asked to meet is Sax Rohmer's "Dr. Fu Manchu" and another is the Baroness Orczy's "The Scarlet Pimpernel." These are hardly detectives, and one wonders why Orczy was not asked to discuss her series involving Bill Owen, the Old Man in the Corner.

In all, 15 characters are described, the majority of whom are forgotten except to specialists: Rupert Grayson's Gun Cotton, Sydney Horler's Tiger Standish, Francis D. Grierson's Professor Wells, Andrew Soutar's Phineas Spinnet, G. D. H. and Margaret Cole's Superintendent Wilson, and Anthony Wynne's Dr. Eustace Hailey. A few names might be recognizable to readers of the Golden Age. Leslie Charteris has a piece describing the genesis of The Saint, Sapper describes the creation of Bull-Dog Drummond, and there are essays by H. C. Bailey, E. C. Bentley, and R. Austin Freeman describing, respectively, Mr. Fortune, Trent, and Dr. Thorndyke.

Forgotten though the majority of these writers are, their essays tend remain alive and readable, albeit not particularly deep or insightful, occasionally revealing more than their creators intended: Sapper created Drummond because he could not kill a golfer with an annoying sniff, and Horler, very fond of his Standish, complains about "women's ideas" and states that his character "appeals to the heart of the boy which is in every man—every man who *is* a man," providing a number of excerpts from his fiction that will (more than likely) fail to convince most contemporary readers of Standish's likeability.

Enjoyable, but now a work for completists and specialists.

663. Mattson, E. (Ed) Christian, and Thomas (Tom) B. Davis. **A Collector's Guide to Hardcover Boy's Series Books; or, Tracing the Trail of Harry Hudson**. Newark, DE: MAD Book, 1997. viii, 578 p. Paperback. Indexes.

The second printing (1997) is described.

This monumental guide lists the boys' series books published in hardcover between 1872 and 1993. Researchers and determined collectors of boys' series books should read section A, "Collecting Information," which contains numerous subsections and includes discussions of the history of boys' series books, collecting boy's series books, book and dustjacket grading, cleaning and repairing books, reference periodicals, hunting for series books, using the MAD (Mattson and Davis) numbering system, logging your collection, rare series and rare books, research on Altemus series books, and additions or corrections for future editions of this book. Important and useful though this material is, it is not necessary to read section A in order to use the *Guide* at a basic level.

Following the introduction and acknowledgments, the contents are A) collecting information; B) author listing (alphabetical—cross-referenced by MAD number); C) series listing (alphabetical—cross-referenced by MAD number); D) publisher listing (alphabetical—cross-referenced by MAD number); E) artist listing (alphabetical—cross-referenced by MAD number); F) subject listing (alphabetical—cross-referenced by MAD number); G) miscellaneous series listing (alphabetical, no cross-references); H) additional information: non-series books by popular authors (alphabetical by author) and a listing of phantom titles (alphabetical—cross-referenced by MAD number); and I) illustrators (by publishers—cross-referenced by MAD number).

The entries in section C comprise the majority of the volume. Listings are alphabetical by series name. Within each series, the titles are listed in their publication order, followed by artist's name, author, and publication date. Accompanying each reference are checklists for condition, dustwrappers, and plates that can be used by collectors. Numerous notes are provided, as are comments on variants, spinoffs, and renumberings. Information is clearly presented and accessible. Only the first printing of each series is documented; the discussions of the individual series in no way approach the bibliographical convolutions of works such as Farah (q.v.).

Collectors of boys' mysteries from the "Adventure and Mystery Series" to the Young Reporter Series will welcome the *Guide*. It belongs next to the University of Minnesota's *Girls Series Books* (q.v.) in all research libraries.

664. Nichols, Victoria, and Susan Thompson. **Silk Stalkings: When Women Write of Murder: A Survey of Series Characters Created by Women Authors in Crime and Mystery Fiction**. Berkeley, CA: Black Lizard Books, 1988. xviii, 522 p. Paperback. Index. LC 88-10491. ISBN 0-88739-096-X.

Nichols and Thompson—who between them have more than 60 years of mystery reading experience—have compiled a partially annotated bibliography of the series characters created by women authors. Nearly 600 characters appearing in more than 3,000 British and American works between 1867 and 1987 are listed in what is described as the "Master List." It is organized alphabetically by author's name (autonym), listing the series characters created by each author, titles featuring the character, and book's year of publication. The authors appearing in the Master List include not only women but also men writing under female pseudonyms and writing teams; numerous cross-references are provided.

The Master List does not open the book, however. Instead, the first section consists of 15 chapters in which a selection of series characters are first grouped thematically by profession, vocation, setting, or inclination, and then described in depth. The thematic groupings include detectives who are (or who are involved with) academics; police detectives; aristocrats; religion; medicine; the stage, television, and motion pictures; business and finance; the law; writers and journalists; curators, bibliophiles, and art experts; the visual arts; professional detectives; the military; wives and other significant others; and unexpected detectives. The descriptions list the series character's name, years in which the character flourished, number of books in which he or she appeared, character's nationality, and author's name. A "biography" of the character is then provided, along with explanations of how the character functions and evolves from novel to novel; often included are relevant quotations from the books.

Sections following the Master List provide a chronology of series characters, a pseudonym to autonym index, and an index that links series characters to their authors.

Nichols and Thompson deserve commendations for compiling an extraordinarily useful reference book. There are some odd omissions (Lillian de la Torre's Dr. Sam: Johnson among them), and more seriously, short stories are sometimes listed as books, and title changes are not always noted. These bibliographic shortcomings do not significantly detract from the virtues of the book, which are many. It belongs in academic and public libraries.

665. Pate, Janet. **The Book of Sleuths**. Chicago: Contemporary Books, 1977. 124 p. LC 77-75843. ISBN 0-8092-7838-3 (hc); 0-8092-7837-5 (pb).

Pate's heavily illustrated guide focuses on the detectives, not on the novels in which they appeared. In order to show the development of the detective novel in relation to the changing social times, she has arranged her 40 entries roughly chronologically, dividing them into three separately titled sections, "Classical Beginnings," "The Heyday," and "Goodbye to the Gentleman." Each detective's entry opens with a quotation (or quotations) describing the detective, followed by a lengthier description of the detective's life and achievements. A concluding bibliography lists the first editions of the books in which the detective appeared as well as the films and theater productions featuring the detective. There are some surprises in Pate's choices of detectives, for in addition to the names one would expect (Dupin, Holmes, Poirot, Marlowe, Spade, etc.), she has described such figures as Sexton Blake, Bulldog Drummond, Rin Tin Tin (!), J. G. Reeder, Batman, Inspector Clouseau, and Theo Kojak.

Whimsical choices of detectives aside, Pate's writing occasionally flags, and her entries lack the depth found in such works as Otto Penzler's *The Great Detectives* (q.v.). Nevertheless, Pate's argument about the detective tending to reflect changing social times is valid (if obvious), and though it is less than it could be, this work is more than a coffee-table book.

666.　Penzler, Otto, ed. **The Great Detectives**. Boston: Little, Brown, 1978. xvii, 281 p. LC 77-25487. ISBN 0-316-69883-0.

Though it has not traditionally been listed as a reference book, this collection of 26 essays describing the creation of significant detectives is as important as the *Detectionary, Silk Stalkings*, or such volumes as Maxim Jakubowsky's *100 Great Detectives* (q.q.v.). With two arguable exceptions, the essays have been written by the creators of the detectives, who more often than not reveal the processes that went into the creation and development of their characters. The list begins with Ngaio Marsh discussing her Roderick Alleyn; concludes with Nicholas Freeling discussing his Inspector Van der Valk; and includes such joys as Ross Macdonald discussing Lew Archer, Ed McBain revealing his intentions to kill off Carella, H. R. F. Keating providing a somewhat bemused look at his Inspector Ghote through the eyes of a colleague, and "Maxwell Grant" (Walter Gibson) surveying the life and adventures of the Shadow. Donald Hamilton's essay reveals the almost inadvertent creation of Matt Helm; John Ball's essay is written as if he and Virgil Tibbs were sharing a dinner in Pasadena; Brett Halliday's essay explains that Michael Shayne was based on a real person; and Chester Gould's essay surveys the development and evolution of Dick Tracy. All essays are delightful, and the majority contain information useful to researchers; all conclude with a facsimile of their writer's signature. (The arguable exceptions are Gibson's article on the Shadow and "Carolyn Keene's" [Harriet Stratemeyer Adams's] description of Nancy Drew. Although Gibson created the character and wrote 282 novels in the series, 43 books were written by others; and although "Keene" wrote and rewrote many Nancy Drew mysteries, they were created by her father, Edward Stratemeyer, and written by a stable of authors, including Mildred Wirt Benson.)

Concluding the volume are a bibliography and filmography. The former is occasionally incomplete, lists only books, and provides only their year of publication and publisher, whereas the latter merely lists the year in which the film appeared and the studio that released it.

The majority of the authors who contributed essays on their characters are now dead, making the contents of this volume historically valuable and important for the study of some of the more significant detectives of the twentieth century. A follow-up volume would be most useful.

667. Penzler, Otto, and others. **Detectionary: A Biographical Dictionary of Leading Characters in Detective and Mystery Fiction, Including Famous and Little-Known Sleuths, Their Helpers, Rogues Both Heroic and Sinister, and Some of Their Most Memorable Adventures, As Recounted in Novels, Short Stories, and Films.** Lock Haven, PA: Hammermill Paper, Lock Haven Division, 1971. xi, 290 p. Indexed. Paperback. LC 74-179410.

668. Penzler, Otto, and others. **Detectionary: A Biographical Dictionary of Leading Characters in Detective and Mystery Fiction, Including Famous and Little-Known Sleuths, Their Helpers, Rogues Both Heroic and Sinister, and Some of Their Most Memorable Adventures, as Recounted in Novels, Short Stories, and Films.** Revised and expanded ed. New York: Overlook Press, 1977. xi, 299 p. LC 75-27326. ISBN 0-87951-041-2.

The 1st edition of this volume was published as a private limited edition intended by Hammermill Paper to demonstrate its printing capabilities. Many copies of this edition were accidentally destroyed, and those that survived became collectible rarities. The 2d edition of the *Detectionary* is physically larger, contains a new preface, and somewhat expands the concluding author index, but the contents are largely similar to those of the 1st edition.

The history and monetary value of the various editions aside, Penzler and his colleagues have created a dictionary to the characters and the cases of detective and mystery fiction. These are arranged into four sections: detectives, rogues and companions in crime, cases, and detective and mystery motion pictures. Each section is arranged alphabetically. The first two sections identify the character, name his or her creator, and give his or her background. The third and fourth sections list and describe the cases and the actors and actresses who played the detectives and villains. Symbolic "clues" are used to facilitate cross-reference between sections; a star is used for detectives, a bullet for rogues and helpers, a square for cases, and a triangle for movies. In addition, the volume is illustrated throughout with stills from motion pictures that have nothing to do with the text on the page on which they appear and whose citations provide only the title of the motion picture, the year in which it appeared, and the studio that made it; actors and actresses are not listed. The book concludes with an author index that lists the detectives, rogues and helpers, and the titles in which these characters appeared.

It is obvious that an enormous amount of effort went into compiling the *Detectionary*, and the contents of the first two sections provide data on some obscure characters. The weaker third and fourth sections are not as comprehensive and are less useful. As a reference work, the *Detectionary* is idiosyncratic and occasionally frustrating, but despite its age and eccentricities, it remains useful.

669. Pringle, David. **Imaginary People: A Who's Who of Modern Fictional Characters**. London and Glasgow: Grafton Books, 1987. x, 515 p. GB 87-32384. ISBN 0-246-12968-9; New York: World Almanac, 1988. x, 518 p. LC 88-60375. ISBN 0-88687-364-9.

670. Pringle, David. **Imaginary People: A Who's Who of Fictional Characters from the Eighteenth Century to the Present Day**. 2d ed. Aldershot, England: Scolar/Ashgate Press, 1996. x, 296 p. Index. LC 95-43986. ISBN 1-85928-162-1.

The 2d edition of *Imaginary People* provides information on more than 1,400 modern fictional characters created between 1719 (Daniel Defoe's Robinson Crusoe) and the early 1990s (Forrest Gump is mentioned); a sizable percentage of these characters appeared in detective and mystery stories. The characters are listed in alphabetical order under the best-known form of his or her name; last names precede first names except when the last name is unknown or rarely used. (The Continental Op, for example, is listed under "C.") The character's name is given in boldface type, after which a biography is provided. The character's creator is named, and the character's attributes are described; the date of the character's first print appearance is given, and later appearances are selectively mentioned. When the character has been adopted for motion pictures, data on these—year of release, director, star—are provided. There is coverage of sequels and pastiches written by "other hands," and there are numerous cross-references, a bibliography of sources, and an index to the characters' creators.

The characters described are well chosen and varied; the first letter of the alphabet contains biographies of Uncle Abner, Hilda Adams, Nick Adams, Roderick Alleyn, Pepper Anderson, John Appleby, and Lew Archer, and those of a number of characters from the related genres of thrillers and espionage. Though additional bibliographic data would have been welcome, this is a well-done and often useful volume.

671. Rovin, Jeff. **Adventure Heroes: Legendary Characters from Odysseus to James Bond**. New York: Facts on File, 1994. vi, 314 p. Index. LC 93-46603. ISBN 0-8160-2881-8 (hc); 0-8160-2886-9 (pb).

Rovin's guide is a companion of sorts to his *Encyclopedia of Superheroes*, but in this volume he eschews characters with superpowers to describe more than 500 comic book, television, motion picture, and literary characters who have no superpowers but whose behavior is nevertheless heroic. A significant percentage of these characters are detectives.

The arrangement of *Adventure Heroes* is alphabetical by the name of the hero, or by the name of the group in which the hero functioned (e.g., the Impossible Missions Force). Each entry provides a one- or two-letter code indicating whether the hero is found in comic books, comic strips, folklore, literature, mythology, a motion picture, an opera, the radio, the stage, a toy, trading cards, television, or a video game. The first appearance of the hero is noted, followed by a biography of the hero and his sidekicks, cohorts, and cases; a comment on the hero concludes each entry, and a brief bibliography and an index conclude the volume.

Rovin's arrangement is idiosyncratic and occasionally makes locating information on a character time-consuming. Characters are listed by their first names; for example, Philip Marlowe's entry may be found under "P" rather than under "M," and Sam Spade's entry is found in the first part of "S" rather than the latter. Additional confusion is caused by Rovin alphabetizing by titles: Mr. and Mrs. North are listed under "M," Sergeant Joe Friday is listed under "S," and cross-references are not provided. Nor are data in Rovin's entries consistently correct.

The worst problem with *Adventure Heroes* is simply that its 500 entries are inadequate; the book should have been at least three times its present length. Collectors of comic books might want *Adventure Heroes*, but the volume contains little that is not available elsewhere.

672.   Tucker, Sara. **Murder by Occupation**.

Available as part of the archives maintained by the DorothyL listserv, and through the Miss Lemon website (http://www.iwillfollow.com/lemon.htm), this list indexes detectives by their profession/occupation, omitting those detectives who are police officers, lawyers, and private investigators and stipulating that the detective must actually practice the profession. The list is arranged alphabetically by character's profession, beginning with "Actor" and concluding with "Writer, Travel," and each entry provides the author's name and the name of the character. Nearly 200 characters are identified.

673.   University of Minnesota, Children's Literature Research Collections. **Girls Series Books: A Checklist of Hardback Books Published 1900–1975**. Minneapolis, MN: Children's Literature Research Collections, University of Minnesota Libraries, 1978. ix, 121 p. Paperback. Index. LC 78-623834.

674.   University of Minnesota, Children's Literature Research Collections. **Girls Series Books: A Checklist of Titles Published 1840–1991**. 2d ed. Minneapolis, MN: Children's Literature Research Collections, University of Minnesota Libraries, 1992. x, 347 p. Paperback. Index.

The 2d edition is described. As its title indicates, the focus is on the hardcover series books published between 1840 and 1991 that were produced (predominantly) for girls; a significant number of these series featured girls solving mysteries. Arrangement is alphabetical by series name. The title of each series is given in boldface capital letters; on separate lines beneath it are the name of the stated series author and the publisher. If the author is a known pseudonym, the real name is given in parentheses, and if the book originally appeared in paperback, the publisher's name is accompanied by (PB). Separately numbered beneath these are the titles of the books in their series order, with the date of first publication given. Renumberings are indicated (as in the Wanderer Books reprints of the Bobbsey Twins series); cross-references indicate related titles and spinoffs; and an asterisk indicates that the title is in the Children's Literature Research Collection. Citations do not reference reprint publishers.

Successive sections provide an author index, a publisher index, and a chronological index; this last is arranged alphabetically within decade divisions.

Although more information on the contents of the book would have been welcome, this volume is nicely produced and essential for the collectors of juvenile series ranging from Patricia Giff's "Abby Jones, Junior Detective" to Hilda Stahl's "Wren House." It belongs next to the Mattson and Davis *A Collector's Guide to Hardcover Boy's Series Books* (q.v.) in all research libraries.

SPECIFIC CHARACTERS

Black Bat

675. Brown, Michael Rogero, and Nicholas Sauer. **The Black Bat.** http://sflovers.rutgers.edu/archive/bibliographies/black-bat.txt

Although this file is maintained in the Sf-Lovers archives at Rutgers University, the Black Bat was a character appearing in 62 issues of *Black Book Detective Magazine* from July 1, 1939, until Winter 1953. Brown's index lists the issue number in which the Black Bat appeared, followed by title of adventure, initials of author's name, date of publication, magazine's volume, and story's number in the Hanos reprint series. The key to the authors' full names is given at the bottom of the file. More data would have been welcome, but what Brown and Sauer provide is very capably presented.

Note: *Black Book Detective Magazine* is also indexed through the first series of Leonard Robbins's *The Pulp Magazine Index* and through Michael Cook and Steve Miller's *Mystery, Detective, and Espionage Fiction* (q.q.v.).

Cherry Ames

676. Mikucki, Eleanor. **The Cherry Ames Page**. http://www.geocities.com/Athens/3777/

Devoted to Cherry Ames, the quick-witted nurse-sleuth, this delightful website provides links to information about her: her name, childhood, family, friends, adversaries, patients, home, apartment, job history, and birthday. An alphabetical index of characters is given, as are also links to scholarly analyses of the Cherry Ames series, summaries of the books, and information about other books written by the authors. Related material—information about the Cherry Ames board game, links to sites featuring nurse sleuths, biographical information on the authors of the books, and descriptions of the Cherry Ames *Book of First Aid and Home Nursing*—is accessible, and numerous cover reproductions are given. All information is clearly presented and thorough; the site is an affectionate and well-done tribute.

Dan Fowler

677. Johnson, Tom. **Dan Fowler: Ace of the G-Men**. Seymour, TX: Fading Shadows, 1997. 52 p. Paperback.

From 1935 through 1953, Dan Fowler was the lead character in some 112 issues of the pulp magazine *G-Men* (later *G-Men Detective*). Because the stories were published under the house pseudonym "C. K. M. Scanlon," authorship of the individual stories remains in doubt, though George F. Eliot, Edward Churchill, D. L. Champion, Whit Ellsworth, and Manly Wade Wellman all appear to have written Fowler's adventures.

Johnson's self-published annotated bibliography provides extensive story summaries of Fowler's first 53 adventures. Johnson begins with a discussion of the characters, after which there is a chronological list of the stories along with date of issue, volume and issue number, and a guess as to the author's identity. These data are followed by individual descriptions of the 53 issues. Each issue is numbered, and data given above are repeated. Each citation lists the story's settings and characters, provides a detailed synopsis, and concludes with notes. Johnson end his list with a list of the "Top Ten and a Stinker," after which is a reprint of "Diamonds Across the Atlantic," which first appeared in the Winter 1946 issue of *G-Men Detective*. The back page of the book is a chronological checklist of all 112 issues; titles are given, as are the volume and issue number and the month and year of issue.

Doc Savage

678. Farmer, Philip José. **Doc Savage: His Apocalyptic Life As the Archangel of Technopolis, As the Golden-eyed Hero of 181 Supersagas, As the Bronze Knight of the Running Board, Including His Final Battle Against the Forces of Hell Itself**. Garden City, NY: Doubleday, 1973. 226 p. LC 72-96236. ISBN 0-385-08488-9.

Biographies of fictional characters have not been included in this work, but Farmer's life of Doc Savage is mentioned here for its three concluding sections. The first, "The Fabulous Family Tree of Doc Savage (Another Excursion into Creative Mythography)," provides a lengthy history of Doc Savage and all of his ancestors. Farmer's coverage starts in 1795, when a meteor in Wold Newton, Yorkshire, England, irradiated the genes of the inhabitants, enabling their descendants to become such supermen as Captain Blood, Tarzan, Micah Clarke, Solomon Kane, Alan Quatermain, Sherlock Holmes, Wolf Larsen, Mr. Moto, and Doc Savage, and such supervillains as Professor Moriarty and Fu Manchu. This section—which has taken on a life of its own—is essential reading for anybody who wants to understand what is sometimes referred to as the "Wold Newton" mythology.

The second and third sections are more germane to the subject of this section. Addendum 2 is a lengthy chronology of the life and career of Doc Savage, as related in the adventures described in *Doc Savage*. Arranged chronologically by adventure, each reference provides the month of publication, duration of the adventure, and issue (or issues) in which it was described.

Finally, the "List of Doc Savage Stories" lists all 181 *Doc Savage* stories in order of publication. Clark's *The Author Index to the Doc Savage Magazine* (q.v.) not being generally accessible, this is the closest thing to a readily obtainable index to *Doc Savage*. Farmer's introductory material to this section is nevertheless not completely reliable, for he was unaware of the contributions of Ryerson Johnson.

679. Lai, Rick. **The Bronze Age: An Alternate Doc Savage Chronology**. Seymour, TX: Fading Shadows, 1992. 60 p. Paperback. (100 copies printed.)

Written partially to expand upon the chronology of Doc Savage's life presented by Farmer in *Doc Savage: His Apocalyptic Life* (q.v.), Lai has proposed an alternative chronology for Doc Savage's life and adventures. Drawing upon the researches of Farmer and such Doc Savage scholars as Will Murray, Lai presents a chronology of Doc Savage's life and adventures from 1918 onward, as recorded in the pulp magazines and books. Each adventure is separately numbered; its date is given, as is the number of days it involved. The title of the magazine or book printing the adventure is given (in capital letters), followed by its author and first publication date. A description of each adventure appears.

This is a worthy alternative to Farmer's work, but it is for specialists.

680. Sines, Jeff. **Doc Savage Unchained!** http://users.aol.com/jsines233/private/DocSavage.htm

The most comprehensive collection of Doc Savage images currently available via the Web, this website provides images of the covers of all the pulp magazines and paperback editions of Doc Savage. The section devoted to paperbacks reprints the material from the books' back covers, gives the date of the first magazine publication, and provides images of the covers of Bantam editions, new novels, and omnibus editions. The section devoted to the pulps provides cover images, arranged chronologically, as well as images for the early book reprints. Images of the covers of *Doc Savage* comic books are posted, as are also the lyrics to the theme song from the 1975 motion picture. Finally, there are numerous links to other Doc Savage sites.

681. Smalley, Rob. **Doc Savage: The Supreme Adventurer**. http://members.netvalue.net/robsmalley

This website provides significant information about the character of Doc Savage and his adventures; in addition, information about Doc Savage's associates and lairs is given. Especially useful is a comprehensive listing of Doc Savage's adventures. The magazine's original publication date is provided, as are the Bantam paperback reprint number and the title of the adventure. A number of the titles are linked to reproductions of the paperback covers and are accompanied by synopses of the stories. Clark Savage's final message to Doc is provided, and there are links to other Doc Savage sites, including the Doc Savage WebRing (http://www.webring.org/cgi-bin/webring?ring=docsavagering;list), a meta-site devoted to Doc Savage. Smalley's website is obviously a labor of love and is well done.

The Hardy Boys

682. Carpentieri, Tony. **Frank and Joe Turn Blue**. Rheem Valley, CA: SynSine Press, 1993. 234 p. Spiralbound. LC 94-173259. ISBN 0-9639949-2-1.

683. Carpentieri, Tony. **Frank and Joe Turn Blue**. 2d ed. Rheem Valley, CA: SynSine Press, 1994.

684. Carpentieri, Tony. **Frank and Joe Turn Blue**. 3d ed. Rheem Valley, CA: SynSine Press, 1994. 248 p. Spiralbound. ISBN 0-9639949-9-9.

This description is based on the 3d edition.

Frank and Joe Turn Blue lists every known printing of the first 58 *Hardy Boys* books, from the appearance of *The Tower Treasure* in 1927 until the 1979 publication of *The Sting of the Scorpion*. In addition, printings for all known Grosset & Dunlap library bindings are described. Entries for each book provide information on cover/dustjacket artists, front and back cover styles, material on the endpapers, information on the spine, and all the relevant data that can be used to differentiate the numerous different printings of each title.

Thorough though Carpentieri is, his work is almost unusable, for he presents the data of each citation through a complex series of abbreviations. These abbreviations are keyed to a lengthy list given only at the book's beginning, and until readers have internalized Carpentieri's system, they will remain baffled by page after page of entries akin to 17 (yel)//e-2/eb/blx2/syn/pf/tp3.1/cp(loc,isbnt,isbn1)/tc/bl/c1/176/blx3/BT(48) of/HB#1-58 of (eb)/e-2//nn.

Like Farah's guide to the *Nancy Drew* series (q.v.), this volume is a labor of love. Its coverage is greater than that in Heffelfinger's *The Bayport Companion* (q.v.), but it is nonetheless very specialized and very difficult to use.

685. Finnan. R. W. **Series Book Central (Hardyboy01's Home Page)**. http://members.aol.com/Hardyboy01/index.html

The most comprehensive website devoted to series books, this one offers links to the sites devoted to Judy Bolton, Hardy Boys, Nancy Drew, and Doc Savage, among others series. The Hardy Boys FAQ (Frequently Asked Questions) page—http://members.aol.com/Hardyboy01/hb3.htm—provides a history of the Hardy Boys excerpted from Charles Heffelfinger's *The Bayport Companion* (below) and information on "Franklin W. Dixon," scarce editions, characters, revision history, and types of dustjackets.

686. Heffelfinger, Charles. **The Bayport Companion**. Tampa, FL: Midnight Press, 1992. 93 p. Paperback. OCLC 30750970.

687. Heffelfinger, Charles. **The Bayport Companion**. 2d ed. Tampa, FL: Midnight Press, 1994. 102 p. Paperback. OCLC 33364572.

This description is based on the 2d edition.

The Bayport Companion lists every known printing of the first 40 *Hardy Boys* books, from the 1927 appearance of *The Tower Treasure* until the 1961 publication of *The Mystery of the Desert Giant*. In addition, Heffelfinger discusses Hardy Boys comics, record albums, games, and collectibles. Entries for each separate printing of each book provide year of publication and information on cover/dustjacket artists, number of books listed on the front flap, color of the spine of the dust jacket, frontispiece artists, color of the endpapers, color of the binding, rear flap ad, and back cover ad.

Thorough though Heffelfinger is, he has consciously modeled the format for his citations after those used by Farah (q.v.), and the result is equally unusable to the uninitiated. There are page after page of citations akin to gf;tp+;cp,HB1-8, TSc1-10;tc;tc(t);;HB1-14,16;WS1-16;HG(9);TOA(7);b1;b1; and the only key is at the beginning of the volume.

Like Farah's guide to the Nancy Drew series and the guide to the Hardy Boys compiled by Carpentieri (q.v.), this volume is an obvious labor of love. Collectors of the Hardy Boys series will probably be satisfied with Carpentieri's effort, but the information provided by this volume should not be discounted.

688. Johnston, Gerald Hankins. **The Hardy Boys Mystery Stories**.

Available as part of the archives maintained by the DorothyL listserve, and also through the Miss Lemon Website (http://www.iwillfollow.com/lemon.htm), this list of mysteries featuring the Hardy Boys is arranged chronologically. Each citation gives the book's title and its years of publication and revision; notes indicate which titles were not set in Bayport. Data are current through 1993. Johnston has also compiled a similar list for Nancy Drew (q.v.).

Judy Bolton

689. Finnan, R. W. **Judy Bolton Series Books**. http://members.aol.com/ Hardyboy01/bolton.html

Finnan provides a list of the 38 Judy Bolton mysteries written by "Margaret Sutton," from the 1932 *The Vanishing Shadow* to the 1967 *The Secret of the Sand Castle*. Apart from the date of first publication, no bibliographic data are provided, but the list is clearly presented.

The Moon Man

690.   Brown, Michael Rogero. **The Moon Man**. http://sflovers.rutgers.edu/archive/
        bibliographies/moon-man.txt

Created by pulp writer Frederick Davis, the Moon Man was one of the
more popular characters to appear in *Ten Detective Aces*. Brown's index to the 39
appearances of the Moon Man is arranged by issue. The story's title is given, followed by Davis's initials and date of the story's publication; volume and number
of the magazine are not known. Separate reprints are noted, and a note makes
reference to *The Night Nemesis*, the first of a proposed two-volume reprinting of
the collected Moon Man.

Nancy Drew

691.   Farah, David. **Farah's Guide**. Pasadena, CA: Farah's Books, 1985–.
        Various pagings. Spiralbound. Numerous editions.

The following annotation describes the 10th (1994) edition.

In what must have been an extraordinary labor of love, Farah describes
every known printing of every volume featuring the character of Nancy Drew
published between 1930 and 1994. Grosset and Dunlap issued the regular editions of Nancy Drew in some 20 different formats, and Farah's bibliography arranges its contents according to these formats. Each entry provides print run,
number of printings, price of the book in good condition in a dustjacket, data on
the dustjacket front flap, cover art, spine, back flap, reverse, pre-text pages, and
post-text pages. Furthermore, he provides biographical information on the
authors and writers of Nancy Drew.

Unfortunately, these data are presented in highly abbreviated form, and
the key to these data is given only at the beginning of the volume. Until they have
internalized Farah's system, users will remain baffled by page after page of entries
akin to 5050,ND#1-19,110-150/1/1f/ML#1-8/DG#1-10 / pwt/pf/tp+/cp,ND#1-18/
tc/b1/pwt/b1 (t)//b1.

Devout Nancy Drew fans and collectors will want this book. The rest of
the world will not.

692.   Finnan, R. W. **Nancy Drew—The Original Series**. http://members.aol.
        com/Hardyboy01/nd3.htm

This site provides a list of the first 56 Nancy Drew stories, from the 1930
publication of *The Secret of the Old Clock* to the 1979 *The Thirteenth Pearl*. Beneath
each title are listed the author of the original text, the person who provided the
outline, the author of the revised text, and the date of revision. It is continued by
"Nancy Drew in Paperback" (below).

693. Finnan, R. W. **Nancy Drew in Paperback**. http://members.aol.com/ Hardyboy01/nd4.htm

A continuation of "Nancy Drew—The Original Series" (above), this site provides lists of the of the various Nancy Drew series. Volumes 57 (*The Triple Hoax*) to 139 (*The Secret of Candlelight Inn*) of the original Nancy Drew series are provided, after which the eight volumes in the Nancy Drew/Hardy Boys Be a Detective Mystery Stories series are listed, as are also the 33 volumes of the Nancy Drew & Hardy Boys Super Mysteries, the 16 volumes in the River Heights Series, the 21 volumes in the Nancy Drew Notebooks, the 23 volumes in the Nancy Drew on Campus Series, and the 123 volumes in the Nancy Drew Files.

An incredible series of lists.

694. Johnston, Gerald Hankins. **The Nancy Drew Mystery Stories**.

Available as part of the archives maintained by the DorothyL listserv, and also through the Miss Lemon website (http://www.iwillfollow.com/lemon.htm), this list of mysteries featuring Nancy Drew is arranged chronologically. Each citation gives the book's title and its years of publication and revision; notes indicate which titles were written by Mildred Wirt Benson and when the setting is not River Heights. Data are current through 1993. Johnston has also compiled a similar list for the Hardy Boys (q.v.).

The Phantom/Phantom Detective

695. Halegua, Mark S. **Phantom Detective**. http://www.mindspring.com/ ~phantom21/phantom.htm

Halegua's site provides information about the character the Phantom (in the series, nobody ever referred to him as the Phantom Detective). In addition, a subsection titled "The Phantom Detective Index" (http://www.mind-spring.com/~phantom21/PD-Index.html) lists the 170 *Phantom Detective* novels in chronological order, giving for each its issue number, title, publication date, and volume and issue number. A nicely done site, although Tom Johnson's *Phantom Detective: The Original Masked Marvel* (below) is more comprehensive.

696. Johnson, Tom. **Phantom Detective: The Original Masked Marvel**. Seymour, TX: Fading Shadows, 1996. 86 p. Paperback. Index.

From 1933 through 1953, the Phantom Detective—the lethal alter ego of rich playboy, dilettante, and disguise expert Richard Curtis Van Loan—was the lead character in some 170 stories appearing in the pulp magazine *The Phantom Detective*. Because the stories were published under the house pseudonym "G. Wayman Jones," authorship of the individual stories remains in doubt, though D. L. Champion, C. S. Montayne, Emil Tepperman, and Norman Daniels all appear to have written stories about the Phantom Detective.

Johnson's self-published annotated bibliography provides extensive story summaries of all 170 adventures of the Phantom Detective. Johnson begins with a history of the characters, who first appeared in 1932, after which there are descriptions of the individual adventures. Each entry is numbered, and the date of the issue and volume and number are given, along with a guess as to the author's identity. Each citation lists the story's settings and characters, provides a detailed synopsis, and concludes with notes about the story. Concluding the book is a chronological list of the stories that is misidentified as a title index.

The Shadow

697.   Lai, Rick. **Chronology of Shadows**. Seymour, TX: Fading Shadows, 1995. 94 p. Paperback. (100 copies printed.)

In *Chronology of Shadows*, Lai proposes a chronology for the life and adventures of the Shadow. The contents: 1) Introduction; 2) The Shadow's Early Years; 3) Chronology of the Shadow's Early Years; 4) Chronology of Recorded Exploits; 5) Afterword: Apocryphal Shadows.

Lai's chronology of the Shadow's early years begins in 1892 with the birth of Kent Allard and concludes in 1929, the year in which the Shadow begins to impersonate Lamont Cranston. In the chronology of recorded exploits, publications are separately numbered. The date of the adventure is given, as are the number of days the adventure involved. The title in which the adventure was published is given in italics, followed by the date of its first publication; a note indicates when the adventure was written by an author other than Walter Gibson. A brief description of the adventure follows.

Lovers of the Shadow will appreciate Lai's efforts.

SECONDARY LITERATURE

> **SCOPE NOTE:** Included in this section are bibliographies of literature written about mystery and detective fiction. Primary and secondary bibliographies devoted to individual authors are listed in the author section.

698. Adams, Donald K., ed. **The Mystery & Detection Annual**. Beverly Hills, CA: Donald Adams, 1972–1973. xii, 264 p. LC 72-87432. ISBN 0-913288-00-4 (1972).

699. Adams, Donald K., ed. **The Mystery and Detection Annual**. Beverly Hills, CA: Donald Adams, 1973[–1974]. xii, 337 p. ISBN 0-913288-01-2. ISSN 0000-0302.

Though it lasted but two years, this annual nevertheless contains excellent and incisive articles, criticism, and reviews. The volume for 1972 is dedicated to Edgar Allan Poe, and several of its essays discuss aspects of Poe's detective fiction. It also has articles about detective and mystery fiction written during the nineteenth century or by authors born during the nineteenth century. The volume's focus is not limited to the nineteenth century, however, and there are articles on such writers as Horace McCoy, Dashiell Hammett, and Ross Macdonald. A surprising inclusion is Lawrence D. Stewart's "Gertrude Stein and the Vital Dead." A section devoted to reviews provides informed criticism on several significant mystery and detective studies published from 1969 until 1972. Julian Symons takes the first edition of Barzun and Taylor's *A Catalog of Crime* to task for bibliographical inaccuracy; Wilbur Jordan Smith discusses Ordean Hagen's deficiencies in listing nineteenth-century titles in *Who Done It?*; and there are additional reviews of such significant works as Symons's *Mortal Consequences* and la Cour and Mogensen's *The Murder Book*. In addition, a number of primary works are reviewed.

Although Adams had hoped to dedicate the 1973 volume of *The Mystery and Detection Annual* to Arthur Conan Doyle, his contributors chose to write on different subjects, and the volume has as its theme "The Southern California

Scene." Nevertheless, historical subjects are treated. There are articles on James Hogg's *The Private Memoirs and Confessions of a Justified Sinner*, Poe, and William Godwin. The discussion of the moderns includes an interview with, and an article about, Ross Macdonald; the first publication of Horace McCoy's "Death in Hollywood"; Raymond Chandler; and F. Scott Fitzgerald's *The Great Gatsby*. There also are articles on Georges Simenon, Paul Bowles, and Dorothy L. Sayers. The critical reviews are diverse, discussing books as varied as *Graham Greene on Film: Collected Film Criticism 1935–1940; Chandler Before Marlowe: Raymond Chandler's Early Prose and Poetry, 1908–1912;* and *The Ghost Stories of Edith Wharton*. As before, a number of primary works are reviewed.

It is to be regretted that this series lasted only two years. Its contents are of consistently high quality.

700. Albert, Walter. **Detective and Mystery Fiction: An International Bibliography of Secondary Sources**. Madison, IN: Brownstone Books, 1985. xii, 781 p. Index. ISBN 0-941028-02-X.

701. Albert, Walter. **Detective and Mystery Fiction: An International Bibliography of Secondary Sources**. San Bernardino, CA: Brownstone Books/Borgo Press, 1997. 672 p. Index. (Brownstone Mystery Guides, vol. 10). LC 95-5335. ISBN 0-941028-15-1 (hc); 0-941028-16-X (pb).

Intended as a comprehensive list of secondary material in the area of crime, detective, and mystery fiction, and suspense and espionage fiction, the second edition references more than 7,700 books, chapters, journal and magazine articles, dissertations, dealer catalogues, an occasional newspaper article, an enormous amount of fan literature, and such ephemera as calendars, trade reports, and company publications. The contents include numerous Swedish, German, French, and Spanish publications as well as (romanized) references to Japanese sources. Excluded are materials on Sherlock Holmes and publications dealing solely with film, television, radio, and stage adaptations.

The 2d edition of *Detective and Mystery Fiction* contains six sections: A) Reference Works: Bibliographies, Dictionaries, Encyclopedias, and Checklists (282 citations); B) General Historical and Critical Works: Books (678 citations); C) General Historical and Critical Works: Articles (1,369 citations); D) Dime Novels, Juvenile Series, and the Pulps (859 citations); E) Works on Specific Authors (4,490 citations); and F) Magazines (58 citations). Each section numbers its citations consecutively; all citation numbers and author names are in boldface type. Sections A–C are arranged alphabetically by critic's last name. Section D contains subsections for materials studying the dime novels and juveniles, and the pulps, and further divides the contents by offering sections on general works and on works studying specific publications. The general sections are alphabetical by author; the sections dealing with specific publications are alphabetical by publication name. Section E is alphabetical by the subject's name; section F is alphabetical by title. Virtually all entries are annotated, occasionally at length, and many are signed, for some 23 experts assisted Albert in the collection of data, including such notables as Robert C. S. Adey, John L. Apostolou, Everett F. Bleiler, Robert E. Briney, J. Randolph Cox, Iwan Hedman, Deidre Johnson, Will Murray, John Nieminski, and Robert Sampson. Internal cross-references are given in parentheses. Data are complete as of 1990. The index provides access by the names of author, monographic titles, and major character.

Detective and Mystery Fiction is almost unbelievably comprehensive, and it is remarkably accurate. The occasional errors and omissions tend to be trivial. All academic libraries and researchers should hold this volume.

702. Bloom, Harold, ed. **Classic Crime and Suspense Writers**. New York: Chelsea House, 1995. xii, 188 p. (Writers of English: Lives and Works). LC 93-22607. ISBN 0-7910-2206-4 (hc); 0-7910-2231-5 (pb).

The first sentence of this book claims that it "provides biographical, critical, and bibliographical information on the thirteen most significant crime and suspense writers of the first half of the twentieth century." It does not. One of the writers (E. W. Hornung) had a career that began prior to the twentieth century; four of the writers (Ian Fleming, John D. MacDonald, Ross Macdonald, and Jim Thompson) did not publish significantly until the latter half of the twentieth century; and although the remaining eight names include Eric Ambler, John Buchan, James M. Cain, Raymond Chandler, Daphne du Maurier, Graham Greene, Dashiell Hammett, and Cornell Woolrich, it would hardly be accurate to state that these few are the "most significant crime and suspense writers."

Prior to the start of the "biographical, critical, and bibliographical information" is Bloom's essay on "The Life of the Author." It contains such sentences as "Beckett was perhaps the least egoistic post-Joycean, post-Proustian, post-Kafkan of writers," and has nothing whatsoever to do with detective and mystery fiction.

Each chapter of the book is devoted to one of the authors named above and consists of three parts: a biography, a selection of critical extracts about the author, and a bibliography of the author's published books. The biographies are often inadequate; for example, Hammett's Continental Op is erroneously described as "a hired gunman," and Hammett first appeared in *Black Mask* in 1922, not 1923. The critical extracts tend to be brief, in the 250- to 400-word range, and the bibliographies provide only the dates of book publication, with no indication whether the work is fiction, nonfiction, poetry, play, essay collection, short story collection, or novel.

The thematically similar work compiled by Bruce Cassiday (q.v.) is superior.

703. Bloom, Harold, ed. **Classic Mystery Writers**. New York: Chelsea House, 1995. xii, 188 p. (Writers of English: Lives and Works). LC 94-5882. ISBN 0-7910-2210-2 (hc); 0-7910-2235-8 (pb).

A companion to Bloom's *Classic Crime and Suspense Writers* (above), this volume is only marginally better. Its introduction states that it "provides biographical, critical, and bibliographical information on the thirteen most significant writers of mystery and detective fiction through the 1920s." These 13 include Wilkie Collins, Arthur Conan Doyle, Edgar Allan Poe, and Melville Davisson Post (dead or inactive prior to the conclusion of the 1920s), but the majority of the book is devoted to Anthony Berkeley, G. K. Chesterton, Agatha Christie, Freeman Wills Crofts, R. Austin Freeman, Mary Roberts Rinehart, Dorothy L. Sayers, S. S. Van Dine, and Edgar Wallace, virtually all of whom were active after the 1920s.

As in the other volume, Bloom's essay on "The Life of the Author" precedes the "biographical, critical, and bibliographical information," and has nothing whatsoever to do with classic mystery writers, the ostensible subject of this volume.

Each chapter is devoted to one of the authors listed above and consists of three parts: a biography, a selection of critical extracts about the author, and a bibliography of the author's published books. The biographies are cleanly written and reasonably accurate, though not without errors; to state that Christie's "*Murder on the Orient Express* (1934), *The A. B. C. Murders* (1936), and *The Body in the Library* (1942) . . . established the 'cozy' British mystery" is to be unaware of literary history. The critical extracts tend to be brief, in the 250- to 400-word range, and the bibliographies provide only the dates of book publication, with no indication whether the work is fiction, nonfiction, poetry, play, essay collection, short story collection, or novel.

Again, the thematically similar work compiled by Bruce Cassiday (q.v.) is preferable.

704. Breen, Jon L. **The Girl in the Pictorial Wrapper: An Index to Reviews of Paperback Original Novels in the New York Times' "Criminals at Large" Column, 1953–1970**. Carson, CA: California State College, Dominguez Hills Library, 1972. 46 leaves.

From 1953 until his death in 1968, Anthony Boucher regularly reviewed paperback original novels in the *New York Times Book Review* in his column "Criminals at Large"; he was succeeded by noted bibliographer Allen J. Hubin. The majority of these reviews are not listed in the *New York Times Index*, which until relatively recently did not index "Criminals at Large." This in turn has made it virtually impossible for researchers to locate contemporary reactions to authors as diverse as Chester Himes, William Bradford Huie, MacKinlay Kantor, John D. MacDonald, Jim Thompson, and Cornell Woolrich.

The index is arranged alphabetically by author's name (given in capital letters); beneath each name (also in capital letters) are titles of books that were reviewed. Also provided are publisher, date of the review in highly abbreviated form (e.g., 7Jul63, 3Nov57), and page of the *New York Times Book Review* upon which the review appeared.

Breen's citations are accurate and models of brevity, and it is unfortunate that this index was not printed in hardcover and made more widely available, for it deserves wider circulation and belongs in all academic libraries.

Note: The bibliographic data provided above occur nowhere in the index itself and are taken from Breen's *What About Murder?* A revised and expanded 2d edition has not been accessible to me.

705. Breen, Jon L. **What About Murder? A Guide to Books About Mystery and Detective Fiction**. Introduction by Ellery Queen. Metuchen, NJ: Scarecrow Press, 1981. xviii, 157 p. Index. LC 81-645. ISBN 0-8108-1413-7.

Despite its brevity, *What About Murder?* is a gold mine, an expertly annotated and beautifully arranged bibliography of 239 (predominantly) English-language books about detective and mystery fiction published during the twentieth century. The volume begins with an excellent introduction in which Breen provides the criteria he used to choose his contents. In brief, he opted for comprehensiveness except in the case of Sherlock Holmes materials, books on motion pictures, dealer and exhibition catalogues, publicity materials, and works on individual authors who were significant *outside* the mystery field.

The bibliography itself contains seven sections: general histories; reference books; special subjects; collected essays and reviews; technical manuals; coffee-table books (not meant pejoratively); and works on individual authors. Each entry provides the book's author, title, and publication data (place of publication, publisher, and date of publication for the first English-language edition and the first American edition if it is different). Pagination of these books is provided, as are the names of others who appear on the title page (e.g., illustrator, translator, editor, introduction writer), the book's series (if any), and whether the book has illustrations, a bibliography, and an index. Finally, Breen has recorded if the book's title was changed upon reprinting. All citations are arranged alphabetically by author except for the citations on individual authors, which are grouped alphabetically under the author being studied. An excellent author-title index concludes the volume.

Breen's annotations may be browsed with enormous pleasure, for he is neither afraid to damn nor reluctant to praise, and his tastes are quite reliable. One may occasionally cavil at Breen's choices, for he has referenced such books as Donald McCormick's *Who's Who in Spy Fiction* and James Robert Parish and Michael Pitts's *Great Spy Pictures*, titles that are completely out of place in a volume such as this. Also, although Geoffrey Household was indeed as fine a stylist as Breen says, he was primarily a thriller writer, writing neither mysteries nor detective stories, and his autobiography really does not need to be referenced in the section devoted to individual authors, especially as Breen references neither the autobiography nor any publication concerning the equally significant thriller writer John Buchan.

These complaints are minor. Although the citations in this volume are included in Walter Albert's work (q.v.), Breen's annotations are of enduring value and quite reliable. *What About Murder?* and its successor volume, *What About Murder? 1981–1991* (below), belong in all libraries in which there is an interest in studies of mystery and detective fiction.

706. Breen, Jon L. **What About Murder? 1981–1991. A Guide to Books About Mystery and Detective Fiction**. Metuchen, NJ: Scarecrow Press, 1993. xi, 376 p. Index. LC 92-34547. ISBN 0-8108-2609-7.

Like Breen's earlier *What About Murder*, *What About Murder? 1981–1991* is exemplary, an annotated bibliography whose 565 entries survey English-language books about mystery and detective fiction that were published primarily between 1981 and 1991. A few citations, such as #198, David Madden's *James M. Cain*, were published earlier (1970 in this instance), and #330, J. Kenneth Van Dover's *Polemical Pulps: The Martin Beck Novels of Maj Sjöwall and Per Wahlöö*, was not published until 1992.

As in the earlier volume, Breen has grouped his material by subject, but he has altered his subject headings, in part to acknowledge the increasing number of publications about mystery and detective fiction. He has dropped the section devoted to "Coffee-Table Books," describing it as "a somewhat amorphous and artificial category to begin with and one to which few if any of the new entries would properly belong," and he has expanded his divisions. The present volume thus contains nine sections: general histories; reference books; special subjects; collected essays and reviews; technical manuals; works on individual authors; anthologies whose editorial matter contains material of reference value; new editions and supplements of volumes included in the original *What About Murder?*; and addendum.

Citations in these sections are arranged alphabetically by author's name except in the case of the works on individual authors, where they are listed alphabetically under their subject's name. Each citation provides the book's author, title, and publication data (place of publication, publisher, and date of publication for the first English-language edition and the first American edition if it differs). Pagination of these books is provided, as are the names of others who appear on the title page (e.g., illustrator, translator, editor, introduction writer), the book's series (if any), and whether the book has illustrations, a bibliography, and an index. Title changes are noted, and an excellent author-title index concludes the volume.

As before, the annotations in *What About Murder? 1981–1991* are pithy and knowledgeable, providing clear and cogent commentary. However, as in the previous volume, Breen has referenced a number of titles surveying espionage fiction. This volume belongs next to its predecessor in all libraries in which there is an interest in the study of mystery and detective fiction.

707. Cassiday, Bruce, ed. **Modern Mystery, Fantasy and Science Fiction Writers**. New York: Continuum/Frederick Ungar, 1993. x, 673 p. Index. (Library of Literary Criticism). LC 92-33859. ISBN 0-8264-0583-8.

Modern Mystery, Fantasy and Science Fiction Writers contains approximately 800 critical citations to the works of 88 writers of mysteries, fantasies, and science fiction. The majority of these writers are Anglo-Americans active during the twentieth century, but some significant nineteenth-century and international writers have been included. A comprehensive list of the mystery writers included would be lengthy, but there are few disappointments and some pleasant surprises: Mary Higgins Clark, Friedrich Dürrenmatt, Dick Francis, Sue Grafton, Edward D. Hoch, Elmore Leonard, Ed McBain, Marcia Muller, Bill Pronzini, and Phyllis Whitney rub shoulders with Eric Ambler, E. C. Bentley, Lawrence Block, James M. Cain, John Dickson Carr, Raymond Chandler, Agatha Christie, Sir Arthur Conan Doyle, Dashiell Hammett, and Chester Himes; and criticism is available on Michael Innes, P. D. James, John D. MacDonald, Ross Macdonald, Ngaio Marsh, Ellery Queen, Ruth Rendell, Mary Roberts Rinehart, Dorothy L. Sayers, Rex Stout, Josephine Tey, S. S. Van Dine, and Donald E. Westlake. The volume is arranged alphabetically by the subject's name, and the criticism is generally arranged chronologically.

The annotations are not the work of the compiler but are excerpted from the published criticism, and Cassiday has taken pains to ensure that the selections and excerpts are acute, leading to a greater understanding of the work. Furthermore, a gratifyingly large percentage of the criticism excerpted by Cassiday has been written by professional authors active within or knowledgeable about the genre whose writers they are criticizing: John Dickson Carr, Julian Symons, Edmund Wilson, W. H. Auden, Jacques Barzun, and Ian Fleming (among others) provide criticism of the works of Raymond Chandler; G. K. Chesterton, Dorothy L. Sayers, Graham Greene, and Rex Stout (among others) provide commentary on the works of Arthur Conan Doyle; and Victoria Nichols and Susan Thompson, Jacques Barzun and Wendell Taylor, Maureen T. Reddy, Kathleen Klein, Sue Feder, and Carolyn G. Heilbrun (among others) provide criticism on the works of Sara Paretsky. Each citation is thoroughly documented, allowing ready access to the original source.

The volume concludes with a list of works mentioned and an index to the criticism. One can cavil that criticism of more writers should have been provided, and indeed, there are no entries for such notables as R. Austin Freeman, Arthur Upfield, and Robert van Gulik. One may also argue that certain entries should have included more criticism, for Lawrence Block is underrepresented with only two citations. Nevertheless, for providing an excellent assortment of criticism on a significant number of the major writers of the twentieth century, one could hardly ask for more than Cassiday has provided. This volume belongs in all academic and public libraries.

708. Cox, J. Randolph. **Masters of Mystery and Detective Fiction: An Annotated Bibliography**. Pasadena, CA; Englewood Cliffs, NJ: Salem Press, 1989. xvi. 281p. Index. (Magill Bibliography). LC 89-10987. ISBN 0-89356-652-7.

Compiled by a librarian and noted scholar of mystery and detective fiction, this annotated bibliography provides data on 74 important writers of mystery and detective fiction. Despite the limitation implied by the title, a number of women writers are among those included. Following an introduction to the history and development of the genre, the book is arranged alphabetically by subject, beginning with Margery Allingham and concluding with Cornell Woolrich. Three notable writers of the nineteenth century (Edgar Allan Poe, Wilkie Collins, and Charles Dickens) are among those profiled, but the majority of the writers are of the twentieth century and include such contemporaries as

Amanda Cross, Tony Hillerman, Harry Kemelman, Elmore Leonard, and Robert Parker. The focus is predominantly on Anglo-American writers, but Arthur Upfield, Maj Sjöwall and Per Wahlöö, Georges Simenon, and Robert van Gulik are also accorded entries.

Each author's entry contains two sections, the first annotating biographical data and the second annotating the critical commentary. Although Cox's preference is to cite books and essays in books, a number of his subjects have never been the recipients of such, and the journals Cox uses range from *Time*, *Newsweek*, and *The New Republic* to *The Armchair Detective* and *Clues: A Journal of Mystery and Detection*. When even journal articles are lacking or inadequate, Cox cites feature stories from the *New York Times*. Cox's citations are accurate, and his annotations are brief and nonevaluative. The volume concludes with a very good index to the critics.

This bibliography is not intended to be comprehensive, for the Magill Bibliographies are intended for undergraduate and novice audiences, and exhaustiveness is not their intent. Its contents are now somewhat dated, but the book offers researchers a good starting place.

709. Hanrahan, Rita M. **Detective Fiction: An Annotated Bibliography of Critical Writings**. San Jose, CA: San Jose State University, 1976. 114 p. Unpublished M.A. thesis.

Not seen. Though it is cited in Albert's *Detective and Mystery Fiction* (q.v.), in 1997 the libraries at San Jose State University were unable to verify its existence.

710. Johnson, Timothy W., and Julia Johnson. **Crime Fiction Criticism: An Annotated Bibliography**. New York: Garland, 1981. xii, 423 p. Index. (Garland Reference Library of the Humanities, vol. 233). LC 80-8497. ISBN 0-8240-9490-5.

Crime Fiction Criticism is an annotated bibliography listing (in separate sections) 1,810 books, book chapters, dissertations, and periodical articles that offer criticism of detective and mystery fiction as a genre or that study its more influential authors. The first section of the volume surveys general works, with different chapters devoted to describing reference works, full-length books, dissertations, and articles and book chapters. The second section contains the secondary literature on some 250 notable authors, though in the case of such authors as Dickens, Doyle, and Poe the Johnsons were of course selective. Each chapter is arranged alphabetically by author; when the work is anonymous, it is listed by title. Cross-references abound, and a cumulative index to the critics concludes the book.

The Johnsons' effort is more comprehensive than that of the Skene Melvins' (q.v.), but their work has its own lacunae and shortcomings. Apart from indexing materials published in *The Armchair Detective*, they have deliberately ignored all fan materials, and they have similarly ignored most book reviews and all publications about crime fiction for television, radio, and motion pictures. The citations tend to be for Anglo-American publications, although a few foreign-language publications have been included. The contents of essay collections are separately annotated in their respective subjects, but these separately listed annotations are neither numbered nor accessible through the index. In addition, one wonders why the second section contains entries for criticism on William Hope Hodgson and Arthur Machen, neither of whom wrote significant amounts of crime fiction. Finally, the volume lacks a title index.

With the publication of Walter Albert's bibliography (q.v.), this work has been effectively superseded.

711. Lindsay, Ethel. **Here Be Mystery and Murder: Reference Books in the Mystery Genre, Excluding Sherlockiana**. Privately published, 1982. Various paginations. Paperback. OCLC 9663628. (100 copies printed.)

According to Lindsay's preface, she was inspired to begin her list of mystery works by the work of Derek Adley, but after assembling more than 800 file cards, she obtained copies of *The World Bibliography of Sherlock Holmes* and *The International Sherlock Holmes* (q.q.v.), realized that she was duplicating the efforts of de Waal, and decided to focus her efforts on "all the main classic mystery reference books . . . also . . . books about mystery writers, non-fiction books by mystery writers, biographies and autobiographies. There is also a sampling of books about true crimes . . . the history of the police, forensic medicine, codes, poisons and even a book about comics." In all, Lindsay has referenced 748 titles. The contents are reproduced from typescript.

There are two sections to *Here Be Mystery and Murder*. The first is a title index. Books are listed by title (in capital letters), and citations provide author, publisher, publication year, pagination, and (often) a brief note on the relevant contents; places of publication are occasionally given. The second section is an author index; the author's last name is given in capital letters, and beneath it are titles of the works cited in the title index.

Though this work is legendarily rare, the lack of focus indicated above renders the contents of no particular value. Researchers interested in the secondary literature surrounding mystery and detective fiction will do better with the works of Walter Albert, Jon Breen, and Norbert Spehner and Yvon Allard (q.q.v.).

712. Skene Melvin, David, and Ann Skene Melvin. **Crime, Detective, Espionage, Mystery, and Thriller Fiction & Film: A Comprehensive Bibliography of Critical Writing Through 1979**. Westport, CT: Greenwood Press, 1980. xx, 367 p. Index. LC 80-1194. ISBN 0-313-22062-X.

First, despite the promises of the subtitle, this book is not a "comprehensive bibliography." Not included are writers who deal with crime who are accepted literati; Holmesiana; discussions of Buchan and Greene beyond those items that "discuss their thrillers and entertainments"; articles dealing with techniques for writers; picaresque literature; studies of pre-1841 crime, detective, espionage, mystery, and thriller literature; studies of the macabre, fantasy, ghosts, supernatural, gothic, and science fiction; and incidental or casual references to crime literature. Also excluded is fan literature.

Reasonable though these criteria for exclusion are, they appear to have been applied on a wholesale basis rather than selectively. To fail to cite material written about literati is to presume not only that a fixed literary canon exists but also that no new readings of these writers is possible. To exclude the criticism of gothic fiction is to overlook that the gothic frequently involves a crime that must be righted and a mystery (or mysteries) that must be solved, and the criticism of the gothic has often noted this. Similarly, though it can be deplorably written, fan literature can also contain significant material that is not elsewhere accessible.

The problems of its comprehensiveness and philosophical focus aside, *Crime, Detective, Espionage, Mystery, and Thriller Fiction & Film* contains 1,628 numbered citations to books, chapters, and journal articles; dissertations are also referenced. The citations are arranged alphabetically by author or editor's last name, and all are numbered; there are numerous cross-references. Materials published in languages as varied as Norwegian, Afrikaans, Japanese, and Czechoslovakian are present, but none of the citations has been annotated, and it will be the exceptional researcher who is able to judge a book such as Manji Gonda's *Shukumei no Bigaku* by its title. There are separate title and subject indexes, and the materials published in languages other than English are also accessible through a separate appendix. The volume has been reproduced from clearly typed copy, but the contents of the indexes and the appendix are double-spaced and give the book an undeservedly amateurish appearance.

The citations are accurate and valid, and the Skene Melvins should be commended for being among the first to document the secondary literature dealing with mystery and detective fiction. Nevertheless with the publication of Walter Albert's *Detective and Mystery Fiction* and Timothy W. Johnson and Julia Johnsons's *Crime Fiction Criticism* (q.q.v.), *Crime, Detective, Espionage, Mystery, and Thriller Fiction & Film* has been effectively superseded.

713. Skinner, Robert E. **The Hard-Boiled Explicator: A Guide to the Study of Dashiell Hammett, Raymond Chandler and Ross Macdonald**. Metuchen, NJ: Scarecrow Press, 1985. x, 125 p. Index. LC 84-20246. ISBN 0-8108-1749-7.

Intended as "a starting point for those interested in these writers or for those interested in hard-boiled writing in general," this volume begins with an engaging 24-page introduction in which Skinner provides biographical data and a discussion of the importance of his three subjects. The guide is divided into four sections—articles and essays, books and monographs, fugitive material, and book reviews—and contains 646 citations. Each section is arranged alphabetically by the critic's last name, although anonymous works are listed at the beginning of each section under "anonymous" rather than alphabetically by their titles. The citations in the first three sections are briefly annotated, as are some of the book reviews, and the volume concludes with a brief subject index.

Although the citations are generally accurate, Skinner's arrangement and indexing do much to hamper this volume's usefulness. The alphabetical arrangement hinders rather than enhances access to the material, and researchers interested in the criticism written about a specific author will be unable to locate it without having to work through the wholly inadequate subject index. There is no index to the critics being cited.

Skinner's citations are duplicated in Walter Albert's substantially more comprehensive work (q.v.); his volume is necessary only for completists.

714. Spehner, Norbert, and Yvon Allard. **Écrits sur le Roman Policier: Bibliographie Analytique et Critique des Études & Essais sur le Roman et le Film Policiers.** Longueuil, PQ: Les Éditions du Préambule, 1990. 769 p. Paperback. Index. (Collection Paralittératures. Sér. Études et Références). C 90-096350-6. ISBN 2-81933-121-4.

Although publications in languages other than English have generally not been included in this work, *Écrits sur le Roman Policier* has been described here because a sizable majority of its more than 5,000 citations are in English. Furthermore, the arrangement of this bibliography is such that the contents are very accessible. One need not know French to be able to use this volume profitably.

Écrits sur le Roman Policier is a selectively annotated bibliography of the studies of detective and mystery stories and motion pictures that were published in English and French (and occasionally in other languages) between 1900 and December 1989. Prior to the citations is the transcription of a telephone call in which the authors discuss the history and development of the detective and mystery story. This is followed by an introduction that explains the grounds used for selecting material and offers definitions of terms used in discussing the detective and mystery story.

The bibliography contains eight sections and several subsections. Each section and subsection is separately lettered and numbered, and the first element of all citations (the author's last name or the title) is in capital letters. The contents of all sections except the last are in alphabetical order; occasional lists and the volume's last section are in chronological order.

The bibliography's contents (in English): I) descriptions and citations of the journals and relevant special issues of journals; II) citations to reference books and bibliographies; III) citations to books and articles (and a few historically important texts) that discuss the theory, history, themes, and generalities of detective and mystery fiction; IV) citations to books and articles that discuss the technique of writing works of detective and mystery; V) citations to books and articles studying detective and mystery motion pictures, with descriptions of special issues of journals; VI) citations to books and articles providing comparative studies and analyses of multiple authors; VII) citations to books and articles studying individual authors; and VII) citations to lists and studies of the best detective and mystery stories. The volume concludes with separate indexes to authors of the criticism and to the subjects of the studies.

Though many of its entries duplicate those in Walter Albert's *Detective and Mystery Fiction* (q.v.), *Écrits sur le Roman Policier* is more selective in its coverage, and its contents are therefore more accessible. It belongs in academic libraries.

CATALOGUING GUIDES

715. Burgess, Michael. **Mystery and Detective Fiction in the Library of Congress Classification Scheme**. San Bernardino, CA: Borgo Press, 1987. 184 p. (Borgo Cataloging Guides, no. 2). LC 84-12344. ISBN 0-89370-818-6 (hc); 0-89370-918-2 (pb).

Noted cataloguer and bibliographer Burgess has prepared a guide to the cataloguing of mystery and detective novels, espionage fiction, and suspense stories under the classification system used by the Library of Congress. The first two sections deal with the application of subject headings and the creation of Library of Congress classification numbers; the last three sections deal with the creation of Library of Congress main entries and classification numbers for Motion Pictures, Television Programs, and Comic Strips. However, the majority of the volume is devoted to listing the writers of genre fiction and providing the call numbers that would probably be (or have been) assigned to them under the Library of Congress classification system. The list of authors is derived primarily from the 2d edition of Allen J. Hubin's *Crime Fiction, 1749–1980* (q.v.).

All too often the Library of Congress does not know the identities behind pseudonymous works or collaborative efforts, and because Burgess derived his material from the Library of Congress, his classification scheme for genre writers has the same problems as its model. "Clifford Ashdown," for example, was a collaborative pseudonym used by R. Austin Freeman and John James Pitcairn, but the Library of Congress does not appear to know this and thus assigns different call numbers to the works of these writers: Freeman's is PR6011.R43; Ashdown's is PR6001.S42. Pitcairn is not accorded a number, and no cross-referencing exists. Gerard Fairlie and Henry Cyril McNeile both wrote as "Sapper," the former continuing the Bulldog Drummond series after McNeile's death in 1937, but despite the continuity of the character, there is no cross-referencing between the two men, whose Library of Congress call numbers are PR6011.A43 and PR6025.A317; no entry for "Sapper" is provided. Similar problems exist with contemporary writers. William DeAndrea occasionally wrote as Philip DeGrave, but the Library of Congress numbers do not collocate the works: DeAndrea's are PS3554.E174, and DeGrave's are PS3554.E416.

These problems, however, are relatively minor, for despite its occasional lapses, the Library of Congress is generally reliable, as is this presentation of its classification scheme. Nevertheless, with the relative accessibility of online data, this guide is not likely to be particularly useful to most academic libraries, although cataloguers working extensively with mystery, detective, espionage, and suspense fiction may occasionally benefit from having it. Mystery aficionados who visit different academic libraries may find the listings of call numbers useful.

ARTIST STUDIES

716. Cooper, John, and B. A. Pike. **Artists in Crime: An Illustrated Survey of Crime Fiction First Edition Dustwrappers, 1920–1970**. Aldershot, England; Brookfield, VT: Scolar Press, 1995. xiv, 203 p. plus 12 unnumbered pages of colored plates. Index. LC 95-14558. ISBN 1-85928-188-5.

Several illustrated histories of mystery fiction are available, but this is the only one devoted entirely to the dustwrappers of the older books. As its title indicates, the authors concentrate on works published between 1920 and 1970. Cooper and Pike class the subjects of the dustwrappers into 18 categories: Damsels in Distress, Distraught Men, Scene of the Crime, Deadly Demesnes, The Watchers, The Killers, The Victims, A Variety of Weapons, An Inquiry, Arm of the Law, The Detectives, The Clues, Murder on the Move, Murder in the Past, Creatures in Crime, Scent of Death, Pastimes in Purgatory, and Old Bones. Each chapter contains black-and-white illustrations of dustwrappers accompanied by the title of the book, author, publisher of the first English edition, and name of the artist (when known). These data are followed by a brief appreciative description of the contents of the book. In addition, each chapter contains a number of references to the colored plates. A nineteenth chapter provides biographical information on 30 significant artists and lists their works that have been reproduced here. The book concludes with separate indexes to artists and authors.

In all, approximately 300 black-and-white illustrations of dustwrappers are reproduced and described according to the format above. However, it is never explained why these particular dustwrappers were selected. There is also the question of balance. Why are Raymond Chandler and Dashiell Hammett represented by one dustwrapper apiece, whereas John Dickson Carr is represented by 19 and Agatha Christie is represented by 17? Why is Rex Stout represented by seven dustwrappers and the infinitely less important G. D. H. and M. Cole by eight? There is no discernible arrangement in the contents of each of the 18 chapters; no bibliographic measurements or data that can be used for identifying the dustwrappers of first editions; and no references from the color plates to the prose discussions.

In their *Detective Fiction: The Collector's Guide* (q.v.) Cooper and Pike state that they "are amateurs in bibliography, with no training or specialized knowledge of this field," and this lack of bibliographical background is evident here, for this book is more appreciation than scholarship. A bibliographically rigid work on dustwrappers and the artists that produced them remains to be done.

MEDIA
CATALOGUES
and GUIDES

SCOPE NOTE: Included in this chapter are guides to motion pictures, television programs, and radio shows, as well as guides to specific programs and series. Additional information on these subjects can be found in the encyclopedias, readers' guides, and studies of individual authors.

GENERAL

717.   Harmon, Jim. **Radio Mystery and Adventure and Its Appearances in Film, Television and Other Media**. Jefferson, NC: McFarland, 1992. xvi, 286 p. Index. LC 92-54086. ISBN 0-89950-663-1.

Data on the early mystery and adventure radio programs are scarce, and in *Radio Mystery and Adventure* Harmon provides the histories of 14 notable radio mystery and adventure programs, describing their adaptations by television, motion pictures, and other media. Each program is described in a separate chapter. The 14 radio programs described are *The Air Adventures of Jimmie Allen, Captain Midnight, Challenge of the Yukon* (Sergeant Preston of the Yukon), *Dick Tracy, Green Hornet, I Love a Mystery, Jack Armstrong, Little Orphan Annie, The Lone Ranger, The Shadow, Sherlock Holmes, Sky King, Superman*, and *Tom Mix*.

Harmon starts each chapter with background information that provides the date of the first and last broadcasts, listing the sponsors and the dates of their coverage. The names of scriptwriters, producers, directors, and actors are listed. Following this, a history of the production is given, containing information on actors and actresses responsible for defining the characters; data on work environments are also provided. This is followed by discussions of motion picture, television, comic book, and (in several cases) magazine and book adaptations of the character. Each chapter concludes with a list of the various premiums given to those who responded to radio advertisements, and their probable values (in 1992 dollars); the book concludes with an index.

There are occasional typos, and the indexing is unfortunately less than comprehensive, but Harmon's writing is clear, and he provides a wealth of information about each show that is accessible nowhere else. This volume should be held by all academic libraries.

718. Howard, Tom. **More Movie Thrillers**. Sydney, Australia: John Howard Reid, 1993. 218 p. (Reid's Film Index, 10). ISBN 0-949149-87-X (hc); 0-949149-86-1 (pb).

The tenth in the heavily illustrated (black-and-white) Australian filmographies, this volume ostensibly examines the thriller movie. Despite the implications of its title, an earlier volume devoted to thrillers does not seem to exist, although Howard's brief introduction makes reference to his earlier *Tom Howard on Mystery Movies* (q.v.), referring to it as *Movie Mysteries*. As in that volume, the salient characteristics of a thriller are never defined, and Howard, in addition to discussing the various film adaptations of Agatha Christie's *And Then There Were None* and a number of detective and mystery movies, discusses such films as Laurel and Hardy's *A-Haunting We Will Go,* James Cagney's *Blonde Crazy*, Charles Laughton's *Hunchback of Notre Dame*, and Marlon Brando's *Viva Zapata!*

Like the other volumes in this series, *More Movie Thrillers* is arranged alphabetically by movie title; its first entry is the 1942 *Across the Pacific,* and its last is the 1963 *Yellow Canary.* Each entry provides the name of the actors (in boldface type) and the characters they played; credits are provided, with the names of the people responsible for creating the film also given in boldface type. The dates of production and release in the United States, England, and Australia are listed, as are the names of the production and distribution companies, running time, and movie's length (in feet). A one- or two-sentence synopsis describes the crux of the movie, and often lengthy notes provide histories, evaluations, and critical commentary on all aspects of the movie, though solutions are not revealed. Approximately 200 "thrillers" are treated in this volume.

Howard clearly knows his subject and offers occasionally shrewd insights, but the volume is not as useful as the similar work of Parish and Pitts (q.v.). Furthermore, many of the photos are not captioned, and the volume lacks indexes. It is not a necessary acquisition.

719. Howard, Tom. **Suspense in the Cinema**. Wyong, Australia: John Howard Reid, 1995. 219 p. Index. (Reid's Film Index, 13). ISBN 0-949149-80-2 (hc); 0-949149-79-9 (pb).

The thirteenth in this heavily illustrated (black-and-white) series of Australian filmographies, this volume begins with an index to the previous 12 volumes, after which it offers surveys of approximately 100 suspense films. The elements that make up a suspense film are never defined, but in a very brief introduction, Howard states that he has "concentrated on mysteries and thrillers, but . . . have not neglected spies, spoofs, romances, even westerns." The mystery movies discussed thus include *The Adventure of Sherlock Holmes' Smarter Brother, Charlie Chan in Panama, Dial M for Murder,* and *The Lady in the Lake,* although these movies are discussed in conjunction with such films as *The Adventures of Tom Sawyer, Anna Christie, Invaders from Mars,* and *Mummy's Boys* (a 1936 comedy).

As in the other volumes in this series, *Suspense in the Cinema* is arranged alphabetically by movie title. Its first entry is the 1946 *Abilene Town* and its last is the 1945 *Shanghai Cobra*. Each entry provides the name of the actors (in boldface type) and the characters they played; credits are provided, with the names of the people responsible for creating the film also given in boldface type. The dates of production and release in the United States, England, and Australia are listed, as are the names of the production and distribution companies, running time, and movie's length (in feet). A one- or two-sentence synopsis describes the movie, and occasionally lengthy notes provide histories, evaluations, and critical commentary, though solutions are not revealed.

Howard clearly loves his subject and offers occasionally shrewd insights, but the volume is not as useful as the similar work of Parish and Pitts (q.v.).

720.   Howard, Tom. **Tom Howard on Mystery Movies**. Sydney, Australia: John Howard Reid, [1992]. 220 p. (Reid's Film Index, 8). ISBN 0-949149-92-6 (hc); 0-949149-91-8 (pb).

This Australian volume is the eighth in a series of heavily illustrated (black-and-white photographs) filmographies. Previous volumes have examined "Memorable Films of the Forties," "Popular Films of the Forties," "Academy Award-Winning Films of the Thirties," and "Academy Award Winning Films 1940–1947," and have provided such thematic approaches as "A Feast of Films," "Unique Black-and-White," and "Movies as Entertainment."

Tom Howard on Mystery Movies is arranged alphabetically by movie title, the first entry being the 1941 *Among the Living* and the last being the 1959 *The Wreck of the Mary Deare*. Major series discussed include Charlie Chan, Sherlock Holmes, and Mr. Moto. Each entry provides the name of the actors (in boldface type) and the characters they played; credits are provided, with the names of the people responsible for creating the film also given in boldface type. The dates of production and release in the United States, England, and Australia are given, as are the names of the production and distribution companies, running time, and movie's length (in feet). A one- or two-sentence synopsis describes the crux of the movie, and often lengthy notes provide histories, evaluations, and critical commentary on all aspects of the movie, though solutions are not revealed. Approximately 220 mystery movies are treated in this volume, which closes with two title indexes: The first covers volumes 1–4 in this series; the second, volumes 5–7.

Although Howard clearly knows his subject and offers occasionally shrewd insights, the volume is not as useful as the similar work of Parish and Pitts (q.v.). The means by which Howard chose his movies is not given and appears arbitrary, for he has included espionage movies, thrillers, Westerns, and such adventures as the 1954 *Valley of the Kings,* while ignoring such movies as *The Maltese Falcon* (and its earlier incarnations), *Farewell My Lovely*, and all adaptations of the work of Agatha Christie. A substantial number of the photographs are not captioned, and the indexing covers only movie titles. Though an amiable publication, *Tom Howard on Mystery Movies* is not a necessary acquisition.

721. Martindale, David. **Television Detective Shows of the 1970s: Credits, Storylines and Episode Guides for 109 Series**. Jefferson, NC: McFarland, 1991. xii, 563 p. Index. LC 90-53508. ISBN 0-89950-557-0.

As its title indicates, this is a lengthy guide to the credits, storylines, and episodes of 109 detective and mystery television series broadcast on American television during the 1970s. As television shows do not conveniently terminate with the advent of a new decade, the book's chronological coverage starts with programs from the 1960s and concludes with those from the 1980s; the factor that determined a show's inclusion was (in Martindale's words) "if the series had new network-televised episodes during the 1970s, regardless how many, the series is included." Furthermore, Martindale has defined "detective" broadly, including not only the television shows featuring police and private detectives but also those featuring lawyers and crime-solving reporters (e.g., *Kolchak: The Night Stalker*). Espionage shows, nondetective newspaper dramas, rescue shows, sitcoms, and traditional Westerns are not included.

Martindale's list is arranged alphabetically, beginning with *Adam-12* and concluding with *The Young Lawyers*. For each of the series he provides a brief broadcast history that includes the network responsible, length of the episode, air date (starting and concluding), usual broadcast time, number of episodes produced, cast and credits, and a discussion of the detective and the environment in which he, she, or they functioned. Individual shows are then profiled: The title, air date, guest stars, and a brief (one to three sentences) summary are given. A gratifyingly thorough index lists all names given in the body of the volume (cast, credits, guest stars, series names, and production companies). Numerous stills enhance the volume.

Martindale's discussions of the shows tend to be more enthusiastic than critical, and the volume contains a few factual errors, though these are rarely significant. A chronology and an index to the shows by their network would have been useful. These complaints are minor, however; *Television Detective Shows* is an impressive achievement.

722. Meyers, Richard. **TV Detectives**. San Diego: A. S. Barnes, 1981. xii, 276 p. LC 91-3576. Index. ISBN 0-498-02576-4 (hc); 0-498-02236-6 (pb).

TV Detectives consists of a year-by-year historical survey of the detective series that appeared on American television from 1947/1948 until 1980/1981. Written in essay form rather than as encyclopedia entries, each year's contents describe—in occasionally hilarious detail—the detective series that premiered during the course of the year. Excluded from the history are one-shot specials, movies, anthology shows, and shows that featured crimes and crime-solving but were advertised as something else (e.g., Westerns). Also excluded from the history—to its occasional detriment—are significant lists of casts and credits and consistent information on guest stars (if any), the show's producer and executive producers, the creator, the person responsible for the music, and the show's play time. The volume concludes with a nicely done index listing names and titles.

TV Detectives is a thoroughly enjoyable volume. It is heavily illustrated, and more important, Meyers is an engaging and witty writer, not afraid to share his opinions. He offers lengthy and occasionally poignant discussions of such shows as *The Man from U.N.C.L.E.*, *Get Smart*, and *Barney Miller*, and he opens his discussion of *The Avengers* by stating that "if a list of the greatest entertainment ever provided to us by Britain were compiled, *The Avengers* would have to rank high—somewhere between The Beatles and *Secret Agent*." Meyers is equally lavish in his assessment of the ludicrous, and never before have so many bad detective shows been described so cheerfully and so well: "A mystery show does not have to have violence, but it has to have something besides pretty girls and atrocious dialog. The makers of *Charlie's Angels* did not seem to think so."

Meyers followed *TV Detectives* with *Murder on the Air: Television's Great Mystery Series* (New York: Mysterious Press, 1989), but rather than providing a chronological summary of the field, this volume contains essays on only a few mystery series.

723. Mulay, James J., Daniel Curran, Jeffrey H. Wallenfeldt, eds. **Spies and Sleuths: Mystery, Spy and Suspense Films on Videocassette**. Evanston, IL: CineBooks, 1988. xx, 211 p. Indexes. Paperback. (CineBooks Home Library Series, no. 1). LC 88-71573. ISBN 0-933997-18-3.

Derived in part from the 12 volumes of CineBooks's *The Motion Picture Guide*, *Spies and Sleuths* provides descriptions of the approximately 400 mystery, detective, and espionage movies that were available on videocassette as of 1988. It is arranged alphabetically by the film's title (in boldface), and each entry provides a star rating (from zero to five, with five being a masterpiece), the year the film was made, the producing/releasing company, whether it was black-and-white (bw) or color (c), if it had an additional title, a list of the cast and characters, a plot synopsis, and the production credits; entries conclude with the parental recommendation and the film's MPAA rating. There are indexes listing the films by star rating, by parental recommendation, by year, by series, and offering access through the actors, cinematographers, directors, editors, music composers, producers, screenwriters, and source authors.

The indexing is superb, but this is best considered a historical document, offering far fewer descriptions than Sennett's *Murder on Tape* (q.v.).

724. Parish, James Robert, and Michael R. Pitts. **The Great Detective Pictures**. Metuchen, NJ: Scarecrow Press, 1990. xiii, 616 p. LC 90-8551. ISBN 0-8108-2286-5.

This volume is a continuation of an unnumbered series, The Great . . . Pictures, where the ellipses may be replaced by the words "Gangster," "Hollywood Musical," "Spy," "Cop," "Animal," and "Science Fiction." A recurrent and unanswered question throughout this series has been the use of the word "Great" in the titles of the volumes, for a great many of the motion pictures included are far from great—in fact, are mediocre at best. In their introduction to the present volume, Parish and Pitts explain that the word "Great" refers to the specific genre being covered, "and *not* to all of the titles included as we continue to run the gamut from the very best to the very worst, with lots of selections in between."

Approximately 400 detective motion pictures and television films are described in this volume. The listings are arranged alphabetically by the picture's title, which is given in capitals and is accompanied by information on producing studio, year in which the picture was released, and running time. These data are followed by extensive lists of cast and credits for the picture. In several instances, these lists are longer than the actual descriptions of the pictures, which provide the plot, cross-references to similar films, and critical commentary. In at least one instance, the film described no longer exists, though intriguing stills survive. In the case of significant remakes, the different versions of the movies are compared. A great many obscure films have been resurrected, and effort has been made to describe the films that featured women as detectives.

There are four appendixes. The first two list radio and television detective programs. Each entry includes the studio that produced the program, date on which the program premiered, date on which the last program aired, and writers; crime and police shows are not included on these lists. The third is a chronology of the described films that starts with the 1905 *Adventures of Sherlock Holmes* and concludes with the 1988 *Without a Clue*; these entries provide only titles. Finally, T. Allan Taylor provides a two-page bibliography of detective fiction sources.

The Great Detective Pictures is not without errors. In discussing the 1940 *The Missing People,* Parish and Pitts state erroneously that "Edgar Wallace . . . had few continuing characters in his works," which is far from the case. Greater flaws include Dorothy L. Sayers's *Busman's Honeymoon* being misidentified as "Busman's Holiday" in the discussion of the 1940 *Haunted Honeymoon.* Similarly, names of actors and actresses are also on occasion misidentified. The volume's most serious flaw, however, is not in its presentation of data but in its lack of indexes to the casts and credits of the pictures being discussed.

Overall, those who know the title of the picture in which they are interested will find this volume full of information not readily accessible elsewhere. It belongs in the libraries of all aficionados of detective and mystery films.

725. Pitts, Michael R. **Famous Movie Detectives**. Metuchen, NJ: Scarecrow Press, 1979. ix, 357 p. LC 79-17474. ISBN 0-8108-1236-3.

726. Pitts, Michael R. **Famous Movie Detectives II**. Metuchen, NJ: Scarecrow Press, 1991. viii, 349 p. LC 90-9083. ISBN 0-8108-2345-4.

Although Pitts's introduction to the first volume never defines the criteria that constitute a "famous movie detective," his purpose is to trace the celluloid careers of movie detectives, excluding Sir Arthur Conan Doyle's Sherlock Holmes and Raymond Chandler's Philip Marlowe. Seventeen detectives are profiled at length, with Pitts devoting lengthy chapters to the cinematic realizations of Boston Blackie, Bulldog Drummond, Charlie Chan, Crime Doctor, Dick Tracy, Ellery Queen, the Falcon, Hildegard Withers, the Lone Wolf, Michael

Shayne, Mr. Moto, Mr. Wong, Philo Vance, the Saint, Sam Spade, the Thin Man, and Torchy Blane. A briefer concluding chapter examines the cinematic realizations of seven additional detectives: Bill Crane, Craig Kennedy, J. G. Reeder, Lemmy Caution, Nancy Drew, Nero Wolfe, and Nick Carter. The entries for all 24 detectives provide sometimes lengthy histories and the successes and failures of the various films and their lead characters. Each concludes with a filmography that lists (in chronological order) the title of the film, the studio that made it, its running time, the director, the screenwriter, and the cast. The number of chapters are given when the film is a serial, as are the titles of the individual chapters. There are a number of stills. The volume concludes with a bibliography listing novels about the fictional detectives treated in the text and a well-done name and title index.

The second volume is similar in arrangement, although it adds a useful chapter titled "Additions and Corrections to the Base Volume," a page-by-page listing of addenda and corrigenda that users of the first volume must consult. In the second volume, 14 chapters provide the cinematic histories and realizations of detectives Arsene Lupin, Hercule Poirot, Inspector Clouseau, Inspector Maigret, Mike Hammer, Miss Jane Marple, Nurse Sarah Keate, Perry Mason, Philip Marlowe, Raffles, Sexton Blake, the Shadow, and the Whistler. A briefer concluding chapter discusses the cinematic careers of Bill and Sally Reardon, C. Auguste Dupin, Duncan MacLain, Father Brown, Flash Casey, Frank Cannon, Hank Hyer, Inspector Hornleigh, Jack Packard and Doc Long, Joe Dancer, Joel and Garda Sloane, Kitty O'Day, Kojak, Lew Archer, Lord Peter Wimsey, Philip Trent, the Roving Reporters, Russ Ashton, Shaft, Thatcher Colt, Tony Rome, Travis McGee, and Wally Benton. Entries for Philip Marlowe and Sherlock Holmes are not exhaustive but are recountings of the films involving those characters that appeared since the publication of the first volume. Filmographies for all detectives have been expanded and now provide chronological lists that include the title of the film, studio that made it, running time, director, assistant director, technical director, art director, music director, producer, executive producer, associate producer, production manager, photographer, editor, screenwriter, special effects, and number and titles of chapters for serializations; the cast of the movies is also listed. The volume includes a number of stills, and a bibliography lists novels about the fictional detectives covered in the text. The volume concludes with a name, title, and photograph index.

Despite occasional errors, these volumes are labors of love, well written and full of information that cannot be readily located elsewhere. They belong in the libraries of all aficionados of detective and mystery films.

727. Sennett, Ted. **Murder on Tape: A Comprehensive Guide to Murder and Mystery on Video**. New York: Billboard Books, 1997. 238 p. Paperback. LC 97-15711. ISBN 0-8230-8335-7.

Describing itself as "the first comprehensive video guide to movies on crime and punishment," this guide provides annotations to more than 1,000 motion pictures, filmed from the early 1930s until 1997, all of which are available on videotape (as of 1997). Arrangement is alphabetical by movie title. Each movie is rated (from one half to four stars). Data include the name of the producing or releasing company, "c" or "b/w" if the film is in color or black-and-white, running time, director name, screenplay author(s), and principal cast members. The annotations that follow are rarely more than 75 words, but Sennett's succinctness is one of the great strengths of this shrewd and genial guide. In addition, there are numerous stills, lists of great movie moments, and biographical data on some of the great noir actresses.

There are some surprising omissions (no *Silence of the Lambs?*) and odd entries (*Death Wish II* is annotated, but not the original *Death Wish*), and there are a few errors in dates and descriptions, but the biggest problem with this guide is that it has no indexes. This in no way prevents the contents of *Murder on Tape* from being accessible, and one hopes that it receives frequent updates.

728. Tibballs, Geoff. **The Boxtree Encyclopedia of TV Detectives**. London: Boxtree, 1992. 458 p. Paperback. ISBN 1-85238-129-4.

Despite its title, this is not an encyclopedia of television detectives; a researcher looking for information on the television careers of "Fletcher, Jessica Beatrice" or "Tibbs, Virgil" will be sorely disappointed. This is instead an alphabetical list of television detective series. Tibballs, who makes no claims for comprehensiveness, documents approximately 500 detective series that have appeared on British and American television since World War II. Miniseries, television movies, and single plays are not included, nor are the majority of the television series that featured animal detectives, secret agents, superheroes, and lawyers and courtrooms. In these, it is similar to Richard Meyers's earlier *TV Detectives* (q.v.).

Tibballs's list begins with *Ace Crawford, Private Eye* and concludes with *Zero One*. Each entry describes the detective and his or her methodology and friends; the regular cast is listed, and seasonal changes of cast are noted. Additional information often includes the show's producer and executive producers, creator, person responsible for the music, show's play time, premiere date, and television networks on which it played. A section called "Detective Notes" lists such information as the longest-running detective shows, stars who made it big after playing detectives, and the best (and worst) dressed detectives. A chronology listing the major events in the history of television detective series concludes the volume.

It is regrettable that Tibballs did not include indexes for cast and detective and did not provide a full chronology, for without these, this book is accessible only if one wants information on a specific television series. Whatever its shortcomings as a reference book, however, it is a delight to read. Tibballs is a witty writer, and his descriptions of such shows as *The Pursuers* ("the series flopped miserably because not only was the dog more intelligent than the two policemen, it was also a better actor") are probably better than the programs themselves.

SPECIFIC SHOWS AND CHARACTERS

Alfred Hitchcock Presents

729. McCarty, John, and Brian Kelleher. **Alfred Hitchcock Presents: An Illustrated Guide to the Ten-Year Television Career of the Master of Suspense.** New York: St. Martin's Press, 1985. xiv, 338 p. Index. LC 84-22887. ISBN 0-312-01710-3 (hc); 0-312-01711-1 (pb).

For 10 years, from 1955 until 1965, Alfred Hitchcock was the witty host—and occasionally the director—of two television shows, the half-hour *Alfred Hitchcock Presents* (266 shows) and its successor, *The Alfred Hitchcock Hour* (93 shows.) The television series adapted some excellent short stories by such authors as Robert Bloch, John Cheever, John Collier, Roald Dahl, Stanley Ellin, Talmage Powell, Henry Slesar, Lawrence Treat, and Roy Vickers. The stars who appeared in the dramatizations included such notables as Mary Astor, Charles Bronson, Peter Lorre, Steve McQueen, Vincent Price, Claude Rains, Robert Redford, William Shatner, Jessica Tandy, and Fay Wray.

Starting with a discussion of Hitchcock's blackly humorous *The Trouble with Harry* (1955) and Hitchcock's Shamley Production Company's contributions to *Suspicion* (1957/1958), the authors of *Alfred Hitchcock Presents* provide a summary of each of the television shows. Arrangement is chronological by air date; each entry provides the show's title, director, author of the teleplay, and author of the story. The summarization includes the name of the lead actors and/or actresses and concludes with the initial air date. A number of small photographs are sprinkled throughout, and an index offers access to the shows by their titles but not by their cast and credits.

Alfred Hitchcock Presents is an engaging and chatty guide that is delightful to browse. It has a few flaws—McCarty and Kelleher claim that *Alfred Hitchcock's Mystery Magazine* started in 1955, at the same time as the television show, whereas its first issue was in fact dated December 1956—but these do not seriously affect the content of the volume. More data could have been provided, for several descriptions do not even name the cast, and the credits are occasionally incomplete, but this volume is an excellent survey of one of the most influential television series.

Charlie Chan

730. Hanke, Ken. **Charlie Chan at the Movies: History, Filmography, and Criticism.** Jefferson, NC: McFarland, 1989. xvi, 270 p. Index. LC 89-42718. ISBN 0-89950-427-2.

As its title indicates, this is a filmography devoted to Charlie Chan, the sympathetic Chinese detective and the most durable creation of novelist Earl

Derr Biggers. Hanke's arrangement is essentially chronological. Starting with Warner Oland, "the most prestigious Charlie Chan the movies ever had," Hanke lists the cast and credits of each picture and provides commentary and an elaborate summary of the plot (without revealing the solution). The volume is illustrated with black-and-white stills from the pictures under discussion.

Later sections provide the same attention to detail for the Charlie Chans acted by Sidney Toler for 20th Century-Fox and Monogram, and for the Charlie Chan played by Roland Winters ("the curious thing about much of the criticism of Winters's portrayal lies in the fact that in many ways his characterization is far closer to Earl Derr Biggers' original than either Oland's . . . or Toler's"). A section titled "Imitations and Offshoots" discusses Mr. Moto and Mr. Wong, the latter of whom is one of Boris Karloff's less-memorable screen ventures. A well-done index concludes the volume.

Hawaii Five-O

731. Rhodes, Karen. **Booking Hawaii Five-O: An Episode and Critical History of the 1968–1980 Television Detective Series**. Foreword by Rose Freeman. Jefferson, NC: McFarland, 1997. viii, 333 p. Index. LC 96-39668. ISBN 0-7864-0171-0.

As its title indicates, this is a comprehensive guide to the once-popular *Hawaii Five-O* television series. The arrangement is chronological, with the first chapter summarizing the pilot movie and listing its cast and credits. Episodes are numbered consecutively. Different chapters provide a season-by-season breakdown of each episode of the show, providing original air date, teleplay author, story author, director, composer, cast, credits, and summary. Appendixes discuss *Hawaii Five-O* collectibles and the show as a cultural icon, provide a glossary of Hawaiian words and phrases used in the television show, and list the episodes in order of filming. The index is thorough, and there are numerous illustrations.

Heartbeat

732. Tangled Web. **Heartbeat TV Series**. http://www.twbooks.co.uk/authors/ heartbeat.html

Heartbeat is a popular British television drama series featuring the activities of a young constable in rural Yorkshire. It is based on a series of novels written by Peter Walker using the name Nicholas Rhea (q.v.). This website provides a discussion of the series with photographs of the recurrent character. Particular emphasis is given to the books: Cover reproductions of five novels are posted, accompanied by the material from the back covers and excerpts from positive reviews. The concluding bibliography lists all the titles in the Constable series.

Mystery!

733.   Miller, Ron. **Mystery! A Celebration. Stalking Public Television's Greatest Sleuths**. Foreword by P. D. James. San Francisco, CA: KQED Books, 1996. xv, 304 p. Paperback. Index. LC 96-42130. ISBN 0-912333-89-8.

Although the lavishly illustrated *Mystery! A Celebration* is not a filmography akin to the other works in this section, it nevertheless deserves mention, for it is an engaging and affectionate survey of the enormously popular series that has appeared on public television from 1980 through the present (1997). Initially hosted by Gene Shalit, then by Vincent Price, and currently by Diana Rigg, and featuring wonderfully macabre drawings by Edward Gorey, *Mystery!* presented often first-rate adaptations of the works of such luminaries as Dornford Yates, Agatha Christie, Arthur Conan Doyle, John Mortimer, Dick Francis, Ellis Peters, Margery Allingham, Ngaio Marsh, and Dorothy L. Sayers.

Miller introduces *Mystery! A Celebration* by providing a brief history of the series and biographical sketches of the hosts. Following this, he takes a broadly thematic approach to his subject, dividing his material into sections devoted to "The Investigators" and "The Cases for Investigation." The division is unnecessary, for the information contained in each section is essentially the same. The author is profiled and, when possible, interviewed; the chief players are described and often interviewed; summarizations occasionally reveal the solutions; and there are photographs, brief bibliographies, and numerous sidebars. In addition, a list of the shows by season is provided, and there is a 100-question trivia quiz. A series of appendixes provide the complete production credits for each show (arranged alphabetically) and a (highly selective) state-by-state list of dealers specializing in crime and mystery fiction. The volume is well indexed.

Fans of the television series—and those who are curious about why the series has such devoted adherents—will find this book a delight.

734.   **Mystery! Home Page**. http://www.pbs.org/wgbh/mystery/

This delightful site makes use of Edward Gorey's artwork to inform viewers about the long-running public television series. There are links offering information about the season's programming schedule, and there are links providing well-illustrated information about the detectives featured in past Mystery! series. The curious may browse an enjoyable Mystery! History!, take a Mystery! Quiz!, and read a murder story. In addition, one can learn about past programs, purchase Mystery! memorabilia, and leave feedback. Though lighthearted, this is a very informative site.

CALENDARS

SCOPE NOTE: Although a number of calendars listing anniversaries in mystery and detective fiction have been published, only the publication below provides these data in a cumulative and nonrestrictive fashion.

---

735. Malloy, William. **The Mystery Book of Days**. New York: Mysterious Press, 1990. Unpaged. Index. LC 90-43560. ISBN 0-89296-422-7.

Malloy has compiled a day-by-day listing of events that are significant (or amusing) and that are somehow related to detective and mystery literature. The arrangement begins with January 1 and concludes with December 31; events occurring on the same date are listed chronologically. A few days have nothing listed for them, and either the Leap Year has not been taken into consideration or nothing of significance has occurred on February 29. The entries are amusing and informative, and virtually every page of the book contains photographs, illustrations from books and magazines, or stills from motion pictures. The calendar concludes with an index listing names, titles, and illustrations.

There a few minor errors, but this is generally reliable as a reference book. More significant, it is a delightful volume to browse. It should be updated every five or six years.

DIRECTORIES OF DEALERS and THEIR PRICE GUIDES

SCOPE NOTE: Here are directories of publishers, bookstores, and booksellers specializing in mysteries and detective fiction. Many readers' guides also provide lists of bookstores and booksellers.

DIRECTORIES

736. Collingwood, Donna, and Robin Gee, eds. **Mystery Writer's Sourcebook: Where to Sell Your Manuscripts**. Cincinnati, OH: Writer's Digest Books, 1993– . ISSN 1081-6747.

Published biennially, the *Sourcebook* is intended to serve several markets. For the putative mystery writer, the *Sourcebook* offers discussions on trends in crime fiction and ways in which mysteries can be written; lists of reference books (many published by Writer's Digest Books) are provided. For the writer who has completed a manuscript, the *Sourcebook* offers examinations of the markets for short stories and novels, describing interests and requirements of publishers that issue mystery lines and agents who represent authors to these publishers. For the mystery fan, the *Sourcebook* offers information about mystery conventions, book clubs, bookstores, and awards. Finally, there are glossaries of mystery terms, information about the authors who contributed sections to the *Sourcebook*, and indexes to the categories of mystery that publishers tend to issue and that agents tend to like.

Though the different editions of the *Sourcebook* contain errors—the glossary persistently states that the "hard-boiled detective" is "a detective character type popularized in the 1940s and 1950s"—novice writers will be greatly assisted by the information it offers. Lovers of mysteries should be aware that Sharon Villines's *The Deadly Directory* (q.v.) lists significantly more information about bookstores and conventions and provides reference to electronic resources, but the two publications cannot otherwise be compared. The *Sourcebook* belongs in all libraries.

Note: The title of this publication's first edition was *Mystery Writer's Marketplace and Sourcebook* (ISSN 1068-8528).

737. Villines, Sharon. **The Deadly Directory**. New York: Deadly Serious Press, 1995– . Unpaged. Paperback. Index.

The Deadly Directory lists bookstores and booksellers, organizations, publications, conventions, online services, and unique mystery product vendors in one alphabetic sequence, then presents these data separately. The alphabetical sequence provides a note about the organization and contact information, including owner's name, address, telephone and fax number, and e-mail address (when available). In addition, entries are graphically coded, the illustration indicating the focus of the organization. A cat indicates bookstores specializing in new mystery, detective, and crime fiction; an angel, booksellers specializing in rare, out-of-print, and first-edition mysteries; an eagle, general bookstores with strong mystery collections; standing cows (*pace* Gary Larson), organizations; elephants, publications; a badge labeled "fun," conventions; an electrical symbol, online services and bulletin boards; and a package, the unique mystery product vendors. This information is as accurate as can be hoped, but the format for its presentation is initially frustrating. The names and telephone numbers are separated from the rest of the information by a line, and the key at the beginning must be constantly checked until the meanings of the codes are internalized.

A series of indexes rearrange the data from the first section. Bookstores and booksellers are listed geographically by state and city. There are separate sections with alphabetical listings for organizations, publications, conventions, online bulletin boards, and the unique mystery product vendors. The 1997–1998 edition of *The Deadly Directory* lists 107 bookstores, 149 rare and used mystery booksellers, 23 conferences, 26 organizations, 63 author and character pubs and clubs, 75 mystery publications, 36 special collections, 10 online mystery discussion groups, and 31 significant websites.

The paper edition of Villines's directory is useful and helpful; it is updated biennially and belongs in all libraries. In addition a constantly updated website, the Deadly Serious Press page, offers additions and corrections. Its URL: http://www.deadlyserious.com

PRICE GUIDES

SCOPE NOTE: Included below are collectors' and dealers' guides to prices that can be asked for mystery and detective fiction. Lists of specialty bookstores and booksellers can be found in the section for directories; in addition, readers' guides frequently provide lists of bookstores and booksellers.

---

738. Pappas, Nick. **Bloody Dagger Reference: A Price Guide to Mystery-Crime-Detection**. San Diego, CA: Bloody Dagger Books, annual. 438 p. Comb bound.

The 1997 edition of the *Bloody Dagger Reference* lists more than 22,000 books written by more than 3,900 authors. Like Marshall Snow (q.v.), Pappas cumulated dealers' catalogues to get these references, but the entries in the *Bloody Dagger Reference* are briefer and provide different information. In particular, Pappas enables users to see the prices that individual dealers charge for books. Pappas's entries are arranged alphabetically by author's last name; pseudonyms are revealed and cross-referenced. The book's title is provided, as are year of publication and publisher; the publisher's name is often given in highly abbreviated form (e.g., L/B for Little, Brown). A note indicates whether the work is an advance review copy, an uncorrected proof, or a limited edition, and whether it is a British edition or an American edition. Additional information describes the book's condition, states if there is anything unique about the title, and gives the price being asked. Finally, abbreviations indicate the name of the dealer and the month and year of the catalogue in which the price was found. It is not uncommon to find five or six prices quoted for the same book in different conditions.

Earlier editions contain a number of typos, but Pappas is making a conscientious effort to correct and eliminate them. Dealers and collectors of mystery and detective fiction will find the *Bloody Dagger Reference* consistently useful.

739. Snow, Marshall. **A Comprehensive Price List of Crime, Mystery, Thriller and Detective Fiction**. South Grafton, MA: Mostly Murder, Mystery & Mayhem Publications, 1995– . Comb bound.

Snow compiled his price guide by cumulating the entries appearing in more than 1,000 sale catalogues issued by more than 150 dealers. The more than 40,000 entries are arranged alphabetically by author; each provides the name as it appears on the book, followed by the author's real name (when applicable) and dates (if the author is dead). A note indicates relevant pseudonyms, and the name of the author's principal series character is indicated. The titles are listed alphabetically in italics, followed by the first edition's place of publication, publisher, and year of publication. An abbreviation indicates whether the book is a Crime Club edition, a paperback original, a collection of short stories, one of the Queen's Quorum titles, the only mystery written by that author, the author's first book, the first hardcover edition, or a reissue that contains new material of some kind. A note is provided indicating whether the book had a dustwrapper, was signed or inscribed, was an advance reading copy or an uncorrected proof, or was in some way a special edition. Finally, the low and high asking prices are given.

Snow has clearly put enormous effort into his work. However, it has a number of typos (e.g., "Godon Holmes," "Gingerbraed Man," "Exectioner's Song," "Frederic Brown," and so forth). Worse yet, the sources from which Snow derived his data were occasionally in error, and his comments perpetuate those errors. For example, the 1977 Mycroft and Moran edition of M. P. Shiel's *Prince Zaleski* is not a reprint of the 1895 edition; *The Eiger Sanction* is the first book appearing under the "Trevanian" pseudonym, but it is not Whitaker's first book. Equally seriously, the most recent edition of the *Price List* does not indicate the condition of its listings, necessitating guesswork and estimates.

Snow is constantly revising and updating his entries—the 1996 edition contained 25 percent new material—and it is probable that later editions will be corrected and expanded. Dealers specializing in antiquarian and used mystery and detective fiction will need this book.

ELECTRONIC SOURCES

SCOPE NOTE: The number of websites concerned with aspects of mystery and detective fiction is enormous and constantly growing, and the following list is highly selective.

---

740. Derie, Kate. **ClueLass Homepage: A Mystery Lover's Notebook.** http://www.cluelass.com

The ClueLass Homepage contains a wide variety of predominantly contemporary information about virtually all aspects of detective and mystery fiction. It offers extensive lists of the nominees and winners of various genre awards, with information provided on the Agathas, the Anthonys, the Arthur Ellis Awards, the CWA Daggers, the Edgars, the Hammett Prize, the Lambda Awards, the Macavity Awards, the Ned Kelly Awards, and the Shamus Awards, among others. In addition, information about conferences, conventions, classes, and other mystery-related events is provided. There are links to mystery groups for writers and fans, to groups intended to help aspiring writers succeed, to lists of frequently asked questions about detective and mystery fiction, to information about new and forthcoming releases, to lists of mystery magazines and newsletters (including electronic publications), to dealers in and publishers of mystery fiction, to factual sites about crime and investigation (including law enforcement and forensics), and to other websites that are relevant to fans of detective and mystery fiction. Very well designed, with well-chosen icons and helpful colors, this site is recommended for all novices to the Web.

741. Kimura, Jiro. **Gumshoe Site.** http://www.nsknet.or.jp/~jkimura/

Devoted to news about detective fiction, this attractive Japanese site offers information about recent book and motion picture releases, with numerous graphics accompanied by lengthy reviews. Though no attempt is made at comprehensiveness, a gratifying amount of information is present.

742. Magic Dragon Multimedia. **Ultimate Mystery/Detective Web Guide.**
http://www.magicdragon.com/UltimateMystery/Mystery-Index.html

Despite its name, this website is not as comprehensive as some of the other sites considered in this section, but it is nevertheless an impressively large compilation, offering links to information about detective and mystery authors, book reviews, movies and television shows, magazines, games and software, publishers, bookstores, recent news, and stories and hypertext fiction. The author section references some 905 authors not known to be on the Web and has links to 443 websites, but many of these latter are entries in the reading list compiled by Michael Grost (q.v.). Similarly, the material in the section devoted to book reviews appears to have been based on voluntary submission rather than on any consistent basis, and the lists of movies and television shows appear to have been chosen randomly. Despite these and other inadequacies, this site has links not readily locatable elsewhere, and it cannot be dismissed.

743. Murray, Bill. **Hardboiled: The Online Reference Site for All Things Noir.** http://www.voicenet.com/~bmurray/

As its name indicates, this website is devoted to all aspects of hard-boiled and noir fiction. Its opening screen offers links to sound files from recent hard-boiled/noir/action movies, to discussion groups on various related subjects, and to other crime- and mystery-related sites. The contents are excellent, and the links are uniformly good. The major drawback to this site is that its design permits only the lower right third of the screen to be used.

744. Mystery Writers of America. **Mystery Writers of America.** http://www. mysterynet.com/mwa

The home page of the Mystery Writers of America offers lists of the winners of MWA awards and links to information about the MWA, to lists of MWA presidents, and to information about regional chapters. There is a calendar of crime and information about membership. A section titled "Mystery Links" provides connections to recommended sites, specific author websites, booksellers specializing in mysteries, and mystery review sources. Though not as comprehensive as some of the other websites considered in this section, the importance of the MWA as an organization makes their site significant.

745. Sisters in Crime. **Sisters in Crime Internet Chapter.** http://www. lit-arts.com/sinc_chap1/

The website of the Internet Chapter of the Sisters in Crime offers access to private message boards, meeting rooms, file areas, e-mail aliases, and research sources. It answers the question of whether the Sisters in Crime is only for women, offers lists of publications written by chapter members, provides a "spotlight profile" page about selected members, lists the currently elected officers, and provides information on joining the Sisters in Crime.

746. Steffensen, Jan B. **The Mysterious Home Page: A Guide to Mysteries and Crime Fiction on Internet** [sic]. http://www.webfic.com/mysthome/

A librarian in Aalborg, Denmark, Jan Steffensen has created one of the finest detective and mystery websites. Not only are its contents gratifyingly thorough, its arrangement and layout facilitate access to these contents, which are available in a frame and a nonframe version. In both versions, Steffensen provides an introduction to the site, and the left side of the page provides the table of contents, offering access to general guides; specific authors; specific characters; themes in mystery fiction; newsgroups and mailing lists; conferences, conventions, and seminars; mystery organizations; mystery awards; publishers; book people; book dealers; mystery reviews; mystery magazines; electronic mystery magazines; film and TV; the pulps; mystery games and interactive fiction; Sherlockiana electronic texts; miscellanea; popular fiction and culture on the Internet; and related topics. Furthermore, Steffensen has striven for comprehensiveness; the section for general guides offers links to more than 50 different sites, and the list of electronic mystery magazines links to numerous different sources.

747. Tangled Web. **Tangled Web UK.** http://www.twbooks.co.uk/

This British site offers an engaging potpourri of information about all aspects of detective and mystery fiction. It provides links to sections devoted to individual authors, to lists of awards, to information about motion pictures and television, to bookstores specializing in genre fiction, and to current news. Though the Tangled Web provides information on events and happenings in the United Kingdom, including information about many writers whose works are not published or readily available in this country, it lacks the depth provided by such websites as Steffensen's and ClueLass (q.q.v.). Furthermore, its bibliographies are rarely comprehensive and are often inconsistent in their presentation of data. Nevertheless, the Tangled Web remains a significant and often useful site.

748. Villines, Sharon. **The Archives of Detective Fiction.** http://www.esc.edu/Archives

The Archives of Detective Fiction is headquartered in New York City's Mercantile Library, a noted private library. Villines's website includes a well-done bibliography of reference books about mystery and detective fiction. This list contains two sections, one devoted to bibliographies, dictionaries, and encyclopedias, and the other to works of history, theory, and criticism. Each section is arranged alphabetically by author, and each citation provides the book's title in boldface type, place of publication, publisher, publication year, and pagination. Indexes and bibliographies are noted, and each citation is capably annotated.

Villines is the author of *The Deadly Directory* (q.v.), and her site provides corrections and additions to the 1997/1998 edition. As of this writing, someone else is now maintaining the site.

In addition, Villines provides links to mystery and detective fiction websites, and there are lists of award-winning mysteries from conferences and organizations that present awards. The section referred to as the "Archives" is intended "to build a comprehensive database on all authors and aspects of mystery, detective, and crime fiction"; it provides links to information about the authors of mystery and detective fiction. Well written and clearly organized.

749.   XX. **Mysterious Strands**. http://www.idsonline.com/userweb/cwilson/mystery.htm

Compiled by the Newsletter for the Chesapeake Chapter of Sisters in Crime, this website contains eight sections. "The Authors" offers links to several dozen single-author websites. "Mystery Reference Sources" has links to lists of mysteries by genre, to *Twists, Slugs, & Roscoes* (q.v.), and to the home pages of a number of relevant professional organizations. Other sections cover mystery readers' & writers' organizations; magazines, newsletters, and online guides/reviews; and bookstores, publishers, and other related sites. "The Characters" links to websites devoted to a single character; "Mysterious TV Pages" offers access to websites devoted to television crime series; and "Other Mysterious Homepages & Mysterious Fun on the Web" offers an engaging miscellany including links to the ClueLass Homepage, the Mysterious Home Page, and the Tangled Web (q.q.v.). Though not as comprehensive as some of the other websites in this section, Mysterious Strands nevertheless remains a significant and useful resource.

CORE PUBLICATIONS

Only two regularly published mystery and detective periodicals are indexed through the *MLA International Bibliography*. Both routinely contain articles, essays, criticism, reviews, and bibliographies.

The Armchair Detective (1967–1997;
        currently inactive but may be restarted.)
P.O. Box 929
Bound Brook, NJ 08805-0929
0004-217X

Clues: A Quarterly Journal of Detection (1980–)
Popular Press
Bowling Green State University
Bowling Green, OH 43403
0742-4248

Numerous periodicals contain reviews and articles, and the following list of currently published titles is highly selective:

Dime Novel Round-up (1931–)
P.O. Box 226
Dundas, MN 55019
0012-2874

The Drood Review of Mystery (1982–)
Box 50267
Kalamazoo, MI 49005
0893-0252

Mean Streets (1990–)
c/o What Goes on Pty Ltd.
214 Hat Hill Road
Blackheath, N.S.W. 2785
Australia
1035-9761

Murder Is Academic (1992–)
c/o English Department
Hunter College
695 Park Ave.
New York, NY 10021
1076-8471

The Mystery Readers [of America] Journal (1981–)
c/o Mystery Readers International
Box 8116
Berkeley, CA 94707
1043-3473

The Mystery Review (1992–)
c/o C. Von Hessert & Associates
P.O. Box 233
Colborne, ON KOK ISO
Canada
1192-8700

Mystery Scene (1985–)
c/o Mystery Enterprises
Box 669
Cedar Rapids, IA 52406

Paperback Parade (1986–)
c/o Gryphon Publications
P.O. Box 280-209
Brooklyn, NY 11228

The Brownstone Mystery Guides (1985–) are an irregularly issued monographic series. The focus of the series tends toward criticism rather than bibliography, but both editions of Walter Albert's *Detective and Mystery Fiction: An International Bibliography of Secondary Sources* (q.v.) appeared as part of this series.

Brownstone Mystery Guides
c/o Borgo Press
P.O. Box 2845
San Bernardino, CA 92406
1055-6859

Dragonby Books is the publisher of four series: British Paperback Checklists (1986–), Dragonby Bibliographies (1990–), British Author Checklists (1990–), and British Hardback Checklists (1987–). The series are reproduced from word-processed typescript; their focus is on the bibliography.

Richard Williams
c/o Dragonby Books
15 High Street, Dragonby
Scunthorpe, North Lincolnshire
DN15 OBE
England

Galactic Central bibliographies tend to concentrate on science fiction and fantasy writers, but several of these have had significant careers as writers of detective and mystery fiction. The focus is on the bibliography. These titles are available in the United States from:

Chris Drumm Books
P.O. Box 445
Polk City, Iowa 50226

Allen and Patricia Ahearn, owners of Quill and Brush, have published numerous author price guides to contemporary authors, a significant percentage of whom are mystery and detective writers. Their focus is on the bibliography.

Quill and Brush
P.O. Box 5363
Rockville, MD 20848

Ultramarine Publishing Company, Inc., has published numerous checklists devoted to contemporary authors. The majority of their checklists are devoted to science fiction and fantasy authors, but a significant percentage document contemporary mystery and detective authors. The focus is on the bibliography.

Christopher P. Stevens
c/o Ultramarine Publishing Company, Inc.
P.O. Box 303
Hastings-on-Hudson, NY 10706

PROFESSIONAL ORGANIZATIONS

Organizations devoted to celebrating the works of specific authors are listed under that author's name in the body of the book. The following list is highly selective.

Crime Writers' Association (CWA)
c/o Richard Grayson
5 Highgate Close
London N6 4SD
England
> Awards the CWA Daggers

Crime Writers of Canada (CWC)
3007 Kingston Road, Box 113
Scarborough, ON M1M 1P1
Canada
> http://www.swifty.com/cwc/cwchome.htm
> Awards the Arthur Ellis Awards

International Association of Crime Writers (IACW)
Benjamin Hill 242-244
Colonia Condesa
Mexico City, DF
Mexico
> Awards the Alexei Tolstoi Awards

Mystery Writers of America (MWA)
17 East 47th Street, 6th Floor
New York, NY 10017
> http://www.bookwire.com/mwa/about
> Awards the Edgar Awards and the Grand Master Award

Sisters in Crime
c/o Beth Wasson, Executive Secretary
P.O. Box 442124
Lawrence, KS 66044
> http://www.lit-arts.com/sinc_chap1/

Index

In addition to being an author-title index, this lists personal names referenced in the body of citations and the names of critics mentioned in the abstracts. Names beginning with "Mac" and "Mc" are filed at the beginning of the "M" sequence. Titles beginning with numbers are treated as if the numbers were words; the exception is *1257 Förteckning över Deckare, Thrillers, Faktaböcker, Memoarer, Kolportageromaner*, which is carried as though the first words of its title were pronounced "Twelve Fifty-Seven." Names and titles beginning with "St." are treated as though they were not abbreviated and were spelled "Saint."

A. E. Marston (Tangled Web), 514

A to Z of the Novels and Short Stories of Agatha Christie, An (Morselt), 318

ACD: The Journal of the Arthur Conan Doyle Society, 393

Adams, Abby, 45

Adams, Donald K., 698, 699

Adams, Harriet Stratemeyer, 666

Adey, Robert C., 85, 86, 701

Adley, Derek, 305, 627

Adventure Heroes: Legendary Characters from Odysseus to James Bond (Rovin), 671

African American Mystery Page (Daniels), 48

Afrikaanse speurverhale uitgegee tot die einde van 1950: 'n Bibliografie (Miller), 129

Agatha Award Winners (Foxwell), 149

Agatha Christie (Jonasson), 317

Agatha Christie (Yaffe), 331

Agatha Christie: Murder in Four Acts. A Centenary Celebration of "The Queen of Crime" on Stage, Film, Radio, and Television (Haining), 315

Agatha Christie: Official Centenary Edition, 1890–1990 (Underwood), 327

Agatha Christie A to Z: The Essential Reference to Her Life and Writings (Sova), 325

Agatha Christie Chronology, An (Wynne), 330

Agatha Christie Companion, The (Fitzgibbon), 314

Agatha Christie Companion, The: The Complete Guide to Agatha Christie's Life and Work (Saunders and Lovallo), 323, 324

Agatha Christie Society, 331a

Agatha Christie Trivia (Ryan), 321

Agatha Christie Who's Who, The (Toye), 326

Ahearn, Allen and Patricia, 279, 285, 295, 301, 313, 340, 347, 405, 421, 426, 449, 458, 465, 480, 490, 505, 529, 592, 603

Ahearn, Patricia. *See* Ahearn, Allen and Patricia

Aimée and David Thurlo (Thurlo), 606

Albatross Modern Continental Library 1932–1949 (Williams and Jollans), 155

Albert, Walter, 199, 700, 701

Alderson, Martha, 242

Alexandersson, Jan, 302

Alfred Hitchcock Presents: An Illustrated Guide to the Ten-Year Television Career of the Master of Suspense (McCarty and Kelleher), 729

Allard, Yvon, 714

Allen, Bonnie J., 600

Altshuler, Harry, 280

Amazing Pulp Heroes (Hullar and Hamilton), 659

Amazing Pulp Heroes: A Celebration of the Glorious Pulp Magazines (Hamilton and Hullar), 660

Ambler, Eric, 25

America's Secret Service Ace: The Operator #5 Story (Carr), 232

American Detective, The: An Illustrated History (Siegel), 97

American Private Eye, The: The Image in Fiction (Geherin), 95

Amos, William, 651, 652

And Then There Were Nine . . . More Women of Mystery (Bakerman), 242

Andrew, R. V., 334

Andrew Taylor (Tangled Web), 601

Androski, Helene, 66, 103

Ann Granger (Tangled Web), 424

Anne Perry and Charlotte and Thomas Pitt (Tangled Web), 533

Anne Perry's Pitt Series, 533

Années "Série Noire" Bibliographie, Critique, d'Une Collection Policière, Les (Mesplède), 185

Annotated Guide to the Work of Dorothy L. Sayers, An (Harmon and Burger), 565

Annotated Sherlock Holmes, The: The Four Novels and Fifty-Six Short Stories Complete, with an Introduction, Notes, and Bibliography (Baring-Gould), 384

Another Shirt Ruined: The Amelia Peabody Page (Knauff and Speckhardt), 536

Anthology Listings (Denton), 189

Anthony Berkeley Cox Files, The: Notes Towards a Bibliography (Johns/Locke), 344

Apostolou, John L., 701

April, Jo, 46

Arbuckle, H. C., 649

Arbur, Rosemarie, 275

Archives of Detective Fiction, The (Villines), 748

Ardai, Charles, 273

Arens, Arnold, 570

Armchair Detective Book of Lists, The: A Complete Guide to the Best Mystery, Crime, and Suspense Fiction (Stine), 153

Armchair Detective Book of Lists, The: A Complete Guide to the Best Mystery, Crime & Suspense Fiction (Strosser), 152

Armchair Detective Index, Volumes 1–10, 1967–1977, The (Stilwell), 210

Armchair Detective Index, Volumes 1–20, 1967–1987, The (Deeck and Stilwell), 211

Armour, Richard, 21

Art of the Mystery Story, The: A Collection of Critical Essays (Haycraft), 20, 21

Artists in Crime: An Illustrated Survey of Crime Fiction First Edition Dust-wrappers, 1920–1970 (Cooper and Pike), 716

Asdell, Philip T., 611

Asian American Mysteries List (Marple), 50

Asimov, Isaac, 45

At Wolfe's Door: The Nero Wolfe Novels of Rex Stout (Van Dover), 597

Aubrey, Irene E., 106

Auden, W. H., 24, 359, 707

August Derleth (1909–1971): A Bibliographical Checklist of His Works (Dutch), 368

August Derleth: A Bibliography (Wilson), 369

August Derleth: Thirty Years of Writing, 1926–1956 (Derleth), 366

August Derleth: Twenty Years of Writing, 1926–1946 (Derleth), 364

August Derleth: Twenty-Five Years of Writing, 1926–1951 (Derleth), 365

Australian Crime Fiction: A Bibliography 1857–1993 (Loder), 118

Author Index to the Doc Savage Magazine, The (Clark), 219

Author Price Guides: Agatha Christie (Ahearn), 313

Author Price Guides: Chester Himes (Ahearn), 458

Author Price Guides: Dick Francis (Ahearn), 405

Author Price Guides: Elmore Leonard (Ahearn), 480

Author Price Guides: Fredric Brown (Ahearn), 279

Author Price Guides: James Crumley (Ahearn), 347

Author Price Guides: James Lee Burke (Ahearn), 285

Author Price Guides: John D. MacDonald (Ahearn), 490

Author Price Guides: Leslie Charteris (Ahearn), 301

Author Price Guides: Martha Grimes (Ahearn), 426

Author Price Guides: P. D. James (Ahearn), 465

Author Price Guides: Patricia Cornwell (Ahearn), 340

Author Price Guides: Raymond Chandler (Ahearn), 295

Author Price Guides: Rex Stout (Ahearn), 592

Author Price Guides: Robert B. Parker (Ahearn), 529

Author Price Guides: Ross Macdonald [Kenneth Millar] (Ahearn), 505

Author Price Guides: Ross Thomas (Ahearn), 603

Author Price Guides: Sue Grafton (Ahearn), 421

Author Price Guides: Tony Hillerman (Ahearn), 449

Avenger, The (Finnan), 212

Avenger/Justice, Inc., The (Vaisala), 214

Avon Mystery (Cox), 156

Avram Cohen Mystery Series, The (Rosenberg), 554

Avram Davidson (Wessells), 352

Ayres, E. C., 265

Babcock, John, 146

Bagley, Desmond, 25

Bailey, H. C., 662

Baird, Newton, 280

Baker, Robert A., 94

Baker, Susan, 242

Baker Street Connection: A Sherlock Holmes Collection (Carroll), 390

Bakerman, Jane S., 242, 243

Ball, John, 666

Ballinger, John, 52

Bantam Doubleday Dell, 417, 473

Barbara Parker (Parker), 528

Barbara Paul's Home Page (Paul), 531

Barbara Vine (Tangled Web), 622

Barbara Wilson (Tangled Web), 642

Barer, Burl, 303

Bargainnier, Earl F., 243, 244

Baring-Gould, William S., 384

Barkocy, Muffy, 593

Barnard, Robert, 25

Barnes, Melvyn, 5, 6, 25

Barnett, Sandy, 7

Barzun, Jacques, 8, 9, 10, 108, 707

Baseball Mysteries List (Gants), 51

Bates, Susannah, 261

Battered Silicon Dispatch Box, 393

Baudou, Jacques, 167

Bayport Companion, The, 686, 687

Bedell, Jeanne F., 243, 244

Bedside, Bathtub & Armchair Companion to Agatha Christie, The (Riley and McAllister), 319

Bedside Companion to Crime, The (Keating), 24

Beetz, Kirk H., 335

Benbow-Pfalzgraf, Taryn, 260

Benson, Gordon, Jr., 276, 277, 517, 609, 620, 621

Benstock, Bernard, 245, 246, 247

Bentley, E. C., 662

Berro, Mike, 278

Best Detective Fiction: A Guide from Godwin to the Present (Barnes), 5

Biblio-Mysteries (Ballinger), 52

Bibliographical Catalogue of the Writings of Sir Arthur Conan Doyle, 1879–1928, A (Locke), 373

Bibliographie der Kriminalliteratur 1945–1984 im deutschen Sprachraum (Walkhoff-Jordan), 124

Bibliographie der Kriminalliteratur 1985–1990 im deutschen Sprachraum (Walkhoff-Jordan), 125

Bibliographie des Éditions Originales de Georges Simenon y Compris les OEuvres Publiées sous des Pseudonymes (Menguy), 574

Bibliography, Chronological Listing, and Comments on the Works of Major Percival Christopher Wren, I.A.R (Arbuckle), 649

Bibliography of A. Conan Doyle, A (Green and Gibson), 374

Bibliography of Christmas Mysteries, A (Wolfe), 58

Bibliography of Crime Fiction 1749–1975, The: Listing All Mystery, Detective, Suspense, Police, and Gothic Fiction in Book Form Published in the English Language (Hubin), 110

Bibliography of Dr. R. H. van Gulik (Litt), 615

Bibliography of Erle Stanley Gardner (Moore), 414

Bibliography of Mysteries from the 1920's and 1930's (Mercantile Library), 113

Bibliography of the Published Works of John D. MacDonald, with Selected Biographical Materials and Critical Essays, A (Shine), 498

Bibliography of the Works of Dorothy L. Sayers, A (Gilbert), 564

Bibliomysteries (McCurley), 53

Bigger Than Life: The Creator of Doc Savage (Cannaday), 361

Bill Pronzini: Mystery and Suspense Writer and Editor, 542

Black Bat, The (Brown and Sauer), 675

Blake, Nicholas, 21

Blei, Norbert, 368

Bleiler, E. F., 386, 701

Blixt, Johan, 635

Bloch, Robert, 15

Block, Lawrence, 15, 273

Bloody Dagger Reference: A Price Guide to Mystery-Crime-Detection (Pappas), 738

Bloom, Harold, 702, 703

Bloomsbury Good Reading Guide to Murder, Crime Fiction, and Thrillers (McLeish), 27

Boardman Crime and Science Fiction 1942–1967, A Checklist of the First Editions, with a Guide to Their Value (Greenslade, Lesser, Williams, and Spurrier), 157

Bob's Your Uncle: A Dictionary of Slang for British Mystery Fans (Turner-Lord), 4

Bodenheimer, Daniel, 304

Boettcher, Bonna J., 90

Book Binder, Author Sandra West Prowell, The (Prowell), 543

Book of Prefaces to Fifty Classics of Crime Fiction 1900–1950, A (Barzun and Taylor), 10

Book of Sleuths, The (Pate), 665

Booking Hawaii Five-O: An Episode and Critical History of the 1968–1980 Television Detective Series (Rhodes), 731

Books by Barbara D'Amato (D'Amato), 351

Boucher, Anthony, 21

Bourgeau, Art, 11

Boxtree Encyclopedia of TV Detectives, The (Tibbals), 728

Boys in the Black Mask, The: An Exhibit in the UCLA Library, January 6–February 10, 1961 (Smith), 116

Bradd, Sid, 222

Branche, Cal, 491

Breen, Jon L., 15, 60, 65, 153, 248, 450, 704, 705, 706

Brett, Simon, 15

Briggs, Matt, 518

Briney, Robert, 701

British Bibliography of Edgar Wallace, The (Lofts and Adley), 627

British Museum in Fiction, The: A Check-List (Ellis), 82

British Mystery and Thriller Writers Since 1940, First Series (Benstock and Staley), 247

British Mystery Writers, 1860–1919 (Benstock and Staley), 245

British Mystery Writers, 1920–1939 (Benstock and Staley), 246

Bronze Age, The: An Alternate Doc Savage Chronology (Lai), 679

Brown, Elizabeth, 280

Brown, Fredric, 280

Brown, Michael R., 231, 233

Brown, Michael Rogero, 218, 235, 236, 241, 653, 675, 690

Brown, Watson 1945–1957 (Holland), 159

Bruccoli, Matthew J., 296, 297, 506, 507
Bruno Fischer (Williams), 403
Buckholtz, Eileen, 650
Budd, Elaine, 249
Bullard, Scott R., 381
Bullets and Beer: The Spenser Home Page
(Loux), 530
Bunson, Matthew E., 381
Burger, Margaret A., 565
Burgess, Michael, 715
Burkey, Alisa Mueller, 145
By a Woman's Hand: A Guide to Mystery
Fiction by Women (Swanson and
James), 255, 256

Cadfael Companion, The: The World of Brother
Cadfael (Whiteman), 539, 540
Cail, Carol, 291
Camp, Roswell Anthony, 560
Campbell, Frank D., Jr., 492
Campbell, Heather, 81
Campion List ("Father Brown"), 263
Canadian Crime Fiction: An Annotated Com-
prehensive Bibliography of Canadian
Crime Fiction from 1817 to 1996 and
Biographical Dictionary of Canadian
Crime Writers, with an Introductory
Essay on the History and Development
of Canadian Crime Writings (Skene
Melvin), 120
Cannaday, Marilyn, 361
Cannell, Dorothy, 15
Caribbean Soulman, 493
Carmichael, Ian, 45
Carol Cail's Home Page (Cail), 291
Carol O'Connell and Kathy Mallory (Tangled
Web), 527
Carolyn G. Hart List (Johnston), 442
Carpentieri, Tony, 682, 683, 684
Carr, John Dickson, 21, 707
Carr, Nick, 222, 232, 654
Carr, Wooda Nick. *See* Carr, Nick
Carroll, David, 390
Carroll John Daly Online! (Pulp Fiction
Central), 350
Carter, D. F, 406
Carter, John, 21, 114
Carter, Steven F., 243

Case of the Missing Detective Stories, The: A
List of Books Desired in the Detective
Fiction Collection of the University of
North Carolina Library (Gribbin),
18
Casey, Robert J., 21
Cassiday, Bruce, 47, 320, 707
Cataio, Joseph, 12
Catalogue of Crime [Being a Reader's Guide to
the Literature of Mystery, Detection,
& Related Genres], A (Barzun and
Taylor), 8, 9
Catherine Lucille Moore and Henry Kuttner: A
Marriage of Souls and Talent (Utter,
Benson, and Stephenson-Payne),
517
Cavolina, Jane, 14
Celia Fremlin (Tangled Web), 409
Chandler, Raymond, 21
Charles Willeford (Denton), 638
Charles Willeford (Tangled Web), 639
Charlie Chan at the Movies: History,
Filmography, and Criticism
(Hanke), 730
Charteris, Leslie, 662
Chassie West (West), 633
Checklist of Arthur Upfield, A (Stephens),
612
Checklist of David Goodis, A (Stephens),
419
Checklist of Detective Short Stories, A
(Mundell), 191
Checklist of Detective Short Stories, A:
Supplement One (Mundell), 192
Checklist of Elmore Leonard, A (Stephens),
481
Checklist of Fredric Brown, A (Stephens),
281
Checklist of Loren D. Estleman, A (Stephens),
400
Checklist of Percival Christopher Wren, A
(Stephens), 649
Checklist of Ross Thomas, A (Stephens), 604
Checklist of the Publications of Dennis
McMillan, A (Stephens), 178
Checklist of Wilson Tucker, A (Stephens),
608
Cherry Ames Page, The (Mikucki), 676
Cherry Tree Books 1937–1953 (Williams),
160

Chester Himes (Daniels), 459

Chester Himes: An Annotated Primary and Secondary Bibliography (Fabre, Skinner, and Sullivan), 460

Chester, John, 602

Chesterton, G. K., 21, 307, 308, 707

Chesterton Continued: A Bibliographical Supplement, Together with Some Uncollected Prose and Verse by G. K. Chesterton (Sullivan), 309

Chesterton Society, G. K., 311a

Chesterton Three: A Bibliographical Postscript (Sullivan), 310

Chittenden, Meg, 312

Choi, Soon Y., 78

Chouteau, Neysa, 242

Christ, Jay Finley, 376

Christie, Agatha, 46

Christie in Order (Santangelo), 322

Christie List, The (Ho), 316

Christie Society, Agatha, 331a

Christmas Mysteries, 56

Christopher West (Tangled Web), 634

Chronology of Shadows (Lai), 697

Clark, Mary Higgins, 14, 332

Clark, Meera, 244

Clark, William J., 219, 428, 496

Clarke, Stephan P., 563

Classic Crime and Suspense Writers (Bloom), 702

Classic Mystery Writers (Bloom), 703

Cleveland, Carol, 242

ClueLass Homepage: A Mystery Lover's Notebook (Derie), 740

Cockrum, Kurt, 618

Cohn, Jan, 243

Cole, G. D. H. and Margaret, 662

Cole, Margaret. *See* Cole, G. D. H. and Margaret

Collecting Bibliomysteries (Ballinger), 52

Collecting Shane Stevens a.k.a. J. W. Rider (Legg), 591

Collecting Tony Hillerman: A Checklist of the First Editions of Tony Hillerman, with Approximate Value and Commentary (Hieb), 451

Collector's Book of Detective Fiction, The (Quayle), 38

Collector's Guide to Hardcover Boy's Series Books, A; or, Tracing the Trail of Harry Hudson (Mattson and Davis), 663

College Mystery Novels: An Annotated Bibliography, Including a Guide to Professorial Series-Character Sleuths (Kramer), 64

Collingwood, Donna, 736

Collins, Max Allan, 248

Collins, Michael Leo, 380

Collins, William, 327

Collins Crime Club: A Checklist of the First Editions, with a Guide to Their Value (Foord, Williams, and Spurrier), 161

Collins White Circle Books 1936–1959 (Williams), 162

Companion to the Mystery of Edwin Drood, The (Jacobson), 371

Complete Maigret, The: From Simenon's Original Novels to Granada's Much Acclaimed TV Series (Haining), 572

Complete Robert Bloch, The: An Illustrated, International Bibliography (Larson), 271

Comprehensive Index to Black Mask, 1920–1951, A: With Brief Annotations, Preface, and Editorial Apparatus (Hagemann), 215

Comprehensive Michael Innes List (McAllister), 464

Comprehensive Price List of Crime, Mystery, Thriller and Detective Fiction, A (Snow), 739

Conan Doyle Bibliography: A Bibliography of the Works of Sir Arthur Conan Doyle, M.D., LL.D. (1859–1930) (Goldscheider), 373

Condon, Richard, 14

Conquest, John, 655

Contento, William G., 188, 197

Cook, Michael L., 180, 181, 198, 199, 200, 201

Cooper, John, 13, 716

Copperfield Checklist of Mystery Authors, The: The Complete Crime Works of 100 Distinguished Writers of Mystery and Detective Fiction (Granovetter), 16

Copperfield Checklist of Mystery Authors, The: The Complete Crime Works of 100 Distinguished Writers of Mystery and Detective Fiction (McCallum and Granovetter), 17

Corgi and Scottie Books 1951–1960 (Williams), 163

Cornell Woolrich (William Irish, George Hopley). A Catalogue of First and Variant Editions of His Work, Including Anthology and Magazine Appearances (Stewart), 648

Corpus Delecti of Mystery Fiction: A Guide to the Body of the Case (Herman and Stiel), 253

Counselman, Mary E., 269

Cox, J. Randolph, 156, 166, 199, 224, 226, 227, 228, 229, 230, 231, 418, 701, 708

Cozies: A Selective List (Antroski), 66

Crespi, Camilla T., 345

Crider, Bill, 248

Crime, Detective, Espionage, Mystery, and Thriller Fiction & Film: A Comprehensive Bibliography of Critical Writing Through 1979 (Skene Melvin), 712

Crime Fiction: 1749–1980: A Comprehensive Bibliography (Hubin), 111

Crime Fiction II: A Comprehensive Bibliography 1749–1990 (Hubin), 112

Crime Fiction Criticism: An Annotated Bibliography (Johnson), 710

Crimes of the Scene: A Mystery Novel Guide for the International Traveler (King and Winks), 135

Critical Survey of Mystery and Detective Fiction (Magill), 29

Cross, Robert S., 463

Crossen, Ken, 21

Crown Crime Companion, The: The Top 100 Mystery Novels of All Time, Selected by the Mystery Writers of America (Penzler, Friedman, Ginna, and Cavolina), 14

Cuppy, Will, 21

Curran, Daniel, 723

Curtis Warren and Grant Hughes (Holland), 164

Cyril Hare (1900–1958), 441

D'Amato, Barbara, 351

D. G. Compton and Alex Duncan (Tangled Web), 339

Daheim, Mary, 349

Dale, Alzina Stone, 138, 141, 145, 146

Dale, Kenneth Herrick, 141

Dale Furutani (Furutani), 412

Dan Fowler: Ace of the G-Men (Johnson), 677

Dana Stabenow's Home Page (Stabenow), 585

Daniel Woodrell (Tangled Web), 647

Daniels, Valarie, 48, 459, 520

Dashiell Hammett (Denton), 432

Dashiell Hammett: A Casebook (Nolan), 439

Dashiell Hammett: A Descriptive Bibliography (Layman), 435

Dashiell Hammett and Raymond Chandler: A Checklist and Bibliography of Their Paperback Appearances, Raymond Chandle (Lovisi), 300, 436

Dashiell Hammett Tour (Herron), 143

David Lindsey: On-line with the Best Selling Author (Lindsey), 484

David Williams (Tangled Web), 640

Davidson, Lionel, 25

Davies, Linda, 354

Davis, Dorothy Salisbury, 15

Davis, Thomas (Tom) B., 663

Day, Dianne, 357

Day-Lewis, the Poet Laureate: A Bibliography (Handley-Taylor and Smith), 359

de la Mare, Walter, 308

de Waal, Ronald Burt, 368, 377, 378, 379

Deadly Directory, The (Villines), 737

DeAndrea, William L., 1

Deeck, William F., 153, 211, 225

Deighton, Len, 25

Dell Great Mystery Library, The (Cox), 166

Dell Paperbacks 1942 to Mid-1962: A Catalog-Index (Lyles), 165

DellaCava, Frances A., 656

DeMarr, Mary Jean, 244

Denise Dietz Wiley (Wiley), 637

Denton, William, 2, 189, 288, 292, 298, 432, 494, 508, 638

Derek Wilson's Tim Lacy Artworld Mysteries (Tangled Web), 643

Derie, Kate, 142, 740

Derleth, August, 364, 365, 366, 367, 368

Derteth Societies, August, 370a

Detecting Men: Pocket Guide (Heising), 88

Detecting Women: A Reader's Guide and Checklist for Mystery Series Written by Women (Heising), 250

Detecting Women 2: A Reader's Guide and Checklist for Mystery Series Written by Women (Heising), 251

Detecting Women 2: Pocket Guide: A Checklist for Mystery Series Written by Women (Heising), 104

Detection in Science Fiction & Fantasy (Herald), 99

Detectionary: A Biographical Dictionary of Leading Characters in Detective and Mystery Fiction, Including Famous and Little-Known Sleuths, Their Helpers, Rogues Both Heroic and Sinister, and Some of Their Most Memorable Adventures, As Recounted in Novels, Short Stories, and Films (Penzler), 667, 668

Detective and Mystery Fiction: An International Bibliography of Secondary Sources (Albert), 700, 701

Detective and the Toga, The (Heli), 77

Detective Fiction: A Reader's Guide (Stevenson), 42

Detective Fiction: An Annotated Bibliography of Critical Writings (Hanrahan), 709

Detective Fiction: The Collector's Guide (Cooper and Pike), 13

Detective Mystery Crime Magazines (Mundell), 205

Detective Short Story, The: A Bibliography (Queen), 194, 195

Detective Short Story, The: A Bibliography and Index (Mundell and Rausch), 193

Detektiver på Frimärken (Hedman), 101

Deveny, Jack, 222

Dick Francis (Messall), 407

Digging for Clues: Mysteries in the Garden (St. Charles Public Library), 67

Digit Books 1956–1966 (Holland and Williams), 168

Dime Detective Index (Traylor), 217

Dime Novel Round-Up: Bibliographic Listing (Cox), 224, 228, 229, 230

Doc Savage (Brown), 218

Doc Savage (Finnan), 220

Doc Savage: His Apocalyptic Life As the Archangel of Technopolis, As the Golden-eyed Hero of 181 Supersagas, As the Bronze Knight of the Running Board, Including His Final Battle Against the Forces of Hell Itself (Farmer), 678

Doc Savage: The Supreme Adventurer (Smalley), 681

Doc Savage Unchained! (Sines), 680

Donald E. Westlake (Blixt), 635

Dorothy L. Sayers: A Reference Guide (Youngberg), 566

Double Trouble: A Bibliographic Chronicle of Ace Mystery Doubles (Jaffery), 154

Doubleday Crime Club Compendium 1928–1991 (Nehr), 169

Douglas, Carole Nelson, 372

Dove, George N., 242, 244

Doyle, Arthur Conan, 384

Drew, Bernard A., 89, 199, 657

Drood Review's 1989 Mystery Yearbook, The (Huang), 109

Duende History of The Shadow Magazine, The (Murray), 239

Dutch, William, 368

E. C. Ayres Homepage (Ayres), 265

Écrits sur le Roman Policier: Bibliographie Analytique et Critique des Études & Essais sur le Roman et le Film Policiers (Spehner and Allard), 714

Ed McBain (King), 486

Eden, Dorothy, 25

Edgar Awards (Slavin), 151

Edgar Wallace: A Filmography (Williams), 628

Edgar Wallace: First American Editions (Kiddle and Williams), 626

Edgar Wallace British Magazine Appearances (Fiction) (Williams), 629

Edgar Wallace Index (Williams), 630

Edgar Wallace Index (Books and Fiction), The (Williams), 631

Edgar Wallace Paperbacks: A Bibliographic Checklist by Imprint. With Valuations (Williams and Kiddle), 632

Edmund Crispin Archive, The (Needblake), 346

Edward D. Hoch Bibliography, 1955–1991 (Moffatt, Nevins, and Lachman), 461

87th Precinct (Stybr), 487

Eisgruber, Frank, Jr., 237

Elizabeth Daniels Squire (Squire), 584

Elizabeth George (Bantam Doubleday Dell), 417

Elizabeth Peters (James), 535

Elizabeth Quinn's Homepage (Quinn), 546

Ellery Queen (Gideon), 544

Ellin, Stanley, 25

Ellis, Edward F., 82

Ellis Peters/Edith Pargeter (Johnston), 538

Ellison, Harlan, 269

Ellroy Confidential (Perani), 398

Elmore Leonard (Tangled Web), 482

Elspeth Huxley: A Bibliography (Cross, Perkin, and Huxley), 463

Encyclopaedia Sherlockiana, The; or, A Universal Dictionary of the State of Knowledge of Sherlock Holmes and His Biographer John H. Watson, M.D (Tracy), 383

Encyclopedia Mysteriosa: A Comprehensive Guide to the Art of Detection in Print, Film, Radio, and Television (DeAndrea), 1

Encyclopedia of Mystery and Detection (Steinbrunner and Penzler), 3

Encyclopedia Sherlockiana: An A-to-Z Guide to the World of the Great Detective (Bunson), 381

Enes Smith (Smith), 581

Engel, Madeline H., 656

EQMM 350: An Author/Title Index to Ellery Queen's Mystery Magazine Fall 1941 Through January 1973 (Nieminski), 221

Erle Stanley Gardner: A Checklist (Mundell), 415, 416

Erle Stanley Gardner: The Case of the Real Perry Mason (Hughes), 414

Erle Stanley Gardner Home Page, The (Miller), 413

Erle Stanley Gardner's Ventura (Senate), 413

Ernest Bramah Bibliography: Books (Berro), 278

Estleman, Loren D., 248

Evanovich, Janet, 401

Ewart, Gawain, 24

Excursions in Victorian Bibliography (Sadleir), 335

F and SF Mystery (Frants), 98

Fabre, Michel, 460

Famous Movie Detectives (Pitts), 725

Famous Movie Detectives II (Pitts), 726

Fantasms: A Bibliography of the Literature of Jack Vance (Levack and Underwood), 617

Fantasms II: A Bibliography of the Works of Jack Vance (Cockrum, Levack, and Underwood), 618

Farah, David, 691

Farah's Guide (Farah), 691

Farmer, Philip José, 363, 678

Fatal Art of Entertainment, The: Interviews with Mystery Writers (Herbert), 252

"Father Brown," 263

Feder, Sue, 707

Female Detectives in American Novels: A Bibliography and Analysis of Serialized Female Sleuths (DellaCava and Engel), 656

Feminine Perspective, The: Crime Fiction by and About Women (James), 105

Fiddy, Dick, 306

Fifty Foreign Firsts: A Tony Hillerman Checklist (Hieb), 452

File of Mystery Authors and Their Pseudonyms (Kenner), 262

Financial Thrillers by Linda Davies (Davies), 354

Finch, Jim, 658

Fine Art of Murder, The: The Mystery Reader's Indispensable Companion (Gorman), 15

Finnan, R. W., 212, 220, 685, 689, 692, 693

First Hundred Years of Detective Fiction, The. 1841–1941. By One Hundred Authors on the Hundred Thirtieth Anniversary of the First Publication in Book Form of Edgar Allan Poe's "The Murders in the Rue Morgue" Philadelphia, 1843 ([Randall?]),115

First You Dream, Then You Die (Nevins), 648

Fisher, Benjamin Franklin, IV, 264

Fitzgibbon, Russell H., 314

Flanagan, Graeme, 269

Fleming, Ian, 707

Flora, Kate, 404

Flying Spy, The: A History of G-8 (Carr), 222

Foord, Peter, 161, 571

Four Square Books 1–322 (1957–1960) (Williams), 170

Foxwell, Beth, 149

Francis Listing (Carter), 406

Frank and Joe Turn Blue (Carpentieri), 682, 683, 684

Frank Gruber Index, The (Clark), 428

Frants, Marina, 98

Frederick Irving Anderson (1877–1947): A Biobibliography (Fisher), 264

Fredric Brown: British and American Books and Films: A Checklist (Williams), 282

Freeling, Nicholas, 666

Freeman, R. Austin, 21, 662

Fremont Jones: A Few Words from the Author (Day), 357

Friedland, Susan, 130

Friedman, Mickey, 14

Friedman, Philip, 273

Furlong, Leslie, 605

Furutani, Dale, 412

G. K. Chesterton (Ward), 311

G. K. Chesterton: A Bibliography, with an Essay, on Books, by G. K. Chesterton (Sullivan), 308

G. K. Chesterton Society, 311a

Gaiman, Neil, 660

Gaines, Elizbeth A., 450

Gangland's Doom (Eisgruber), 237

Gants, Susan E., 51

Gardner, Erle Stanley, 21

Gardner, John, 14, 25

Gaskill, Rex W., 242

Gay and Lesbian Characters and Themes in Mystery Novels: A Critical Guide to over 500 Works in English (Slide), 68

Gee, Robin, 736

Geherin, David, 95

Gendai Kaigai Misuteri Besuto (Jinka), 127

Georges Simenon: A Bibliography of the British First Editions in Hardback and Paperback and of the Principal French and American Editions, with a Guide to Their Value, edited by Richard Williams and Sally Swan (Foord, Swan, and Williams), 571

Georges Simenon: A Checklist of His "Maigret" and Other Mystery Novels and Short Stories in French and English Translation (Young), 578

Georges Simenon's Inspector Maigret (Trussel), 577

Gertrude Stein and the Vital Dead (Stewart), 698

Gibbs, Rowan, 512

Gibson, John Michael, 374

Gibson, Walter B., 238, 666

Gideon, David, 544

Gilbert, Colleen B., 564

Gilbert, Michael, 25

Ginna, Peter, 14

Girl in the Pictorial Wrapper, The: An Index to Reviews of Paperback Original Novels in the New York Times' "Criminals at Large" Column, 1953–1970 (Breen), 704

Girls Series Books: A Checklist of Hardback Books Published 1900–1975 (University of Minnesota, Children's Literature Research Collections), 673

Girls Series Books: A Checklist of Titles Published 1840–1991 (University of Minnesota, Children's Literature Research Collections), 674

Glick, Ruth, 650

Glover, Dorothy, 114

Goldscheider, Gaby, 373

Golf Murders Collection, The: A Reader's and Collector's Illustrated Guide to Golf Mystery Fiction (Taylor), 70

Golf Mysteries (Leininger), 69

Gollancz Crime Fiction 1928–1988, a Checklist of the First Editions, with a Guide to Their Value (Williams and Spurrier), 171

Gonda, Manji and Nakajima, 127

Gonda, Nakajima. *See* Gonda, Manji and Nakajima

Gorman, Ed, 15, 248

Gothic Novels of the Twentieth Century: An Annotated Bibliography (Radcliffe), 71

Gotwald, Frederick G., 594

Goulart, Ron, 72

Gould, Chester, 666

Grafton, Sue, 14, 422

Graham, Philip, 25

Gramol Group 1932–1937, The (Holland and Williams), 172

Granovetter, Pamela, 16, 17

Gray Nemesis, The (Hopkins), 213

Grayson, Rupert, 662

Great Detective Pictures, The (Parrish and Pitts), 724

Great Detectives, The (Penzler), 666

Great Women Mystery Writers: Classic to Contemporary (Klein), 254

Green, Joseph, 658

Green, Richard Lancelyn, 374

Greenberg, Martin H., 60, 188, 248, 450

Greene, Douglas, 153

Greene, Graham, 114, 374, 707

Greenslade, Lyndsey, 157

Gribbin, Lenore S., 18, 107

Grierson, Francis D., 662

Griffith, Thomas H., 87

Grigg, David R., 336

Grilley, Kate, 425

Grimes, Larry E., 244

Grimes, Terris McMahan, 427

Grobius Shortling's John Dickson Carr Page (Shortling), 294

Grost, Michael E., 19, 408

Guide to Classic Mystery and Detection, A (Grost), 19

Guide to the First Editions of Edgar Wallace, A (Kiddle), 625

Guilty Parties: A Mystery Lover's Companion (Ousby), 34

Gumshoe Site (Kimura), 741

Gun in Cheek: A Study of "Alternative" Crime Fiction (Pronzini), 35

Gunnison, John P., 202

Guy N. Smith (Tangled Web), 582

Gwendoline Butler (Tangled Web), 290

Gwinn, Nancy E., 82

H. R. F. Keating (Tangled Web), 468

Hagemann, E. R., 199, 215

Hagen, Ordean, 108

Hager, Jean, 429

Hailey, J. P., 430

Haining, Peter, 315, 387, 388, 389, 572

Halegua, Mark S., 695

Hall, Alison, 83

Hall, Graham M., 270

Hall, Parnell, 430

Halliday, Brett, 666

Hamilton, Donald, 666

Hamilton, Frank, 659, 660

Hamilton, Lyn, 431

Hamilton and Panther Books 1945–1956 (Holland and Williams), 173

Hammer, Diane, 450

Hammett, Dashiell, 21

Hammett and His Continental Op, 433

Hammett-List WWW Page, The (Johnson), 434

Handley-Taylor, Geoffrey, 359

Hanke, Ken, 730

Hannah Wakefield and Dee Street (Tangled Web), 623

Hanrahan, Rita M., 709

Hardboiled: The Online Reference Site for All Things Noir (Murray), 743

Hardboiled America (O'Brien), 73

Hard-Boiled Dick, The: A Personal Check-List (Sandoe), 74

Hardboiled Dicks, The (Goulart), 72

Hardboiled Era, The: A Checklist, 1929–1958 (O'Brien), 73

Hard-Boiled Explicator, The: A Guide to the Study of Dashiell Hammett, Raymond Chandler and Ross Macdonald (Skinner), 713

Hardeen, George, 450

Hardy Boys Mystery Stories, The (Johnson), 688

Harmon, Jim, 717

Harmon, Robert B., 565

Harper, Carol, 61

Harper, Katherine, 289

Harry Stephen Keeler Home Page (Poundstone), 471

Harry Stephen Keeler Society (Polt), 470

Hart, Carolyn G., 15

Hasnes, Geir, 307

Hatchards Crime Companion, The: 100 Top Crime Novels Selected by the Crime Writers' Association (Moody), 32

Haycraft, Howard, 20, 21, 22, 23, 153

Hayne, Barrie, 243, 244

Hayter, Sparkle, 444

Heartbeat TV Series (Tangled Web), 732

Hecht, Ben, 21

Hedman, Iwan. *See* Hedman-Morelius, Iwan

Hedman-Morelius, Iwan, 101, 131, 132, 302, 701

Heffelfinger, Charles, 686, 687

Heilbrun, Carolyn G., 707

Heising, Willeta L., 88, 104, 250, 251

Heli, Rick, 77

Hendershott, Barbara Sloan, 145, 146

Henderson, Lesley, 259

Herald, Diana Tixier, 99

Herbert, Rosemary, 252

Here Be Mystery and Murder: Reference Books in the Mystery Genre, Excluding Sherlockiana (Lindsay), 711

Herman, Linda, 253

Hermans, Willy, 119

Hero Pulp Index, The (McKinstry and Weinberg), 203

Hero Pulp Index, The (Weinberg and McKinstry), 204

Hero Pulp Reprint Index (Thom), 196

Heroines: A Bibliography of Women Series Characters in Mystery, Espionage, Action, Science Fiction, Fantasy, Horror, Western, Romance and Juvenile Novels (Drew), 657

Herron, Don, 143

Hess, Joan, 15

Hewett, Jerry, 619

Hieb, Louis A., 451, 452, 453, 454, 455, 456

Highsmith, Patricia, 25

Hill, Reginald, 24, 25, 660

Hillich, Reinhard, 123

Historical Mystery Bibliography (James and Choi), 78

History of the Mystery, The: An Interactive Journey (Barnett), 7

Ho, Dora, 316

Hoch, Edward D., 15, 60

Hodder and Stoughton 1926–1960 (Williams), 174

Holland, Stephen, 159, 164, 168, 172, 173, 177, 179, 184, 186, 187, 548

Honce, Charles, 586

Hopkins, Howard, 213

Horler, Sydney, 662

Hornsby, Wendy, 273, 525

Howard, Tom, 718, 719, 720

Howe, Gerry, 408

Huang, Jim, 109

Hubin, Allen J., 108, 110, 111, 112

Hughes, Dorothy B., 25, 414

Hughes, Matt, 462

Hullar, Link, 659, 660

Humorous Mysteries (Wittman), 80

Hundred Best Crime Stories, The (Symons), 44

Husby, Noralf, 307

Hutchinson Group Post-War Numbered Series, Later Arrow Books 1949–1960 (Williams), 175

Huxley, Elspeth, 463

Hvem Begik Hvad? Dansk Kriminalliteratur indtil 1979: En Bibliografi København [i.e., Copenhagen] (Nielsen), 121

Ian Rankin in His Own Words (Tangled Web), 547

Illustrierte Geschichte der Kriminalliteratur (Woeller), 47

Imaginary People: A Who's Who of Fictional Characters from the Eighteenth Century to the Present Day (Pringle), 670

Imaginary People: A Who's Who of Modern Fictional Characters (Pringle), 669

Index des Personnages de Georges Simenon (Lemoine), 573

Index of Black Mask, An (Mundell), 216
Index of Small Hero Pulps from Dell [and others] (Brown and Sauer), 653
Index to Crime and Mystery Anthologies (Contento and Greenberg), 188
Index to the JDM Bibliophile, An (Shines), 223
Index to the Universal Sherlock Holmes (de Waal), 379
Informal Reading List, An (Goulart), 72
Ingravallo, Ciccio, 126
Insight Guide: Native America (Hardeen), 450
International Sherlock Holmes, The: A Companion Volume to the World Bibliography of Sherlock Holmes and Dr. Watson (de Waal), 378
Irish Mystery (Ingravallo), 126

J. C. Masterman (Tangled Web), 515
Jack Vance: A Fantasmic Imagination (Stephensen-Payne and Benson), 620
Jack Vance: A Fantasmic Imagination, A Working Bibliography (Stephensen-Payne and Benson), 621
Jackie Manthorne (Manthorne), 511
Jacobson, Wendy S., 371
Jacovetty, Vincent L., 561
Jaffery, Sheldon, 154
Jakubowsky, Maxim, 661
James Ellroy (Tangled Web), 399
James Lee Burke and Dave Robicheaux (Tangled Web), 287
James Lee Burke Internet Guide, The (Steffensen), 286
James M. Cain (Denton), 292
James M. Cain (King), 293
James Sallis (Tangled Web), 559
James, Dean, 78, 105, 255, 256, 535
James, Russell, 466
Janet Evanovich Online (Evanovich), 401
Janice Law (Law), 478
Jarvis, Mary J., 102
Jay Russell (Russell), 556
Jay Russell (Tangled Web), 557

JDM Master Checklist, The: A Bibliography of the Published Writings of John D. MacDonald (Moffatt and Clark), 496
JDM Quotations (Rufener), 497
Jean Hager (Hager), 429
Jeffery Deaver (Tangled Web), 360
Jinka, Katsuo, 127
Joe R. Lansdale (Lansdale), 476
Joe R. Lansdale (Tangled Web), 477
John Baker (Tangled Web), 267
John D. MacDonald (Denton), 494
John D. MacDonald: A Checklist of Collectible Editions and Translations with Notes on Prices (MacLean), 495
John D. MacDonald: A True Bibliophile (Shine), 499
John D. MacDonald and the Colorful World of Travis McGee (Campbell), 492
John D. MacDonald Homepage, The (Branche), 491
John Mortimer Page (Briggs), 518
John Sandford (Camp), 560
John Sandford (Jacovetty), 561
John Straley and Cecil Younger, PI (Tangled Web), 598
Johns, Ayresome, 344
Johnson, Deidre, 791
Johnson, Joseph M., 434
Johnson, Julia, 710
Johnson, Timothy W., 710
Johnson, Tom, 677, 696
Johnston, Gerald Hankins, 538, 442, 688, 694
Jollans, Alastair, 155
Jonasson, Ragnar, 317
Jonathan and Faye Kellerman: American and English Publications, 1972–1996 (Seels), 472
Jonathan Kellerman (Bantam Doubleday Dell), 473
Joseph Hansen and Dave Brandstetter (Tangled Web), 440
Joyner, Nancy C., 243
Judith Cutler (Tangled Web), 348
Judith Hawkes (Tangled Web), 443
Judy Bolton Series Books (Finnan), 689

Julian Symons: A Bibliography with Commentaries and a Personal Memoir by Julian Symons and a Preface by H. R. F. Keating (Walsdorf and Allen), 600

Junot, Jim, 341

Kate Flora's Home Page/Kate's Lair (Flora), 404

Katherine Ross Home Page, The (Ross and Wicker), 555

Keating, H. R. F., 14, 15, 24, 25, 45, 153, 600, 666

Keegan, Alex, 469

Keene, Carolyn, 666

Kelleher, Brian, 729

Kellerman, Faye, 472

Kellerman, Jonathan, 472

Kelley, George, 248

Kemelman, Harry, 60

Kemper, Lisa, 410

Kenner, Pat, 262

Kenneth Millar/Ross Macdonald: A Checklist (Bruccoli), 506

Key to Fredric Brown's Wonderland, A: A Study and an Annotated Bibliographical Checklist with Reminiscences by Elizabeth Brown and Harry Altshuler and "It's Only Everything" by Fredric Brown (Baird), 280

Kiddle, Charles, 625, 626, 632

Kienzle, William X., 60

Killer Beside Me, The: The Jim Thompson Resource Page (Furlong), 605

Kimura, Jiro, 741

King, David J., 272, 293, 299, 423, 486, 509

King, Nina, 135

King, Stephen, 15, 46

King, Tabitha, 46

Kinky Friedman (Kuilder), 411

Kinky Friedman Site, The (Kemper), 410

Klein, Kathleen Gregory, 242, 243, 254, 707

Knauff, Margie, 536

Knepper, Marty, 244

Knox, Ronald A., 21, 34

Kobayashi, Susumu, 284

Kramer, John E., Jr., 64

Kramer, John E., III, 64

Kriminaliteratur der DDR 1949–1990, Die: Bibliografie (Hillich and Mittmann), 123

Kriminallitteratur på Svenska 1749–1985 (Hedman-Morelius), 131

Kriminallitteratur på Svenska 1986–1990 (Hedman-Morelius), 132

Kristick, Laurel, 62, 92

Kuilder, Gerrit, 411

Kumagai, Kasho, 137

la Cour, Tage, 26, 190

Lachman, Marvin, 49, 153, 248, 461

Lai, Rick, 679, 697

Landmark Publications in Mystery and Detective Fiction (Sutherland), 117

Lang, Roger, 46

Langton, Jane, 46

Lansdale, Joe R., 476, 477

Larson, Randall D., 269, 271

Last Bookman, The (Ruber), 588, 589

Lauren Henderson (Tangled Web), 445

Laurie R. King (Tangled Web), 474

Law, Janice, 478

Lawmen in Scarlet: An Annotated Guide to Royal Canadian Mounted Police in Print and Performance (Drew), 89

Lawrence, Martha C, 479

Lawrence Block (King), 272

Lawrence Block: Bernie Rhodenbarr and Evan Tanner (Tangled Web), 274

Lawrence Block: Bibliography 1958–1993 (Seels), 273

Lawson, Janet, 136

Layman, Richard, 435

Leacock, Stephen, 21

Legal Thrillers (Campbell), 81

Legg, John, 591

Leiber, Fritz, 269

Leigh Brackett & Edmond Hamilton: The Enchantress & The World Wrecker: A Working Bibliography (Benson), 277

Leigh Brackett, Marion Zimmer Bradley, Anne McCaffrey: A Primary and Secondary Bibliography (Arbur), 275

Leigh Douglas Brackett and Edmond Hamilton: A Working Bibliography (Benson), 276

Leininger, John, 69

Lemoine, Michel, 573

Leo Bruce Homepage (Kobayashi), 284

Leslie Charteris och Helgonet under 5 Decennier en Bio-Bibliographi (Alexandersson and Hedman), 302

Lesser, Tom, 157

Lester Dent: The Man Behind Doc Savage (Weinberg), 363

Lester Dent: The Man, His Craft and His Market (McCarey-Laird), 362

Levack, Daniel J. H., 617, 618

Levine, Paul, 483

Lewis, Paul, 337

Lia Matera's Web Site (Matera), 516

Library Mysteries: A Halloween Sampler (Gwinn), 82

Library Mysteries Bibliography (Hall), 83

Linda Davies (Tangled Web), 355

Lindkvist, Karl-Erik, 510

Lindsay, Ethel, 711

Lindsey, David, 484

Lindsey Davies (Tangled Web), 356

Lingblom, Hans E., 133

Lion Books and the Lion Library: A Checklist (Stephens), 176

List Nero, 595

List of Married (Fictional) Sleuths, A (Griffith), 87

List of the Original Appearances of Dashiell Hammett's Magazine Work, A (Mundell), 437, 438

Literary Symbiosis, A: Science Fiction/ Fantasy Mystery (Pierce), 100

Literature of Crime and Detection, The: An Illustrated History from Antiquity to the Present (Woeller and Cassiday), 47

Liza Cody: Anna Lee & Eva Wylie (Tangled Web), 333

Lochte, Dick, 248

Locke, George, 344

Locke, H., 373

Locked Room Murders and Other Impossible Crimes (Adey), 85, 86

Loder, John, 118

Lofts, W. O. G., 305, 627

Lord Peter Wimsey Companion, The (Clarke), 563

Loux, Mike, 530

Lovallo, Len, 323, 324

Lovesey, Peter, 14

Lovisi, Gary, 100, 300, 375, 436

Luber, Philip, 485

Lucas, E. V., 21

Lundin, Bo, 131

Lyles, William H., 165

Lyn Hamilton (Hamilton), 431

Lynn S. Hightower (Tangled Web), 447

MacDonald, John D., 15

Macdonald, Ross, 666, 699

MacDonald Potpourri . . . Being a Miscellany of Post-Perusal Pleasures of the John D. MacDonald Books for Bibliophiles, Bibliographers and Bibliomaniacs, A (Shine), 500

MacLean, David C., 495

MacLeod, Charlotte, 15

McAllister, Jill, 464

McAllister, Pam, 319, 320

McBain, Ed, 35, 666

McCallum, Karen Thomas, 17

McCarey-Laird, M. Martin, 362

McCarty, John, 729

McCurley, Marsha, 53

McDonald, Gregory, 14, 25

McKinstry, Lohr, 203, 204

McLeish, Kenneth and Valerie, 27

McLeish, Valerie. *See* McLeish, Kenneth and Valerie

Mackler, Tasha, 28

Madden, Cecil, 662

Magdalen Nabb (Tangled Web), 523

Magic Dragon Multimedia, 742

Magill, Frank N., 29

Magnet Detective Library (Cox), 224

Mallett, Daryl F., 619

Malloy, William, 735

Man of Magic and Mystery: A Guide to the Works of Walter B. Gibson (Cox), 418

Manthorne, Jackie, 511

Marcia Muller: Mystery and Suspense Writer and Editor, 521

Marcia Muller and Sharon McCone (Tangled Web), 522

Marele Day and Claudia Valentine PI (Tangled Web), 358

Marian Babson (Tangled Web), 266

Maron, Margaret, 14, 15

Marple, Laura, 50

Marsh, Ngaio, 666

Martha C. Lawrence (Lawrence), 479

Martin Edwards (Tangled Web), 396

Martindale, David, 721

Mary Daheim Page (Daheim), 349

Mary Higgins Clark (Clark), 332

Mary Willis Walker (Tangled Web), 624

Mary Wings and Emma Victor (Tangled Web), 645

Mask of Midas, with a Father Brown Bibliography by John Peterson, The (Chesterton and Hasnes), 307

Masters of Mystery and Detective Fiction: An Annotated Bibliography (Cox), 708

Matera, Lia, 516

Matt Hughes (Hughes), 462

Mattson, E. Christian, 663

Maxine O'Callaghan: Bibliography 1974–1995 (Seels), 525

Maxine O'Callaghan's Home Page (O'Callaghan), 526

Mechele, Tony, 306

Medieval and Renaissance Mysteries (Orgelfinger), 79

Meet Rebecca York (Glick and Buckholtz), 650

Meet the Detective (Madden), 662

Meg Chittenden's Web Page (Chittenden), 312

Menendez, Albert J., 30, 31, 57

Menguy, C., 574

Mercantile Library, 113

Mesplède, Claude, 185

Messall, Mary, 407

Metamorphoses de la Chouett, Les e (Baudou and Schleret), 167

Meyers, Ric, 153

Meyers, Richard, 722

Michael Pearce (Tangled Web), 532

Midnight Louie, Esq. (Douglas), 372

Mike Ripley and Fitzroy Maclean Angel (Tangled Web), 551

Mikucki, Eleanor, 91, 676

Miller, Anita, 129

Miller, Elizabeth V., 338

Miller, John Anthony, 413

Miller, Ron, 733

Miller, Stephen T., 201

Mistletoe Malice: The Life and Times of the Christmas Murder Mystery (Menendez), 57

Mittmann, Wolfgang, 123

Modern Fiction 1945–1958 (Holland), 179

Modern Mystery, Fantasy and Science Fiction Writers (Cassiday), 707

Moffatt, June M., 461, 496

Moffatt, Len, 496

Mogensen, Harald, 26

Monthly Murders: A Checklist and Chronological Listing of Fiction in the Digest-Size Mystery Magazines in the United States and Canada (Cook), 198

Moody, Susan, 32

Moon Man, The (Brown), 690

Monro, Gabriel, 38

Moorcock, Michael, 660

Moore, Ruth, 414

Moran, Peggy, 242

More Movie Thrillers (Howard), 718

More Mysteries, 55

Morselt, Ben, 318

Mulay, James J., 723

Muller, Marcia, 37, 525

Mundell, E. H., 191, 192, 193, 205, 216, 415, 416, 437, 438

Murder . . . by Category: A Subject Guide to Mystery Fiction (Mackler), 28

Murder Book, The: An Illustrated History of the Detective Story (la Cour and Mogensen), 26

Murder by Mail: Inside the Mystery Book Clubs with Complete Checklist (Cook), 180. 181

Murder by Occupation (Tucker), 672

Murder for Pleasure: The Life and Times of the Detective Story (Haycraft), 22, 23

Murder in Print: A Guide to Two Centuries of Detective Fiction (Barnes), 6

Murder Ink: The Mystery Reader's Companion (Winn), 45

Murder off the Rack: Critical Studies of Ten Paperback Masters (Breen and Greenberg), 248

Murder on Tape: A Comprehensive Guide to Murder and Mystery on Video (Sennett), 727

Murderess Ink: The Better Half of the Mystery (Winn), 46

Murphy, Warren, 15

Murray, Bill, 743

Murray, Will, 199, 239, 248, 363, 701

Musgrave Papers, 393

Music/Musicians/Musical Mysteries
(Boettcher), 90

Mysteries, 54

Mysteries Involving Libraries, Librarians, Etc.
(Schwartz), 84

Mysteries of Africa (Schleh), 130

Mysterious Home Page, The: A Guide to Mysteries and Crime Fiction on Internet
(Steffensen), 746

Mysterious Strands, 749

Mysterium and Mystery: The Clerical Crime Novel (Spencer), 63

Mystery! A Celebration. Stalking Public Television's Greatest Sleuths (Miller), 733

Mystery and Adventure in Canadian Books for Children and Young People/Romans Policiers et Histoires D'Aventures Canadiens pour la Jeunesse (Aubrey), 106

Mystery & Crime: The New York Public Library Book of Answers. Intriguing and Entertaining Questions and Answers About the Who's Who and What's What of Whodunits (Pearsall), 150

Mystery and Detection Annual, The (Adams), 698, 699

Mystery and Detective Fiction in the Library of Congress Classification Scheme (Burgess), 715

Mystery Book of Days, The (Malloy), 735

Mystery by Region (Lawson and Orr), 136

Mystery Checklist (Cataio), 12

Mystery, Detective, and Espionage Fiction: A Checklist of Fiction in U.S. Pulp Magazines, 1915–1974 (Cook and Miller, 201)

Mystery, Detective, and Espionage Magazines (Cook), 199

Mystery Fancier, The: An Index to Volumes I–XIII, November, 1976–Fall, 1992 (Deeck), 225

Mystery Fanfare: A Composite Annotated Index to Mystery and Related Fanzines 1963–1981 (Cook), 200

Mystery! Home Page, 734

Mystery Index: Subjects, Settings, and Sleuths of 10,000 Titles (Olderr), 33

Mystery Lover's Companion, The (Bourgeau), 11

Mystery Magazine Index: 1980–1997 (Contento), 196

Mystery Reader's Walking Guide: Chicago (Dale), 138

Mystery Reader's Walking Guide: England (Dale and Hendershott), 145

Mystery Reader's Walking Guide: London (Dale and Hendershott), 146

Mystery Reader's Walking Guide: New York (Dale), 141

Mystery Writers of America, 744

Mystery Writers of America, 744

Mystery Writer's Sourcebook: Where to Sell Your Manuscripts (Collingwood and Gee), 736

Nakajimi, Kawataro, 127

Nancy Drew in Paperback (Finnan), 693

Nancy Drew Mystery Stories, The (Johnston), 694

Nancy Drew—The Original Series (Finnan), 692

Nash, Ogden, 21, 24

Nedblake, William, 346

Nehr, Ellen, 169

Nero Wolfe (Barkocy), 593

Nero Wolfe Companion, The (Gotwald), 594

Nevins, Francis M., Jr., 461, 648

New Bedside, Bathtub & Armchair Companion to Agatha Christie, The (Riley and McAllister) (Riley and McAllister), 320

New Hard-Boiled Dicks, The: A Personal Checklist (Skinner), 75

New Hard-Boiled Dicks, The: Heroes for a New Urban Mythology (Skinner), 76

New Magnet Library (Cox), 226

New Nick Carter Weekly (Cox), 227

Newbury, Jenny, 391

Newfront Productions, 7

Newman, Sharan, 524

Ngaio Marsh (Tangled Web), 513

Ngaio Marsh: A Bibliography of English Language Publications in Hardback and Paperback, with a Guide to the Value of the First Editions (Gibbs and Williams), 512
Nicholas Rhea (Peter N. Walker) (Tangled Web), 549
Nichols, Victoria, 664, 707
Nick Carter Library (with Notes and Commentary on the Rest of the Saga), The (Cox), 228
Nick Carter Stories and Other Series Containing Stories About Nick Carter (Cox), 229, 230
Nicole St. John/Norma Johnston (St. John), 558
Nicolson, Marjorie, 21
Niebuhr, Gary Warren, 96
Nielsen, Birger, 342, 616
Nielsen, Bjarne, 121
Nieminski, John, 221, 234, 701
Nietzel, Michael T., 94
Night Master, The (Sampson), 240
Nihon Suiri Shosetsu Jiten (Nakajimi), 127
XIX Century Fiction: A Bibliographic Record Based on His Own Collection (Sadleir), 335
Nixon, Joan Lowery, 15
Nolan, William F., 439
Norfolk-Hall, 587
nouvelisste et le conteur, Le, 575
Novel Verdicts: A Guide to Courtroom Fiction (Breen), 65
Nuns in Mysteries (Harper), 61
Nurse Sleuths (Mikucki), 91

O'Brien, Geoffrey, 73
O'Callaghan, Maxine, 525, 526
O'Donnell, Peter, 45
O och A. Detektivromaner på Svenska under 1900–talet (Tullberg), 134
Official Alex Keegan Home Page, The (Keegan), 469
Official Sharyn McCrumb Website, The, 488
Olderr, Steven, 33
Oleksiw, Susan, 59
O'Marie, Carol Anne, 60
On Collecting Hillerman (Hieb), 453
100 Books by August Derleth (Derleth), 367

100 Great Detectives; or, The Detective Directory (Jakubowsky), 661
1001 Midnights: The Aficionado's Guide to Mystery and Detective Fiction (Pronzini and Muller), 37
Operator #5 (Brown), 231
Orbit, The: The Official Drive-in Theatre of Champion Mojo Storyteller Joe R. Lansdale (Lansdale), 476
Orczy, Baroness, 662
Orgelfinger, Gail, 79
Originals, The: An A-Z of Fiction's Real-Life Characters (Amos), 651
Originals, The: Who's Really Who in Fiction (Amos), 652
Orr, Cynthia, 136
Osborne, Eric, 114
Other Detective Pulp Heroes, The (Carr), 654
Ousby, Ian, 34

Palmer, Jerry, 25
Pan Books 1945–1966. A Bibliographical Checklist with a Guide to Their Value (Williams), 182
Pappas, Nick, 738
Parish, James Robert, 724
Park, Orlando, 382
Parker, Barbara, 528
Parker, Robert B., 137
Parnell Hall's Mystery Page (Hall), 430
Parrish, M. L., 338
Pate, Janet, 665
Patricia Cornwell (Tangled Web), 343
Patricia Cornwell Bibliography (Nielsen), 342
Patricia Cornwell Web Site, The (Junot), 341
Paul, Barbara, 531
Paul Levine (Levine), 483
Paul Renin: A Bibliographical Checklist (Holland and Williams), 548
Paula Gosling (Tangled Web), 420
Pauline Bell (Tangled Web), 268
PBS Adult Learning Service, 457
PBS Adult Learning Service Presents an Online Q&A with Tony Hillerman, 457
Pearsall, Jay, 150
Pederson, Jay P., 260
Pendex, The: An Index of Pen Names and House Names in Fantastic, Thriller, and Series Literature (Bates), 261

Penguin Crime Fiction 1935–1990: A Biblio-graphical Checklist with a Guide to Their Value (Williams), 183

Penny Sumner and Victoria Cross (Tangled Web), 599

Penzler, Otto, 3, 14, 153, 666, 667, 668

Peralez, Jon, 607

Perani, Jérôme, 398

Perkin, Michael, 463

Peter Robinson (Robinson), 552

Peter Robinson and DCI Alan Banks (Tangled Web), 553

Peter Turnbull (Tangled Web), 610

Peters, Ellis, 60, 539, 540

Peters Fan Club, Elizabeth, 537a

Peters Fan Club, Ellis, 540a

Petit Dictionnaire des Auteurs Belges de Litté-rature Policière (Hermans), 119

Phänomen Simenon, Das: Einführung in das Werk: Bibliographie (Verzeichnis der Werke und der Sekundärliteratur) (Arens), 570

Phantom, The (Sauer and Brown), 233

Phantom Detective (Halegua), 695

Phantom Detective: The Original Masked Marvel (Johnson), 696

Philip Luber's Home Page (Luber), 485

Philmore, R., 21

Phoebe Atwood Taylor (Chester), 602

Piccadilly Novels (Holland), 184

Pickard, Nancy, 15

Pierce, Hazel Beasley, 101

Pike, B. A., 13, 716

Piron, Maurice, 576

Pitts, Michael R., 724, 725, 726

Planet Sparkle (Hayter), 444

Police Detectives (Kristick), 92

Polly Whitney (Whitney), 636

Polt, Richard, 470

Porter, Thomas E., 244

Poundstone, William, 471

Powell, Talmage, 541

Praed Street Irregulars, 370

Pringle, David, 669, 670

Private Eyes: One Hundred and One Knights: A Survey of American Detective Fiction 1922–1984 (Baker and Nietzel), 94

Pronzini, Bill, 15, 35, 36, 37

Provisional Descriptive Bibliography of First Editions of the Works of Arthur Upfield (Asdell), 611

Prowell, Sandra West, 543

Pulp Fiction Central, 350

Pulp Magazine Index, The: First Series (Robbins), 206

Pulp Magazine Index, The: Fourth Series (Robbins), 209

Pulp Magazine Index, The: Second Series (Robbins), 207

Pulp Magazine Index, The: Third Series (Robbins), 208

Quayle, Eric, 38

Queen, Ellery, 21, 39, 40, 153, 194, 195, 707

Queen's Quorum: A History of the Detective-Crime Short Story As Revealed by the 106 Most Important Books Published in This Field Since 1845 (Queen), 39, 40

Quinn, Elizabeth, 546

R. & L. Locker/Harborough Publishing Co. Ltd./Archer Press (1944–1954) (Holland), 177

R. Austin Freeman (Grost), 408

Radcliffe, Elsa J., 71

Radio Mystery and Adventure and Its Appear-ances in Film, Television and Other Media (Harmon), 717

Randall, David A., 115

Rauch, Nancy V., 613

Rausch., G. Jay, 193

Rave or Rage: The Critics & John D. MacDonald (Shine), 501

Raymond Chandler (Denton), 298

Raymond Chandler (King), 299

Raymond Chandler: A Checklist (Bruccoli), 296

Raymond Chandler: A Descriptive Bibliography (Bruccoli), 297

Raymond Chandler's Los Angeles (Ward and Silver), 140

Reader's Guide to the American Novel of Detec-tion, A (Lachman), 49

Reader's Guide to the Classic British Mystery, A (Oleksiw), 59
Reader's Guide to the Police Procedural, A (Vicarel), 93
Reader's Guide to the Private Eye Novel, A (Niebuhr), 96
Reader's Guide to the Suspense Novel, A (Jarvis), 102
Reading List for Mystery Lovers! Mysteries on Location. Scene of the Crimes, A (Stone), 139, 144, 147, 148
Reddy, Maureen T., 707
Redmond, Christopher, 385, 392
Redmond, Donald A., 376, 386
Reginald Hill and Dalziel & Pascoe (Tangled Web), 448
Reid, Sharon, 354
Reilly, John M., 243, 257, 258
Rennison, Nick, 41
Revised Descriptive Bibliography of First Editions of Arthur W. Upfield, A: Australian, British, and U.S. (Asdell) 611
Rex Stout: An Annotated Primary and Secondary Bibliography (Townsend), 596
Rhodes, Karen, 731
Rice, Carig, 21
Rick Riordan (Riordan), 550
Rikoskirjallisuuden Bibliografia, 1864–1984: Eli 120 Vuoden Aikana Suomeksi Limestyneet Jännitysromaanit (Sjöblom), 122
Riley, Dick, 319, 320
Riordan, Rick, 550
Rita Mae Brown (Wicker), 283
Robbins, Leonard A., 206, 207, 208, 209
Robert Bloch: A Bio-Bibliography (Flanagan), 269
Robert Bloch Bibliography (Hall), 270
Robert van Gulik Bibliography (Nielsen), 616
Robert Wilson (Tangled Web), 644
Robinson, Peter, 552
Rohmer, Sax, 662
Romans Policiers et Histoires D'Aventures Canadiens pour la Jeunesse (Aubrey), 106
Rosenberg, Robert, 554
Ross, Katherine, 555
Ross Macdonald (Denton), 508

Ross Macdonald (King), 509
Ross Macdonald Files, The (Lindkvist), 510
Ross Macdonald/Kenneth Millar: A Descriptive Bibliography (Bruccoli), 507
Rovin, Jeff, 671
Ruber, Peter, 368, 588, 589
Rufener, S., 497
Rumpole Home Page, The (Schott), 519
Russell James (Tangled Web), 467
Russell James Website, The (James), 466
Russell, Jay, 556
Ruth Dudley Edwards (Tangled Web), 397
Ryan, Richard T., 321

Sadleir, Michael, 335
Saint, The (Mechele and Fiddy), 306
Saint, The: A Complete History in Print, Radio, Film and Television of Leslie Charteris's Robin Hood of Modern Crime, Simon Templar, 1928–1992 (Barer), 303
Saint and Leslie Charteris, The (Lofts and Adley), 305
Saint and Leslie Charteris, The: A Collection (Bodenheimer), 304
St. Charles Public Library, 67
St. James Guide to Crime & Mystery Writers (Pederson), 260
St. John, Nicole, 558
Saint Magazine Index, Authors and Titles, Spring 1953–October 1967, The (Nieminski), 234
St. Mary Mead Public Library: An Agatha Christie Booklist (Wilson), 328
Saintly Sleuths (Kristick), 62
Salongsbödlarna (Lundin), 131
Sampson, Robert, 199, 239, 240, 241, 363, 701
Sandoe, James, 21, 74, 153
Sandra Scoppettone (Scoppetone), 568
SanFran Sleuths: San Francisco Bay Area Mysteries (Derie), 142
Santangelo, Elena, 322
Sarah Dreher and Stoner McTavish (Tangled Web), 394
Satterthwait, Walter, 562
Sauer, Nicholas, 233, 653, 675
Saunders, Dennis, 323, 324
Sayers, Dorothy L., 21, 707

Sayers Society, Dorothy L., 567

Scandinavian Mysteries in English (Steffensen), 128

Schleh, Eugene, 130

Schleret, Jean Jacques, 167

Schott, Brian, 519

Schwartz, Candy, 84

Science Fiction Detective Tales: A Brief Overview of Futuristic Detective Fiction in Paperback (Lovisi), 100

Scoppettone, Sandra, 568

Secret Agent 'X' (Brown), 235

Seels, James T., 273, 472, 525

Sekai no Suiri Shosetsu Sokaisetsu (Gonda), 127

Senate, Richard, 413

Sengo Suiri Shosetsu Somokuroku (Nakajima), 127

Sennett, Ted, 727

Series Book Central (Hardyboy01's Home Page) (Finnan), 685

Sexton Blake Library (Third and Fifth Series), The (Holland and Williams), 186

Shadow, The (Brown), 236

Shadow Scrapbook, The (Gibson), 238

Sharan Newman Home Page (Newman), 524

Sharon Gwyn Short (Tangled Web), 569

Shaw, John Bennett, 375

Shepard, Richard, 41

Sheridan, Monica, 537

Sherlock Comes to America (Christ), 376

Sherlock Holmes: A Study in Sources (Redmond), 389

Sherlock Holmes: The Great Detective in Paperback (Lovisi), 375

Sherlock Holmes Among the Pirates: Copyright and Conan Doyle in America 1890–1930 (Redmond), 376

Sherlock Holmes Encyclopedia (Park), 382

Sherlock Holmes, Esq., and John H. Watson, M.D.: An Encyclopaedia of Their Affairs (Park), 382

Sherlock Holmes Fan Clubs and Societies, 393a

Sherlock Holmes Gazette, 393

Sherlock Holmes Handbook, A (Redmond), 385

Sherlock Holmes International (Newbury), 391

Sherlock Holmes Journal, 393

Sherlockian Holmepage, A (Redmond), 392

Sherlockian Tidbits, 393

Sherman, Michael, 393

Shine, Jean and Walter, 223, 498, 499, 500, 501, 502, 503, 504

Shine, Walter. *See* Shine, Jean and Walter

Short Detective Story 1925–1982, The: A Personal Checklist (la Cour), 190

Shortling, Grobius, 294

Siegel, Jeff, 97

Silk Stalkings: When Women Write of Murder: A Survey of Series Characters Created by Women Authors in Crime and Mystery Fiction (Nichols and Thompson), 664

Silver, Alain, 140

Silverberg, Robert, 619

Sines, Jeff, 680

Sisters in Crime, 745

Sisters in Crime Internet Chapter (Sisters in Crime), 745

Sjöblom, Simo, 122

Skene Melvin, Ann, 712

Skene Melvin, L. David St. C., 120, 712

Skillman, Trish Macdonald, 579

Skinner, Robert E., 75, 76, 460, 713

Slavin, Charlie, 151

Sleuths, Sidekicks and Stooges: An Annotated Bibliography of Detectives, Their Assistants and Their Rivals in Crime, Mystery and Adventure Fiction, 1795–1995 (Green and Finch), 658

Slide, Anthony, 68

Slip F-18/John D. MacDonald's Travis McGee (Warble), 493

Slung, Michele, 25

Smalley, Rob, 681

Smith, Barbara Burnett, 580

Smith, Enes, 581

Smith, Ralph B., Jr., 370

Smith, Timothy D'Arch, 359

Smith, Wilbur Jordan., 116, 698

Snow, Marshall, 739

Solar Pons Page, The (Smith), 370

Son of Gun in Cheek (Pronzini), 36

Soos, Troy, 583

Soutar, Andrew, 662

South African Detective Stories in English and Afrikaans from 1951–1971 (Friedland), 130

Sova, Dawn B., 325

Special Confidential Report, The (Shine), 502

Special Confidential Report: Subject: Travis McGee (Shine), 503, 504

Speckhardt, Lisa, 536

Spehner, Norbert, 120, 714

Spencer, William David, 63

Spenser's Boston (Parker), 137

Spider, The (Brown), 241

Spies and Sleuths: Mystery, Spy and Suspense Films on Videocassette (Mulay, Curran, and Wallenfeldt), 723

Spurrier, Ralph, 157, 161, 171

Squire, Elizabeth Daniels, 584

Stabenow, Dana, 585

Staley, Thomas F., 245, 246, 247

Starrett, Vincent, 21, 195

Steeves, Harrison R., 21

Steffensen, Jan B., 128, 286, 746

Steinbrunner, Chris, 3, 238

Stella Duffy and Saz Martin (Tangled Web), 395

Stephens, Christopher P., 176, 178, 281, 400, 419, 481, 604, 608, 612, 649

Stephensen-Payne, Phil, 517, 609, 620, 621

Stern, Philip Van Doren, 21

Steven Knight (Tangled Web), 475

Stevenson, W. B., 42

Stewart, Enola, 590, 648

Stewart, Lawrence D., 698

Stiel, Beth, 253

Stilwell, Steven A., 43, 210, 211

Stine, Kate, 153

Stone, Ben, 138

Stone, Carolyn K., 139, 144, 147, 148

Stout, Rex, 21, 707

Stout Fan Clubs, Rex, 597a

Street & Smith's Hero Pulp Checklist (Gunnison), 202

Strickland, William Bradley, 244

Strosser, Edward, 152

Stubbs, John Heath, 24

Stybr, Denise, 487

Subject Is Murder, The: A Selective Subject Guide to Mystery Fiction (Menendez), 30, 31

Sue Grafton (King), 423

Sue Grafton's Web Site (Grafton), 422

Sullivan, Eleanor, 25, 545

Sullivan, John, 308, 309, 310

Sullivan, Lester, 460

Suspense in the Cinema (Howard), 719

Sutherland, Michael C., 117

Swan, Sally, 571

Swanson, Jean, 255, 256

Swedish Crime Story, The (Lundin), 131

Symons, Julian, 24, 26, 44, 153, 319, 320, 600, 707

Synod of Sleuths: Essays on Judeo-Christian Detective Fiction (Breen and Greenberg), 60

T. V. Boardman 1942–1957 (Williams), 158

Talburt, Nancy Ellen, 243, 244

Talmage Powell, Author (Powell), 541

Tangled Web, 266, 267, 268, 274, 287, 290, 333, 339, 343, 348, 355, 356, 358, 360, 394, 395, 396, 397, 399, 402, 409, 420, 424, 440, 441, 443, 445, 447, 448, 467, 468, 474, 475, 477, 482, 489, 513, 514, 515, 522, 523, 527, 532, 533, 547, 549, 551, 553, 557, 559, 569, 582, 598, 599, 601, 610, 622, 623, 624, 634, 639, 640, 641, 642, 643, 644, 645, 647, 732, 747

Tangled Web UK (Tangled Web), 747

Taylor, T. Allan, 724

Taylor, Thomas, 70

Taylor, Wendell Hertig, 8, 9,10, 707

Television Detective Shows of the 1970s: Credits, Storylines and Episode Guides for 109 Series (Martindale), 721

Television Sherlock Holmes, The (Haining), 387, 388, 389

10 Women of Mystery (Bargainnier), 243

Terris McMahan Grimes Presents Sister Sleuth (Grimes), 427

13 Mistresses of Murder (Budd), 249

Thom, William, 196

Thompson, Susan, 664, 707

Thomson, H. Douglas, 21

Thurlo, Aimée and David, 606

Thurlo, David. *See* Thurlo, Aimée and David

Tibballs, Geoff, 728

Timothy Williams (Tangled Web), 641

Tollin, Anthony, 238

Tom Howard on Mystery Movies (Howard), 720

Tonik, Al, 199

Tony Fennelly (Tangled Web), 402

Tony Hillerman: A Bibliography (Hieb), 454

Tony Hillerman: From the Blessing Way to Talking God: A Bibliography (Hieb), 455

Tony Hillerman Abroad: An Annotated Checklist of Foreign Language Editions (Hieb), 456

Tony Hillerman Companion, The: A Comprehensive Guide to His Life and Work (Greenberg), 450

Townsend, Guy M., 596

Toye, Randall, 326

Tracy, Jack, 383

Traylor, James L., 217

Trish Macdonald Skillman (Skillman), 579

Trouble Is Their Business: Private Eyes in Fiction, Film and Television, 1927–1988 (Conquest), 655

Trouble with Simona Griffo, The (Crespi), 345

Troy Soos Home Page (Soos), 583

Trussel, Steve, 577

Tucker, Sara, 672

Tullberg, Sigurd, 134

Turner-Lord, Jann, 4

Turow, Scott, 14

TV Detectives (Meyers), 722

Twelve Englishmen of Mystery (Bargainnier), 244

1257 Förteckning över Deckare, Thrillers, Faktaböcker, Memoarer, Kolportageromaner, 133

Twentieth-Century Crime and Mystery Writers (Henderson), 259

Twentieth-Century Crime and Mystery Writers (Reilly), 257, 258

Twists, Slugs and Roscoes: A Glossary of Hardboiled Slang (Denton), 2

221B Baker Street (Sherman), 393

Ultimate Mystery/Detective Web Guide (Magic Dragon Multimedia), 742

Underwood, Lynn, 327

Underwood, Tim, 617, 618

L'Univers de Simenon: Guide des Romans et Nouvelles (1931–1972) de Georges Simenon (Piron), 576

Universal Sherlock Holmes, The (de Waal), 379

University of Minnesota, Children's Literature Research Collections, 673, 674

Unofficial Carl Hiaasen Webpage, The (Zelzer), 446

Unofficial Diane Mott Davidson Webpage, The (Reid), 353

Unofficial Elizabeth Peters Page/The Unofficial Barbara Michaels Page/The Unofficial Barbara Mertz Page, The (Sheridan), 537

Unofficial Quiller Web Site, The (Pcralez), 607

Upfield Mysteries (Rauch), 613

Utter, Virgil, 517

Vachss, Andrew, 614

Vaisala, 214

Val McDermid (Tangled Web), 489

Van Dine, S. S., 21

Van Dover, J. Kenneth, 597

Vance, Jack, 619

Vance, Norma, 619

Vanderburgh, George A., 368, 379

Veendam, S. S., 21

Véry, Pierre, 21

Vicarel, Jo Ann, 93

Victorian Detective Fiction: A Catalogue of the Collection Made by Dorothy Glover & Graham Greene (Osborne), 114

Viking/W[orld] D[istributors]L[td.]/Consul 1949–1966 (Holland and Williams), 187

Villines, Sharon, 737, 748

Vincent Starrett: A Catalogue of First and Variant Editions of His Work, Including Books Edited by Him and Those with Introductions, Prefaces, Afterwords, or Anthologized Contributions (Stewart), 590

Vincent Starrett Catalogue, A: First Editions, Books By and About, Fine Association Copies & Ephemera (Norfolk-Hall), 587

Vincent Starrett Library, A: The Astonishing Result of Twenty-Three Years of Library Activity (Honce), 586

W. R. Burnett (Denton), 288

W. R. Burnett (Harper), 289

Walkhoff-Jordan, Klaus-Dieter, 124, 125

Wallace, Penelope, 45

Wallace Fan Club, Edgar, 632a

Wallenfeldt, Jeffrey H., 723

Walsdorf, John J., 600

Walter Mosley (Daniels), 520

Walter Satterthwait Homepage, The (Satterthwait), 562

Wambaugh, Joseph, 14

Ward, Christopher, 21

Ward, Elizabeth, 140

Ward, Martin, 311

Waterstone's Guide to Crime Fiction (Rennison and Shepard), 41

Waugh, Hillary, 25

Web Companion to Agatha Christie, The (Woodbury), 329

Weinberg, Robert, 203, 204, 237, 269, 363

Welcome to Kate Grilley's Web Site (Grilley), 425

Welcome to Purple Sage (Smith), 580

Wells, Betty and George, 379

Wells, George. *See* Wells, Betty and George

Werremeier, Friedhelm, 124, 125

Wessells, Henry, 352

West, Chassie L., 633

Westlake, Donald E., 248

What About Murder? A Guide to Books About Mystery and Detective Fiction (Breen), 705

What About Murder? 1981–1991. A Guide to Books About Mystery and Detective Fiction (Breen), 706

What Mystery Do I Read Next? A Reader's Guide to Recent Mystery Fiction (Stilwell), 43

Whiteman, Robin, 539, 540

Whitney, Polly, 636

Who's Who in Sherlock Holmes (Bullard and Collins), 380

Who's Whodunit (Gribbin), 107

Who Done It? A Guide to Detective, Mystery and Suspense Fiction (Hagen), 108

Whodunit: A Biblio-Bio-Anecdotal Memoir of Frederic Dannay, "Ellery Queen," (Sullivan) 545

Whodunit? A Guide to Crime, Suspense and Spy Fiction (Keating), 25

Wicker, Gene, 283, 555

Wiley, Denise Dietz, 637

Wilkie Collins (Lewis), 337

Wilkie Collins: A Critical Survey of His Prose Fiction with a Bibliography (Andrew), 334

Wilkie Collins: An Annotated Bibliography, 1889–1976 (Beetz), 335

Wilkie Collins and Charles Reade: First Editions (with a Few Exceptions) in the Library of Dormy House, Pine Valley, New Jersey (Parrish and Miller), 338

Wilkie Collins Appreciation Page (Griggs), 336

Williams, Richard, 155, 157, 158, 160, 161, 162, 163, 168, 170, 171, 173, 174, 175, 182, 183, 186, 187, 282, 403, 512, 548, 571, 626, 628, 629, 630, 631, 632

Wilson, Alison M., 368, 369

Wilson, Edmund, 21, 565, 566, 707

Wilson, Michael, 328

Wilson "Bob" Tucker: Wild Talent (Stephensen-Payne and Benson), 609

Winks, Robin, 135, 153

Winn, Dilys, 45, 46

Wittman, Pat, 80

Woddis, Roger, 24

Woeller, Waltraud, 47

Wolfe, S. J., 58

Wolfe Packe, 597

Womack, Steven, 646

Womack Web, The (Womack), 646

Women Mystery Writers: Strong, Independent Female Lead Characters (Androski), 103

Woodbury, Roger, 329
*Work of Jack Vance, The: An Annotated
    Bibliography & Guide* (Hewett and
    Mallett), 619
*World Bibliography of Sherlock Holmes and
    Dr. Watson, The: A Classified and
    Annotated List of Materials Relating
    to Their Lives and Adventures*
    (de Waal), 377
Wynne, Anthony, 662
Wynne, Nancy Blue, 330

Yaffe, Ben, 331
Yaffe, James, 60
Yorke, Margaret, 15
Young, Trudee, 578
Youngberg, Ruth Tanis, 566

Zelzer, Marcus, 446
*Zero, The: The Official Home Page of Andrew
    Vachss* (Vachss), 614